HELENA:

EMPRESS AND SAINT

BY

HANS A. POHLSANDER

ARES PUBLISHERS, INC.
CHICAGO, ILLINOIS
MCMXCV

Copyright 1995
ARES PUBLISHERS, INC.
Chicago, Illinois 60626
Printed in the United States of America
International Standard Book Number
0-89005-562-9

Frontispiece:

Helena adoring the Cross, illuminated initial from
a 15th century Lombard gradual. Cornell University MSS Bd.
Rare BX C36 6737++ (formerly MS B 50++), fol. 28,v.
Photo Cornell University.

Uxori carissimae meae

amoris causa

CONTENTS

ACKNOWLEDGEMENTS

This book would not have been possible without the generous support of many institutions and individuals. The University at Albany, State University of New York, granted me a sabbatical leave for the spring of 1989. I have received grants-in-aid from the University at Albany, State University of New York, the United University Professions, the National Endowment for the Humanities, and the American Philosophical Society. I have enjoyed the hospitality and assistance of the American Academy in Rome, the Cyprus American Archaeological Research Institute, the American Numismatic Society, the Pierpont Morgan Library, the Franz Joseph Dölger-Institut of the University of Bonn, and, repeatedly, the University of Trier.

Parts of the manuscripts were read and suggestions for improvement were made by Professors Randall T. Craig, Mojmir S. Frinta, Warren S. Ginsberg, Mary G. Goggin, George S. Hastings, K. Drew Hartzell, Louis W. Roberts, Michael R. Werner, and Mary Beth Winn, all of them my colleagues at the University at Albany, State University of New York; also by Dr. Winfried Weber, director of the Bischöfliches Dom- und Diözesanmuseum in Trier, and by Dr. Stephan Borgehammar of Uppsala University. Professor Charles Odahl of Boise State University has read the entire manuscript and shared with me his own recent and forthcoming pertinent publications. Professor Heinz Heinen of the University of Trier has read parts of the manuscript and, beyond that, has been a never-failing source of assistance and encouragement. Professor Franz J. Ronig, the diocesan conservator of the Catholic diocese of Trier, has taken a kind and personal interest in this work.

To all those listed above St. Helena and I express sincere thanks. Others, too numerous to mention here, who have assisted with the clarification of specific points, are recognized in the notes.

July 28, 1994   Hans A. Pohlsander

ABBREVIATIONS

I. Periodicals

AA	*Archäologischer Anzeiger*, see *JDAI*.
AAS	*Acta Apostolicae Sedis*.
AAWW	*Anzeiger der österreichischen Akademie der Wissenschaften in Wien, phil.-hist. Klasse.*
AHVNrh.	*Archiv des historischen Vereins für den Niederrhein.*
AIPHOS	*Annuaire de l'Institut de philologie et d'histoire orientales et slaves.*
AJA	*American Journal of Archaeology.*
Anal. Boll.	*Analecta Bollandiana.*
AncW	*The Ancient World.*
Arch. Class.	*Archeologia Classica.*
Arctos	*Arctos: Acta Philologica Fennica.*
ArtB	*Art Bulletin.*
ASE	*Anglo-Saxon England.*
BAB	*Bulletin Antieke Beschaving.*
BASOR	*Bulletin of the American Schools of Oriental Research.*
BCH	*Bulletin de correspondance hellénique.*
BdA	*Bollettino d'arte.*
BGDSL	*Beiträge zur Geschichte der deutschen Sprache und Literatur.* Also cited as *PBB* (Tübingen).
BHR	*Bibliothéque d'Humanisme et Renaissance.*

BIFAO	*Bulletin de l'Institut Français d'Archéologie Orientale.*
BJ	*Bonner Jahrbücher.*
BNJ	*Byzantinisch-neugriechische Jahrbücher.*
BLE	*Bulletin de littérature ecclésiastique.*
BRL	*Bulletin of the John Rylands Library.*
Bull.	*Soc. des Antiq. Bulletin de la Société des Antiquaires de France.*
BZ	*Byzantinische Zeitschrift.*
Cah. Arch.	*Cahiers Archéologiques.*
CHR	*Catholic Historical Review.*
DOP	*Dumbarton Oaks Papers.*
EHR	*English Historical Review.*
EO	*Échos d'Orient.*
Eph. Lit.	*Ephemerides Liturgicae.*
Et. Cl.	*Études classiques.*
GGA	*Göttingische gelehrte Anzeigen.*
GRBS	*Greek, Roman, and Byzantine Studies.*
HThR	*Harvard Theological Review.*
JBAA	*Journal of the British Archaeological Association.*
JbAC	*Jahrbuch für Antike und Christentum.*
JbNum.	*Jahrbuch für Numismatik und Geldgeschichte.*

ABBREVIATIONS

JBAS	*Journal of the British Archaeological Society.*
JDAI	*Jahrbuch des Deutschen Archäologischen Instituts.*
JEGP	*Journal of English and Germanic Philology.*
JEH	*Journal of Ecclesiastical History.*
JHS	*Journal of Hellenic Studies.*
JMRS	*Journal of Medieval and Renaissance Studies.*
JÖB	*Jahrbuch der österreichischen Byzantinistik.*
JRH	*Journal of Religious History.*
JRS	*Journal of Roman Studies.*
JThS	*Journal of Theological Studies.*
JWarb.	*Journal of the Warburg and Courtauld Institutes.*
MÆ	*Medium Ævum.*
MEFR	*Mélanges d'archéologie et d'histoire de l'École française de Rome.*
MémAcInscr.	*Mémoires de l'Académie des Inscriptions et Belles-Lettres.*
MemPontAcc.	*Memorie della Pontificia Accademia Romana di Archeologia.*
MIÖG	*Mitteilungen des Instituts für österreichische Geschichtsforschung.*
MLN	*Modern Language Notes.*
MMJ	*Metropolitan Museum Journal.*

NBAC	*Nuovo bullettino di archeologia cristiana.*
NC	*Numismatic Chronicle.*
N. Circ.	*Spink & Son's Numismatic Circular.*
NM	*Neuphilologische Mitteilungen.*
NZ	*Numismatische Zeitschrift.*
OA	*Oriens Antiquus.*
OCP	*Orientalia Christiana Periodica.*
ÖJh.	*Jahreshefte des österreichischen archäologischen Instituts in Wien.*
Or. Chr.	*Oriens Christianus.*
PMLA	*Publications of the Modern Language Association of America.*
QDAP	*Quarterly of the Department of Antiquities in Palestine.*
RACrist.	*Rivista di Archeologia Cristiana.*
RArts	*Revue des Arts.*
RBPhil.	*Revue belge de philologie et histoire.*
RDAC	*Report of the Department of Antiquities, Cyprus.*
REB	*Revue des études byzantines.*
Rev. Bibl.	*Revue Biblique.*
Rev. Or. Chr.	*Revue de l'Orient chrétien.*
RHDFE	*Revue historique de droit français et étranger.*

ABBREVIATIONS

RHE	*Revue d'histoire ecclésiastique.*
RN	*Revue numismatique.*
Röm. Mitt.	*Mitteilungen des Deutschen Archäologischen Instituts, Römische Abteilung.*
RömQ	*Römische Quartalschrift für christliche Altertumskunde und für Kirchengeschichte.*
SPFB	*Sborník Prací Filosofické Fakulty Brenské Univerzity.*
SZG	*Schweizerische Zeitschrift für Geschichte.*
TAPS	*Transactions of the American Philosophical Society.*
TU	*Texte und Untersuchungen zur altchristlichen Literatur.*
TxSE	*Texas Studies in English.*
TZ	*Trierer Zeitschrift.*
Vet. Chr.	*Vetera Christianorum.*
Vig. Chr.	*Vigiliae Christianae.*
WS	*Wiener Studien.*
ZChrK	*Zeitschrift für Christliche Kunst.*
ZDA	*Zeitschrift für deutsches Altertum und deutsche Literatur.*
ZHT	*Zeitschrift für die historische Theologie.*
ZKG	*Zeitschrift für Kirchengeschichte.*
ZNTW	*Zeitschrift für die neutestamentliche Wissenschaft.*
ZRG	*Zeitschrift der Savigny-Stiftung für Rechtsgeschichte.*

K. Abt.	*Kanonistische Abteilung.*
R. Abt.	*Romanistische Abteilung.*

II. Editions of Texts

ACO — Acta Conciliorum Oecomenicorum, ed. Eduard Schwartz, Berlin and Leipzig 1914 ff.

Acta Sanct. — Acta Sanctorum Bollandistarum, Brussels 1643 ff.; repr. 1965 ff.

AGCC — Anthologia Graeca Carminum Christianorum, edd. Wilhelm von Christ and Matthios Paranikas, Leipzig 1871; repr. Hildesheim 1963.

AHMA — Analecta Hymnica Medii Aevi, edd. Guido Maria Dreves and Clemens Blume, Leipzig 1886-1922; repr. New York 1961.

CC — Corpus Christianorum.

Ser. Lat. — Series Latina, Turnhout 1953 ff.

Cont. Med. — Continuatio Mediaevalis, Turnhout 1971 ff.

CSEL — Corpus Scriptorum Ecclesiasticorum Latinorum, Vienna, Prague, and Leipzig 1866 ff.

CSCO — Corpus Scriptorum Christianorum Orientalium, Paris and Louvain 1903 ff.

Script. Arab. — Scriptores Arabici.

CSHB — Corpus Scriptorum Historiae Byzantinae, Bonn 1828-1897.

EETS — Early English Text Society.

OS	*Original Series*, London 1864-1962.
ES	*Extra Series*, London 1867-1920.
SS	*Supplementary Series*, London 1970 ff.
FHG	Carl Müller, *Fragmenta Historicorum Graecorum*, Paris 1841-1938; repr. Frankfurt 1975.
FP	*Florilegium Patristicum*, Bonn 1904.
Franz. Quellenschr.	*Franziskanische Quellenschriften*, Werl, Westphalia, 1951 ff.
GCS	*Die griechischen christlichen Schriftsteller der ersten [drei] Jahrhunderte*, Berlin 1897 ff. Note: the most recent volumes in this series are without sequential numbers.
Mansi	Giovanni Domenico Mansi, *Sacrorum Conciliorum Nova et Amplissima Collectio*, Florence and Venice 1757 ff.; repr. Paris 1901-1927; repr. Graz 1960-1961.
Mart. Rom.	*Martyrologium Romanum*, ed. Cesare Baronio, (ed. 1586) Rome 1586.
MGH	*Monumenta Germaniae Historica*.
AA	*Eutropius* *Auctores Antiquissimi*, Hannover 1877 ff.
Chron. Min.	*Chronica Minora* = vols. IX, XI, and XIII of the *Auctores Antiquissimi*.
Dipl.	*Diplomata Imperii*, Hannover 1872.
Dipl. Karol.	*Diplomata Karolinorum (Die Urkunden der Karolinger)*, Hannover 1906 ff.

Dt. Chron.   *Deutsche Chroniken und andere Geschichtsbücher des Mittelalters* or *Scriptores qui vernacula lingua usi sunt*, Hannover 1877 ff.

Epist.   *Epistolae*, Berlin 1887 ff.

GPR   *Gesta Pontificum Romanorum*, Berlin 1898.

Poet. Lat.   *Poetae Latini Medii Aevi*, Leipzig 1881 ff.

Script.   *Scriptores*, Hannover 1826 ff.

SRGS   *Scriptores Rerum Germanicarum in usum scholarum*, Hannover 1866 ff.

SRM   *Scriptores Rerum Merovingicarum*, Hannover 1885 ff.

Migne, *PG*   J. P. Migne, *Patrologia, Series Graeca*, Paris 1857 ff.

Migne, *PL*   J. P. Migne, *Patrologia, Series Latina*, Paris 1844 ff.

RIS   *Rerum Italicarum Scriptores*, ed. L. A. Muratori, Milan 1723-1754; 2nd ed. Bologna 1900.

Rolls Series   *Rerum Britannicarum Medii Aevi Scriptores* or *Chronicles and Memorials of Great Britain and Ireland during the Middle Ages*, London 1857 ff.

SC   *Sources Chrétiennes*, Paris 1855 ff.

Script.   *Scriptores Rerum Suecicarum Medii Aevi*,
Rer. Suec.   Uppsala 1818-1876; repr. Graz 1968.

III. Other Works

ANRW   *Aufstieg und Niedergang der römischen Welt*, edd. Hildegard Temporini and Wolfgang Haase, Berlin and New York 1972 ff.

Bächtold-Stäubli	Hanns Bächtold-Stäubli, *Handwörterbuch des deutschen Aberglaubens*, Berlin 1927-1942; repr. 1986.
BHG [3]	*Bibliotheca Hagiographica Graeca, Subsidia Hagiographica* 47, 3rd ed., ed. François Halkin, Brussels 1957.
BHL	*Bibliotheca Hagiographica Latina Antiquae et Mediae Aetatis, Subsidia Hagiographica* 6, edd. Socii Bollandiani, Brussels 1898-1901 and 1911.
Bibl. Sanct.	*Bibliotheca Sanctorum*, Rome 1961-1970.
CBM	*Corpus der byzantinischen Miniaturenhandschriften*, ed. Otto Demus, Stuttgart 1977 ff.
CIG	*Corpus Inscriptionum Graecarum*, Berlin 1828-1877.
CIL	*Corpus Inscriptionum Latinarum*, Berlin 1863 ff.
Cohen	Henry Cohen, *Description historique des monnaies frappées sous l'empire romain*, 2nd ed., 8 vols., Paris 1880-1892; repr. Graz 1955.
Copt. Enc.	*The Coptic Encyclopedia*, ed. Aziz S. Atiya, New York 1991.
DACL	*Dictionnaire d'archéologie chrétienne et de liturgie*, edd. Fernand Cabrol and Henri Leclercq, Paris 1907 ff.
DDrC	*Dictionnaire de droit canonique*, Paris 1935-1965.
DHGE	*Dictionnaire d'histoire et de géographie ecclésiastique*, Paris 1912 ff.
ILCV [2]	*Inscriptiones Latinae Christianae Veteres*, ed. Ernst Diehl 1925 ff.; 2nd ed. Jacques Moreau, Berlin 1961.
ILS	*Inscriptiones Latinae Selectae*, ed. Hermann Dessau, Berlin 1892-1916; repr. Berlin 1962.

LCI   *Lexikon der christlichen Ikonographie,* edd. Engelbert Kirschbaum and Wolfgang Braunfels, Freiburg 1968-1976.

Literatur-   *Literaturlexikon: Autoren und Werke deutscher Sprache,*
lexikon   ed. Walther Killy, Gütersloh and Munich 1988 ff.

LTHK [2]   *Lexikon für Theologie und Kirche,* 2nd ed., Freiburg 1957 ff.

Manitius   Max Manitius, *Geschichte der lateinischen Literatur des Mittelalters, Handbuch der Altertumswissenschaft* IX.2.1-3, Munich 1911-1931.

NCE   *New Catholic Encyclopedia,* New York 1967-1979.

ODB   *The Oxford Dictionary of Byzantium,* ed. Alexander P. Kazhdan, Oxford 1991.

Platner-Ashby Samuel Ball Platner and Thomas Ashby, *A Topographical Dictionary of Ancient Rome,* London 1929.

PLRE   *The Prosopography of the Later Roman Empire,* edd. A. H. M. Jones, J. R. Martindale, and J. Morris, Cambridge 1971-1980.

RAC   *Reallexikon für Antike und Christentum,* edd. Theodor Klauser and Ernst Dassmann, Stuttgart 1941 ff.

RBK   *Reallexikon zur byzantinischen Kunst,* edd. Klaus Wessel and Marcell Restle, Stuttgart 1966 ff.

RE   Pauly-Wissowa, *Real-Encyclopädie der klassischen Altertumswissenschaft,* Stuttgart 1893 ff.

Réau,   Louis Réau, *Iconographie de l'art chrétien,* Paris
Iconographie 1955-1959.

RIC VI   *The Roman Imperial Coinage*, vol. VI: *From Diocletian's Reform (A.D. 294) to the Death of Maximinus (A.D. 313)*, by C. H. V. Sutherland, London 1967.

RIC VII   *The Roman Imperial Coinage*, vol. VII: *Constantine and Licinius, A.D. 313-337*, by Patrick M. Bruun, London 1966.

RIC VIII   *The Roman Imperial Coinage*, vol. VIII: *The Family of Constantine I, A.D. 337-364*, by J. P. C. Kent, London 1981.

Roscher,   Wilhelm Heinrich Roscher, *Ausführliches Lexikon der*
Lexikon   *griechischen und römischen Mythologie*, Leipzig 1884-1921; repr. Hildesheim 1965.

Thieme-   Ulrich Thieme and Felix Becker, *Allgemeines Lexikon*
Becker,   *der bildenden Künstler*, Leipzig 1907-1950.
Künstler-Lexikon

TRE   *Theologische Realenzyklopädie*, edd. Gerhard Krause and Gerhard Müller, Berlin 1976 ff.

Verfasser-   *Die deutsche Literatur des Mittelalters: Verfasser-*
lexikon[2]   *lexikon*, 2nd ed., ed. Kurt Ruh, Berlin 1977 ff.

IV. Ancient Authors

The standard abbreviations have been used in citing ancient authors.

Chapter I.
Introduction

It is the purpose of this book to provide accurate and in-depth information on the various aspects of the life and legacy of the Roman empress Helena, mother of the emperor Constantine I (306-337) and Christian saint. Such information will be of use, it is hoped, to students and scholars in a wide range of academic disciplines: Roman history, Byzantine history, ecclesiastical history, hagiography, liturgical studies, art history, medieval literature and history, modern English literature, folk lore, and women's studies.

It has been asserted that "in the history of Europe there is no more dramatic moment than the reign of Constantine."[1] That assertion is subject to challenge, of course, but the reign of Constantine certainly was an eventful and highly dramatic one. It is not surprising, therefore, that we have an abundance of books on the life and reign of Constantine. Much less had been written, until recently, on the lady Flavia Julia Helena, one of the most remarkable women in all of ancient history.[2] But it is clear from all accounts that she played an important role in the dynastic, ecclesiastical, and political affairs of the empire and that she dominated the court of her son, who outlived her by only eight years. She, as well as her son, must be counted among those personalities of Late Antiquity who laid the foundations of post-classical European civilization. We will welcome, therefore, the recent appearance of two very fine contributions to the subject: Stephan Borgehammar, *How the Holy Cross was Found: From Event to Medieval Legend*,[3] and Jan Willem Drijvers, *Helena Augusta: The Mother of Constantine the Great and the Legend of Her Finding of the True Cross.*[4]

These two studies do, I hope to show, leave room for a third effort. Borgehammar's book limits itself to an exhaustive examination

---

[1]Alistair Kee, *Constantine versus Christ* (London 1982) 1.

[2]There were earlier studies by Paul Lucot (1876), A.-M. Rouillon (1908), Remi Couzard (1911), Jules Maurice (1930), Karl L. Mackes (1956), Hans-Henning Lauer (1967), Josef Dietz (1972), and Richard Klein (1988). These showed a continuing interest in the subject, but did not by any means exhaust it, serving, as they did, different and more limited purposes. Richard Klein's article, in *RAC*, has been the most thorough of these studies.

[3]Uppsala University dissertation (Stockholm 1991).

[4]Leiden 1992. A revision and translation of the author's doctoral dissertation: *Helena Augusta: Waarheid en Legende* (Groningen 1989).

of one aspect of our subject, namely the *inventio* of the Holy Cross, and Drijvers devotes more than one half of his book to that same aspect. In my own study this aspect has received less emphasis, and the conclusions which I have reached differ from both those of Borgehammar and those of Drijvers. I have given, conversely, much attention to aspects which Borgehammar and Drijvers have chosen to examine only in passing or not at all, such as: Helena's special role in the traditions of the German Rhineland, of England, and of Constantinople; the development of her cult; the saga of her relics; and her place in religious literature and ecclesiastical art.

Helena was born in humble circumstances, but rose to the rank of Augusta; that in itself is remarkable. Moreover she appears to have been a woman of grace, beauty, intellect, and faith. Her conversion to Christianity, no less than her son's, was a historical event the importance of which can hardly be overrated. In the Christian tradition she was remembered for her piety, but there is need to explore other aspects of her life and personality as well. She was credited with having found the True Cross of Christ's passion, an achievement which most modern scholars assign to legend rather than to history. Medieval hagiography and art never tire of telling how she undertook a pilgrimage to the Holy Land, how she forced the Jew Judas to reveal to her the location of the True Cross, how she ordered it to be dug up, and how it was verified. And thus Saint Helena has tended to overshadow the empress Helena.

The evidence for the life of Helena is scattered over a wide range of sources, and some of it is not trustworthy; the legendary and the historical have to be separated. We have the lady's likeness on ancient coins and in ancient sculptures. She has given her name to several cities and islands and to an entire province, not to mention chapels and churches. She is the subject of a medieval *vita* and of a modern novel. This account must, and does, cover a span of more than 1600 years of history, religion, literature, and art.

Chapter II.
The Obscure Years

The Byzantine historian Procopius, in the course of describing the building activities of the emperor Justinian,[1] tells us that Helena was born in Helenopolis in Bithynia:

There is a certain city in Bithynia which is named after Helena, the mother of the emperor Constantine; for it is said that Helena hailed from this city, which previously was a village not worth mentioning. But Constantine, paying the debt for her nurture, bestowed on this place the name and rank of a city.

It is to be noted that Procopius modifies his statement by 'it is said,' thereby introducing an element of doubt. Other sources, both ancient and medieval,[2] report that this city is the former Drepanum[3] and that in 327 Constantine changed its name in honor of his mother; they do not specifically say that Helena was born there.

It is difficult, however, to think of any other reason that might have prompted Constantine to bestow such great honor on a place said to be quite insignificant otherwise, unless it were this: Jerome,[4] while reporting that Constantine changed the name of Drepanum to Helenopolis, also tells us that Constantine did so 'in honor of the martyr Lucian who is buried there.' It is difficult to see, however, how that change of name gave honor to the saint. Philostorgius[5] adds that Helena was fond of Drepanum because the body of Lucian the martyr was carried there

---

[1]*Aed* 5.2.1-2.

[2]Euseb.-Hieron. *Chron.* Olymp. 276 (ed. Fotheringham 313; ed. Helm[2] [*GCS* XLVII] 231). Socrates, *Hist. Eccl.* 1.17 and 1.18 (Migne, *PG*, LXVII 117 and 124; ed. Bright[2] 35 and 39). Sozomen, *Hist. Eccl.* 2.2.5 (Migne, *PG* LXVII 936; ed. Bidez-Hansen [*GCS* L] 51; ed. Bidez [*SC* CCCVI] 234-36). Cassiodorus, *Hist. Eccl. Trip.* 2.18.7 (Migne, *PL* LXIX 936; ed. Jacob-Hanslik [*CSEL* LXXI] 114). Philostorgius, *Hist. Eccl.* 2.12 (Migne, *PG* LXV 476; ed. Bidez-Winkelmann [*GCS* XXI] 24). Prosper Tiro, or Prosper of Aquitaine, *Epit. Chron.* 1023 (*MGH, AA* IX = *Chron. Min.* I 450). Johannes Malalas, *Chron.* 13.12 (Migne, *PG* XCVII 484; ed. Dindorf [*CSHB* VIII] 323), who, however, refers to Helenopolis as the former Souga in Bithynia. *Chronicon Paschale* Olymp. 276, ad annum 327 (Migne, *PG* XCII 708; ed. Dindorf [*CSHB* XVI] I 527). Bede, *Chron.* 423-24 (*MGH, AA* XIII = *Chron. Min.* III 296).

[3]Located on the Propontis in western Bithynia and not to be confused with like-named places in Sicily, the Peloponnese, and Crete; sometimes called Drepana, today Yalova.

[4]See n. 2 above.

[5]See n. 2 above.

by a dolphin. But why did Helena revere Lucian in the first place? A reasonable answer certainly would be that Helena was fond of Lucian because of his association with Drepanum, not vice versa, and that Drepanum was her place of birth.[6] Drepanum, in any event, has found wide acceptance as Helena's place of birth.[7] The late and highly

---

[6]Lucian was a presbyter at Antioch, who was martyred at Nicomedia in 312, a victim of the persecutions of Maximinus, and buried at Drepanum = Helenopolis; see Euseb. *Hist. Eccl.* 8.13.2 and 9.6.3 and Hieron. *De Vir Ill.* 77 (Migne, *PL* XXIII 685 [ed. 1845] or 723 [ed. 1865]; ed. Richardson [*TU* 14] 41-42; ed. Herding 49). His feast day is January 7 in the West and October 15 in the East. The story of the dolphin was told more fully in an early *vita* of the saint which was rewritten in the tenth century by the Byzantine hagiographer Simeon Metaphrastes (*BHG*[3] 997; Philostorgius, *Hist. Eccl.*, ed. Bidez-Winkelmann [*GCS* XXI] 184-201; Migne, *PG* CXIV 397-416; Latin translation only in *Acta Sanct.* Ian. I [ed. 1643] 359-62). See also Hippolyte Delehaye, *The Legends of the Saints* (New York 1962) 147-50.

The Vatican Library's manuscript of the Menologion of Basil II (Byzantine emperor 976-1025; text in Migne, *PG* CXVII) contains among its 430 illuminations one which shows on the left St. Lucian confined in a prison and on the right an executioner casting the body of the saint into the sea (Cod. Vat. Grec. 1613, p. 115; facsimile ed., Turin 1907, II 115). For a description of this MS see Cyrus Giannelli, *Codices Vaticani Graeci: Codices 1485-1683* (Vatican City 1950) 276-78, and Jacqueline Lafontaine-Dosogne, *Histoire del'art byzantin et chrétien d'Orient* (Louvain-La-Neuve 1987) 133. For the date of this MS, ca. 979-986, see Sirarpie Der Nersessian, "Remarks on the Date of the Menologium and Psalter Written for Basil II," *Byzantion* 15 (1940-1941) 104-25, esp. 111 and 115. For other illustrations and additional sources see *Bibl. Sanct.* VIII 262-65, *LCI* VII 420, and Timothy D. Barnes, *Constantine and Eusebius* (Cambridge, Massachusetts, 1981) 194.

On Lucian's (supposed) links to Arianism see *LThK*[2] VI (1961) 1211-12; also Glanville Downey, *A History of Antioch in Syria* (Princeton 1961) 337-42. Adolf von Harnack, *Lehrbuch der Dogmengeschichte,* 4th ed. (Tübingen 1909-1910) II 187, called Lucian "Arius vor Arius," while Ramsey MacMullen, *Constantine* (New York 1969) 224, called him 'the grandfather of Arianism.' Gustave Bardy, *Recherches sur Saint Lucien d'Antioche et son école* (Paris 1936), held that there were two Lucians. More recently Lucian's links to Arianism have been put into question:

David S. Wallace-Hadrill, *Christian Antioch* (Cambridge 1982) 81-84. Rowan D. Williams, *Arius: Heresy and Tradition* (London 1987) 162-67. R.P.C. Hanson, *The Search for the Christian Doctrine of God: The Arian Controversy 318-381* (Edinburgh 1988) 79-83. Hanns Christof Brennecke, "Lucian von Antiochien," in *TRE* XXI (1991) 474-79.

[7]Jules Maurice, *Numismatique Constantinienne* (Paris 1908-1912) I 89; id., *Sainte Hélène* (Paris 1930) 5. MacMullen, *Constantine* 190. *PLRE* I 410. Barnes, *Constantine and Eusebius* 3. Timothy D. Barnes, *The New Empire of Diocletian and Constantine* (Cambridge, Massachusetts, 1982) 36. Richard Klein, "Helena II (Kaiserin)," in *RAC* XIV (1988) 355-75 at 355. Procopius' report is, however, discounted and Helena's place of birth left open to question by some others: Karl L. Mackes, "Das Werden der (continued...)

unlikely claims of other cities in Asia and Europe will be discussed shortly.

It is apparent that Helena was of low social status. St. Ambrose[8] reports that she was a *stabularia,* a maid in a tavern or inn. He emphasizes that she was a good *stabularia.* Perhaps this is the ultimate source of the many tales which were once current among the people of Trier about Helena the good maid.[9] Nothing whatsoever is known about Helena's parents, although it is assumed by some that they owned or operated the inn in which their daughter was employed.

The date of Helena's birth can be reconstructed only from what we know about her death. Eusebius tells us that she was 80 years old at the time of her death;[10] this is confirmed by Sozomen (5th c.).[11] Neither author, unfortunately, gives us the year of her death. Since she is known to have undertaken her pilgrimage to the Holy Land after the deaths of Crispus and Fausta in 326 and to have died not too long after her return, i.e. in ca. 328-330, she must have been born in 250 or shortly before.[12]

[handwritten annotations: "ethnocentric thinking" but proposed other "his dates for her birth. (pg 11) It is possible (?) Const. met H. ... Drep. ... that a/h that she followed him on his military assignments.]

[11](...continued)
Helenalegende," in *Aus der Vor-, Früh-, und Siedlungsgeschichte der Stadt Viersen* (Viersen 1956) 182-202 at 182 and 189. Joseph Vogt *Constantin der Grosse und sein Jahrhundert,* 2nd ed. (Munich 1960) 140. Mika Kajava, "Some Remarks on the Name and Origin of Helena Augusta," *Arctos* 19 (1985) 41-54 at 49 and 54. Ingemar König, *Origo Constantini: Anonymus Valesianus, Teil 1: Text und Kommentar* (Trier 1987) 60. Drijvers, *op. cit.* 9-12. Hans-Henning Lauer, *Kaiserin Helena: Leben und Legenden* (Munich 1967) 8-9, prefers Drepanum but is reluctant to commit himself. A. H. M. Jones, *The cities of the Eastern Roman Provinces,* 2nd ed. (Oxford 1971) 164, is certainly wrong in stating that Constantine founded Helenopolis in A.D. 318.

[8]*De Obitu Theodosii* 42 (Migne, *PL* XVI 1399 [ed. 1845] or 1463 [ed.1866]; ed. Mannix 59; ed. Faller [*CSEL* LXXIII] 393).

[9]Hans-Henning Lauer, op. cit. 60-61. Josef Dietz, "St. Helena in der rheinischen Überlieferung," in *Festschrift Matthias Zender* (Bonn 1972) I 356-83 at 357-358.

[10]*Vita Const.* 3.46.1 (Migne, *PG* XX 1105; ed. Winkelmann [*GCS*] 103). On the *Vita Constantini* of Eusebius see the following: Andreas Alföldi, *The Conversion of Constantine and Pagan Rome* (Oxford 1948; 1969 impression) VII-VIII with bibliographical note. Friedhelm Winkelmann, "Zur Geschichte des Authentizätsproblems der Vita Constantini," *Klio* 40 (1962) 147-243. Barnes, *Constantine and Eusebius* 265-71 with n. 66.

[11]*Hist. Eccl.* 2.2.4 (Migne, *PG* LXVII 936; ed. Bidez-Hansen [*GCS* L] 51; ed. Bidez [*SC* CCCVI] 234).

[12]Fully discussed in chapters VIII and XI below.

Joseph Vogt has examined the relationship of Christianity to Judaism in the fourth century.[13] Was Helena perhaps of Jewish birth or background? Very cautiously Vogt says that "the meager sources do not exclude this possibility."[14] In this context it is of interest what the legend of St. Sylvester reports: Helena was on the verge of accepting the Jewish faith when she received word of her son's conversion to Christianity.[15] That, of course, implies that she was *not* Jewish by birth or background. It is not likely that this part of the legend would have arisen if Helena had been Jewish by birth or background.[16] Helena's long-lasting relationship with Constantius also argues strongly against her having been Jewish, given Constantius' rank and Roman attitudes towards Jews.

In the narthex of Cologne's Church of St. Gereon, which medieval tradition erroneously believed to have been founded by Helena,[17] there was once a wooden inscription which asserts that Helena was of Jewish birth. The text, in Latin hexameters, reads as follows:

REGIBUS EXEMPLUM SACROQUE CARISMATE PLENA
CONDIDIT HOC TEMPLUM S. GEREONIS HELENA
PAGANA NATA JUDAEA FIT INDE RENATA
INVENTRIX S. CRUCIS ALMO PNEUMATE FLANTE
SEPTUAGINTA DUO COLLEGIA FUNDAT AMOENA
DONANS PERPETUO THEBEIS MATER HELENA.[18]

---

[13]"Helena Augusta, das Kreuz und die Juden: Fragen um die Mutter Constantins des Grossen," *Saeculum* 27 (1976) 211-222.

[14]*Ibid.* 219. Rejected by Wolf Steidle, "Die Leichenrede des Ambrosius für Kaiser Theodosius und die Helena-Legende," *Vig. Chr.* 32 (1978) 94-112 at 100, n. 26; also by Kajava, *op. cit.* 50, Robin Lane Fox, *Pagans and Christians* (New York 1987) 775, n. 5, Richard Klein in *RAC* XIV 357, and Drijvers, *op. cit.* 36.

[15]Wilhelm Levison, *Aus rheinischer und fränkischer Frühzeit* (Düsseldorf 1948) 402.

[16]The legend of St. Sylvester will be considered at greater length in chapter III.

[17]See chapter V below.

[18] As an example to kings and full of holy grace, Helena founded this Church of St. Gereon. Born a pagan Jewess, then reborn, she became the finder of the Holy Cross, through the inspiration of the Holy Spirit. Seventy-two beautiful churches Mother Helena established, giving them forever to the Thebans. Franz Xaver Kraus, *Die christlichen Inschriften der Rheinlande* (Freiburg 1890-1894) II 265, no. 562, says that the inscription is of unknown date and no longer extant. Hugo Rahtgens, *Die Kunstdenkmäler der Stadt Köln* II.1 (Düsseldorf 1911) 40, dates the inscription to the 15th century and reports that it has been placed in the crypt of the church.

In the absence of any corroborating evidence we have no reason to believe that Helena was of Jewish birth or background, it seems to me. Of interest – and no credit to the anonymous author of the inscription – is also the statement that Helena established 72 churches. The number 72 has too many numerological associations to be of any historical value.[19]

In the ninth century the monk Altmann (or Almann; of Hautvillers, near Reims) wrote a *vita* of St. Helena.[20] He claims that Helena was a native of Trier: *oriunda Trevirensis*.[21] This claim was repeated in the early twelfth century by the author of the *Gesta Treverorum*,[22] who refers to Helena as *Trebirorum nobilissima*.[23] How little trust we may place in this assertion is indicated by the fact that the author, in the preceding sentence, reports that the emperor Constantius Chlorus was buried in Trier, confusing him with a certain *comes* Constantius, who died in 421.[24] Not much later it is said in the *Inventio S. Mathiae* – this *inventio* took place in 1127 – that Helena was *indigena civitatis Trevericae*.[25] The idea of Helena's being a native of Trier once enjoyed

---

[19]In Luke 10.1 Christ chooses 70 or 72 disciples (the manuscripts give both readings). And Eucherius, who was the first bishop of Trier, was said to have been one of them; see *Gesta Trev.* 14 (Migne, *PL* CLIV 1117; *MGH, Script.* VIII 145). The Septuagint is said by Jewish tradition to be the work of 72 translators.

[20]*BHL* 3772; see further chapter XVI below.

[21]1.9 (*Acta Sanct.* Aug. III [ed. 1867] 583).

[22]Manitius III 516-18. Heinz Thomas, *Studien zur Trierer Geschichtsschreibung des 11. Jahrhunderts, insbesondere zu den Gesta Treverorum* (Bonn 1968), esp. 139-52. Heinz Thomas, "Gesta Treverorum," in Verfasserlexikon² III (1981) 34-37.

[23]18 (Migne, *PL* CLIV 1133; ed. Georg Waitz [*MGH, Script.* VIII] 151).

[24]See the comments of Waitz ad locum.

[25]*BHL* 5697. *Acta Sanct.* Febr. III (ed. 1865) 441. *MGH, Script.* VIII 228.

considerable popularity in Trier,[26] but lacks all basis in fact and is now universally rejected or simply ignored.[27]

Constantius campaigned in Britain and died at York; there, too, Constantine was proclaimed Augustus by his troops. These historical associations could readily give rise to the tradition which will have us believe that Constantine and Helena both were natives of Britain. Furthermore, on the occasion of Constantine's marriage to Fausta in 307 a panegyrist referred to Constantius and Constantine, respectively, thus: *Liberavit ille Britannias servitute; tu etiam nobiles illic oriendo fecisti.*[28] We shall do well to be skeptical of the rhetorical flourishes and fulsome flatteries of the panegyrist, when much more sober evidence, to be considered shortly, tells us that Constantine was born at Naissus (Nish) in Moesia Superior. Furthermore, *oriendo* could reasonably be understood as a reference to Constantine's rise to power rather than to his birth. An enthusiastic but unconvincing defense of Constantine's and Helena's British birth was given by Cardinal Cesare Baronio (1538-1607) in his *Annales Ecclesiastici.*[29] Modern scholarship rightly rejects these claims.[30]

---

[26]Dietz, "St. Helena," 358. Thomas Grünewald, "'Constantinus Novus': Zum Constantin-Bild des Mittelalters," in Giorgio Bonamente and Franca Fusco, edd., *Costantino il Grande dall'antichità all'umanesimo* (Università degli studi di Macerata, *Publicazioni della facoltà di lettere e filosofia* 67; Macerata 1992) I 461-85 at 466-68. It was known also outside of Trier. In the middle of the 12th century Otto of Freising writes uncommittingly: *Hanc Helenam ex pago Treverorum oriundam dicunt. Chron.* 3.45 in ed. Wilmans (*MGH, Script.* XX) 190; 3.45 in ed. Hofmeister (*MGH, SRGS* XLV) 175; 3.43 in ed. Lammers 282.

[27]Johann Leonardy, *Geschichte des Trierischen Landes und Volkes,* 2nd ed. (Trier 1877) 204-205. Heinrich Volbert Sauerland, *Trierer Geschichtsquellen des XI. Jahrhunderts* (Trier 1889) 72. Theodor Konrad Kempf, "Das Haus der heiligen Helena," *Neues Trierisches Jahrbuch* 1978, Beiheft, 1-16 at 5, n. 11, holds that Altmann and other medieval sources failed to distinguish between Helena, the mother of Constantine, and Helena, the wife of Constantine's son Crispus, and that it is the latter who was a native of Trier.

[28]He freed Britain from servitude, but you enobled it by being born here *or* by rising to power here. *Pan. Lat.* 7.4.3 (edd. Baehrens, Mynors) or 6.4.3 (ed. Galletier).

[29]Ad annum 306, ed. Augsburg 1738, III 416-17. On Baronio, Vatican Librarian from 1597 to 1607, see Hubert Jedin, *Kardinal Caesar Baronius: Der Anfang der katholischen Kirchengeschichtsschreibung im 16. Jahrhundert* (Münster 1978).

[30]Leonardy, *op. cit.* 204. Christopher Bush Coleman, *Constantine the Great and Christianity* (New York 1914) 120. Gordon Home, *Roman York* (London 1924) 84-87. Winifred Joy Mulligan, "The British Constantine: An English Historical Myth," *JMRS* 8 (1978) 257-79 at 258. Charles Thomas, *Christianity in Roman Britain to AD 500*

(continued...)

The claims of Colchester, the ancient Camulodunum, require special attention. Between 1136 and 1139 Geoffrey – or Galfred – of Monmouth wrote his *Historia Regum Britanniae* or *Historia Britonum*, a collection of anecdotes and legends, especially Arthurian legends, rather than a history.[31] Here we find this remarkable statement:

Quo defuncto insigniuit se Constantius regni diademate duxitque filiam Coel cui nomen erat Helena. Pulcritudo eius provinciales puellas superabat nec uspiam adeo decora reperiebatur. Caruerat pater alia sobole que solio regni potiretur unde eam ita docere laboraverat ut regimen patrie post obitum suum facilius tractare quiuisset. Cum igitur illam in societate thori recepisset Constantius generavit ex ilia filium vocavitque Constantinum.[32]

In claiming that Helena was the daughter of the British king Coel ('Old King Cole' or 'Good King Cole' of the nursery rhymes) Geoffrey

---

[30](...continued)
(London 1981) 41. John Frederick Matthews, "Macsen, Maximus and Constantine," *The Welsh Historical Review* 11 (1983) 431-48 at 439 and 445. Grünewald, "Constantinus Novus," 466. W. Gurney Benham, "Legends of Coel and Helena," *JBAS*, N.S. 25 (1919) 229-44 at 241, does not succeed very well in his efforts to rescue at least part of the tradition.

[31]Gustav Gröber, *Übersicht über die lateinische Litteratur* (ed. Munich 1963?) 312-13. Edmond Faral, *La légende Arthurienne* (Paris 1929) II 10-28. Manitius III 475-79. Robert W. Hanning, *The Vision of History in Early Britain* (New York 1966) 121-72. Albert C. Baugh in Albert C. Baugh, ed., *A Literary History of England,* 2nd ed. (New York 1967) 160-70. Charles Sears Baldwin, *Three Medieval Centuries of Literature in England, 1100-1400* (New York 1968) 66-69. Antonio Gransden, *Historical Writing in England* I (Ithaca 1974) 200-10. Erich Köhler in Henning Krauss, ed., *Europäisches Hochmittelalter* (Wiesbaden 1981) 257; Joachim Ehlers *ibid.* 449. John Frederick Matthews, "Macsen, Maximus and Constantine" 439-40.

[32]Upon the death of Coel Constantius assumed the crown of his kingdom and married his daughter, who was named Helena. Her beauty outranked the local girls, and nowhere was any girl found as beautiful as she. Her father was without other offspring who might obtain the throne of the kingdom; hence he had endeavored to bring her up in such a way that after his death she might more easily manage the government of the country. Thus, when Constantius had received her in marriage, he begot by her a son and named him Constantine. 5.6 in ed. J. A. Giles (London 1844; repr. New York 1967) 82. 5.6 in ed. Acton Griscom (New York 1929) 338-39. 5.5, with variant text, in ed. Jacob Hammer (Cambridge, Massachusetts, 1951) 90. Cf. also 5.11 in ed. Giles 88, 5.11 in ed. Griscom 347, or 5.10 in ed. Hammer 95.

was neither the first nor alone,[33] and several later English historians followed in his steps.[34] The idea found acceptance even in the territory of Trier, although Trier, as we have seen, had its own traditions in this matter.[35]

Since Colchester was, supposedly, Coel's city, it followed readily enough that it should be the place of Helena's birth. And thus it is claimed in the city's 14th century chronicle,[36] in the legend of its earliest seal,[37] and in an illuminated initial **H** in a charter granted to the city by King Henry V in 1413.[38] The tradition has remained alive even into our own century,[39] and a 12-foot high bronze statue of Helena was put in place in 1902 as the crowning element of the tower of Colchester's new town hall.[40] The entire legend is, of course, without historical value.

London has a church named St. Helen's Bishopsgate, but this church cannot be shown to have existed, at the earliest, before the year

---

[33]Francis Bond, *Dedications and Patron Saints of English Churches* (Oxford 1914) 75. Benham, "Legends" 241. Josef Giesen, "Die HELENA DE BRITANIA des Meisters von St. Severin," *Jb. des Kölnischen Geschichtsvereins* 25 (1950) 145-52 at 148.

[34]Giesen, "HELENA" 149.

[35]Leonardy, *op. cit.* 204.

[36]Part of the town's 'Oath Book,' folio 20r (IIIr), for AD 242; MS in the Colchester Branch of the Essex Record Office. W. Gurney Benham, *The Oath Book or Red Parchment Book of Colchester* (Colchester 1907) 27. Benham, "Legends" 232-34. Giesen, "HELENA" 150. David Stephenson, *The Book of Colchester* (Chesham 1978) 37. I am indebted to Mr. P. R. J. Coverley, Branch Archivist, for his kind assistance.

[37]*Quam crux insignit Helenam Colcestria gignit.* Helena is seen holding a cross in her right hand and three nails in her left hand. A cast of the seal is on display in Colchester's Castle Museum. Benham, *Oath Book,* title p. and 227. Benham, "Legends" 229-230, dates this seal to ca. 1189-1200. Giesen, "HELENA" 150 and ill. following p. 146. Stephenson, *op. cit.* 34. In another seal of Colchester, dating from ca. 1413, Helena is also seen holding a large cross and three nails: Benham, "Legends" 231. Giesen, "HELENA" 150 and ill. following p. 146. Stephenson, *op. cit.* 11. Charles Kightly, *Folk Heroes of Britain* (London 1982) 64.

[38]*Sancta Elena - nata fuit in Colcestria - mater Constantini fuit - et sanctam crucem invenit - Elena.* The charter is kept in Colchester's Castle Museum. *Colchester: The Charters and Letters Patent Granted to the Borough by Richard I and Succeeding Sovereigns* (Colchester 1904), Introductory. Benham, "Legends" 230-231. Giesen "HELENA" 150. Stephenson, *op. cit.* 34 and 51. Kightly, *op. cit.* 72, ill. 16. Geoffrey Ashe, *Mythology of the British Isles* (London 1990), ill. 80.

[39]Giesen, "HELENA" 150-152.

[40]Geoffrey Howard Martin, *The Story of Colchester* (Colchester 1959) 107. Stephenson, *op. cit.* 34 and 124.

1010.[41] There are all together 135 churches and chapels of St. Helena in England, 34 in Yorkshire alone.[42] They testify to the popularity of her cult; they do not lend historicity to the claims of legend. We shall return to the subject in chapter VI.

The tradition of Helena's being a native of Trier and the tradition of her being a native of Britain have one thing in common: far from being the *stabularia* of which St. Ambrose reports, Helena has now become a lady of nobility. One must assume that her humble background was felt to be an embarrassment.

Some English chroniclers, as we have seen, maintained that Helena was born in their province of the empire. Some Arab authors, engaging in similarly ethnocentric thinking, put Helena's birthplace in the far eastern regions of the empire or even beyond its borders. In the tenth century the Arab author Hamza ibn al-Hasan (Hamza al-Isfahani)[43] tells us that Helena was brought from Edessa (Syrian Edessa, named after Macedonian Edessa; now the Turkish city of Urfa) as a captive by Constantius. Perhaps he confused Helena, the first century queen of Adiabene, with Helena, the mother of Constantine.[44] He also says that Constantine professed the Christian faith in the first year of his reign and that Helena undertook her pilgrimage in the seventh year of his reign. Thus he hardly inspires confidence.[45] That Helena was a native of Edessa can be read also in the writings of the historian al-Mas'udi, a contemporary of Hamza al-Isfahani.[46] A third Arabic author of the

[41]Wilberforce Jenkinson, *London Churches before the Great Fire* (London 1917) 105-10. Royal Commission on Historical Monuments, England, *An Inventory of the Historical Monuments in London IV: The City* (London 1929) 19-24. Elizabeth and Wayland Young, *Old London Churches* (London 1956) 87-89. Malcolm and Esther Quantrill, *Monuments of Another Age: The City of London Churches* (London 1975) 34-35. Mervyn Blatch, *A Guide to London's Churches* (London 1978) 78-84.

[42]Bond, *Dedications* 72 and 75. A slightly different set of figures is given by Frances Arnold-Forster, *Studies in Church Dedications* (London 1899) III 16. See also *ibid.* I 181-89.

[43]*Annales* 2.4 (Arabic text and Latin trans. J. M. E. Gottwaldt [St. Petersburg and Leipzig 1844-1848] I 73 and II 55). Mackes, *op. cit.* 189. Hans-Henning Lauer, *op. cit.* 9.

[44]J. B. Segal, *Edessa: 'The Blessed City'* (Oxford 1970) 41, 51, and 68.

[45]He receives high praise, however, from Franz Rosenthal in *The Encyclopedia of Islam* III^2 (Leiden 1978) 156; see *ibid.* for further literature.

[46]D. M. Dunlop, *Arab Civilization to A.D. 1500* (London, New York, and Beirut 1971) 99-114, especially 107. The pertinent passage from the *Tanbih* (Admonition) can be found in a French translation in Bernard Carra de Vaux, *Le Livre de l'avertissement*

(continued...)

same century, known in Greek as Eutychius of Alexandria and in Arabic as Sa'id ibn Batriq,[47] claims to know that Helena was a native of Caphar Phacar in Roha (Edessa) and was already a Christian when she met Constantius.[48]

In the course of recording Constantine's parentage, a number of authors, from Jerome to Bede,[49] tell us that Helena was Constantius' concubine. Zosimus (ca. 500), who is consistently hostile to Constantine, does not use the word 'concubine,' but says that Helena was "not respectable and not legally married to the emperor Constantius."[50] Aurelius Victor, Socrates, and Sozomen simply report that Helena was

---

[46](...continued)
et de la revision (Paris 1896) 198. I owe the references to the kindness of Professor Karl K. Barbir.

[47]877-940; elected patriarch of Alexandria in 933. He wrote in Arabic a history of the world from the creation to the year 937. The Arabic text, under the Latin title *Annales,* edited by L. Cheikho, is available in *CSCO* L-LI = *Scriptores Arabici* VI-VII. A translation into Latin by Edward Pocock (Oxford 1658) was reprinted in Migne, *PG* CXI 907-1156. See Georg Graf, *Geschichte der christlichen arabischen Literatur* (Vatican City 1944-1953) II 32-38.

[48]The pertinent passage, *CSCO* L = *Script. Arab.* VI 117-18 or Migne, *PG* CXI 999, has this to say: When he (Constantius) had come to parts of Mesopotamia and Roha and had stopped in a certain city of Roha, called Caphar Phacar (the potters' quarter), he saw there a very beautiful woman, named Helena. She had been converted to the Christian faith by Barsicas, the bishop of Roha, and she had learned to read. Constantius obtained her from her father and made her his wife, and she became pregnant by him. Then, when Constantius had returned to Byzantium, Helena gave birth to a beautiful, gentle, and intelligent son, Constantine, who was educated in Roha and learned the wisdom of the Greeks.

Roha, or better al-Ruha, is the Arabic name for Edessa; see Segal, *op. cit.* 255 with n. 2. I have not been able to locate Caphar Phacar (or Kafr Fakhar). Mackes, *op. cit.* 189, and Hans-Henning Lauer, *op. cit.* 9, simply refer to "Caphar Phacar in Mesopotamia."

[49]Euseb.-Hieron. *Chron.* Olymp. 271 (ed. Fotheringham 310; ed. Helm² [*GCS* XLVII] 228). Repeated in Prosper Tiro 976 (*MGH, AA* IX = *Chron. Min.* I 447). Orosius 7.25.16 (Migne, *PL* XXXI 1128; ed. Zangemeister [*CSEL* V] 493). *Chronica Gallica Anni DXI* 445 (*MGH, AA* IX = *Chron. Min.* I 643). Cassiodorus, *Chron.* 1035 (Migne, *PL* LXX 1239; *MGH, AA* XI = *Chron. Min.* II 150). *Chronicon Paschale* Olymp. 271, sub anno 304 (ed. Dindorf I [*CSHB* XVI] 517). Aldhelm, *De Virginitate* (prose version) 48 (Migne, *PL* LXXXIX 148; ed. Ehwald [*MGH, AA* XV] 302). Bede, *Hist.* 1.8. Bede, *Chron.* 411 (*MGH, AA* XIII = *Chron. Min.* III 295). Also additamentum II, s.v. Galerius (ibid. 337).

[50]2.8.2; similarly 2.9.2.

Constantine's mother, but do not specify her legal or social status.[51] Eutropius says that Constantine hailed *ex obscuriore matrimonio*.[52] The fourth century account known as the *Anonymus Valesianus* or the *Origo Constantini Imperatoris* refers to Helena as Constantius' wife *(uxor)*, but adds immediately that she was a very low *(vilissima)* woman.[53] Other passages, namely in Jerome[54] and Aurelius Victor,[55] and two inscriptions,[56] would indicate that Helena and Constantius were joined in a legitimate marriage. It is to be noted that Jerome, in the two passages cited, contradicts himself. When taken together these sources leave no doubt about Helena's lower-class background, especially when St. Ambrose's statement, considered above, is added. The legal status of Helena's and Constantius' relationship, on the other hand, remains subject to question, and later Byzantine authors are of little help on this point.[57]

Most modern scholars do not think that Helena was legally married to Constantius. Otto Seeck thinks that references to Helena as Constantius' wife are mere flattery.[58] Hans-Henning Lauer simply speaks of concubinage,[59] and Thomas Grünewald of Constantine's il-

[51] Aur. Vic. *Epit.* 41.2; Socrates, *Hist. Eccl.* 1.17 and 1.18 (Migne, *PG* LXVII 117 and 124; ed. Bright² 35 and 39). Soz. *Hist. Eccl.* 2.1.2 and 2.2.1 (Migne, *PG* LXVII 929 and 933; ed. Bidez-Hansen [*GCS* L] 47 and 50; ed. Bidez [*SC* CCCVI] 226 and 232-34).

[52] 10.2.2. (ed. Droysen [*MGH, AA* II] 170; ed. Santini 65). Repeated in Landolfus Sagax 170 (*MGH, AA* II 322).

[53] *Anon. Val.* 1.1-2.2 (ed. Mommsen [*MGH, AA* IX = *Chron. Min.* I] 7; ed. Moreau-Velkov 1; ed. König [Trier 1987] 34).

[54] Euseb-Hieron. *Chron.* Olymp. 267 (ed. Fotheringham 308; ed. Helm² [*GCS* XLVII] 225-26). Similarly Prosper Tiro 942 (*MGH, AA* IX = *Chron. Min.* I 445).

[55] *Caes.* 39.25; *Epit.* 39.2.

[56] *CIL* X 517 = *ILS* 708, and *CIL* X 1483.

[57] Some of these refer to the circumstances of Constantine's birth in unflattering terms indeed; see Alexander P. Kazhdan, "Constantin imaginaire," *Byzantion* 57 (1987) 196-250 at 213 and 214. The twelfth century chronicler Zonaras in one passage, *Ann.* 13.1 (Migne, *PG* CXXXIV 1097; ed. Dindorf III 172), acknowledges that his sources give divided testimony on this point; but in two other passages, *Ann.* 12.31 and 12.33 (Migne, *PG* CXXXIV 1084 and 1092; ed. Dindorf III 160 and III 167), he ignores the problem by simply calling Helena Constantius' wife.

[58] *RE* IV.1 (1900) 1041 and *RE* VII.2 (1912) 2821. Cf. also *Geschichte des Untergangs der antiken Welt* I⁴ (Stuttgart 1921) 47.

[59] *Op. cit.* 11.

legitimate birth.[60] Maurice, Vogt, and Karl Baus point out that a legally recognized marriage between Helena and Constantius was precluded by law.[61] In 336 Constantine instituted a law which prevented the children born to a *vir perfectissimus,* such as a *tribunus,* and a lower-class woman, such as a *stabularia,* from inheriting their father's property.[62] Such unions, therefore, must have been invalid in the eyes of the law, even before that date. Eugen Ewig deems it not a coincidence that Gregory of Tours, the Frankish chronicler 'Fredegar,' and Isidore of Seville say nothing about Helena's early years.[63] Ingemar König believes that Constantinian propaganda tried to cover up Constantine's illegitimate birth.[64] Drijvers thinks that *uxor,* when applied to Helena, has the same meaning as *concubina.*[65] But Barnes proposes a different solution: Constantius must have married Helena before he attained the rank of *tribunus.*[66] The problem of Helena's legal status is thus linked to the question of when she met Constantius and when she gave birth to Constantine.

My own judgment is that the relationship between Helena and Constantius was not that of legitimate marriage. It is unlikely that reports of an illegitimate relationship would have arisen without some basis in fact. On the other hand it is much likelier that such a relationship would be covered up by those who deemed it an embarrassment.

No ancient source, unfortunately, tells us when and where Constantius took up his relationship with Helena. Writing in the 14th century but drawing on earlier hagiographic material, the Byzantine author Nikephoros Kallistos Xanthopoulos[67] describes at length how

[60]Grünewald, "Constantinus Novus" 466.

[61]Maurice, *Numismatique Constantinienne* I 89, n. 3; *Sainte Hélène* 6. Vogt, *Constantin der Grosse*[2] 102 and 140-41; "Helena Augusta" 211, with less assurance: "perhaps concubinage." Baus, *Handbuch der Kirchengeschichte,* ed. Hubert Jedin, I (Freiburg 1962) 455.

[62]*Cod. Theod.* 4.6.3 (ed. Mommsen-Meyer I.2 176).

[63]"Das Bild Constantins des Grossen im abendländischen Mittelalter," *Hist. Jb. der Goerres-Gesellschaft* 75 (1955) 1-46 at 23. So also Richard Klein in *RAC* XIV 359.

[64]*Origo Constantini* 61. In the next generation Constantine's relationship with Minervina was to provide an interesting parallel; see Hans A. Pohlsander, "Crispus: Brilliant Career and Tragic End," *Historia* 33 (1984) 79-106 at 80.

[65]*Op. cit.* 17-19.

[66]*New Empire* 36.

[67]Karl Krumbacher, *Geschichte der byzantinischen Litteratur,* 2nd ed. (Munich 1897) I 291-93. Hans-Georg Beck, *Kirche und theologische Literatur im byzantinischen Reich* (Munich 1959) 705-706. Kazhdan, "Constantin imaginaire," 201-203 and 212-15.

Constantius met Helena at Drepanum in her father's inn, begot the future emperor Constantine, and some time later summoned Helena and Constantine to Rome.[68] The whole account is quite absurd and was refuted already by Baronio.[69]

That Constantius and Helena first met at Drepanum remains a possibility – but no more than that –, simply because most people in antiquity did not move far from their places of birth. After their first meeting, wherever and whenever that may have been, Helena must have accompanied Constantius on his military assignments, for she gave birth to Constantine at Naissus in Moesia Superior.[70]

It is ironic that reliable evidence should provide us with the month and day of Constantine's birth, namely February 27, but deny us the year. Literary sources furnish us an approximate age at the time of death.[71] The discussion must begin with Eusebius. In his *Vita Constantini* Eusebius saw fit to make some comparisons – quite unfair to Alexander – between Alexander the Great and Constantine.[72] At the beginning of the next chapter he states 1. that Constantine began his reign at that point in life at which Alexander died; 2. that Constantine lived twice as long as Alexander; and 3. that Constantine reigned three times as long as Alexander.

According to the first of these statements Constantine would have been born in 273 or 274 (since Alexander died at the age of 33, or almost 33, and Constantine's reign began in 306). According to the second statement Constantine would have been born between 271 and 273 (337 - 66 = 271; 337 - 64 = 273). The third of Eusebius' statements is demonstrably false: Alexander reigned for 13 years, or just short of that number. But Constantine reigned for 30 years and 10 months – from July 25, 306, to May 22, 337 –, not for 39 or even 36 years. It is quite clear that Eusebius is interested in rhetorical effect and that his data are only approximate. In another passage of the *vita* he tells us, again quite inaccurately, that Constantine reigned for 32 years, minus

---

[68]*Hist. Eccl.* 7.18 (Migne, *PG* CXLV 1241-44).

[69]*Op. cit.* III 415-19. In maintaining that Constantine and Helena were natives of Britain, as we have seen above, Baronio is, of course, substituting one error for another.

[70]*Anon. Val.* 2.2 (ed. Mommsen [*MGH, AA* IX = *Chron. Min.* I] 7; ed. Moreau-Velkov 1; ed. Konig [Trier 1987] 34). Firmicus Maternus, *Math.* 1.10.13 (ed. Kroll-Skutsch-Ziegler I 38). Seeck, *RE* VII.2 (1912) 2821. *PLRE* I 223. Barnes, *New Empire* 39.

[71]*CIL* I², pp. 255, 258, and 259.

[72]1.7 (Migne, *PG* XX 917-20; ed. Winkelmann [*GCS*] 18).

some months and days, and lived twice that long; this, again, would place his birth in 273 (337 - 64 = 273).[73]

Other ancient sources are more precise but at variance one with another; they assign to Constantine a life span of 60, 62, 63, ca. 64, or 65 years and thus place his birth between 272 and 277.[74] Again we are denied a specific year and must be content with a range of years; this range agrees roughly with the data provided by Eusebius. The many scholars who, on very weak evidence, have placed Constantine's birth in the 280's are refuted by Barnes and rightly so.[75] Nothing that we know about the circumstances of Constantine's birth, it would seem, allows any conclusions about the legal status of Helena's and Constantius' relationship.

On March 1, 293, Constantius was appointed to the rank of Caesar.[76] Several ancient sources record that *on this occasion* Constantius was required to divorce Helena and marry Theodora, the stepdaughter (or daughter) of Maximian. In Eutropius we can read:

> Diocletianus Maximianum Herculium ex Caesare fecit Augustum, Constantium et Maximianum Caesares,.... Atque ut eos etiam adfinitate coniungeret, Constantius privignam Herculi Theodoram accepit,..., Galerius filiam Diocletiani Valeriam, ambo uxores quas habuerant repudiate compulsi.[77]

Also, Jerome reports:

> Constantius et Galerius Maximianus Caesares adsumuntur in regnum ... atque, ut eos Diocletianus etiam adfinitate coniungeret, Constantius privignam Herculii Theodoram accepit,..., Galerius filiam Diocle-

---

[73]4.53 (Migne, *PG* XX 1204; ed. Winkelmann [*GCS*] 142).

[74]Barnes, *New Empire* 40.

[75]*New Empire* 40-42. Barnes' list of errant scholars, while by no means complete, includes such well-known names as Otto Seeck and Joseph Vogt. The latter's "Streitfragen um Konstantin den Grossen," *Röm. Mitt.* 58 (1943) 190-203, at 190-195 should be noted. Barnes' calculations are accepted by Drijvers, *op. cit.* 13-15.

[76]Seeck in *RE* IV.1 (1900) 1041; also *Geschichte* I[4] 31. *PLRE* I 228. Barnes, *New Empire* 4.

[77]Diocletian promoted Maximian Herculius from Caesar to Augustus and appointed Constantius and (Galerius) Maximianus Caesars, ... And in order that he might tie them to himself also by the bonds of family, Constantius received in marriage Theodora, the stepdaughter of Herculius, and Galerius received in marriage Valeria, the daughter of Diocletian; both men were compelled to dismiss the wives whom they already had. 9.22.1 (ed. Droysen [*MGH, AA* II] 162-64; ed. Santini 62).

tioni Valeriam, ambo uxores quas habuerant repudiare compulsi.[78]
Aurelius Victor makes an interesting comparison:

Prior [Constantius] Herculi privignam, alter [Galerius] Diocletiano editam sortiuntur diremptis prioribus coniugiis, ut in Nerone Tiberio ac Iulia filia Augustus quondam fecerat.[79]

Yet another source, the so-called *Anonymus Valesianus,* has this to say:

Iste [Constantius] cum Galerio a Diocletiano Caesar factus est. Relicta enim Helena priore uxore, filiam Maximiani Theodoram duxit uxorem.[80]

The *enim* of this passage strongly suggests that Constantius' marriage to Theodora was a precondition of his appointment to the rank of Caesar. And would we not expect to read *duxerat* rather than *duxit* if that marriage had taken place several years earlier?

On the other hand a panegyric addressed to Maximian offers this passage:

Tu quidem certe, imperator, tantum esse in concordia bonum statuis ut etiam eos qui circa te potissimo funguntur officio necessitudine tibi et affinitate devinxeris, id pulcherrimum arbitratus adhaerere lateri tuo non timoris obsequia, sed vota pietatis.[81]

---

[78]Constantius and Galerius Maximianus were appointed to rule as Caesars ... and, in order that Diocletian might join them to himself even by the bonds of family, Constantius received in marriage Theodora, the stepdaughter of Herculius, ... and Galerius received in marriage Valeria, the daughter of Diocletian; both men were compelled to dismiss the wives whom they already had. Euseb.-Hieron. *Chron.* Olymp. 267 (ed. Fotheringham 307-308; ed. Helm [*GCS* XLVIII] 225-26). A similar reading is found in Prosper Tiro, *Epit. Chron.* 942 (*MGH, AA* IX = *Chron. Min.* I 445).

[79]Before this one man (Constantius) received the daughter of Herculius and the other man (Galerius) the daughter of Diocletian, while their earlier wives had been taken from them, just as Augustus had once done in the case of Nero Tiberius and his daughter Julia. *Caes.* 39.25. The *Epitome,* 39.2., is less specific.

[80]He (Constantius), together with Galerius, was appointed Caesar by Diocletian. For, having given up Helena, his previous wife, he married Theodora, the daughter of Maximian. *Anon. Val.* 1.1 (ed. Mommsen [*MGH, AA* IX = *Chron. Min.* 1] 7; ed. Moreau-Velkov 1; ed. König [Trier 1987] 34).

[81]You, emperor, indeed value harmony so highly that you have tied to yourself by family relationships even those who fill the highest offices around you; for you deem this the greatest blessing that loyal devotion rather than obedience born of fear be offered to you. *Pan. Lat.* 10.11.4 (edd. Baehrens, Mynors) or 2.11.4 (ed. Galletier).

This panegyric can be dated to April 21, 289;[82] and numerous scholars have interpreted it as a reference to Constantius and have assumed that he was married to Theodora already by that date,[83] while a few have held otherwise.[84] The latter are, I believe, correct. The passage in the panegyric admits another interpretation.[85] The testimony of the other sources cited is straightforward and not rendered invalid by Jerome's evident use of Eutropius. Furthermore, an alternate date for Galerius' marriage to Valeria will also have to be found if 293 is abandoned as the date of Constantius' marriage to Theodora.

We do not know where or under what circumstances Helena lived after her separation from Constantius.[86] Nothing at all suggests that their paths ever crossed again. And we can only guess at the hurt which Helena must have suffered.

[82]*Pan. Lat.*, ed. Galletier I 7-9 and 21.

[83]Seeck, *RE* IV.1 (1901) 1041; *Geschichte* I⁴ 29. Vogt, *Constantin der Grosse*² 102 and 141. Hans-Henning Lauer, *op. cit.* 15. Ingemar König, "Die Berufung des Constantius Chlorus und des Galerius zu Caesaren," *Chiron* 4 (1974) 567-76 at 574. Vogt, "Helena Augusta," 211. Barnes, *New Empire* 37 and 125-26. Stephen Williams, *Diocletian and the Roman Recovery* (New York 1985) 64. König, *Origo Constantini* 62. Alexander Demandt, *Die Spätantike: Römische Geschichte von Diocletian bis Justinian, 284-565 n. Chr.* (Munich 1989) 48. Drijvers, op. cit. 19 and 21.

[84]Maurice, *Sainte Helene* 6. *PLRE* I 228. That Constantius should have married Theodora at the earlier time is a mere possibility to Frank Kolb, *Diocletian und die Erste Tetrarchie* (Berlin 1987) 68, n. 181, and 70.

[85]*PLRE* I 407-408 suggests that it may refer to the marriage of Maximilian to Eutropia, the future mother of Maxentius and Fausta.

[86]I see no justification at all for the statement made by Ludwig Voelkl, *Der Kaiser Konstantin* (Munich 1957) 17, that Helena was tolerated at the court but deprived of all rights and honors.

Chapter III.
A Position of Honor
and Religious Conversion

We do not know in what year or at what age Constantine was separated from his mother. It is possible that they did not see each other between 293 and 306. But it is clear that there existed between mother and son strong bonds of affection which survived the separation. Constantine's filial devotion was much praised by Eusebius and has been noted also by modern authors.[1]

After the death of Constantius, and only then, Helena emerged from the obscurity to which a cruel fate had subjected her and attained a position of honor by the side of her son. It is, however, highly unlikely that she joined him while he was still in Britain. In spite of a multitude of legends which associate her with various sites in Britain, there is no evidence that she ever set foot on British soil. Constantine was proclaimed Augustus by his troops on July 25, 306, and before the end of the year he was already in Trier.[2] It is not likely that Helena could have left her place of exile, wherever that may have been, and traveled safely before Constantine's position had been recognized by Galerius and a measure of stability had been established. That Helena was at Constantine's court in Trier cannot be doubted, but when she joined him there we do not know.[3] Helena's residence in Trier will be the subject of another chapter.

When Constantine came to power in 306 he was already a seasoned soldier. Helena, on the other hand, cannot have had much understanding of the affairs of the empire, given her humble background and the years of seclusion. It is not to be supposed, therefore, that Constantine depended on her; she was not an Agrippina, and he was not a Nero. Nevertheless, his devotion to her must have allowed her to

---

[1]Euseb. *Vita Const.* 3.47.2 (Migne, *PG* XX 1108; ed. Winkelmann [*GCS*] 103); Seeck, *Geschichte* I 48; Henri Leclercq, "Hélène, impératrice," in *DACL* VI.2 (1925) 2126-46 at 2127; Franziskus Maria Stratmann, *Die Heiligen und der Staat* (Frankfurt 1949-1958) II 149 and 153; Joseph Vogt, "Heiden und Christen in der Familie Constantins des Grossen," in *Eranion: Festschrift fur Hildebrecht Hommel* (Tübingen 1961) 149-68 at 155 and 158; Hans-Henning Lauer, *op. cit.* 20-21. MacMullen, *Constantine* 216.

[2]Barnes, *New Empire* 68-69.

[3]Drijvers, *op. cit.* 30, questions whether Helena ever lived in Trier at all. But where then would she have lived from 306 to 312 or later?

wield some influence, especially in family affairs. Vogt has called her 'the dominating figure in Constantine's house.'[4] But when Julian the Apostate referred to Helena as the 'wicked stepmother' of his own father Julius Constantius, who was the son of Constantius and Theodora and thus Constantine's half-brother, he surely was not an unbiased judge.[5]

The careers of two nephews of Constantine, Dalmatius and Hannibalianus, may be of interest in this regard. These two brothers were the sons of the elder Dalmatius, who was also Constantine's half-brother. Both were kept away from the imperial court and out of public life. MacMullen has suggested that this was due to 'the jealous affection of Helena' (for her own grandsons).[6] In 335, five or more years after Helena's death, these two young men were at last given recognition. Dalmatius was appointed Caesar, while Hannibalianus was married to Constantina, Constantine's daughter, and made *rex regum et Ponticarum gentium*.[7] The timing of these events does not support MacMullen's suggestion, unless we wish to assume that Constantine respected his mother's wishes long after her death. The public career of the elder Dalmatius, it may be noted, began long before Helena's death, either in 321 or in 324.[8] Should Helena not have been jealous of the father as well as of the sons?

Until the year 324 Helena and also Constantine's wife Fausta carried the title *nobilissima femina*.[9] The rank of *nobilissimus* was reserved for the most immediate members of the emperor's family.[10]

Constantine heaped great honors on his mother especially during the last few years of her life, when she was in her seventies. He granted

---

[4]*Constantin der Grosse*[2] 248; similarly "Heiden und Christen" 158 and 164. See also Richard Klein in *RAC* XIV 361, Drijvers, *op. cit.* 43, and Rudolf Leeb, *Konstantin und Christus* (Berlin 1992) 162.

[5]Libanius, *Orat.* 14.30. W. H. C. Frend, *The Rise of Christianity* (Philadelphia 1984) 595.

[6]*Constantine* 218.

[7]Vogt, "Heiden und Christen" 164; Patrick M. Bruun in *RIC* VII 26; *PLRE* I 241 and 407; J. P. C. Kent and K. S. Painter, edd., *Wealth of the Roman World: Gold and Silver AD 300-700* (London 1977) 166, introduction and n. 395.

[8]*Cod. Theod.* 12.17.1 (ed. Mommsen-Meyer I.2 732). *PLRE* I 241.

[9]Seeck, *RE* VII.2 (1912) 2821; Maurice, *Numismatique Constantinienne* I 89-91; Patrick M. Bruun in *RIC* VII 26.

[10]Dessau ad *ILS* 666 and 667; Maria R. Alföldi, "Helena nobilissima femina," *JbNum.* 10 (1959/60) 79-90 at 80-81.

to her, as well as to Fausta, the title *Augusta*.[11] This was not too long after the defeat of Licinius.[12] It has been suggested that it was specifically on November 8 of 324,[13] the same day on which Constantius II was appointed Caesar.[14] But it has also been argued that it was not until 325.[15] The honor itself, it seems to me, is more significant than the specific date. From 325 on Constantine no longer wore a laurel wreath but a diadem.[16] From that year on Helena and Fausta, too, seem to have worn a diadem, although the evidence is not entirely clear.[17]

Constantine even granted to his mother the right to dispense funds from the imperial treasury.[18] This enabled her to dispense charity and to sponsor the construction of churches. We have already seen that Drepanum in Bithynia was renamed Helenopolis by Constantine in honor of his mother. There was a second Helenopolis in Palestine.[19] Con-

[11]Euseb. *Vita Const.* 3.47 (Migne, *PG* XX 1108; ed. Winkelmann [*GCS*] 103). Sozomen, *Hist. Eccl.* 2.2.4 (Migne, *PG* LXVII 936; ed. Bidez-Hansen [*GCS* L] 51; ed. Bidez [*SC* CCCVI] 234). *RIC* VII, index of obverse legends. *CIL* VI 1134 = *ILS* 709, VI 1135, VIII 1633, X 517 = *ILS* 708, and X 1483-84.

[12]Vogt, *Constantin der Grosse*[2] 249; MacMullen, *Constantine* 218; Barnes, *New Empire* 9. Helene Homeyer, in *LThK*[2] V (1960) 208, states erroneously that Helena attained the rank of Augusta when Constantine came to power in 306.

[13]Patrick M. Bruun, *RIC* VII 26 and 77. Rejected by Drijvers, *op. cit.* 41, n. 10.

[14]Seeck, *Regesten der Kaiser und Päpste* (Stuttgart 1919) 174; *PLRE* I 226; Barnes, *New Empire* 85.

[15]*PLRE* I 410.

[16]Maurice, *Numismatique Constantinienne* I 97; Seeck, *Geschichte* I 72 and 439; Richard Delbrueck, *Spätantike Kaiserporträts* (Berlin 1933) 54-55 and 58; Andreas Alföldi, *Die monarchische Repräsentation im römischen Kaiserreiche* (Darmstadt 1970) 3 and 138.

[17]Maurice, *Numismatique Constantinienne* I 90; Seeck, *RE* VII.2 (1912) 2821; Delbrueck, *Spätantike Kaiserporträts* 63. Vogt, "Heiden und Christen," 158; Dietz, "St. Helena," 356. But Maria R. Alföldi, *Die constantinische Goldprägung* (Mainz 1963) 144f., contends that the supposed diadem of Helena and Fausta is only part of the coiffure and not a sign of rank or status.

[18]Euseb. *Vita Const.* 3.47.3 (Migne, *PG* XX 1108; ed. Winkelmann [*GCS*] 103); Sozomen, *Hist. Eccl.* 2.2.4 (Migne, *PG* LXVII 936; ed. Bidez-Hansen [*GCS* L] 51; ed. Bidez [*SC* CCCVI] 234); Vogt, *Constantine der Grosse*[2] 249; *PLRE* I 410.

[19]Sozomen, *Hist Eccl.* 2.2.5 (Migne, *PG* LXVII 936; ed. Bidez-Hansen [*GCS* L] 51; ed. Bidez [*SC* CCCVI] 234-36); Albert Strobel in *LThK*[2] V (1960) 209; Michael Avi-Yonah, *The Holy Land from the Persian to the Arab Conquests (536 B.C. to A.D. 640): A Historical Geography* (Grand Rapids, Michigan, 1966) 123, 127, and maps 9 and 11; Felix-Marie Abel, *Géographie de la Palestine*, 3rd ed. (Paris 1967) 205; A.H.M. Jones,

(continued...)

stantine also gave the name of Helenopontus, again in honor of his mother, to one of the provinces of the diocese of Pontus in Asia Minor.[20] Coins minted by her or in her name, statues of her in public places, and her costly burial must be added to the list of honors, but will be considered separately. Constantine's final show of devotion to his mother occurred during the last few weeks of his life, between April 3 (Easter) and May 22 (Pentecost and the day of his death) of 337: he visited Drepanum = Helenopolis and prayed at the shrine of his mother's favorite saint, the martyr Lucian.[21]

The year 326 was one of tragedy for Constantine and his family; for in that year Constantine ordered the execution first of his son Crispus and then of his wife Fausta.[22] These events also cast the only shadow on the relationship between mother and son, since two of our sources report some involvement of Helena. The *Epitome* of Aurelius Victor reports:

> At Constantinus obtento totius Romani imperii mira bellorum felicitate regimine Fausta coniuge, ut putant, suggerente Crispum filium necari iubet. Dehinc uxorem suam Faustem in balneas ardentes coniectam interemit, cum eum mater Helena dolore nimio nepotis increparet.[23]

And in Zosimus, who is distinctly hostile to Constantine, we read:

---

[19](...continued)
The Cities of the Eastern Roman Provinces 279; Michael Avi-Yonah, *Gazetteer of Roman Palestine* (Jerusalem 1976) 64.

[20]*Cod. Iust. Nov.* 28.1 (ed. Schöll-Kroll, *Corpus Iuris Civilis* III 213); Johannes Malalas, *Chron.* 13.12 (Migne, *PG* XCVII 484; ed. Dindorf [*CSHB* VIII] 323); Walter Ruge in *RE* VII.2 (1912) 2844; Seeck in *RE* VII.2 (1912) 2821.

[21]Euseb. *Vita Const.* 4.61.1 (Migne, *PG* XX 1212; ed. Winkelmann [*GCS*] 145); Seeck, *Regesten* 184; Carl Schneider, *Geistegeschichte des antiken Christentums* (Munich 1954) I 734. On the shrine of St. Lucian see Pierre Maraval, *Lieux saints et pélerinages d'Orient* (Paris 1985) 367.

[22]See my "Crispus," 99-106. To the secondary literature there listed must be added François Paschoud, *Cinq études sur Zosime* (Paris 1975) 24-39.

[23]When Constantine had seized control of the whole Roman empire by miraculous success in war he ordered, upon the urging of his wife Fausta, it is believed, the execution of his son Crispus. Then, when his mother Helena reproached him exceedingly for the loss of her grandson, he had his wife Fausta placed in an overheated bath and thus caused her death. *Epit.* 41.11-12. Repeated in Landolfus Sagax 11.174 *(MGH, AA* II 326). The passage is misinterpreted by John Julius Norwich, *Byzantium: The Early Centuries* (London 1988) 59.

When all the power devolved on Constantine alone he no longer hid the evil nature that was within him, but allowed himself to do all things as he pleased.... His son Crispus, who had been honored with the rank of Caesar, as previously mentioned, came under suspicion of being involved with his stepmother Fausta; Constantine destroyed him without any regard to the laws of nature. When Constantine's mother Helena was disturbed by these events and was taking the loss of the young man very hard, Constantine, as if to console her, corrected one evil by an even greater evil: he ordered an unbearably hot bath to be prepared, had Fausta placed in it, and had her taken out only when she was dead.[24]

It is to be noted that Helena is not accused by either report of having intrigued against Fausta; we are told that Helena was disturbed by the death of Crispus and reproached Constantine on account of it. Our numerous other sources do not mention Helena in this context. Thus there are no grounds on which the responsibility for Fausta's death can be shifted from Constantine to Helena. But Helena may have felt that Constantine condemned Crispus rashly, and, indeed, there seem to have been no judicial procedures at all. There may well have been rivalries and jealousies between Helena and Fausta beyond those tensions that commonly exist between mother-in-law and daughter-in-law. Fausta must have resented the domination of Constantine's court by Helena. Helena may have been possessive of Constantine and may have resented Fausta as the half-sister of Theodora, who had replaced Helena as the consort of Constantius.[25] Constantine may have thought that Fausta's death would please Helena.

None of this would convict Helena in a court of law, but the suspicions remain. It has been suggested that Helena undertook her pilgrimage to the Holy Land as an act of expiation, either for her own sins[26] or those of Constantine.[27] The case remains open.

---

[24]2.29.1-2.

[25]*PLRE* I 895.

[26]MacMullen, *Constantine* 187; Diana Bowder, *The Age of Constantine and Julian* (London 1978) 33 and 62; E. D. Hunt, *Holy Land Pilgrimage in the Later Roman Empire AD 312-460* (Oxford 1982) 32-33.

[27]Walter Schulten, *Die Heilige Stiege auf dem Kreuzberg zu Bonn* (Düsseldorf 1964) 89; Stratmann, *op. cit.* II 158.

The close relationship between Constantine and Helena also affected their religious beliefs. Eusebius tells us that Helena was converted to Christianity by Constantine; he does not, unfortunately, give particulars.[28] There is no reason to question Eusebius' statement, and it has won wide acceptance.[29]

In the seventh century the Frankish chronicler who erroneously became known as Fredegar asserted that Constantine was converted by Helena.[30] He writes:

Constantinus cum matrem Helenam crucem Domini nostri Jesu Christi Hierusolimis invenit, effectusque est Christianus ab Helena ... Constantinus per signum crucis omnes gentes superat.[31]

'Fredegar' distinguishes himself neither by his command of Latin syntax nor by his knowledge of history. His assertion that Helena converted Constantine, rather than vice-versa, is not based on facts and can readily be dismissed.[32]

---

[28]*Vita Const.* 3.47.2 (Migne, *PG* XX 1108; ed. Winkelmann [*GCS*] 103).

[29]Seeck, *RE* VII.2 (1912) 2821; Seeck, *Geschichte* I[4] 48; Maurice, *Sainte Hélène* 10; Kurt Aland, "Die religiose Haltung Kaiser Konstantins," in *Studia Patristica* I (Berlin 1957) 549-600 at 577; Vogt, *Constantin der Grosse*[2] 249; Vogt, "Heiden und Christen" 158 and 166; Baus in Jedin, *op. cit.*, I 455; Hans-Henning Lauer, *op cit.* 21; MacMullen, *Constantine* 217; *PLRE* I 410; Vogt, "Helena Augusta," 217-18; André Wankenne, "Constantin et Hélène à Trèves," *Et. Cl.* 52 (1984) 313-16 at 314; Richard Klein in *RAC* XIV 357; Demandt, *op. cit.* 62. For a dissenting view see Agostino Amore, in *Bibl. Sanct.* IV (1964) 989, who thinks that Eusebius is merely flattering Constantine.

[30]Gröber, *op. cit.*, 109; Manitius I 221-27; Walter Goffart, "The Fredegar-Problem Reconsidered," *Speculum* 38 (1963) 206-41; Franz Brunhölzl, *Geschichte der lateinischen Literatur des Mittelalters* I (Munich 1975) 140-41.

[31]Constantine, with his mother Helena, found the cross of our Lord Jesus Christ in Jerusalem and was made a Christian by Helena .... In the sign of the Cross Constantine conquered all peoples. *Chron.* 2.42 (ed. Krusch [*MGH*, *SRM* II] 66).

[32]Coleman, *op. cit.* 152; Ewig, "Das Bild Constantins," 23; John Frederick Matthews, "Macsen, Maximus and Constantine" 445. Theodoret, *Hist. Eccl.* 1.17 in Migne, *PG* LXXXII 957-58, 1.18.1 in ed. Parmentier-Scheidweiler [*GCS* XLIV] 63, and Gelasius of Cyzicus, *Hist. Eccl.* 3.6.1 (ed. Loeschke-Heinemann [*GCS* XXVIII] 144-45), do not say that Helena raised Constantine as Christian, only that she raised him 'in piety.' Drijvers, *op. cit.*, 35, n. 5, misinterprets these passages. There are, however, some liturgical sources of later date which credit Helena with having converted Constantine; see Amnon Linder, "The Myth of Constantine the Great in the West," *Studi Medievali*, 3rd ser. 16 (1975) 43-95 at 89, n. 266.

ATLA?

Helena's conversion, then, certainly did not take place before the eventful year of 312 and perhaps not until a number of years after 312.[33] Nothing is known about the place or circumstances, nor do we know what Helena's earlier religious beliefs were or what kind of religious experience led to her conversion. Certainly we cannot place any trust at all in the so-called *Vita S. Silvestri*, or *Actus S. Silvestri*, of the fifth century,[34] which attributes numerous miracles to Pope Sylvester and credits him with having baptized not only Constantine[35] but also Helena.[36] It has long been recognized as having little or no historical value,[37] but enjoyed much popularity through the centuries.[38] It has also provided subject matter for numerous works of art. Of these we may conveniently mention here two of the frescoes in the Raphael stanze of the Vatican ("The Baptism of Constantine," i. e. his supposed baptism by Sylvester, not his historical baptism by Bishop Eusebius of Nicomedia; and "The Donation of Constantine") and the series of frescoes which Pope Clement VIII (1592-1605) ordered for the transept of the Basilica of St. John Lateran. And

---

[33]Mackes, *op. cit.* 184, thinks that it did not take place until the last decade of her life.

[34]*BHL* 7725-35. The complete text is found in Boninus Mombritius (Bonino Mombrizio), *Sanctuarium seu Vitae Sanctorum,* ed. Paris 1910, II 508-31 (*ed. princeps* Milan 1480). I have not had access to François Combefis, *Illustrium Christi Martyrum Lecti Triumphi* (Paris 1660) 258-336. A partial text is provided by Coleman, op. cit. 217-27. For the history of this text see Levison, *Frühzeit* 396-425, especially 396 and 409, Joseph Vogt, "Constantinus der Grosse," in *RAC* III (1957) 306-79 at 374-376, and Kazhdan, "Constantin imaginaire," 209-10 and 239.

[35]Mombritius, *op. cit.,* II 512-13; Coleman, *op. cit.,* 223. More briefly, but clearly dependent on the *vita,* the *Liber Pontificalis,* Silvester 2 (ed. Mommsen [*MGH, GPR* I.1] 47; ed. Duchesne² I 170); see P. Schaskolsky "La leggenda di Constantino il Grande e di Papa Silvestro," *Roma e l'Oriente* 6 (1913) 12-25 at 16, and Vogt, "Constantinus der Grosse" 376.

[36]Mombritius, *op. cit.* II 528.

[37]Baronio, *op. cit.* III 595, ad annum 315. Franz Joseph Dölger, "Die Taufe Konstantins und ihre Probleme," in his *Konstantin der Grosse und seine Zeit (RömQ,* Suppl. 19; Freiburg 1913) 377-447, especially 394-416. Schaskolsky, *op. cit.,* especially 23; Erich Caspar, *Geschichte des Papsttums* (Tübingen 1930-1933) I 123-24 and 127-28; Ewig, "Das Bild Constantins," 13; Baus and Ewig in Jedin, *op. cit.* II.1 256.

[38]Dölger, "Die Taufe Konstantins," Schaskolsky, *op. cit.,* 13-14; Levison, *Frühzeit* 396-97; Arnold Ehrhardt, "Constantine, Rome, and the Rabbis," *BRL* 42 (1959-1960) 280-312 at 289.

finally this legend made possible the famous eighth century forgery known as the Donation of Constantine.[39]

The circumstances leading to Helena's conversion are described thus in the *Vita S. Silvestri*: Helena is living in Bithynia, together with her grandsons Constans and Constantius. She is at the point of converting to Judaism and writes a letter to Constantine urging that he, too, should accept Judaism rather then Christianity. In his response Constantine announces that a disputation is to be held, in his presence, between representatives of the two faiths. The disputation takes place in the palace in Rome, in the presence of both Constantine and Helena. The Jewish side is represented by 132 rabbis and scholars; the Christian side by 75 bishops, with Sylvester at their head. Two upright and honest pagans, Crato and Zenophilus, serve as judges.[40]

The disputation is then described at great length: Sylvester himself proves superior to eleven of his Jewish opponents.[41] A twelfth opponent, named Zambri, kills a bull by magic; Sylvester miraculously restores the bull to life. Three thousand Jews, Helena "with all her sons and daughters," all the servants, and even the two judges are converted and baptized.[42]

The modern mind finds it difficult to understand how an account as obviously fictitious as this one could ever enjoy the acceptance and popularity which it did. We must also reject what Johannes Malalas,[43] a Byzantine chronicler of the sixth century, has to say:

> Immediately (after entering the city of Rome) he (Constantine) destroyed the shrines and all the temples of the Greeks and opened the churches of the Christians, sending letters everywhere that the churches of the Christians be opened. And when he had fasted and received instruction he was baptized by Sylvester, the bishop of Rome, both he himself

---

[39]Levison, *Frühzeit* 390-465; Judith Herrin, *The Formation of Christendom* (Princeton 1987) 385-87. Text in Coleman, *op. cit.*, 228-37; also ed. Horst Fuhrmann (*MGH, Fontes Iuris Germanici Antiqui in Usum Scholarum Separatim Editi* X) Hannover 1968; repr. 1984. For earlier editions see Vogt, "Constantinus der Grosse" 376.

[40]Mombritius, *op. cit.* II 515-16.

[41]Mombritius, *op. cit.* II 516-28.

[42]Mombritius, *op. cit.* II 528; Schaskolsky, *op. cit.*, 15-16; Levison, *Frühzeit* 402; Ehrhardt, "Constantine, Rome, and the Rabbis" 296-297.

[43]*Chron.* 13.2 (Migne, *PG* XCVII 476; ed. Dindorf [*CSHB* VIII] 317). Krumbacher, *op. cit.* I 325-34; Herbert Hunger, *Die hochsprachliche profane Literatur der Byzantiner* (Munich 1978) I 319-325.

and his mother Helena, all his relatives and friends, and a large number of other Romans. And the emperor Constantine himself became a Christian.

Constantine did not at this time destroy pagan temples; Sylvester did not become bishop of Rome until 314 (succeeding Miltiades); and Helena is not likely to have accompanied Constantine in the war against Maxentius. There have been mistaken efforts in recent years to show that Constantine was a Christian even before 312.[44] Rather, Constantine made his basic commitment to Christianity in 312,[45] but postponed baptism until shortly before his death.[46] It is not unreasonable to assume that his support of the church, however generous, was motivated at least in part by political considerations. His religious thinking was at times quite confused, and he does not seem to have grasped some of the most basic tenets of the Christian faith.[47] On numerous occasions he displayed

[44]These efforts have been summarized and cogently refuted by Thomas Grünewald, *Constantinus Maximus Augustus: Herrschaftspropoganda in der zeitgenössischen Überlieferung* (Stuttgart 1990) 80-86.

[45]Vogt, "Die Bedeutung des Jahres 312 für die Religionspolitik Konstantins des Grossen," *ZKG*, 3rd ser. 61 (1942) 171-90; Vogt, "Constantinus der Grosse" 318-30; Henry Chadwick, "Conversion in Constantine the Great," *Studies in Church History* 15 (1978) 1-13 at 11; Roger Scott in Paul Magdolino, ed., *The New Constantines* (Aldershot, Hampshire, 1994) 59.

[46]Euseb. *Vita Const.* 4.61-62 (Migne, *PG* XX 1212-17; ed. Winkelmann [*GCS*] 145-46); Euseb.-Hieron. *Chron.* Olymp. 279 (ed. Fotheringham 316; ed. Helm [*GCS* XLVII] 234).

[47]The debate over Constantine's religious beliefs and attitudes continues. Among the more recent contributions to the already extensive and still growing literature on the subject one may note especially two: Paul Keresztes, *Constantine: A Great Christian Monarch and Apostle* (Amsterdam 1981), and Alistair Kee, *Constantine versus Christ* (London 1982). The provocative titles of both books serve notice to us that a consensus on the subject has not yet been achieved. Even Keresztes, *op. cit.* 8, must admit that Constantine was 'not ... always well-informed in matters of doctrine.' Similarly *ibid.* 123. Kee, *op. cit.* 15, goes much further, of course: 'He (Constantine) was now a devotee of God, the God of the Christians, but he did not confess faith in Christ.' Similarly, *ibid.* 147. That 'the dogmatic foundations of Christianity remained a mystery to him' (Constantine) is the conclusion of Andreas Alföldi, *The Conversion of Constantine* 21; see also *ibid.* 57. Similarly Vogt, "Constantinus der Grosse" 363f., and

(continued...)

a mean spirit and a cruel nature.[48]

Helena, on the other hand, appears to have been more spiritually minded than her son. Her piety was more intense and her conduct more pure. She understood and practiced the Christian virtues of humility and charity. Her life, much more than that of her son, came to be dominated by the Christian faith. On her pilgrimage to the Holy Land she helped the poor, freed some from prisons or mines, and mingled with the worshipers, wearing simple and modest clothes, according to Eusebius.[49] St. Ambrose reports that Helena was a *stabularia* as we have seen. But this is no cause for embarrassment to him; rather he praises her piety and humility. Helena is *sanctae memoriae*, he says, and was a *magna femina;* Constantine was blessed to have such a mother, and Christ raised her from her lowly condition.[50] He praises Helena more than he does Constantine.[51] Rufinus tells us that Helena

[47](...continued)
Hans-Henning Lauer, *op. cit.* 26 and 28. A more favorable assessment of Constantine's understanding of the Christian faith is given by Charles Odahl, "Constantine's Epistle to the Bishops at the Council of Arles: A Defense of Imperial Authorship," *JRH* 17 (1993) 274-89, and id., "God and Constantine: Divine Sanction for Imperial Rule in the First Christian Emperor's Early Letters and Art," *CHR* 81 (1995) 327-52.

[48]It is well known that Constantine was responsible in varying degrees and in various ways for the deaths of some of his nearest kin. Just as revealing is some of the legislation instituted by him. With much attention to detail he decreed that certain types of offenders be sewed into a leather bag together with serpents, be burned alive, or have molten lead poured into their mouths; see *Cod. Theod.* 9.15.1, 9.16. 1, and 9.24.1 (ed. Mommsen-Meyer I.2 458-59 and 476-77). In another case he even prescribed crucifixion; see *Cod. Theod.* 9.5.1 (ed. Mommsen-Meyer I.2 443-44). On the other hand Aurelius Victor, *Caes.* 41.4, and Sozomen, *Hist. Eccl.* 1.8.13 (Migne, *PG* LXVII 881; ed. Bidez-Hansen [*GCS* L] 19; ed. Bidez [*SC* CCCVI] 146-48), report that Constantine forbade the use of crucifixion as a means of execution; this, we may be sure, was not for humanitarian reasons.

Not everyone will agree with Ramsay MacMullen, *Christianizing the Roman Empire* (New Haven 1984) 50 with nn. 36 and 37, that 'the empire had never had on the throne a man given to such bloodthirsty violence as Constantine.' In his barbarous cruelty Constantine was not alone; see Macmullen, *Corruption and the Decline of Rome* (New Haven 1988) 140-41. Barnes, *Constantine and Eusebius* 220, calls Constantine's morals legislation 'morbid and unwholesome.' On Constantine's legislation see further Arnold Ehrhardt, "Constantin d. Gr. Religionspolitik und Gesetzgebung," *ZRG, R. Abt.* 72 (1955) 127-90.

[49]*Vita Const.* 3.44-45 (Migne, *PG* XX 1105; ed. Winkelmann [*GCS*] 102-103).

[50]*De Obitu Theodosii* 40-42 (Migne, *PL* XVI 1399-1400 [ed. 1845] or 1462-63 [ed. 1866]; ed. Mannix 59; ed. Faller [*CSEL* LXXIII] 392-93).

[51]Steidle, *op. cit.* 97.

humbly waited on the consecrated virgins whom she met In Jerusalem.[52] Paulinus of Nola, in one of his letters to his friend Sulpicius Severus, says of Constantine that he deserved to be 'prince of Christian princes' no more by his own faith than by that of his mother Helena.[53] The tenth century *Suda*, while noting Helena's service to the consecrated virgins, credits her with 'Christ-like humility.'[54] In modern times Helena's devoutness has received high marks not only from the authors of devotional literature but also from historians.[55]

Helena gave the most visible evidence of her piety by establishing churches in many locations. It will be our task in subsequent chapters to distinguish those actually founded by her from those merely attributed to her by tradition. There are, however, two foundations attributed to Helena which it will be convenient to consider now. The first is a church in honor of St. Lucian at Drepanum = Helenopolis. Simeon Metaphrastes (tenth century) reports that Helena founded Helenopolis after her return from Jerusalem, settled it with people from the neighboring territory, and built a large church in honor of her favorite saint.[56] This report has been accepted by a number of scholars, but there is no archaeological evidence.[57] A Monastery of St. Lucian is attested for the year 787.[58] The second is the Church of St. Stephen at Besançon. Our only evidence in this case is the medieval

[52]*Hist. Eccl.* 1.8 in Migne, *PL* XXI 477-78; 10.8 in ed. Mommsen (*GCS* IX.2) 970-71. Similarly Socrates, Sozomen, and Theodoret.

[53]*Epist.* 31.4 (Migne, *PL* LXI 327; ed. Hartel [*CSEL* XXIX] 271). In this letter Paulinus reports Helena's discovery of the True Cross; we shall give more attention to it in chapter IX below. Baronio, *op. cit.* III 594, ad annum 315, erroneously interprets this passage as meaning that Helena became a Christian before Constantine did.

[54]S. v. ʹΕλένη (ed. Ada Adler [Leipzig 1929-1938] II 242-43). The *Suda* also claims to know that Helena established a convent in Jerusalem and provided for its maintenance: s. v. ʹΕστιάδες (ed. Adler II 429); see also E. D. Hunt, *op. cit.* 44.

[55]A.-M. Rouillon, *Sainte Hélène* (Paris 1908) 49-51; Stratmann, *op. cit.* II 168-69; Elena Ianulardo, *Santa Elena* (Foggia 1958) passim. Ekkart Sauser, *Heilige und Selige im Bistum Trier* (Trier 1987) 69-71. Seeck, *Geschichte* I[4] 48: Leclercq in *DACL* VI.2 (1925) 2128; Mackes, *op. cit.* 184-85; Vogt, *Constantin der Grosse* 249; Hans-Henning Lauer, *op. cit.* 21; MacMullen, *Constantine* 21.

[56]*Vita* of St. Lucian 20 (Migne, *PG* CXIV 416; Latin translation only in *Acta Sanct.* Ian. I [ed. 1643] 362).

[57]Baronio, *op. cit.* III 399-400, ad annum 326; Maurice, *Sainte Hélène* 5; A. H. M. Jones, *Constantine and the Conversion of Europe* (London 1948) 149; MacMullen, *Constantine* 179; Leeb, *op. cit.* 162.

[58]Raymond Janin, *Les églises et les monastères des grands centres byzantins* (Paris 1975) 97-98 and 440.

bishop's list of that city – not a document of unquestionable reliability.[59] We must remain skeptical in both cases.

[59]S. v. Hylarius, in *MGH, Script.* XIII 372, or in Louis Duchesne, *Fastes épiscopaux de l'ancienne Gaule* (Paris 1907-1915) III 200.

Chapter IV.
The Historical Links to Trier

It was claimed in the ninth century by the monk Altmann and after him by others that Helena was a native of Trier. In chapter II above that claim has already been considered and rejected. But Helena is linked to Trier in other ways which we must examine.

A list of the bishops of Trier is extant in nine recensions dating from the tenth, eleventh, and twelfth centuries and easily accessible in two editions.[1] The fourth name on this list – or at least in the 'standard' form of this list – is that of Agritius.[2] Fortunately he is authenticated by a much earlier source: the *acta* of the council which was held at Arles in the year 314 record that *Agroecius episcopus ... de civitate Treverorum* was in attendance.[3] We do not know, however, how long he had been in office before he attended the council, nor does any ancient source record the date of his death. Of Maximinus, Agritius' successor, it is said in his *vita* that he became bishop in the 24th year of the reign of Constantine,[4] i.e. between July 25, 329, and July 24, 330.[5] The date provided by the *vita* lacks confirmation but is not inherently improbable. Probably Agritius' tenure as bishop and Helena's residence in Trier overlapped by a number of years (it is not known exactly when Helena transferred her residence to Rome).

An anonymous *vita* of Bishop Agritius was composed in Trier between 1050 and 1072.[6] Its value as a historical source is negligible,[7]

---

[1]Duchesne, *Fastes épiscopaux* III 30-44; *MGH, Script.* XIII 296-301.

[2]Alternate spellings are Acritius, Acratius, Agroetius, and Agroecius.

[3]Jacques Sirmond, ed., *Concilia Antiqua Galliae* (Paris 1629) I 8; Joannes Dominicus Mansi, ed., *Sacrorum Conciliorum Nova et Amplissima Collectio* (ed. Paris 1901) II 469 and 476; Charles Munier, ed., *Concilia Galliae A. 314 - A. 506 (CC, Ser. Lat.* CXLVIII, Turnhout 1963) 4 and 15; Jean Gaudemet, ed., *Conciles Gaulois du IV⁰ siècle* (*SC* CCXLI, Paris 1977) 40 and 60.

[4]*BHL* 5822. *Acta Sanct.* Maii VII (ed. 1867) 21, where XXVII is an erroneous emendation for XXIV.

[5]*PLRE* I 223. Barnes, *New Empire* 5.

[6]*BHL* 178-79. Text in *Acta Sanct.* Ian. I (ed. 1643) 773-81; or Ian. II (ed. 1863) 55-63; and in Sauerland, *op. cit.,* 185-211. For the date see the following: Victor Garenfeld, *Die Trierer Bischöfe des vierten Jahrhunderts* (Diss. Bonn 1888) 20; Sauerland, *op. cit.,* 150; Ernst Winheller, *Die Lebensbeschreibungen der vorkarolingischen Bischöfe von Trier* (Bonn 1935) 139.

[7]Garenfeld, *op. cit.* 24; Sauerland, *op. cit.* 149; Winheller, *op. cit.* 145.

but it probably reflects an actual close relationship between the empress and the bishop. In the first chapter of this *vita* we are told that Helena, *after* the discovery of the True Cross, implored Pope Sylvester to send a suitably holy man to Trier, where the true faith had largely lapsed. Sylvester obliged Helena, and his choice fell upon Agritius, the patriarch of Antioch and the most renowned of all bishops at the time. Agritius accepted the call and became bishop of Trier.

This account must be rejected for several reasons:

1. Agritius was bishop of Trier already in 314, and Helena did not undertake her pilgrimage until many years later. In fact, when Agritius assumed office, in 314 or earlier, Helena in all likelihood had not yet been converted.

2. Sylvester is known to have assumed his office on January 31, 314.[8] It is likely that Agritius had become bishop of Trier already before that date.

3. The bishops (not yet patriarchs) of Antioch are all known to us, and the name Agritius does not appear on the list.[9]

4. The transfer of clerics, especially the transfer of bishops from one see to another, was frowned upon. It was expressly forbidden by the second canon of the Council of Arles[10] and the 15th canon of the Council of Nicaea;[11] Constantine himself is known not to have approved of it.[12] (It did, however, occur. Eusebius of Nicomedia had formerly been bishop of Beirut; he became bishop of Constantinople in 339.)

5. The traditions of Trier ascribed non-native origin also to Eucharius, Valerius, and Maternus, Agritius' predecessors, and to

---

[8]*MGH, AA* IX = *Chron. Min.* I 76; Philipp Jaffé, *Regesta Pontificum Romanorum*, 2nd ed. (Leipzig 1885-1888) 128; Seeck, *Regesten* 162.

[9]*Acta Sanct.* Iulii IV (ed. 1868) IX-X and 38-40; *MGH, AA* XIII = *Chron. Min.* III 557-58; Pius Bonifacius Gams, *Series Episcoporum Ecclesiae Catholicae* (Regensburg 1873) 433; Marius Chaine, *La chronologie des temps chrétiens de l'Égypte et de l'Éthiopie* (Paris 1925) 254-55; Robert Devreesse, *Le Patriarcat d'Antioche* (Paris 1945) 115.

[10]Sirmond, *op. cit.* I 5; Mansi, *op. cit.* II 471; Munier, *op. cit.* 5 and 9; Gaudemet, *op. cit.* 44 and 46; Karl Joseph von Hefele and Henri Leclercq, *Histoire des conciles* (Paris 1907 ff.) I.1 281.

[11]Mansi, *op. cit.*, II 716; Hefele-Leclercq, op. cit. I.1 597-601; Giuseppe Alberigo et al., *Conciliorum Oecumenicorum Decreta* (Freiburg 1962) 12.

[12]Euseb. *Vita Const.* 3.60-62 (Migne, *PG* XX 1128-37; ed. Winkelmann [*GCS*] 112-17).

Maximinus and Paulinus, his successors; a hagiographic topos can be observed here.[13]

The tradition of Agritius' coming to Trier from Antioch at Helena's request, therefore, has not found favor with modern scholars.[14] Nancy Gauthier remarks that it 'does not even merit the benefit of a doubt.'[15] The Monastery of St. Maximinus at Trier laid claim to having been founded by Helena, or by Constantine at Helena's request. This claim is contrary to all that is known about the rise of monasticism in Egypt and its spread first in the East and then in the West. Athanasius' first sojourn at Trier in 335-337 may have given to the churches of the West a first exposure to the ideas of monasticism, but did not lead immediately to the establishment of monasteries and was in any event several years after Helena's death.[16] Thus there cannot have been any monasteries in Trier during Helena's lifetime.[17] The fictitious claim was advanced not only in the quest for prestige but also to support the monastery's aspirations to being free from the control of the archbishops of Trier and subject only to the authority of Emperor and Pope ("Reichsunmittelbarkeit").[18]

In the long struggle the monks of St. Maximinus repeatedly had recourse to forgery. A diploma supposedly issued by the Frankish king Dagobert I in 634, specifically mentioning Helena and confirming all the

[13]Maternus actually was bishop of Cologne and needs to be struck from the list.

[14]Sauerland, op. cit., 84; Winheller, op. cit., 126-27. Hans Hubert Anton, Trier im frühen Mittelalter (Paderborn 1987) 70-71 and 75, keeps the question open.

[15]L'évangélisation des pays de la Moselle (Paris 1960) 45.

[16]For the beginnings of monasticism in Gaul see Friedrich Prinz, Frühes Mönchtum im Frankenreich (Munich 1965), the bibliography in Jedin, Handbuch II.1 389, and Herrin, op. cit., 67-69. Of broader scope: Rudolf Lorenz, "Die Anfänge des abendländischen Mönchtums im 4. Jahrhundert," ZKG 77 (1966) 1-61.

[17]Prinz, op. cit. 197-99; Ernst Gierlich, Die Grabstätten der rheinischen Bischöe vor 1200 (Mainz 1990) 21-22. Gottfried Kentenich, Geschichte der Stadt Trier (Trier 1915) 80, states that there were no monasteries in Trier before the sixth century. But we learn from August. Conf. 8.6.15 that there were individual monks already in the second half of the fourth century; see also Leonardy, op. cit. 269-70, and Heinz Heinen, Trier und das Trevererland in römischer Zeit (Trier 1985) 341-43.

[18]A summary account of the long struggle and its eventual outcome is conveniently provided by Hermann Bunjes et al., Die kirchlichen Denkmäler der Stadt Trier mit Ausnahme des Domes (Düsseldorf 1938) 289; For a more detailed account see Jacob Marx, Geschichte des Erzstifts Trier (Trier 1858-1864) II.1 102-22.

monastery's privileges,[19] has long been recognized as a forgery of the tenth century.[20] Similar diplomas supposedly issued by King Pepin in 765,[21] by Charlemagne in 800,[22] and by Louis the Pious in 814 and 822[23] are also forgeries.[24] Additional forged diplomas, all serving the same purpose, were produced in the 12th century.[25] In 1245 the monastery's claim to being a foundation of Helena was recognized by Archbishop Conrad of Cologne[26] and by Pope Innocent IV.[27]

In the 10th century the chapter hall, or refectory, of the Monastery of St. Maximinus was decorated with a series of 22 or 23 wall paintings which depicted scenes from the life of St. Maximinus and from the history of the monastery. Subsequently one of the monks composed for each of the paintings a descriptive epigram in hexameter verse; in length these epigrams vary from two to 18 verses. The paintings themselves were destroyed long ago, perhaps in 1522 or 1674. The epigrams, however, are extant in a manuscript written in the late 10th or 11th century at Trier in the Monastery of St. Maximinus and now kept in the library of the University of Ghent (no. 528, folio 25 r

[19]Heinrich Beyer, *Urkundenbuch zur Geschichte der ... mittelrheinischen Territorien* I (Koblenz 1860) 2-3, no. 3; *MGH, Dipl.* I 146-47, no. 29 *(spuria)*.

[20]Marx, *Geschichte* II.1 40-43; Sauerland, *op. cit.*, 166-67; Otto Oppermann, *Rheinische Urkundenstudien* II (Utrecht 1951) 16-66; Eugen Ewig, "Kaiserliche und apostolische Tradition im mittelaiterlichen Trier," *TZ* 24-26 (1956-1958) 147-86 at 151-52; Warren Sanderson, "Die frühmittelalterlichen Krypten von St. Maximin in Trier," *TZ* 31 (1968) 7-172 at 11; Erich Wisplinghoff, *Untersuchungen zur frühen Geschichte der Abtei S. Maximin bei Trier von den Anfängen bis etwa 1150* (Mainz 1970) 7; Dietz, "St. Helena" 359; Nancy Gauthier, *L'évangélisation* 45 with n. 51; Gierlich, *op. cit.* 22, n. 55.

[21]*MGH, Dipl. Karol.* I 54-55, no. 39 "unecht"; Beyer, *Urkundenbuch* I 25, no. 20; Johann Friedrich Böhmer and Engelbert Mühlbacher, *Die Regesten des Kaiserreiches unter den Karolingern: 751-918* (Innsbruck 1889) 45.

[22]*MGH, Dipl. Karol.* I 400-11, no. 276 "unecht'; Beyer, *Urkundenbuch* I 52-53, no. 46; Böhmer-Mühlbacher, *op.cit.* 176.

[23]Beyer, *Urkundenbuch* I 53, no. 47, and I 60-61, no. 54; Böhmer-Mühlbacher, *op. cit.*, 271.

[24]Marx, *Geschichte* II.1 104; Oppermann, *op. cit.*, 16-66; Wisplinghoff, op. cit. 13 with n. 57 and 126-42, esp. 127-29 and 142; Dietz, "St. Helena" 359; Nancy Gauthier, *L'évangélisation* 45; Anton, *op. cit.* 71.

[25]Oppermann, *op. cit.* 66-113, esp. 108; Theo Kolzer, "Zu den Fälschungen für St. Maximin in Trier," in *Fälschungen im Mittelalter (MGH, Schriften* 33.I-V, 1988) III 315-26 at 315-317.

[26]Beyer, *Urkundenbuch* III 619-20., no. 829.

[27]*Ibid.* 630, no. 841.

and v). Whether these epigrams were actually inscribed on the walls as *tituli* has been questioned.[28]

The first of the 22 or 23 paintings depicted the purported establishment of the monastery by Constantine, Helena, and Bishop Agritius. The corresponding epigram reads as follows:

DE DEDICATIONE ET CONSTRUCTIONE PRIORIS MONASTERII.
Presul regalem dicat hanc Agricius aedem
Symniste patris summi sub honore Iohannis.
Is locus abbati commendaturque Iohanni.
A Constantini Helena genitrice sereni,
Hortatuque domus sacratur presule cuius.[29]

Neither the paintings nor the epigrams add anything to the credibility of the tradition; they merely show how much this tradition was cherished. We must conclude that any association of Helena with the *Monastery* of St. Maximinus is to be rejected.[30] On the other hand nothing argues against an early Christian cemetery and *church* on the site of the future monastery.[31] The church, the Church of St. John the Evangelist, provided a burial place for Bishop Agritius, i. e. existed already in Constantinian times.[32]

---

[28]Sauerland, *op. cit.* 87; Paul Clemen, *Die romanische Monumentalmalerei in den Rheinlanden* (Düsseldorf 1916) 748 with n. 25; Bunjes, *op.cit.*, 320-22; Manitius II 421; Ewig, "Tradition" 151; Wisplinghoff, *op. cit.*, 7; Dietz, "St. Helena," 359.

[29]Concerning the Dedication and Building of the Former Monastery:
Bishop Agritius dedicated this royal building
In honor of his fellow-priest, great Father John.
This place was entrusted to abbot John
By Helena, the mother of the serene Constantine,
And the house was consecrated with the encouragement of that [bishop].
MGH, Poet. Lat. V 146-52 at 147; Franz Xaver Kraus, *Inschriften* II 180-182, no. 374, at 180. I propose *presulis eius* as an emendation.

[30]Ewig, "Tradition" 152-53; Nancy Gauthier, *Topographie chrétienne des cités de la Gaule des origines au millieu du VIIIᵉ siècle* I: *Province ecclésiastique de Trèves (Belgica Prima)* (Paris 1966) 30; Drijvers, *op. cit.*, 23.

[31]Eugen Ewig, *Trier im Merowingerreich: Civitas, Stadt, Bistum* (Trier 1954) 50; Ewig, "Tradition" 152-53; Hans Erich Kubach and Albert Verbeek, *Romanische Baukunst an Rhein und Maas* (Berlin 1976) II 1128. Excavations have been conducted in the interior of the Church of St. Maximinus since 1978. The excavator, Heinz Cüppers, has provided preliminary reports in Rheinisches Landesmuseum Trier, *Trier: Kaiserresidenz und Bischofssitz* (Mainz 1984) 232-34, and more recently in his *Die Römer in Rheinland-Pfalz* (Stuttgart 1990) 644-46 and ill. 583-84. A comprehensive report is pending.

[32]According to his *vita* 2.10 (*Acta Sanct.* Ian. II [ed. 1863] 57). For additional sources see Ewig, *Trier im Merowingerreich* 49, n. 182.

Our medieval sources report that Helena donated her 'house' in Trier, so that it might become a church, and that Agritius dedicated this church. In Altmann's *vita* of Helena we read:

...domus eius facta ecclesiae pars maxima in honore beati Petri apostolorum principis in sedem episcopalem metropolis dicata, adeo ut vocetur et sit prima sedes Galliae Belgicae, nec non et cubile regiae ambitionis factum in eadem urbe opere mirabili.[33]

The *vita* of Agritius follows:

...domus beatae imperatricis Helenae ... rogatu eiusdem mulieris sanctissimae a beato patriarcha Agricio in honore principis apostolorum Petri in sedem episcopalem metropolis dicata ... est.[34]

Finally the *Gesta Treverorum* offers this text:

In the year of the birth of our Lord 368 St. Agritius was appointed bishop of Trier .... He also dedicated the house of the blessed Helena, from which she herself had excluded all the filth of paganism, in honor of St. Peter and appointed it the head of the church of Trier.[35]

This text hardly inspires confidence. The date of 368 is hopelessly wrong and a good indication of how much history the author of this 'history' actually knows. Also one may observe how the account becomes more embellished as it is passed from the ninth to the eleventh to the twelfth century.[36] It is not surprising, therefore, that scholars, until some forty years ago, have denied that Helena had anything to do

---

[33]... her house became the greater part of a church which was dedicated in honor of the blessed Peter, the chief of the apostles, as a metropolitan episcopal see, so that it might be called and might be the first see of Gallia Belgica, and particularly the bedroom of the royal residence, which had been built in the same city with wondrous workmanship. 1.9 (*Acta Sanct.* Aug. III [ed. 1867] 583; also in *MGH, Script.* VIII 151, n. 57).

[34]... the house of the blessed empress Helena, ..., at the request of the same holy lady, was dedicated by the blessed Bishop Agritius in honor of Peter, the chief of the apostles, as a metropolitan episcopal see. 7 (*Acta Sanct.* Ian. II [ed. 1863] 61).

[35]19 (Migne, *PL* CLIV 1134-35; *MGH, Script.* VIII 152).

[36]The three texts are quoted at length by Jochen Zink in Franz J. Ronig, ed., *Der Trierer Dom* (Neuss 1980) 18-19 with nn. 10-15.

with the beginnings of Trier's cathedral.[37] But a dramatic discovery since then has forced us to reconsider the question.

Archaeological excavations were conducted below the east end of the nave of the cathedral in 1945-1946 and again in 1965-1968 by Theodor Konrad Kempf, then director of Trier's diocesan museum. The first excavations were undertaken in the course of repairing World War Two damage, the second in the course of extensive renovation. These excavations revealed, almost 3 m. below the modern floor of the church, a (slightly irregular) rectangular room measuring ca. 10 x 7 m. The walls of this room, once painted, were standing, in part, to a height of 50-80 cm. The painted ceiling was found in situ but in thousands of fragments. Restoration required many years of painstaking effort and was completed in December of 1983, just in time for the city's 2000th anniversary in 1984. In 1988 the ceiling was transferred from the old to the new diocesan museum. It consists of 15 (5 x 3) panels divided one from another by multi-colored borders.[38] Of the 15 panels eight each depict a pair of Erotes (or, in one case, Cupid and Psyche),[39] three depict male figures,[40] unquestionably poets or philosophers, and the remaining four female figures.[41] Thus far we are on uncontested ground.[42]

[37]Leonardy, *op. cit.*, 222-23; Sauerland, *op. cit.*, 68-74; Kentenich, Geschichte 38; Nikolaus Irsch, *Der Dom zu Trier* (Düsseldorf 1931) 65-69; Winheller, *op. cit.* 130. Gottfried Kentenich, "Die älteste Nachricht über den Trierer Dom: Ein Beitrag zur Kritik Altmanns von Hautevillers," *TZ* 1 (1926) 87-92, supposes extensive interpolation in Altmann's text. Nancy Gauthier, *Topographie chrétienne* I 24, has doubts even now.

[38]Not 21 (7 x 3), as was believed earlier.

[39]Nos. 1, 3, 5, 7, 9, 11, 13, and 15, beginning in the northwest corner of the room and counting from north to south in each row of five. I am following the system employed by Winfried Weber (see n. 42 below), rather than the earlier system of counting the panels in the sequence of their discovery.

[40]Nos. 6, 10, and 12; no. 6 is the least complete of the restorations and therefore questionable.

[41]Nos. 2, 4, 8, and 14.

[42]The excavator published his findings in a large number of separate and partly redundant articles; see the bibliography. The current director of the diocesan museum, Winfried Weber, has provided a very useful summary in his *Constantinische Deckengemälde aus dem römischen Palast unter dem Trierer Dom*, 2nd ed. (Trier 1986). The lack of a final and definitive publication is to be noted.

A coin find prompted the excavator to postulate the year 316 as a *terminus ante quem non* for the construction of the room.[43] A number of years later the room apparently was torn down to make room for other construction, and another coin find convinced him that this was not before 326. This *terminus post quem* must be adjusted to the year 330, I am told by Winfried Weber, the current director of the diocesan museum, who has re-examined the numismatic evidence. The new construction on the site was none other than the north church of the Constantinian double church – the later *Dom*.[44] The new construction was completed by 348.[45] The same dates, 326-348, have been established by Kempf for the construction of the atrium to the west of the church proper.[46]

This reconstruction of events on the basis of archaeological and numismatic evidence receives strong support from an unexpected literary source: Athanasius of Alexandria was in exile at Trier from 335 to 337. He visited Trier again in 343, and may have been present in Trier also

---

[43]Kempf and Wilhelm Reusch, edd., *Frühchristliche Zeugnisse im Einzugsgebiet von Rhein und Mosel* (Trier 1965) 240-41; Kempf, "Die Konstantinischen Deckenmälereien aus dem Trierer Dom," *Archäologisches Korrespondenzblatt* 7 (Mainz 1977) 147-59 at 155; more critically Winfried Weber, *Deckengemälde*[2] 29.

[44]Kempf, "Die vorläufigen Ergebnisse der Ausgrabungen auf dem Gelände des Trierer Domes," *Germania* 29 (1951) 47-58 at 48 and 50; Kempf, "Die Ausgrabungen am Trierer Dom und an der Liebfrauenkirche von 1943 bis 1950," in *Neue Beiträge zur Kunstgeschichte des 1. Jahrtausends I.1: Spätantike und Byzanz = Forschungen zur Kunstgeschichte und christlichen Archäologie* I (Baden-Baden 1952) 103-13 at 104; Kempf, "Die altchristliche Bischofsstadt Trier," in *Trier: Ein Zentrum abendländischer Kultur (Rheinischer Verein für Denkmalpflege und Heimatschutz, Jahrbuch* 1952) 47-64 at 53 and 59; Kempf, "Trierer Domgrabungen 1943-1954," in *Neue Ausgrabungen in Deutschland* (Berlin 1958) 368-79 at 371; Kempf, *Legende-Überlieferung-Forschung: Untersuchungen über den Trierer Hl. Rock* (Trier 1959) 12; Kempf-Reusch, *Zeugnisse* 240-41; Kempf, "Die Konstantinischen Deckenmalereien" (1977) 155; Winfried Weber, *Deckengemälde* 29; Nancy Gauthier, *Topographie chrétienne* 22 and 24.

[45]Kempf, "Die altchristliche Bischofskirche Triers," part III, *Trierer Theologische Zeitschrift, Pastor Bonus* 56 (1947) 118-23; Kempf, "Die vorläufigen Ergebnisse" 48 and 50; Kempf, "Die altchristliche Bischofsstadt Trier," 54; Kempf, "Die Ausgrabungen... von 1943 bis 1950" 104.

[46]Kempf, "Die altchristliche Bischofskirche Triers," part III, 118-23 at 119-20; Kempf in "Jahresbericht 1941 bis 1944," *TZ* 18 (1949) 269-334 at 293-95 and 296. Kempf, "Die Erforschung einer altchristlichen Bischofskirche auf deutschem Boden," *Forschungen und Fortschritte* 26 (1950) 244-47 at 246. But the existence of such an atrium is being put into question by new excavations currently in progress in the same area.

in 346.[47] Some years later he was accused by his adversaries of having held divine services in an unfinished church at Alexandria. Athanasius did not deny it. Instead he pointed out that his predecessor, Bishop Alexander, had done so before him. Furthermore he had seen the same thing being done in Trier and in Aquileia.[48] His reference to Trier has quite reasonably been taken as a reference to the later cathedral, not only by Kempf but also by others.[49] Unfortunately Athanasius does not say in what year or on what occasion he made this observation, but it clearly must have been between 335 and 346. This, of course, agrees fully with the dates proposed by Kempf.

A more specific date, namely 321, has been proposed for the painted ceiling (not necessarily for the room itself). In that year, or at the latest in January of 322, Crispus must have married a woman named Helena but otherwise unknown. A child was born to the young couple evidently in the fall of 322. This was Constantine's first grandchild, and he celebrated the occasion by granting a pardon to many condemned criminals. The decree was received in Rome on October 30, 322.[50] Now, panel 4 of our pointed ceiling shows a young woman wearing a sleeveless purple tunic, perhaps with a golden fibula, and the floral wreath of a Roman bride. This bride, so Maria R. Alföldi suggested, is

[47]Athanasius, *Apol. contra Arianos* or *Apologia Secunda* 9.4 and 87.3-7 (Migne, *PG* XXV 265 and 405-408; ed. Opitz II.1 95 and 166); Socrates, *Hist. Eccl.* 1.35 and 2.3 (Migne, *PG* LXVII 169-72 and 189-92; ed. Bright[2] 58 and 66-67); Sozomen, *Hist. Eccl.* 2.28.14 and 3.2.1-8 (Migne, *PG* LXVII 1017 and 1036-37; ed. Bidez-Hansen [*GCS* L] 93 and 102-103); Euseb.-Hieron. *Chron.* Olymp. 280 (ed. Fotheringham 318; ed. Helm[2] [*GCS* XLVII] 236). Repeated in Prosper Tiro, *Epit. Chron.* 1066 (*MGH, AA* IX = *Chron. Min.* I 453) and in Bede, *Chron.* 429 (*MGH, AA* XIII = *Chron. Min.* III 296).

[48]*Apol. ad Const.* 14-15 (Migne, *PG* XXV 612-13; ed. Szymusiak [*SC* LXVI] 102-104); this can be dated to 357.

[49]Kempf, "Die altchristliche Bischofskirche Triers," part I, 2-9 at 3-4; "Die altchristliche Bischofsstadt Trier" 53; "Trierer Domgrabungen 1943-1954" 368 ; "Das Haus der heiligen Helena" 12. Marx, *Geschichte* I.1 64, long before the excavations of recent decades. Eduard Hegel, "Die rheinische Kirche in römischer und frühfränkischer Zeit," in Victor H. Elbern, ed., *Das erste Jahrtausend: Kultur und Kunst im werdenden Abendland an Rhein und Ruhr* (Düsseldorf 1962-1964) I 93-113 at 101; Edith Mary Wightman, *Roman Trier and the Treveri* (London 1970) 63 and 111; Jochen Zink in Franz J. Ronig, ed., *Der Trierer Dom* (Neuss 1980) 24 and 74, n. 19; Nancy Gauthier, *Topographie chrétienne* 22.

[50]*Cod. Theod.* 9.38.1 (ed. Mommsen-Meyer I.2 496).

the younger Helena.[51]   This interpretation and the date deduced from it have been endorsed by Kempf.[52]

The location of this room, the date of its construction, and the quality of the paintings have convinced the excavator that this room, a 'Prunksaal,' was part of the imperial residence.[53] Altmann and the tradition following him thus would appear to be vindicated at least in part. We may now wish to accept that the Constantinian north church, the later cathedral, was built on a site previously occupied by a part of the imperial residence, 'the house of Helena.' But it is quite impossible that Bishop Agritius should have dedicated this church, which was still under construction during one of Athanasius' stays in Trier; by then Agritius had been succeeded by Maximinus.   And the reference to Trier as a metropolitan see is an anachronism which reflects Trier's later claims on primacy.

Let us now return to the painted ceiling and let us, foregoing any discussion of the Erotes and the three male figures, consider possible interpretations of the four female figures.   We have already seen that questions of interpretation and of date go hand-in-hand.   In his earlier publications Kempf admitted of two possible interpretations: the ladies portrayed in our panels (only three at that time) are either allegorical figures, or else members of the imperial family.[54]   But from the beginning he inclined toward the latter possibility, and with time he pressed

---

[51]"Helena nobilissima femina" 81-82; *Die constantinische Goldprägung* 127.

[52]Kempf-Reusch, *Zeugnisse* 245; "Das Bild einer kaiserlichen Braut," *Kölner Römer-illustrierte* 2 (1975) 175-76; "Die Konstantinischen Deckenmalereien" (1977) 155; "Das Haus der heiligen Helena" 5. Winfried Weber, *Deckengemälde* 27. The most recent restoration omits the lyre and the plectrum which were part of an earlier version.

[53]"Die altchristliche Bischofsstadt Trier" 59; *Legende-Überlieferung-Forschung* 16-18; Kempf-Reusch, *Zeugnisse* 240-41; "Die Konstantinischen Deckenmalereien" (1977) 153-55; "Das Haus der heiligen Helena" 4-6. Winfried Weber, *Deckengemälde* 30. It is the three factors taken together which give strength to Kempf's conclusion, I think. Considered separately they are less convincing. One might observe, for instance, that some private residences in Trier were also decorated with paintings and mosaics of high quality. Kempf's conclusion found favor with Ewig, *Trier im Merowingerreich* 33. Heinz Cüppers, director of the Rheinisches Landesmuseum in Trier, also concludes that the room excavated by Kempf was part of the imperial residence: *Führer zu vor-und frühgeschichtlichen Denkmälern* XXXII: *Trier* (Mainz 1977) 104-105; Ronig, *Dom* 118, and *Trier: Kaiserresidenz und Bischofssitz* 69-72.

[54]"Konstantinische Deckenmalereien aus dem Trierer Dom," *TZ* 19 (1950) 45-51 at 51.

Plate I

The central panel of the painted ceiling from the 'House of Helena' found under the cathedral of Trier. This panel is believed by some to be a likenesss of Helena but by others to be an allegorical figure. Photo Bischöfliches Dom- und Diözesonmuseum, Trier.

this point more firmly.[55] From the beginning he also sensed the special significance of panel 8, even before that panel proved to be the central one in the total composition of the ceiling.[56] This panel shows an older woman, richly adorned, who lifts her veil with her right hand and holds a kantharos in her left hand; on her head she wears a chain of pearls and a golden coronet with three large jewels. As is true of the other three ladies, her head is surrounded by a nimbus. The conclusion that this should be Helena, the mother of Constantine, was a natural one for Kempf.[57]

The attractive suggestion has been made that the painted ceiling was created in honor of Crispus' wedding, which can be dated to the year 321, as we have seen.[58] But if that were so, would one not expect to find the bride *and the groom*, and in the center of the composition? Kempf therefore suggested that the elder Helena's 70th birthday is being celebrated.[59] That, too, is not without attendant difficulties: Helena's 70th birthday should fall in 320, or even in 319 or 318, not in 321.[60]

The remaining two ladies in our ceiling, panels 2 and 14, have been identified by Kempf respectively as Constantia, Constantine's sister, and as Fausta, his wife.[61]

Even before the second phase of the excavations Kempf referred to his find as "the most significant archaeological discovery on German

[55]"Die Ausgrabungen ... von 1943 bis 1950" 110-12; "Die Konstantinische Doppelkirchenanlage in Trier und ihre Baugeschichte von 326-1000," *Kunstchronik* 4 (1951) 107-109; Kempf-Reusch, *Zeugnisse* 244-46, without, however, precluding an allegorical interpretation entirely; "Die Konstantinischen Deckenmalereien" (1977) 155; "Das Haus der heiligen Helena," 4-6. Winfried Weber, *Deckengemälde*[2] 26.

[56]See n. 53.

[57]"Die Ausgrabungen ... von 1943 bis 1950" 112; "Die altchristliche Bischofsstadt Trier" 59; *Legende-Überlieferung-Forschung* 18, crediting Richard Delbrueck. Kempf-Reusch, *Zeugnisse* 244-45, by inference. "Die Konstantinischen Deckenmalereien" (1977) 155, again crediting Richard Delbrueck. "Das Haus der heiligen Helena" 4-5; Winfried Weber, *Deckengemälde*[2] 21-22 and 27.

[58]Maria R. Alföldi, "Helena nobilissima femina" 81-82; Walter N. Schumacher, "Cubile Sanctae Helenae," *RömQ* 58 (1963) 196-222 at 197; Wightman, *Roman Trier* 109-10; Drijvers, *op. cit*,. 28-29.

[59]"Die Konstantinischen Deckenmalereien" 1977) 155-57; "Das Haus der heiligen Helena" 4-6; Winfried Weber, *Deckengemälde*[2] 27.

[60]See chapter II above and chapters VIII and XI below.

[61]"Die Konstantinischen Deckenmalereien" (1977) 157; "Das Haus der heiligen Helena" 5-6. Winfried Weber, *Deckengemälde*[2] 27.

soil since the war."[62]   Certainly the significance of his find was not slow to be recognized by other scholars. Irving Lavin has referred to it as "one of the most spectacular revelations in the field of early Christian archaeology since World War II."[63]

A number of scholars and the present writer have agreed with Kempf in interpreting the four (or three) panels as actual likenesses of imperial ladies, while not necessarily agreeing with all individual identifications.[64] The question was left open by Lavin, who addresses himself chiefly to stylistic matters, Wladimiro Dorigo, Jochen Zink, and Heinz Heinen.[65]

There have been dissenting voices, too. Andreas Rumpf assigns the paintings, on stylistic grounds, to the time of the emperor Gratian (367-383) and asserts that portraits of imperial ladies would never be found in a ceiling.[66] Maria R. Alföldi rightly points out that Rumpf ignores both the archaeological and historical context.[67]   And at Aquileia, according to some views, there are imperial portraits in a mosaic floor.

The comments of Michelangelo Cagiano de Azevedo on our subject are not to be dismissed as readily.[68] Like Kempf, he holds the room to be part of the imperial residence and dates it to the second decade of the fourth century.[69] But the iconography, he insists, is far too uncertain to permit the identification of a Helena or a Fausta or any

---

[62]*Legende-Überlieferung-Forschung* 17.

[63]"The Ceiling Frescoes in Trier and Illusionism in Constantinian Painting," *DOP* 21 (1967) 97-113 at 99.

[64]Andreas Alföldi, "Zur Erklärung der konstantinischen Deckengemälde in Trier," *Historia* 4 (1955) 131-50; Maria R. Alföldi, see n. 51; Heinz Kähler,   *Die Stiftermosaiken in der konstantinischen Südkirche von Aquileia* (Cologne 1962) 12; Walter N. Schumacher, see n. 58; Wilhelm Bernhard Kaiser, "Der Trierer Ada-Kameo," in *Festgabe Wolfgang Jungandreas* (Trier 1964) 24-35 at 33-35; Edith Mary Wightman, *Roman Trier* 109-110, but she leaves the question open in her *Gallia Belgica* (Berkeley 1965) 236; Johannes Deckers, "Die Decke eines Trierer Prunksaals," *Kölner Römer-Illustrierte* 2 (1975) 176-79; Hans Erich Kubach and Albert Verbeek, *op. cit.* II 1086; this writer, "Crispus," 84.

[65]Lavin, "The Ceiling Frescoes in Trier" 99-102; Dorigo, *Late Roman Painting* (New York 1971) 200-201; Zink in Ronig, *Der Trierer Dom* 18; Heinen, *op. cit.*, 269-75.

[66]*Stilphasen der spätantiken Kunst: Ein Versuch* (Cologne 1957) 24.

[67]"Helena nobilissima femina" 81, n. 17.

[68]"Ritratti o personificazioni le figure del soffitto dipinto di Treviri?" *Arch. Class.* 10 (1956) 60-63.

[69]*Ibid.* 60.

other specific person. Rather, he says, the ladies depicted are personifications of imperial virtues and of the beneficial influence of these on the citizens.[70] Raissa Calza also rejects Kempf's interpretation as being based on insufficient evidence; she, too, prefers to recognize only anonymous and allegorical representations.[71] Friedrich Wilhelm Deichmann points out the need to interpret the Trier ceiling in the context of other late classical ceilings; he feels certain also that the pictures of the Trier ceiling form a meaningful and coherent whole.[72] Max Wegner joins those who do not accept Kempf's interpretation.[73]

By far the most serious challenge to Kempf's interpretation has been posed by Hugo Brandenburg. Having voiced his objection in several earlier publications,[74] he has most recently dealt with the subject at considerable length.[75] He gives full credit to the excavator for his discovery and fully recognizes the quality of the paintings,[76] but soon parts company with Kempf on other points. His dissenting views may be summarized as follows:

1. The considerable distance of the site of the discovery from the so-called Basilica and from the 'Kaiserthermen' raises serious doubts about the room being part of the imperial residence. Kempf's regular

---

[70]*Ibid.* 63.

[71]*Iconografia romana imperiale da Carausio a Giuliano* (Rome 1972) 179, no. 95. The same author had previously pointed to the absence of iconographical support for Kempf's interpretation: "Cronologia ed identificazione dell' 'Agrippina' capitolina.," *Mem. della Pont. Accad. Romana di Archeologia* 8 (1955) 107-36 at 133.

[72]'Kassettendecken,' *JÖB* 21 (1972) 83-107 at 103-105.

[73]In Hans Peter L'Orange, *Das spätantike Herrscherbild von Diokletian bis zu den Konstantin-Söhnen: 284-361 n. Chr.* (Berlin 1984) 147. Others are listed by Hugo Brandenburg, "Zur Deutung der Deckenbilder aus der Trierer Domgrabung," *Boreas* 8 (1985) 143-89 at 144, n. 4; additionally, Harald Mielsch, "Zur stadtrömischen Malerei des 4. Jahrhunderts n. Chr.," *Röm. Mitt.* 85 (1978) 151-207 at 174-75.

[74]*Studien zur Mitra* (Münster 1966) 111, n. 118; "Meerwesensarkophage und Clipeusmotiv," *JDAI* 82 (1967) 195-245 at 220, n. 80; "Le pitture del offitto del di Treviri e la loro interpretazione," *Corsi de cultura sull' arte ravennate e bizantina* 25 (1978) 29-32; review of Theodor Kempf, "Die Konstantinischen Deckenmalereien" (1977), in *BZ* 72 (1979) 247.

[75]"Zur Deutung der Deckenbilder."

[76]*Ibid.* 143.

use of the word 'Prunksaal' assumes for too much and is not even justified by the dimensions of the room.[77]

2. The coin finds are poorly documented and yield at best a *terminus post quem*, 326, for the construction of the church; they do not date the painted ceiling, which may be of a somewhat later date.[78]

3. Among those scholars who have seen imperial ladies in the female figures of the ceiling, there has been considerable disagreement about specific identifications. Kempf himself has not been consistent in his identifications. This surely suggests the basic weakness of this entire interpretation.[79]

4. The three male figures cannot by any stretch of the imagination be interpreted as members of the imperial family. The absence of any male imperial portraits in the total composition makes it impossible to interpret the female figures as imperial ladies.[80]

5. The three male figures are placed in positions of equal rank with three of the purported imperial ladies, which creates an additional difficulty.[81]

6. A wide-ranging survey of contemporary monuments shows that ceiling portraits, both of private persons and of officials, can be found.[82]

7. But the gestures and attributes of the four female figures are entirely inappropriate and unparalleled for imperial ladies – why, especially, should Helena be holding a kantharos?[83]

8. The coronets worn by three of the ladies cannot be insignia of imperial rank: 'Helena's coronet is decorated with three large jewels, 'Fausta's' with four, and 'Constantia's' with five; but Helena and Fausta were of equal rank, while Constantia was of lesser rank.[84]

9. Coin portraits offer no parallels for the use of the coronet by the ladies of Constantine's family.[85]

---

[77]*Ibid.* 145-47. In size the room is roughly comparable to the well-known room, in Rome's Terme Museum, from the Villa of Livia at Prima Porta.

[78]*Ibid.* 147f.

[79]*Ibid.* 157-59.

[80]*Ibid.* 159f.

[81]*Ibid.* 160f.

[82]*Ibid.* 161-70.

[83]*Ibid.* 170-72.

[84]*Ibid.* 172f. A minor correction to Brandenburg's argument seems in order: as the wife of Licinius, Constantia was of the some rank as Helena and Fausta.

[85]*Ibid.* 173f.

10. The use of the nimbus is by no means limited to imperial portraits.[86]

11. A comparative study shows the popularity, in late antiquity, of divine figures and personifications in decorative designs.[87]

12. The four female figures in the painted ceiling in Trier are best understood as personifications of an abundant and cultivated life-style. Such interpretation would harmonize with the presence of the three male figures, who represent the life of the mind, and of the Erotes.[88]

The first of these points is not fully convincing. Within the walls of the Roman city of Trier there was ample room for even the most ambitious project; much of the area enclosed by the walls was not built up. Cagiano de Azevedo is right, I think, in envisioning a complex of gardens and separate buildings.[89] Could Helena have had a separate residence, as she later did in Rome?

On the second of these points, Brandenburg is right in pointing out that the coin finds are poorly documented. But Kempf has shown the same dates of construction (326-348) both for the atrium and for the new construction above the room with the pointed ceiling. And since the ceiling was found below the floor of the Constantinion church it can in no way be of a later date, as Winfried Weber rightly points out.[90]

The cumulative evidence of the remaining ten points is, it seems to me, incontrovertible. I conclude that the room excavated by Kempf was part of the imperial residence and that it was taken down to make room for the Constantinian church, but that it is no longer possible to recognize members of the imperial family in the four female figures of the ceiling.

A recent interpretation of the ceiling by Erika Simon does not allow for a portrait of Helena.[91] 'Fausta' becomes a personification of *Sapientia*, 'Constantia' a personification of *Pulchritudo*,[92] and 'Helena'

---

[86]*Ibid.* 175-77.

[87]*Ibid.* 177-84.

[88]*Ibid.* 186-89. Lavin, "The Ceiling Frescoes in Trier" 101, had already observed that "the message, or at least the mood, of the ceiling is one of joy and happiness."

[89]"I palatia imperiale di Treviri, Milano e Ravenna," *Corsi di cultura sull' arte ravennate e byzantina* 25 (1978) 33-44 at 36.

[90]*Deckengemälde*[2] 29.

[91]*Die konstantinischen Deckengemälde in Trier* (Mainz 1986).

[92]*Ibid.* 26-37.

an 'Idealporträt' of Fausta as *Iuventas* and *Salus*.[93] Most readers will be skeptical of this interpretation.

The association of St. Helena with the cathedral of Trier has found eloquent expression through the centuries in the interior appointments of the church.[94]

The *Gesta Treverorum* attributes to Helena the foundation of a second church in Trier:

At that time there was built in Trier, on orders of the blessed Helena, a church which was well appointed and of impressive dimensions, in honor of the Holy Cross and shaped like a cross.[95]

Given the general unreliability of the *Gesta Treverorum*, we should be skeptical. But a chapel or church of the Holy Cross, located just outside the city's south-eastern gate, the Porta Alba , is documented as early as 704. The present Chapel of the Holy Cross was built on the site of an earlier church between 1050 and 1066. It was badly damaged during World War Two but restored in 1957, it is connected with the modern Church of the Holy Cross, immediately to the south, by a corridor.[96]

About three km up the Mosel from Trier, on the left bank of the river, lies the former village of Euren, now an integral part of the city. Here, on August 27, 1075, Archbishop Udo of Trier dedicated a Church of St. Helena.[97] The present building, however, dates only from 1874-

---

[93]*Ibid.* 39-45.

[94]Irsch, *Dom*, passim; Franz Ronig, "Die Ausstattung des Trierer Domes," *Das Münster* 21 (1968) 33-48; Ronig, *Dom, passim.*

[95]19 (*MGH, Script.* VIII 152-53), immediately after reporting the foundation of the Church of St. Peter, the later cathedral. For a fuller account see Bunjes, *op. cit.*, 95-96.

[96]Kentenich, *Geschichte* 130; Egid Beitz, *Das heilige Trier* (Augsburg 1927) 21; Bunjes, *op. cit.*, 95-103, with earlier literature; Ewig, *Trier im Merowingerreich* 50; Kurt Böhner, *Die fränkischen Altertümer des Trierer Landes* (Berlin 1956) II 160; Kubach and Verbeek, *op. cit.* II 1112; Winfried Weber, *Die Heiligkreuz-Kapelle in Trier* (Trier 1982).

[97]Christopher Brower, *Antiquitates et Annales Trevirenses,* ed. Jacob Masen (Liège 1670) I 553; *MGH, Script.* XV.2 1281; Franz Xaver Kraus, *Inschriften* II 201, nos. 423-24; Sauerland, *op. cit.*, 75; Bunjes, *op. cit.*, 380; Ewig, "Tradition" 149; Dietz, "St. Helena" 360; Alois Willems in *Festschrift zur 900-Jahrfeier der Pfarrei St. Helena* (Trier-Euren 1975) 9.

Plate II

A page from the *Missale Trevirense* printed in 1547 by Eucharius Cervicorus in Koblenz. From left to right: St. Matthias, Pope Cornelius (on their relics in Trier see Chapter X), St. Peter (the patron of Trier's cathedral), St. Helena, and Bishop Maternus (third on the list of the bishops of Trier, after Eucharius and Valerius). Reproduced from Joseph Theele, *Rheinische Buchkunst* (Cologne 1925), pl. 41, ill. 62.

Marble statue of St. Helena, in the east choir of the cathedral of Trier. This statue and a companion statue of Constantine are part of a grand design of the high altar by Johann Wolfgang Fröhlicher, shortly before 1700.

1876.[98] It was heavily damaged on December 8, 1944; reconstruction was completed by Christmas of 1948.[99]

In Roman days the site of the church had been occupied by a villa; chance finds have included substantial parts of a mosaic floor. According to local tradition Helena resided in this villa.[100] Not far from the church there is a public fountain, the 'Helenenbrunnen.' It, too, is associated with Helena by local tradition.[101]

In the liturgical calendars of Trier there is no mention of Helena before the 13th century.[102] It would be mistaken, however, to infer from this that Helena did not receive veneration in Trier before the 13th century.[103]

There are, or were, various relics, either of St. Helena or associated with her, which establish further links between her and the city of Trier. These will be considered in chapters X and XII below.

[98]Bunjes, op. cit. 381. The new church was not dedicated until 1883: Alois Willems in Festschrift St. Helena 28. The circumstances surrounding the construction are detailed by Franz J. Ronig, ibid. 84-88.

[99]Alois Willems, op. cit. 36-37.

[100]Bunjes, op. cit. 380; Böhner, op. cit. I 288 and II 154-55; Dietz, "St. Helena" 359; Alois Willems in Festschrift St. Helena 2-3.

[101]Nikolaus Hocker, "Sagen von der Mosel," Zeitschrift für deutsche Mythologie und Sittenkunde 1 (1853) 189-95 at 194; Paul Zaunert, Rheinland Sagen (Jena 1924) II 75; Hans-Henning Lauer, op. cit. 46-47 and 58-59; Dietz, "St. Helena" 359-60; photograph in Festschrift St. Helena 16.

[102]Sauerland, op. cit. 75-77; Peter Miesges, Der Trierer Festkalendar (Trierisches Archiv, Ergänzungsheft 15; Trier 1915) 78.

[103]Ewig, "Tradition" 149.

Chapter V.
The Legends of Cologne, Bonn, and Xanten

Numerous places in the Rhineland are linked to Helena not by historical facts, but by legend and cult. Detailed studies of this subject have been undertaken by others.[1] To report the findings of these studies in every detail would be both distracting and unnecessary in the present context. It seems appropriate, however, to examine the tradition of Helena in three major locations where it has been especially fruitful: Cologne, Bonn, and Xanten.

The site of the Church of St. Gereon in Cologne served as a Christian place of burial and worship from the fourth century on, as archaeological evidence suggests.[2]

Gregory of Tours (d. 594) is the first to tell us of a basilica on the site;[3] this basilica, not yet named after St. Gereon, but called *Ad Sanctos*

---

[1]Mackes, *op. cit.*, and Dietz, "St. Helena."

[2]A carefully detailed and still valuable description of this church is provided by Hugo Rahtgens, *Die Kunstdenkmäler der Stadt Köln* II.1 (Düsseldorf 1911) 1-102; the extensive bibliography (1-8) and inventory of illustrations (8-14) by Johannes Krudewig deserve special mention. See also Paul Clemen, *Die romanische Monumentalmalerei* 132-37. Gertie Gretz and Otto Koch, *St. Gereon zu Köln* (Bonn 1939), is useful but not reliable in all details. There are numerous more recent descriptions which take into account the damage suffered by the church during World War Two and the subsequent explorations and restoration. I have made use of the following: Otmar Schwab, "St. Gereon" in *Frühchristliches Köln* (Cologne 1965) 34-37; Kubach and Verbeek, *op. cit.* I 533-44 and III, pls. 217-26; *Führer zu vor- und frühgeschichtlichen Denkmälern* vol. 38: *Köln* II (Mainz 1980) 191-204 by Hansgerd Hellenkemper and 204-11 by Werner Schäfke; Hiltrud Kier and Ulrich Krings, edd., *Köln: Die romanischen Kirchen* (Cologne 1984-1985) I 278-97 by Werner Schäfke, and III, ill. 295-378; Werner Schäfke, *Kölns romanische Kirchen*, 5th ed. (Cologne 1985) 100-28 and 153-55, color pl. 6-9 and 21, and ill. 24-35; Werner Schäfke, *St. Gereon in Köln* (Cologne 1985). The basic architectural problems posed by the restoration are discussed by Robert Grosche, "Zur Wiederherstellung des Inneren von St. Gereon zu Köln," *Das Münster* 15 (1962) 279-289.

On the Christian place of burial and worship see specifically Rahtgens, *Kd. Köln* II.1 15, 17, and 28, and Schäfke, *Kölns r. Kirchen*[5] 100, or id., *St. Gereon* 2. There is no evidence, however, for the presence of martyrs' graves; see Johannes G. Deckers, "St. Gereon in Köln: Ausgrabungen 1978/79," *JbAC* 25 (1982) 102-31 at 127.

[3]*Liber in Gloria Martyrum* 61 in *MGH, SRM* I.2 530 or I.2 [2] 80; 62 in Migne, *PL* LXXI 761-62; Clemen, *Die romanische Monumentalmalerei* 135 with n.1; Levison, *Frühzeit* 58; Friedrich Wilhelm Oediger, *Die Regesten der Erzbischöfe von Köln im Mittelalter* I: *313-1099* (Bonn 1954) 17-18, no. 19; Otmar Schwab, *op. cit.* 34; Oediger in Eduard Hegel, *Geschichte des Erzbistums Köln* I[2] (Cologne 1972) 29.

Aureos, featured a well, he says, which served as a tomb for fifty members of The Theban Legion who here suffered martyrdom.[4] The whole tradition of this Theban Legion is fraught with many difficulties, especially so the reports of detachments of this legion having been dispatched to Trier, Cologne, and other places.[5] Not much later the church apparently acquired St. Gereon for its patron.[6] St. Gereon, it turns out, is the leader of those Thebans who were sent to Cologne and there martyred. A full account was given by the 10th century anonymous *Passio S. Gereonis et Aliorum Martyrum*.[7]

[4]No trace of this well has ever been found: Otmar Schwab, *op. cit.* 34; Oediger in Hegel, *op. cit.* I² 29; Deckers, "St. Gereon" 126 with n. 91; Schäfke in Kier-Krings, *op. cit.* I 281 and 284; Schäfke, *Kölns r. Kirchen*⁵ 104 and 110, or id., *St. Gereon* 7 and 12. At Trier, too, the bodies of martyrs were supposedly thrown into a well; see the *Gesta Treverorum* 17 (Migne, *PL* CLIV 1131; *MGH, Script.* VIII 149-51).

[5]I do not think that there ever were any Thebans in Trier or in the Rhineland. On Theban martyrs in the Rhineland see also: Wilhelm Neuss, *Die Anfänge des Christentums im Rheinlande*, 2nd ed. (Bonn 1933) 27; Levison, *Frühzeit* 62; Gottfried Kentenich, "Der Kult der Thebäer am Niederrhein," *Rheinische Vierteljahrsblätter* 1 (1931) 339-350, esp. 342; Harald von Petrikovits, *Das römische Rheinland: Archäologische Forschungen seit 1945* (Cologne 1960) 140; Harald von Petrikovits in Petri and Droege, *Rheinische Geschichte* I.1: *Altertum* (Düsseldorf 1978) 254; Hugo Borger, *Xanten: Entstehung und Geschichte eines niederrheinischen Stiftes* (Xanten 1966) 11-13. All these are skeptical. Johannes Christian Nattermann, *Die goldenen Heiligen: Geschichte des Stiftes St. Gereon zu Köln* (Cologne 1960) 18, is more inclined to accept the tradition.

[6]The earliest reference to St. Gereon as patron of this church is in the anonymous *Liber Historiae Francorum* 38 (ed. Krusch [*MGH, SRM* II] 309), in the context of events taking place in the year 612. This text can be dated to the year 727; see Manitius I 227, Brunhölzl, *Geschichte der lat. Lit. des Mittelalters* I 141-42, and John Michael Wallace-Hadrill, *The Frankish Church* (Oxford 1983) 199; Rahtgens, *Kd. Köln* II.1 16; Neuss, *Anfänge* 27; Nattermann, *op. cit.* 21; Oediger in Hegel, *op. cit.* I² 29-30; Kubach and Verbeek, *op. cit.* I 533; Hellenkemper in *Führer Köln* II 203-204; Schäfke in Kier-Krings, *op. cit.* I 296, n. 23; Schäfke, *Kölns r. Kirchen*⁵ 103-104, or id., *St. Gereon* 5.

[7]*BHL* 3446. Text in *Acta Sanct.* Oct. V (ed. 1868) 36-42 and in Migne, *PL* CCXII 759-72. There and elsewhere (Rahtgens, *Kd. Köln* II.1 15; Clemen, *Die romanische Monumentalmalerei* 135, n. 1, 136, and 137, n. 3; Gretz-Koch, *op. cit.* 201, but not 18 or 153; Otmar Schwab, *op. cit.* 34; and Deckers, 'St. Gereon" 119) erroneously attributed to Helinand, a Cistertian monk and chronicler (d. after 1229). Levison, *Frühzeit* 59-60, makes a good case for the *passio* having been written ca. 1000, and this date has been widely accepted; see, e.g., Agostino Amore in *Bibl. Sanct.* III (1963) 923, and Schäfke in Kier-Krings, *op. cit.* I 281 with n. 21. Mackes, *op. cit.* 192-94, however, argues for 1069. Nattermann, *op. cit.* 20, dates the *passio* to ca. 1000, but still attributes it to Helinand, without explaining the contradiction; in another passage, *op. cit.* 49, he attributes it to an unknown author. This text constitutes the first link of Helena with Cologne, but in the liturgical calendars of Cologne, which reach back to the ninth

(continued...)

In this account the number of martyred Thebans has grown to 318, and the well accommodated all of them![8] Above this well, we learn, Helena built the Church of St. Gexon:

> Fecit (Helena) ... super eiusdem sancti martyris et sociorum eius corpora ... insignem neminique prorsus vel sententia sermonis explicabilem vel arte operis imitabilem structurae mirificae sublimis ecclesiam.[9]

The original church building was greatly expanded by Archbishop Anno (1056-1075).[10] The *vita* of this archbishop, completed in 1104 or 1105,[11] again links the church with Helena:

> Verum inter multas antiquitatis structuras, quibus ipsa civitas nobiliter excellit, beati Gereonis olim eximia celebratur fabrica, quam Helena christianissima matrona, Consstantini mater, regiis sumptibus in rotundum erexerat.[12]

---

[7](...continued)
century, there is no mention of Helena before the 12th century; see Georg Zilliken, "Der Kölner Festkalender," *BJ* 119 (1910) 13-157 at 90.

[8]1.14 (*Acta Sanct.* Oct. V [ed. 1868] 38; Migne, *PL* CCXII 765). See also the *Chronicon* of the 13th century monk Alberich (Albericus) of Trois-Fontaines, ad annum 306 (*MGH, Script.* XXIII 685). The number 318 is found already in martyrologies which are older than the *passio*; see Levison, *Frühzeit* 60, n. 3, and 61 with n. 6. Ultimately it may be traced back to other traditions: in Genesis 14.14 Abraham is said to have 318 servants, and the number of bishops attending the Council of Nicaea in 325 reportedly was also 318. See Michel Aubineau, "Les 318 serviteurs d'Abraham et le nombre des Pères au Concile de Nicée," *RHE* 61 (1966) 5-43.

[9](Helena) built ... above the bodies of the same holy martyr and his companions ... a remarkable church of marvelous design, a church which no one, indeed, can explain by power of speech or imitate by skill of hands. 2.19 (*Acta Sanct.* Oct. V [1868] 40; Migne, *PL* CCXII 767).

[10]*Notae S. Gereonis Coloniensis* (*MGH, Script.* XIII 723); Franz Xaver Kraus, *Inschriften* II 262, no. 557; Rahtgens, *Kd. Köln* II.1 17-18; Clemen, *Die romanische Monumentalmalerei* 137 with nn. 4-5; Oediger, *Regesten Köln* I 285, no. 983; *Handbuch des Erzbistums Köln*, 26th ed. (Cologne 1966) I 35; Oediger in Hegel, *op. cit.* I² 32. Kubach and Verbeek, *op. cit.* I 533 and 536; Schäfke in *Führer Köln* II 205; Schäfke, *Kölns r. Kirchen*⁵ 109, or id., *St. Gereon* 9-10.

[11]Rudolf Koepke in *MGH, Script.* XI 463; Manitius III 573.

[12]But among the many ancient buildings for which this city is renowned none is celebrated more than the Church of the blessed Gereon, which that most Christian lady, Helena, the mother of Constantine, had built at royal expense in circular shape. 2.17 (*BHL* 507; Migne, *PL* CXLIII 1555; *MGH, Script.* XI 491); Clemen, *Die romanische Monumentalmalerei* 136, n. 2. But not for the first time; Ewig, "Tradition" 184, is in error.

The development of a legend by accretion can be observed here. Rahtgens is of the opinion that these data have only legendary significance.[13] Hippolyte Delehaye points out that the hagiographers of Cologne were especially imaginative.[14] Réau thinks that the legend of St. Gereon is only a doublet of the legend of St. Ursula.[15] The supposed remains of St. Gereon were raised in 1121 in the presence of Archbishop Frederick I and St. Norbert, formerly of Xanten and later archbishop of Magdeburg.[16]

The claim made by Cologne to have a church founded by Helena is best understood in the context of the intense rivalry which existed for centuries between the church of Cologne and that of Trier. This rivalry manifested itself in many other ways:

1. Maternus, properly a bishop of Cologne in the early fourth century, was appropriated by the church of Trier for the first time in the *vita* of Bishop Maximinus, which dates from the eighth century.[17] Trier's claim on Maternus was stated more expressly in the *vita* of Sts. Eucharius, Valerius, and Maternus, which was produced in Trier during the tenth century.[18]

2. A 'staff of St. Peter,' associated in legend with Maternus, was obtained from Metz by Archbishop Bruno I of Cologne (953-

[13]*Kd. Köln* II.1 15.

[14]*Les origines du culte des martyrs*, 2nd ed. (Brussels 1933) 360.

[15]*Iconographie* III.2 581.

[16]*Epistulae Rodulfi Abbatis* (MGH, Script. X 330); *Vita Norberti* 12 (MGH, Script. XII 682; Migne, *PL* CLXX 1290-91); Richard Knipping, *Die Regesten der Erzbischöfe von Köln im Mittelalter* II:*1100-1205* (Bonn 1901) 29; Oediger in Hegel, *op. cit.* I² 281; Odilo Engels in Petri and Droege, *op. cit.* I.3: *Hohes Mittelalter* (Düsseldorf 1983) 218; Schäfke in Kier-Krings, *op. cit.* I 283; Franz J. Felten in Kaspar Elm, ed., *Norbert von Xanten* (Cologne 1984) 104-108. The diocesan library in Münster (Westphalia) owns an exemplar of a Latin and German *vita* of St. Norbert produced in Antwerp in 1622. It is illustrated with 35 engravings, and no. 16 of these shows the raising of the remains of St. Gereon; see Elm, *op. cit.* 338 and 342.

[17]*Acta Sanct.* Maii VII (ed. 1867) 21-25; Winheller, *op. cit.* 14; Ewig, *Trier* 33.

[18]*BHL* 2655; *Acta Sanct.* Ian. II (ed. 1643) 918-22; or Ian. III (ed. 1863) 533-37; Manitius II 224, n. 2; Winheller, *op. cit.* 40 and 44; Levison, *Frühzeit* 19.

965).[19] One half of this staff was acquired in 980 by Archbishop Egbert of Trier.[20]

3. The *Gesta Treverorum* of the twelfth century reports that upon the death of this same Maternus there was a dispute between the people of Trier and those of Cologne over the possession of the bishop's body and that a manifestation of the divine will resolved the dispute in favor of the people of Trier.[21]

4. A concerted effort was made by the church of Trier to discredit Bishop Euphrates of Cologne, a contemporary of Maximinus of Trier. The *vita* of Maximinus reports that Euphrates was excommunicated at a council of bishops held in Cologne in 346.[22] But many scholars have concluded that no such council was ever held, and rightly so.[23]

During World War Two the Church of St. Gereon suffered extensive damage, especially to its interior and to the northwest side of the decagon.[24] Restoration was begun in the early post-war years.[25] In conjunction with the restoration archaeological excavations and explorations were conducted.[26] These established that the original building can be dated to Roman times, more specifically to the last third of the fourth century.[27] This, of course, is substantially later than Helena. Addi-

---

[19]The *vita* of Bruno 31 (*MGH, Script.* IV 266). *Catalogi Archiepiscoporum Coloniensium* (both I and II; *MGH, Script.* XXIV 339); Oediger, *Regesten Köln* I 143, no. 467.

[20]Oediger, *Regesten Köln* I 163, no. 531; *Chronica Albini Monachi Trium Fontium* ad 953 and 972 (*MGH, Script.* XXIII 766 and 771).

[21]16 (Migne, *PL* CLIV 1125-26; *MGH, Script.* VIII 148); Gröber, *op. cit.* 282; Manitius III 516-18.

[22]1.3 (*Acta Sanct.* Maii VII [ed. 1867] 21).

[23]Two excellent recent examinations of the pseudo-council of Cologne are: Hanns Christof Brennecke, "Synodum congregravit contra Euphratam nefandissimum episcopum: Zur angeblichen Kölner Synode gegen Euphrates," *ZKG* 90 (1979) 176-200; Nancy Gauthier, *L'évangélisation* 447-53.

[24]Kubach and Verbeek, *op. cit.* I 534; photograph in Schäfke, *Kölns r. Kirchen* 124, or id., *St. Gereon*, inside front cover.

[25]Willy Weyres in Wilhelm Neuss, *Rheinische Kirchen im Wiederaufbau* (Mönchen-Gladbach 1951) 12-14.

[26]Armin von Gerkan, *op. cit.* 59-65.

[27]*Ibid.* 59; Armin von Gerkan, "St. Gereon in Köln," *Germania* 29 (1951) 215-18 at 215; id., "Der Urbau der Kirche St. Gereon in Köln," in *Neue Beiträge zur Kunstgeschichte des I. Jahrtausends* I.1: *Spätantike und Byzanz* = *Forschungen zur*

(continued...)

tional excavations undertaken in 1978-1979 have confirmed the earlier conclusions.[28] The tradition of Helena's having founded the Church of St. Gereon has remained strong throughout the centuries. Attentive visitors are reminded of this tradition wherever their steps might lead them. Today we lament the loss of some of the treasures of the church, but many have survived all vicissitudes.[29] An inventory would be a lengthy one and would include objects from eight centuries. Of significance is the constant association of Helena with St. Gereon and Archbishop Anno; i.e., Helena is remembered primarily for having founded the church. There appears to be much less interest in Helena's reported discovery of the True Cross.

Many reminders of St. Helena can be found elsewhere in the city of Cologne: in the churches of St. Severinus, St. Maria Lyskirchen, St. Kunibert, and St. Peter, and in the Wallraf-Richartz-Museum.[30] There is another, less direct link of Helena to the cathedral and to the entire city of Cologne:

Among the relics which Helena is reported to have found are the remains of the Three Kings (or Magi). First taken by her to Constantinople, they were, supposedly, soon transferred by a certain Bishop Eustorgius to Milan. From there, in 1164, Archbishop Reinald von Dassel acquired them for Cologne, as a reward for his services to the emperor Frederick Barbarossa. The arrival of the relics was a most extraordinary event in the history of Cologne; it accounts for the city's

---

[27](...continued)
Kunstgeschichte und christlichen Archäologie I (Baden-Baden 1952) 91-102 at 92; Fritz Fremersdorf, *Ältestes Christentum mit besonderer Berücksichtigung der Grabungsergebnisse unter der Severinskirche in Köln* (Berlin 1956) 5; Otmar Schwab, *op. cit.* 36; Oediger in Hegel, *op. cit.* I[2] 31. Kubach and Verbeek, *op. cit.* I 533 and 534; Hellenkemper in *Führer Köln* II 200-202; Schäfke in Kier-Krings, *op. cit.* I 281; Schäfke, *Kölns r. Kirchen*[5] 100, or id., *St. Gereon* 2. Gretz-Koch, *op. cit.* esp. 21 and 198-200, had already, on structural and comparative grounds, assigned the original structure of St. Gereon to the fourth century, but had gone wrong in assigning it more specifically to the times of Constantine and Helena.

[28]Deckers, "St. Gereon."

[29]Rahtgens, II.1, passim;, Gretz-Koch, *op. cit., passim*; Dietz, "St. Helena," *passim*; Kier-Krings, *op. cit., passim*; Schäfke, *Kölns r. Kirchen*[5], *passim*.

[30]References will be found in the following: Hugo Rahtgens and Hermann Roth, *Die Kunstdenkmäler der Stadt Köln* II.2 (Düsseldorf 1929); Kier-Krings, *op. cit.;* Rahtgens, *Kd. Köln* II.1; Schäfke, *Kölns r. Kirchen*[5];Wilhelm Ewald and Hugo Rahtgens, *Die Kunstdenkmäler der Stadt Köln* I.4 (Düsseldorf 1916); Wallraf-Richartz-Museum, Cologne, *Vollständiges Verzeichnis der Gemäldesammlung* (Cologne 1986).

sometimes being called the 'City of the Three Kings' and for the three crowns in its coat of arms.[31] The famous shrine which houses the relics was built some years later under Reinald's successor by Nicolas of Verdun (mostly) and through the centuries and many vicissitudes has remained a principal treasure of the cathedral.[32] It does not appear that much recognition was given to Helena in this context. But the middle panel of the wall paintings on the south side of the high choir of the cathedral has the legend of the Three Kings for its subject matter. This panel, like the others, consists of seven individual scenes; the fifth one

[31]Knipping, *Regesten Köln* II 132-33, no. 804; Fritz Witte, *Der goldene Schrein: Ein Buch über Köln* (Cologne 1923) 66-72; Andreas Huppertz, *Der Kölner Dom und seine Kunstschätze* (Cologne 1950) 7-9; Joseph Hoster, *Der Dom zu Köln* (Cologne 1965) 12-14; Patrice Boussel, *Des reliques et de leur bon usage* (Paris 1971) 139-40; Oediger in Hegel, *op. cit.* I² 155-56; Matthias Zender, *Räume und Schichten mittelalterlicher Heiligenverehrung*, 2nd ed. (Cologne and Bonn 1973) 202; Hans Hofmann, *Die Heiligen Drei Könige* (Bonn 1975) 80, 96-114, and 302-304; Adolf Klein, *Der Dom zu Köln* (Cologne 1980) 52-54; Stefan Weinfurter and Odilo Engels, *Series Episcoporum Ecclesiae Catholicae Occidentalis* V.1 (Stuttgart 1982) 38; Wallraf-Richartz-Museum, Cologne, *Die Heiligen Drei Könige* (Cologne 1982), passim.

   Meanwhile at Milan, in the Chapel of the Magi of the Church of St. Eustorgius, the visitor can still see the huge sarcophagus which formerly contained the relics of the Magi. In the same church a carved column capital tells the story of the *translatio* to Milan: Ute Wachsmann, *Die Chorschrankenmalereien im Kölner Dom* (Dissertation Bonn 1985) I 141 and II, ill. 183-84. More on the relics of the Magi in chapter X below.

[32]Franz Xaver Kraus, *Inschriften* II 255-59, no. 547; Otto von Falke and Heinrich Frauberger, *Deutsche Schmelzarbeiten des Mittelalters* (Frankfurt/Main 1904) 54-59 and pls. 61-64; Otto von Falke, *Der Dreikönigenschrein des Nikolaus von Verdun im Kölner Domschatz* (Mönchengladbach 1911); Fritz Witte, *Die Schatzkammer des Domes zu Köln* (Augsburg 1927) 9-12 and 44-52, pls. 9-17; Paul Clemen, *Der Dom zu Köln*, 2nd ed. (Düsseldorf 1938) 338-54; Hermann Schnitzler, *Der Dreikönigenschrein* (Bonn 1939); Huppertz, *op. cit.* 102-104 and ill. 141-50; Hoster, *op. cit.* 14-18, color pl. 2, and pls. 40-47; Hermann Fillitz, *Das Mittelalter* I (Berlin 1969) 103, 261-62, and ill. 359-60; good illustration in Hegel, *op. cit.* I², following p. 160; William D. Wixom in Florens Deuchler, ed., *The Year 1200* II (New York 1970) 97 and ill. 111-21; Peter Lasko, *Ars Sacra, 800-1200* (Harmondsworth, Middlesex, 1972) 243-45 and pl. 293; Walter Schulten, *Der Schrein der Heiligen Drei Könige* (Cologne 1975); Walter Schulten, *Der Kölner Domschatz* (Cologne 1980) 68-69 and 113-15, no. 64; Hugo Borger, *Der Dom zu Köln* (Cologne 1980) 16-17; Anton Legner, *Deutsche Kunst der Romanik* (Munich 1982) 101-104 and pls. 422-435; bibliography, 191; Marie-Madeline S. Gauthier, *Les routes de la foi* (Fribourg 1983) 64-66; Rolf Lauer in Anton Legner, ed., *Ornamenta Ecclesiae* (Cologne 1985) II 216-25, no. E18; Walter Schulten, *Der Dom zu Köln*, 7th ed. (Cologne 1986) 20-21 and 32-33.

depicts the *translatio* of the three Kings to Constantinople by St. Helena.[33]

From Cologne let us turn to Bonn. The principal church of Bonn is the Minster.[34] This church was dedicated in memory of Sts. Cassius and Florentius, supposedly members of the Theban Legion martyred together with seven companions at Bonn.[35] Tradition ascribes the foundation of this church, too, to Helena. It appears, however, that in Bonn the tradition is of more recent date than in Cologne.[36] Archaeological evidence shows that a church was first built here ca. 400 – again substantially later than Helena – on the site of an earlier cemetery and *cella memoriae*.[37] The supposed remains of Cassius, Florentius, and Mallusius (another one of the Theban martyrs) were raised in 1166 by

[33]Ludwig Scheibler and Carl Aldenhoven, *Geschichte der Kölner Malerschule* (Lübeck 1902) 25; Arnold Steffens, "Die alten Wandgemälde auf der Innenseite der Chorbrüstungen des Köner Domes," part III, *ZChrK* 15 (1902) 202-203; Paul Clemen, *Die gotiscen Monumentalmalereien der Rheinlande* (Düsseldorf 1930) 185-86 and pls. 38, 42, and 47; Alfred Stange, *Deutsche Malerei der Gotik* I (Berlin 1934) 17-18; Clemen, *Der Dom zu Köln*[2] 167; Huppertz, *op. cit.* 68-70 and ill. 54 and 60; Borger, *Der Dom zu Köln* 36 and 113; Schnütgen-Museum, Cologne, *Rhein und Maas: Kunst und Kultur 800-1400* (Cologne 1972) II 70; Legner, *Deutsche Kunst der Romanik* 88; Walter Schulten, *Der Dom zu Köln*[7] 34; Wachsmann, *op. cit.* I 140-49 and II, ill. 102. The next two scenes depict the *translatio* first to Milan and then to Cologne.

[34]A detailed description, with extensive bibliography, is provided by Paul Clemen, *Die Kunstdenkmäler der Stadt und des Kreises Bonn* (Düsseldorf 1905) 51-108. A more recent description is that of Kubach and Verbeek, *op. cit.* I 107-19 and III, pls. 40-49.

[35]*Passio S. Gereonis,* esp. 1.13 (*Acta Sanct.* Oct. V [ed. 1868] 38; Migne, *PL* CCXII 764-65). In Alberich of Trois-Fontaines, *Chronicon* ad annum 306 (*MGH, Script.* XXIII 685), we read *Cassius Florentius* rather than *Cassius et Florentius.*

[36]Clemen, *Kd. Bonn* 56; Dietrich Höroldt, "Das Stift St. Cassius zu Bonn," *Bonner Geschichtsblätter* 11 (1957) 1-387 at 36; Dietz, "St. Helena" 374.

[37]Hans Lehner und Walter Bader, "Baugeschichtliche Untersuchungen am Bonner Münster," *BJ* 136/137 (1932) 1-216, esp. 210; Johann Peter (Giovanni) Kirsch, "Un cimitero romano cristiano con chiesa cimiteriale del IV° e V° secolo scoperto a Bonn sul Reno," *RACrist.* 9 (1932) 151-58, esp. 157; Theodor Klauser, "Bemerkungen zur Geschichte der Bonner Märtyrergräber," *Bonner Geschichtsblätter* 3 (1947) 35-41; Höroldt, *op. cit.,* 37, n. 16; Harald von Petrikovits, "Die Zeitstellung der ältesten frühchristlichen Kultanlage unter dem Bonner Münster," *Kölner Jb.* 9 (1967-1968) 112-19; Oediger in Hegel, *op. cit.* I[2] 35; Kubach and Verbeek, *op. cit.* I 108; Ewig in Petri and Droege, *op. cit.* I.2: *Frühes Mittelalter* (Düsseldorf 1980) 41; *ibid.,* vol. of ill. 102, nos. 222-23; Albert Verbeek, *Das Münster in Bonn,* 2nd ed. (Cologne 1983) 4; The *cella memoriae* has been transferred to Bonn's Rheinisches Landesmuseum. See Rheinisches Landesmuseum Bonn, *Führer durch die Sammlungen,* 2nd ed. (Cologne 1985) 64 and ill. 49.

Archbishop Reinald Von Dassel.[38] There is no documentary evidence for the existence of a church on the site before 691/692[39] Most of the extant structure can be dated to the 11th and 12th century.[40] This structure suffered heavy damage by wartime events in 1689 and in 1944.[41] Archaeological explorations were undertaken after World War Two in conjunction with restoration work.[42] Bonn's Minster contains, or contained, an impressive number of representations of Helena.[43]

A former 'Kanonikerhaus' (canon's house) in Bonn's Martinsplatz, a stone's throw away from the Minster, contains in its upper story a Romanesque chapel named after St. Helena. Frescoes dating from the year 1760 included a representation of Helena.[44] In World War Two, when an air raid destroyed the roof of the chapel, these frescoes perished almost entirely.[45] Tradition has it that Helena lived in this house while the Minster was being built and that she set up the chapel in the house at that time.[46] The Kirche auf dem Kreuzberge in

[38]Knipping, *Regesten Köln* II 142, no. 834; Höroldt, *op. cit.* 163; Dietz, "St. Helena," 365; Verbeek, *op. cit.* 5; on Mallusius see Bretz-Koch, *op. cit.* 215, and Höroldt, *op. cit.* 200-202.

[39]Wilhelm Levison, "Die Bonner Urkunden des frühen Mittelalters," *BJ* 136/137 (1932) 217-70 at 236-37, no. 5; Höroldt, *op. cit.* 38; Neuss, *Anfänge*[2] 28; Oediger in Hegel, *op. cit.* I[2] 35.

[40]Clemen, *Kd. Bonn* 57; Lehner-Bader, *op. cit.* esp. 210; Oediger in Hegel, *op. cit.* I[2] 36; Kubach and Verbeek, *op. cit.* I 107 and 110-12.

[41]1689: Clemen, *Kd. Bonn* 59; Kubach and Verbeek, *op. cit.* I 108; 1944: Bernhard Gelderblom, "Die Kriegsschäden am Bonner Münster," Bonner Geschichtsblätter 3 (1947) 151-55; Neuss, *Rheinische Kirchen* 31-33; Kubach and Verbeek, *op. cit.* I 108.

[42]Franz Oelmann in *BJ* 149 (1949) 334-35 and 356-61; Neuss, *Rheinische Kirchen* 75-77.

[43]References will be found in the following: Clemen, *Kd. Bonn*; Walter Holzhausen, "Das Innere des Bonner Münsters," *AHVNrh.* 155-156 (1954) 559-67; Dietz, "St. Helena"; Theo Siering, *Das Münster im Herzen der Stadt Bonn* (Bonn 1980); Verbeek, *op. cit.*

[44]Clemen, *Kd. Bonn* 182-83; Felix Hauptmann, "Die St. Helenakapelle in Bonn," *Bonner Archiv* 4 (1912) 60-62; Höroldt, *op. cit.,* 160 and ill. 15; Dietz, "St. Helena," 365-66; Kubach and Verbeek, *op. cit.* I 120-21 and III, pl. 52; Verbeek, *op. cit.* 29 and ill. 32. The actual street address is Am Hof 32-34. The chapel has recently been reopened after renovation.

[45]Walther Zimmermann in Neuss, *Rheinische Kirchen* 84-85.

[46]Josef Dietz, *Aus der Sagenwelt des Bonner Landes* (Bonn 1965) 15-16; Dietz, "St. Helena" 366.

Bonn's Poppelsdorf district dates from 1627-1628.[47]   Tradition has erroneously associated it with St. Helena.[48]

The small city of Xanten is located to the northwest of Cologne in the plain of the lower Rhine. Its name is derived from 'Sankten,' a corruption of the Latin *Ad Sanctos*.[49] Thus the very name of the city suggests a belief in the presence of martyrs' graves.

The city's principal church is the Church of St. Victor, or 'Dom.' Like the Church of St. Gereon in Cologne and Bonn's Minster, this church stands on the site of an ancient Roman cemetery. Archaeological excavations were conducted in the interior of the church in 1933-1934 and intermittently in 1948-1966.[50] A *cella memoriae* first constructed in the late fourth century and twice renewed in the fifth century is of special interest; for it was believed to mark the grave of a martyr. The first church, as distinguished from a *cella memoriae*, on this site was not constructed till the second half of the eighth century and saw substantial expansion and rebuilding within the next one hundred years. This church suffered extensive damage at the hands of the Normans in 863 and in major fires in 1081 and 1109. Most of the structure extant in modern times until 1944 dated from the 12th through the 16th century. Much destruction occured during World War Two, and reconstruction required many years.[51]

[47]Clemen, *Kd. Bonn* 234; Walter Schulten, *Die Hl. Stiege* (1964) 27; Walter Schulten, *Die Heilige Stiege und Wallfahrtsstätte auf dem Kreuzberg in Bonn*, 5th ed. (Cologne 1986) 3.

[48]Dietz, *Sagenwelt* 15; Dietz, "St. Helena" 366 and 375.

[49]Richard Klapheck, *Der Dom zu Xanten und seine Kunstschätze* (Berlin 1930) 7-8; Walter Bader, *Der Dom zu Xanten* I (Kevelaer 1978) 12; Kubach and Verbeek, *op. cit.* II 1264; Ewig in Petri and Droege, *op. cit.* I.2 40.

[50]The numerous excavation reports are listed in Kubach and Verbeek, *op. cit.* II 1274-75; a good summary of the results, II 1264-66. For more detailed accounts see the following: Borger, *Xanten: Entstehung und Geschichte* 13-31; Hugo Borger and Friedrich Wilhelm Oediger, *Beiträge zur Frühgeschichte des Xantener Viktorstiftes* (Düsseldorf 1969) 5-54; Bader, *Der Dom zu Xanten* I 31-55.

[51]Stephan Beissel, *Die Baugeschichte des heiligen Victor in Xanten* (Freiburg 1883), largely superseded; Paul Clemen, *Die Kunstdenkmäler des Kreises Moers* (Düsseldorf 1892) 81-153; Klapheek, *op. cit.* 8 and 12-48: Walter Bader, ed., *Sechzehnhundert Jahre Xantener Dom* (Cologne 1964), esp. 72 ff. by Hugo Borger; Borger and Oediger, *op. cit.* 54-132; Kubach and Verbeek, *op. cit.* II 1264-75 and III, pls. 595-600; Hans Peter Hilger, *Der Dom zu Xanten* (Königstein im Taunus 1984) 5-14; Hans Peter Hilger, *Der Dom zu Xanten*, 3rd ed. (Cologne 1985) 6-8.

A martyr named Victor is briefly mentioned by Gregory of Tours in the context of Theban martyrs.[52] But for a full account we must once again turn to the *Passio S. Gereonis*: While St. Gereon and his companions were martyred at Cologne, St. Victor and 330 companions, so we learn, were cut down at Xanten and their bodies cast into a swamp.[53] But Theban martyrs are no more believable in Xanten than they are in Cologne or Bonn. No less an authority than Hugo Borger concludes that in the eighth century the finding of many burials on the site of the future 'Dom,' in the course of building activities and in the deliberate search for relics, gave rise to the legend of St. Victor and his Theban companions, which subsequently was incorporated in the *Passio S. Gereonis*.[54]

There is no archaeological evidence which would establish a historical St. Victor, one who was the commander of a contingent of Thebans and was martyred during the reign of Diocletian. Rather, the martyrs' grave under the *cella memoriae* mentioned above is a double burial which can be dated to the years 348-363 or, even more specifically, 361-363.[55] The supposed remains of St. Victor were raised

[52]*Liber in Gloria Martyrum* 62 in *MGH, SRM* I.2 530 or I.2² 80; 63 in Migne, *PL* LXXI 762; Peter Weiler, *Urkundenbuch des Stiftes Xanten* I (Bonn 1935) 1, no. 1; Oediger, *Regesten Köln* I 17, no. 18; Oediger in Hegel, *op. cit.* I² 36.

[53]1.15 (*Acta Sanct.* Oct. V [ed. 1868] 38; Migne, *PL* CCXII 766); In Alberich of Trois-Fontanes, *Chronicon* ad annum 306 (*MGH, Script.* XXIII 685), the number of companions is given as 360 rather than 330; Dietz, "St. Helena" 368, also gives 360.

[54]"Die Ausgrabungen unter der Stiftskirche des hl. Viktor zu Xanten in den Jahren 1945-1960 (Vorbericht II)," *BJ* 161 (1961) 396-448 at 423; *Xanten: Entstehung und Geschichte* 10-11.

[55]Walter Bader, "Ausgrabungen unter dem Xantener Dom: Vorbericht," *Germania* 18 (1934) 112-17 at 113; Wilhelm Neuss, "Eine altchristliche Martyrerkirche unter dem Chor der St. Viktorskirche in Xanten," *RömQ* 42 (1934) 177-82; Hugo Borger, "Die Ausgrabungen im Bereich des Xantener Doms," in *Neue Ausgrabungen in Deutschland* (Berlin 1958) 380-90 at 381. Good collection of plans and photographs in Walter Bader, *Die Stiftskirche des Hl. Viktor zu Xanten* I.1 (Kevelaer 1960); Hugo Borger, "Ausgrabungen ... 1945-1960," *BJ* 161 (1961) 396-448 at 403; Walter Bader, "Das Xantener Grab der Märtyrer," *Der Niederrhein* 30 (1963) 168-80 at 169 and 175-78; Hugo Borger, "Die Ausgrabungen unter der Stiftskirche des hl. Viktor und in der Stifts-Immunität zu Xanten," 181-86 at 182; Hugo Borger, "Die Ausgrabungen unter der Stiftskirche des hl. Viktor und in der Stifts-Immunität zu Xanten: Vorbericht," *Kunstchronik* 16 (1963) 117-37 at 119-120; Bader, *Sechzehnhundert Jahre* 54-56; Hugo Borger in Bader, *Sechzehnhundert Jahre* 67-68 and 85-90, pls. 1-6; Borger, *Xanten: Entstehung und Geschichte* 13-19; Oediger in Hegel, *op. cit.* I 39, with commendable caution; Bader, *Der Dom zu Xanten* I 31-48; Petri and Droege, op. cit., vol. of ill. 103, nos. 224-25.

at some time before 863.[56] In that year, just before the city was taken by the Normans, the precious relics were temporarily removed to Cologne.[57] In 1129 they were placed in a gilt shrine which is still among the treasures of the church and contained within the high altar.[58]

Sts. Gereon, Cassius and Florentius, and Victor have shared October 10 as their common feast day since the ninth or tenth century.[59] A hymn, init. *Maiestati sacrosanctae*, to the Theban martyrs was composed in Cologne, probably before the turn of the 12th century.[60] It refers specifically to Gereon with his 319 companions at Agrippina (Cologne), to Victor with his 330 companions at Troia (Xanten), and to Cassius (but not to Florentius) with his seven companions at Verona (Bonn); there is no mention of Helena. The bonds of a common 'Theban' tradition eventually found a practical expression as well. In 1236 the three chapters

[56]Borger, "Ausgrabungen ... 1945-1960," *BJ* 161 (1961) 396-448 at 408 and 424; Borger, "Die Ausgrabungen ... zu Xanten," *Der Niederrhein* 30 (1963) 181-86 at 181; Oediger in Hegel, *op. cit.* I² 40; Bader, *Der Dom zu Xanten* I 91 ff; Kubach and Verbeek, *op. cit.* II 1266-67.

[57]*Annales Xantenses* sub anno 864 (*MGH, Script.* II 230-31). On the *Annales Xantenses* see Friedrich Wilhelm Oediger, *Vom Leben am Niederrhein* (Düsseldorf 1973) 186-201. I owe the reference to the kindness of Custos Herbert van Bebber. Weiler, *Urkundenbuch* I 2, no. 2; Wilhelm Classen, *Das Erzbistum Köln: Archdiakonat von Xanten* I (*Germania Sacra* III.1.1; Berlin 1938) 59; Oediger, *Vom Leben am Niederrhein* 118-20.

[58]Clemen, *Kd. Kreis Moers* 106; Falke and Frauberger, *op. cit.* 24-25 and pls. 25-26; Klapheck, *op. cit.* 120-21; J. H. Schmidt, "Der Schrein des heiligen Viktor," *Xantener Domblätter* 3.2 and 4 (1952) 75-84; Reinhold Honl in Bader, *Sechzehnhundert Jahre* 263; Horst-Johs Tümmers, *Die Altarbilder des älteren Bartholomäus Bruyn* (Cologne 1964) 86; Oediger in Hegel, *op. cit.* I² 39; Lasko, *op. cit.* 174-75 and pl. 184; Dietz, "St. Helena" 369; Kubach and Verbeek, *op. cit.* II 1268 and 1272.

[59]Georg Zilliken, "Der Kölner Festkalender" 104; *Passio S. Gereonis* 2.23 (*Acta Sanct.* Oct. V [ed. 1868] 40; Migne, *PL* CCXII 770-71); Kentenich, "Thebaer" 344; Höroldt, *op. cit.* 36; Oediger in Hegel, *op. cit.* I² 28; The feast of Sts. Gereon, Cassius and Florentinus, and Victor passed into the Martyrologium Romanum of 1584: *Mart. Rom.* (ed. 1586) 469; French trl. by J. Baudot and F. Gilbert (2nd ed., 1953) 376-77; English trl. by J. B. O'Connel (1962) 222.

[60]Franz Joseph Mone, *Lateinische Hymnen des Mittelalters* (Freiburg 1853-1855) III 321-22, no. 950; Joseph Kehrein, *Lateinische Sequenzen des Mittelalters* (Mainz 1873) 401, no. 590; Cyr Ulysse Joseph Chevalier, *Repertorium Hymnologicum* (Louvain and Brussels 1892-1921) II 73, no. 11046; *AHMA* LV 171-72, no. 150. For other hymns to the Theban martyrs see the index in Chevalier, *Repertorium* VI.

joined together in an agreement for mutual aid and protection.[61] And in this document, for the first time, it is asserted that Helena established all three churches:

> Cum itaque unam et eandem ecclesie nostre habuerint fundatricem, beatam videlicet Helenam reginam gloriosam, inter patronos etiam ecclesiarum nostrarum una et vera fuerit societas ....

It is to be noted that for the Church of St. Victor, as for the Minster in Bonn, this claim is made substantially later then it is for the Church of St. Gereon in Cologne. In 1249 Pope Innocent IV makes reference to the 'Dom' of Xanten as the Church of Sts. Victor and Helena.[62]   The *Historia Xantensis* of ca. 1420-1421 embellishes the account by reporting that Helena gathered the remains of the Theban martyrs from the swamp.[63]   In 1629 the founding of all three churches by St. Helena was believed to have taken place about the year 310, a date utterly impossible.[64]

---

[61]Therefore, since one and the same lady has founded our churches, i.e. the blessed and glorious queen Helena, let there be also a single and true association among the patrons of our churches .... P. Joerres, *Urkundenbuch des Stiftes St. Gereon zu Köln* (Bonn 1893) 108-11, no. 106; Kentenich, "Thebaer," 344; Weiler, *op. cit.* I 90-92, no. 120; Classen, *op. cit.* 59; Höroldt, *op. cit.* 36; Ewig, "Tradition," 184; Nattermann, *op. cit.* 175; Dietz, "St. Helen" 368; Oediger in Hegel, *op. cit.* I² 31.

[62]Weiler, *op. cit.* I 111-12, no. 162; Dietz, "St.Helena" 368; Bader, *Der Dom zu Xanten* I 96.

[63]The attribution of the *Historia Xantensis* to Philipp Schoen, canon and doctor of medicine, is erroneous, as he is known to have died on December 1, 1492. See Classen, *op. cit.* 135. Also Oediger in Borger and Oediger, *op. cit.* 207-208. Clemen, *Kd. Kreis Moers* 147, no. 8, apparently misread MCCCCXCII as MCCCCXIII on Schoen's epitaph in the cloister.

The unpublished MS is in the Stiftsarchiv Xanten, H6. Folios 71v-74v give an account, largely dependent on the *Passio S. Gereonis*, of Helena's activities in the Rhineland: Constantine is occupied in the East with the Arian controversy. He commissions Helena to promote Christianity in the western provinces and especially to collect everywhere the remains of the martyrs and to give them proper burial. For this purpose he provides ample funds from the imperial treasury. Helena travels through Italy, Britain, France, and Germany. She reaches Trier and from there Bonn, Cologne, and Xanten, finding and burying the remains of the martyrs in each place. At Cologne the bodies must be recovered from the well, in Xanten from the swamp. The year is 307. Custos Herbert van Bebber kindly provided copies of the pertinent folios; I have also examined the MS.

See also Clemen, *Kd. Kreis Moers* 82, and Oediger in Hegel, *op. cit.* I² 39, n. 42.

[64]Höroldt, *op. cit.* 36.

Not surprisingly, the Church of St. Victor counts among its sculptures, paintings, tapestries, and other artifacts numerous likenesses of Helena.[65] Tradition credits Helena with having built in Xanten not only the Church of St. Victor but also a chapel of St. Gereon.[66] A 'Brotherhood of St. Helena' celebrated its 600th anniversary in 1963.[67]

As one might expect, the cult, legends, and visual representations of Helena did not remain restricted to Trier, Cologne, Bonn, and Xanten. Rather, from these centers they spread to numerous other, less important places in the Rhineland. For the details the reader must be referred elsewhere.[68]

---

[65]References will be found in the following: Clemen, *Kd. Kreis Moers*; Klapheck, *op. cit.*; Bader, *Sechzehnhundert Jahre;* Dietz, "St. Helena;" Hilger, *Der Dom zu Xanten* (1984); Hilger, *Der Dom zu Xanten*³ (1985).

[66]Clemen, *Kd. Kreis Moers* 156; Heinrich Engelskirchen, "Die Xantener Gereonskapelle in den Sümpfen," *AHVNrh.* 162 (1960) 130-34; "Die Xantener Gereonskapelle innerhalb der Stadt," *AHVNrh.* 164 (1962) 197-204; Dietz, "St. Helena" 368-69.

[67]*Gedenkschrift zur Sechshundert-Jahrfeier der St. Helena Bruderschaft Xanten*, Xanten 1963. A collection of "Schützensilber," on which Helena is depicted numerous times, is to be seen in Xanten's Regional-Museum.

[68]Robert Haass, *Die Kreuzherren in den Rheinlanden* (Bonn 1932) 193-201; Mackes, *op. cit.* 197-202; Dietz, "St. Helena" 358, 360, 369-70, and 377-83; Schnütgen-Museum, *Rhein und Maas* II 464-65.

Chapter VI.
The Traditions of Britain

In chapter II above we have already rejected the notion that Helena was of British origin and specifically what Geoffrey of Monmouth has to say on the subject. The tradition of a British Helena, not only in England, but also in Wales, in literature, historiography, and the arts, must now be explored more fully.

This tradition begins with St. Aldhelm in the seventh century.[1] He has occasion to remark that Constantine was born *in Britannia ex pelice Helena*.[2] This could suggest British origin for Helena as well; it does not, however, exclude the possibility that Helena was born elsewhere and followed Constantius on his military assignments. There is no mention yet of King Coel or of Colchester, and the word *pelix* leaves no doubt about Helena's status.

The poet Cynewulf lived in the later part of the eighth century or the earlier part of the ninth century. Little is known about his life. He has left us four poems written not in Latin but in Old English. Of these four poems *Elene* is the finest and, with 1321 lines, the longest. It is divided

---

[1]Aldhelm was abbot of Malmesbury (Wiltshire) and later bishop of Sherborne (Dorset); he died in 709. Grober, *op. cit.*, 108; Manitius I 134-35; Gordon Hall Gerould, *Saints' Legends* (Boston 1916) 97-98; Eleanor Shipley Duckett, *Anglo-Saxon Saints and Scholars* (London 1947) 19-97, esp. 60-64; Robert Howard Hodgkin, *A History of the Anglo-Saxons*, 3rd ed. (London 1952) I 321-26; M.L.W. Laistner, *Thought and Letters in Western Europe, A.D. 500-900*, 2nd ed. (Ithaca 1957) 153-56; John Godfrey, *The Church in Anglo-Saxon England* (Cambridge 1962) 201-206; Kemp Malone in Baugh, *op. cit.* 13-14; Whitney F. Bolton, *A History of Anglo-Latin Literature 597-1066* I: *597-740* (Princeton 1967) 68-72 and 87-93; Brunhölzl, *Geschichte der lat. Lit. des Mittelalters* I 200-201; Michael Lapidge and Michael Herren, *Aldhelm: The Prose Works* (Cambridge and Totowa, New Jersey, 1979), introductory essays; Stanley B. Greenfield and Daniel C. Calder, *A New Critical History of Old English Literature* (New York 1986) 9-13; On St. Aldhelm and William of Malmesbury see Gransden, *op. cit.*, I 175-78.

[2]*De Virginitate* (prose version) 48 (Migne, *PL* LXXXIX 148; ed. Ehwald [*MGH, AA* XV] 302). Aldhelm mentions Helena also in another, less relevant context: *De Virginitate* (prose version) 25 (Migne, *PL* LXXXIX 123; ed. Ehwald [*MGH, AA* XV] 259) and *De Virginitate (carmen)* 613 (Migne, *PL* LXXXIX 249; ed. Ehwald [*MGH, AA* XV] 378). On the two versions of the work see Manitius I 138 and Brunhölzl, *Geschichte der lat. Lit. des Mittelalters* I 203-205.

into 15 cantos (or 'fits') and tells the story of the discovery of the True Cross by Helena.[3] The contents can be summarized thus:

1. In the year 233, i.e. in the sixth year of his reign, Constantine receives his famous vision, prior to battling the Huns on the Danube (not Maxentius on the Tiber).

2. Constantine gains victory, is converted, and receives baptism from men who had been taught by Sylvester.

3. Helena is sent out by Constantine to search for the Holy Cross and arrives in Jerusalem, accompanied by a numerous host.

4-8. Helena assembles the wise men of the Jews and interrogates and chastises them. One of them, named Judas, agrees to cooperate, after he has been confined in a pit without food or water for seven days.

9. Taken to the Hill of Calvary, Judas prays for divine assistance.

10. Having received a divine sign, Judas digs up three crosses. The True Cross of the Savior is revealed when one of the three crosses restores a dead man to life.

11. Judas is victorious in a war of words with Satan.

12. Constantine orders a church to be built where the Cross had been found. Judas is baptized.

13. Judas is ordained bishop of Jerusalem by Eusebius, Bishop of Rome, and Helena changes his name to Cyriacus (or Quiriacus). Upon Helena's request he also finds the nails of Christ's Passion.

14. Helena sends the nails to Constantine, to be fastened into his bridle. She bestows a treasure on Cyriacus and prepares to return to her native land.

---

[3]Gerould, *Saints' Legends* 70-76; E. E. Wardale *Chapters on Old English Literature* (London 1935) 162-71; Charles W. Kennedy, *The Earliest English Poetry* (London 1943) 214-20; Hodgkin, *op. cit.* II 459-60; Laistner, *op. cit.* 372-74; Godfrey, *op. cit.*, 177 and 193-94; Theodor Wolpers, *Die englische Heiligenlegende des Mittelalters* (Tübingen 1964) 125-31; W.L. Renwick and Harold Orton, *The Beginnings of English Literature to Skelton, 1509*, 3rd ed. (London 1966) 170-71; Kemp Malone in Baugh, *op. cit.* 73-74; Robert Stepsis and Richard Rand, "Contrast and Conversion in Cynewulf's *Elene*," *NM* 70 (1969) 273-82; Catharine Regan, "Evangelicalism as the Informing Principle of Cynewulf's *Elene*," *Traditio* 29 (1973) 27-52; Greenfield and Calder, *op. cit.* 171-76; Marie Nelson, *Judith, Juliana and Elene: Three Fighting Saints* (New York 1991) 113-209 (text, translation, and afterword essay). Prof. Nelson had kindly made parts of her book available to me prior to publication. Two recent books on Cynewulf are: Daniel G. Calder, *Cynewulf* (Boston 1981), and Earl R. Anderson, *Cynewulf: Structure and Theme in his Poetry* (London 1983).

15. Cynewulf identifies himself and gives testimony of his faith.[4]

In telling the story of the discovery of the True Cross, Cynewulf follows the Cyriacus version of the legend, rather than the simpler versions of Ambrose, Rufinus, or Paulinus of Nola.[5] Specifically one may note the erroneous date and circumstances given for Constantine's vision, the erroneous mention of Eusebius, Bishop of Rome, and the anti-Semitic tone. A Latin version of the Cyriacus legend must have been available to him; minor variants, however, indicate, that his was not one of the MSS extant today. Nothing suggests that Cynewulf thought of Helena as being a native of Britain; he does not identify her native country.

Another much-admired Old English religious poem is the *Dream of the Rood,* composed by an anonymous poet in Northumbria, probably at the end of the seventh century.[6] The poem, 156 lines long, has for its main subject the Crucifixion. The Invention of the Cross is mentioned, but without naming Helena.[7]

[4]Edd. George Philip Krapp, *The Vercelli Book* (New York 1932) 66-102, F. Holthausen (4th ed., Heidelberg 1936), and Pamela O. E. Gradon (London 1958 and Exeter 1977). Translation by Charles W. Kennedy in his *The Poems of Cynewulf* (London 1910; repr. New York 1949) 87-128 and in his *Early English Christian Poetry* (London 1952) 179-214. For the Vercelli Book (Vercelli, Biblioteca Capitolare CXVII) see Neil R. Ker *Catalogue of Manuscripts Containing Anglo-Saxon* (Oxford 1957) 460-464, no. 394

[5]These versions are discussed in chapter IX below.

[6]Edd. George Philip Krapp, *The Vercelli Book* (see n. 4 above) 61-65, Hans Bütow (Heidelberg 1935), Bruce Dickins and A. S. C. Ross (4th ed., London 1963), and Michael J. Swanton (Manchester 1970). Translations by Charles W. Kennedy in his *Poems of Cynewulf* (see n. 4 above) 306-311 and in his *Early English Christian Poetry* (see n. 4 above) 93-97, and by Kemp Malone in his *Ten Old English Poems* (Baltimore 1941) 3-7.

[7]Gerould, *Saints' Legends* 90-91; Wardale, *op. cit.* 177-82; Charles W. Kennedy, *The Earliest English Poetry* 259-66; Hodgkin, *op. cit.* II 460-61; Laistner, *op. cit.* 363 and 377; Rosemary Woolf, "Doctrinal Influences on the Dream of the Rood," *MAE* 27 (1958) 137-53; John A. Burrow, "An Approach to the Dream of the Rood," *Neophilologus* 43 (1959) 123-33; Godfrey, *op. cit.* 177 and 193-94; Renwick and Orton, *op. cit.* 223-25; Kemp Malone in Baugh, *op. cit.* 78-79; Michael J. Swanton, "Ambiguity and Anticipation in 'The Dream of the Rood'," *NM* 70 (1969) 407-25; Helen Gardner, "The Dream of the Rood," in W. W. Robson, ed., *Essays and Poems Presented to Lord David Cecil* (London 1970) 18-36; Ute Schwab, "Das Traumgesicht vom Kreuzesbaum," in Ute Schwab and Elfriede Stutz, edd., *Philologische Studien: Gedenkschrift für Richard Kienast* (Heidelberg 1978) 131-92, with text and German translation; Gerd Wolfgang

(continued...)

THE TRADITIONS OF BRITAIN 65

It is a chronicle written at Colchester ca. 1120, in St. John's Abbey, which first asserts that Helena was born at Colchester: Est igitur Colcestria civitas in orientali parte Brittaniae posita; ... Traditur tamen Helenam, quondam imperii [sic] matrem, ex hac civitate natam et educatam; quae quanti fuerit, vel eo conjicitur, quod Constantius, Constantini Magni genitor, triennio dicitur hanc obsedisse; nec optinuisse, nisi tandem per Helenae nuptias.[8] Geoffrey of Monmouth has claimed our attention previously. His *Historia Regum Britanniae* enjoyed much popularity and exerted great influence. It is clearly the most prominent of our sources for the legend of Coel and Helena. Geoffrey's contemporary Henry of Huntingdon was at work for many years on his *Historia Anglorum*, but when he died in 1155 it was unfinished.[9] Henry's account of Coel and Helena gives additional detail; he reports that Helena, *Britanniae nobilis alumna*, is said to have built the walls around London and to have embellished Colchester with fine buildings.[10] Henry of Huntingdon merits our trust no more than Geoffrey of Monmouth does.[11]

Another contemporary of Geoffrey of Monmouth was William of Malmesbury, who died in 1142 or 1143.[12] His *De Gestis Regum Ang-*

---

[7](...continued)
Weber in Klaus von See, ed., *Europäisches Frühmittelalter* (Wiesbaden 1985) 289 and 294-95; Greenfield and Calder, *op. cit.* 194-99.

[8]For the city of Colchester is located in the eastern part of Britain; ... Nevertheless it is reported that Helena, the future mother of the emperor, was born and brought up in this city; how this is so can be seen from the fact that Constantius, the father of Constantine the Great, is said to have laid siege to this city for three years but not to have taken it except, finally, by marrying Helena.
The chronicle records the founding of the abbey by Eudo Dapifer in 1096 and Eudo's death in 1120. The MS is in the British Library; Cotton Nero D. VIII. The text is printed in William Dugdale's *Monasticon Anglicanum* IV (ed. London 1823) 607; Martin, *The story of Colchester* 10; Kightly, *op. cit.* 60-61.

[9]Gröber, *op. cit.* 313; Manitius III 481-82; Gransden, *op. cit.* I 193-99. Huntingdon is now in Cambridgeshire, but formerly was a county town; Henry held the post of archdeacon there. I do not know on what grounds Kightly, *op. cit.* 61 , places Henry's *Historia Anglorum* in 1129, before Geoffrey's *Historia Regum Britanniae*.

[10]I.37-38 (Migne, *PL* CXCV 817-18; ed. Petrie [*Monumenta Historica Britannica* I; 1848] 702-703; ed. Arnold [Rolls Series LXXIV] 29-30).

[11]Bond, *Dedications* 75, calls them "two of the worst liars in the Middle Ages."

[12]Gröber, *op. cit.* 313; Manitius III 466-67; Hugh Farmer, "William of Malmesbury's Life and Works," *JEH* 13 (1962) 39-54; Gransden, *op. cit.* I 166-85; (continued...)

lorum, or *Historia Regum Anglorum*, covers the time span of 449-1128; he, nevertheless, has occasion to refer to both Constantine and Helena. He quotes Aldhelm at length, but does not claim British birth for Helena, saying merely that Constantine was born *ex Helena stabularia*.[13] He reports that Duke Hugh of the Franks (whom he calls *rex*) presented to King Aethelstan (or Athelstan) the 'sword of Constantine,' the pommel of which contained one of the four nails of Christ's passion; he does not mention Helena in this context.[14] This event can be dated to the year 926.[15]

Colchester's 14th century chronicle claims, as we have seen in chapter II above, that Helena was born in 242 in Colchester as the daughter of King Coel. Beyond that it offers a strange mixture of facts, erroneous dates, and legend, such as:

Constantine is born at Colchester in 265.

Constantius dies at York in 299.

Constantine is victorious at the Mulvian Bridge in 305.

Constantine is baptized by Pope Sylvester in 306.

The Council of Nicaea is held in 316.

Helena discovers the True Cross on May 5, 319.

Helena, over 80 years old, dies in Britain in 322 and is buried in Rome in the Lateran Church.

A certain monk of St. Edmund's translates Helena's head from Rome to the monastery of Bury St. Edmund's in 1145.[16]

---

[12](...continued)
Erich Köhler in Henning Krauss, *op. cit.* 257; Joachim Ehlers, *ibid.* 448; Rodney Thomson, *William of Malmesbury* (Woodbridge, Suffolk, 1987); On Geoffrey of Monmouth, Henry of Huntingdon, and William of Malmesbury see Mulligan, *op. cit.* 261-62.

[13]4.354 (Migne, *PL* CLXXIX 1308; ed. Hardy [London 1840; repr. Vaduz 1964] II 546; ed. Stubbs [Rolls Series XC.2] 410); William of Malmesbury also wrote a life of Aldhelm (book V of his *Gesta Pontificum*). 1.1 (Migne, *PL* CLXXIX 959; ed. Hardy [London 1840; repr. Vaduz 1964] I 6; ed. Stubbs [Rolls Series XC.1] 5). On this point see Stubbs' preface to XC.2, pp. XVIII-XIX.

[14]2.135 (Migne, *PL* CLXXIX 1102; ed. Hardy [London 1840; repr. Vaduz 1964] I 217; ed. Stubbs [Rolls Series XC.1] 150).

[15]Joseph Armitage Robinson, *The Times of Saint Dunstan* (Oxford 1923) 79-80; C.N.L. (Christopher) Brooke, *The Saxon and Norman Kings* (New York 1963) 135-36; Frank Merry Stenton, *Anglo-Saxon England*, 3rd ed. (Oxford 1971) 345; Linder, "The Myth of Constantine the Great" 67; David W. Rollason, "Relic-cults as an Instrument of Royal Policy, c.900 - c. 1050," *ASE* 15 (1986) 91-103 at 93.

[16]The Colchester "Oath Book," folios 20r-20v (IIIr - IIIv); Benham, *Oath Book* 27; Benham, "Legends" 233-34. Helena's burial will be discussed in chapter XII below.

In Chaucer's Canterbury Tales the host at one point swears "by the croys which that Seint Eleyne fond."[17]

John Capgrave, 1393-1464, was an Augustinian monk at King's Lynn (or simply Lynn; Norfolk), who wrote both in Latin and in English. Among his English writings is a *Chronicle of England*.[18] In this chronicle he reports that Constantius (whom he erroneously calls Constantine) married Helena, the daughter of the king of Colchester (whose name he does not give).[19]

Jean de Waurin, a Flemish nobleman, wrote a chronicle of England from Brutus to the year 1471 and titled it *Recueil des Croniques et Anchiennes Istories de la Grant Bretaigne, a present nomme Engleterre*.[20] He, too, asserts that Helena was the daughter of King Coel.[21] A manuscript of this chronicle in the British Library counts among several illuminations one, of considerable charm, which depicts the marriage of Helena and Constantius and the birth of Constantine.[22]

The Humanist scholar Polydore Vergil completed the first edition of his *Anglica Historia* in 1513, but political circumstances did not allow him to publish it until 1534.[23] To him, too, Constantine was born of a British mother.[24] And William Camden in his *Britannia* of 1586 steadfastly maintained that Helena was the daughter of King Coel of Colchester.[25]

---

[17]The Pardoner's Tale 489.

[18]Henry Stanley Bennett, *Chaucer and the Fifteenth Century* (Oxford 1947) 267; Renwick and Orton, *op. cit.* 356-57; Gransden, *op. cit.* II 389-90.

[19]Anno mundi 5495 (ed. Hingeston [Rolls Series I] 76).

[20]Gransden, *op. cit.* I 288-93.

[21]1.2.44 (ed. Hardy and Hardy [Rolls Series XXXIX] I 166-67).

[22]Royal 15 E IV; Folio 73; Ashe, *op. cit.*, ill. 82.

[23]The second and third edd. appeared in 1546 and 1555 respectively; all three edd. were printed in Basel. Denys Hay, ed., *The Anglica Historia of Polydore Vergil, A.D. 1485-1537* (Camden Series LXXIV; London 1950), pp. XIII-XVII; Denys Hay, *Polydore Vergil, Renaissance Historian and Man of Letters* (Oxford 1952) 79-85; Clive Staples Lewis, *English Literature in the Sixteenth Century, Excluding Drama* (Oxford 1954) 278; Beatrice R. Reynolds, "Latin Historiography: A Survey, 1400-1600," *Studies in the Renaissance* 2 (1955) 7-66 at 46; Tucker Brooke in Baugh, *op. cit.* 316; Mulligan, *op. cit.* 270; Gransden, *op. cit.* II 431-33.

[24]A sixteenth century English translation, ed. Ellis (London 1846) I 90: "Helena, the dowghter of a certain prince Coill."

[25]Lewis, *op. cit.* 631; Mulligan, *op. cit.* 274; Alistair Fowler, *A History of English Literature* (Cambridge, Massachusetts, 1987) 117. Ed. London 1586, p. 247. In his

(continued...)

In *The Faerie Queen* of Edmund Spenser (ca. 1552 - 1599) we find an echo of Geoffrey of Monmouth:

> For Asclepiodate him ouercame,
>
> . . .
>
> . . .
>
> . . . ;
>
> But shortly was by Coyll in battell slaine;
> Who after long debate, since Lucies time,
> Was of the Britons first crownd Soueraine:
> Then gan his Realme renewe her passed prime:
> He of his name Coylchester built of stone and lime.
> Which when the Romanes heard, they hither sent
> Constantius, a man of mickle might,
> With whom king Coyll made an agreement,
> And to him gaue for wife his daughter bright,
> Faire Helena, the fairest liuing wight;
> Who in all godly thewes, and goodly prayse
> Did far exell, but was most famous hight
> For skill in Musicke of all in her dayes,
> Aswell in curious instruments, as cunning layes.
> Of whom he did great Constantine beget,
> Who afterward was Emperour of Rome.[26]

In 1590-1600 Richard Hakluyt published the final edition of his *The Principal Navigations, Voyages, Traffiques and Discoveries of the English Nation.*[27] He writes that Helena was the daughter of King Coel, was a gifted musician and learned in Hebrew, Greek, and Latin, wrote books, and died in Rome in 337;[28] also that her body is preserved in Venice.[29]

---

[25](...continued)
Remains Concerning Britain, ed. R. D. Dunn (Toronto 1904) 84 and 207, respectively, Camden also insisted that Helena and Constantine were of British birth, *pace* Nikephoros Kallistos and Lipsius.

[26]Book II, Canto 10, stanzas 58-60, within a chronicle of British rulers from the mythical Brute to Elizabeth I.

[27]George Bruner Parks, *Richard Hakluyt and the English Voyages* (New York 1928) 187-99; Lewis, *op. cit.,* 649; Ed. Glasgow: Hakluyt Society, 1903-1905, IV 270-72. Apparently confusing Helena with Eudocia, the wife of Theodosius II; see Richard Allen Drake in Tito Orlandi, ed., *Eudoxia and the Holy Sepulchre* (Milan 1980) 149. On Eudocia see chapter XV below, nn. 32-33.

[28]For the time and place of Helena's death see chapter XI below.

[29]For the relics of St. Helena see chapter XII below.

It should be noted that in these traditions of England interest focuses on Helena's purported British birth and her purported discovery of the True Cross. There is no mention of her residence in Trier, of Theban martyrs, or of anything else detracting from her supposed links to England. Local and national pride are being served.

In the traditions of neighboring Wales Helena also occupies a place, albeit a less prominent one. The emperor Magnus Maximus may serve as a point of departure: a man of Spanish birth and humble origin, he rose to become a Roman commander in Britain. In 383 he usurped imperial power from Gratian, but in 388 he was defeated by Theodo-sius.[30]   His role in Welsh traditions is comparable to the role of Constantius in English traditions. His name becomes Maxen (or Macsen) Wledig, and he marries Elen, the daughter of Eudda (or Eudaf), a Welsh chieftain at Caernarvon. She is identified with Elen Luyddog, or Helen of the Hosts, and then with our Helena. Together they become the progenitors of the Dyved dynasty.[31]   Chronology alone deprives this tradition of all historical validity.

British historians of more modern times have not failed to concern themselves with Helena's supposed links to Britain. It is interesting to observe the contrast between Colchester's own historian Philip Morant on the one hand and the celebrated Edward Gibbon on the other. Morant, the rector of St. Mary's Church in Colchester, published his history of Colchester in 1748.[32]   He goes to great lengths in defense of the tradition which holds that Helena was the daughter of King Coel and

[30]*RE* XIV.2 2546-55; Courtenay Edward Stevens, "Magnus Maximus in British History," *Etudes celtiques* 3 (1938) 86-94; *PLRE* I 588; John Frederick Matthews, *Western Aristocracies and the Imperial Court, A.D. 364-425* (Oxford 1975) 95-96, 173-82, and 223-25; John Davies, *A History of Wales* (London 1993) 42 and 53-54.

[31]John Edward Lloyd, *A History of Wales,* 3rd ed. (London 1939) 92-93; Rachel Bromwich, "The Character of the Early Welsh Tradition' in Hector Munro Chadwick et al. *Studies in Early British History* (Cambridge 1954) 83-136 at 93-94, 108-109, and 127, n. 2; Thomas Parry, *A History of Welsh Literature* (Oxford 1955) 80-81; Linder, "The Myth of Constantine the Great" 78; Mulligan, *op. cit.* 259-60; John Frederick Matthews, "Macsen, Maximus and Constantine" 432 and 446; Ashe, *op. cit.* 162-64; Elissa R. Henken, *The Welsh Saints: A Study in Patterned Lives* (Cambridge 1991) 13. Whether three women were conflated into one or there is but one Helena in three different contexts is not very important to us.

[32]*The History and Antiquities of the Most Ancient Town and Borough of Colchester in the County of Essex* (London 1748), repr., with the original pagination, in his *The History and Antiquities of the County of Essex* (London 1763-1768) I.

gave birth to Constantine in Britain.[33] Gibbon, about 30 years later, in his *Decline and Fall of the Roman Empire*, had little regard for a tradition "invented in the darkness of monasteries" and argued that the panegyrist's *oriendo* refers to Constantine's accession rather than to his nativity.[34]   In our own century it is Gibbon's view which has prevailed.[35]

The vitality of the cult of St. Helena in England finds expression in the fact, previously mentioned, that there are approximately 135 churches or chapels dedicated in her memory. We also know of some medieval parish guilds dedicated to St. Helena (as well as of others dedicated to the Holy Cross). The Guild of St. Helen at West Lynn in Norfolk was founded in 1359,[36] that at Binbrooke in Lincolnshire in 1376.[37] At Beverley in Yorkshire, at the Church of the Friars Minor, a Guild of St. Helen and St. Mary was founded in 1378.[38] Annually on the feast day of St. Helen this guild sponsored a procession featuring an old man with a cross, another with a spade, and a youth dressed as Queen Helen, in an obvious allusion to the finding of the True Cross. Colchester's Guild of St. Helen was founded in 1407.[39]

Mention has been made in chapter II above of the large statue of Helena which crowns the tower of the town hall of Colchester. A thoughtful visitor is reminded of Helena also by the ubiquitous arms of the town; these consist of a rough-hewn green cross, with three crowns and three nails, all on a red ground.[40] Colchester also has a small chapel known as St. Helen's Chapel. It stands in Maidenburgh Street, is first mentioned in 1076, but consists mostly of 13th century fabric,

---

[33]*Ibid.*, 28-31; he also accepts (p. 34) without questioning, the story of the discovery of the Cross, dating the event to May 3, 319.

[34]Chapter XIV (Modern Library ed. I 344); see chapter II above.

[35]E. g. H. M. Gwatkin in *The Cambridge Medieval History* I, 2nd ed. (Cambridge 1924) 2; see chapter II above, n. 30, for some others. Mulligan, *op. cit.* 279, makes the interesting point that the myth finally died when it had outlived its usefulness.

[36]H. F. Westlake, *The Parish Guilds of Medieval England* (London 1919) 200.

[37]*Ibid.* 156.

[38]Toulmin Smith and Lucy Toulmin Smith, *English Gilds* (*EETS, OS,* no. 40; Oxford 1870) 148-49; Westlake, *op. cit.* 233.

[39]Morant, *op. cit.,* Appendix 13-14, gives the text of the license granted by King Henry IV. See also Morant, *op. cit.* 149-50.

[40]Benham, "Legends" 243-44; Giesen, "HELENA" 150-51; Martin, *The Story of Colchester* 10.

and is currently used as a storeroom by the museum.[41]   Before the Reformation it was attached to St. John's Abbey, in whose records it is frequently mentioned.[42]   Not surprisingly there is also a school bearing Helena's name.

Throughout England, mostly, of course, in churches and chapels, one can find visual reminders of Helena.   In time these range from the 12th to the 20th century.[43]   Many of them are of considerable artistic merit, but only two shall here be singled out for brief mention.   The first of these is a delicately carved stone cross of the late twelfth century which is to be found in the chancel of the Church of St. Helen in Kelloe (a few miles south-east of Durham).   The shaft of this cross is decorated with three reliefs.   The upper one depicts Constantine's dream, and the lower one the *inventio* of the True Cross.   In the middle one, more difficult to interpret, one sees two crowned female figures, one of whom may reasonably be assumed to be Helena.[44]   For the second of these visual reminders we must visit the Church of St. Michael in Ashton-under-Lyne (Greater Manchester).   Here 18 panels of 15th century glass which give

[41]The Colchester Chronicle, The "Oath Book" of Colchester, folio 20v (IIIv); Morant, *op. cit.* 34 and 153; John Horace Round, *St. Helen's Chapel, Colchester* (London, 1887); Benham, *Oath Book* 28; Royal Commission on Historical Monuments, England, *An Inventory of the Historical Monuments in Essex* II (London 1922) 50; Martin, *The Story of Colchester* 10, 21, and 34; Stephenson, *op. cit.* 34; Geoffrey Haward Martin, *Colchester: Official Guide,* 5th ed. (Colchester 1982) 39.

[42]Stuart Moore, ed., *Cartularium Monasterii Sancti Johannis Baptiste de Colcestria* (London 1897) passim.

[43]References will be found in the following: Edward S. Prior and Arthur Gardner, *An Account of Medieval Figure-Sculpture in England* (Cambridge 1912); Lawrence Stone, *Sculpture in Britain: The Middle Ages,* 2nd ed. (Harmondsworth, Middlesex, 1972); Arthur Gardner, *English Medieval Sculpture* (Cambridge 1951); Philip Nelson, *Ancient Painted Glass in England, 1170-1500* (London 1913); Herbert Read, *English Stained Glass* (London 1926); Christopher Woodforde, *English Stained and Painted Glass* (Oxford 1954); John D. Le Couteur, *English Medieval Painted Glass,* 2nd ed. (London 1978); Brian Coe, *Stained Glass in England: 1150-1550* (London 1981).

[44]Prior and Gardner, op. cit. 117 and 219-20; Arthur Gardner, *English Medieval Sculpture* 85 and fig. 150; Fritz Saxl, *English Sculpture of the Twelfth Century* (Boston 1956) 67-68 and pls.   XCVI-XCVIII; Robert Thomas Stoll and Jean Roubier, *Architecture and Sculpture in Early Britain* (London 1967) 328 and pl. 169; John Betjeman, *Collins Pocket Guide to English Parish Churches: The North* (London 1968) 131; Andreas and Judith A. Stylianou, *By This Conquer* (Nicosia 1971) 49-53 and figs. 28, 28a, and 28b; Karl Adolf Wiegel, *Die Darstellungen der Kreuzauffindung bis zu Piero della Francesca* (Diss. Cologne 1973) 157-58; Nikolaus Pevsner, *The Buildings of England: County Durham,* 2nd ed., rev. by Elizabeth Williamson (Harmondsworth, Middlesex, 1984) 343-44.

us scenes from the lives of Constantine and Helena once occupied the church's great east window, arranged in three registers. Unfortunately they were removed in 1872 and after various vicissitudes are now placed in four windows in the south aisle, in a rather unhappy arrangement.[45] Panels 1-6 give us scenes from Helena's life, up to and including the birth of Constantine. Panels 7-9 depict Constantine's victory at the Mulvian Bridge, his baptism, and the Council of Nicaea. Panels 13-15 tell the story of Helena's conversion, and panels 10-12 and 16-18 the story of the *inventio* and *verificatio* of the True Cross.[46]

Helena's name is perpetuated also on the map of England in a number of place-names. In Lancashire, just east of Liverpool, there is the city of St. Helen's, and a little to the south from there, between Widnes and Warrington, there is St. Helen's Canal.[47] Of the Isles of Scilly, off the coast of Cornwall, one is named St. Helen's. In Norfolk, north of Norwich, we find a village named St. Helena and in the County of Durham one named St. Helen Auckland. Yet another village of St. Helen's is found on the Isle of Wight, at its eastern end, where there was once a priory of St. Helen.[48]

[45]George Augustus Pugh, "The Old Glass Windows of Ashton-under-Lyne Parish Church," *Transactions of the Lancashire and Cheshire Antiquarian Society* 20 (1902) 130-38 at 136; William Farrer and J. Brownbill, *The Victoria History of the County of Lancaster* IV (London 1911) 347; Nelson, *Ancient Painted Glass* 49-50 and 130-31; Philip Nelson, "The Fifteenth Century Glass in the Church of St. Michael, Ashton-under-Lyne," *Archaeological Journal* 70 (N.S.20; 1913) 1-10 at 8; Bond, *Dedications* 75; Andreas and Judith A. Stylianou, *By This Conquer* 60 and 63; Woodforde, *op. cit.*, 25; Nikolaus Pevsner, *The Buildings of England: Lancashire* I (Harmondsworth, Middlesex, 1967) 68; Le Couteur, *op. cit.* 52; Coe, *op. cit.* 48 and 106.

[46]Panels 1-3 are in the first window, panels 4-6 in the second, panels 7-9 in the third, and panels 10-12 in the fourth; for panels 13-15 we return to the first window and for panels 16-18 to the second. The numbering scheme is that of Nelson, *Ancient Painted Glass* 130-31.

[47]The only association with St. Helena appears to be the presence of a Church of St. Helen, first mentioned in 1552. See Forrer and Brownbill, op. cit. III (London 1907) 375.

[48]J. C. Cox in H. Arthur Doubleday and William Page, *A History of Hampshire and the Isle of Wight* II (London 1903) 215-16; David Knowles and R. Neville Hadcock, *Medieval Religious Houses: England and Wales*, 2nd ed. (New York 1972) 98 and 102.

Chapter VII.
Residence in Rome

No ancient source, unfortunately, tells us when Helena left Trier and took up residence in Rome. It has been supposed that by 326 Helena had been living in Rome for many years,[1] or, more specifically, that she took up residence in Rome in 322.[2] She probably resided in Rome when Constantine visited the city for the celebration of his *vicennalia* in July, 326.[3] We know for certain that Helena resided in Rome long enough to sponsor significant building activity, specifically the restoration of a bath building.

Five fragments of a large inscription found in the neighborhood of the Basilica of Santa Croce in Gerusalemme have been convincingly restored and are of considerable interest to us. The restored inscription is displayed in the Vatican Museum, suitably enough in the Sala a Croce Greca,[4] the same room which houses the two famous porphyry sarcophagi associated with Constantine's family. The restored inscription reads as follows:

D(omina) n(ostra) He[lena venerabilis do]mini [n(ostri)
Constantini A]ug(usti) mater e[t] avia beatis[simor(um)
et floren]tis[simor(um) Caesarum nostrorum] therm[as
incendio de]stru[ctas restituit].[5]

---

[1]Barnes, Constantine and Eusebius 220-21.

[2]Kempf, "Das Haus der heiligen Helena" 9.

[3]André Piganiol, *L'empire chrétien (325-395)*, 2nd ed. (Paris 1972) 39.

[4]Museo Pio-Clementino, inv. no. 209.

[5]Our venerable Lady Helena, mother of our Lord Constantine Augustus and grandmother of our most blessed and excellent Caesars, has restored these baths after they had been destroyed by fire. CIL VI 1136; Orazio Marucchi, *Éléments d'archéologie chrétienne* (Paris 1899-1903) III 346; Walter Amelung and Georg Lippold, *Die Skulpturen des Vaticanischen Museums* (Berlin 1903-1956) text III.1 190-91 and pls. III.1 74; Mariano Armellini, *Le chiese di Roma dal secolo IV al XIX*, 3rd ed. (Rome 1942) II 982; Antonio Maria Colini, "Horti Spei Veteris: Palatium Sessorianum," *MemPontAcc.* 8 (1955) 137-77 at 141, 147, and 177; Giuseppe Lugli, *Fontes ad topographiam veteris urbis Romae pertinentes* IV (Rome 1957) 92, no 291; Ernest Nash, *Pictorial Dictionary of Ancient Rome*, 2nd ed. (New York 1968) II 456, fig 1260; Adrian Van Heck, *Breviarium Urbis Romae Antiquae* (Leiden and Rome 1977) 138, no. 66; Arthur E. Gordon, *Illustrated Introduction to Latin Epigraphy* (Berkeley 1983) 169-70, no. 83; Drijvers, *op. cit.*, 47-48.

The inscription is framed by a border of acanthus leaves, with ansae, and was flanked on each side by a winged Nike in relief; these reliefs have survived but are displayed separately.[6] The lack of a date is most regrettable. A date after 325 must, I think, be excluded, because at some time in 324 or 325 Helena was granted the rank of Augusta, which is lacking in this inscription.[7]

The inscription records only a restoration, and we do not know who originally caused these baths to be erected. Nevertheless they are often referred to as the *Thermae Helenae* or *Helenianae*. They have been almost completely obliterated; only some of the water reservoirs still exist. We have plans of the building drawn in the 16th century. These baths were located in the fifth region of the city, north-west of the Basilica of Santa Croce in Gerusalemme and south-west of the Porta Maggiore, between today's via di Santa Croce in Gerusalemme and via Eliniana.[8]

It has been asserted that the last of Rome's aqueducts was built by Alexander Severus.[9] The *Scriptores Historiae Augustae* mention an aqueduct built by this emperor and called the *Aqua Alexandriana* (or *Alexandrina*),[10] and this has been identified with the aqueduct which

---

[6]Inv. nos. 586 and 591.

[7]See chapter III above; *Aug.* surely must be read *Augusti*, in apposition to *Constantini. PLRE* I 410 is in error.

[8]Rodolfo Lanciani, *Forma Urbis Romae* (Milan 1893-1901), sheets 31-32; Rodolfo Lanciani, *The Ruins and Excavations of Ancient Rome* (New York 1897) 398-400; Platner-Ashby 530; Giuseppe Lugli, *I monumenti antichi di Roma e suburbio* (Rome 1931-1940) II 67; Colini, *op. cit.* 140-47; Nash, *op. cit.* II 454-57 with figs. 1257-59 and 1261-62; Giuseppe Lugli, *Itinerario di Roma antica* (Milan 1970) 518-19. Filippo Coarelli, *Roma* (Rome 1980) 231-32; L. Richardson, Jr., *A New Topographical Dictionary of Ancient Rome* (Baltimore 1992) 393.

[9]Rodolfo Lanciani, *Topografia di Roma antica: I comentarii di Frontino* (Rome 1880) 185; Lanciani, *Ruins* 56; Lugli, *I monumenti* II 402; Esther Boise Van Deman, *The Building of the Roman Aqueducts* (Washington 1934) 18-19; Thomas Ashby, *The Aqueducts of Ancient Rome* (Oxford 1935) 14-15; Lugli, *Itinerario* 118. Ultimately this assertion can be traced back to Raphael Fabretti, *De Aquis et Aquaeductibus Veteris Romae* (Rome 1680) 147-49.

[10]Alexander Severus 25.3; Lanciani, *Topografia*, 168; Platner-Ashby 20; Donald R. Dudley, *Urbs Roma* (London 1967) 24; Lugli, *Itinerario* 117; Van Heck, *op. cit.* 31, no. 8.23. Alexander Severus is credited with the construction of this aqueduct also by a list, found in some MSS of the *Notitia Dignitatum* (after 395), *De Montibus et Aquis Urbis Romae*; see Roberto Valentini and Giuseppe Zucchetti, *Codice Topografico della Città di Roma* I (Rome 1940) 295, or, as excerpted by Polemus Silvius, *MGH*, AA IX = *Chron. Min.* I 546.

served the *Thermae Helenae*.[11] This identification has not been substantiated by epigraphical evidence.[12]

A different solution has been proposed by Joseph Francis Merriman. He suggested that the aqueduct supplying the *Thermae Helenae* was really the *Aqua Augustea* and was in fact built by Helena.[13] His argument rests primarily on a new interpretation of a well-published and well-preserved inscription which was found in the late 16th century in a vineyard belonging to the Basilica of Santa Croce in Gerusalemme and now is to be seen in the Basilica's Cappella Gregoriana:

Dominae nostrae Fl(aviae) Iul(iae) Helenae piissimae Aug(ustae), genetrici d(omini) n(ostri) Constantini Maximi Victoris clementissimi semper Augusti, aviae Constantini et Constanti beatissimorum ac florentissimorum Caesarum, Iulius Maximilianus v(ir) c(larissimus) comes pietati eius semper dicatis(simus).[14]

The Iulius Maximilianus who set up this inscription is probably identical with the Iulius Maximilianus who held the post of *consularis aquarum* in the year 330 but is called a *comes* in this inscription.[15] The inscription should therefore, Merriman suggests, be assigned a date after 330.[16] From the phrase *pietati eius semper dicatissimus* it is clear that this inscription is a commemorative one and was set up after Helena's

---

[11]Platner-Ashby 530; Van Deman, *op. cit.* 342; Nash, *op. cit.* II 454.

[12]Merriman, *op. cit.* (see n. 13) 438.

[13]"The Empress Helena and the Aqua Augustea," *Arch. Class.* 29.2 (1977) 436-46.

[14]To our Lady Flavia Julia Helena, the most pious Augusta, mother of our Lord Constantinus Maximus Victor, always the most gentle Augustus, and grandmother of the most blessed and excellent Caesars Constantine and Constantius, (this statue was set up by) Julius Maximilianus, of senatorial rank and a count, always most devoted to her memory. *CIL* VI 1134 = *ILS* 709; Raimondo Besozzi, *La storia della basilica di Santa Croce in Gerusalemme* (Rome 1750) 70; Marucchi, *op. cit.* III 346; Armellini, *op. cit.* II 982; Colini, *op. cit.* 147 with fig. 12; Voelkl, *Der Kaiser Kontantin*, ill. 92; Lugli, *Fontes* IV (1957) 107, no. 74; Irving Lavin, "An Ancient Statue of the Empress Helena Reidentified?" *ArtB* 49 (1967) 58 and fig. 2; Hans-Henning Lauer, *op. cit.* 35; Walther Buchowiecki, *Handbuch der Kirchen Roms* (Vienna 1967-1974) I 624; Sergio Ortolani, *S. Croce in Gerusalemme*, 2nd ed. (Rome 1969) 15 and fig. 6; Drijvers, *op. cit.* 45-46 and 189.

[15]*Cod. Theod.* 15.2.1 (ed. Mommsen-Meyer 1.2 814); Ernst Kornemann in *RE* IV.2 (1901) 1787; *PLRE* I 575; In Rodolfo Lanciani, *Wanderings through Ancient Roman Churches* (Boston 1924) 219, the name is erroneously given as Fulvius Maximianus. On the office of *consularis aquarum* see A. H. M. Jones, *The Later Roman Empire* (Oxford 1964) I 691. On the rank of *comes, ibid.* 104-105.

[16]*Op. cit.* 442.

death. Since Constans is not mentioned among the Caesars it is also clear that the incription cannot be assigned to a date after 333.[17] This inscription has allowed the restoration of the text of another, three fragments of which were found also in the neighborhood of the *Thermae Helenae* but are now lost.[18] This inscription, too, appears to have been set up by Iulius Maximilianus in honor of Helena, and the same arguments concerning the date apply.

The existence (or former existence) of two such inscriptions - and statues belonging with them — suggests to Merriman "that the empress initiated some major project related to the city's water supplies," i.e. sponsored the construction of the aqueduct which served the baths, the *Aqua Augustea*.[19] The suggestion is attractive but remains problematic. What aqueduct supplied water to the baths before Helena commissioned a new aqueduct? Merriman dates Helena's death to the year 330, but she may have died already in 329 or even in 328, i.e. before Maximilianus served as *consularis aquarum*.[20] And how would her pilgrimage to the Holy Land fit into this time frame?[21]

A third inscription commemorating Helena, found in the area of the Lateran but now lost, was erected by a certain Pistius, *praepositus rerum privatarum*.[22] I do not believe that it sheds light on our problem. All that we can safely conclude is that Helena's memory was suitably honored in the city of Rome.

---

[17]A faulty chronology (372 for 327?) is given by Armellini, *op. cit.* II 982, and by Carlo Cecchelli, his editor. The dates, 317-322, given by Richard Krautheimer, *Corpus Basilicarum Christianarum* I (Vatican City 1937) 167 with n. 2, are based on a misinterpretatation of the inscription. Guiseppe Bovini, *Edifici cristiani di culta d'età costantiana a Roma* (Bologna 1968) 104, appears to follow in Krautheimer's footsteps. Buchowiecki, *op. cit.*, I 624, incorrectly: "Mitte bis Ende des 4. Jahrhunderts." More correctly Irving Lavin, "An Ancient Statue" 58. On *pietatis causa, ex pietate*, and similar formulae see the dictionaries. On the elevation of Constans to the rank of Caesar see Otto Seeck in *RE* IV.1 (1900) 948, Seeck, *Regesten* 182, *PLRE* I 220, or Dietmar Kienast, *Römische Kaisertabelle* (Darmstadt 1990) 307.

[18]*CIL* VI 36950 (*PLRE* I 575 erroneously: 36980); Colini, *op. cit.* 147, n. 31; Lugli, *Fontes* IV (1957) 107, no. 75.

[19]*Op. cit.* 442-43.

[20]See chapter XI below.

[21]See chapter VIII below.

[22]*CIL* VI 1135; Colini, *op. cit.* 147, n. 31; Drijvers, *op. cit.* 46-47.

Plate III

Helena's residence in Rome, the Sessorian Palace, seen from the southwest.

The facade of Rome's Basilica of Santa Croce in Gerusalemme. Of the statues on the roof that of St. Helena is the first from the left.

Helena's residence in Rome was the Sessorian Palace, as we may learn from the *Liber Pontificalis*,[23] and as is suggested by the numerous associations of the area with Helena. Substantial remains of this palace can still be seen directly north of the Basilica of Sante Croce in Gerusalemme, in the courtyard of the Granatieri barracks.[24] Within this palace Constantine established a basilica, or so the Liber tells us.[25] Although the Liber clearly identifies Constantine, not Helena, as the builder, the basilica was sometimes called the *Basilica Heleniana*.[26] The new basilica required little new construction; the builders converted the aula of the palace and added an apse.[27] The *Liber* further says that Constantine placed a piece of the Holy Cross in this basilica and that for

---

[23]Migne, *PL* VIII 810; ed. Mommsen (*MGH, GPR* I) 67; ed. Duchesne^2 I 183; Lugli, *Fontes* IV (1957) 107, no. 72.

[24]Lanciani, *Ruins* 397, where Maximilianus must be read for Maximianus; Lanciani, *Wanderings* 216-20; Joseph Wilpert, *Die römischen Mosaiken und Malereien der kirchlichen Bauten vom IV. bis XIII. Jahrhundert*, 3rd ed. (Freiberg 1924) I.1 338; Platner-Ashby 487-88; Lugli, *Monumenti* III 486-90; Krautheimer, *Corpus* I 167; Colini, *op. cit.* 137-40., 154-68, and 170-77; Nash, *op. cit.* II 384-86 with figs. 1169-73; Lugli, *Itinerario* 518; Coarelli, *op. cit.* 231; L. Richardson, Jr., *op. cit.* 361-62; Charles Odahl, *Early Christian Latin Literature: Readings from the Ancient Texts* (Chicago 1993) 142, n. 51; Charles Odahl, "The Christian Basilicas of Constantinian Rome," *AncW* 26 (1995) 3-28 at 13.

[25]Migne, *PL* VIII 807; ed. Mommsen (*MGH, GPR* I) 61; ed. Duchesne^2 I 179; Lanciani, *Wanderings* 225; Christian Hülsen, *Le chiese di Roma nel medio evo* (Florence 1927) 243, no. 29; Valentini and Zucchetti, *op. cit.* II (1942) 231; Colini, *op. cit.* 173; Lugli, *Fontes* IV (1957) 105, no. 58; Odahl, *Early Christian Latin Literature* 142.

[26]Duchesne in his ed. of the *Liber* I^2 196, n. 75; Wilpert, *Die römischen Mosaiken* I.1^3 338; Lanciani, *Wanderings* 225; Krautheimer, *Corpus* I 168; Armellini, *op. cit.* II 981; Bovini, *Edifici cristiani* 105.

[27]August Stegenšek, "Architektonische Untersuchung von S. Croce in Gerusalemme in Rom," *RömQ* 14 (1900) 177-86 at 186; Wilpert, *Die römischen Mosaiken* I.1^3 339; Lanciani, *Wanderings* 226. The most thorough architectural description of the basilica is that of Krautheimer, *Corpus* I 165-95. Subsequent accounts have been briefer: Armellini, *op. cit.*, II 981-69 and 1282; Friedrich Wilhelm Deichmann, *Frühchristliche Kirchen in Rom* (Basel 1948) 30-31; Buchowiecki, *op. cit.* I 613-25; Bovini, *Edifici cristiani* 101-25; Ortolani, *S. Croce in Gerusalemme*^{2}; Charles Pietri, *Roma Christiana* (Paris 1976) I 14-17; Hugo Brandenburg, *Roms frühchristliche Basiliken des 4. Jahrhunderts* (Munich 1979) 160-69; Richard Krautheimer, *Rome: Profile of a City, 312-1308* (Princeton 1980) 24, excellent map *ibid.*, fig. 28; Roloff Beny and Peter Gunn, *The Churches of Rome* (New York 1981) 100-102; Odahl, "The Christian Basilicas" 13.

this reason it is called Hierusalem.[28] These last two statements of the *Liber* are repeated by Bede.[29]

But we have reason to be skeptical. The limited reliability of the *Liber* – a compilation begun in the 6th century – was recognized by both Mommsen and Duchesne and has been pointed out by others after them.[30] The earliest reference to relics of the True Cross does not occur until the middle of the 4th century, a decade or more after Constantine's death.[31] It is thus impossible for Constantine to have possessed such a relic.[32] Furthermore, Richard Krautheimer, having carefully examined the brickwork of the apse of the Basilica, concluded at one time that it should be dated to the middle of the 4th century rather than to earlier decades.[33] If this is correct, the establishment of a basilica in the Sessorian Palace would have to be attributed to one of Constantine's sons rather than to Constantine himself.

As one might expect, the Basilica is rich in works of art celebrating Helena and the legend of the True Cross. On the balustrade of the Baroque facade, which dates from 1743, there are six statues; from left to right: Helena with a large cross, the evangelists Luke, Matthew, John,

[28]*Loc. cit.* (n. 25).

[29]*Chron.* 417 (*MGH, AA* XIII = *Chron. Min.* III 296); Lugli, *Fontes* IV (1957) 106, no. 64.

[30]Mommsen's ed. (*MGH, GPR* I) VII-XVIII; Duchesne's ed., I² CLII and CLXI; Louise Ropes Loomis, *The Book of the Popes* (New York 1916) X-XI; Henri Leclercq in *DACL* IX.1 (1930) 354-60; Caspar, *op. cit.* II 314-20; Raymond Davis, *The Book of the Pontiffs* (*Liber Pontificalis*) (Liverpool 1989), introduction. Élie Griffe, "Le *Liber Pontificalis* au temps du pape saint Grégoire," *BLE* 57 (1956) 65-70, discusses the date of the *Liber*.

[31]See chapter IX below.

[32]Caspar, *op. cit.* I 126; Krautheimer, *Corpus* I 167 with n. 3; Richard Klein in *RAC* XIV 367.

[33]Krautheimer, *Corpus* I 191-92; similarly Deichmann, *Frühchristliche Kirchen* 30-31. The arguments of Brandenburg, *Roms frühchristliche Basiliken* 164, for a date prior to 324 seem less compelling. Krautheimer's conclusion was challenged by Pietri, *op. cit.*, I 15, n. 3; but Krautheimer himself had already withdrawn it in his "The Constantinian Basilica," *DOP* 21 (1967) 115-40 at 130, n. 49; in his *Early Christian and Byzantine Architecture*, 4th ed. (Harmondsworth, Middlesex, 1986) 50, Krautheimer is much less critical. Finally, in his *Three Christian Capitals* (Berkeley 1983) 129, n. 16, he sees "no reason to doubt the tradition of Helena's having brought to her palace the relic of the cross from her pilgrimage to the Holy Land." Richard Klein in *RAC* XIV 367: "wohl noch im 4. Jh."

and Mark, each with the appropriate attribute, and Constantine with a lance.[34]

In the nave there is a large ceiling painting by Corrado Giaquinto (1703-1765), datable to 1744. We see Helena presenting Constantine to the Virgin, who in turn presents both Helena and Constantine to the Holy Trinity above.[35] The fresco in the half-dome of the apse is probably the work of Antoniazzo Romano (but it has also been attributed to several other painters) and dates from ca. 1485-1495. It is divided into two zones. In the upper zone there is a Christ in a mandorla. In the lower zone a vast panorama unfolds. In a landscape of mountains, trees, a river, and cities the legend of the True Cross is told.[36]

Behind the apse, at a lower level, there are two chapels, the Gregorian Chapel and the Chapel of St. Helena. The former, as we have seen, houses an inscription which is of considerable importance in our

[34]Buchowiecki, op. cit. I 611; Ortolani, S. Croce in Gerusalemme² 44 and fig. 17; Beny and Gunn, op. cit. 101 and 237; Giovanni Paolo Tesei, Le chiese di Roma (Rome 1986) 440-41.

[35]Besozzi, op. cit. 50-51; Marisa Volpi, "Corrado Giaquinto e alcuni aspetti della cultura figurativa del' 700 in Italia," BdA 43 (1958) 263-82 at 271-72 with n. 46; Mario d'Orsi, Corrado Giaquinto (Rome 1958) 63 and fig. 65; Buchowiecki, op. cit. 614; Ortolani, S. Croce in Gerusalemme² 58-60 with fig. 26; Sandra Vasco Rocca in Pietro Amato, ed., Corrado Giaquinto (1703-1766) (Molfetta 1985) 104-105. Preliminary sketches and modelli for this ceiling painting are to be found in the Museo di San Martino in Naples, the Necchi Collection in Portalupa (Pavia) , the Musée Vivant-Denon in Chalon-sur-Saône, and the Saint Louis Art Museum: D'Orsi, op. cit. 63-64 and figs. 63-64; Myron Laskin, "Corrado Giaquinto's St. Helena and the Emperor Constantine Presented by the Virgin to the Trinity," Museum Monographs 1 (1968) 28-40, with corrections to d'Orsi; The St. Louis Art Museum, Handbook of the Collections (St. Louis 1975), inv. no. 31: 1963 (from the estate of Albert S. Ludlow of Waukesha, Wisconsin); Pierre Rosenberg and Arnauld Brejon de Lavergnée in Amato, op. cit. 79, no. 12, and fig. 15; Yale University Art Gallery, A Taste for Angels: Neopolitan Painting in North America, 1650-1750 (New Haven, Connecticut, 1987) 308-11, no.42. I am grateful for information provided by Ms. Mary Ann Lenhard of the Saint Louis Art Museum.

[36]Besozzi, op. cit. 34-35; Adolfo Venturi, Storia dell'arte italiana VII.2 (Milan 1913) 280-86 with figs. 220-23; Piero Mazzoni, La leggenda della croce nell'arte italiana (Florence 1914) 134-40 with pls. XI-XII; Joseph A. Crowe and Giovanni Battista Cavalcaselle, A History of Painting in Italy V (London 1914) 387 (attribution to Pinturicchio); Maurice, Sainte Hélène 36-37; Raimond van Marle, The Development of the Italian Schools of Painting XV (The Hague 1934) 270-72 with fig. 166; Carlo Grigioni, Marco Palmezzano (Faenza 1956) 742-43, no. 33 (rejects attribution to Marco Palmezzano); Buchowiecki, op. cit. I 616; Ortolani, S. Croce in Gerusalemme² 50-56 with figs. 22-25; George Kaftal, Saints in Italian Art: Iconography of the Saints in the Painting of North East Italy (Florence 1978) 395-402 with fig. 498 (attribution to Marco Palmezzano); Beny and Gunn, op. cit. 102.

context. The latter must be considered now. Above the altar, facing the Gregorian Chapel, there is a large statue of St. Helena holding an even larger cross in the right hand and two nails in the left hand. Irving Lavin has identified this statue as an ancient one which was found at Santa Croce in the mid-16th century and which in fact belongs to the base now in the neighboring Gregorian Chapel.[37] It was placed in its present position in the 17th century after a painting of St. Helena by Rubens had been removed.[38] Heavily restored, it resembles both the figure of St. Helena in the Rubens painting and the statue of Helena by Bolgi.[39]

In the 5th century the chapel was provided with mosaics by the young emperor Valentinian III (425-455), his regent-mother Galla Placidia, and his sister Honoria.[40] These mosaics were reworked extensively and repeatedly in the late 15th and 16th century. In the center of the vaulted ceiling, in a medallion, there is a half-figure of Christ, and in the corners there are ovals with figures of the four Evangelists. In the spandrels between the ovals there are four scenes of the legend of the True Cross: the *inventio*, the exaltation of the Cross, the division of the Cross into three parts by Helena, and, the return of the Cross by Heraclius. In the barrel-vaulted arch above the altar there are figures of Sts. Peter and Paul. In a second barrel-vaulted arch, in the passage to the Gregorian Chapel, there are figures of Pope Sylvester and of St. Helena; at Helena's feet is a kneeling Cardinal Carvajal, the donor of the mosaic.[41]

In the staircase which leads from the right transept down into the chapel there are some inscriptions on terracotta tiles which date from

---

[37]"An Ancient Statue" 58 and figs. 1-4; Rodolfo Lanciani, *Storia degli scavi di Roma* (Rome 1902-1907) III 163.

[38]Besozzi, *op. cit.* 83-84. For the Rubens painting see chapter XVII below, where it is discussed in the context of French and Flemish art.

[39]Lavin, "An Ancient Statue" 58 and figs. 1, 3, and 4; Drijvers, *op. cit.* 190, n. 5. The Bolgi statue will be considered shortly. Others have seen in our St. Helena a reused statue of Juno: Lanciani, *Wanderings* 249; Mazzoni, *op. cit.* 134; Buchowiecki, *op. cit.* I 622; Ortolani, *S. Croce in Gerusalemme*² 76 with fig. 36; Beny and Gunn, *op. cit.* 102.

[40]Krautheimer, *Corpus* I 168.

[41]Lanciani, *Wanderings* 250; Mazzoni, *op. cit.* 134; Wilpert, *Die römischen Mosaiken* I.1³ 340-43 with fig. 111; Adolfo Venturi, *Musaici cristiani in Roma* (Rome 1925) 57 and fig. 77; Edgar Waterman Anthony, *A History of Mosaics* (Boston 1935) 240; Armelini, *op. cit.* 986 and 1282; Bovini, *Edifici cristiani* 108-12 with fig. 19; Buchowiecki, *op. cit.* I 621-22; Ortolani, *S. Croce in Gerusalemme*² 74-76 with fig. 35; Giuseppe Bovini, *Mosaici paleocristiani di Roma* (Bologna 1971) 115-17; Pietri, *op. cit.* I 503; Beny and Gunn, *op. cit.* 102; Richard Klein in *RAC* XIV 367.

Plate IV

The main altar of the Chapel of St Helena in Rome's Basilica of Santa Croce in Gerusalemme.

Statue of St. Helena by Andrea Bolgi, completed in 1639, in the crossing of St. Peter's Basilica, Rome.

1495 and provide information on the history of the chapel and of the entire church. One of these inscriptions claims to know that Helena had soil from Mount Calvary shipped to Rome and put into the chapel, which was formerly her cubiculum, and that for this reason the chapel and the entire church is called "Jerusalem."[42]

The famous relics of the church, housed in the modern (1930) Chapel of the Relics, will be considered in chapter X. We must now turn our attention to other monuments in the city of Rome which are associated with Helena.

A short distance from the Basilica of St. John Lateran, in the Piazza San Giovanni in Laterano, we find the Scala Santa, a building erected by Domenico Fontana under Pope Sixtus V (1585-1590). It is a place of pilgrimage, where the faithful ascend the central stairs of the building only on their knees. The 28 marble steps of these stairs were salvaged from the original Lateran Palace. According to tradition they were brought by Helena from the palace of Pontius Pilate in Jerusalem. This tradition can be traced back no further than the 13th century.[43]

Nor is St. Peter's Basilica without its links to Helena. The *Liber Pontificalis* reports that Constantine placed a huge cross of pure gold above the tomb of St. Peter, and records, however imperfectly, the inscription of this cross.[44] This inscription indicates that Constantine and Helena were the joint donors. The existence of such a cross on the

[42]Besozzi, *op. cit.* 76; Lanciani, *Wanderings* 246 and 250-51; Buchowiecki, *op. cit.* I 618-21. J.C.J. Metford, *Dictionary of Christian Lore and Legend* (London 1983) 118, erroneously states that Helena is reported to have brought earth from Jerusalem to Rome's Church of S. Maria in Ara Coeli.

[43]Hülsen, *Le chiese* 291, no. 23; Achille Petrignani, *Il santuario della Scala Santa* (Vatican City 1941) 16 and 20-21; Schulten, *Die Hl. Stiege* (1964) 111-15; Buchowiecki, *op. cit.* I 94-97.

[44]Migne, *PL* VIII 805; ed. Mommsen (*MGH, GPR* I) 57; ed Duchesne[2] I 176; Giovanni Battista De Rossi, *Inscriptiones Christianae Urbis Romae* II (Rome 1888) 199. Only an incomplete text of the inscription is provided in the 12th century by Pietro Mallio in his *Descriptio Basilicae Vaticanae*; see Valentini and Zucchetti, *op. cit.* III (1946) 384; Marucchi, *op. cit.* III 117; Bernhard Kötting, *Perigrinatio Religiosa* (Münster 1950) 231; Rudolf Egger, "Das Goldkreuz am Grabe Petri," *AAWW* 96 (1959) 182-202; Engelbert Kirschbaum, *The Tombs of St. Peter and St. Paul* (London 1959) 61 and 152; James Lees-Milne, *Saint Peter's* (Boston 1967) 77; Pietri, *op. cit.* I 51-52 and 68; Achim Arbeiter, *Alt-St. Peter in Geschichte und Wissenschaft* (Berlin 1988) 56, 60, 216, and ill. 132; Odahl, "The Christian Basilicas" 16, n. 26. That the cross was a donation of Constantine and Helena is denied by Leeb, *op. cit.* 5, n. 14.

tomb of St. Peter is confirmed by the carvings on the rear side of a fifth century ivory casket found at Samagher near Pola in Istria.[45] A second link of St. Peter's Basilica to St. Helena is both more certain and more visible. In the crossing, under the dome, four colossal statues were placed into niches in the four mighty piers by the design of Bernini: St. Longinus in the northeast pier, St. Andrew in the southeast pier, St. Veronica in the southwest pier, and St. Helena in the northwest pier. (This is not, however, their original arrangement.) The St. Helena can be dated to the year 1639 and is the work of Andrea Bolgi, one of Bernini's pupils, who labored on it for ten years. Helena holds a large cross in her right hand and three nails in her left hand.[46]

Nothing would indicate that Helena returned to Rome after her pilgrimage or even that she had any desire to do so; she probably pre-

[45]Formerly in the Museo civico in Pola. Since 1960 in the Museo archeologico in Venice; inv. no. 278, kindly supplied by the museum. Pietro Toesca, *Il medioevo* (Turin 1927) I 328-330, 337, and fig. 192.III; John Ward Perkins, "The Shrine of St. Peter and Its Twelve Spiral Columns," *JRS* 42 (1952) 21-33 at 22 and pl. I.1; Jocelyn Toynbee and John Ward Perkins, *The Shrine of St. Peter* (New York 1957) 203-204 with fig. 21; Kirschbaum, *op. cit.* 60 and pl. 10; Frederik van der Meer, *Early Christian Art* (Chicago 1967) 71, 134, and pl. 18a; John Beckwith, *Early Christian and Byzantine Art* (Harmondsworth, Middlesex, 1970) 12 and 21; Wolfgang Friedrich Volbach, *Elfenbeinarbeiten der Spätantike und des frühen Mittelalters*, 3rd ed. (Mainz 1976) 85, no. 120; Victor H. Elbern in Kurt Weitzmann, ed., *Age of Spirituality: Late Antique and Early Christian Art, Third to Seventh Century* (New York 1979) 594 and fig. 83; Arbeiter, *op. cit.* 171 and ill. 117; Odahl, "The Christian Basilicas," ill. 22. Robert L. Milburn, *Early Christian Art and Architecture* (Berkeley 1988) 95-96 with ill. 56, erroneously places the casket at Pola. Alexander Coburn Soper, "The Italo-Gallic School of Early Christian Art," *ArtB* 20 (1938) 145-92 at 154 and fig. 2, interprets this panel as a wedding.

[46]Maurice, *Sainte Hélène* 48; Howard Hibbard, *Bernini* (Harmondsworth, Middlesex, 1965) 80-85; Rudolf Wittkower, *Gian Lorenzo Bernini: The Sculptor of the Roman Baroque*, 2nd ed. (London 1966) 17, 34, cat. no. 28, and pl. 41; Maurizio and Marcello Fagiolo dell'Arco, *Bernini: Una introduzione al gran teatro del barocco* (Rome 1967) 140-41, schedario 57-58, and pl. IV; Buchowiecki, *op. cit.* I 154-55; Irving Lavin, *Bernini and the Crossing of Saint Peter's* (New York 1968) 19-22, 32-37, and figs. 49-52; Hans Kaufmann, *Giovanni Lorenzo Bernini* (Berlin 1970) 97-108; John Pope-Hennessy, *Italian High Renaissance and Baroque Sculpture*, 2nd ed. (London 1970) 108-10 and 442; Rudolf Wittkower, *Art and Architecture in Italy 1600-1750*, 3rd ed. (Harmondsworth, Middlesex, 1973) 201; Irving Lavin, *Bernini and the Unity of the Visual Arts* (New York and London 1980) I 21 and II, figs. 8-11; Franco Borsi, *Bernini* (New York 1984) 60, 270, and ill. 44-50; Beny and Gunn, *op. cit.* 246 and 255; Tesei, *op. cit.* 549. It is clear that Bolgi's St. Helena does not fare well in a comparison with Bernini's St. Longinus, but Lees-Milne, *op. cit.* 254, goes too far in calling Bolgi's work "dismal." The St. Andrew is by Francois Duquesnoy, and the St. Veronica by Francesco Mochi.

ferred to be close to Constantine in the East. In chapters XI and XII
below we shall consider Helena's death and burial, and in that context
we shall be very much concerned with Rome again.

Chapter VIII.
Pilgrimage to the Holy Land

Nothing that Helena did in her life did more to shape later traditions than her pilgrimage to the Holy Land.[1] Helena undertook this pilgrimage not as a private person but as the representative of her son and as Augusta; μεγαλοπρεπείᾳ βασιλικῆς ἐξουσίας is Eusebius' phrase.[2]

None of our sources says specifically when Helena set out on her pilgrimage, how many months or years she spent traveling, or when she returned. Helena would not, however, have traveled in the eastern half of the empire before Constantine became master of it in September of 324. Sozomen, moreover, places her pilgrimage after the Council of Nicaea, which closed on July 25 of 325.[3] We know from Eusebius that she was "advanced in years" at the time and died shortly after her return.[4] Numismatic evidence points to her death in or about 329.[5] A number of scholars have linked Helena's pilgrimage to the tragic events which took place in Constantine's family in 326, and rightly so.[6] We will not be too far off the mark in assuming that Helena began her journey *after* the deaths of Crispus and Fausta and her own possible

---

[1]MacMullen, *Constantine* 188, is wrong in claiming that Helena was the first Christian pilgrim to the Holy Land. This is pointed out by Fergus Millar, *JRS* 60 (1970) 216, and by E. D. Hunt, *op. cit.* 28, n. 1. See also the following: Max von Wulf, *Über Heilige und Heiligenverehrung in den ersten christlichen Jahrhunderten* (Leipzig 1910) 476; Kötting, *op. cit.* 91; Günter Stemberger, *Juden und Christen im Heiligen Land* (Munich 1987) 77; Stefan Heid, "Der Ursprung der Helenalegende im Pilgerbetrieb Jerusalems," *JbAC* 32 (1989) 41-71 at 47-48; Peter Walker, *Holy City, Holy Places?* (Oxford 1990) 11-13; Norwich, *op. cit.* 70, commits the same error.

[2] "in the splendor of her royal position." *Vita Const.* 3.44 (Migne, *PG* XX 1105; ed. Winkelmann [*GCS*] 102). Cf. Richard Klein in *RAC* XIV 366, Heid, "Der Ursprung" 54, Drijvers, *op. cit.* 62-63, and Leeb, *op. cit.* 88 ("Staatswallfahrt").

[3]*Hist. Eccl.* 2.1.1 (Migne, *PG* LXVII 929; ed. Bidez-Hansen [*GCS* L] 47; ed. Bidez [*SC* CCCVI] 226).

[4]*Vita Const.* 3.42.; 46.

[5]To be considered in chapter XI below.

[6]See chapter III above, nn. 26-27, and especially E. D. Hunt, *loc. cit.* A different perspective is offered by Drijvers, *op. cit.* 67.

involvement in the family tragedy.[7] A journey of two years duration would not be unreasonable given Helena's apparently busy schedule of activities and the slowness of travel in the ancient world. Thus all of our data are in agreement.

Nor are we told by any ancient author whether Helena set out on her journey from Trier, Rome, Nicomedia, or some other place; we do not even know whether she traveled by land or by sea.[8] If she travelled by land, in either direction, it is most likely that she passed through Syrian Antioch. Her presence in the area contributed, in any event, to the downfall of Eustathius, the bishop of Antioch.[9]

Several ancient sources report that Eustathius was driven from his see. Eusebius of Caesarea could have succeeded to the vacant see,

---

[7]326 has found widespread acceptance; see, e.g., Hans-Henning Lauer, *op. cit.* 28, *PLRE* I 410, Dietz, "St. Helena" 357, Barnes, *Constantine and Eusebius* 221, idem, *New Empire* 9, n. 40, Lane Fox, *op. cit.* 670-71 and 674, and Leeb, *op. cit.* 157; Maurice, *Sainte Hélène* 14, thinks that Helena arrived in the Holy Land in 327; Krautheimer, *Early Chr. and Byz. Architecture* (ed. 1981) 62, gives no justification for 325. Karl Künstle, *Ikonographie der christlichen Kunst* (Freiburg 1926-1928) II 295, J. H. Geiger in *NCE* VI (1967) 1000, and J. N. D. Kelly, *Jerome* (New York 1975) 118, erroneously give 324. John Wilkinson in Yoram Tsafrir, ed., *Ancient Churches Revealed* (Jerusalem and Washington, D.C., 1993) 23, erroneously gives 329. The chronology offered by Seeck, *RE* VII.2 (1912) 2821-22, is wrong in regards to both Helena's pilgrimage and her death (after 330). So is Steidle, *op. cit.* 97, n. 14. Seeck's error is pointed out by Marie Vodová, "La chronologie de la vie d'Hélène, mère de l'empereur Constantin, et ses portraits," *SPFB* 24 (1979) 63-72. I do not know on what grounds J.P.V.D. Balsdon, *Roman Women* (New York 1962) 166, states that Helena undertook her pilgrimage at the age of 73 and survived "by some years." The chronology offered by Borgehammar, *op. cit.* 139-42, will be considered in chapter IX.

[8]Barnes, *Constantine and Eusebius* 221, says that she set out from Rome; similarly id., *New Empire* 9, n. 40. Maurice, *Sainte Hélène* 14, supposes that she traveled by sea and was detained by winter storms on Cyprus. There is also a late and untrustworthy tradition which holds that Helena, on her way to the Holy Land, was obliged by a storm to seek shelter on the island of Paros and, in fulfillment of a vow, sponsored there the construction of the Church of the Panagia Hekatontapyliani (or more correctly Katapoliani): Harry Herbert Jewell and Frederick William Hasluck, *The Church of Our Lady of the Hundred Gates in Paros* (London 1920) 1-2; Georgios N. Korres, Ἡ Ἑκατονταπυλιάνη τῆς Πάρου (Athens 1954) 30 and 48; Theologos Chr. Aliprandis and Nikos Chr. Aliprandis, Πάρος - Ἀντίπαρος, 2nd ed. (Athens 1966) 79.

[9]For the bishops of Antioch see chapter IV above, n. 9. On Eustathius see Johannes Quasten, *Patrology* (Westminster 1950) III 302-306. On his ouster see Victor C. De Clerq, *Ossius of Cordova* (Washington, D. C., 1954) 293-95, and Leslie W. Barnard, "Church-State Relations, A.D. 313-337," *Journal of Church and State* 24 (1982) 337-55 at 349-50.

but he declined and won Constantine's praise in the process.[10] Jerome dates this event to the year 328 and attributes Eustathius' fate to the stance which he had taken in the Arian controversy:

... XXIII Eustathius, quo in exilium ob fidem truso usque in praesentem diem Arriani ecclesiam obtinuerunt.[11]

Athanasius also gives Eustathius high marks as a defender of orthodoxy and adds that his enemies had brought false charges against him before Constantine; specifically Eustathius was said to have offered offense to Helena, ὡς τῇ μητρὶ αὐτοῦ ποιήσας ὕβριν.[12] Unfortunately Athanasius does not tell us what the nature of Eustathius' alleged ὕβρις was.

Socrates tells us that Eustathius was deposed by a synod of bishops which met in his own city; he then describes the dissension which prevailed within the church.[13] There is no mention of Helena; neither is there in the parallel accounts of Sozomen and of Theodoret.[14]

Jerome, as previously mentioned, dates Eustathius' exile to the year 328. Henry Chadwick has argued that the council of which Socrates, Sozomen, and Theodoret speak was held in 326.[15] Further refining Chadwick's arguments, Barnes has proposed 327.[16] Any of

---

[10]*Vita Const.* 3.59-62 (Migne, *PG* XX 1125-35; ed. Winkelmann [*GCS*] 111-17).

[11] ... in the year 23 (of Constantine, i.e. in 328 of our era) Eustathius; when he was driven into exile because of his faith, the Arians seized the church and they hold it to this day. Euseb-Hieron. *Chron.* Olymp. 277 (ed. Fotheringham 314; ed. Helm² [*GCS* XLVII] 232). Repeated in Prosper Tiro, *Epit. Chron.* 1027 (*MGH, AA* IX = *Chron. Min.* I 451).

[12]*Hist. Arian.* 4.1 (Migne, *PG* XXV 697-700; ed. Opitz II.1 184-85).

[13]*Hist. Eccl.* 1.24 (Migne, *PG* LXVII 144-45; ed. Bright² 47-48).

[14]Sozomen, *Hist. Eccl.* 2.19 (Migne, *PG* LXVII 981-84; ed. Bidez-Hansen [*GCS* L] 74-76; ed. Bidez [*SC* CCCVI] 306-10). Theodoret, *Hist. Eccl.* 1.20 in Migne, *PG* LXXXII 965-68; 1.21 in ed. Parmentier-Scheidweiler (*GCS* XLIV) 70-72. Theodoret tells how Eustathius' enemies hired a woman to accuse him of having fathered her child; this is hardly a very convincing story. Theodoret calls Eustathius a "champion of truth."

[15]Henry Chadwick, "The Fall of Eustathius of Antioch," *JThS* 49 (1948) 27-35. Chadwick rightly rejects 330, which had become widely accepted, e. g. by Chaine, *op.cit.* 254, and by Robert Victor Sellers, *Eustathius of Antioch* (Cambridge 1928) 39, n. 1. Most recently the date of 330 is given again by Harold W. Attridge and Gohei Hata in the introduction to their *Eusebius, Christianity, and Judaism* (Detroit 1992) 32.

[16]"Emperor and Bishops, A.D. 324-344: Some Problems," *Am. Journ. of Anc. Hist.* 3 (1978) 53-75 at 59-60; Chadwick dates the Council of Serdica to 342, while Barnes holds for 343; Barnes is, I believe, correct. 327 is also the date given by Walker, *op. cit.*

(continued...)

these dates would coincide with Helena's pilgrimage to the Holy Land. Whether Eustathius insulted her to her face or made a disparaging remark in her absence we cannot tell.[17]

Helena's pilgrimage was an act of personal piety, and it is this aspect which is emphasized by Eusebius. She practiced charity and humility; she also offered prayers on behalf of the empire, her son, and her grandsons. Above all, her piety found expression in the building or embellishment of churches at Christendom's most holy places. The emperor and his mother were happily united in a common purpose. But her journey was also a state visit and most likely served secular purposes as well, namely to forestall unrest among the inhabitants of the eastern provinces.[18]

The emperor Hadrian, it is well known, had transformed the Jewish city of Jerusalem into the Roman city of Aelia Capitolina. As part of the program of transformation, a temple of Venus had been built on a platform that was piled up over the very spot which Christians believed to be the site of the Resurrection. After the Council of Nicaea (325) Constantine ordered the removal of the offending pagan temple and even of the platform on which it stood.[19] In the course of the work of removal the tomb which was believed to be - and in all likelihood - is the tomb of Jesus was discovered.[20] Constantine then issued instructions to the "governors of the eastern provinces" and to Macarius, the Bishop of Jerusalem, for the construction of a splendid church – the Church of the Holy Sepulchre.[21] The order was executed speedily.[22] The church

[16](...continued)
27, no. 85, and by Drijvers, op. cit. 71-72; R.P.C. Hanson, "The Fate of Eustathius of Antioch," ZKG 95 (1984) 171-79, argues for 328 or 329; he does not seem to be aware of Barnes' article.

[17]Downey, op. cit. 352; MacMullen, Constantine 179-80; Barnes, Constantine and Eusebius 228; E.D. Hunt, op. cit. 35-36.

[18]This point is emphasized by Drijvers, op. cit. 65-72, who goes too far, however, when he claims that Helena's journey was not a pilgrimage at all.

[19]Euseb. Vita Const. 3.25-27 (Migne, PG XX 1085-88; ed. Winkelmann [GCS] 94-96).

[20]Ibid. 28.

[21]Ibid. 29-32.

[22]Ibid. 33.

was dedicated on September 13 (*not* 17), 335, by an assembly of bishops who were then attending the Council of Tyre.[23]

Constantine's Church of the Holy Sepulchre was a complex of structures laid out on an east-west axis. At the east end a formal gateway or propylaea afforded access from the street to a colonnaded court or atrium. From this atrium, in turn, one could enter, by one of three portals, a five-aisled basilica or Martyrium. Beyond the basilica there was another court which contained on its south side the rock of Calvary or Golgotha. At the west end of this second court there was the sacred tomb, which, some years later according to some authorities, was enclosed by the famous rotunda that became known as the Anastasis. Constantine's complex suffered many vicissitudes through the centuries, and not much of the original construction has survived. The present Church of the Holy Sepulchre is a Crusader church of the 12th century. Our principal source of information on the Constantinian church is Eusebius.[24]

---

[23]*Ibid.* 4.43.1-2 and 4.47 (Migne, *PG* XX 1193 and 1197; ed. Winkelmann [*GCS*] 138 and 140); Athan. *Apol. contra Arian.* = *Apol. Secunda* 84 (Migne, *PG* XXV 397; ed. Opitz II.1 162-63); Socrates, *Hist. Eccl.* 1.33.1 (Migne, *PG* LXVII 164; ed. Bright[2] 56); Sozomen, *Hist. Eccl.* 2.26 (Migne, *PG* LXVII 1008; ed. Bidez-Hansen [*GCS* L] 87-88; ed. Bidez [*SC* CCCVI] 346-48); Theodoret, *Hist. Eccl.* 1.29 in Migne *PG* LXXXII 988; 1.31.1 in ed. Parmentier-Scheidweiler (*GCS* XLIV) 87-88. The *Chronicon Paschale* erroneously dates the event to September 17, 334 (Migne, *PG* XCII 714; ed. Dindorf [*CSHB* XVI] I 531; *MGH, AA* IX = *Chron. Min.* I 234-35); Hefele-Leclercq, *op. cit.* I.2 666 with n. 2; Seeck, *Regesten* 183 (erroneously September 17); John Winter Crowfoot, *Early Churches in Palestine* (London 1941) 9; André Grabar, *Martyrium* (Paris 1943-1946) I 256; Vogt, "Constantinus der Grosse" 369; Charles Coüasnon, *The Church of the Holy Sepulchre in Jerusalem* (London 1974) 15 (erroneously September 17); E.D. Hunt, *op. cit.* 10, 25 with n. 117 (September 17, citing the *Chronicon Paschale*), and 38; Barnes, *Constantine and Eusebius* 248-49; F.E. Peters, *Jerusalem* (Princeton 1985) 139-40; Maraval, *op. cit.* 67; Walker, *op. cit.* 280. Krautheimer, *Early Chr. and Byz. Architecture* (ed. 1981) 62, erroneously gives 336. Borgehammar, *op. cit.* 99-103, corrects the date given by the *Chronicon Paschale*.

[24]*Vita Const.* 3.34-40 (Migne, *PG* XX 1096-1100; ed. Winckelmann [*GCS*] 99-101). Eusebius does not, however, mention the rotunda of the Anastasis or the rock of Golgotha; that he was aware of the latter is apparent from its mention in his *Onomasticon* s. v. Golgouâ (ed. Klostermann [*GCS* XI.1] 74). Only a partial listing of the vast secondary literature will be attempted here: Melchior de Vogüé, *Les églises de la Terre Sainte* (Paris 1860) 118-232, is the first systematic study. August Heisenberg, *Grabeskirche und Apostelkirche* (Leipzig 1908) I; Hugues Vincent and F.- M. Abel, *Jérusalem* (Paris 1912-1926) II.1 89-300; H. T. F. Duckworth, *The Church of the Holy Sepulchre* (London 1923); F.-M. Abel s. v. Jérusalem in *DACL* VII.2 (1927) 2304-74 at 2312-18; Crowfoot, *op. cit.* 9-21; Grabar, *Martyrium* I 257-82; Erik Wistrand,

(continued...)

The Pilgrim of Bordeaux, who visited the Holy Land in 333, does not add much to our knowledge; his brief reference to the site does, however, suggest that the rotunda of the Anastasis had not yet been built at that time.[25] When the pilgrim Egeria visited Jerusalem in ca. 380

[24](...continued)
Konstantins Kirche am Heiligen Grab in Jerusalem nach den ältesten literarischen Zeugnissen (Göteborg 1952); Ludwig Voelkl, "Die konstantinischen Kirchenbauten nach Eusebius," *RACrist.* 29 (1953) 49-66 and 187-206 at 87-89; John Kenneth Conant, "The Original Buildings at the Holy Sepulchre in Jerusalem" *Speculum* 31 (1956) 1-48; J. G. Davies, "Eusebius' Description of the Martyrium at Jerusalem," *AJA* 61 (1957) 171-73; André Parrot, *Golgotha and the Church of the Holy Sepulchre* (New York 1957) 66-83; Joséf Tadeusz Milik, "Notes d'epigraphie et de topographie palestiniennes," *Rev. Bibl.* 67 (1960) 354-67 and 550-91 at 358-59; Bellarmino Bagatti, *L'archeologia Cristiana in Palestina* (Florence 1962) 40-47; P. Testini, "L'Anastasis alla luce delle recenti indagini," *OA* 3 (1964) 263-92; Robert Houston Smith, "The Tomb of Jesus," *Biblical Archaeologist* 30 (1967) 74-90; Asher Ovadiah, *Corpus of the Byzantine Churches in the Holy Land* (Bonn 1970) 75-77, with earlier literature; Yoram Tsafrir s. v. Jerusalem in *RBK* III (1972-1978) 588-600; Coüasnon, *op. cit.*; Magen Broshi, "Evidence of Earliest Christian Pilgrimage to the Holy Land Comes to Light in Holy Sepulchre Church," *Biblical Archaeology Review* 3 (1977) 42-44; John Wilkinson, *Egeria's Travels to the Holy Land,* rev. ed. (Jerusalem and Warminster, England, 1981) 39-46 and 164-71; Virgilio C. Corbo, *Il Santo Sepolcro di Gerusalemme: Aspetti archeologici dalle origini al periodo crociato* (Jerusalem 1982); E.D. Hunt, *op. cit.* 7-14; Peters, *op. cit.* 132-37; Maraval, *op. cit.* 252-57; Dan Bahat, "Does the Holy Sepulchre Church Mark the Burial of Jesus?" *Biblical Archaeological Review* 12:3 (May/June 1986) 26-45; Heribert Busse and Georg Kretschmar, *Jerusalemer Heiligtumstraditionen in altkirchlicher und frühislamicher Zeit* (Wiesbaden 1987) 29-68; Stemberger, *op. cit.* 54-60; Walker, *op. cit.* 235-81; Joseph Patrich in Tsafrir, *Ancient Churches Revealed* 100-17. Principal controversies have concerned the date of the Anastasis and the shape of the west end of the Martyrium. Corbo's work has been much criticized by Bahat. Summary descriptions of the Constantinian church are provided, among others, by the following: William L. MacDonald, *Early Christian and Byzantine Architecture* (New York 1962) 20-21; Jack Finegan, *The Archeology of the New Testament: The Life of Jesus and the Beginning of the Early Church* (Princeton 1969) 163-65; John Gray, *A History of Jerusalem* (New York 1969) 199-200 and fig. VIII; Michael Avi-Yonah in *Encyclopedia of Archaeological Excavations in the Holy Land* (Englewood Cliffs, New Jersey, 1975-1978) II 614; Krautheimer, *Early Chr. and Byz. Architecture* (ed. 1981) 62-64; Milburn, *op. cit.* 100-102 with fig. 61; Yoram Tsafrir, "Ancient Churches in the Holy Land," *Biblical Archaeology Review* 19:5 (September/October, 1993) 26 and 37-39; Tsafrir, *Ancient Churches Revealed* 10-11.

[25]*Itinerarium Burdigalense* 593-94 (Migne, *PL* VIII 791; ed. Geyer [*CSEL* XXXIX] 22-23; ed. Cuntz 97; *CC, Ser. Lat.* CLXXV 17). Odahl, *Early Christian Latin Literature* 155. Wilkinson, *op. cit.* 158, n. 7; Peters, *op. cit.* 145. On the Pilgrim of Bordeaux see further: Kötting, *op. cit.* 92-93 and 351-54; Wilkinson, *op. cit.* 153-63; E.D. Hunt, *op. cit.* 55-58; and Peters, *op. cit.* 143-45.

she took a special interest in the liturgical practices of the Jerusalem church and in the Encaenia, the feast of the dedication of the Church of the Holy Sepulchre;[26] she was less interested in the buildings but refers specifically both to the Martyrium and to the Anastasis.[27]

It is Constantine, according to Eusebius' account, who took the initiative in the building of the Church of the Holy Sepulchre; Eusebius makes no mention of Helena in this regard.[28] Athanasius, who certainly was in a position to know, similarly makes no mention of Helena.[29] Sozomen also attributes the initiative to Constantine.[30] But Socrates reports that it was Helena who ordered the destruction of the pagan temple, found the tomb, and then had the church built.[31] Socrates is linking and intermingling two traditions, the foundation of the church and the Invention of the True Cross. A measure of his lack of accuracy may be seen in his saying that Helena built two other churches *after the completion* of the "New Jerusalem," i.e. the Church of the Holy Sepulchre; but we know that that church was not dedicated until 335. Helena certainly did not stay long enough in the Holy Land to see its completion. And Theodoret will have us believe that Helena delivered Constantine's letter to Bishop Macarius; he also fuses the discovery of

[26]*S. Silviae, quae fertur, Peregrinatio ad Loca Sancta* 24.1-49.3 [55-74] (ed. Geyer [*CSEL* XXXIX] 71-101; ed. Pétré [*SC* XXI] 188-266; ed. Franceschini-Weber [*CC, Ser. Lat.* CLXXV] 67-90; ed. Maraval [*SC* CCXCVI] 235-318); this is almost half of the extant text. Odahl, *Early Christian Latin Literature* 161-67. The same feast day, she claims to know, commemorates the dedication of the church, the Invention of the True Cross, and the dedication of Solomon's Temple. Odahl, *Early Christian Latin Literature* 159-60.

[27]*Ibid.*, 48.1 [74]. On Egeria, or Etheria, or Silvia, see the following: Kötting, *op. cit.* 354-57; Wilkinson, *op. cit.*, with bibliography 334-37; Hagith Sivan, "Who was Egeria?" *HThR* 81 (1988) 59-72. The date of her pilgrimage is problematic; see Kötting, *op. cit.* 157, n. 398, ed. Maraval 27-39, and esp. Paul Devos, "La date du voyage d'Égérie," *Anal. Boll.* 85 (1967) 165-94.

[28]This is emphasized by Harold Allen Drake in Orlandi, *Eudoxia and the Holy Sepulchre* 134-35, and by E.D. Hunt, *op. cit.* 37-38 and 48. See also Richard Klein, "Das Kirchenbauverständnis Constantins d. Gr. in Rom und in den östlichen Provinzen," in Christoph Börker and Michael Donderer, edd., *Das antike Rom und der Osten* (Erlangen and Nuremberg 1990) 77-101, and Leeb. *op. cit.* 88, n. 13.

[29]*Apol. contra Arian.* = *Apol. Secunda* 84 (Migne, *PG* XXV 397; ed. Opitz II.1 162-63).

[30]*Hist. Eccl.* 2.1.1 (Migne, *PG* LXVII 929; ed. Bidez-Hansen [*GCS* L] 47; ed. Bidez [*SC* CCCVI] 226).

[31]*Hist. Eccl.* 1.17 (Migne, *PG* LXVII 117-21; ed. Bright[2] 35-37).

the tomb and the Invention of the True Cross into a single event.[32] I cannot think of any reason why one should believe Socrates and Theodoret, who do not fully agree with each other, rather than Eusebius and Athanasius, who were close to the events which they report, and Sozomen. The pilgrim Egeria states in one place that the church was built by Constantine and in another that it was decorated by Constantine *sub praesentia* of his mother.[33] She is undoubtedly merely reporting what she was told locally.

The Crusaders' Church of the Holy Sepulchre features an extension off the east choir and accessible from the ambulatory of the choir by means of a staircase. This extension is called the Chapel of St. Helena, and off it is a smaller chapel, really a cistern, called the Chapel of the Invention of the Cross.[34] The existence of these chapels proves neither that Helena ordered the construction of the church nor that she discovered the True Cross.

The Gospel narrative of the birth of Jesus says that Mary placed her new-born son in a manger (φάτνη).[35] To generations of Bible readers in the West this has suggested that Mary and Joseph had found shelter in a *stable*. But in the Near East caves have always provided shelter to animals and to men, even to this day, and in numerous Byzantine works of art the setting of the nativity is a cave. Thus there is no need to reject reports which place the birth of Jesus in a *cave* near Bethlehem. We have two such reports, both from the second century: Justin Martyr's *Dialogue with Trypho*[36] and the apocryphal Protevangelium of James.[37] And in the third century Origen reports that the cave in which Jesus was born is pointed out at Bethlehem.[38] Over and around this cave or grotto the Church of the Nativity was built.

[32]*Hist. Eccl.* 1.17 in Migne, *PG* LXXXII 957-61; 1.18 in ed. Parmentier-Scheidweiler (*GCS* XLIV) 63-64.

[33]*Peregrinatio* 25.1 [58] (ed. Geyer [*CSEL* XXXIX] 74; ed. Pétré [*SC* XXI] 198; ed. Franceschini-Weber [*CC, Ser. Lat.* CLXXV] 70); 25.9 [59].

[34]Vincent and Abel, *Jérusalem* II.1 131-34; Parrot, *op. cit.* 80-81; Robert Houston Smith, *op. cit.* 78; Coüasnon, *op. cit.* 41-43; Bahat, *op. cit.* 42-44.

[35]Luke 2.7.

[36]78 (Migne, *PG* VI 657; ed. Archambault II 18-20).

[37]18.1 (ed. Tischendorf[2] 33; ed. Rauscher[2] [*FP* III] 76; ed. de Strycker [*Subsidia Hagiographica* XXXIII] 146).

[38]*Contra Celsum* 1.51 (Migne, *PG* XI 756; ed. Koetschau [*GCS* III] I 102). Similarly Eusebius, *Dem. Evang.* 3.2.47 and 7.2.15, amended (Migne, *PG* XXII 180 and 540; ed. Heikel [*GCS* XXIII] 103 and 330); Kelly, op. cit. 118; Walker, *op. cit.* 171-72.

Eusebius is once again a vital source of information although his language is vague and even contradictory. In his *Laus Constantini* of 336 he tells us that Constantine chose three places distinguished by their mystic grottoes and decorated them with "rich constructions": the place of the Nativity, the place of the Ascension, and the Sepulchre.[39] There is no mention here of Helena. A year later, in the *Vita Constantini*, Eusebius uses very similar language in reference to the place of the Nativity and the place of the Ascension. But this time he adds in one passage[40] that thus Constantine honored the memory of his mother, and in another that Helena erected and "dedicated" these two churches, while Constantine offered costly presents.[41]

Eusebius' language does not make clear, then, what specific roles Constantine and Helena respectively played in the construction of these two churches.[42] A joint interest and endeavor do not at all seem unreasonable. Jerome Murphy-O'Connor writes that the first Church of the Nativity was dedicated by Helena on May 31, 339.[43] This can in no way be correct, since Helena's death had occured some ten years earlier; we do not know, in fact, when this church was completed or when it was dedicated.

The Pilgrim of Bordeaux makes only brief reference to the Church of the Nativity.[44] "Here a basilica was built on orders of Constantine," he says. There is no mention of Helena, and the impression is left that the church was completed at the time of his visit. The pilgrim Egeria refers to the church twice but very briefly, without describing its architectural design or mentioning its founders.[45] St.

---

[39]9.17 (Migne, *PG* XX 1369-72; ed. Heikel [*GCS* VII] 221). On caves as holy places see Robert L. Wilken, *The Land Called Holy* (New Haven 1992) 88-89, and in Attridge and Hata, *op. cit.* 743-44.

[40]3.41 (Migne, *PG* XX 1101; ed. Winkelmann [*GCS*] 101).

[41]*Ibid.* 43; Richard Klein, "Das Kirchenbauverständnis Constantins d. Gr." 94.

[42]On this point see Wilkinson, *op. cit.* 46. Finegan, *op. cit.* 96, finds Eusebius' language "slightly confusing" in another regard. Walker, *op. cit.* 187, concludes that the Church of the Holy Sepulchre, the Church of the Nativity, and the Church of the Eleona are rightly associated with Constantine but that the latter two must also be associated directly with Helena. Drijvers, *op. cit.* 64, considers Helena's contribution a minor one.

[43]*The Holy Land*, 2nd ed. (Oxford 1986) 167.

[44]*Itinerarium Burdigalense* 598 (Migne, *PL* VIII 792; ed. Geyer [*CSEL* XXXIX] 25; ed. Cuntz 98; *CC, Ser. Lat.* CLXXV 20). Odahl, *Early Christian Latin Literature* 156.

[45]*Peregrinatio* 25.12 [60] and 42 [70] (ed. Geyer [*CSEL* XXXIX] 77 and 93; ed. Pétré [*SC* XXI] 206 and 246; ed. Franceschini-Weber [*CC, Ser. Lat.* CLXXV] 72 and

(continued...)

Jerome mentions that there was once a grove of Thammuz (Adonis) on the site.[46] In the sixth century the Constantinian Church of the Nativity was replaced with a slightly larger one by the emperor Justinian, and it is Justinian's church which stands to this day.[47] Excavations in the 1930's revealed the foundation walls of the earlier church and a mosaic floor which is of a somewhat later date but clearly antedates Justinian's church. Like the Church of the Holy Sepulchre, so the Church of the Nativity is a memorial church, and there are similarities in the original designs of the two churches. Both churches were laid out on an axis, but a visitor to the Church of the Nativity advanced from west to east, not from east to west. First there was an enclosed atrium, then a square, five-aisled basilica without transept, and finally an octagonal structure which housed the grotto of the Nativity.[48]

---

[45](...continued)
84; ed. Maraval [SC CCXCVI] 254 and 296-98); Paul Devos, "Égérie à Bethléem," Anal. Boll. 86 (1968) 87-108.

[46]Epist. 58.3, to Paulinus of Nola. Cf. Paulinus, epist. 31.3 (Migne, PL LXI 326; ed. Hartel [CSEL XXIX] 270).

[47]Procopius in his De Aedificiis is silent about it. We depend for this information on the Annales of Eutychius, the tenth century patriarch of Alexandria: ed. Cheikho (CSCO L = Script. Arab. VI) 201 or Migne, PG CXI 1070; on Eutychius cf. ch. II above, n. 47; Gregory T. Armstrong, "Fifth and Sixth Century Church Buildings in the Holy Land," Greek Orthodox Theological Review 14 (1969) 17-30 at 24-26.

[48]Again only a partial listing of the secondary literature is here provided: Vogüé, op. cit. 46-117; Hugues Vincent and F.-M. Abel, Bethléem: Le sanctuaire de la Nativité (Paris 1914); Henri Leclercq s. v. Bethléem in DACL II.1 (1925) 828-37; Robert William Hamilton, "Excavations in the Atrium of the Church of the Nativity, Bethlehem," QDAP 3 (1934) 1-8; William Harvey, Structural Survey of the Church of the Nativity, Bethlehem (London 1935); E. T. Richmond, "Basilica of the Nativity: Discovery of the Remains of an Earlier Church," QDAP 5 (1936) 75-81; E.T. Richmond, "The Church of the Nativity: The Plan of the Constantinian Church," QDAP 6 (1938) 63-66, and "The Church of the Nativity: The Alterations Carried out by Justinian," ibid. 67-72; Crowfoot, op. cit. 22-30; Grabar, Martyrium I 245-51; Robert William Hamilton, The Church of the Nativity, Bethlehem (Jerusalem 1947); Bellarmino Bagatti, Gli antichi edifici sacri di Betlemme in seguito agli scavi e restauri praticati dalla Custodia di Terra Santa (1948-51) (Jerusalem 1952); Alfons Maria Schneider s. v. Bethlehem in RAC II (1954) 224-28 at 225-26; Milik, op. cit. 572-73; Bagatti, L'Archeologia Cristiana 47-53; Marcel Restle s. v. Bethlehem in RBK I (1966) 599-612; Gregory T. Armstrong, "Imperial Church Building in the Holy Land in the Fourth Century," Biblical Archaeologist 30 (1967) 90-102 at 92-94; Ovadiah, op. cit. 33-37, with earlier literature; Michael Avi-Yonah in Encyclopedia of Archaeological Excavations in the Holy Land I 199-205; Wilkinson, op. cit. 46-49; E.D. Hunt, op. cit. 14-15 and 20-21; Walker, op. cit. 171-88. Summary
(continued...)

A third Constantinian church in the Holy Land was the Church of the Eleona, or Church on the Mount of Olives, located on the Mount of Olives, a little below its summit. Although this church was associated with the event of the Ascension, it must be distinguished from the somewhat later Church of the Ascension, or Inbomon Church, now a mosque, which is located at the very summit of the mount. The Church of the Eleona was a memorial church laid out on a west-east axis. A visitor would pass through a portico into an atrium, and from the atrium into a three-aisled basilica ca. 30 m. long. At the eastern end of the basilica there was an apse, and below this apse there was a crypt or cave, in which Christ was believed to have taught his disciples.[49] Only the foundation trenches and small segments of the foundation walls remain today.[50]

We have already seen that Eusebius does not tell us specifically how Constantine and Helena respectively were involved in the establishment of this church. The Pilgrim of Bordeaux says only that "here a basilica was built on orders of Constantine."[51] The pilgrim

[48](...continued)
descriptions of Helena's church are provided by others: MacDonald, *op. cit.* 21; Finegan, *op. cit.* 20-22; Krautheimer, *Early Chr. and Byz. Architecture* (ed. 1981) 60-62; Maraval, *op. cit.* 272-73; Stemberger, *op. cit.* 61; Milburn, *op. cit.* 90-100 and fig. 60; Tsafrir, "Ancient Churches in the Holy Land" 35 and 37; Tsafrir, *Ancient Churches Revealed* 7, 8-9, and 13.

[49]Matthew 24.3 and Mark 13.3.

[50]Again only a partial listing of the secondary literature is attempted: Vogüé, *op. cit.* 315-22; Vincent and Abel, *Jérusalem* II.1 337-60; F.- M. Abel s. v. Jerusalem in *DACL* VII.2 (1927) 2318-20; Crowfoot, *op. cit.* 30-34; Grabar, *Martyrium* I 282-91; Hugues Vincent, "L'Éléona, sanctuaire primitif de l'ascension," *Rev. Bibl.* 64 (1957) 48-71; Milik, *op. cit.* 555-56; Bagatti, *L'Archeologia Cristiana* 54-56; Armstrong, "Imperial Church Building in the Holy Land in the Fourth Century" 94-95; Ovadiah, *op. cit.* 82-83, with earlier literature; Yoram Tsafrir s. v. Jerusalem in *RBK* III (1972-1978) 605-606 with ill. 30; Wilkinson, *op. cit.* 49-51; Walker, *op. cit.* 199-213. Briefer descriptions of the site are provided by others: Finegan, *op. cit.* 95-97; Avi-Yonah in *Encyclopedia of Archaeological Excavations in the Holy Land* II 614; E. D. Hunt, *op. cit.* 15; Maraval, *op. cit.* 265; Stemberger, *op. cit.* 61; Milburn, *op. cit.* 104; Tsafrir, "Ancient Churches in the Holy Land" 33, 34, and 36; Tsafrir, *Ancient Churches Revealed* 2 and 7-8.

[51]*Itinerarium Burdigalense* 595 (Migne, *PL* VIII 791; ed. Geyer [*CSEL* XXXIX] 23; ed. Cuntz 97; *CC, Ser. Lat.* CLXXV 18). Odahl, *Early Christian Latin Literature* 155.

Egeria clearly distinguishes between the church and the Imbomon, the summit.[52] Neither pilgrim mentions Helena.

There is no need to consider in this context a fourth Constantinian church in the Holy Land, the basilica at Mamre, since no ancient source associates it with Helena.

Architecturally the Constantinian church foundations in the Holy Land invite comparison with those in Trier (?), Rome, and Constantinople.[53] The atrium appears to have been of considerable significance in early Christian architecture.[54] Such an atrium was a feature also of the post-Constantinian Church of St. Gereon in Cologne, and Rome's Church of S. Clemente has retained its atrium to this day.

We have previously, in chapter II above, had occasion to consider the *Historia Ecclesiastica* of the 14th century Byzantine author Nikephoros Kallistos Xanthopoulos – and have found it wanting. Nikephoros appears to be dependent, at least in part, on a source of the tenth century.[55] In this tenth century source Helena is credited with 28 church foundations in the Holy Land,[56] while Nikephoros himself speaks of "more than 30."[57] Yet another late tradition attributes to Helena 48 church foundations in the Holy Land; the number 48, as a multiple of 12, is at once suspect.[58] None of these reports seems creditable.[59] Just as the churches of Gaul competed one with another in claiming to be apostolic foundations, so one may imagine that the churches of the Holy Land vied one with another in claiming to be foundations of Helena.

---

[52]*Peregrinatio* 31.1 [64] (ed. Geyer [*CSEL* XXXIX] 83; ed. Pétré [*SC* XXI] 220-22; ed. Franceschini-Weber [*CC, Ser. Lat.* CLXXV] 77; ed. Maraval [*SC* CCXCVI] 272-74).

[53]Vogt, "Constantinus der Grosse" 369; Wightman, *Roman Trier* 110; but see now chapter IV above, n. 46; Krautheimer, *Early Chr. and Byz. Architecture* (ed. 1981) 66.

[54]Suzanne Spain Alexander, "Studies in Constantinian Church Architecture," *RACrist.* 47 (1971) 281-300 and 49 (1973) 33-44; E.D. Hunt, *op. cit.* 20.

[55]Krumbacher, *op. cit.* I 247 and 291; François Nicolas Nau, "Les constructions palestiniennes dues à Sainte Hélène," *Rev. Or. Chr.* 10 (1905) 162-68.

[56]Nau, op. cit. 168.

[57]*Hist. Eccl.* 8.30 (Migne, *PG* CXLVI 117).

[58]Armstrong, "Imperial Church Building" 99, without identifying his source.

[59]Drijvers, *op. cit.* 64, dismisses such reports as "unreliable late-antique and medieval legendry."

Quite apart from the number of churches founded, Helena's pilgrimage was clearly a memorable event. Shortly after 400 Paulinus of Nola writes enthusiastically to Sulpicius Severus:

She (Helena) was divinely inspired, as events have shown, when she came to know Jerusalem. She was then reigning together with her son and held the title of Augusta. She asked her son to support her plans: all the places where our Lord had set foot and which are marked by the remembrances of divine works for us she intended to cleanse, by destroying temples and idols, from every contamination with profane impiety and to return them to the true faith, so that at last the church might be glorified in the land of its own origin. Helena, the emperor's mother and Augusta, readily obtained the permission of her son the emperor, the treasuries were opened for the holy purpose, and she used up the entire household. With all the expense and care of which she was capable and which piety advised, she covered and embellished, by building churches, all the places in which our Lord and Savior had fulfilled the saving mysteries of his love by the sacraments of the incarnation, passion, resurrection, and ascension.[60]

Paulinus must be exaggerating slightly; it is to be doubted that Helena's activities drained the imperial treasury and that Constantine would have allowed this to happen. But it is clear that Helena's activities had Constantine's blessing and support.

Helena's itinerary apparently was not limited to the holy sites of Palestine. Rather, she toured "the East," as Eusebius expressly states twice.[61] Unfortunately Eusebius does not provide more specific information. Late and untrustworthy sources bequeath upon us only a welter of legendary material.

One place in the East which is linked by tradition to Helena is St. Catherine's Monastery in the Sinai. The extant part of Egeria's *Peregrinatio* begins with a lengthy account of her visit to Mt. Sinai.[62] Here she found a community of monks living in cells, a small church on

---

[60]*Epist.* 31.4 (Migne, *PL* LXI 327-28; ed. Hartel [*CSEL* XXIX] 271).

[61]*Vita Const.* 3.42 and 44 (Migne, *PG* XX 1105; ed. Winkelmann [*GCS*] 101 and 102).

[62]1-5 [31-37] (ed. Geyer [*CSEL* XXXIX] 37-45; ed. Pétré [*SC* XXI] 97-118; ed. Franceschini-Weber [*CC, Ser. Lat.* CLXXV] 37-45).

the summit of Jebel Mousa, another church at the foot of the mountain, and the Burning Bush in a well-watered garden in front of the latter church. The famous monastery, originally named not St. Catherine's but St. Mary's, did not yet exist. It was built on orders of Justinian, as Procopius reports, and can be dated more specifically to the years 548-565, thanks to two inscriptions on the roof beams of the monastery's church.[63] The building of the monastery is attributed to Justinian also by Eutychius of Alexandria in his *Annales*.[64] Nektarios, a patriarch of Jerusalem in the 17th century, reports that Helena had built a small chapel on the site of the later monastery.[65] This is accepted by some at face value, while others have been skeptical.[66] The latter are surely right, given the late date of our source and the claims sometimes made by the patriarchs of Jerusalem on St. Catherine's Monastery.

[63]Procopius, *Aed.* 5.8.4-5. Hyacinth Louis Rabino, *Le monastère de Sainte-Cathérine du Monte Sinaï* (Cairo 1938) 18, wrongly dates the death of Theodora to the year 561. Henri Leclercq s. v. Sinai in *DACL* XV.1 (1950) 1463-90 at 1476; Ihor Ševčenko, "The Early Period of the Sinai Monastery in the Light of its Inscriptions," *DOP* 20 (1966) 255-64 at 256 and 262, nos. 4 and 5; George H. Forsyth, "The Monastery of St. Catherine at Mount Sinai: The Church and Fortress of Justinian," *DOP* 22 (1968) 1-19 at 9; Ihor Ševčenko in George H. Forsyth and Kurt Weitzmann, *The Monastery of St. Catherine at Mount Sinai: The Church and Fortress of Justinian* I: Plates (Ann Arbor 1973) 19 and pls. 80-81; Kurt Weitzmann in John Galey, *Sinai and the Monastery of St. Catherine* (Garden City, New York, 1980) 82.

[64]Ed. Cheiko [*CSCO* L = *Script. Arab.* VI] 202-203 or Migne, *PG* CXI 1071-72. On certain differences between Procopius' account and Eutychius' account see the following: Robert Devreesse, "Le christianisme dans la péninsule sinaïtique des origenes à l'arrivée des musulmans," *Rev. Bibl.* 49 (1940) 205-23 at 212-13. Philip Mayerson, "Procopius or Eutychius on the Construction of the Monastery at Mt. Sinai: Which is the More Reliable Source?" *BASOR* 230 (1978) 33-38.

[65]'Επιτομὴ τῆς ἱεροκοσμικῆς ἱστορίας (ed. Venice 1805) 95-96.

[66]E. H. Palmer, *The Desert of the Exodus* (New York 1872) 58; George Ernest Wright in *The Interpreter's Dictionary of the Bible* IV (1962) 376; Burton Bernstein, *Sinai: The Great and Terrible Wilderness* (New York 1979) 10 and 147; Paul Huber, *Heilige Berge*, 2nd ed. (Zürich 1982) 22 and 24. Lina Eckenstein, *A History of Sinai* (London 1921) 99; André Guillou, "Le monastère de la Théotokos au Sinaï," *MélRome* 67 (1955) 217-58 at 221, remarks that almost every Greek monastery claims to have been founded by Helena; he gives the impossible date of 337 for her visit. Heinz Skrobucha, *Sinai* (London 1966) 19, points out that the journey would have been far too strenuous for the aged empress. Maraval, *op. cit.* 300-309, makes no mention of Helena. Tsafrir, *Ancient Churches Revealed* 1 and 327, rejects the association of Helena with Mt. Sinai.

The memory of Helena is kept alive at St. Catherine's to this day by a Chapel of Sts. Constantine and Helena in the monastery church.[67] Constantine and Helena are also represented on some of the monastery's icons.[68]

In the Lebanese village of Maghdushi, or Maghdouche, a little south of Sidon, there is a Christian cave-chapel called Sayidet al-Mantara, i.e. Our Lady of the Awaiting. According to tradition, Mary waited here for Jesus while he preached in Tyre and Sidon.[69] When Helena passed through the area and was told of the tradition, she reportedly arranged for a chapel to be set up in the cave.[70] A more modest version of the story claims only that Helena donated a precious icon.[71] The icon, after various vicissitudes, until recently graced the cave-chapel.[72] The ultimate source of this tradition I have not been able to discover.[73]

Tradition also attributes to Helena the building of a church, which later perhaps became the cathedral, in Aleppo.[74] This can be traced back to a 15th century Arab author, Muhammad Ibn al-Shina.[75] One scholar who rejected the tradition remarks rightly that "in the East almost every church believed to be ancient is attributed to the empress Helena."[76] There are scanty remains of this church, and these date

[67]The second chapel, from the west, off the north aisle; Rabino, op. cit. 19 and 29; Forsyth, op. cit. 11 and figs. 2 and 19; Forsyth in Forsyth and Weitzmann, op. cit. I 8-9 and pl. 93A; Forsyth in Galey, op. cit. 59-61.

[68]Georgios and Maria Sotiriou, Icones du Mont Sinaï (Athens 1956-1958).

[69]Mark 7.24-31 reports that Jesus on one occasion extended his ministry into southern Lebanon, but says nothing about Mary's accompanying him.

[70]Bruce Condé, See Lebanon (Beirut 1960) 265-73.

[71]Colin Thubron, The Hills of Adonis (Boston 1968) 18.

[72]The area of Maghdouche has been the scene of heavy fighting during the Lebanese civil war. The icon is now missing, I have been informed.

[73]Condé, op. cit., and Thubron, op. cit., unfortunately do not cite their sources. Joseph Goudard, La Sainte Vierge au Liban (Paris 1908) 52-59, gives a charming account of the chapel and of various miracles associated with it, but there is no mention of St. Helena.

[74]Robin Fedden, Syria and Lebanon, 3rd ed. (London 1965) 42.

[75]Al-Durr al muntakhab litarikh Halab (ed. Beirut 1909) 61.

[76]S. Guyer, "La Madrasa al-Halâwiyya à Alep," BIFAO 11 (1914) 217-31 at 219.

Plate V

Interior of the cove-chapel of Sayidet al-Mantara at Maghdushi,
near Sidon, Lebanon.

from the sixth rather than the fourth century.[77] Other Arab writers give Helena credit also for having built Aleppo's water-supply system - another most unlikely story.[78]

In the year 324 the island of Cyprus and other parts of the East were struck by a severe drought and famine.[79] This event underwent considerable embellishment at the hands of various Cypriot chroniclers, who attribute to the calamity a duration of 17 or 36 years.[80] Only divine intervention finally brought an end to the suffering of the people, we are told. The tenth century Byzantine hagiographer Simeon Metaphrastes reports that the heavens responded to the fervent prayers of St. Spyridon.[81] But the 15th century chronicler Leontios Macheiras gives credit for the divine intervention to Helena and the precious relics which she carried with her on her way back from the Holy Land. And on a precipitous mountain ca. ten miles west of Larnaca she established Stavrovouni Monastery, he tells us; to this monastery and to the villages

[77]Guyer, op. cit. 224; Howard Crosby Butler, *Early Churches in Syria* (Princeton 1929) 170-71; René Dussaud, Paul Deschamps, and Henri Seyrig, *La Syrie antique et médiévale illustrée* (Paris 1931), pl. 74; Jean Sauvaget, *Alep* (Paris 1941) text vol. 59; Jean Lassus, *Sanctuaires chrétiens de Syrie* (Paris 1947) 153.

[78]Heinz Glaube und Eugen Wirth, *Aleppo* (Wiesbaden 1984) 179.

[79]Theophanes (died ca. 817), *Chronographia*, ad annum mundi 5824 = A.D. 324 (Migne, *PG* CVIII 117; ed. de Boor I 29; Kyriakos Chatziioannou, Ἡ ἀρχαία Κύπρος εἰς τὰς Ἑλληνικὰς πήγας I² [Nicosia 1985] 386-89, no. 129.1). Victor Chapot, *La frontière de l'Euphrate de Pompée à la conquéte arabe* (Paris 1907) 213; Downey, *A History of Antioch* 336-37. But Kedrenos (or Georgius Cedrenus, 11/12th century), in his *Compendium Historiarum*, dates the same events to 334 (Migne, *PG* CXXI 564-65; ed. Bekker [*CSHB* XXVI-XXVII] I 519; Chatziioannou, op. cit., I² 388-89, no. 129.2).

[80]Chatziioannou, op. cit. I² 388-89, no. 129.3; John Hackett, *A History of the Orthodox Church of Cyprus* (London 1901) 8-9; Sir George Hill, *A History of Cyprus* I (Cambridge 1940) 246.

[81]*Vita S. Spyridonis* 4-6 (Migne, *PG* CXVI 420-24). St. Spyridon was bishop of the Cypriot city of Tremithus (or Trimythus), although he is now patron saint of Corfu. While his attendance at the Council of Nicaea is not well attested, he certainly did attend the Council of Serdica in 343. Hackett, op. cit. 382-86; Hippolyte Delehaye, "Saints de Chypre," *Anal. Boll.* 26 (1907) 161-297 at 239-41; Johann Georg, Herzog zu Sachsen, *Der heilige Spyridon, seine Verehrung und Ikonographie* (Leipzig 1913); Hill, op. cit. 248 and 250; Paul van den Ven, *La légende de S. Spyridon, évéque de Trimithonte* (Louvain 1953), provides a collection of primary source material; Réau, *Iconographie* III.3 (1959) 1234-35; *Bibl. Sanct.* XI (1968) 1354-59; *LCI* VIII (1976) 387-89. Another collection of primary source material is found in Chatziioannou, op. cit. I² 368-79, no. 121.

of Lefkara and Tokhni (about half-way between Larnaca and Limassol) she gave pieces of the True Cross.[82]

The accounts of Simeon Metaphrastes and of Leontios Machairas can in no way be reconciled with each other. Furthermore that of Leontios Machairas is inconsistent within itself. It says that the drought lasted for 36 years until the baptism of Constantine.[83] But Constantine's baptism – whether the legendary one by Pope Sylvester or the historical one by Eusebius of Nicomedia - did not coincide with Helena's pilgrimage and any possible visit to Cyprus. Such a visit is no more than a mere possibility.[84]

[82]Leontios Machairas, *Chronikon Kyprou* 1.3-8 (ed. Miller-Sathas I 4-6; ed. Dawkins I 2-8; Chatziioannou, *op. cit.* I² 391-94, no. 130); Hacket, *op. cit.* 9-10, 433-35, and 454; Eugen Oberhummer, *Die Insel Cypern* I (Munich 1903) 155 and 214; Hill, *op. cit.* 246; Doros Alastos, *Cyprus in History* (London 1955) 111; Gordon Home, *Cyprus Then and Now* (London 1960) 150-51; Anatole Frolow, *La relique de la Vraie Croix* (Paris 1961) 558, no. 862; Stylianou, *By This Conquer* 98; Constantinos Spyridakis, *A Brief History of Cyprus*, rev. ed. (Nicosia 1974) 91 and 108. In 1727 the Russian mont Basil Barsky (Vasyl' Bars'kyi) visited Stavrovouni Monastery and learned about St. Helena's visit and the relic of the True Cross. See Andreas Stylianou, Αἱ περιηγήσεις τοῦ Βάρσκου ἐν Κύπρῳ, Κυπριακαὶ Σπουδαί 21 (1957) 1-158 at 36. A facsimile edition of Barsky's manuscript and a new English translation have been prepared by Professor Alexander Grishin of the Australian National University, Canberra, and are forthcoming.

[83]*Chronikon Kyprou* 1.3.

[84]Nevertheless some writers quite uncritically accept the legendary reports as if they were historical facts: Rupert Gunnis, *Historic Cyprus* (London 1936) 428-29 and 439-41; Philip Newman, *A Short History of Cyprus*, 2nd ed. (London 1953) 64.

Chapter IX.
The Discovery of the True Cross

The most glorious achievement of Helena's pilgrimage was not the establishment of this church or that monastery, but rather the *inventio,* or discovery, of the True Cross, if we wish to accept the tradition. This tradition, which enjoyed tremendous popularity through the centuries, must now be examined in detail.

It has often been noted that Eusebius is silent on Helena's discovery of the True Cross.[1] Eusebius' silence by itself does not, of course, prove that the event did not take place. But in this case the *argumentum ex silentio* is unusually persuasive, because Eusebius would have had every reason and ample opportunity to mention such a glorious event. He produced the final revision of his *Ecclesiastical History* in or after 326, i.e. while Helena was in the East.[2] The *Laus Constantini* of 336 (including the treatise on the Church of the Holy Sepulchre) would have been another opportunity. Finally, in the *Vita Constantini* of 337, Eusebius described the Church of the Holy Sepulchre in detail and praised Helena at length, again without mentioning the discovery of the Cross.[3] As bishop of Caesarea he certainly knew well whatever transpired in near-by Jerusalem. We might conclude from Eusebius' silence that the event did not happen in his lifetime. But other explanations have been advanced and must be considered.

Eusebius did preserve for us Constantine's letter to Macarius, and in it Constantine speaks of τὸ γνώρισμα τοῦ ἁγιωτάτου ἐκείνου [τοῦ σωτῆρος] πάθους, long hidden under the ground but now found.[4] Within the last decade several scholars have interpreted this phrase as a

---

[1]Henri Leclercq s. v. Croix (invention et exaltation de la vraie) in *DACL* III.2 (1914) 3131-39 at 3137; *idem* s. v. Hélène, impératrice, in *DACL* VI.2 (1925) 2130; Bond, *op. cit.* 73; Mackes, *op. cit.* 187; Vogt, "Constantinus der Grosse" 373; *PLRE* I 410; Vogt, "Helena Augusta," 212 and 217; E.D. Hunt, *op. cit.* 38; Peters, *op. cit.* 137; Wilken, *op. cit.* 295, n. 63.

[2]Barnes, *Constantine and Eusebius* 150.

[3]3.25-40 (Migne, *PG* XX 1085-1100; ed. Winkelmann [*GCS*] 94-101). 3.42-47. Cf. Richard Klein in *RAC* XIV 359-60 and Walker, *op. cit.* 188-89.

[4]... the token of the suffering of that most holy one (the Savior), ... See chapter VIII above, n. 21. *Vita Const.* 3.30.1 (Migne, *PG* XX 1089; ed. Winkelmann [*GCS*] 97).

reference to the actual Cross.[5]   But the vagueness of Constantine's circumlocution, it seems to me, demands a measure of skepticism.

The same scholars endeavor to explain Eusebius' silence. They agree one with another that Eusebius' silence was deliberate, but they are not in agreement on why he kept silence: Rubin explains Eusebius' silence in terms of ecclesiastical politics, i. e. the rivalry between the see of Caesarea and Eusebius on the one hand and the see of Jerusalem and Macarius on the other hand.[6] Drake points to Eusebius' imprecise language and his tendency to stress the symbolic over the physical nature of the Cross.[7] He suggests that Eusebius did not desire "the very heart and soul of the faith (to be) fettered to an imperial standard."[8] But he concludes that "in a purely formal sense discovery in the reign of Constantine of wood taken to be that of the True Cross has not been proved" ... and that "the possibility must remain open that Eusebius said nothing about such a discovery simply because one did not take place."[9]

Walker holds that Eusebius as historian, as theologian, and as bishop of Caesarea did not approve of the *inventio* of the True Cross and hence was silent about it.[10] As a historian he might have questioned the authenticity of the find, as a theologian he wished to stress Christ's resurrection rather than his death and the spiritual nature of Christianity rather than physical relics, and as the bishop of Caesarea he would have been concerned about the growing aspirations of the Jerusalem church. Borgehammar attributes Eusebius' silence to his concerns as a theologian and an apologist and perceives a difference between Eusebius' and Constantine's attitudes to the Cross.[11] Drijvers surveys the pertinent arguments of Rubin, Drake, and Walker and concludes confidently that "the Cross was indeed found during Constantine's reign in the 320's."[12] The

---

[5]Ze'ev Rubin, "The Church of the Holy Sepulchre and the Conflict between the Sees of Caesarea and Jerusalem," in L. I. Levine, ed., *The Jerusalem Cathedra* II (Jerusalem 1982) 79-105 at 82-83; Harold Allen Drake, "Eusebius on the True Cross," *JEH* 36 (1985) 1-22 at 9-10; Walker, *op. cit.* 128; Borgehammar, *op. cit.* 105-107; Drijvers, *op. cit.* 85 and 128-29. But Leeb, *op. cit.* 91, thinks that the phrase refers to the rock of Golgotha.

[6]*Op. cit.* 91-95; This is rejected by Wilken, *op. cit.* 295, n. 62.

[7]"Eusebius on the True Cross" 15.

[8]*Ibid.* 20.

[9]*Ibid.* 21.

[10]*Op. cit.* 126-30.

[11]*Op. cit.* 115-20, esp. 119.

[12]*Op. cit.* 86-89.

Plate VI

The *inventio* of the Cross; Helena is crowned and nimbed. Colored pen drawing in a manuscript produced ca. 1460 in the workshop of Diebert Lauber in Hagenau, Alsace. Cod. pal. germ. 137, folio 137r.

Photo Universitätsbibliothek Heidelberg (pending).

divergence of these explanations is to be noted. The silence of Eusebius, in my estimation, continues to be a formidable obstacle to considering the question settled.

The Pilgrim of Bordeaux in his hurried account mentions Golgotha, the tomb, Constantine's basilica, the cisterns, and the baptistry, but not the True Cross or Helena.[13] Again it is difficult to explain such silence, or such priorities.[14]

The 24 catechetical lectures of Cyril of Jerusalem, which are commonly dated to 348 or 350, give us the earliest explicit reference to the wood of the Cross, although nothing is said about its discovery.[15] Cyril remarks no fewer than three times that particles of the wood of the cross have filled almost the entire earth.[16] We also have a letter addressed by Cyril to the emperor Constantius in the year 351. In the course of this letter Cyril declares that the salvation-bringing wood of the cross was found in Jerusalem in the days of Constantius' father Constantine, because divine grace granted to *him* who was rightly seeking ($τ\hat{ω}$ ... $ζητο\hat{υ}ντι$) piety the discovery of the hidden holy places.[17] This intends to say, it would seem, that Constantine himself had a major part In the discovery of the Cross; it is silent about Helena, and it does not assign the discovery to a particular date.

Cyril's references to the particles of the wood of the cross are not idle talk. He is borne out by a Mauretanian inscription which dates

[13]See chapter VIII above, n. 25.

[14]Gibbon, *Decline and Fall* chapter XXIII (Modern Library ed. I 777, n. 65), scoffed, "The silence of Eusebius and the Bordeaux pilgrim, which satisfies those who think, perplexes those who believe." Quoted by Drake, "Eusebius on the True Cross" 2, and by Borgehammar, *op. cit.* 92; Mackes, *op. cit.* 187; E.D. Hunt, *op. cit.* 38.

[15]Otto Bardenhewer, *Geschichte der altkirchlichen Literatur* III² (Freiburg 1923) 273-74; Quasten, *op. cit.* III 364; Antoine Paulin, *Saint Cyrille de Jérusalem, catéchète* (Paris 1959) 25; Berthold Altaner and Alfred Stuiber, *Patrologie,* 8th ed. (Freiburg 1978) 312.

[16]*Catecheses* 4.10, 10.19, and 13.4 (Migne, *PG* XXXIII 469, 685-88, and 776; ed. Reischl-Rupp I 100, I 284, and II 54); Borgehammar, *op. cit.* 88-90; Drijvers, *op. cit.* 81-82; Rubin, *op. cit.* 98, on the authenticity of these references.

[17]*Epist. ad Constantium* 3 (Migne, *PG* XXXIII 1168; ed. Reischl-Rupp II 436); Ernest Bihain, "L'épître de Cyrille de Jèrusalem à Constance sur la vision de la croix (*BHG³* 413)," *Byzantion* 43 (1973) 264-96 at 287; Borgehammar, *op. cit.* 90-92; Drijvers, *op. cit.* 82-83 and 134-36. The authenticity of this letter has been questioned by some, *e.g.* Hans-Henning Lauer, *op. cit.* 45, but has been defended by Vogt, "Berichte über Kreuzeserscheinungen aus dem 4. Jahrhundert n. Chr.," *AIPHOS* 9 (1949) 593-606 at 596. Vogt, *ibid.* 602-603, dates this letter to 353; this does not matter in our context. Rubin, *op. cit.* 98, specifically refrains from using this letter in support of his position.

from the year 359; here we find the phrase *de lignu crucis* on a stone slab which once covered a large reliquary box.[18] Gregory of Nyssa reports in 379 that his sister, St. Macrina (the Younger), wore a locket containing a particle of the True Cross.[19]

At the time of Egeria's visit the Invention of the Cross was celebrated in Jerusalem as part of the Encaenia and the wood exposed for veneration on Good Friday, but Egeria makes no mention of Helena in either context.[20]

St. John Chrysostom (died 407) reports in one place that three crosses were found and that the True Cross could be identified because it was in the middle position and still bore the *titulus*.[21] He mentions in another place that there are many, both men and women, who wear a golden locket containing a particle of the True Cross.[22] But there is nothing in either passage about Helena.

The discovery of the True Cross must have been known to Jerome, since he repeatedly speaks of the *lignum crucis* or the nails in his

[18]*CIL* VIII 20600 = *ILCV* I 2068, now in the Louvre, inv. no. Ma 3023. 9830492 AGR; Henri Leclercq in *DACL* I.1 (1907) 827-29; Paul Monceaux, "Enquête sur l'épigraphie chrétienne d'Afrique," *MémAcinscr.* 12 (1908) 161-399 at 298-302; Franz Joseph Dölger, "Das Anhängekreuzchen der hl. Makrina und ihr Ring mit der Kreuzpartikel," *Antike und Christentum* 3 (1932) 81-116 at 102-104 and pl. 10; Frolow, *La relique* 158-59, no. 3; Anatole Frolow, *Les reliquaires de la Vraie Croix* (Paris 1965)117; Yvette Duval, *Loca Sanctorum Africae* (Rome 1982) I 331-37, no. 157; Drijvers, *op. cit.* 89-90. For the conversion of the *annus provinciae* see *ILCV²* III 269 and Duval, *op. cit.* I 336. A second Mauretanian inscription mentioning the wood of the Cross is less helpful, as it is not dated and now lost: *CIL* VIII 9255 = *ILCV²* I 1822; Monceaux, *op. cit.* 303-305; Frolow, *La relique* 159, no.4; Frolow, *Les reliquaires* 117; John Frederick Matthews, "Mauretania in Ammianus and the Notitia," *British Archaeological Reports, Supplementary Series* 15 (1976) 157-86 at 174-75; Duval, *op. cit.* I 351-53, no. 167; Drijvers, *op. cit.* 90.

[19]*Vita St. Macr.* (Migne, *PG* XLVI 989; ed. Jaeger VIII.1 404; ed. Maraval [*SC* CLXXVIII] 240); Dölger, "Das Anhängekreuzchen" 81-116; Frolow, *La relique* 159, no. 5; Drijvers, *op. cit.* 90.

[20]In September; see chapter VIII above, nn. 23 and 26; Matthew Black, "The Festival of Encaenia Ecclesiae in the Ancient Church," *JEH* 5 (1954) 78-85 at 78-80; Wilken, *op. cit.* 97. For the feasts of the Invention of the Cross and the Exaltation of the Cross see below, this chapter, with nn. 88-90. *Peregrinatio* 37.1-2; Drijvers, *op. cit.* 91-92.

[21]*In Ioannem Homil.* 85.1 (Migne, *PG* LIX 461); Drijvers, *op. cit.* 95.

[22]*Contra Iudaeos et Gentiles, quod Christus Sit Deus* 10 (Migne, *PG* XLVIII 826); Drijvers, *op. cit.* 91.

biblical commentaries and in his letters.[23] But he does not mention it in his chronicle, nor do fifth and sixth century chroniclers dependent on him.[24] And he does not mention Helena.

The first extant text to link the name of Helena with the discovery of the True Cross is a lengthy digression in the oration which Ambrose of Milan delivered on February 25, 395, in honor of the recently deceased emperor Theodosius.[25] Having declared that Helena was guided by the Holy Spirit,[26] he proceeds to tell that she found three crosses in a confused state, but was able to distinguish the cross of Jesus from those of the two thieves by the famous *titulus,* found still in place, *Iesus Nazarenus Rex Iudaeorum.*[27] She also found the nails (apparently two) with which Jesus was fastened to the cross. One of these she had worked into a horse's bridle and the other (*alterum,* not *alium*) she had built into a diadem; she then sent both of these objects to Constantine.[28]

[23]*Tractatus de Psalmo XCV,* ad vers. 10 (Migne, *PL* XXVI 1114 [ed. 1845] or 1181 [ed. 1866]; ed. Morin [*CC, Ser. Lat.* LXXVIII] 154). Psalm 95 of Jerome's Vulgate and the Catholic tradition becomes Psalm 96 of Protestant Bible translations; E.D. Hunt, *op. cit.* 39, n. 62; *In Zach.* ad vers. 14.20 (Migne, *PL* XXV 1540; ed. Adriaen [*CC, Ser. Lat.* LXXVIA] 898); *In Math.* ad vers. 23.5 (Migne, *PL* XXVI 168; ed. Hurst and Adriaen [*CC, Ser. Lat.* LXXVII] 212). Finally, writing in the name of his associates Paula and Eustochium, Jerome mentions the *lignum crucis* in his letter to Marcella *Epist.* 46.12 in Migne, *PL* XXII 491; 46.13 in ed. Hilberg (*CSEL* LIV) 343 and in ed. Labourt II 113. On this letter see further Kelly, *op. cit.* 124 and 141; But in his *Epitaphium Sanctae Paulae, Epist.* 108.9 (Migne, *PL* XXII 883; ed. Hilberg [*CSEL* LV] 315; ed. Labourt V 167), cited by Borgehammar, *op. cit.* 87, n. 2, and by Drijvers, *op. cit.* 92 with n. 49, he is probably referring to the commemorative cross on Golgotha. See Kelly, *op. cit.* 122, n. 3, and further 277-79. Bovini, *Edifici cristiani* 128, Drijvers, *op. cit.* 92, n. 49, and Borgehammar, *op cit.* 87, n. 2, cite as evidence also a letter addressed by Jerome to a certain Desiderius in 393. But the pertinent phrase, *quasi recentia nativitatis et crucis ac passionis ... vestigia,* while it may imply, does not, it seems to me, explicitly state that there are particles of the Cross. *Epist.* 47.2 (Migne, *PL* XXII 493; ed. Hilberg [*CSEL* LIV] 346; ed. Labourt II 115). On this letter see Kelly, *op. cit.* 180.

[24]Ewig, "Das Bild Constantins" 21; Drijvers, *op. cit.* 92, n. 49.

[25]*BHL* 4163. *De Obitu Theodosii* 41-48 (Migne, *PL* XVI 1399-1402 [ed. 1845] or 1462-65 [ed. 1866]; ed. Mannix 59-61; ed. Faller [*CSEL* LXXIII] 393-97); Borgehammar, *op. cit.* 60-66; Drijvers, *op. cit.* 108-113.

[26]*De Ob. Theod.* 43.

[27]*Ibid.* 45-46.

[28]*Ibid.* 47.

A more elaborate version of the story is offered only a few years later by Rufinus.[29] The *titulus* did not suffice for positive identification of the True Cross. Macarius, bishop of Jerusalem, ordered the three crosses taken to the house of a gravely ill lady. Then, having asked in prayer for a divine sign, he ordered each of the three crosses in turn to be applied to the ill lady's body. Nothing at all happened on the first or second try, but on the third try the lady at once regained her full strength, and thus the True Cross was revealed. Helena ordered a church to be built on the spot where the crosses had been found. The nails (the number is not specified) she took to Constantine, who had some fashioned into a bridle and others into a helmet. Of the Cross, too, she took one part to Constantine, the other she had placed in a silver chest and left behind.

At about the same time Paulinus of Nola, writing to Sulpicius Severus, gives a somewhat more miraculous account.[30] Helena inquired of learned men, both Christians and Jews, as to the location of Jesus' passion; she then ordered digging to commence, and the three crosses soon come to light. The *verificatio* of the True Cross was accomplished by it being applied to the body not of an ill lady but of a dead man. And this was on the initiative of Helena, not on that of Bishop Macarius, of whom no mention is made. The *titulus* is not mentioned either.

The account given by Sulpicius Severus is clearly dependent on the report which he had received from Paulinus: Helena made inquiry and assembled a crew of diggers.[31] Once the three crosses had been found, a dead man served to test them and identify the True Cross. The *titulus* and Bishop Macarius are left out of the account. Sulpicius Severus is not an independent witness to the events which he describes.[32] It should be noted that Ambrose, Rufinus, Paulinus, and Sulpi-

---

[29]*Hist. Eccl.* 1.7-8 in Migne, *PL* XXI 475-76; 10.7-8 in ed. Mommsen (*GCS* IX.2) 969-71; Borgehammar, *op. cit.* 21-23; Drijvers, *op. cit.* 79-80 and 101-102; Drijvers deems Rufinus' account the closest to the original version.

[30]*Epist.* 31.5 (Migne, *PL* LXI 328-29; ed. Hartel [*CSEL* XXIX] 272-73). The letter accompanied the most precious gift of a particle of the True Cross, which had been brought to him from the Holy Land by the lady Melania the Elder. The Cross remains intact, he says *ibid.* 31.6, although small pieces are taken away from it. Nora K. Chadwick, *Poetry and Letters in Early Christian Gaul* (London 1955) 79-80; Borgehammar, *op. cit.* 66-71; Drijvers, *op. cit.* 113-16 and 121-22.

[31]*Chron.* 2.34 (Migne, *PL* XX 148; ed. Halm [*CSEL* I] 88); Drijvers, *op. cit.* 116-117.

[32]On the date and value of his chronicle see Bardenhewer, *op. cit.* III² (1923) 422, Altaner-Stuiber, *op. cit.* 231 and Quasten, *op. cit.* IV (1986) 538-39.

cius Severus are all Western authors writing in Latin at the end of the fourth century and the beginning of the fifth century. It does not, however, follow that the legend originated in the West, to the contrary, there is good reason to believe that it originated in Jerusalem.[33] Rufinus, who for many years resided in a monastery on Jerusalem's Mount of Olives before returning to Italy, is certain to have used an Eastern source, namely the lost *Ecclesiastical History* of Gelasius of Caesarea.[34]

Gelasius became bishop of Caesarea in 367. At the request of Cyril of Jerusalem, his uncle, he wrote in ca. 390 an *Ecclesiastical History* covering the years 302-378. Rufinus, Socrates, Sozomen, Theodoret, and Gelasius of Cyzicus all can be shown to have used this text. Building on the pioneering work of Friedhelm Winkelmann, Stephan Borgehammar has carefully and convincingly reconstructed the narrative of the *inventio* of the Cross by Helena: Helena came to Jerusalem, driven by the desire to find the wood of the Cross. She found three crosses buried deep in the ground, but was unable to tell which of them was the True Cross. Bishop Macarius identified the True Cross by applying all three crosses to the body of a gravely ill woman. Helena then found the holy nails as well; two of these she had put into the emperor's hel-met, and the others she had worked into a bit for his horse. Of the Cross she took one part to her son and left the other in a silver casket in Jerusalem. She also humbly served the consecrated virgins of Jerusalem.[35]

This account is already a fully developed legend. It differs on a number of points from the independent account of St. Ambrose, which says nothing of Bishop Macarius or of a miraculous *verificatio*.

The Eastern historians Socrates, Sozomen, and Theodoret, in that order, wrote of the same event a generation or two later, around the

---

[33]Heid, "Der Ursprung der Helenalegende," especially 43, 47, 57, and 62; Stefan Heid, "Zur frühen Protonike- und Kyriakoslegende," *Anal. Boll.* 109 (1991) 73-108 at 95 with n. 107, specifically rejecting the suggestion of Demandt, *op. cit.* 76, n. 75, that Ambrose freely invented the story of the discovery of the Cross.

[34]Altaner-Stuiber, *op. cit.* 225-26; Heid, "Der Ursprung der Helenalegende" 63-64; Heid, "Zur frühen Protonike- und Kyriakoslegende" 75; Borgehammar, *op. cit.* 21-23; Drijvers, *op. cit.* 95-99.

[35]Winkelmann, *Untersuchungen zur Kirchengeschichte des Gelasios von Kaisereia (Sb. der deutschen Ak. der Wissensch. zu Berlin* 1965:3; Berlin 1966); "Charakter und Bedeutung der Kirchengeschichte des Gelasios von Kaisareia," *Byzantinische Forschungen* 1 (1966) 346-385. Borgehammar, *op. cit.* 31-55 and 57-60.

middle of the fifth century. Socrates follows the account of Rufinus;[36] Sozomen and Theodoret in turn follow Socrates, although the former betrays some acquaintance, direct or indirect, also with Paulinus' version.[37] Cassiodorus has nothing to add.[38] Sozomen's account contains another new element:

> The place was revealed and the fraud surrounding it detected. Some say that a Jew, a resident of the East, provided the information from a document in the possession of his family. But it is closest to the truth to think that God showed the way through signs and dreams.[39]

Sozomen is here apparently rejecting the legend of Cyriacus or Quiriacus. This legend exists in various Syriac, Greek, and Latin versions;[40] it came into being some time after the reign of Julian the Apostate, probably in the first half of the fifth century.[41] The pertinent aspects of this legend can be summarized as follows:

[36]*Hist. Eccl.* 1.17 (Migne, *PG* LXVII 117-21; ed. Bright[2] 35-37); Drijvers, *op. cit.* 102-104.

[37]Sozomen, *Hist. Eccl.* 2.1 (Migne, *PG* LXVII 929-33; ed. Bidez-Hansen [*GCS* L] 47-50; ed. Bidez [*SC* CCCVI] 226-32); Drijvers, *op. cit.* 104-107. Theodoret, *Hist. Eccl.* 1.17 in Migne, *PG* LXXXII 957-61; 1.18 in ed. Parmentier-Scheidweiler (*GCS* XLIV) 63-65; Drijvers, *op. cit.* 107-108.

[38]*Hist. Eccl. Trip.* 2.18.7-11 (Migne, *PL* LXIX 936-37 ed. Jacob-Hanslik [*CSEL* LXXI] 114-15).

[39]See n. 37.

[40]Johannes Straubinger, *Die Kreuzauffindungslegende* (Paderborn 1912), provides a useful synopsis of these (pp. 15-49) as well as a complete listing of all printed editions available at the time of his writing (pp. 4-7). The most important of these editions shall here be named: Two of the Syriac versions were edited and translated into German by Eberhard Nestle, *De Sancta Cruce* (Berlin 1889) 7-36 and 39-64. Three of the Greek versions have been edited, respectively, by Karl Wotke in *WS* 13 (1891) 302-11, Eberhard Nestle in *BZ* 4 (1895) 324-31, and Alessandro Olivieri in *Anal. Boll.* 17 (1898) 414-20. The Latin texts are available in the following editions: Mombritius, *op. cit.* (ed. 1910) I 376-79; *Acta Sanct.* Maii I (ed. 1866) 450-52; Alfred Holder, *Inventio Sanctae Crucis* (Leipzig 1889) 1-13; Borgehammer, *op. cit.* 201-302, and English translation 154-61. Drijvers, *op. cit.* 165-71, provides an English translation from a Syriac manuscript.

[41]Straubinger, *op. cit.* 75 and 76; Amnon Linder, "Jerusalem as a Focal Point in the Conflict between Judaism and Christianity," in Benjamin Z. Kedar, ed., *Jerusalem in the Middle Ages* (Jerusalem 1979) 5-26 at 18 (in Hebrew); Borgehammar, *op. cit.* 146-47; Drijvers, *op. cit.* 174-75. But Heid, "Zur frühen Protonike- und Kyriakoslegende" 99-102, argues for a somewhat earlier date.

In the year 233 the Holy Spirit prompted the empress Helena to undertake a search for the Holy Cross.[42] When the Jews whom she was interrogating failed to cooperate she threatened to have them cast into a fire. They then delegated one Judas as their spokesman. He, too, although he was privy to special knowledge passed on to him by his father, was unwilling to share his knowledge with the empress. Thereupon she had him thrown into a dry well and deprived of food. After seven days in the well Judas relented, and a pleasant odor guided him to the right location. He personally dug up the three crosses and brought them to Helena. He also tested them and identified the True Cross by applying them to the body of a just-deceased young man. Fully converted by now to the Christian faith, he was baptized by the bishop of Jerusalem (whose name is not given except in later interpolations). Shortly thereafter the bishop of Jerusalem died, and Helena prevailed on Pope Eusebius, who was with her, to ordain Judas the next bishop of Jerusalem; she also changed his name to Cyriacus (Κυριακός = the Lord's own). In response to another request of the empress, Cyriacus also found the Holy Nails, the location of which was pointed out to him by a bolt of lightning. Helena, before dying peacefully, ordered all the Jews to be driven from Judaea.

The apocryphal nature of this story is obvious. The dates given are impossible. Pope Eusebius occupied the Holy See only briefly in the year 309 and certainly did not travel to Jerusalem.[43] No other source mentions a contemporary bishop of Jerusalem by name of Cyriacus or Quiriacus.[44] Tradition knows, however, other saints by the name of Cyriacus, which has added to the confusion.[45] Eusebius of Caesarea

---

[42]This is the date given by three of the Greek and one of the Latin versions; the same Latin version adds "in the sixth year of the reign of Constantine." See Straubinger, *op. cit.* 15 and 50, and Borgehammar, *op. cit.* 255. A possible explanation is offered by Borgehammar, *op. cit.* 181-82, and another one by Drijvers, *op. cit.* 173-74, but the date remains puzzling. It can refer to the Christian era only by later interpolation.

[43]Philipp Jaffé, *op. cit.* I 26-27.

[44]Gams, *Series Episcoporum* 452; Theodore Edward (Archdeacon) Dowling, "The Episcopal Succession in Jerusalem," *Palestine Exploration Fund for 1913*, pp. 164-77; Chaine, *op. cit.* 260; Drijvers, *op. cit.* 177. There is no need in this context to investigate the supposed martyrdom of a Cyriacus or Quiriacus under Julian the Apostate.

[45]Réau *Iconographie* III.1 (1958) 365-66; *Bibl. Sanct.* III (1963) 1292-1308; *LCI* VI (1974) 14-18. In the traditions of the Italian city of Ancona the Cyriacus who is associated with St. Helena, the Cyriacus who reportedly suffered martyrdom under Julian the Apostate, and a third Cyriacus, bishop of Ancona, merge into a single S. Ciriaco, the patron saint of the city; the city's *duomo* is dedicated in his memory, and his *corpus* rests in the crypt in that splendid church.

lists a Judas as the fifteenth bishop of Jerusalem, but this Judas was in office when the Second Jewish Revolt erupted in 132.[46] A strong anti-Jewish element in the story should also be noted.[47]

The Syriac and Latin versions of this legend appear to be derived from the Greek version.[48] The original home of this legend is in the East, but it soon found acceptance in the West. The compiler of the first redaction of the *Liber Pontificalis* (ca. 532) is clearly familiar with it:

Sub huius (Eusebii) temporibus inventa est crux domini nostri, Iesu Christi V Non. Mai. et baptizatus est Iudas qui et Cyriacus.[49]

But the author of the so-called Gelasian Decree, in the same century, has reservations about the *scriptura de inventione crucis dominicae*; quoting the Apostle Paul, he advises: *omnia probate, quod bonum est tenete.*[50]

Gregory of Tours (died in 594) reports in one place that the True Cross was revealed to Helena by "the Jew Judas, who after his baptism was called Quiriacus."[51] A second reference to the True Cross is less specific and less helpful.[52] The number of nails found by Helena has grown to four. She fashions two into the emperor's bridle and has the third cast into the Adriatic Sea to calm it; "of the fourth they say that it was placed in the head of Constantine's statue."[53]

The legend of the *inventio* of the True Cross by Helena, if any legend ever, clearly is one which developed by accretion, and the dif-

---

[46]*Hist. Eccl.* 4.5.

[47]Heid, "Der Ursprung der Helenalegende" 64, even suggests that the legend of Cyriacus owed its popularity to this anti-Jewish tone; similarly Drijvers, *op. cit.* 165, 177-79, and 187-88.

[48]Borgehammar, *op. cit.* 149. Straubinger, *op. cit.* 66 and 75, thought that the Greek and Latin versions were derived from the Syriac version; Drijvers, *op. cit.* 172.

[49]In his (Eusebius') days the cross of our Lord Jesus Christ was found on May 3, and Judas, who is also known as Cyriacus, was baptized. Ed. Mommsen [*MGH, GPR* I] 45; ed. Duchesne[2] I 167; Drijvers, *op. cit.* 175.

[50]Examine all things, retain what is good. *Decretum Gelasianum de libris recipiendis et non recipiendis;* Migne, *PL* LIX 173; ed. Dobschütz (*TU* 38.4 [1912]) 10. On the Gelasian Decree see Straubinger, *op. cit.* 73, Bardenhewer, *op. cit.* IV (1924) 626, and Altaner-Stuiber, *op. cit.* 463; more extensively Henri Leclercq in *DACL* VI.1 (1924) 722-47; Heid, "Zur frühen Protonike- und Kyriakoslegende" 102; Drijvers, *op. cit.* 175.

[51]*Hist. Franc.* 1.34 in Migne, *PL* LXXI 179; 1.36 in *MGH, SRM* I.1 51 or I.1[2] 27; Drijvers, *op. cit.* 175.

[52]*Liber in Gloria Martyrum* 5 (Migne, *PL* LXXI 709; *MGH, SRM* I.2 489 or I.2[2] 39).

[53]*Ibid.* 6.

ferent stages of development can readily be identified. The point of departure is given by the historical facts of Helena's pilgrimage and the construction of the Church of the Holy Sepulchre. Thus in the first stage Eusebius is well informed on these two points, but he reports nothing about the discovery of the True Cross by Helena or by anyone else. In the second stage Cyril, Egeria, Chrysostom, and Jerome know about the wood of the Cross, but do not mention Helena. Only in the third stage do Gelasius, Ambrose, Rufinus, and Paulinus attribute the discovery of the Cross to Helena. The Cyriacus story is developed from the Helena story and thus constitutes a fourth stage.[54]

There is yet another legend of the discovery of the Cross, which originated in Syria but never found acceptance in the West. According to this legend the Cross was found already by a certain Protonike, the supposed wife of the emperor Claudius.[55] This is, of course, quite fantastic but explains why the Syriac versions of the Cyriacus legend speak of Helena's discovery of the Cross as a second discovery.[56]

When all of our sources have been fully exploited and all arguments carefully considered, which elements of the tradition remain? Helena's pilgrimage, the construction of the church subsequently known as the Church of the Holy Sepulchre, and the discovery of the tomb believed to be that of Jesus are incontestable facts. And at some time before the middle of the fourth century, when Cyril wrote his *Catecheses* the wood believed to be that of the True Cross had been found. But the more specific time of the precious find remains open to question, and any part of Helena in such find seems quite unlikely to me.

The legend of the discovery of the True Cross by Helena plays a large role in mediaeval literature; this we shall consider in chapter XVI. It remains now to survey, without aiming at completeness, the rather extensive secondary literature on the subject.

Baronio, with whom this survey may suitably begin, examines the sources, duly notes Eusebius' silence, but concludes, somewhat predictably, that there can be no doubt about Helena's having found the

---

[54]The growth of the legend is similarly descibed by Mary-Catherine Bodden, ed., *The Old English Finding of the True Cross* (Cambridge 1987) 24-27. Drijvers, *op. cit.* 139, also holds that the legend developed in phases; but Borgehammar, *op. cit.* 9 and 126, strongly objects, and so does Heid, "Zur frühen Protonike- und Kyriakoslegende" 106.

[55]Bodden, *op. cit.* 82-103; Henri Leclercq in *DACL* III.2 (1914) 3133-34; Heid, "Zur frühen Protonike- und Kyriakoslegende" 73-98; Drijvers, *op. cit.*, 147-63.

[56]Straubinger, *op. cit.* 15; Linder, "Jerusalem as a Focal Point" 18.

Cross.[57] Similarly the renowned Tillemont is aware of Eusebius' silence but concludes that "one cannot call the discovery of the Cross by Helena in question."[58]

In the 19th century Franz Xaver Kraus, with his accustomed thoroughness, undertook his own survey of the primary sources and, while not rejecting the *inventio* of the Cross as such, concluded that Helena had no part in it, notwithstanding the testimonies of Ambrose, Rufinus, Sozomen, and the like.[59]

A much less critical writer, the Abbé Paul Lucot, writing in 1876 at the request of the bishop of Châlons, accepts Ambrose's account of the discovery of the Cross without question and without reference to other sources.[60]

Another French churchman, A.-M. Rouillon, employs better judgment and concludes his lengthy investigation thus:

The wisest and surest way is to attest, texts in hand, to the existence and consequently, until proven otherwise, to the discovery of the Cross in the first half of the fourth century, while separating it from the various circumstances and attributes in which we find it dressed in the course of history.[61]

Rouillon's book was published in 1908. Three years later the Abbé Remi Couzard either did not know of Rouillon's work or chose to ignore the warning; his account is as rich in imagination as it is lacking in critical judgment.[62]

With Henri Leclercq we return to historical scholarship. He observes the development of the legend by successive increments and concludes thus:

In short, there is no proof that the true cross had been discovered in 326. One can suspect with great likelihood that it had not yet been found in 333, or even in 335, the year when Eusebius came to Jerusalem for the dedication of the Church of the Resurrection. Without

---

[57]*Ad annum* 326, *op. cit.* IV 174-178; 175.

[58]*Mémoires* (Paris 1693-1712) VII 638-39.

[59]*Der heilige Nagel in der Domkirche zu Trier* (Trier 1868) 50-59; 69-70.

[60]*Sainte Hélène, mère de l'empereur Constantin* (Paris 1876) 27-31. The same author, *ibid.* 28-29, credulously accepts what the *Vita S. Silvestri* reports on the baptism of Constantine.

[61]*Op. cit.* 171, in an appendix. Translation mine.

[62]*Sainte Hélène d'après l'histoire et la tradition* (Paris 1911) 154-64.

question the discovery must be placed before 347, since Cyrillus attests to the veneration of which it has been the object since then. The *inventio,* then, took place between 335 and 347, but we do not know under what circumstances.[63]

In the course of surveying the use of the cross in early Christian art, Max Sulzberger says of the *inventio* of the True Cross by Helena: "Cela n'a aucun fondement historique."[64]

To Jules Maurice the discovery of the True Cross is a historical event, at least as far as St. Ambrose tells it.[65] The publication of this event was suppressed, he says, by the tyrannical Constantius II, who hated the memory of his grandmother. Maurice's argument can be disarmed simply by pointing out that Constantius did not come to power in the East until 337 and in the West until 351 and died in 361, that is, he had only limited opportunity to prevent the publication of this event. Furthermore the commemorative coins with which Helena was honored during Constantius' reign do not at all suggest that he hated her.[66] With Rufinus' version, Paulinus' version, and even more the story of Cyriacus, Maurice admits, we enter the realm of legend.

Stratmann's account is neither complete nor sufficiently critical.[67] Mackes, on the other hand dismisses the entire tradition, a little too rashly, as "Fabeleien."[68] Vogt deals with the tradition under the heading of "Legenden und Erfindungen."[69] Réau remarks that "this whole story was invented."[70] To Hans-Henning Lauer the discovery of the True Cross by Helena is a mere legend, even in the form in which Ambrose presents it.[71]

Two excellent studies by Anatole Frolow have for their subject not the Invention of the Cross but the cult and the relics of the True

[63]In *DACL* III.2 (1914) 3134; similarly in *DACL* VI.2 (1925) 2129-31. In *DACL* III.2 (1914) 3137. Translation mine. Similarly in *DACL* VI.2 (1925) 2130. 348 or 350 would be more correct, see n. 90.

[64]"Le symbole de la croix," *Byzantion* 2 (1925) 337-448 at 428.

[65]*Sainte Hélène* 15-31.

[66]See chapter XI below, nn. 45 and 47.

[67]*Op. cit.* II 161-165.

[68]*Op. cit.* 186.

[69]"Constantinus der Grosse" 371-74.

[70]*Iconographie* II.2 505.

[71]*Op. cit.* 45.

Cross.[72] Nevertheless Frolow remarks that "the legend which makes Helena intervene ... is no older than the end of the fourth century" and that "the oldest texts mark the stages of a period of development."[73] His account of the source material is exceedingly thorough.[74]

Henri Chirat gives a reasonable account of the sources but concludes that "the finding of the cross must have taken place on September 13 between 325 and 334."[75] This interpretation appears to be based on a misreading of Egeria's text.

Carl Andresen wonders whether the legend of the *inventio* of the True Cross was part of the dynastic propaganda of Constantine's sons.[76] Maria Vodová traces the development of the legend (without mentioning the work of Straubinger) and stresses the dependence of Sulpicius Severus on Paulinus and of Socrates, Sozomen, and Theodoret on Rufinus; it is impossible, she says, to bring the discovery of the Cross into connection with Helena.[77] Wilkinson deems it "extremely improbable" that Egeria attributed the discovery of the True Cross to Helena.[78] Barnes thinks that the story of Helena's discovery of the Cross was "invented."[79] E.D. Hunt asserts that "there is nothing in history to link Helena with the discovery of the true cross."[80] Kajava finds "nothing to persuade one that Helena was the discoverer of the *lignum crucis*."[81] And Richard Klein concludes that the legends have no claim on history.[82]

Walker, while he believes that the *inventio* of the True Cross took place, or was claimed to have taken place, shortly after 325, does

[72]*La relique de la Vraie Croix* (Paris 1961) and *Les reliquaires de la Vraie Croix* (Paris 1965).

[73]*La relique de la Vraie Croix* 55.

[74]*Ibid.* 155-70.

[75]S. v. Cross, Finding of the Holy, in *NCE* IV (1967) 479-82.

[76]*Die Kirchen der alten Christenheit* (Stuttgart 1971) 515.

[77]"L'impératrice Hélène et l'invention de la Sainte-Croix," *SPFB* 25 (1980) 235-40; 236.

[78]*Op. cit.* 241.

[79]*Constantine and Eusebius* 382, n. 130.

[80]*Op. cit.* 28.

[81]*Op. cit.* 51.

[82]In *RAC* XIV 371.

not believe that Helena was involved in it, despite the many later legends.[83]

Drijvers although he believes that the Cross was found in the 320's, denies to Helena any part in such a find.[84] Borgehammar, on the other hand, endeavors to show that Helena did indeed find the Cross, and did so in 325, and to this end proposes a new chronology for her pilgrimage: Helena left Bithynia late in 324, reached the Holy Land in 325, and was back in Italy in 326, in time to participate in Constantine's *vicennalia.*[85] But our sources clearly indicate that she undertook her journey after the Council of Nicaea and that she died shortly after her return; furthermore her journey must be correlated with the fall of Eustathius of Antioch.[86] I find the proposed chronology quite unlikely.[87]

Helena's pilgrimage remains a historical event of considerable interest and is in no way called in question.

The Feast of the Invention of the Cross was previously observed in the West on May 3 but was suppressed by Pope John XXIII in 1960.[88] In some Eastern calendars the Invention of the Cross is noted

[83]See this chapter, above, n. 10. *Op. cit.* 277, n. 149.

[84]See this chapter, above, n. 12. *Op. cit.* 1, 81, 93, 140, and 142.

[85]*Op. cit.* 133-42.

[86]Sozomen, especially, *Hist. Eccl.* 2.1.1, places her journey after the Council. For her death see chapter XI below, and for the fall of Eustathius chapter VIII above, nn. 9-17.

[87]For my own chronology see chapter VIII above, nn. 8-7.

[88]Martyrology of Bede ad V Non. Mai. (Migne, *PL* XCIV 900; Henri Quentin, *Les martyrologes historiques du moyen âge,* 2nd ed. [Paris 1908] 51). Martyrology of Hrabanus Maurus (ca. 780-856) ad V Non. Mai. (Migne, *PL* CX 1142; ed. McCulloh [*CC, Cont. Med.* XLIV] 42). Martyrology of Ado of Vienne (858) ad V Non. Mai. (Migne, *PL* CXXIII 256-59; Quentin, *op. cit.* 619). Martyrology of Usuard (ca. 875) ad V Non. Mai. (*Acta Sanct.* Iunii VI.2 [ed. 1714] 250; Migne, *PL* CXXIV 15-16; ed. Dubois (*Subsidia Hagiographica* 40] 223); *Breviarium Romanum* of 1568 (ed. Turin 1952, II [Spring] 1003-19; *Mart. Rom.* (ed. 1586) 194; French trl. by J. Baudot and F. Gilbert (2nd ed., 1953) 175; English trl. by J. B. O'Connell (1962) 88; Louis Duchesne, *Christian Worship: Its Origin and Evolution,* 5th ed. (London 1949) 274-75; Bertrand Cornet, "La fete de la croix du 3 mai," *RBPhil.* 30 (1952) 637-48; Sacra Congregatio Rituum, "Instructio de Calendariis Particularibus," *Eph. Lit.* 75 (1961) 143-54 at 149; Pierre Jounel, "Le culte de la croix dans la liturgie romaine," *Le Maison-Dieu* 75 (1963) 68-91 at 72-74; Joseph Pascher, *Das liturgische Jahr* (Munich 1963) 445-46; Polycarpus Radó, *Enchiridion Liturgicum* (Rome 1966) II 1307; Adam Adolf, *The Liturgical Year* (New York 1981) 182.

on March 6.[89] The Exaltation of the Cross (or Triumph of the Cross) is observed on September 14, in both the East and the West; this feast commemorates the recovery of the Cross from the Persians by the emperor Heraclius in 629 as well as the Invention of the Cross.[90] Changes in the calendar have gone hand-in-hand, of course, with changes in the Mass. Thus the Introit formerly used on May 3 – *Nos autem gloriari oportet in Cruce Domini nostri Jesu Christi...*-is now used on September 14.

[89]Juan Mateos *Le Typicon de la Grande Église* (Rome 1962-1963) I 244; Heinrich Ferdinand Wüstenfeld, translator, *Synaxarion, das ist Heiligen-Kalender der Coptischen Christen* (Gotha 1879) 30-32; I.-H. Dalmais, "La glorification de la Sainte Croix dans l'église copte," *La Maison-Dieu* 75 (1963) 109-18 at 110; Aziz S. Atiya, "Synaxarion, Copto-Arabic: The List of Saints," in *Copt. Enc.* VII 2173-90 at 2182, "apparition" presumably in error for "Invention", since the apparition (of the Cross in Jerusalem) is commemorated on May 7- see *ibid.* 2185; March 6 = Baharmet 10; May 7 = Bashans 12.

[90]For the East, see Aleksei Dmitrievskii, *Opisanie liturgitseskich rukopiesej* I (Kiev 1895) 5; Alexios von Maltzew, *Menologion der Orthodox-Katholischen Kirche des Morgenlandes* (Berlin 1900-1901) I 81-83; *Synaxarium Constantinopolitanum*, ed. Delehaye *(Acta Sanct.,* Propylaeum Nov. [ed. 1902]) 43; Sirarpie Der Nersessian, "La fête de l'exaltation de la Croix," in *Mélanges Henri Grégoire* II (1950) 193-98; Mateos, *op. cit.* I 29-33; René Bornert, "La célébration de la sainte croix dans le rite byzantin," *La Maison-Dieu* 75 (1963) 92-108 at 97-99; Wüstenfeld, *loc. cit.,* Dalmais, *op. cit.* 110; Atiya, "Synaxarion, Copto-Arabic" 2175; September 14 = Tut 17. For the West, see Martyrology of Bede ad XVIII Kal. Oct. (Migne, *PL* XCIV 1044; Quentin, *op. cit.* 54); Martyrology of Hrabanus Maurus (ca. 780 - 856) ad XVIII Kal. Oct. (Migne, *PL* CX 1168; ed. McCulloh [*CC, Cont. Med.* XLIV] 92-93); Martyrology of Ado of Vienne (858) ad XVIII Kal. Oct. (Migne, *PL* CXXIII 556-57; Quentin, *op. cit.* 506); Martyrology of Usuard (*ca.* 875) ad XVIII Kal. Oct. *(Acta Sanct.* Iunii VII [ed. 1717] 532-33; Migne, *PL* CXXIV 467-68; ed. Dubois [*Subsidia Hagiographica* 40] 302); *Breviarium Romanum* of 1568 (ed. Turin 1952, IV [Autumn] 543-58); *Mart. Rom.* (ed. 1586) 414; French trl. by J. Baudot and F. Gilbert (2nd ed., 1953) 342; English trl. by J. B. O'Connell (1962) 199; Duchesne, *Christian Worship* 274-75; Jounel, *op. cit.* 75-77; Sacra Congregatio Rituum, *Calendarium Romanum* (Vatican City 1969) 29, 103, and 138; Sacra Congregatio Rituum, "Calendarium Romanum Generale," *Eph. Lit.* 83 (1969) 202-23 at 209; United States Catholic Conference, *The Roman Calendar: Text and Commentary* (Washington, D. C., 1976) 39, 60, 92, and 125. I wish to acknowledge the kind assistance of the Rev. Ronald F. Krisman, Executive Director, Secretariat for the Liturgy, National Conference of Catholic Bishops, Washington, D. C. For the recovery of the Cross by Heraclius see the following: Anatole Frolow, "La Vraie Croix et les expéditions d'Héraclius en Perse," *REB* 11 (1953) 88-105; Venance Grumel, "La reposition de la vraie Croix à Jérusalem par Heraclius: Le jour et l'année," *Byzantinische Forschungen* 1 (1966) 139-49; Herrin, *op. cit.* 197-206.

Chapter X.
A Rich Harvest of Holy Relics

It is a measure of Helena's popularity that so many holy relics are said to have been brought by her from the Holy Land or are otherwise associated with her. In modern church life relics are not of the same importance as they once were, and the modern mind is inclined towards skepticism more than towards credulity. In this chapter I shall inquire not whether these relics be authentic or not, but rather whether they can be associated with Helena or not. The two questions cannot, however, be separated entirely from each other – an answer to one will have a bearing on the other.

We have seen in chapter IX above that Helena cannot have had a part in any *inventio* of the True Cross. Nevertheless the relics of the True Cross must be the first to be considered here. A complete account of these is neither possible nor necessary in the present context, and Anatole Frolow has already provided such an account with his excellent *Le relique de la Vraie Croix*. But it must be said that the relics of the True Cross and Helena's fame spread together throughout Christendom. Wherever a church possessed a relic of the Cross, there one might very well find a reliquary, a fresco, an altar painting, a statue, or a stained glass window depicting and honoring Helena: Florence's Church of Santa Croce, Bonn's Kreuzbergkirche, Cologne's cathedral, and countless others.

How many relics of the True Cross are there or were there? Frolow gathered 1150 'pieces justificatives,' and that number may astonish us.[1] At the same time the large number of relics of the Cross cannot be used as an argument against their authenticity, since each one is only a small particle.[2] An exception would be the fairly large piece

---

[1] *La relique.*

[2] A single beam of wood measuring 4"x6"x60" could yield 1440 particles of one cubic inch each. And a cross, one might imagine, would have consisted of a horizontal beam measuring 5' and a vertical beam measuring 10'. There is no reason, then, to take John Calvin very seriously when he sarcastically remarks: "What audacity is that to fill the earth with pieces of wood in such quantity that 300 men would not be able to carry it?" *Traité des reliques*, ed. Francis M. Higman (London 1970) 61. In one of the *colloquia* of Erasmus, the *Peregrinatio Religionis Causa*, one of the interlocutors remarks that, if all the pieces of the Cross were brought together, they would fill a whole freight ship: *Opera Omnia*, ed. Halkin et al., I.3 (Amsterdam 1972) 478. But Charles Rohault de

(continued...)

which Egeria saw during her pilgrimage in Jerusalem's Church of the Holy Sepulchre. This would be the same piece that the emperor Heraclius recovered from the Persians in 629 but which no longer exists today. Artists, of course, have preferred to depict the emperor carrying an entire cross. The large number of relics of the Cross gives testimony of their value and desirability, as do the splendid reliquaries in which so many of them are enclosed.

Among several relics of the True Cross in the Vatican three deserve to be mentioned here. The first of these is kept in the pier of St. Helena in the crossing of St. Peter's Basilica, with the napkin of St. Veronica, the spear of St. Longinus, and, until 1964, the head of St. Andrew in the other three piers. The four relics relate, of course, to the four colossal statues which were placed in the crossing by Pope Urban VIII (1623-1644).[3] The four relics were placed there by the same Pope, as an inscription records in each case; the relic of the Cross had been, prior to that, in the Church of Santa Croce in Gerusalemme.[4] Another fragment of the True Cross is contained in the silver-gilt Crux Vaticana, which was a gift from the emperor Justin II (565-578) and is now kept in St. Peter's treasury.[5] Our third fragment is contained in an enameled

[2](...continued)
Fleury, *Mémoire sur les instruments de la passion de N.-S. J.-C.* (Paris 1870) 163, calculated the total volume of all particles of the True Cross known to him at 3,941,975 cubic millimeters. That translates into 240.55 cubic inches, a mere fraction of what the total volume of the Cross must have been. On the remarks of Calvin and Erasmus see also Borgehammar, *op. cit.* 2. When Procopius, Pers. 2.11.14-20, reports that the people of Syrian Apamea possessed a piece of the Cross one cubit long we must be very skeptical. Frolow, *La relique* 184-85, no. 42.

[3]See chapter VII above, n. 46.

[4]Émile Mâle *L'art religieux après le Concile de Trente* (Paris 1932) 105-106; Frolow, *La relique* 632, no. 1049; Frolow, *Les reliquaires* 86 and 217; Buchowiecki, *op. cit.* I 155; Irving Lavin, *Bernini and the Crossing of St. Peter's* 20-21; Irving Lavin, *Bernini and the Unity of the Visual Arts* I 20.

[5]Ormonde M. Dalton, *Byzantine Art and Archaeology* (Oxford 1911) 548 and figs. 336-37; Ormonde M. Dalton, *East Christian Art* (Oxford 1925) 220, 331, and pl. LXI; Charles Diehl, *Manuel d'art byzantin*, 2nd ed. (Paris 1925-1926) I 310 and ill. 155; Louis Bréhier, *La sculpture et les arts mineurs byzantins* (Paris 1936) 37; Joseph Braun, *Die Reliquiare des christlichen Kultes und ihre Entwicklung* (Freiburg 1940) 459, 470, and ill. 532; Francesco Saverio Orlando, *Il tesoro di San Pietro* (Milan 1958) 74-75 and pls. 90-94; *ICLV²* I 379, no. 1954; David Talbot Rice, *The Art of Byzantium* (New York 1961) 305 and pl. 71; Frolow, *La relique* 180-81, no. 34; *Frühchristliche Kunst aus Rom* (exhibition catalogue, Essen 1962) 221, no. 463; Maurizio Calvesi, *Treasures of the Vatican* (New York 1962) 13 and 15; David Talbot Rice, *Art of the Byzantine Era* (continued...)

ninth century cross of Roman origin, formerly in the Sancta Sanctorum of the Lateran but now in the Museo Sacro of the Vatican Library.[6] Reliquary crosses are, as one might expect, quite common; but not every cross is a reliquary, and a reliquary cross may contain a relic other than one of the True Cross. A reliquary crown, containing a particle of the True Cross as well as some other relics, was given in 1267

[5](...continued)
(London 1963) 62-63 with ill. 50; Frolow, *Les reliquaires* 187 and fig. 95; André Grabar, *The Golden Age of Justinian* (New York 1967) 306 and pl. 359; Charles Delvoye, *L'art byzantin* (Paris 1967) 85, 140-41, and ill. 70; Angelo Lipinsky, "Crux Vaticana, Kaiser Justinus' II Kreuz," *RömQ* 63 (1968) 185-203; Wolfgang Fritz Volbach and Jaqueline Lafontaine-Dosogne, *Byzanz und der christliche Osten* (Berlin 1968) 194 and ill. 69; John Beckwith, *The Art of Constantinople*, 2nd ed. (London 1968) 46 and fig. 55; Beckwith, *Early Christian and Byzantine Art* 43 and pl. 83; Sabine G. MacCormack, *Art and Ceremony in Late Antiquity* (Berkeley 1981) 84-85 and pl. 24; Lafontaine-Dosogne, *Histoire de l'art byzantin* 71. For a different view see Christa Belting-Ihm, "Das Justinuskreuz in der Schatzkammer der Peterskirche zu Rom," *Jb. des Römisch-Germanischen Zentralmuseums, Mainz* 12 (1965) 142-66.

[6]Inv. no. 1216; Hartmann Grisar, *Die römische Kapella Sancta Sanctorum und ihr Schatz* (Freiburg 1908) 62-65 with ill. 31-32, 74-80 with ill. 33-35 and pls. I-II; Dalton, *Byzantine Art and Archaeology* 508-10 with fig. 305; Charles Diehl, *Manuel d'art byzantin*[2] I 307 and ill. 153; Carlo Cecchelli, "Il tesoro del Laterano II: Oreficiere, argenti, smalti,' *Dedalo* 7 (1926) 231-56 at 234-40; Bréhier, *op. cit.* 40, 89, and pl. LXI. Attribution to sixth century Byzantine provenience has been rejected by more recent scholarship. An inscription firmly dates the cross to the time of Pope Paschal I (817-824). Charles Rufus Morey, "The Inscription on the Enameled Cross of Paschal I" *ArtB* 19 (1937) 595-96 and figs. 1-2; Yvonne Hackenbroch, *Italienisches Email des frühen Mittelalters* (Basel 1938) 15-16 and ill. 1; W. Frederick Stohlman, *Gli smalti del Museo Sacro Vaticano* (Vatican City 1939) 19; Joseph Braun, *Die Reliquiare* 459, 470, and ill. 534; Paul Thoby, *Le crucifix des origines au concile de Trente* (Nantes 1959) 60 and pl. XXVIII, no. 67; Frolow, *La relique* 215-16, no. 88; Calvesi, *op. cit.* 13-14; Frolow, *Les reliquaires* 95 and fig. 99; Wessel, *Byzantine Enamels* 46-50, no. 7; Fillitz, *op. cit.* 160 and pl. XXIII; Jean Hubert, Jean Porcher, and Wolfgang Friedrich Volbach, *The Carolingian Renaissance* (New York 1970) 217 and fig. 198; Klaus Wessel in *RBK* II (1971) 105-106; Marie-Madeline S. Gauthier, *Émaux du moyen age occidental*[2] 319, no. 13; Lasko, *op. cit.* 55 and pl. 49; Leonard von Matt, Georg Daltrop, and Adriano Prandi, *Art Treasures of the Vatican Library* (New York 1974) pls. 75-77; Marie-Madeline S. Gauthier, *Les routes de la foi* 142, no. 84; Anton Legner, ed., *Ornamenta Ecclesiae* (Cologne 1985) III 82-84, no. H9; Lafontaine-Dosogne, *Histoire de l'art byzantin* 104. This cross is often compared with the so-called Beresford Hope Cross in London's Victoria and Albert Museum, inv. no. 265-1886.

by Saint Louis to the Dominican convent of Liège and is now in the Louvre.[7]

Of those writers who attribute to Helena the *inventio* of the True Cross several say that she took or sent part of it to her son Constantine: Rufinus, Socrates, Sozomen, and Theodoret; but Ambrose, Paulinus, and Sulpicius Severus do not mention this.[8] Socrates adds that Constantine placed his part of the Cross within a statue of himself that was erected in Constantinople's Forum of Constantine on a column of porphyry.[9] Before the events of 1204 the Church of St. Sophia, the Grand Palace, and some of the monasteries in Constantinople claimed to possess relics of the True Cross.[10]

Three English chroniclers, Roger of Wendover (died 1236), repeating him Matthew Paris (died 1259), and Ralph of Coggeshall (died 1228) all report how one piece of the True Cross which was formerly in Constantinople reached England.[11] There it was accquired by the Clu-

---

[7]*OA* 8445; Frolow, *La relique* 441, no. 563; Frolow, *Les reliquaires* 84 and fig. 36; Maximilien Gauthier, *The Louvre: Paintings* (New York 1964) 14; Joan Evans, *A History of Jewellery 1100-1870,* 2nd ed. (London 1970) 48 and pl. 9b; Ernst A. and Jean Heiniger, *The Great Book of Jewels* (Lausanne 1974) 180 and 195.

[8]Rufinus, *Hist. Eccl.* 1.8 in Migne, *PL* XXI 477; 10.8 in ed. Mommsen (*GCS* IX.2) 970; Socrates, *Hist. Eccl.* 1.17 (Migne, *PG* LXVII 120; ed. Bright[2] 36-37); Sozomen, *Hist. Eccl.* 2.1.8-9 (Migne, *PG* LXVII 933; ed. Bidez-Hansen [*GCS* L] 49; ed. Bidez [*SC* CCCVI] 230); Theodoret, *Hist. Eccl.* 1.17 in Migne, *PG* LXXXII 960; 1.18 in ed. Parmentier-Scheidweiler (*GCS* XLIV) 65.

[9]This detail is repeated by Cassiodorus, *Hist. Eccl. Trip.* 2.18.12 (Migne, *PG* LXIX 937; ed. Jacob-Hanslik [*CSEL* LXXI] 115); Frolow, *La relique* 167-68, no. 13. On the column of porphyry and the statue of Constantine see the following: Theodor Preger, "Konstantinos-Helios," *Hermes* 36 (1901) 457-69, esp. 458, n. 4; Richard Delbrueck, *Antike Porphyrwerke* (Berlin 1932) 26, 140-45 with ill. 57-59, and pl. 68; Voelkl, *op. cit.* 165; Raymond Janin, *Constantinople byzantine,* 2nd ed. (Paris 1964) 77-80; Michael Maclagan, *The City of Constantinople* (New York 1968) 23 and 26; Gilbert Dagron, *Naissance d'une capitale* (Paris 1974) 38-39; Wolfgang Müller-Wiener, *Bildlexikon zur Topographie Istanbuls* (Tübingen 1977) 255-57; Krautheimer, *Three Christian Capitals* 55-56, figs. 51-53, and 137, n. 21, for primary sources; Averil Cameron and Judith Herrin, edd., *Constantinople in the Early Eighth Century: The Parastaseis Syntomoi Chronikai* (Leiden 1984) 219 and 263-64 with reference to primary sources. The statue was thrown down by a storm on April 5, 1106. Part of the column, the "Burnt Column," survives.

[10]Frolow, *La relique* 185, no. 43; 194-95, no. 66; 222, no. 106; 238, no. 143; 251, no. 164; 265, no. 203; 362, nos. 405-406; and 387, no. 461.

[11]Roger of Wendover, *Flores Historiarum* ad annum 1223 (ed. Hewlett [Rolls Series LXXXIV.2] 274-76); Matthew Paris, *Chronica Maiora* ad annum 1223 (ed. Luard [Rolls
(continued...)

niac priory of Bromholm in Norfolk, and here it remained until the priory was suppressed in 1537.[12] Another Constantinopolitan piece of the True Cross was carried off by a German knight and, together with its splendid enameled reliquary dating from 964 or 965, found its way by way of the Augustinian convent of Stuben (Mosel) eventually to the cathedral treasury of Limburg/Lahn.[13] Mention must be made here also of the relic of the True Cross which Baldwin II, the Latin emperor of Constantinople, ceded to St. Louis of France and which would enhance the fame of Paris' Sainte-Chapelle.[14] Of considerable interest also is the

[11](...continued)
Series LVII] 3.80-81). On Roger of Wendover and Matthew Paris see the following: Vivian Hunter Galbraith, *Roger Wendover and Matthew Paris* (Glasgow 1944); Gröber, *op. cit.* 316; Renwick and Orton, *op. cit.* 358, with further literature; Gransden, *op. cit.* I 356-79. Ralph of Coggeshall, *Chronicon Anglicanum*, ed. Stevenson (Rolls Series LXVI) 201-203. On Ralph (Radulf) of Coggeshall see Gröber, *op. cit.* 312-13, and Gransden, *op. cit.* 322-31.

[12]J. C. Cox in William Page, ed., *The Victoria History of the County of Norfolk* (London 1906) II 361; Francis Wormald, "The Rood of Bromholm," *JWarb.* 1 (1937-1938) 31-45; Frolow, *La relique* 414-15, no. 505.

[13]Inv. no. S 1; Franz Xaver Kraus, *Inschriften* II 312-14, no. 3; Ferdinand Luthmer, *Die Bau- und Kunstdenkmäler des Lahngebietes* (Frankfurt 1907) 103-106 with fig. 86; Dalton, *Byzantine Art and Archaeology* 522-24 with fig. 311; Dalton, *East Christian Art* 341-42; Charles Diehl, *Manuel d'art byzantin*[2] II 690-91 with ill. 341; Bréhier, *op. cit.* 89-90 and pl. LXII; Joseph Braun, *Die Reliquiare* 263; Jakob Rauch, E. Schenk zu Schweinsberg, and Johann Michael Wilm, "Die Staurothek von Limburg," *Das Münster* 8 (1955) 201-40; Hermann Schnitzler, *Rheinische Schatzkammer* (Düsseldorf 1957) 24, no. 12, and pls. 38-47; Marvin C. Ross, "Basil the Proedros: Patron of the Arts," *Archaeology* 11 (1958) 271-75; David Talbot Rice, *The Art of Byzantium* 56, ill. 124-26, and pl X; Frolow, *La relique* 233-37, no. 135; David Talbot Rice, *Art of the Byzantine Era* 110 and ill. 101; Herbert Hunger, *Reich der neuen Mitte* (Graz 1965), pl. 5 and p. 442; Frolow, *Les reliquaires,* figs. 38a, 38b, and 39 and passim; Delvoye, *op. cit.,* 291-92 and ill. 166; Wessel, *Byzantine Enamels* 75-76, no. 22; Beckwith, *The Art of Constantinople*[2] 87-92 and figs. 114-16; Volbach and Lafontaine-Dosogne, *op. cit.,* 198 and ill. 81b; Margaret Frazer in Deuchler, *The Year 1200* II, ill. 221; Beckwith, *Early Christian and Byzantine Art* 97-98 and pl. 179; Klaus Wessel in *RBK* II (1971) 106 and 111-12; Lord Kinross, *Hagia Sophia* (New York 1972) 77-79; Hans Wolfgang Kuhn, "Zur Geschichte des Trierer und des Limburger Domschatzes," *Archiv für mittelrheinische Kirchengeschichte* 28 (1976) 155-207 at 199-204; Walter Michel, "Die Inschriften der Limburger Staurothek,' *Archiv für mittelrheinische Kirchengeschichte* 28 (1976) 23-43; Joachim Pick, *Dom und Domschatz in Limburg an der Lahn -- Lubentiuskirche in Dietzkirchen,* 3rd ed. (Königstein im Taunus 1986) 28-31.

[14]Matthew Paris, *Chronica Maiora* ad annum 1241 (ed. Luard [Rolls Series LVII] 4.90; Frolow, *La relique* 427-30, no. 530, with earlier literature; Frolow, *Les reliquaires* 87, 147-48, 217, and 219; Margaret Wade Labarge, *Saint Louis: Louis IX, Most*
(continued...)

relic of the True Cross which Philippe de Mézières, Grand Chancellor of Cyprus, presented in 1370 to Venice's Scuola Grande di San Giovanni Evangelista and which was subsequently credited with numerous miracles. Some of these miracles are the subject of a series of paintings now in the Accademia.[15]

If we deny to Helena a part in any *inventio* of the True Cross, then we must also deny to her a part in any *inventio* of the holy nails or other relics of the Passion. The problems surrounding the holy nails are even more difficult than those surrounding the True Cross. How many nails had been used to crucify Jesus? Two, three, or four? Franz Xavier Kraus has carefully considered this question and concluded that there were four.[16] More recent scholarship has agreed with him.[17] In Byzantine depictions of the crucifixion one regularly sees four nails employed, i.e. Jesus' feet are side by side and each is fixed to the shaft or the *suppadaneum* of the cross with its own nail. In the West, from the 13th century on, one generally sees only three nails employed, i.e. Jesus' feet are placed one above the other and a single large nail is used to fix both feet to the cross.[18] Correspondingly, when the holy nails are depicted, their number never exceeds three. We can observe this in the tympanum of the west-central portal (the Portal of the Last Judgment) of Paris' Cathedral of Notre Dame and elsewhere.[19]

---

[14](...continued)
Christian King of France (Boston 1968) 65-66; William Chester Jordan, *Louis IX and the Challenge of the Crusade* (Princeton 1979) 107-109. Five years earlier Louis had acquired the Crown of Thorns, also from Baldwin.

[15]Giulio Lorenzetti, *La 'Scuola Grande' di S. Giovanni Evangelista* (Venice 1929) 7, 11-12, and 54-55; Luigi Coletti, *Pittura veneta del Quattrocento* (Novara 1953), p. LVII and pls. 124-28; Frolow, *La relique* 519, no. 752, and 555-56, no. 855; John Steer, *A Concise History of Venetian Painting* (London 1970) 63-65 and ill. 44, 45, and 47; Kenneth M Setton, *The Papacy and the Levant (1204-1571)* I (Philadelphia 1976) 283-84; Sibilla Symeonides, *Fourteenth and Fifteenth Century Paintings in the Accademia Gallery, Venice* (Florence 1977) 191-210 with figs. 78-83; Patricia Fortini Brown, *Venetian Narrative Painting in the Age of Carpaccio* (New Haven 1988) 45, 60-63, and pls. 20 and 31; also 282-86 with pertinent pls; Norbert Huse and Wolfgang Wolters, *The Art of Renaissance Venice* (Chicago 1990) 203-204 with fig. 176 and pls. 2-3.

[16]*Der heilige Nagel* 18-42. Arguments to the contrary, offered by Thoby, *op. cit.* 4-5, are not convincing, especially so since they assume the authenticity of the Shroud of Turin.

[17]Josef Blinzler in *LThK²* VI (1961) 621-22.

[18]Thoby, *op. cit.* 4, 156, 184, 211, and 230.

[19]Bottineau, *op. cit.* ill. 12.

In reading what the ancient authors have to say on the *inventio* of the Cross one gains the impression that the *inventio* of the nails is an afterthought. And there is no agreement on the number of nails supposedly found by Helena or on other details. Ambrose mentions only two nails: Helena had one fashioned into a bridle, the other into a diadem, and sent both of these items to Constantine.[20] Rufinus says, without specifying the number, that Helena *carried* to her son the nails with which Christ's body had been fixed to the cross; also that Constantine made a bridle out of some and a helmet out of others.[21] Socrates reports that Helena *sent* to Constantine the nails, presumably two, with which Christ's hands were fixed to the cross and that Constantine made a bridle and a helmet out of them; this does not exclude the possibility that Helena had found, but did not send, additional nails.[22] Sozomen agrees with Rufinus.[23] In Theodoret once again the number of nails is not specified, but it is Helena who has them worked into a bridle and a helmet.[24] Cassiodorus does not help us to solve our problem.[25]

What Gregory of Tours reports is different yet: Helena has two nails made into a bridle, and there is no mention of a diadem or a helmet.[26] A third nail she casts into the Adriatic Sea to calm its stormy water, and of a fourth one he has heard that it was placed on the head of Constantine's statue in the Forum of Constantine in Constantinople. If Gregory does not merit our trust, neither does his contemporary, John Malalas, with whom the number of nails found by Helena has grown to five.[27] Following John Malalas, the Armenian historian Moses of Chorene (or Moses Khorenats'i) also says that Helena found five nails.[28]

---

[20]*De Obitu Theodosii* 47 (Migne, *PL* XVI 1401 [ed. 1845] or 1464-65 [ed. 1866]; ed. Mannix 61; ed. Faller [*CSEL* LXXIII] 396).

[21]See n. 8 above.

[22]See n. 8 above.

[23]See no. 8 above.

[24]*Hist. Eccl.* 1.17 in Migne, *PG* LXXXII 960; 1.18 in ed. Parmentier-Scheidweiler (*GCS* XLIV) 64.

[25]*Hist. Eccl Trip.* 2.18.11-12 (Migne, *PL* LXIX 937; ed. Jacob-Hanslik [*CSEL* LXXI] 115).

[26]*Liber in Gloria Martyrum* 6 (Migne *PL* LXXI 710; *MGH, SRM* I.2 491 or I.2² 41).

[27]*Chron.* 13.5 (Migne, *PG* XCVII 477; ed. Dindorf [*CSHB* VIII] 319).

[28]*History of Armenia* 2.87 (English trl. by Robert W. Thomson [Cambridge, Massachusetts, 1978] 242). This historian has erroneously been assigned to the fifth century; so, e.g., by Franz Xaver Kraus, *Der Heilige Nagel* 58-59, and by M. Chahin
(continued...)

The holy nails, like other relics, multiplied. Boussell counted 32 nails which in various places and at various times were venerated.[29] Kraus, including some possible duplications, counted 36.[30] The most famous of these is contained in the "Iron Crown" of Lombardy, in the cathedral (Basilica di S. Giovanni Battista) of Monza.[31] Two others will be considered shortly, and the remainder need not detain us.

The Chapel of the Relics in Rome's Church of Santa Croce in Gerusalemme contains a remarkable collection of eight relics, six of which are relics of Christ's passion:

    1.   Three particles of the True Cross.

[28](...continued)
The Kingdom of Armenia (London 1987; New York 1991) 31, 201, and 304. For the correct assignment to the eighth or ninth century see the following: Krumbacher, op. cit. I 406; Vahan Inglisian, "Die armenische Literatur," in *Handbuch der Orientalistik* I.7 (Leiden 1963) 156-250 at 177-79; Charles Burney and David Marshall Lang, *The Peoples of the Hills: Ancient Ararat and Caucasus* (New York 1971) 233. For Moses' use of Malalas see the following: Auguste Carrière, *Nouvelles sources de Moïse de Khoren* (Vienna 1893; supplement 1894); Robert W. Thomson, *op. cit.* 22-23 and 242; Hunger, *Die hochsprachliche profane Literatur* I 325.

[29]*Op. cit.* 167.

[30]Franz Xaver Kraus, *Der Heilige Nagel* 81-100.

[31]Lodovico Antonio Muratori, *De Corona Ferrea* (Milan 1719); Franz Xaver Kraus, *Der Heilige Nagel* 81-84; Adolfo Venturi, *Storia dell'arte italiana* II (1902) 72 and fig. 70; Dalton, *Byzantine Art and Archaeology* 519; Toesca, *Il medioevo* I 345-47 and fig. 208; Hackenbroch, *op. cit.* 21-23 and ill. 8; Augusto Merati, *Storia architettonica del duomo di Monza* (Monza 1962), fig. 3; Percy Ernst Schramm and Florentine Mütherich, *Denkmale der deutschen Könige und Kaiser* (Munich 1962) 128-29, no. 39; Magda von Bárány-Oberschall, *Die eiserne Krone der Lombardei und der lombardische Königsschatz* (Vienna 1966) 47-49; Augusto Merati, *Il tesoro del duomo di Monza*, 2nd ed. (Monza 1969) 26-27 with figs. 25 and 26; Guido Gregorietti, *Jewelry through the Ages* (New York 1969) 150-51; Joan Evans, *A History of Jewelry*[2] 41, n. 4; Lasko, *op. cit.* 55-56 and pl. 50; Heiniger, *op. cit.* 184 and 192; Margaret Frazer in Roberto Conti, *Il duomo di Monza*, 2nd ed. (Milan 1989) II 47-48, with bibliography. The crown is kept inside the altar of the north apsidal chapel, or cappella teodelindea, and shown on request; a replica is displayed above the altar. In the tympanum of the portal there is a 14th century relief in which Queen Theodelinda is seen offering the crown to John the Baptist, the patron of the church: Francis Oppenheimer, *Frankish Themes and Problems* (London 1952) 105-70 with pls. 4 and 14; Saverio Lomartire in Conti, *op. cit.* I 101-103 with ill. 62. Photographs in Merati, *Storia architettonica del duomo di Monza*, fig. 102, and in Roberto Cassanelli, ed., *Monza anno 1300: La basilica di S. Giovanni Battista e la sua fasciata* (Monza 1988), ill. 26. Of the pinnacles which crown the facade one, the second from the right, houses a seated statue of St. Helena with a large cross; it was placed there in the course of restoration work in 1906; see Cassanelli, *op. cit.* 33 and 155, and id. in Conti, *op. cit.* I 65.

2.   Half of the *titulus*, in three alphabets and in retrograde.
3.   One of the holy nails.
4.   Two thorns of Christ's Crown of Thorns.
5.   Particles of the Holy Sepulchre.
6.   Particles of the column of Christ's Passion.
7.   A finger of St. Thomas (*the* finger: John 20.24-29).
8.   Particles of the manger of the baby Jesus.[32]

The *Liber Pontificalis* reports that Constantine deposited a piece of the True Cross in the Church of Santa Croce, and we have already rejected that statement.[33] An additional consideration is that Constantine did not visit Rome after 326.[34] Would he have allowed someone else to deposit such a precious relic on his behalf?

Even more serious objections can be raised against the *titulus*, or rather the one-half of it. Two witnesses report having seen (and even handled and kissed) a *titulus* (presumably an entire one, not a divided one) in Jerusalem, not in Rome: Egeria in ca. 380, and a certain pseudo-Antoninus (Antoninus Placentinus, the Anonymous of Piacenza) in ca. 560-570.[35] And our confidence in the Roman *titulus* is not strengthened when we learn that it was lost and then found again in 1492.[36]

In the 18th century Raimondo Besozzi, as abbot of the Monastery of Santa Croce and Procurator General of the Cistercian order, had a special interest in defending the relics of his church against charges or suspicions of spuriousness. He asserts specifically that the three particles of the Cross were deposited by Helena and Constantine; he also maintains the authenticity of the nail.[37] Another Cistercian, Balduino Bedini,

---

[32]Buchowiecki, *op. cit.* I 625; less accurately Beny and Gunn, *op. cit.* 102.

[33]See chapter VII above, n. 25; see chapter VII above.

[34]Barnes, *New Empire* 77-80.

[35]Egeria, *Peregrinatio* 37.1-3 (ed. Geyer [*CSEL* XXXIX] 88); ed. Pétré [*SC* XXI] 232-34; ed. Franceschini-Weber [*CC, Ser. Lat.* CLXXV] 80-81; ed. Maraval [*SC* CCXCVI] 284-86. Antoninus Placentinus, *Itinerarium* 20 (Migne, *PL* LXXII 906; ed. Geyer [*CSEL* XXXIX] 172 and 204; ed. Geyer [*CC, Ser. Lat.* CLXXV] 139 and 164); Boussel, *op. cit.* 164-65. On Antoninus Placentinus, see the following: Umberto Moricca, *Storia della letteratura latina cristiana* III.2 (Turin 1934) 1387-89; Kötting, *op. cit.* 361-62; Altaner-Stuiber, *op. cit.* 245-46.

[36]Stegenšek, *op. cit.* 181; Frolow, *La relique* 328, no. 333; Buchowiecki, *op. cit.* I 608; Bovini, *Edifici cristiani* 125; Boussel, *op. cit.* 165-66.

[37]*Op. cit.* 139-43 and 143-45.

also has defended the traditional account in a booklet which is devotional rather than historical in nature and lacking in critical judgement.[38]

More critically Giuseppe Bovini surveys the primary sources for the *inventio* of the True Cross and concludes that the relics were deposited not by Constantine but by one of his sons.[39] That, of course, excludes Helena.

That Helena returned to Rome after her pilgrimage and brought sacred relics with her has sometimes been asserted rather rashly.[40] The statement has been expressed also in painting. An example is a painting by the Netherlandish painter Bernart van Orley in which Helena is seen presenting herself to the Pope; the painting can be dated to 1515-1520 and is housed in Brussels' Musées royaux des Beaux-Arts.[41]

Since Trier was Helena's residence for a substantial number of years and claimed to be Helena's place of birth it is not surprising that the same city should claim a fair number of relics associated with her. These we must examine next.

The ninth century *vita* of St. Helena by Altmann was first mentioned in chapter II above and will be considered more fully in chapter XVI below. We have already rejected what it has to say on Helena's birth in Trier. In this same *vita* we have the first reference to Helena's sending holy relics to her "native" city:

> Helena ... de diversis martyrum reliquiis composuit thecam: in qua etiam cultellum recondidit, quo Dominus noster Jesus Christus usus est in sacratissimo coenae convivio. Qua dignitate admirabili et optanda volebat munire et insignire suam regionem, ut, quae erat toto mundo columna restitutionis per inventionem sanctae crucis, esset et decus speciale aliquatenus patriae suae.[42]

---

[38]*Le reliquie sessoriane della passione del Signore*, 3rd ed. (Rome 1967) passim.

[39]*Edifici cristiani* 125-31.

[40]Giuseppe Ricciotti, *The Age of Martyrs* (Milwaukee 1959) 199; Lees-Milne, *op.cit.* 63.

[41]Inv. no. 4999; Musées royaux des Beaux-Arts de Belgique, Département d'art ancien, *Catalogue inventaire de la peinture ancienne* (Brussels 1984) 217; Max J. Friedländer, *Early Netherlandish Painting* (New York 1967) VIII 57-59, 104-105, no. 99, and pl. 98.

[42]Helena ... filled a chest with various relics of martyrs; in this chest she also placed the knife which our Lord Jesus Christ used at that most holy meal. With this wonderful and desirable distinction she wished to strengthen and to mark her (native) district, in

A *cultellus*, believed to be the "Abendmahlsmesser" of Christ, once belonged to the treasury of the Monastery of St. Maximinus. In Napoleonic times it was removed, along with other relics, to the Church of St. Martin in Pfalzel, across the Mosel from Trier; it is today in the possession of the parish of St. Mary and St. Martin in Pfalzel. A small silver tablet attached to it proclaims *cultellus quo dominus Jesus Christus usus fuit in cena*. It appears to be of 12th century workmanship and thus fails to prove Altmann's claim.[43]

Two centuries later the anonymous *vita* of Bishop Agritius expands the account.[44] On his way from Antioch to Trier Agritius visited Rome and there received from Helena several holy relics, namely the remains of the Apostle Matthias, recently transferred from Judaea, one of the holy nails, and the *cultellus* first mentioned by Altmann. In chapter IV above we have already seen that this *vita* is of little historical value and that Helena cannot have had a role in Agritius' succession to the bishop-ric in Trier. In chapter VII above we have found nothing to suggest to us that Helena was ever present in Rome after her pilgrimage. Even more damning is the introduction of a forged diploma, the so-called Diploma of Sylvester.[45] This diploma supposedly granted to the church of Trier primacy over all of Gaul and Germany; it again mentions the remains of St. Matthias and the nail, but not the knife. It is clearly an invention in support of the ecclesiastical policy of the bishops of Trier.[46]

---

[42](...continued)
order that what was a column of restitution (?) to the whole world through the finding of the Holy Cross might also be the special glory, in some measure, of her own country. 4.43 (*Acta Sanct.* Aug. III [ed. 1867] 592).

[43]Handwritten chronicle of the parish, dated 1856, p. 53; Franz Xaver Kraus, *Inschriften* II 203, no. 429; Ernst Wackenroder and Heinrich Neu, *Die Kunstdenkmäler des Landkreises Trier* (Düsseldorf 1936) 281-82 and ill. 187; Thomas van Zanten in Andrea Bidinger, ed., *Pfalzel: Geschichte und Gegenwart* (Trier: Arbeitsgemeinschaft Pfalzeler Chronik, 1989) 151. Through the courtesy of Pfarrer Thomas van Zanten I was able to inspect both the chronicle and the knife in August, 1985.

[44]1.5-6 (*Acta. Sanct.* Ian. II [ed. 1863] 56); Sauerland, *op. cit.* 82 and 187.

[45]*Ibid.* 1.7.

[46]The diploma or *privilegium* has been judged to be a forgery by many: Johann Nikolaus von Hontheim, *Historia Treverensis Diplomatica et Pragmatica* (Augsburg 1750) I 17; Franz Xaver Kraus, *Der heilige Nagel* 113-15; Leonardy *op. cit.* 220; Philip Diel, *Die St. Matthias-Kirche bei Trier und ihre Heligthümer* (Trier 1881) 89-90 and 149-53; Sauerland, *op. cit.* 88; Manitius III 517; Winheller, *op. cit.* 126; Mackes, *op. cit.* 192. The shortest and presumably oldest version of the diploma is known to us only
(continued...)

Beyond his election, as reported in Acts 1, there is a dearth of reliable information on St. Matthias. Some late traditions report that he preached and died in some far-away place such as perhaps Ethiopia or Cappodocia.[47] *If* there be any substance to these traditions then Helena cannot, of course, have found his remains in the Holy Land.

The remains of St. Matthias were, *mirabile dictu,* found in Trier a first time in 1053 and a second time in 1127.[48] The Church of St. Matthias (formerly St. Eucharius) in Trier takes great pride in containing the tomb of the Apostle Matthias, the only tomb of an Apostle north of the Alps.[49] At the same time the head of the Apostle is venerated in the Church of S. Maria Maggiore in Rome.[50] Nevertheless the treasury of Trier's cathedral once contained a head reliquary of St. Matthias, dating from ca. 1390.[51]

It can be shown that the Church of Trier claimed already in the tenth century, i. e. long before the *vita* of Agritius was composed, to possess one of the holy nails.[52] The treasury of Trier's cathedral contains the portable altar of St. Andrew, made on orders of Archbishop Egbert (977-993) and hence also known as the Egbert-shrine. It contained, among other things, this nail, which is now, together with its cover, displayed to view outside the shrine.[53] In 1792-1844 the nail was

---

[46](...continued)
from Brower, *op. cit.* I 215, quoted by Franz Xaver Kraus, *Der heilige Nagel* 107, and by Sauerland, *op. cit.* 88. It mentions neither Helena nor any relics sent by her to Trier.

[47]Franz Mussner in *LThK*² VII (1962) 179-80; A. le Houllier in *NCE* IX (1967) 503.

[48]Marx, *Geschichte* II.1 188-90; Diel, *op. cit.* 86-95 and 97-99; Kentenich, *Geschichte* 130; Bunjes, *op. cit.* 215-16; Rudolf M. Kloos, *Lambertus de Legia: De vita, translatione, inventione ac miraculis sancti Matthiae Apostoli libri quinque* (Trier 1958) 17-28; Joachim Schiffhauer in August Leidl, ed., *Bistumspatrone in Deutschland* (Munich 1984) 117-20 ("eine Fiktion") and bibliography 126-27; Winfried Weber in *Zwischen Andacht und Andenken* (Trier 1992) 104; See also n. 84 below.

[49]Diel, *op. cit.* 104-106; Beitz. *Das heilige Trier* 54 and ill. 109; Bunjes, *op. cit.* 244-46; Winfried Weber in *Zwischen Andacht und Andenken* 104-106.

[50]Diel, *op. cit.* 95-97.

[51]Irsch, *Dom* 365, no. 11, and pl. XV.

[52]Franz Xaver Kraus, *Der heilige Nagel* 150.

[53]Falke-Frauberger, *op. cit.* 6, 123, and pl. 2; Beitz, *Das heilige Trier* 18 and ill. 19; Peter Weber, *Der Domschatz zu Trier* (Augsburg 1928) 14-15 and ill. 13; Irsch, *Dom* 334-35 and fig. 219; Joseph Braun, *Die Reliquiare* 452 and ill. 526; Schnitzler, *Rheinische Schatzkammer* 22, no. 5, and pl. 23; Hanns Swarzenski, *Monuments of Romanesque Art,* 2nd ed. (Chicago and London 1967) 41-42 and pl. 27, fig. 61; Lasko,
(continued...)

Plate VII

Figure of St. Matthias over the main portal of the Church of St. Matthias in Trier. The church contains the Apostle's tomb.

absent from Trier, being in the possession of Prince Metternich, the Austrian Chancellor, during much of this time.[54]

In the early 12th century, about half a century after the *vita* of Agritius was written, the author of the *Gesta Treverorum* gives us another version of the diploma; it contains an expanded list of relics:

... quam ipsa felix per apostolum Matthiam Judea translatum cum tunica et clavo Domini et dente sancti Petri et scandaliis [sic] sancti Andreae apostoli et capite Cornelii papae ceterisque reliquiis magnifice ditavit specialiterque provexit.[55]

The same relics are listed as Helena's gifts to her native city by the *Kaiserchronik*.[56] This immense chronicle, in Early Middle High German, was composed around the middle of the 12th century by an anonymous cleric, or perhaps a group of clerics, at Regensburg and is considered the first historical work in the German language. It consists of 17,283 verses; its chronological scope, after a brief summary of earlier history, is from Julius Caesar to the year 1147. It contains many episodes which are legendary, rather than historical, or even fantastic.[57] The author, or authors, would appear to have been acquainted with the *Gesta Treverorum*. The two lists do not, of course, establish the authenticity or ultimate provenience of the relics listed but only their presence in Trier in the 12th century.

The *tunica* which is claimed for Trier both by the *Gesta Treverorum* and by the *Kaiserchronik* is none other than the Seamless Robe of

---

[53](...continued)
op. cit. 97 and pl. 91; Hiltrud Westermann-Angerhausen, *Die Goldschmiedearbeiten der Trierer Egbertwerkstatt* (Trier 1973) 32-34 and ill. 13; Petri and Droege, *op. cit.*, vol. of ill. 303, no. 520; Ronig in *Schatzkunst Trier* 97-98, no. 24.

[54]Franz Xaver Kraus, *Der heilige Nagel* 170-72.

[55]. . . which (the city of Trier) the blessed lady herself generously endowed and specially promoted by (the body of) the apostle Matthias, translated from Judaea, together with the tunic and the nail of the Lord, the tooth of St. Peter, the sandals of St. Andrew, the head of Pope Cornelius, and other relics. 18 (Migne, *PL* CLIV 1134; *MGH, Script.* VIII 152); Hontheim, *op. cit.* I 17; Beyer, *Urkundenbuch* I 1, no. 1; Franz Xaver Kraus, *Der heilige Nagel* 111-12; Sauerland, *op. cit.* 92; Philipp Jaffé, *op. cit.* I 29.

[56]Verses 10387-99 (Ed. Edward Schröder [*MGH, Dt. Chron.* I.1] 272).

[57]Ewald Erb, *Geschichte der deutschen Literatur von den Anfängen bis 1160* II (Berlin 1965) 717-24; Joachim Ehlers in Henning Krauss, *op. cit.* 427-28; Eberhard Nellmann, "Kaiserchronik," in *Verfasserlexikon²* IV (1982-1983) 949-64; Ernst Hellgardt, "Kaiserchronik," in *Literaturlexikon* VI (1990) 193-95.

Christ (John 19.23), Trier's famous "Heiliger Rock." But Gregory of Tours, writing more than 500 years earlier and in an excellent position to know, associates the Seamless Robe neither with Helena nor with Trier. He says of it:

> Ferunt autem in civitatem Galateae, in basilica quae ad sanctos archangelos vocitatur, retineri. Est enim haec civitas ab urbe Constantinopolitana quasi milibus 150, in qua basilica est cripta abditissima, ibique in arca lignea hoc vestimentum habetur inclausum.[58]

Similarly in the next century "Fredegar" knows nothing of the Seamless Robe having been sent to Trier by Helena. To the contrary, he writes that in the 30th year of the Frankish king Guntram, i.e. in A. D. 590, the robe was found *in civitatem Zafad procul a Hierusolima in arca marmorea* and brought to Jerusalem by the bishops Gregory of Antioch, Thomas of Jerusalem, and John of Constantinople.[59] The accounts given by Gregory and by "Fredegar" present their own problems and can be reconciled neither with each other nor with the traditions of Trier.

On May 6, 1012, the cathedral of Bamberg was dedicated in the presence of King Henry II by an assembly of 45 bishops. Among the relics deposited in the Altar of the Holy Cross was a particle of the Seamless Robe of Christ.[60] This is our first mention of the robe in the West. Since Archbishop Megingaud of Trier was one of the bishops who participated in the dedication, Kempf was certain that the particle of the robe had been brought as a gift by him from Trier, i.e. that the robe was then in Trier.[61] Kempf's conclusion is attractive but not compelling; it was anticipated and rejected by Erwin Iserloh.[62]

---

[58]But it is said that it (the Seamless Robe) is kept in a city of Galatia (?), in the basilica which is called the basilica of the Holy Archangels. For this city is about 150 miles distant from Constantinople. In this basilica there is a very remote crypt, and there this garment is kept locked away in a wooden chest. *Liber in Gloria Martyrum* 8 (Migne, *PL* LXXI 711-12), or 7 (*MGH, SRM* I.2 492-93 or I.2² 42-43). *civitas Galateae* is questionable; Henri Leclerq in *DACL* XV.2 (1953) 2821-22.

[59]*Chron.* 4.11 (*MGH, SRM* II 126-27). Zafad remains unexplained; Henri Leclerq in *DACL* XV.2 (1953) 2822-23.

[60]*Dedicatio Ecclesiae S. Petri Babenbergensis* (*MGH, Script.* XVII 635-36); Johann Looshorn, *Die Geschichte des Bisthums Bamberg* I (Bamberg 1886) 185-87.

[61]*Legende-Überlieferung-Forschung* 7.

[62]"Der heilige Rock und die Wallfahrt nach Trier," *Geist und Leben* 32 (1959) 271-79 at 272, n. 4.

Some years later, between 1029 and 1039, on a September 8, the main altar of the principal church of Freising was dedicated. Among the relics deposited was again a particle of the Seamless Robe.[63] There is no mention of Trier this time.

In the second half of the 11th century the anonymous author of the *vita* of Agritius does not mention the robe among the relics sent to Trier by Helena, as we have seen. He does, however, refer to it in another context: there was, he says, in Trier a reliquary box in which Agritius had placed relics of Christ, perhaps the robe. In the days of a certain bishop, after a three-day fast, a certain monk was chosen because of his righteousness to open the box. When he did he was immediately struck blind – a sure sign from heaven that no one was supposed to open the box and see its holy contents.[64] In this story, surely apocryphal, Kempf also sees evidence for the presence of the robe in Trier in the 11th century.[65]

We finally reach firm ground at the end of the 12th century. On May 1, 1196, under Archbishop Johann I (1190-1212), the Seamless Robe was removed from the west choir of Trier's cathedral and transferred to the main altar.[66] It does not emerge into history again until April 14, 1512. On that day it was inspected by Emperor Maximilian, who was then in Trier on the occasion of an imperial diet.[67] It was publicly displayed and became the object of pilgrimages in 1655, 1810, 1844, 1891, 1933, and 1959 (but not in 1984 when Trier celebrated the 2000th anniversary of its foundation).[68] It will next be displayed – so

[63]*Nota Dedicationis Frisingensis (MGH, Script. XXX.2 769).*

[64]4.17 *(Acta Sanct.* Jan. II [ed. 1863] 58); Sauerland, *op. cit.* 195-96; Franz J. Ronig in *Zwischen Andacht und Andenken* 120.

[65]*Legende-Überlieferung-Forschung* 5.

[66]*Gesta Treverorum Continuata, Additamenta (MGH, Script.* XXIV 396); Kentenich, *Geschichte* 155-56; Irsch, *Dom* 112; Ronig, *Dom* 275 and 339; Franz J. Ronig in *Zwischen Andacht und Andenken* 120-21.

[67]Leonardy, *op. cit.* 596; Kentenich, *Geschicte* 119 and 323-24; Ronig, *Dom* 253 and 339; Franz Rudolf Reichert in Franz J. Ronig, ed., *Schatzkunst Trier: Forschungen und Ergenbnisse* (Trier 1991) 168-69; Franz J. Ronig in *Zwischen Andacht und Andenken* 122.

[68]Jacob Marx, *Geschichte des heiligen Rockes in der Domkirche zu Trier* (Trier 1844); Leonardy, *op. cit.* 1007-1008; Kentenich, *Geschichte* 518 and 806; Irsch, *Dom* pl. XV; Ronig, *Dom* 234 and ill. 22; Emil Zenz, *Geschichte der Stadt Trier im 19. Jahrhundert* (Trier 1979-1980) I 25 and 120-23; Emil Zenz, *Die Stadt Trier im 20. Jahrhundert: 1. Hälfte 1900-1950* (Trier 1981) 346-47; Gunther Franz in Düwell and

(continued...)

it was recently announced – in May, 1996, i.e. 800 years after its *depositio* in the main altar of the cathedral. It was temporarily removed to Cologne in 1648 in a dispute between the cathedral chapter and the Elector Philipp Christoph von Sötern.[69] In 1667-1759, 1765-1790, and 1792-1810 it was again absent from Trier for security reasons, being kept most of this time in Ehrenbreitstein, where it was displayed in 1765.[70] A large (4.66 x 2.50m) and ornate silver shrine, made in 1729-1732, once housed the robe but was melted down during the French Revolution. When its doors were closed the front of this shrine was dominated by a life-size figure of St. Helena holding the robe in her arms. Two engravings in Trier's Stadtbibliothek depict the lost shrine.[71] Today the Seamless Robe, still the most renowned of all of Trier's relics, is contained in a wooden shrine which is in turn kept in a glass case in the "Heiltumskapelle" or "Heilig-Rock-Kapelle" at the eastern end of the cathedral.[72]

Not surprisingly the authenticity of the Seamless Robe has often been challenged and often been defended. A vast amount of literature has been generated, most recently on the occasion of the display of the robe in 1959. The problem must remain outside of the scope of the present study.[73] A rival robe of Christ at Argenteuil (near Paris) seems to

---

[68](...continued)
Irsigler, *op. cit.* 332; Manfred Heimers *ibid.* 417; Reinhard Bollmus *ibid.* 530; Guido Gross in *Zwischen Andacht und Andenken* 88; Franz J. Ronig *ibid.* 125-33; Michael Embach *ibid.* 137-53; Markus Gross-Morgen *ibid.* 248-53.

[69]Kentenich, *Geschichte* 509.

[70]Leonardy, *op. cit.* 1007; Kentenich, *Geschichte* 518; Peter Weber, *op. cit.* 8; Ronig, *Dom* 295; Gunther Franz in Düwell and Irsigler, *op. cit.* 332; Markus Gross-Morgen in *Zwischen Andacht und Andenken* 247-48. For the return to Trier in 1810 see Hans Wolfgang Kuhn, *op. cit.* 187.

[71]Beitz, *Das heilige Trier* 51 and pl. XII; Peter Weber, *op. cit.* 7 and ill. 2; Irsch, *Dom* 250-51, 367, no. 54, and fig. 92; Ronig, "Ausstattung" 40; Ronig, *Dom* 284, 295 and ill. 159-60; Henryk Dziurla in Ronig, *Dom* 367 and 369; Norbert Jopek in *Schatzkunst Trier* 248-49, no. 212; Gunther Franz in Düwell and Irsigler, *op. cit.* 354 and 369; Markus Gross-Morgen in *Zwischen Andacht und Andenken* 390-91, no. B 286.1 and 2.

[72]Ronig, *Dom* 327, 330, and ill. 113.

[73]A suitable starting point would be Erwin Iserloh in *LThK*² VIII (1963) 1348-50. Today the controversy is no longer along confessional lines, as it once was. (Both Luther and Calvin denied the authenticity of the Seamless Robe.) It is to be noted that a Catholic scholar, writing in a Catholic journal, can now conclude that the Seamless Robe is not genuine but is nevertheless of value as a symbol of the unity of the Church; see Iserloh's article (n. 62 above) 278 and 271 respectively.

be of very questionable authenticity, there being no witness for it before the 12th century.[74]

A reliquary containing a tooth of St. Peter, dating from 1347 and documented for 1655 and 1776, was melted down during the French Revolution.[75]

The "sandals of St. Andrew" have given their name to the portable altar of St. Andrew mentioned above, an object of extraordinary interest and value.[76]

Pope Cornelius died in exile at Centumcellae (Civitavecchia) in 253.[77] His body was subsequently taken to Rome, and his tomb can be seen to this day in the crypt of Lucina in the cemetery of Callistus.[78] According to one tradition his body was removed in the ninth century to the Church of S. Maria in Trastevere.[79] ccording to another tradition the Frankish king Charles the Bald (840-877) took the body to France.[80] And the same king is said to have presented the saint's head to the Benedictine Monastery of Kornelimünster (originally *monasterium ad Indam*), near Aachen.[81] Nevertheless the treasury of Trier's cathedral contained

---

[74]André Lesort in *DHGE* IV (1930) 32-36; Henri Leclercq in *DACL* XV.2 (1953) 2823; Boussel, *op. cit.* 147-50.

[75]Irsch, *Dom* 365, no. 9, and pl. XV.

[76]Franz Xaver Kraus, *Inschriften* II 172, no. 353; Beitz, *Das heilige Trier* 16-17 and ill. 20-23; Peter Weber, *op. cit.* 12-15 and ill. 9-12; Irsch, *Dom* 329-34 and pl. XVI; Schnitzler, *Rheinische Schatzkammer* 21-22, no. 4, and pls. 14-22; Hanns Swarzenski, *Monuments*[2] 42 and pl. 27, fig. 62; Lasko, *op. cit.* 96-98 and pl. 89; Westermann-Angerhausen, *Goldschmiedearbeiten* 21-32, pls. A and B, and ill. 1-12; Hiltrud Westermann-Angerhausen, "Überlegungen zum Trierer Egbertschrein," *TZ* 40-41 (1977-78) 201-20; Ronig in *Schatzkunst Trier* 96-97, no. 23.

[77]*Liber Pontificalis* ed. Mommsen (*MGH, GPR* I) 28-31; ed. Duchesne² I 150-51. But what the *Liber* tells about Cornelius being martyred under Decius is to be rejected.

[78]Giovanni Battista De Rossi, *Rome Sotterranea* I (Rome 1864) 274-87; Josef Wilpert *La cripta de Papi e la capella di santa Cecilia* (Rome 1910) 26-28 and 34-35; Paul Styger, *Die römischen Martyrergrüfte* (Berlin 1935) I 97-108 with pl. III; II, pls. 50-52; Johann Peter Kirsch, *The Catacombs of Rome* (Rome 1946) 137-38 and fig. 49; Renzo U. Montini, *Le tombe de papi* (Rome 1957) 77-79; Louis Reekmans, *La tombe du papei Corneille et sa région cemeteriale* (Vatican City 1964).

[79]Montini, *op. cit.* 79; This church was at one time called the Church of Sts. Callistus and Cornelius: Hülsen, *Le chiese* 371, no. 91.

[80]Alberich of Trois Fontaines (13th century), *Chron.* sub anno 876 (ed. Scheffer-Boichorst [*MGH, Script.* XXIII] 742).

[81]Emil Pauls, "Beiträge zur Geschichte der grösseren Reliquien und der Heiligtumsfahrten zu Cornelimünster bei Aachen," *AHVNrh* 52 (1891) 157-74 at 157 and

(continued...)

a head reliquary of Cornelius made in 1515 and melted down at the time of the French Revolution.[82] Also, Trier's Church of St. Paulinus owns, but does not currently (1993) have on display, a painting by Jean Louis Counet (of Liège, active in Trier in 1700-1721) which depicts the (supposed) martyrdom of Pope Cornelius; apparently Cornelius was of some interest in Trier.[83]

Later in the 12th century, probably soon after 1131, there was produced another text to enhance the reputation and strengthen the claims of the Monastery of St. Eucharius.[84] It again confidently asserts that Helena was a native of Trier, that through Agritius she sent to Trier the body of St. Matthias, and that the latter was put to rest next to the bodies of Sts. Eucharius, Valerius, and Maternus. The author of this text even knows when Helena sent the remains of St. Matthias to Trier: in 368! And his source of information is a letter addressed to Agritius by Pope Sylvester![85]

To sum it all up:

1. Altmann, in the ninth century, is the first to claim that Helena sent relics to Trier, just as he is the first to claim that Helena was a native of Trier. After Altmann the legend grows in increments.

2. It is impossible for Helena and Agritius to have met in Rome after Helena's pilgrimage; it is very unlikely that their paths ever crossed again after Helena left Trier to take up residence in Rome.

3. When the relics supposedly sent to Trier by Helena are considered individually nothing at all is found that would substantiate any association with Helena and serious questions arise concerning the authenticity of some of them.

The oldest of all the items in the cathedral's treasury is a Roman amethyst bowl, dating from the third or fourth century and measuring

---

[81](...continued)
166; Heribert Reiners, *Die Kunstdenkmäler der Landkreise Aachen und Eupen* (Düsseldorf 1912) 68 with fig. 46; August Franzen in *DGHE* XIII (1956) 895-97; Basilius Senger in *LThK*[2] VI (1961) 557; Leo Hugot, *Aachen-Kornelimünster*, 2nd ed. (Cologne 1979) 8, 21, and ill. 17. The cult of St. Cornelius flourishes at Kornelimünster to this day, especially in the former abbey church, today's Probsteikirche.

[82]Irsch, *Dom* 366, no. 38, and pl. XV.

[83]Bunjes, *op. cit.* 356; Gunther Franz in Düwell and Irsigler, *op. cit.* 365-66.

[84]Sauerland, *op. cit.* 113; *De Inventione Beati Mathiae Apostoli* (*Acta Sanct.* Febr. III [ed. 1865] 441-45, *MGH, Script.* VIII 226-31).

[85]*Ibid.* 1.

14.9 cm. in diameter. It has long, but for no good reason, been called the "drinking bowl of St. Helena."[86]

Finally, because of a tenuous link to Helena, another object in the treasury of Trier's cathedral must be considered here. This is a carved ivory panel which measures 13.1x26.1 cm and probably once decorated the lid or one of the sides of a reliquary box.[87] It is commonly presumed to be of Byzantine provenience, and it has been suggested, not unreasonably, that it came to the West in the wake of the sack of Constantinople by the Crusaders in 1204. It was acquired by the cathedral chapter in 1849, but possibly had been part of the cathedral treasury at some earlier time. This possibility gave rise, in turn, to the speculation that our panel decorated the box which contained the Seamless Robe. The date of our panel is difficult to determine, and estimates have ranged from the fifth to the seventh century. A half-figure of Christ, cruciform-nimbed, in the upper left-hand corner certainly would indicate a date before iconoclasm (726). The carvings depict, against an elaborate architectural background, a *translatio* of relics. Two bishops (or perhaps a bishop and an assistant), court officials, an emperor, and an empress are participating; the latter holds a large cross in her left hand. Some have fondly imagined that the locale is Trier and that the emperor and empress

---

[86]Peter Weber, *op. cit.* 9-10 and ill. 3; Irsch, *Dom* 319; Anita Büttner, "Die Trinkschale der Kaiserin Helena im Domschatz zu Trier," in *Festschrift Eugen von Mercklin* (Waldsassen, Bavaria, 1964) 27-31 and pls. 15-16; Kempf and Reusch, *Frühchristliche Zeugnisse* 248-49, no. 47; Winfried Weber in *Schatzkinst Trier* 77, no. 1, and color pl. 1. But more recently the bowl has been dated to the 14th century; see Ronig, *Schatzkunst Trier: Forschungen und Ergebnisse* 17, no. 1.

[87]Dalton, *Byzantine Art and Archaeology* 211 and fig. 127; Peter Weber, *op. cit.* 10-12 and ill. 8; Richard Delbrueck, *Die Consulardiptychen und verwandte Denkmäler* (Berlin and Leipzig 1929) 261-70, no. 67; Neuss, *Anfänge*[2] 53; Irsch, *Dom* 319-23, with extensive bibliography, and figs. 207-208; Grabar, *Martyrium* II 352, n. 4, and pl. LXX; Joseph Natanson, *Early Christian Ivories* (London 1953) 33 and ill. 51; Schnitzler, *Rheinische Schatzkammer* 21, no. 1, and pls. 1-5; David Talbot Rice, *The Art of Byzantium* 305 and pl. 70; Peter Metz, *Elfenbein der Spätantike* (Munich 1962) 31 and ill. 48; Kempf and Reusch, *Frühchristliche Zeugnisse* 220-21, no. 22; Volbach and Lafontaine-Dosogne, *op. cit.,* 200 and pl. 93; Beckwith, *Early Christian and Byzantine Art* 40 and pl. 74; Johannes Kollwitz in *RAC* IV (1959) 1133; Volbach, *Elfenbeinarbeiten der Spätantike*[3] 95-96, no. 143, and pl. 76; Christopher Walter, *Art and Ritual of the Byzantine Church* (London 1982) 83 and 145-46; Legner, *Deutsche Kunst der Romanik* 89 and ill. 34; Winfried Weber in *Schatzkunst Trier* 80-81, no. 5; Hans-Werner Hegemann, *Das Elfenbein in Kunst und Kultur Europas* (Mainz 1988), color pl. 14. For additional literature see Ronig, *Schatzkunst Trier: Forschungen und Ergebnisse* 17, no. 5.

are Constantine and Helena.[88] No one holds to this erroneous interpretation today, and other, far more plausible interpretations have been offered.[89] The locale, several observers now agree, is Constantinople, but the specific occasion has proved more elusive.

We return to the relics of the Magi, or Three Kings, which have briefly occupied us in chapter V above. The Gospel account of the Magi does not call them kings, does not give their number, does not assign them names, and says that they returned to their homes.[90] Tertullian[91] is the first to call them kings, Origen[92] is the first to give their number as three (because they brought three gifts, it is assumed),[93] and their names, Caspar, Melchior, and Balthasar, are not found until the seventh

[88]Franz Xaver Kraus, *Der heilige Nagel* 135-41, rejects this interpretation. Beitz, *Das heilige Trier* 14, seems open to it. Irsch, *Dom* 322, withholds judgment. More recently (see following note) this interpretation has simply been ignored.

[89]Stylianos Pelekanides, "Date et interpretation de la plaque en ivoire de Trèves," in *Mélanges Henri Grégoire* IV = *AIPHOS* 12 (1952) 361-71; Venance Grumel, "A propos de la plaque d'ivoire de Trèves," *REB* 12 (1954) 187-90. Balthasar Fischer, "Die Elfenbeinfafel des Trierer Domschatzes: Zu ihrer jüngsten Deutung durch Stylianos Pelekanides, 1952," *Kurtrierisches Jahrbuch* 9 (1969) 5-19; Suzanne Spain, "The Translation of Relics Ivory, Trier," *DOP* 31 (1977) 279-304; Kenneth G. Holum and Gary Vikan, "The Trier Ivory, *Adventus* Ceremonial, and the Relics of St. Stephen," *DOP* 33 (1979) 113-33; Winfried Weber, "Die Reliquienprozession auf der Elfenbeintafel des Trierer Domschatzes und das kaiserliche Hofzeremoniell," *TZ* 42 (1979) 135-51; John Wortley, "The Trier Ivory Reconsidered," *GRBS* 21 (1980) 381-94; Kenneth G. Holum, *Theodosian Empresses* (Berkeley 1982) 104-109 with fig. 15; Winfried Weber in *Spätantike und frühes Christentum* (exh. cat. Frankfurt 1983) 676-77, no. 251; Laurie J. Wilson, "The Trier Procession Ivory: A New Interpretation," *Byzantion* 54 (1984) 602-14.

[90]Matthew 2.1-12.

[91]*Adv. Iud.* 9.12 (Migne, *PL* II 619 [ed. 1844] or 659 [ed. 1878]; ed. Kroymann [*CSEL* LXX] 291, ed. Kroymann [*CC, Ser. Lat.* II] 1367-68; ed. Tränkle 22); *Adv. Marc.* 3.13.8. (Migne, *PL* II 339 [ed. 1844] or 367 [ed. 1878]; ed. Kroymann [*CSEL* XLVII] 398; ed. Kroymann [*CC, Ser. Lat.* I] 525; ed. Moreschini 128; ed. Evans I 208).

[92]In his *In Gen. hom.* (Latin transl. by Rufinus) 14.3 (Migne, *PG* XII 238; ed. Baehrens [*GCS* XXIX] 124-25; ed. Doutreleau [*SC* VII²] 340-44) Origen likens the Magi to Abimelech, Ahuzzath, and Phichol of Gen. 26.26, who in turn represent rational, natural, and moral philosophy.

[93]Origen dwells at length on these gifts in *Contra Celsum* 1.60 (Migne, *PG* I 771; ed. Koetschau [*GCS* II] 111; ed. Borret [*SC* CXXXII] 240); In Roman catacomb paintings the number of the Magi varies from two to four; see Réau, *Iconographie* II.2 237, and James Stevenson, *The Catacombs* (London 1978) 87. It would appear then that three became the canonical number only with the passing of time.

or eighth century in the *Excerpta Latina Barbari*.[94] That Helena collected the remains of the Magi from their separate tombs, that she carried them to Constantinople, and that, with the permission of the emperor, Bishop Eustorgius of Milan translated them to that city, all that is reported for the first time by a brief *vita* of that same bishop. This *vita* is by a nameless author, of uncertain date, and highly suspect; it exists in numerous textual variants.[95] It is to be noted that we are not told where Helena made her find.[96] In Milan the relics of the Magi were not discovered until 1158.[97] The relics contained in Cologne's Shrine of the Three Kings were officially and carefully examined in 1864 – 700 years after their arrival in Cologne. The results of this examination have been summarized by Walter Schulten, who concludes that 'in the remains of the Three Kings Cologne possesses the best-documented relics of Biblical times.'[98] Yet, that Helena had anything at all to do with their *inventio* or with their *translatio* to Constantinople remains a legend without historical foundation.[99]

In the early eleventh century a Venetian author, Johannes Diaconus Venetus, claimed that the emperor Heraclius had given to the city of Grado (on the Bay of Venice and once the see of the patriarchate) the cathedra of St. Mark, and furthermore that this cathedra had originally

---

[94]Bibliothèque Nationale, Paris, Ms. lat. 4884, folio 52; Bibliothèque Nationale, Paris, *Catalogus Codicum Manuscriptorum Bibliothecae Regiae* (Paris 1739-1744) IV 13; Ed. Mommsen (*MGH, AA* IX = *Chron. Min.* I) 278; Edmund Weigand, "Zur Datierung der kappadokischen Höhlenmalereien." *BZ* 36 (1936) 337-97 at 363. In the mosaics of S. Apollinare Nuovo at Ravenna the Magi are identified by inscriptions above their heads, but these must be assigned not to the sixth century original work but to a later restoration.

[95]I have consulted the version which Aegidius of Orval included in his *Gesta Episcoporum Leodiensium* (ca. 1250), ed. Heller (*MGH, Script.* XXV) 107-108. Hans Hofmann provides, *op. cit.* 77, a synopsis and, *op. cit.* 80-64, a list of the MSS.

[96]Walter Schulten, "Kölner Reliquien," in Legner, *Ornamenta Ecclesiae* II 61-87 at 75, points out: "To this day we have learned nothing of a tomb of the Three Kings from which St. Helena, according to the legend, might have removed the three bodies."

[97]Hans Hofmann, *op. cit.* 75-76 and 94-95. Hofmann, *op. cit.* 94, deems it likely that our anonymous *vita* was composed only after this event and that before then there was in Milan a well-developed cult of St. Eustorgius, but not of the Three Kings.

[98]*Op. cit.* (n. 109 above) II 72-74; 75.

[99]Boussel, *op. cit.* 139-40, rejects the entire account.

been taken from Alexandria by Helena.[100]   But it is most unlikely that Helena included Alexandria in the itinerary of her pilgrimage.

According to a late (ca. 1480) and curious tradition Helena brought to Rome, specifically to the area then taken up by the Circus of Nero but now known as the Campo Santo Teutonico, earth from Jerusalem's Akeldama or Potter's Field (*not* from Mt. Calvary).[101]   We have seen in chapter VII above that she is also supposed to have brought earth from Mt. Calvary to Rome's Church of Santa Croce in Gerusalemme. Both traditions date from the late 15th century.

---

[100]*Chronicon Venetum* (*MGH, Script.* VII 5; Migne, *PL* CXXXIX 878; ed. Giovanni Monticolo in *Fonti per la storia d'Italia* IX = *Chronache Veneziane antichissime* [Rome 1890] I 62-63); Manitius II 246-49; Kurt Weitzman, "The Ivories of the so-called Grado Chair," *DOP* 26 (1972) 43-91 at 52.

[101]German ed. of the *Mirabilia Romae*, ca. 1480, near the end (facsimile ed. Berlin 1907); Paul Maria Baumgarten, *Cartularium Vetus Campi Sancti Teutonicorum de Urbe* (Rome 1908) 39, n. 1; Albrecht Weiland, *Der Campo Santo Teutonico in Rom und seine Grabdenkmäler* (Rome 1988) 40-43. I owe the reference to the courtesy of Prälat Erwin Gatz; August Schuchert, in *Frühchristliche Kunst aus Rom* 17, is in error. A similar tradition holds that earth from Mt. Calvary was shipped to Pisa's Camposanto.

Chapter XI.
Possible Residence in Constantinople and Death

Very shortly after his victory over Licinius, before the year 324 had come to an end, Constantine forged ahead with his plans for 'the new Rome,' and the new city was dedicated on May 11, 330.[1] None of our sources states specifically that Helena ever resided in the new city. It is most unlikely that she set foot in it before her pilgrimage to the Holy Land. On the other hand it is a reasonable assumption that she spent some time in the city between her return and her death.

Concerning the foundation of Constantinople's Church of the Holy Apostles there are two traditions in our sources and in modern scholarship.[2] One of these holds that the church was built by Constantine, or at least begun by him; the other holds that it was built by Constantius II.[3] There is also a report which associates Helena with her son in the construction of this church. It is this report which we must investigate.

---

[1]*MGH, AA* IX = *Chron. Min.* I 233 and 643.

[2]The Church of the Holy Apostles was taken down by the Turks in 1461, and on its site a mosque was erected, the Fatih Mosque or Mosque of Muhammed the Conqueror. The literature on the churches of Constantinople is voluminous. Among more recent works one should note the following: Raymond Janin, *La géographie ecclésiatique de l'empire byzantin* I.3, 2nd ed. (Paris 1969); Thomas F. Mathews, *The Early Churches of Constantinople: Architecture and Liturgy* (University Park, Pennsylvania, 1971); Thomas F. Mathews, *The Byzantine Churches of Istanbul: A Photographic Essay* (University Park, Pennsylvania, 1976).

[3]Heisenberg, *op. cit.* II 97-117; Alfons Maria Schneider, *Byzanz* (Berlin 1936) 52-53; Agathe Kaniuth, *Die Beizetzung Konstantins des Grossen* (Breslau 1941) 10-12; Grabar, *Martyrium* I 227-34; Jean Ebersolt, *Constantinople: Recueil d'études d'archéologie et d'histoire* (Paris 1951) 31-33; Glanville Downey, "The Builder of the Original Church of the Apostles at Constantinople," *DOP* 6 (1951) 51-80; Joseph Vogt, "Der Erbauer der Apostelkirche in Konstantinopel," *Hermes* 81 (1953) 111-17; Philip Grierson, "The Tombs and Obits of the Byzantine Emperors (337-1042)," *DOP* 16 (1962) 1-60 at 4-5; Richard Krautheimer, "Zu Konstantins Apostelkirche in Konstantinopel," in *Mullus: Festschrift Theodor Klauser, JbAC,* suppl. 1 (1964) 224-29; Janin, *op. cit.* (n. 2 above) 42; Dagron, *Naissance d'une capitale* 401-409; Müller-Wiener, *op. cit.* 405; Krautheimer, *Early Chr. and Byz. Architecture*[4] 69-70; Krautheimer, *Three Christian Capitals* 56-60; Cyril Mango, *Le développement urbain de Constantinople (IVe-VIIe siècles)* (Paris 1985) 27; Marcell Restle, "Konstantinopel," in *RBK*, fasc. 27/28 (1989) 366-639 and fasc. 29/30 (1990) 641-737 at 370 and 377.

A Byzantine text of the tenth century, the *Patria Konstantinoupoleos* of pseudo-Codinus mentions three times that Constantine and
Helena built the Church of the Holy Apostles in a joint effort, adding in
one case that Constantine and Helena both lie buried there.[4] But if
Constantine built the church at all he did so shortly before his death,
perhaps in 336.[5] By then Helena had been dead for a number of years.[6]
Thus any report of Helena's participation in the construction of this
church must be rejected.[7]

The same text gives credit to Helena for having founded several
other churches or monasteries in Constantinople. These are:

    1.   The Church of St. Mocius (jointly with Constantine).[8]
    2.   The Monastery of Bethlehem.[9]
    3.   The Monastery of the Gastria.[10]

---

[4]1.50, 3.1, and 4.32 (Migne, *PG* CLVII 457, 548, and 632; ed. Preger II 140, 214,
and 286); Jean Paul Richter, *Quellen der byzantinischen Kunstgeschichte* (Vienna 1897)
102, no. 133; Heisenberg, *op. cit.* II 103 and 106. On this text see the following:
Krumbacher, *op. cit.* I 423-24; Hunger, *Die hochsprachliche profane Literatur* I 536-37;
Gilbert Dagron, *Constantinople imaginaire* (Paris 1984) 21-22; Albrecht Berger,
Untersuchungen zu den Patria Konstantinoupoleos (Bonn 1988).

[5]Euseb. *Vita Const.* 4.58-60 (Migne, *PG* XX 1209-12; ed. Winkelmann [*GCS*] 144-
45); Heisenberg, *op. cit.* II 97 and 110; Ebersolt, *Constantinople* 31.

[6]See below, this chapter; Heisenberg, *op. cit.* II 110, does not take into account the
correct date of Helena's death.

[7]Janin, *La géographie ecclésiastique* I.3² 42; Maclagan, *op. cit.* 50.

[8]*Patria* 3.3 (Migne *PG* CLVII 548; ed. Preger II 215); Jean Paul Richter, *op. cit.*
120-22, nos. 180-87; Ebersolt, *Constantinople* 74-76; Janin, *La géographie ecclésiastique*
I.3² 354-58; Maraval, *op. cit.* 407. Other sources, cited by Janin, *loc. cit.* attribute the
church to Constantine alone. The church no longer exists.

[9]*Patria* 3.4 (Migne, *PG* CLVII 548; ed. Preger II 215); Jean Paul Richter, *op. cit.*
132, no. 218; Janin, *Constantinople byzantine*² 322; Janin, *La géographie ecclésiastique*
I.3² 63. The location and history of this monastery are not known.

[10]*Patria* 3.4 (Migne, *PG* CLVII 548; ed. Preger II 215); Jean Paul Richter, *op. cit.*
132-33, no. 218; Alexander Van Millingen, *Byzantine Churches in Constantinople*
(London 1912) 268; Raymond Janin, "Les couvents secondaires de Psamathia," *EO* 32
(1933) 325-39 at 332-37; Janin, *Constantinople byzantine*² 353-54; Janin, *La géographie
ecclésiastique* I.3 67-68; Γαστρία is derived, according to the *Patria* from γάστραι,
"pots" or "vases." In these pots or vases Helena supposedly planted various plants which
she brought with her from Jerusalem. The church of this monastery was converted into
a mosque, called Sandjakdar Mesdjid, or Mosque of the Standard Bearer.

4.   The Church of St. Theodore of Claudius.[11]
5.   The Church of St. Romanus.[12]
6.   The Monastery of Sts. Carpus and Papylus.[13]
All these attributions must be rejected for a number of reasons:
1.   There certainly were no monasteries in Constantinople in Helena's lifetime.[14]
2.   Helena's stay in Constantinople certainly was too short to allow for much such activity.
3.   Local ambition and disregard for historical facts not infrequently prompted fictitious attributions, both in the West and the East. Alleged Constantinian foundations are especially suspect.[15]

[11]*Patria* 3.5 (Migne, *PG* CLVII 548; ed. Preger II 216); Jean Paul Richter, op. cit. 132, no. 216; Raymond Janin, "Les églises byzantines des saints militaires," *EO* 34 (1935) 56-70 at 60-61; Janin, *La géographie ecclésiastique* I.3² 149. There were numerous other churches of St. Theodore; hence the peculiar name. See Van Millingen, *op. cit.* 244; The same passage credits Helena with having founded the palace of Psomathea and a nursing home (γηροκομεῖον); Jean Paul Richter, *op. cit.* 376, no. 1002; Christian Gnilka, "Altersversorgung" in *RAC,* suppl. 1-2 (1985) 266-89 at 287. But the γηροκομεῖον of Helena was founded by Helena, the wife of Constantine VII Porphyrogenitus; see the following: Jean Paul Richter, *op. cit.,* 234, no. 605; Janin, *Constantinople byzantine²* 355; Demetrios J. Constantelos, *Byzantine Philanthropy and Social Welfare,* 2nd ed. (New Rochelle, New York, 1991) 163 and 170-71; Janin, *La géographie ecclésiastique* I.3² 554; Arnold Toynbee, *Constantine Porphyrogenitus and His World* (London 1973) 223.

[12]*Patria* 3.81 (Migne, *PG* CLVII 577; ed. Preger II 245); Jean Paul Richter, *op. cit.* 131-32, no. 215; Janin, *La géographie ecclésiastique* I.3² 448-49. The church no longer exists.

[13]*Patria* 3.82 (Migne, *PG* CLVII 577; ed. Preger II 245); Jean Paul Richter, *op. cit.* 134, no. 223. Alfons Maria Schneider, *Byzanz* 1-4, gives a possible location. Janin, *La géographie ecclésiastique* I.3² 279; Müller-Wiener, *op. cit.* 187; Restle, "Konstantinopel" 377-78.

[14]Wulf, *op. cit.* 357; Hans-Georg Beck, *Kirche und theologische Literatur* 213; Hunger, *Reich der neuen Mitte* 248; Gilbert Dagron, "Le moines et la ville: Le monachisme à Constantinople jusqu'au concile de Chalcédoine (451)," *Travaux et Mémoires* 4 (1970) 229-76 at 229-30; A.H.M. Jones, *The Later Roman Empire* II 929-30; Karl Baus and Eugen Ewig, *Handbuch der Kirchengeschichte,* ed. Hubert Jedin, II.1 (Freiburg 1973) 384; Dagron, *Naissance d'une capitale* 513-15; Cyril Mango, *Byzantium* (New York 1980) 110-11; Hans-Georg Beck, "Constantinople: The Rise of a New Capital in the East," in Kurt Weitzmann, ed., *Age of Spirituality: A Symposium* (New York 1980) 29-37 at 31; Frend, *op. cit.* 747 with n. 32.

[15]Raymond Janin, "Églises et monastères de Constantinople byzantine," *REB* 9 (1951) 143-53 at 147-48.

The existence of a monastery of St. Helena in Constantinople, whether founded by her or merely named after her, is also to be questioned, as it is reported only by a single, late, and Latin source.[16]

Procopius, in the course of reporting the events of 532, mentions "a palace named after Helena."[17] This palace can probably be identified with the Helenianae.[18] This latter name has also been applied, perhaps erroneously, to the quarter in which the palace was located.[19] It is not claimed by our sources that Helena built this palace or resided in it. Within this palace there were baths called the Heleniana. These are mentioned repeatedly in the context of events transpiring in 498.[20]

The city was well provided with statues of Helena, as it was with statuary in general. It is, however, impossible, because of the inadequacy of our sources, to determine their correct number or to learn very much about them.

The Milion in the center of Constantinople was a small structure, probably a tetrapylon, from which all distances were measured and from which several major roads took their departure. It was thus comparable to the Miliarium Aureum in the Forum of Rome. Two Byzantine texts, the *Parastaseis Syntomoi Chronikai* of the early eighth century and the

---

[16]See chapter XII below, nn. 27-29.

[17]*Pers.* 1.24.30; Jean Paul Richter, *op. cit.* 377, no. 1005.

[18]Charles du Fresne du Cagne, *Constantinopolis Christiana* (Paris 1680) II 130; Janin, *Constantinople byzantine*² 131.

[19]*Ibid.* 355-56; Victor Tiftixoglu, "Die Helenianai nebst einigen anderen Besitzungen im Vorfeld des frühen Konstantinopel," in *Studien zur Frühgeschichte Konstantinopels,* ed. Hans-Georg Beck (Munich 1973) 49-120 at 49-54.

[20]*Chronicle* of Victor, ad annum 498 (Migne, *PL* LXVIII 949; *MGH, AA* XI = *Chron. Min.* II 193). Victor reports that a certain Olympius, an Arian and a blasphemer, died while bathing in these baths. Victor was bishop of Tunnuna or Tonnenna (?) in North Africa; his chronicle covers the years 444-566. See the following: Gröber, *op. cit.* 100; Bardenhewer, *op. cit.* V 329-30; Manitius I 215; Altaner-Stuiber, *op. cit.* 233. A more elaborate version of Olympius' death is found in Theodorus Lector (Theodoros Anagnostes), *Hist. Eccl.* 4, fr. (Migne, *PG* LXXXVI 221-23; ed. Hansen [*GCS*] 131-33). On Theodorus Lector, of the sixth century, see the following: Bardenhewer, *op. cit.* V 117-18; Altaner-Stuiber, *op. cit.* 228-29. In the eighth century the account given by Theodorus Lector was utilized by St. John Damascene, *De Imaginibus* 3 (Migne, *PG* XCIV 1389); Jean Paul Richter, *op. cit.* 148, no. 273; Cyril Mango, *Art of the Byzantine Empire, 312-1453* (Englewood Cliffs, New Jersey, 1972) 35-36. On St. John Damascene see the following: Albert Ehrhard in Krumbacher, *op. cit.* 168-71; Bardenhewer, *op. cit.* V 51-66; Hans-Georg Beck, *Kirche und theologische Literatur* 476-86; Altaner-Stuiber, op. cit. 526-32. The episode is mentioned briefly also by Theophanes (Homologetes or Confessor, of the eighth century), *Chronographia*, ad annum mundi 5991 (Migne, *PG* CVIII 341; ed. de Boor I 142); Jean Paul Richter, *op. cit.* 377, no. 1008.

Patria Konstantinoupoleos, cited above, report that the Milion was topped by statues of Constantine and Helena, with a cross between them.[21] There was a second statuary group of Constantine and Helena in the Forum of Constantine, again with a cross between them.[22] In the *Forum Bovis* or Βοῦς, there was a third such group.[23] These groups, however, cannot have been of Constantinian date, since they are obviously inspired by the post-Constantinian legend of the True Cross.[24]

In the square called Philadelphion there stood individual statues of Constantine, his mother, and two of his sons. There was also a statuary group of two of his sons embracing each other; from this group, which has been identified with the tetrarchs at St. Mark's in Venice, the square derived its name. Since Fausta and Crispus had been eliminated in 326 and Constans was not appointed a Caesar until 333, we may assume that the two sons represented were Constantine and Constantius and that all of the statues were put in place between 326 and 333.[25]

---

[21]Krumbacher, *op. cit.* I 424; ed. Averil Cameron and Judith Herrin (Leiden 1984) 17. Gabriel Millet, "*Parastaseis Syntomoi Chronikai:* Essai sur la date," *BCH* 70 (1946) 393-402, attempted to date this text more specifically to 742-746. Dagron, *Constantinople imaginaire* 29-48, examines this text at length; Kazhdan, "*Constantine imaginaire*" 249-50, deems it a "work of burlesque, a bouffonade, a parody." *Parastaseis Syntomoi Chronikai* 34 (Migne, *PG* CLVII 676; ed. Preger I 38; ed. Cameron and Herrin 94-95 and 208); *Patria* 2.29 (Migne, *PG* CLVII 492; ed. Preger II 166); André Grabar, *L'empereur dans l'art byzantin* (Paris 1936) 38; Cyril Mango, *The Brazen House* (Copenhagen 1959) 47-48; Janin, *Constantinople byzantine*[2] 104; André Grabar, *L'art de la fin de l'antiquité et du moyen âge* (Paris 1968)) I 258; Maclagan, op. cit. 23; Rodolphe Guilland, *Études de topographie de Constantinople byzantine* (Amsterdam 1969) II 28; Christopher Walter, *L'iconographie des conciles dans la tradition byzantine* (Paris 1970) 230; Beckwith, *Early Christian and Byzantine Art* 77; Dagron, *Naissance d'une capitale* 37; George M. A. Hanfmann, *From Croesus to Constantine* (Ann Arbor 1975) 86 and fig. 178; Müller-Wiener, *op. cit.* 216.

[22]*Parastaseis Syntomoi Chronikai* 16 (Migne, *PG* CLVII 665; ed. Preger I 30-31; ed. Cameron and Herrin 78-81 and 192); Pseudo-Codinus, *Patria Konstantinoupoleos* 2.16 and 2.102 (Migne, *PG* CLVII 484; ed. Preger II 158 and 205); Janin, *Constantinople byzantine*[2] 63.

[23]*Parastaseis Syntomoi Chronikai* 52 (Migne, *PG* CLVII 700; ed. Preger I 54; ed. Cameron and Herrin 126-27 and 239-40); Janin, *Constantinople byzantine*[2] 69-71.

[24]So, correctly, Cameron and Herrin. edd., *Parastaseis Syntomoi Chronikai* 37 and 193.

[25]*Parastaseis Syntomoi Chronikai* 58 (Migne, *PG* CLVII 704; ed. Preger I 58; ed. Cameron and Herrin 134-35 and 247); Delbrueck, *Antike Porphyrwerke*, pp. XX, 26, and 117; Janin, *Constantinople byzantine*[2] 410; Mango, *Le développement urbain* 28-29; Restle, "Konstantinopel" 402 and 697-98; Pseudo-Codinus, *Patria Konstantinoupoleos*

(continued...)

In the Constantinian Church of St. Sophia there stood, among other statues, three statues of Helena: one of porphyry, one of silver on a bronze column, and one of ivory. Whether they were placed there by Constantine or by one of his successors is not reported; they were eventually taken elsewhere by Justinian.[26]

The Senate House which stood in the Augusteum was destroyed by a fire in 404, during the reign of Arcadius (395-408).[27]   A badly garbled account blames this fire on Theodosius II (408-450) and reports that statues of Constantine, Fausta (the daughter of Diocletian!), and Helena were saved. The account does not inspire confidence.[28]

An open court in Constantinople, the *Augusteum*, was so called in honor of the *Augusta* Helena, and in it Constantine erected a porphyry column topped by a statue of his mother.[29]

[25](...continued)
2.50 (Migne, *PG* CLVII 508; ed. Preger II 178), mentions only the statues of Constantine's sons, but not those of Constantine and Helena. On the Philadelphion see Müller-Wiener, *op. cit.* 266-67.

[26]*Parastaseis Syntomoi Chronikai* 11 (Migne, *PG* CLVII 661; ed. Preger I 27; ed. Cameron and Herrin 70-73 and 184); Pseudo-Codinus, *Patria Konstantinoupoleos* 2.96 (Migne, *PG* CLVII 537; ed. Preger II 202); Jean Paul Richter, *op. cit.* 13-14, no. 39; Delbrueck, *Antike Porphyrwerke*, pp. XXI and 118.

[27]Mango, *The Brazen House* 56; Dagron, *Naissance d'une capitale* 139; Müller-Wiener, *op. cit.* 248. The same building was destroyed by fire again in 532, in the course of the famous Nika Revolt; see J. B. Bury, *History of the Later Roman Empire* (London 1923) II 40-41, Dagron, *loc. cit.,* and Müller-Wiener, *loc. cit.* There was a second Senate House in the Forum of Constantine.

[28]*Parastaseis Syntomoi Chronikai* 43 (Migne, *PG* CLVII 692; ed. Preger I 50-51; ed. Cameron and Herrin 118-21 and 230-32); Delbrueck, *Antike Porphyrwerke*, p. XX.

[29]Hesychius Illustris (of Miletus, 6th century), *Patria Konstantinoupoleos* 40 (*FHG* IV 154; ed. Preger I 17); *Chronicon Paschale* Olymp. 277, sub anno 328 (Migne, *PG* XCII 709; ed. Dindorf [*CSHB* XVI] I 528-29; *MGH, AA* IX = *Chron. Min.* I 233); Pseudo-Codinus, *Patria Konstantinoupoleos* 1.44 and 2.15 (Migne, *PG* CLVII 456 and 484, ed. Preger II 138 and 158); Jean Paul Richter, *op. cit.* 394, no. 1073. On Hesychius see Krumbacher, *op. cit.* I 323-25, and Hunger, *Die hochsprachliche profane Literatur* I 536; Johannes Malalas, *Chron.* 13.8 (Migne, *PG* XCVII 480-81; ed. Dindorf [*CSHB* VIII] 321); Mango, *The Brazen House* 46; Janin, *Constantinople byzantine*[2] 59-60 and 73; Maclagan, *op. cit.* 65; Beckwith, *The Art of Constantinople*[2] 7; Guilland, *op. cit.* II 44; Mango, *Art of the Byzantine Empire, 312-1453* 10; Dagron, *Naissance d'une capitale* 374, n. 6; Müller-Wiener, *op. cit.* 248; Dagron, *Constantinople imaginaire* 58.

In an area known as the Kontaria Constantine reportedly built a church of the Theotokos, "portraying himself and his mother and Jesus and the Virgin."[30]

In that quarter of the city which came to be known as the Dihippion the emperor Phocas (602-610) erected two statues of Constantine and Helena respectively.[31]

Reinhold Lubenau, a German traveler who visited Constantinople in 1587, claimed to have seen in the Church of St. Sophia, in one of the galleries, a mosaic depicting Constantine, Helena, and Fausta.[32] We have reason to be skeptical and, in any event, do not learn the date of the mosaic.

The evidence assembled here fails to establish that Helena ever resided in Constantinople. On the other hand I do not think that all of these traditions are without some basis in fact. And it appears that Helena was held in high regard not only by Constantine but also by his successors and by the people. Let us next consider the time and place of Helena's death.

It is clear from our ancient sources that Helena died shortly after her return from the Holy Land and in the presence of her son, but we are given neither a specific year nor a specific place. Eusebius tells us that Helena died in her 80th year, that she had liberally provided in her will for her son and her grandsons, and that Constantine was at her side.[33] Socrates and Sozomen simply say that she was about 80 years old at the time of her death.[34] The text of Theodoret suggests that she

[30]*Parastaseis Syntomoi Chronikai* 53 (Migne, *PG* CLVII 700; ed. Preger I 55; ed. Cameron and Herrin 128-29 and 240); Pseudo-Codinus, *Patria Konstantinoupoleos* 2.66 (Migne, *PG* CLVII 520; ed. Preger II 187).

[31]Cyril Mango, "Le Diippion: Étude historique et topographique," *REB* 8 (1950) 152-61; Guilland, *op. cit.* I 393. Pseudo-Codinus, *Patria Konstantinoupoleos* 2.35 (Migne, *PG* CLVII 496; ed. Preger II 169-70); Janin, *Constantinople byzantine²* 342-43.

[32]Cyril Mango, *Materials for the Study of the Mosaics of St. Sophia at Istanbul* (Washington, D. C., 1962) 119-20.

[33]*Vita Const.* 3.46 (Migne, *PG* XX 1105; ed. Winkelmann [*GCS*] 103).

[34]*Hist. Eccl.* 1.17 (Migne, *PG* LXVII 121; ed. Bright² 37). *Hist. Eccl.* 2.2.4 (Migne, *PG* LXVII 936; ed. Bidez-Hansen [*GCS* L] 51; ed. Bidez [*SC* CCCVI] 234).

died at Constantine's court.[35] Mediaeval chronicles, not surprisingly, are of little or no assistance.[36]

Since Helena undertook her pilgrimage, as we have seen, in 326 and since this pilgrimage must have required many months, most scholars place Helena's death in 328, 329, or even 330.[37] The year 327 has also been proposed.[38] A full examination of the numismatic evidence by Patrick Bruun points to 329 as the year of Helena's death.[39]

In the years 335-337, supposedly, the imperial mints of Rome, Constantinople, and Trier issued coins of the type *nummus centenionalis* which bear on the reverse a figure of Peace with the legend PAX PVB-LICA and on the obverse a bust of Helena with the legend FL(aviae) IVL(iae) HELENAE AUG(ustae).[40] Otto Seeck assumed that such coins could have been issued only while Helena was alive and dated Helena's death to 336.[41] In fact these coins are part of a commemora-

[35]*Hist. Eccl.* 1.17 in Migne, *PG* LXXXII 961-62; 1.18.9 in ed. Parmentier-Scheidweiler (*GCS* XLIV) 65.

[36]The *Chronicon* of Alberich of Trois-Fontaines (13th century; *MGH, Script.* XXIII 685) places Constantine's baptism and the *inventio* of the Cross both in 318 and Helena's death in 332.

[37]Chapter VIII above. Maurice, *Numismatique Constantinienne* I, pp. CXLI and CXLVIII; Maurice, *Sainte Hélène* 14 and 55: 329; Voelkl, *op. cit.* 177: 329; Réau, *Iconographie* III.2: 329; Vogt, *Constantin²* 249: 329; Vogt, "Heiden und Christen" 159: 329; Mackes, *op. cit.* 185: 328 or 329; Hans-Henning Lauer, *op. cit.* 32: 328 or 329; MacMullen, *Constantine* 187: 329 or 330; Andreas Alföldi, *The Conversion of Constantine* 104: 330; *PLRE* I 411: 330; Dietz, "St. Helena" 357: 328 or 329; Vodová, "La chronologie" 68 and 71: 328 or 329; Richard Klein in *RAC* XIV 358: 328 or 329; Drijvers, *op. cit.* 73: 328 or 329.

[38]Barnes, *Constantine and Eusebius* 221 and *New Empire* 9. But Barnes finds it necessary to move the refoundation of Drepanum as Helenopolis from 327 (Euseb.-Hieron. *Chron.; Chronicon Paschale*) to January 7, 328 (the feast day of St. Lucian) and to *assume* that this act was in memory of Helena *after her demise*. I have not been convinced. On the practice of giving dynastic names to cities see A. H. M. Jones *The Later Roman Empire* I 719-20.

[39]*RIC* VII 72-73 with n. 6; also *ibid.* 233 and 420.

[40]Cohen VII² (1888) 95, nos. 4 and 6 (no date assigned); Maurice, *Numismatique Constantinienne* I 261, no. I (Rome); I 495, no. II, 498, no. III, and pl. XXIII, nos. 21 and 23 (Trier); II 535, no. VI (Constantinople); Delbrueck, *Spätantike Kaiserporträts* 86 and pl. 11, no. 14; Raissa Calza, *Iconografia romana* 169 and pl. LI, no. 160.

[41]*RE* VII.2 (1912) 2822.

tive issue of the years 337-340.[42] The three Augusti, Constantine II, Constantius II, and Constans, must have been in agreement on this, since one mint, the mint at the imperial residence, in each part of the empire participated. At the same time Theodora, Helena's one-time rival, was also honored by a commemorative issue of coins; the same three mints participated. Theodora's coins bear on the reverse the legend PIETAS ROMANA and an allegorical figure holding two children.[43]

As for the place of Helena's death a reasonable case can be made for Nicomedia or Constantinople, but not for some place in southern

---

[42]R. A. G. Carson, P. V. Hill, and J. P. C. Kent, *Late Roman Bronze Coinage* (London 1960), part I, nos. 104, 112, 119, 128 (Trier), 616, 621 (Rome), and 1046-47a (Constantinople); Vittorio Picozzi, *La monetazione imperiale Romana* (Rome 1966) 97; Richard Reece, *Roman Coins* (London 1970) 151 and pl. 56, nos. 895-96 (Trier); less precisely J. P. C. Kent, *Roman Coins* (London and New York 1978) 53; *RIC* VIII 143-44, nos. 42, 47, 55, 63-64, 78, and 90, and pl. 1, no. 63 (Trier); 250-51, nos. 27 and 53 (Rome); 449-450, nos. 33-35, 38, and 48-49, and pl. 21, no. 33 (Constantinople); David Van Meter, *The Handbook of Roman Imperial Coins* (Nashua, New Hampshire, 1991) 293. For the mint of Trier specifically see the following: Peter N. Schulten, *Die römische Münzstätte Trier von der Wiederaufnahme ihrer Tätigkeit unter Diocletian bis zum Ende der Folles-Prägung* (Frankfurt 1974) 30; Karl-Josef Gilles, *Münzprägung im römischen und mittelalterlichen Trier* (Trier 1983) 11 and 13, no. 15. Gilles' list is reproduced also in Rheinisches Landesmuseum Trier, *Trier: Kaiserresidenz und Bischossitz* 54-55, and in Heinen, *Trier und das Trevererland* 214-15. Seeck's thinking on the date of Helena's death is specifically rejected by the following: Wilhelm Kubitscheck, "Gedächtnismünzen der Kaiserinnen Helena und Theodora," *NZ*, N. F. 8 (1915) 180-84; Andreas Alföldi, *The Conversion of Constantine* 104; Vodová, "La chronologie" 68 and 72; Richard Klein in *RAC* XIV 358 and 363. Seeck's date is accepted, however, by Deichmann, "Untersuchungen" 739, and by Krautheimer, *Corpus* II (1959) 202. Most recently Timothy E. Gregory, s. v. "Helena" in *ODB* I 909, cites both *PLRE* and Seeck, apparently not wishing to commit himself to either date.

[43]Cohen VII[2] (1888) 98-99, nos. 3-5; Maurice, *Numismatique Constantinienne* I 261, no. II, and pl. XVIII, no. 18 (Rome); I 495-96, no. III, 498, no. IV, and pl. XXIII, no. 22 (Trier); II 536, no. VII, and pl. XVI, no. 6 (Constantinople); Kubitschek, *op. cit.*; Carson, Hill, and Kent, *op. cit.* part I, nos. 105, 113, 120, 129 (Trier), 617, 622 (Rome), 1048-49, and 1050 (Constantinople); Picozzi, *op. cit.* 97; Reece, *op. cit.* 151 and pl. 56, nos. 897-98 (Trier); J. P. Callu, "Pietas Romana: Les monnaies de l'impératrice Théodora," in *Melanges P. Boyancé* (Rome 1974) 141-51; Kent, *Roman Coins* 53; *RIC* VIII 143-44, nos. 43, 48, 56, 65, 79, and 91, and pl. 1, no. 43 (Trier); 250-51, nos. 28 and 54 (Rome); 449-50, nos. 36 and 50-51, and pl. 21, no. 51 (Constantinople). For the mint of Trier specifically see again Peter N. Schulten, loc. cit., and Gilles, *op. cit.* 11 and 13, no 21. Drijvers, *op. cit.* 44, holds that these commemorative coins of Helena and Theodora were issued in 337 only, between May 22, when Constantine died, and September 9, when his sons assumed the rank of Augustus; furthermore that these coins reflect the problems surrounding the succession.

Italy, Rome, the Holy Land, or Trier.[44] Since we know – I see no reason to question Eusebius on this point – that Helena died in Constantine's presence, it is necessary to correlate all reports of Helena's death with Constantine's itinerary during the years in question. Not enough attention has been paid to this in the past. Constantine was in the East throughout the year 327 and until March, 328. The rest of 328 he spent in the Balkans, at Trier, and on the Rhine frontier. in 329 he was in the Balkans again, and only in the spring of 330 did he return to the East.[45] At no time during these years was he in southern Italy, in Rome, or in the Holy Land; thus Helena cannot have died in any of these places. It is doubtful that she traveled extensively after her return from the Holy Land; this further restricts our options.

[44]Nicomedia: Barnes, *Constantine and Eusebius* 221. Constantinople: Richard Klein, *op. cit.* 358. Southern Italy: Hans-Henning Lauer, *op. cit.* 34. Rome: *PLRE* I 411; P. Van den Bosch, "Sancta Helena, nobilissima femina," *Clairlieu* 38 (1980) 71-88 at 75, 79, and 88; Wankenne, *op. cit.* 316; Kienast, *op. cit.* 300; Timothy E. Gregory, s. v. "Helena" in *ODB* I 909. The Holy Land: David Hugh Farmer, *The Oxford Dictionary of Saints* (Oxford 1982) 188; Metford, *op. cit.* 118; Norwich, *op. cit.* 70.   Trier: Drijvers, *op. cit.* 73.

[45]Seeck, *Regesten* 178-80; *RIC* VII 77-78; Barnes, *New Empire* 77-78.

Chapter XII.
Burial and Scattered Remains

Eusebius reports that Constantine had his mother's body conveyed under military escort to "the royal city" and there placed in the royal tomb.[1] Eusebius refers to Rome as the "royal city" elsewhere, but in the next century Socrates misunderstood Eusebius as referring to Constantinople, the "new Rome."[2] That Socrates was mistaken and that Helena was buried in Rome was recognized already by Baronio, and many others since Baronio have reached the same conclusion.[3] Nevertheless Socrates' error has been perpetuated by some scholars.[4]

The *Liber Pontificalis* reports that Constantine erected a basilica in honor of the martyrs Marcellinus and Peter *in territurio inter duos* (or

---

[1]*Vita Const.* 3.47.1 (Migne, *PG* XX 1108; ed. Winkelmann [*GCS*] 103).

[2]*Vita Const.* 3.7.2 (Migne, *PG* XX 1061; ed. Winkelmann [*GCS*] 84); Socrates, *Hist. Eccl.* 1.17 (Migne, *PG* LXVII 121; ed. Bright[2] 237).

[3]Baronio, *op. cit.* III 401, ad annum 326, ch. 62; Henri de Valois (Henricus Valesius) ad Euseb. *Vita Const.* 3.47.1 (Paris 1659; repr. in Migne, *PG* XX 1107, n. 31); Theodor Mommsen, *Liber Pont.* (*MGH, GPR* I), p. XXVII; Louis Duchesne, *Liber Pont.*[2] I 198, n. 90; Seeck in *RE* VII.2 (1912) 2822; Rudolf Egger, "Die Begräbnisstätte des Kaisers Konstantin," *ÖJh* 16 (1913) 212-30 at 225-26; Pio Petro Franchi de' Cavalieri, "I funerali ed il sepolcro di Constantino Magno," *MEFR* 36 (1916-1917) 205-61 at 245-46; Maurice, *Sainte Hélène* 55-57; Erik Sjöqvist and Alfred Westholm, "Zur Zeitbestimmung der Helena- und Constantiasarkophage," in Swedish Institute in Rome, *Opuscula Archaeologica* I (Lund 1935) 1-46 at 1-3; Kaniuth, *op. cit.* 33; Deichmann, *Frühchristliche Kirchen* 19; Deichmann, "Untersuchungen" 738-39 with n. 2; Voelkl, *op. cit.* 177; Friedrich Wilhelm Deichmann and Arnold Tschira, "Das Mausoleum der Kaiserin Helena und die Basilika der heiligen Marcellinus und Petrus vor Rom," *JDAI* 72 (1957) 44-110 at 76 with n. 90; Vogt, "Heiden und Christen" 159; Andreas Alföldi, *The Conversion of Constantine* 104; Piganiol, *op. cit.* 44, n. 2; Pietri, *op. cit.* I 32, no. 5; E. D. Hunt, *op. cit.* 31, n. 21; Jean Guyon, *Le cimetière aux deux lauriers* (Vatican City 1987) 257; Richard Klein, *op. cit.* 358; Demandt, *op. cit.* 68 and 380. Borgehammar, *op. cit.* 72; Drijvers, *op. cit.* 74. *PLRE* I 411 misinterprets Eusebius as saying that Helena died at Rome and ignores Socrates' reference to Constantinople. One important argument against Socrates' interpretation is that Constantinople's Church of the Holy Apostles would not yet have been ready to receive Helena's burial. In an interesting parallel Constantina, Constantine's daughter, died in 354 in Bithynia, but was buried in the well-known mausoleum on the Via Nomentana in Rome; see *PLRE* I 222.

[4]Rodolfo Lanciani, *Pagan and Christian Rome* (London 1892) 198; Mackes, *op. cit.* 186; Dietz, "St. Helena" 357.

duas) lauros, and also a mausoleum, where his mother Helena Augusta is buried, on the Via Labicana, at the third milestone.[5] The ancient Via Labicana is today's Via Casilina, which leads southeast from the city into the Roman Campagna. And on this road indeed, three miles from the Porta Maggiore, behind the Church of Sts. Marcellinus and Peter and adjacent to the catacombs of Peter and Marcellinus, we find substantial remains of a large ancient structure. This structure is popularly known as Tor Pignattara, from the clay pots ("pignatte") which are built into its vault and are plainly visible. The structure was a vaulted rotunda, and, with an interior diameter of 20 m., of imposing dimensions. A house and a small church were built within the ancient ruins in the 17th century. This, then, is the mausoleum to which the *Liber Pontificalis* refers. The rotunda was linked by means of a rectangular entrance hall to the east end of the ancient basilica, of which only some foundation walls have survived. This kind of arrangement was employed a few years later in the Church of the Holy Sepulchre at Jerusalem, the Church of the Nativity at Bethlehem, and the Church of the Holy Apostles at Constantinople. A rectangular niche in the mausoleum wall, facing the entrance, accommodated the sarcophagus which is now in the Sala a Croce Greca of the Vatican Museum.[6]

---

[5]Migne, *PL* VIII 809; ed. Mommsen (*MGH, GPR* I) 65-66; ed. Duchesne[2] I 182. Sjöqvist and Westholm, *op. cit.* 4, also citing Anastasius Bibliothecarius; Valentini and Zucchetti, *op. cit.* II (1942) 232; Deichmann and Tschira, *op. cit.* 74; Bovini, *Edifici cristiani* 162; Odahl, *Early Christian Latin Literature* 150.

[6]Antonio Bosio, *Roma sotterranea* (edd. Rome 1650 and 1710) 342-43; Hülsen, *Le chiese* 261-62, no. 3, and 419-20, no. 17; Carlo Cecchelli and Edoardo Persico, *SS. Marcellino e Pietro* (Rome 1936) 48, 53-54, and 72; Friedrich Wilhelm Deichmann, "Untersuchungen an spätrömischen Rundbauten in Rom und Latium," *JDAI, AA* 1941, pp. 733-48 at 735-37 and ill. 1-3; Armellini, *op. cit.* II 1094-97; Deichmann, *Frühchristliche Kirchen* 19-21, 79, ill. 3-4, and plan 2; Deichmann and Tschira, *op. cit.* 46-81; Voelkl, *op. cit.* 154 and ill. 58; Krautheimer, *Corpus* II (1959) 191-204, after Deichmann and Tschira, *op.cit.;* Bovini, *Edifici cristiani* 160-62 and 172-74; Pietri, *op. cit.* I 29-33; Brandenburg, *Roms frühchristliche Basiliken* 60-71; Guyon, *op. cit.* 207-63. Odahl, "The Christian Basilicas" 20 and ill. 33-35. Deichmann and Tschira, *op. cit.* 64 and 74, and Brandenburg, *Roms frühchristliche Basiliken* 69, have shown that the basilica was built first and then the mausoleum; Krautheimer, *Corpus* II (1959) 202, agrees. Voelkl, *op. cit.* 154, and Vogt, "Constantinus der Grosse" 370, less carefully assume the reverse. The basilica had its apse in the west and its narthex in the east. The use of terracotta amphorae in the construction of the vault, which accounts for the modern popular name of the mausoleum, has a parallel in the Church of St. Gereon in Cologne. See the following: Hellenkemper in *Führer Köln* II 194, 195 and 200; Deckers, "St. Gereon" 104; Schäfke, *Kölns r. Kirchen*[5] 101, or id., *St. Gereon* 3.

Plate VIII

The Mausoleum of St. Helena, now called the 'Tor Pignattara,' on Rome's ancient *Via Labicana.*

The porphyry sarcophagus of St. Helena, now in the Sala a Croce Greco, Vatican Museum.

That the mausoleum on the Via Labicana was the site of Helena's burial is confirmed in the seventh century by two itineraries, *Notitia Ecclesiarum Urbis Romae* (or *Itinerarium Salisburgense*) and *De Locis Sanctorum Martyrum Quae Sunt Foris Civitatis Romae* (or *Epitome Salisburgensis*), at the time of Charlemagne by the *Itinerarium Einsidlense*, and in the ninth century by the Martyrology of Usuard.[7] It was also known to William of Malmesbury in the first half of the 12th century.[8] Bede very specifically refers to the sarcophagus of porphyry.[9]

It is generally and correctly, it seems to me, assumed that the sarcophagus and/or the mausoleum were originally intended for Constantine himself; and the wording of the *Liber Pontificalis* does not preclude this.[10]

---

[7]Migne, *PL* CI 1361; De Rossi, *Roma sotterranea* I 139 and 178; Cecchelli and Persico, *op. cit.* 50-51; Valentini and Zucchetti, *op. cit.* II (1942) 83; Deichmann and Tschira, *op. cit.* 78; Krautheimer, *Corpus* II (1959) 193; Ed. Glorie (*CC, Ser. Lat.* CLXXV) 307. On the sole MS, once in Salzburg, now in Vienna, and on the date see Valentini and Zucchetti, *op. cit.* II (1942) 69, and Kötting, *op. cit.* 364, n. 11. Migne, *PL* CI 1364; De Rossi, *Roma sotterranea* I 142 and 178; Cecchelli and Persico, *op. cit.* 50-51; Valentini and Zucchetti, *op. cit.* II (1942) 113; Krautheimer, *Corpus* II (1959) 194; Ed. Glorie (*CC, Ser. Lat.* CLXXV) 318; Bovini, *Edifici cristiani* 177. On the MSS, two of which were formerly in Salzburg but are now in Vienna, and on the date see Valentini and Zucchetti, *op. cit.* II (1942) 101-103, and Kötting, *op. cit.* 365, n. 120. *Codex Einsidlensis* 326 (at the monastery of Einsiedeln in Switzerland), folios 82v-83r; Henri Jordan and Christian Hülsen, *Topographie der Stadt Rom im Alterthum* II (Berlin 1871) 652-53; De Rossi, *Roma sotterranea* I 179; Rodolfo Lanciani, *L'itinerario die Einsiedeln e l'ordine di Benedetto canonico* (Rome 1891) 11-12; Christian Hülsen, *La pianta di Roma dell'anonimo einsidlense* (Rome 1907) 28 and pl. III; Valentini and Zucchetti, *op. cit.* II (1942) 194; Kötting, *op. cit.* 366. Lugli, *Fontes* IV (1957) 31, no. 15; Ed. Glorie (*CC, Ser. Lat.* CLXXV) 338; Gerold Walser, *Die Einsiedler Inschriftensammlung und der Pilgerführer durch Rom* (Stuttgart 1987) 150-51 and 166-89. August 18 (Migne, *PL* CXXIV 373-74; ed. Dubois [*Subsidia Hagiographica* 40] 285); Guyon, *op. cit.* 468, n. 53.

[8]*Gesta Regum Anglorum* 4.352 (Migne, *PL* CLXXIX 1305, ed. Hardy [London 1840; repr. Vaduz 1964] II 541-42; ed. Stubbs [Rolls Series XC.2] 406); De Rossi, *Roma sotterranea* I 179; Valentini and Zucchetti, *op. cit.* II (1942) 146; Kötting, *op. cit.* 365-66; Ed. Glorie (*CC, Ser. Lat.* CLXXV) 326.

[9]*Chron.* 420 (*MGH, AA* XIII = *Chron. Min.* III 296).

[10]Maurice, *Sainte Hélène* 56-57; Deichmann, "Untersuchungen" 740 and *Frühchristliche Kirchen* 19; Deichmann and Tschira, op. cit. 64, 74, and 77; Krautheimer, *Corpus* II (1959) 202; Bovini, *Edifici cristiani* 174; Andreas Alföldi, *The Conversion of Constantine* 104; MacMullen, *Constantine* 142; Buchowiecki, *op. cit.* II 332; Brandenburg, *Roms frühchristliche Basiliken* 70; Krautheimer, *Rome: Profile of a City* 25, 28, and 213; Krautheimer, *Three Christian Capitals* 23; Guyon, *op. cit.* 257-
(continued...)

Pope Anastasius IV (1153-1154) ordered the great sarcophagus to be moved to the Lateran Basilica, where it was to serve as his own tomb.[11] Finally, under Pope Pius VI (1775-1799), it was taken to the Vatican.[12] Because of its size, history, and prominent display it is one of the best-known monuments of late antiquity. But its value to art historians is diminished by the fact that it was severely damaged in the 17th century and was extensively restored over a period of no less than nine years (1778-1787).[13] The battle scenes which decorate all four sides certainly

[10](...continued)
58; Richard Klein, op. cit. 358; Demandt, op. cit. 68 and 380; Drijvers, op. cit. 75. It has also been suggested, less convincingly, that the sarcophagus belonged really to Constantius Chlorus: Jean Ebersolt, "Sarcophages impériaux de Rome et de Constantinople," BZ 30 (1929-1930) 582-87 at 586; Delbrueck, Antike Porphyrwerke 215-16; Hunger, Reich der neuen Mitte 88; Sjöqvist and Westholm, op. cit. 33-42, assign the sarcophagus to the second century. Barnes, Constantine and Eusebius 221 , is wrong, it seems to me, in suggesting that the sarcophagus was constructed in the East on the occasion of Helena's death and then transported to Rome. Milburn, op. cit. 77, goes too far in questioning whether the sarcophagus ever contained Helena's body.

[11]Liber Pont., ed. Duchesne² II 388 with n. 3; Johannes Diaconus Romanus (ca. 1170), Liber de Ecclesia Lateranensi or Descriptio Lateranensis Ecclesiae (Migne, PL CXCIV 1553); Sjöqvist and Westholm, op. cit. 6; Valentini and Zucchetti, op. cit. III (1946) 351; Acta Sanct. Aug. III (ed. 1867) 606; Graphia Aurea Urbis Romae 27 (supplementing the Mirabilia Romae; ed. Gustav Parthey [Berlin 1869] 29; ed. Ida Ferrante Corti [Albano Laziale 1930] 31 [text], 95 [translation], and 246 [commentary]); Jordan-Hülsen, op. cit. II 628; see apparatus; Valentini and Zucchetti, op. cit. III (1946) 86. On the Mirabilia Romae and the Graphia Aurea Urbis Romae, both of the 12th century, see Jordan-Hülsen, op. cit. II 357 ff., Manitius III 245-48, and Valentini and Zucchetti, op. cit. III 3-16 and 67-76; Delbrueck, Antike Porphyrwerke, p. XVII; Ferdinand Gregorovius, History of the City of Rome in the Middle Ages IV.2 (London 1896) 524, n. 1; Sergio Ortolani, S. Giovanni in Laterano (Rome 192-?) 20; Horace K. Mann, Lives of the Popes in the early Middle Ages IX (London 1925) 229-30; Deichmann and Tschira, op. cit. 81; Buchowiecki, op. cit. I 65; Bovini, Edifici cristiani 178; Brandenburg, Roms frühchristliche Basiliken 68 (erroneously 11th century); Krautheimer, Rome: Profile of a City 213; Drijvers, op. cit. 75.

[12]Inv. no. 238; Gregorovius, loc. cit. (n. 11 above); Ludwig von Pastor, The History of the Popes XXXIX, ed. E. F. Peeler (repr. London 1952) 70 and 74; Sjöqvist and Westholm, op. cit. 9. Pius VI also, in 1788, moved the sarcophagus of Constantina from the mausoleum on the Via Nomentana to the Vatican Museum.

[13]Adolfo Venturi, Storia dell'arte italiana I (1901) 435-36 and figs. 172-75; Dalton, Byzantine Art and Archeology 131-32 with fig. 76; Costanza Gradara, "I sarcofagi Vaticani di Sant'Eleno e di Santa Costanza," NBAC 20.3-4 (1914) 43-49 at 43-46; Pio Petro Franchi de' Cavalieri, "Il sarcofago di S. Elena prima dei restauri del secolo XVIII," NBAC 27 (1921) 15-38 and pls. 7-8; Gerhard Rodenwaldt, "Der Belgrader
(continued...)

suggest that it originally was intended for a male member of the imperial family.[14]

Later Byzantine authors insist that Helena was buried in Constantinople, but vary considerably on details. In the eighth century Theophanes states that Helena was the first to be buried in the Church of the Holy Apostles; he says nothing about her sarcophagus.[15] From the tenth century we have the so-called *Ceremonial Book of Constantine Porphyrogenitus* (Constantine VII Porphyrogenitus, emperor 913-959).[16] Here, in the course of a description of the imperial porphyry sarcophagi, we find the statement that Constantine and Helena rest in the same sarcophagus in the Church of the Holy Apostles.[17] In the 11th century Georgius Cedrenus reports that Helena died at the age of eighty and that Constantine, Helena, and Fausta were buried in a single porphyry sarcophagus in Constantinople's Church of the Holy Apostles.[18] He is quite

---

[13](...continued)
Kameo," *JDAI* 37 (1922) 17-38 at 31-35; Dalton, *East Christian Art* 181-82; Henri Leclercq in *DACL* VI.2 (1925) 2139-42 and fig. 5615; Delbrueck, *Antike Porphyrwerke* 27, 215, and pls. 100-101; Sjöqvist and Westholm, *op. cit.* 7-9, 12-33, and pls. I-V; Gerhard Rodenwaldt, "Zum Sarkophag der Helena," in *Scritti in onore di Bartolomeo Nogara* (Vatican City 1937) 389-93 and pls. LIV-LVI; Amelung and Lippold, *op. cit.*, text III.1 195-205, no. 589, and pls. III.1 69-73; Bernard Andreae in Wolfgang Helbig, *Führer durch die öffentlichen Sammlungen klassischer Altertümer in Rom*, 4th ed., I (Tübingen 1963) 20-21, no. 25; Friedrich Wilhelm Deichmann, Giuseppe Bovini, and Hugo Brandenburg, *Reportorium der christlich-antiken Sarkophage* (Wiesbaden 1967) 105-108, no. 173, and pls. 37-40; Bovini, *Edifici cristiani* 174-76; Diana E. E. Kleiner, *Roman Sculpture* (New Haven 1992) 455-457 with ill. 418.

[14]See n. 10 above.

[15]Theophanes Homologetes or Confessor, *Chronographia* ad annum mundi 5817 (Migne, *PG* CVIII 113; ed. de Boor I 27); Jean Paul Richter, *op. cit.* 107, no. 149.

[16]On this important treatise see the following: Krumbacher, *op. cit.* I 254-55; J. B. Bury, "The Ceremonial Book of Constantine Porphyrogennetos," *EHR* 22 (1907) 209-27 and 417-39; Georg Ostrogorsky, *History of the Byzantine State*, 2nd ed. (New Brunswick, New Jersey, 1969) 279-80; Arnold Toynbee, *op. cit.* 575-81; Hunger, *Die hochsprachliche profane Literatur* I 364-65.

[17]*De Ceremonis Aulae Byzantinae* 2.42 (ed. Reiske [*CSHB*] I 642; Migne, *PG* CXII 1189-92); Jean Paul Richter, *op. cit.* 108, no. 150; Delbrueck, *Antike Porphyrwerke*, p. X; Alexander Alexandrovich Vasiliev, "Imperial Porphyry Sarcophagi in Constantinople," *DOP* 4 (1948) 1-26 at 8; Glanville Downey, "The Tombs of the Byzantine Emperors at the Church of the Holy Apostles in Constantinople," *JHS* 79 (1959) 27-51 at 30, 32, and 34.

[18]*Compendium Historiarum* (ed. Becker [*CSHB* XXVI-XXVII] I 499 and 519; Migne, *PG* CXXI 544 and 565); Delbrueck, *Antike Porphyrwerke*, p. IX.

unaware of Fausta's unhappy fate and thus hardly inspires confidence.[19] In ca. 1200 Nicolaus Mesarites, describing the mausoleum of Constantine, mentions a *logos* that Constantine and Helena are buried together;[20] he does not vouch for the veracity of this *logos*.[21] Two brief lists, both anonymous, of the sarcophagi in the Church of the Holy Apostles also mention, in almost identical wording, that Constantine and Helena are buried in the same sarcophogus.[22] But Nikephoros Kallistos, in the 14th century, says that Helena was originally buried in Rome and transferred to Constantinople's Church of the Holy Apostles two years later, together with the sarcophagus.[23] We have had occasion previously to question this author's trustworthiness, and an attempt to show his credibility in the present context has not succeeded.[24]

Russian visitors to Constantinople in the 13th, 14th, and 15th century report having seen the sarcophagus of Constantine and Helena in the

[19]The work of Georgius Cedrenus is a world chronicle from the creation to the year 1057. It is a compilation from earlier sources and lacks independent value. See Krumbacher, *op. cit.* I 368-69, and Hunger, *Die hochsprachliche profane Literatur* I 393.

[20]*Description of the Church of the Holy Apostles at Constantinople* 39 (ed. Downey, *TAPS* n. s. 47.6 [1957] 891 and 915); Heisenberg, *op. cit.* II 82; Delbrueck, *Antike Porphyrwerke*, pp. XVII and 222; Vasiliev, "Imperial Porphyry Sarcophagi" 9.

[21]This work of Nicolous Mesarites was unknown until the MS was discovered in 1898.

[22]The *terminus post quem* for the compilation of both lists is 1028; for their relationship to each other and to the *Ceremonial Book* of Constantine VII see Downey, "The Tombs of the Byzantine Emperors" 28-29. For the pertinent passage in the first list see the following: Du Cagne, *Constantinopolis Christiana* IV 109; Delbrueck, *Antike Porphyrwerke*, p. XII; Vasiliev, "Imperial Porphyry Sarcophagi" 8; Downey, "The Tombs of the Byzantine Emperors" 37. For the pertinent passage in the second list see the following: Codinus, *Excerpta de Antiquitatibus Constantinopolitanis*, ed. Becker (*CSHB* XIV; Bonn 1843) 203; Migne, *PG* CLVII 725; Downey, "The Tombs of the Byzantine Emperors" 40.

[23]*Hist. Eccl.* 8.31 (Migne, *PG* CXLVI 120); Delbrueck, *Antike Porphyrwerke* p. XVII.

[24]See chapter II above. Ebersolt, "Sarcophages impériaux." Alfons Maria Schneider, review of K. Hönn, *Konstantin der Grosse, GGA* 202 (1940) 208-10 at 210, agrees with Ebersolt. Vasiliev, "Imperial Porphyry Sarcophagi" 22-23, does not refer to Nikephoros, but postulates a similar sequence of events. Helene Homeyer, in *LThK*[2] V (1960) 208, appears to follow Nikephoros. Nikephoros is specifically refuted by Sjöqvist and Westholm, *op. cit.* 3-4.

Church of the Holy Apostles.[25] But in 1432 a French traveler, Bertrandon de la Broquière, will have us believe that the tombs (plural!) of Helena and Constantine are to be seen in the Church of the Pantocrator, rather than in the Church of the Holy Apostles.[26] The contradictory Byzantine traditions of Helena's burial must, I think, yield to the Roman traditions, which are not only earlier but also consistent.

There is also a Venetian tradition which holds that Helena's body was removed from Constantinople to Venice in 1212. The Doge Andrea Dandolo (1343-1354) wrote in Latin a chronicle which encompasses events from the days of the Apostles, particularly St. Mark, to the year 1280.[27] In this chronicle we read that in the eighth year (of the Doge Pietro Ziani, 1205-1229) a Venetian *canonicus* named Aicardo took the body of St. Helena by stealth from the Monastery of St. Helena in Constantinople and deposited it in the [future] Monastery of St. Helena in Venice.[28] If, as I believe, Helena's body never was in Constantinople, then, obviously, this *translatio* can never have taken place. Additionally, we may be suspicious of this tradition for the following reasons:

1. Dandolo is writing more than a century after the supposed event, and there is no earlier reference to it in either Byzantine or Venetian sources; also, he is writing for the glory of his city.
2. A Monastery of St. Helena in Constantinople is not known from other sources.[29]

[25]Paul Édouard Didier Riant, *Exuviae Sacrae Constantinopolitanae* II (Geneva 1878) 225; Sofia Khitrovo, *Itinéraires russes en Orient* I.1 (Geneva 1899) 101, 162, and 203; Vasiliev, "Imperial Porphyry Sarcophagi" 16-18; George P. Majeska, *Russian Travelers to Constantinople in the Fourteenth and Fifteenth Centuries* (Washington, D.C., 1984) 148-49, 160-63, 184-85, 299-300, and 304-305.

[26]*Voyage d'Outremer*, ed. Charles Schefer (Paris 1892) 161; Delbrueck, *Antike Porphywerke*, pp. IX and 220; Majeska, *op. cit.* 305, n. 105. For the Church of the Holy Apostles see chapter XI above. The Church of the Pantocrator, founded in the 12th century by the empress Irene, still stands, but has been converted to a mosque, Zeïrik Kilissi Jamissi (or Zeyrek Kilise Camii). It contained four imperial burials, two of the 12th century, and two of the 15th century. Our traveler apparently was misinformed.

[27]Gröber, *op. cit.* 294; Heinrich Kretschmayr, *Geschichte von Venedig* I (Gotha 1905) 391; Girolamo Arnaldi, "Andrea Dandolo Doge-Cronista," in Agostino Pertusi, *La Storiografia Veneziana fino al secolo XVI* (Florence 1970) 127-252; Donald M. Nicol, *Byzantium and Venice* (Cambridge 1988) 280-82.

[28]*Chronica* 10.4 (ed. Pastorello [*RIS*[2] XII.1] 285); Flaminio Cornaro (Corner), *Ecclesiae Venetae* IX (Venice 1749) 175-77; Riant, *op. cit.* II 262; Janin, *La géographie ecclésiastique* I.3[2] 109.

[29]Janin, *op. cit.* 109-110; Nicol, *op. cit.* 185.

3. Visitors to Constantinople continue to refer to the sarcophagus of Constantine and Helena in the Church of the Holy Apostles; they do not mention that it has been disturbed.[30]   Only Bertrandon de la Broquiére is aware of the Venetian tradition.[31] (The Venetians, he says, also attempted to open the sarcophagus of Constantine, but did not succeed.)

It should be noted also that Dandolo speaks of a *corpus,* presumably entire, not a relic. We are not permitted, therefore, to resolve the difficulty by assuming that the remains were divided, part remaining in Constantinople and part being taken to Venice.[32]   The Venetians did take, however, an impressive number of other relics from Constantinople.[33]

In the ecclesiastical calendars of Venice Helena's *translatio* is noted on May 21.[34]   Venice's Church of St. Helena, with attached monastery, stands to this day on the Island of St. Helena. This church was originally built in the 13th century to receive the presumed body of St. Helena; it was rebuilt in the 15th century.   Over the doorway of the church's western facade there is a larger-than-life sculpture group by Antonio Rizzo: Admiral Vittorio Cappello (died 1467) is kneeling before St. Helena; the two figures once held a cross between them. In the 19th century, after the Church of St. Helena had been suppressed, this group was removed first to the Church of SS. Giovanni e Paolo and then to the Church of S. Aponal. It was returned to its original location in 1929, when the Church of St. Helena was rededicated.[35] In the chancel of the

---

[30]See n. 25 above.

[31]See n. 26 above.

[32]In 1385 a pilgrim claimed specifically to have seen "the body entire" of St. Helena in Venice, and a second pilgrim on the same occasion reported to have seen her "body." See Theophilus Bellorini and Eugene Hoade, translators, *Visit to the Holy Places of Egypt, Sinai, Palestine, and Syria in 1384 by Frescobaldi, Gucci and Sigoli* (Jerusalem 1948) 33 and 200.

[33]Kretschmeyr, *op. cit.* 312; Rodolfo Gallo, *Il tesoro di San Marco e la sua storia* (Venice 1967) 9-13; Nicol, *op. cit.* 185-88.

[34]Flaminio Cornaro, *op. cit.* IX 181; Riant, *op. cit.* II 294. May 21 is the feast day of Sts. Constantine and Helena in the Greek Orthodox tradition; see chapter XV below. The choice of this date is surely more than coincidence.

[35]Francesco Sansovino, *Ventia città nobilissima et singolare* (ed. Venice 1663) 212-13; Adolfo Venturi, *Storia dell'atre italiana* VI (1908) 1061 and fig. 721; Paul Schubring, *Die italienische Plastik des Quattrocento* (Berlin 1919) 244; Leo Planiscig, *Venezianische Bildhauer der Renaissance* (Vienna 1921) 36 and 64; John Pope-Hennessy,

(continued...)

Plate IX

The main portal of the Church of St. Helena, Venice. Note the figures of Admiral Vittorio Cappello and St Helena, by Antonio Rizzo, in the tympanum.

church, on the north wall, there is a panel painting which concerns us. This was painted at the end of the 15th century or the beginning of the 16th century by Bernardino da Murano, who is otherwise not very well known. In this panel Helena stands on a pedestal, wearing a crown and holding a large cross in her right hand; she is flanked by St. Geminianus on the left and St. Menna on the right.[36]

There is yet another tradition which is more worthy of our attention. The monk Altmann has left us, in addition to his *vita* of St. Helena, a lengthy account, according to which Helena's remains were brought in the year 840 by a monk named Theogisus from Rome to Altmann's own monastery, the Benedictine abbey of Hautvillers near Reims.[37] Theogisus, Altmann reports, entered the church where Helena was buried at the time of evening prayers, stole the remains under cover

---

[35](...continued)
Italian Renaissance Sculpture, 2nd ed. (London 1971) 336; Robert Munman, "The Monument to Vittore Cappello of Antonio Rizzo," *Burlington Magazine* 113 (1971) 138-45 with figs. 21-32; Umberto Franzoi and Dina di Stefano, *Le chiese de Venezia* (Venice 1976) 20 and 534-35 with ill. 777-80; John McAndrew, *Venetian Architecture of the Early Renaissance* (Cambridge, Massachussetts, 1980) 63 and 72-75 with fig. 6.9; Ralph Lieberman, *Renaissance Architecture in Venice, 1450-1540* (New York 1982), pl. 27. The attribution of this work to Rizzo is not assured; it has also been attributed to Niccolò di Giovanni Florentino: Anne Markham Schulz, *Niccolò di Giovanni Florentino and Venetian Sculpture of the Early Renaissance* (New York 1978) 27ff. and passim; Anne Markham Schulz, *Antonio Rizzo* (Princeton 1983) 188-91; Huse and Wolters, *op. cit.* 134-35 with fig. 112.

[36]St. Geminianus was a bishop of Modena; his feast day is January 31. St. Menna, or Menas, was an Egyptian soldier-saint; his feast day is November 11, and his shrine, Abu Mina or Menapolis, was southwest of Alexandria, while his cult spread to Greece and Constantinople. Whether or how these two saints are associated with St. Helena I do not know. The panel was originally in Venice's Church of S. Geminiano, until that church was suppressed in 1807 (or 1810?). From 1838 to 1919 it was in the Gemäldegalerie der Akademie der bildenden Künste in Vienna (former inv. no. 15). In 1919 it was returned to Venice and consigned to the Accademia (inv. no. 1009; cat. no 949). Between 1932 and 1947 it was in the Museo di Murano, and since 1947 it has been in the Church of St. Helena. Walter Bombe in Thieme-Becker, *Künstler-Lexikon* III (1909) 442; Maurice, *Sainte Hélène* 38; Von Marle, *op. cit.* XVII (1935) 476-80; Berenson, *Italian Pictures of the Renaissance, Venetian School* I 74 (attribution to Benedetto Diana); Sandra Moschini Marconi, *Gallerie dell'Accademia di Venezia: Opere d'atre del secolo XVI* (Rome 1962) 30-31, no. 54, and ill. 54. Additional information was kindly provided by Dr. Renate Trnek, Gemäldegalerie der Akademie der bildenden Künste, Vienna.

[37]*Historia Translationis [S. Helenae] ad Coenobium Altivillarense; BHL* 3773; *Acta Sanct.* Aug. III (ed. 1867) 601-603; Jean Baptiste Manceaux, *Histoire de l'abbaye et du village d'Hautvillers* (Epernay 1880) I 202-32.

of night, and returned with them to Hautvillers. When doubts arose about the authenticity of the precious relics, three other monks were sent to Rome to investigate. These returned, bringing with them not only the desired proof but also the relics of other saints! Altmann does not say just how they accomplished their assignment.[38] Additionally care was taken to authenticate the relics by ordeal, after the appropriate three-day fast.

Altmann's account was drawn upon by Flodoard, the tenth century abbot, historian, and archivist of Reims, in his *History of the Church of Reims*.[39] The *translatio* is mentioned briefly and erroneously assigned to the year 849 by Sigebert, a monk in the Benedictine monastery of Gembloux (Belgium), in his *Chronicle*, which encompasses events between 381 and 1112.[40] Several mediaeval martyrologies list Helena's *depositio* in Hautvillers under February 7.[41] Even John Capgrave (1393-1469) mentions Helena's *translatio* in his *Chronicle of England*.[42]

Great value was attached to relics in the Carolingian realm at this time, and it is not at all to be thought that Altmann made up the story of Helena's *translatio*.[43] He was writing only a few decades after the event and had access to all the sources of information. The date which he gives, 840, certainly is to be preferred to 849, given by Sigebert, because he correctly reports that the see of Reims was vacant at the

---

[38]A difficult, if not impossible assignment, as Patrick J. Geary, *Furta Sacra* (Princeton 1978) 65-66, points out.

[39]*Historia Remensis Ecclesiae* 2.8 (Migne, *PL* CXXXV 108-111; ed. Heller and Waitz [*MGH, Script.* XIII] 456-57). On Flodoard's *Historia Remensis Ecclesiae* see the following: Gröber, *op. cit.* 145; Philippe Lauer, *Les annales de Flodoard* (Paris 1905), pp. XIII-XVIII; Georges Boussinesq and Gustav Laurent, *Histoire de Reims* (Reims 1933) I 103, n.; Manitius II 160-66; René Aigrain, *L'hagiographie, ses sources, ses méthodes, son histoire* (Paris 1953) 309.

[40]*Chronicon*, ad annum 849 (Migne *PL* CLX 162; ed. Bethmann [*MGH, Script.* VI] 339); Sjöqvist and Westholm, *op. cit.* 6. On this important and influential chronicle see Gröber, *op. cit.* 269 and 303-304, Manitius III 344-46, and Aigrain, *L'hagiographie* 310. Similarly the erroneous date of 849 is found in the *Chronicon Turonense*, which records events to the year 1246; see Edmond Martène and Ursinus Durand, *Veterum Scriptorum Amplissima Collectio* (Paris 1724-1733) V 966-67. On this chronicle see Gröber, *op. cit.* 307.

[41]*Acta Sanct.* Aug. III (ed. 1867) 600; Maurice, *Sainte Hélène* 60; Linder, "The Myth of Constantine the Great" 88.

[42]Anno mundi 6025 (ed. Hingeston [Rolls Series I] 108).

[43]For other *translationes* of relics in the ninth century, mostly from Italy, see Hanns Leo Mikoletzky, "Sinn und Art der Heiligung im frühen Mittelalter," *MIÖG* 57 (1949) 83-122 at 99-102.

time.2[44] But Altmann is writing hagiography, not history. We are not assured by the long list of miracles which, so Altmann writes, took place in the course of the *translatio* and after the *depositio* of the remains.[45] The manner in which Theogisus supposedly removed the body of St. Helena is a hagiographical topos.[46] The model had been provided only a few years earlier by the *Translatio Sanctorum Marcellini et Petri* of Einhart, Charlemagne's biographer and secretary.[47] Would Theogisus have been able to lift the heavy lid of Helena's sarcophagus? Would the theft not have been promptly discovered? Is it not possible that Theogisus perpetrated a hoax? I am very much inclined to think so.[48]

Let us now return to Helena's mausoleum in Rome. By the 12th century the building had fallen into neglect, and thieves took valuable objects from the sarcophagus, breaking the lid in the process. Pope Innocent II (1130-1143) then ordered Helena's remains to be transferred

[44]Duchesne, *Fastes épiscopaux* III 87-88; Boussinesq and Laurent, *op. cit.* I 171-72 and II.2 930. The erroneous date of 849 is repeated by Baronio, *op. cit.* XIV 374, Mackes, *op. cit.* 191, and Dietz, "St. Helena" 364. Ewig, "Tradition" 153 and 156, correctly gives 840. So does Pierre-André Sigal, "Les miracles de Sainte-Hélène a l'abbaye d'Hautvillers," *Assistance et assistés jusqu'à 1610* (Paris 1979) 499-513 at 500.

[45]*Miracula [S. Helenae]; BHL* 3774-75; *Acta Sanct.* Aug. III (ed. 1867) 612-18; repeated by Flodoard, *loc. cit.* (n. 38 above); Sigal, *op. cit.*

[46]Geary, *Furta Sacra*, pp. IX-X, 32, and 100.

[47]*BHL* 5233; *Acta Sanct.* Iun. I (ed. 1695) 181-206; Migne, *PL* CIV 537-94; ed. Waitz (*MGH, Script.* XV 1) 238-64; Baronio ad annum 826, *op. cit.* XIV 103-10; Patrick J. Geary, "The Ninth-Century Relic Trade," in James Obelkevich, ed., *Religion and the People 800-1700* (Chapel Hill 1979) 8-19 at 16-18. On Einhart and the impact of his *Translatio* see the following: Gröber, *op. cit.* 141; Marguerite Bondois, *La translation des saints Marcellin et Pierre: Étude sur Einhard et sa vie politique de 827 à 834* (Paris 1907); Manitius I 639-40 and 644-45; Aigrain, *L'hagiographie* 190 and 308; Eleanor Shipley Duckett, *Carolingian Portraits* (Ann Arbor 1962) 74-84; Peter Llewellyn, *Rome in the Dark Ages* (London 1971) 186-90; Brunhölzl, *Geschichte der lat. Lit. des Mittelalters* I 320-21; Geary, *Furta Sacra* 52-53, 143-45, and 148, n. 9. Martin Heinzelmann, *Translationsberichte und andere Quellen des Reliquienkultes* (Turnhout 1979) 56-57 with n. 43; Jean Décarreaux, *Moines et monastères à l'époque de Charlemagne* (Paris 1980) 112-13; John Michael Wallace-Hadrill, *op. cit.* 202-203.

[48]Lanciani, *Wanderings* 224, thinks that the story of this *translatio* is "hardly worth repeating." Bovini, *Edifici cristiani* 177, deems it not very likely. Émile Mâle, *Early Churches of Rome* (London 1960) 95, in this context, refers to Helena's "supposed" tomb on the Via Labicana; thus he appears to question the original burial rather than the *translatio*.

to the Church of S. Maria in Ara Coeli.[49] The Church of S. Maria in Ara Coeli, on the Capitoline Hill, certainly was a safer depository than the mausoleum outside the walls of the city.

The *translatio* to Hautvillers in 840 and the *translatio* ordered by Innocent II 300 years later cannot be reconciled with each other, of course, except again by expediently assuming that in each case only a part of the relics were involved.[50] The later *translatio* is, I think, far more believable than the earlier one.[51] In any event, when Anastasius IV appropriated the great sarcophagus for himself it was already empty.

The Church of S. Maria in Ara Coeli (formerly S. Maria de Capitolio), originally erected in the fifth century, contains in the center of the left transept the so-called Chapel of St. Helena or Santa Cappella. This is a round structure of eight columns first built in the 17th century, destroyed by the French in 1798, and rebuilt in the early 19th century. In the center of this structure there is an urn of porphyry which, as an inscription proclaims, contains the relics of St. Helena.[52]

The supposed relics of Helena in Hautvillers were repeatedly disturbed; the tomb was opened in 1095, 1120, 1235, 1410, 1518, and 1602.[53] On these occasions and perhaps others, we must assume, some of the relics were removed to be sent elsewhere. This would account for the fact that numerous churches and monasteries in Germany, France, Belgium, and Luxembourg claim to possess relics of Helena.

In the year 952 two crypts, an upper one and a lower one, were dedicated in the Church of St. Maximinus at Trier. On this occasion relics of St. Helena were deposited in one of the altars of the lower

---

[49]*Acta Sanct.* Aug. III (ed. 1867) 606. In the second half of the 14th century the church is known as the place of Helena's burial to the anonymous author of the *Memoriale de mirabilibus et indulgentiis quae in urbe Roma existunt;* see Valentini and Zucchetti, *op. cit.* IV (1953) 83-84. In the 17th century Jean Mabillon, *Museum Italicum* (Paris 1687-89) I.1 135, recognizes that the claims of Hautvillers and those of the Church of S. Maria in Ara Coeli conflict with each other.

[50]Thus Deichmann and Tschira, *op. cit.* 80, and Drijvers, *op. cit.* 75.

[51]This is also the conclusion of Bovini, *Edifici cristiani* 177.

[52]Marucchi, *op. cit.* III 241; Arduino Colasanti, *S. Maria in Aracoeli* (Rome 1923?) 7 and ill. 20; Armellini, *op. cit.* I 669; Buchowiecki, *op. cit.* II 511; Bredan J. Gross, "De H. Helena in de Aracoelikerk te Rome," *Clairlieu* 38 (1980) 101-103.

[53]*Acta Sanct.* Aug. III (ed. 1867) 604-605; Sigal, *op. cit.* 500-501. Slightly different Manceaux, *op. cit.* III 449.

Plate X

Chapel of St. Helena in the Church of Santa Maria in Ara Coeli, Rome.

crypt, an altar dedicated to the Holy Virgins.[54] This is the first mention of relics of St. Helena at Trier, and it is reasonable to assume that they were obtained from Hautvillers.[55]

The monk Otloh of the Monastery of St. Emmeram in Regensburg lived from ca. 1010 to ca. 1070. Between 1062 and 1066, while residing at Fulda, he wrote his *Liber Visionum*.[56] In this work, in the context of events having taken place in his youth, before 1033, he mentions a church of St. Helena at Würzburg.[57] This is the first mention of a church of St. Helena on German soil.[58] The church would, of course, have possessed relics of its patron saint.

Between 1029 and 1039, on a September 8, in the presence of three bishops, the main altar of the principal church of Freising was dedicated. Relics of St. Helena, together with those of numerous other saints, were deposited at that time; also a piece of the True Cross and a piece of the Seamless Robe of Christ.[59]

At Echternach in Luxembourg, famous for its associations with St. Willibrord, there are no fewer than three relics of St. Helena. One of these, the one in the Oratory of St. Michael, was acquired in 1039 from the Monastery of St. Maximinus at Trier. There also are two pieces of the True Cross.[60]

An altar dedicated in 1064 in the Monastery of St. Emmeram in Regensburg contained relics of St. Helena.[61] Given the close connections of this monastery with the Monastery of St. Maximinus in Trier, it is likely that these relics were obtained from the latter place.[62]

At the monastery of Gorze (near Metz) Archbishop Udo of Trier dedicated a Church of St. Peter in 1068, and Bishop Hermann of Metz

---

[54]*Notae S. Maximini Treverensis* (*MGH, Script.* XV.2 967) or *Notae Dedicationum S. Maximini Treverensis* (ibid. 1270-71); Bunjes, *op. cit.* 294-95; Mackes, *op. cit.* 192; Ewig, "Tradition" 149. Sanderson, *op. cit.* 13-14; Dietz, "St. Helena" 364.

[55]Sauerland, *op. cit.* 86-87; Ewig, "Tradition" 150; Dietz, "St. Helena" 364.

[56]Manitius II 83-85 and 90-91.

[57]*Visio Sexta* (Migne, *PL* CXLVI 359-60; *MGH, Script.* XI 379-80).

[58]Mackes, *op. cit.* 192; Ewig, "Tradition" 149; Dietz, "St. Helena" 365.

[59]*Nota Dedicationis Frisingensis* (*MGH, Script.* XXX.2 769).

[60]*Notitiae Dedicationum Ecclesiae Epternacensis* (*MGH, Script.* XXX.2 771, 772, and 774); Ewig, "Tradition" 149.

[61]*Notae S. Emmerami II* (*MGH, Script* XV.2 1097).

[62]Marx, *Geschichte* II.1 76-78.

dedicated a Church of the Apostles in 1077. On both occasions relics of Helena are mentioned, along with numerous others.[63]

The Church of St. Helena in Trier-Euren, although the present building dates only from the 19th century, was established in 1075 by Archbishop Udo; relics of St. Helena are specifically mentioned.[64]

By 1132 relics of St. Helena, as well as a piece of the Cross, were owned by the Monastery of St. Amandus (near Tournai in Belgium).[65]

In 1135 relics of St. Helena reached Bonn, whence a portion of them was soon transferred to the Church of St. Gereon in Cologne and placed in the so-called *Corona S. Helenae*.[66] More relics of St. Helena reached Cologne in 1219, and in 1220 Xanten.[67]

In 1228, or 1278, the Cathedral of Sainte-Croix in Orléans received relics of St. Helena from Hautvillers, and henceforth February 7 was observed as the feast day of St. Helena in Orléans as it was in Hautvillers. But the relics received in the 13th century perished in the course of the religious upheavals of the 16th century. A second *translatio* of relics of St. Helena from Hautvillers to Orléans took place in 1602 at the request of King Henry IV of France.[68]

The emperor Charles IV took a keen interest in holy relics.[69] When

---

[63]*Notae Gorzienses (MGH, Script.* XV.2 975 and 976); Ewig, "Tradition" 149.

[64]*Notae Dedicationum Dioeceseos Treverensis II (MGH, Script.* XV.2 1281); Brower-Masen, *Antiquitates* I 553; Saueriand, *op. cit.* 75. Ewig, "Tradition" 149; Dietz, "St. Helena" 360.

[65]*Notitia S. Amandi (MGH, Script.* XXX.2 785-86).

[66]Rahtgens, *Köln* II 99; Clemen, *Die romanische Monumentalmalerei* 560, n. 16; Mackes, *op. cit.* 194; Nattermann, *op. cit.* 217. Dietz, "St. Helena" 365 and 367.

[67]Mackes, *op. cit.* 195; Dietz, "St. Helena" 367.

[68]*Acta Sanct.* Aug. III (ed. 1867) 605; François Lemaire, *Histoire et antiquitez de la ville et duché d'Orleans* 2nd ed. (Orléans 1648) I, "Histoire et antiquitez de la ville & duché d'Orleans" 200; II, "Antiquitez de l'eglise & diocese d'Orleans" 37; Manceaux, *op. cit.* II 196-98; Linder, "The Myth of Constantine the Great" 88, n. 254. Of the eleven chapels in the cathedral's ambulatory the third one from the right is that of St. Helena; see Georges Louis Chenesseau, *Monographie de la cathédrale d'Orléans* (Orléans 1925) 89. François Noel Alexandre Dubois, *Notice historique et description de l'église cathédrale de Sainte-Croix d'Orléans* (Orléans 1818) 27, reports that in the 17th century the cathedral possessed bells named after Cyriacus, Constantine, and Helena.

[69]In the Lady Chapel of Karlstein Castle near Prague, on the south wall, a three-part fresco, perhaps by Nicolaus Wurmser, depicts Charles receiving various relics and then depositing them in a reliquary cross: Vlasta Dvoraková, *Gothic Mural Painting in Bohemia and Moravia, 300-1378* (London 1964) 89-92 and pls. 84-85; Vlasta Dvoraková and Dobroslava Menclová, *Karlstejn* (Prague 1965) 76 and 79-83 with ill. 79, 81-83 and

(continued...)

he visited Trier in 1354 he took a number of relics for the Cathedral of St. Vitus, which was then being built in Prague, his capital. Among these was a piece of the "staff of St. Peter."[70] But on a later occasion he gave to Kuno von Falkenstein, Archbishop of Trier (1362-1388), the head of St. Helena; the archbishop, in turn, donated the relic to Trier's cathedral chapter.[71] The treasury of the cathedral holds a small silver shrine, probably of Byzantine workmanship and dating from the 13th century. According to an inventory of 1776 this shrine contained the head of Helena, but the *Designatio* of 1655 says of the same shrine that it contained the head of Lazarus.[72] A silver bust or head reliquary of

---

[69](...continued)
85; Helga Wammetsberger, "Individium und Typ in den Porträts Kaiser Karls IV," *Wissenschaftliche Zeitschrift der Friedrich-Schiller-Universität Jena, Gesellschafts- und sprachwissenschaftliche Reihe* 16 (1967) 79-95 at 82, 89, no. 25, and ill. 4; Michael Eschborn, *Karlstein: Das Rätsel um die Burg Karls IV* (Stuttgart 1971) 100, 185, 192, and ill. 60; Johanna von Herzogenberg in Ferdinand Seibt, ed., *Bohemia Sacra* (Düsseldorf 1974) 471-72 and 49, pl. III; Gerhardt Schmidt in Erich Bachmann, ed., *Gothic Art in Bohemia* (New York 1977) 47 and ill. 120; Herzogenberg in Ferdinand Seibt, ed., *Kaider Karl IV: Staatsman und Mäzen,* 2nd ed. (Munich 1978) 331; Wolfgang Braunfels, *Die Kunst im Heiligen Römischen Reich* V (Munich 1985) 105 with ill. 105; Georges Duby, *History of Medieval Art, 980-1440* 2nd ed. (Geneva 1986) III 69-70 and 74; Emanuel Poche, *Böhmen und Mähren* (Munich 1986) 119 and 393; Mária Prokopp, *Italian Trecento Influence on Murals in East Central Europe, particularly Hungary* (Budapest 1963) 130. In the adjacent Chapel of St. Catherine, above the entrance, there is another contemporary fresco which depicts the emperor and his (third) wife with the same reliquary cross between them: Dvořaková, *op. cit.* 92 and pl. 78; Dvořaková and Menclová, *op. cit.* 97-99 with ill. 96 and 97; Wammetsberger, *op. cit.* 82 and 69, no. 26; Eschborn, *op. cit.* 186 and ill 63; Rudolf Chadraba, *Starometská mostecká vez a triumfální symbolika v umení Karla IV* (Prague 1971) 69 and ill. 65; Seibt, *Bohemia Sacra,* ill. 104; Gerhard Schmidt in Bachmann, *op. cit.* 47 and ill. 105. Herzogenberg in Seibt, *Kaiser Karl IV: Staatsman und Mäzen²* 332; Poche, *op. cit.* 393; Prokopp, *op. cit.* 130.

[70]Ferdinand Seibt, *Karl IV: Ein Kaiser in Europa, 1346-1378* (Munich 1978) 243-44; Franz Machilek in Seibt, *Kaiser Karl IV: Staatsman und Mäzen* 90 and ill. 45-47; Ronig in *Schatzkunst Trier* 150, no. 92; *ibid.* for earlier literature.

[71]Adam Goerz, *Regesten der Erzbischöfe zu Trier von Hetti bis Johann II, 814-1503* (Trier 1861) 101. I am indebted for this reference to Prof. Franz J. Ronig, Trier. I have examined the pertinent document, dated December 20, 1367, at Ehrenbreitstein, in the Landeshauptarchiv Koblenz (Best. 1 D Nr. 617). See also Dietz, "St. Helena" 371.

[72]Peter Weber, *op. cit.* 16 and ill. 15; Irsch, *Dom* 324-26, with fig. 212, and pl. XV; Ronig in *Schatzkunst Trier* 143, no. 82; *ibid.* for earlier literature; also 246, no. 210; Hans-Walter Stork in Ronig, *Schatzkunst Trier: Forschungen und Ergebnisse* 184-86. The *Designatio Sacratissimarum Quarundarum Reliquiarum* etc. is a leaflet printed in

(continued...)

St. Helena, dating from 1380, was once among the treasures of the cathedral, but was melted down during the French Revolution. Here Helena was shown with a cross in her right arm and three nails in her left hand.[73] On August 19, 1990, the relic was deposited in a new large reliquary fashioned of bronze by the sculptor Theo Heiermann.[74] The new reliquary, which was placed in a niche of the east crypta, features a bust of St. Helena, with a cross in her right arm and three nails in her left hand, on top of a model of the cathedral as it is believed to have appeared in the fourth century. The inscription reads: *Ave caput ecce sanctae Helenae/ fundatricis verae ecclesiae/ cathedralis vetustae Treverensis.*

When, in 1760, the Chapel of St. Helena in Bonn was re-dedicated, relics of St. Helena were deposited in the altar.[75]

In 1791, in the midst of the French Revolution, the relics of Helena still remaining at Hautvillers were removed by a pious cleric (Dom Jean-Baptiste Grossard, the last abbot), who was intent on saving them. Subsequently, on November 29, 1819 (or 1820?), they were deposited by the Confraternity of the Holy Sepulchre in the high altar of Paris' Church of Saint-Leu (Saint-Leu-Saint-Gilles).[76] In the ambulatory of this church there is a stained-glass window, dating from 1861, which depicts St. Helena.[77] She is shown with crown and scepter, but without the usual cross; in her left hand she holds a disk with the image of Christ. The Abbey of Hautvillers, like others in France, fell victim to

---

[72](...continued)
Cologne in 1655 as a "Wallfahrtsblatt" for the display of the Seamless Robe in that year. An exemplar owned by Trier's diocesan seminary is on display in the treasury of the cathedral; a second exemplar is owned by the diocesan museum (Inv. Nr. G 216). See Markus Gross-Morgen in *Zwischen Andacht und Andenken* 257-58, no. B 1.

[73]Irsch, *Dom* 318, no. 4; 365, no. 12; fig. 237a; and pl. XV; Dietz, "St. Helena" 371; Schnütgen-Museum, Cologne, *Rhein und Maas* I 141; Franz J. Ronig in *Schatzkunst Trier* 246, no. 210.

[74]*Paulinus: Trierer Bistumsblatt*, no. 34, August 26, 1990.

[75]Hauptmann, *op. cit.*, 61.

[76]Paul Lucot, *Sainte Hélène, mère de l'empereur Constantin* (Paris 1876) 45-52; Manceaux, *op. cit.* III 427-36; Maurice, *Sainte Hélène* 61; Maurice Vimont, *Histoire de l'église et de la paroisse Saint-Leu-Saint-Gilles à Paris* (Paris 1932) 43 and 168; Piganiol, *op. cit.* 44, n. 2; Stephen Wilson, "Cults of Saints in the Churches of Central Paris," in Stephen Wilson, ed., *Saints and their Cults* (Cambridge 1983) 233-60 at 236. The church is located at 92, rue Saint-Denis.

[77]Louis Grodecki, Françoise Perrot, and Jean Talaron, *Les vitraux de Paris, de la région Parisienne, de la Pacardie, et du Nord-Pas-de-Calais* (Paris 1978) 51.

Plate XI

New (1990) head reliquary of St. Helena in the cathedral of Trier.

secularization; the former abbey church now serves the local parish. Part of the relics were returned to Hautvillers from Paris in 1827 and deposited in a reliquary which is displayed in the north aisle of this church. The main altar of the church features an 18th century statue of St. Helena.[78]

Records of the Barberini family show that in 1636 Francesco Barberini, Cardinal and Vatican Secretary of State, sent a valuable reliquary containing relics of St. Helena as a gift to the queen of England.[79] At that time Maffeo Barberini, Francesco's uncle, was occupying the Holy See as Urban VIII (1623-1644), and it is he who had the statue of St. Helena placed in the crossing of St. Peter's Basilica.[80] The queen of England at that time was Henrietta Maria, the beautiful, French-born, and Catholic wife of the unfortunate Charles I (1625-1649). The gift, we may assume, was to encourage her in, and to reward her for, her efforts for her co-religionists in Protestant England.[81] We do not learn, unfortunately, the provenience of the relics. Were they taken from Rome's Church of S. Maria in Ara Coeli? The reliquary was the work of Francesco Spagna, following a design by Bernini.

We must mention, only to reject it, a report contained in the Colchester "Oath Book."[82] According to this not very trustworthy source, a certain monk by name of John, a Roman by nation, translated the head of St. Helena from Rome to the monastery of Bury St. Edmunds in Suffolk. The date given for this supposed *translatio* is 1145. It is impossible to reconcile this report with any of the other accounts which we have considered. Not surprisingly there is no mention of this *translatio* in the records of the Abbey of Bury St. Edmunds.[83]

A number of Greek churches and monasteries claim to possess relics of St. Helena; these are:

    1. Kykko Monastery in the Troodos Mountains of Cyprus.

---

[78]A complete but uncritical history of the abbey is provided by Manceaux, *op. cit.*, A concise summary, by Reine Renoux, is found in the *Dictionnaire des églises de France* VB 64-65.

[79]Marilyn Aronberg Lavin, *Seventeenth-Century Barberini Documents and Inventories of Art* (New York 1975) 6, document no. 42.

[80]See chapter VII above.

[81]For other dealings between the cardinal and the queen see Pastor, *op. cit.* XXIX (1938) 332-33, and the various biographies of Henrietta Maria.

[82]Folio 20v (IIIv); cf. chapter VI, n. 16; Benham, *Oath Book*, 27.

[83]*Memorials of St. Edmund's Abbey*, ed. Thomas Arnold (Rolls Series XXCVI), 3 vols., London 1890-1896.

2. The Monastery of St. Panteleimon at Mt. Athos.

3. The Monastery of Xenophon at Mt. Athos.

4. The Church of Sts. Constantine and Helena at Hagios Konstantinos in Phthiotis.

5. The Monastery of Hagia Lavra near Kalavrita in the northern Peloponnese.

6. The Monastery of St. John the Theologian (the Sublime) at Mytilene on Lesbos.

7. The Monastery of the Panagia Tourliane on Mykonos.

8. The Church of St. Lazarus at Kophinas on Chios.

9. The Monastery of the Koimesis of the Panagia Phaneromeni near Gournia on Crete.[84]

All of these relics must be rejected as spurious if I am correct in concluding that Helena's body never rested in Constantinople.[85]

---

[84]Otto Meinardus, "A Study of the Relics of Saints of the Greek Orthodox Church," *Or. Chr.* 54 (1970) 130-278 at 190.

[85]Only upon the completion of my own investigation did I become aware of Mark J. Johnson, "Where Were Constantius I and Helena Buried?" in *Latomus* 51 (1992) 145-50. Johnson and I have independently reached the same conclusion on nearly every point.

Plate XII

Medallion of Constantine and his family, dating from 326-330 and found in the Loire River in 1922. Photo Musée Dobrée, Nantes.

Chapter XIII.
Image in Roman Art

Constantine and members of his family are represented, as one would expect, in numerous pieces of contemporary art. But the identification of Helena in specific works of Roman art varies in degree of probability from the quite certain to the very unlikely, leaving us at times on uncertain ground.

In chapter IV above we examined the painted ceiling from the cathedral of Trier and concluded, with a sense of disappointment, that the central panel of that ceiling offers us an allegorical figure, not a likeness of Helena. Fortunately there are some other works of art which give us portraits of Helena in the company of other members of the imperial family.

Let us consider first a small but important and readily interpreted object of art. This is a copper (or bronze?) medallion which came to light in 1922 in the course of dredging operations in the Loire River and is now kept in the Musée Dobrée in Nantes.[1] It features portrait busts of Constantine (left) and Helena (right) facing each other. The identification is assured by comparison with coin types and by a Chi-Rho monogram between and slightly above the two imperial personages. Three smaller effigies below them have been identified, less securely, as Constantia (Constantine's sister and *nobilissima femina*), Constantine II, and Constantius II (left to right), or, alternatively, as the three sons remaining to Constantine after the death of Crispus. The absence of Fausta and of Crispus allows us to date the medallion to 326 or later, while the presence of Helena, of course, demands a date before 330. Constantine's youngest son, Constans, was not given the rank of Caesar until 333. The use of the Chi-Rho monogram reflects Constantine's religious policy during the later years of his reign.[2]

---

[1]Inv. no. 2211.

[2]Jean Lafaurie, "Médaillon Constantinien," *RN*, 5th ser. 17 (1955) 227-50 at 227-38 and pl. IX.1; Jean Lafaurie, "Un médaillon conservé au Musée Thomas Dobrée à Nantes," *Bull. Soc. des Antiqu. de France* 1956, pp. 20-21 and pl. I; Vogt, "Heiden und Christen" 163-64; Calza, *Iconografia romana* 175, no. 87; 238-40, no. 151; pls. LVIII, no. 181, and LXXXIII, no. 293; L'Orange, *Das spätantike Herrscherbild* 132-33; Kleiner, *op. cit.* 442. But Max Wegner, *ibid.* 145, and Drijvers, *op. cit.* 194, prefer to identify the imperial couple as Constantine and Fausta.

The great mosaic floor in the cathedral of Aquileia (once the south church of a Constantinian double church) is divided into ten compartments, two of which concern us here. Entering the church by a doorway on the north side, the ancient visitor came immediately upon the north compartment on the second (from the west) north-south axis of the floor. In this compartment the empress Fausta and Constantine's four sons are depicted; a date of 325 has been assigned.[3] In the compartment which is adjacent to the south and thus on the central west-east axis one finds portraits of the emperor Constantine and four female members of his family. One of these is Helena, while the other three are less securely identified.[4] The bishop's chair, the altar, a figure of Victory, the portrait of Helena, and the portrait of Constantine are all on the same axis. There are no inscriptions to accompany the portraits, and identification is based on context and iconography; we look in vain for physiognomic detail.

The Stadtbibliothek of Trier owns an eighth-century evangeliary which once belonged to Ada, the sister of Charlemagne, and is therefore commonly known as the Ada Codex. The cover of this manuscript is graced by a large and beautiful sardonyx cameo. The cameo shows two eagles with spread wings and above them, behind a balustrade, five portrait busts, obviously members of an imperial family. This imperial family has been identified erroneously as that of Augustus, Claudius, or

[3]Kähler, *Die Stiftermosaiken* 13 and ill. 2-6, was the first to offer this interpretation, and others have followed: Theodor Klauser, review of Kähler, *Die Stiftermosaiken,* in *JbAC* 7 (1964) 158-61 and pl. 11; Jörgen Bracker, "Zur Ikonographie Constantins und seiner Söhne," *Kölner Jb.* 8 (1965-66) 12-23 at 12-16; Heinz Kähler, *Die frühe Kirche: Kult und Kultraum* (Berlin 1972) 51-52 and color pl.B; Klaus Wessel, "Kaiserbild," in *RBK* III (1972-1978) 722-854 at 780; Pohlsander, "Crispus" 90-91; Klaus Wessel, "Konstantin u. Helena" in *RBK,* fasc. 27/28 (1989) 357-66 at 359; Richard Klein in *RAC* XIV 364. Objections were raised, however, by the following: Andrea Carandini, review of Kähler, *Die Stiftermosaiken* in *Arch. Class.* 14 (1962) 310-13; Raissa Calza, *Iconografia romana* 179-80, no. 96, and pl. LX, no. 191; Giuseppe Bovini, *Le antichità cristiane di Aquileia* (Bologna 1972) 159-61; L'Orange, *Das spätantike Herrscherbild* 119.

[4]Kähler, *Die Stiftermosaiken* 12-14 and ill. 1 and 7-10; Klauser, review of Kähler, *Die Stiftermosaiken* (see n. 3 above); Friedrich Gerke, *Spätantike und frühes Christentum* (Baden-Baden 1967) 73; Kähler, *Die frühe Kirche* 52 and color pls. A and D; Wessel, "Kaiserbild" 780; Walter N. Schumacher, *Hirt und 'Guter Hirt': Studien zum Hirtenbild in der römischen Kunst vom 2. bis zum Anfang des 4. Jahrhunderts = RömQ,* suppl. 34 (Freiburg 1977) 217-303 at 293; Wessel, "Konstantin und Helena" 359.

Theodosius.[5] Correctly identified, the five imperial personages are, from left to right, Helena, Constantine, Constantine II, Fausta, and Crispus, and the most plausible date would appear to be 317.[6] Facial features in this cameo are, unfortunately, devoid of individual fidelity.

In Cologne's Römisch-Germanisches Museum there is a cameo fragment which claims our attention. This fragment constitutes approximately one-fourth of the original whole cameo, which must have been oval in shape; it provides us with the upper-right portion of a border frieze and a small segment of the oval center. Of the male portrait head which took up the center only the nose and forehead, in profile, are extant. In the border frieze there are three female portrait heads and a very small part of a fourth one; the ladies' coiffure is that which was fashionable at Constantine's court. It has been argued convincingly that the cameo was carved in Constantinian times in a local workshop, that Constantine's image took up the center, that Constantine's four sons were presented in the lost left side of the frieze, and that the four ladies on the

[5]Lafaurie, "Médaillon Constantinien" 238-41; Adolf Furtwängler, *Die antiken Gemmen* (Leipzig 1900) III 323-24; Gerda Bruns, *Staatskameen des 4. Jahrhunderts nach Christi Geburt* (Berlin 1948) 29-31 with ill. 24; Gerda Bruns, "Der grosse Kameo von Frankreich," *Röm. Mitt.* 6 (1953) 71-115 at 84-86; Wilhelm von Sydow, *Zur Kunstgeschichte des spätantiken Porträts im 4. Jahrhundert n. Chr.* (Bonn 1969) 58.

[6]Anna Maria Cetto, "Der Trierer Caesaren-Cameo: Eine neue Deutung," *Der kleine Bund* 30, no. 39 (Bern, Sept. 30, 1949, when the cameo was on exhibit in Bern); J.M.C. Toynbee, "Der römische Kameo der Stadtbibliothek Trier," *TZ* 20 (1951) 175-77; Maria R. Alföldi, *Die constantinische Goldprägung* 127-28; Kaiser, *op. cit.* 24-35; A. N. Zadoks-Josephus Jitta, "Imperial Messages in Agate, II," *BAB* 41 (1966) 91-104 at 98-99; Pohlsander, "Crispus" 93-95 and ill. 9; Dagmar Stutzinger in *Spätantike und frühes Christentum* 432-33, no. 45; Winfried Weber in *Schatzkunst Trier* (exhibition catalogue, Trier 1984) 77-78, no. 2; Kleiner, *op. cit.* 441-442 with ill. 403. Somewhat divergent interpretations are those of Andreas Alföldi, "Der grosse römische Kameo der Trierer Stadtbibliothek," *TZ* 19 (1950) 41-44, and of Kempf, "Die altchristliche Bischofsstadt Trier" 52, n. 15. Alföldi's interpretation, which does not affect the identification of Helena and Constantine, was accepted by Wessel, "Kaiserbild" 780-81, and by Richard Klein in *RAC* XIV 364, but rejected by Josef Engemann, "Glyptik," in *RAC* XI (1981) 270-313 at 303. Kempf's interpretation retains Constantine but eliminates Helena, following an earlier interpretation of Felix Hettner. Raissa Calza, *Iconografia romana* 180, no. 97; 240-41, no. 152; and pl. LXXXIII, no. 292, questions the identifications (and, p.180, but not p. 240, erroneously places the cameo in Trier's cathedral). Whether the cameo was originally carved in the 1st century and then reworked in the 4th century cannot be decided here, but I think not.

right were members of Constantine's family. But it is not possible to say which of the four ladies might be Helena.[7]

A much more impressive piece is a large (21.1 x 29.7 cm.) sardonyx cameo in the Royal Coin Cabinet formerly in The Hague, but now in Leiden.[8] It is described by Gisela M. A. Richter[9] as follows:

> An emperor and his family, in a chariot drawn by two
> bearded Centaurs. Beneath one of the Centaurs is an
> upturned krater; beneath the other are two vanquished
> enemies. A Victoria is flying toward the emperor,
> holding out a wreath in both hands. The emperor wears
> a tunic and a paludamentum, and has a laurel wreath on
> his head, as well as sandals on his feet. In his right
> hand he holds a thunderbolt, being likened to Jupiter; his
> left arm is placed round the shoulders of the woman by
> his side, who also wears a laurel wreath, and so must be
> a member of the imperial family. In her left hand she
> held ears and a poppy, being likened to Ceres. She
> wears a chiton and a himation, brought up to the
> back of her head, also a diadem and a necklace. Behind
> the emperor appears a young woman, likewise with a
> laurel wreath, and with her hair tied at the back. As a
> fourth occupant of the chariot is seen a little boy,
> wearing a cuirass and a helmet, his left hand lowered to
> his sword.

Several scholars have associated this cameo with Constantine and his family and, more specifically, have identified the young woman behind the emperor as Helena.[10] While the Constantinian association is

---

[7]Inv. no. N 5392. Jörgen Bracker, "Eine Kölner Kameenwerkstatt im Dienste konstantinischer Familienpolitik,' *JbAC* 17 (1974) 103-108 at 103-105 and pl. 8a. Bracker's interpretation was accepted by Wessel, "Kaiserbild" 781, and by Richard Klein in *RAC* XIV 364, but rejected by Hugo Brandenburg in *BZ* 69 (1976) 605 and by Antje Krug, *Antike Gemmen im Römisch-Germanishen Museum Köln* (Frankfurt 1981) 184-85, no. 61, and pl. 75, no. 61. Engemann, *op. cit.* 304, remains skeptical.

[8]Furtwängler, *op. cit.* I, pi. LXVI, no. 1, and II 304-305. A fine color photograph is found in Michael Grant, *The Fall of the Roman Empire: A Reappraisal* (Radnor, Pennsylvania, 1976) 207.

[9]*The Engraved Gems of the Romans* (London 1971), no. 600.

[10]Bruns, *Staatskamen* 8-16; Zadoks-Josephus Jitta, "De grote camee in het Kon. Penningkabinet," *Hermeneus* 22 (1951) 182-85; Vogt, "Heiden und Christen" 158-59; Gisela M. A. Richter, *loc. cit.* (n. 9 above); Engemannn, *op. cit.* 304-305. Richard Klein in *RAC* XIV 364 reserves judgment. For a variant interpretation see Frédéric Louis Bastet, "Die grosse Kamee in Den Haag," *BAB* 43 (1968) 2-22.

probably correct, the identification of Helena is, in my opinion, impossible: Helena appears *much* too young, even girlish, and nowhere else in Roman art is she relegated to such inferior position. The pagan iconography of this cameo presents additional difficulties.[11]

We return now to Helena's porphyry sarcophagus, in the Vatican Museum, which was discussed in chapter XII above. On the two long sides of this sarcophagus (A and C), in the upper corners, there are portrait busts which are clearly apart from the narrative reliefs below them. Of the two busts in front the one on the right, a woman wearing a diadem, has been identified as an ancient portrait of Helena;[12] the identification is supported by a slightly curved nose, a small mouth, and a generally youthful appearance. But it has also been held that this bust is part of the restorations of 1778-1787.[13] Its value as a true likeness of Helena is therefore quite limited. The identification of the other portrait busts presents similar problems.

It is known from the literary and epigraphical evidence previously considered that statues were erected to Helena in Rome, Constantinople, and elsewhere. We would be surprised if it were not so. Many of Helena's statues have perished, of course, and the identification of some others is questionable.

In the Sala degli Imperatori of Rome's Capitoline Museum there is a seated statue of a woman, made of Greek marble and based on a Greek prototype of the fifth century.[14] Once believed to be a work of the first century A.D. and to represent Agrippina the Elder, it is now recognized to represent Helena.[15] We may observe a curved nose, a

---

[11]Pohlsander, "Crispus" 96-97; Drijvers, *op. cit.* 192-93. We cannot even exclude the possibility that the cameo is a work of the 17th century; see Dagmar Stutzinger in *Spätantikes und frühes Christentum* 435-37, no. 47.

[12]Raissa Calza, "Cronologia ed identificazione" 133-34 with figs. 22 and 22a; Raissa Calza, *Iconografia romana* 173, no. 84, and pl. LVI, nos. 173-74.

[13]Sjöqvist and Westholm, *op. cit.* 21 and 25; Amelung and Lippold, op.cit., text III.1 195-96; Bernard Andreae in Wolfgang Helbig, *op. cit.* I⁴ 20-21, no. 25; Max Wegner in L'Orange, *Das Spätantike Herrscherbild* 146; Drijvers, *op. cit.* 190.

[14]Loc. no. 59; inv. no. 496.

[15]Johann Jakob Bernoulli, *Römische Ikonographie* (Stuttgart 1882-1894) II.1 245-47 with fig. 44; Henry Stuart Jones, *A Catalogue of the Ancient Sculptures Preserved in the Municipal Collections of Rome: The Sculptures of the Museo Capitolino* (Oxford 1912) 214-15, no. 84, and pl. 53; Raissa Calza, "Cronologia ed identificazione" 107-36; Raissa Calza, "Elena," in *Enciclopedia dell'arte antica* III (1960) 297-99 at 299; Hans Peter L'Orange, "Der subtile Stil," *Antike Kunst* 4 (1961) 68-74 at 72 and pl. 30, ill. 3 and 4; Helga von Heintze in Wolfgang Helbig, *op. cit.* II⁴ 153-54, no. 1326; Irving Lavin, "An
(continued...)

172 IMAGE IN ROMAN ART

small mouth, and a hairstyle familiar from her coin images. The diadem which she wears allows us to date the statue – or at least the head, which is inserted – to 325 or later. The identification is practically assured by a striking resemblance to the bronze medallion of Helena in the British Museum.[16] It may be of some interest also that this statue served Antonio Canova as a model for his statue of "Madame Mére" (Letizia Ramolino, the mother of Napoleon Bonaparte).[17]

Another seated statue of Helena is in the Uffizi Gallery in Florence.[18] In pose, style, and features it is quite similar to, but not a replica of, the one in Rome; it is of Roman provenience.[19] Also, a portrait bust, of unknown provenience, in the Vatican's Palazzo del Governatorato is so similar to the head of the seated Helena in the Capitoline Museum that it has been regarded by some as an ancient likeness of Helena and by others as a modern copy.[20]

[15](...continued)
Ancient Statue" 59 with n. 13; Erika E. Schmidt, *Römische Frauenstatuen* (n. p., 1967) 171-74; Helga von Heintze, "Ein spätantikes Mädchenporträt in Bonn," *JbAC* 14 (1971) 61-91 at 64, no. 2, 66, and pl. 3c; Raissa Calza, *Iconografia romana* 170-71, no. 80, and pl. LII, nos. 161-63; Marianne Bergmann, *Studien zum römischen Porträt des 3. Jahrhunderts n. Chr.* (Bonn 1977) 199; Klaus Fittschen and Paul Zanker, *Katalog der römischen Porträts in den Capitolinischen Museen und den anderen kommunalen Sammlungen der Stadt Rom* III (Mainz 1983) 35-36, no. 38, and pls. 47-48; Richard Klein in *RAC* XIV 365; Max Wegner in L'Orange, *Das spätantike Herrscherbild* 146; Drijvers, *op. cit.* 191; Kleiner, *op. cit.* 442 and ill. 404. But Vodová, "La chronologie de la vie d'Hélène" 69-70, 71, and pl. IX, raises objections; so does Wessel, "Konstantin u. Helena" 358.

[16]To be considered in chapter XIV below.

[17]Devonshire Collection, Chatsworth, England. Giulio Carlo Argan, *Antonio Canova* (Rome 1969) 130; Mario Praz and Giuseppe Pavanello, *L'opera completa del Canova* (Milan 1976) 110, nos. 147-48, and pls. XXXII and XXXIII; Fred Licht and David Finn, *Canova* (New York 1983) 37, 39, and 143-44.

[18]Inv. no. 1914.171. Bernoulli, *op. cit.* II.1 384.

[19]Raissa Calza, "Cronologia ed identificazione" 115 and ill. 11, 14, and 14a; Guido A. Mansuelli, *Galleria degli Uffizi: Le sculture* (Rome 1958-1961) II 131, no. 171, and pl. 168a-c; Erika E. Schmidt, *loc. cit.* (n. 15); Helga von Heintze, "Ein spätantikes Mädchenporträt" 64, no. 3, and 66; Raissa Calza, *Iconografia romana* 171-72, no. 81, pl. LIII, no. 164, and pl. LIV, nos. 167-68; Bergmann, *Studien zum römische Porträt* 199; Max Wegner in L'Orange, *Das spätantike Herrscherbild* 144. Wessel, *loc. cit.* (n. 15) again objects.

[20]Inv. no. 19152. Raissa Calza, "Cronologia ed identificazione" 126 and ill. 18 and 18a; Rassa Calza, *Iconografia romana* 172, no. 82, and pl. LIV, nos. 165-66; Dagmar Stutzinger in *Spätantikes und frühes Christentum* 429-30, no. 41; Max Wegner in
(continued...)

Plate XIII

Detail from the sarcophagus of Helena (the upper right-hand corner of the front), a likeness of Helena, but of questionable date.

Head of a seated statue once believed to represent Agrippina the Elder, now recognized as Helena. Note the diadem. Sala degli Imperatore, Capitoline Museum, Rome.

There are several Roman sculptures which *possibly* are portraits of Helena. One such, in the Museum of Fine Arts, Boston, is a head which has been identified as Helena, Fausta, or a lady of the Theodosian period. The facial features are youthful; in the absence of a diadem a date before 325 will have to be assumed, if indeed this is Helena.[21] Another, in Berlin's Pergamon-Museum, is a bust so heavily restored as to make assessment difficult.[22] A third, not very strong, possibility is a head in the Ny Carlsberg Glyptotek in Copenhagen.[23]

In 1924 the Kunsthistorisches Museum of Vienna acquired a marble portrait head of unknown provenience, of no more than average quality, and in slightly damaged condition. The portrait is that of an older woman, whom Julius Bankó has identified as St. Helena.[24] This identifi-

[20](...continued)
L'Orange, *Das spätantike Herrscherbild* 146-47; Drijvers, *op. cit.* 191. Helga von Heintze, "Ein spätantikes Mädchenporträt" 67, n. 16; Marianne Bergmann, "Fälschung, Umarbeitung oder eigener Stil: Beobachtungen zu einer konstantinischen Porträtbüste," *Städel-Jb.*, n. s. 10 (1905) 45-54 at 45-50.

[21]Accession no. 62.662; acquired in Rome. "Recent Museum Acquisitions," *Apollo* 77 (1963) 348, fig. 1; Cornelius C. Vermeule, "Greek, Etruscan, and Roman Sculptures in the Museum of Fine Arts, Boston," *AJA* 68 (1964) 323-41 at 339-40 and pl. 106, fig. 34; Von Sydow, *op. cit.* 7-8, n. 19, and 161; Jaroslav T. Folda in *Ancient Portraits* (exh. cat.; Chapel Hill, N.C., 1970), no. 24; Museum of Fine Arts, Boston, *Greek and Roman Portraits, 470 BC - AD 500* (Boston 1972), no. 83; Mary B. Comstock and Cornelius C. Vermeule, *Sculpture in Stone: The Greek, Roman, and Etruscan Collections of the Museum of Fine Arts, Boston* (Boston 1976) 242-43, no. 380; James D. Breckenridge in Weitzmann, *Age of Spirituality* 21, no. 14; Max Wegner in L'Orange, *Das spätantike Herrscherbild* 144.

[22]Inv. no. 449 (in storage). Carl Blümel, *Römische Bildnisse in Staatlichen Museen zu Berlin* (Berlin 1933) 50, R 120, and pl. 76; Raissa Calza, "Cronologia ed identificazione" 125-26 and ill. 16 and 16a; Raissa Calza, *Iconografia romana* 172-73, no. 83, and pl. LV, nos. 169 and 171; Max Wegner in L'Orange, *Das Spätantike Herrscherbild* 143-44; Wessel, "Konstantin u. Helena" 358. Differenty Bianca Maria Felletti Maj, "Contributo alla iconografia del IV secolo D.C.: Il ritratto femminile," *Critica d'arte* 6 (1941) 74-90 at 78-79, no. 8.

[23]Inv. no. 1938. Frederik Poulsen, *Catalogue of Ancient Sculptures in the Ny Carlsburg Glyptotek* (Copenhagen 1951) 529, no. 762, and Billedtavler, pl. LXV (4th century); Julius Bankó, "Porträtkopf der heiligen Helena," *Jb. der Kunsthist. Sammlung in Wien*, n.s. 1 (1926) 11-14 at 12; Frederik Poulsen, "Mellem Glyptotekets romerske portraetter," *Kunstmuseets Aarsskrift* 13-15 (1926-1928) 1-55 at 25 and ill. 30; Felletti Maj, "Contributo alla iconografia" 77-78, no. 5; Helga von Heintze, "Ein spätantikes Mädchenbild" 64, no. 1, and pl. 3a; Vagn Poulsen, *Les portraits romains* II (Copenhagen 1974) 192, no. 199, and pls. CCCXXIV-CCCXXV; Max Wegner in L'Orange, *das spätantike Herrscherbild* 144.

[24]Inv. no. I 1497. *Op. cit.* 11-14 and pl. II.

cation is based primarily on comparison with the medallion in the British Museum. The portrait would have to be no later than 325, since Helena does not wear a diadem. Bankó also thought that the physiognomy of this head expressed the "severity and seriousness of the Christian spirit." Bankó's interpretation of this portrait head has been rejected by other scholars.[25]

A head, now mounted on a modern bust, in Rome's Museo Torlonia is of special interest to us because it was found near the Tor Pignattara, Helena's mausoleum. And, indeed, it was first believed to be a portrait of Helena, but later scholarship has been unanimous in holding otherwise.[26]

There are some additional Roman sculptures which one scholar or another, at one time or another, attempted to identify as a portrait of Helena, without evidence strong enough to persuade many others. Thus Jules Maurice thought that he could identify a portrait bust in the Salone of Rome's Capitoline Museum as a portrait of Helena, but this identification has not found favor with other scholars.[27] And in the Musée du

[25]Raissa Calza, "Cronologia ed identificazione" 132; Helga von Heintze, "Ein spätantikes Mädchenporträt" 67, 73, no. 1, and 74; Raissa Calza, *Iconografia romana* 177, no. 91, and pl. LIX, no. 185; Bergmann, *Studien zum römischen Porträt* 200; Karina Türr, *Fälschungen antiker Plastik seit 1800* (Berlin 1984) 214-15; Max Wegner in L'Orange, *Das spätantike Herrscherbild* 147-48; Bergmann, "Fälschung, Umarbeitung, oder eigener Stil" 50-51 with ill. 11; Wessel, "Konstantin u. Helena" 359.

[26]Carlo Lodovico Visconti, *Les monuments de sculpture antique du Musée Torlonia* (Rome 1884) 429, no. 611; reluctantly followed by Bernoulli, *op. cit.* II.3 203; Bankó, *op. cit.* 12; Hans-Henning Lauer, *op. cit.* 13; Delbrueck, *Spätantike Kaiserporträts*, 49 and ill. 20; Felletti Maj, "Contributo alla iconografia" 83, no. 27, and pl. XLVIII, no. 10; Raissa Calza, "Cronologia ed identificazione" 132; Von Sydow, *op. cit.* 67 and pl. 1; Helga von Heintze, "Ein spätantikes Mädchenporträt" 73, no. 5, and pls. 9d and 11b; Ranuccio Bianchi Bandinelli, *Rome: The Late Empire* (New York 1971) 38 and ill. 34 (Eudoxia?); Raissa Calza, *Iconografia romana* 132-33, no. 43, and pl. XXXI, nos. 85-86; Bergmann, *Studien zum römischen Porträt* 199; Max Wegner in L'Orange, *Das spätantike Herrscherbild* 147; Wessel, "Konstantin u. Helena" 359. It has recently been proposed that the Torlonia collection, which has long been inaccessible, be exhibited in the Palazzo Torlonia on the Via della Conciliazione. Under this proposal the head of 'Helena' would be among 114 portraits (Visconti 507-620) to be displayed in the corridor which encompasses the upper floor. See Maria Elisa Tittoni and Sergio Guarino, edd., *Invisibilia: Rivivere i capolavori, vedere i progetti* (exhibition catalogue, Rome 1992) 125-37, esp. 125 and 128. I owe the reference to the kindness of Professor Malcolm Bell, III.

[27]Loc. no. 57; inv. no. 679. Henry Stuart Jones, *The Sculptures of the Museo Capitolino* 304, no. 57, and pl. 75; "Portraits d'imperatrices de l'epoque constantinienne," *NC* 1914, pp. 314-29 at 317-20 with figs. 1-2; Maurice, *Sainte Hélène*
(continued...)

Bardo in Tunis there is a head which Jean Charbonneaux took to represent Helena but which others have assigned to the Antonine Age.[28] And to the some category we must assign the following:
A head in Fasanerie Castle (formerly Adolphseck) near Fulda.[29]
A headless statue in the Museum Carnuntinum in Deutsch Altenburg in Lower Austria.[30]

[27](...continued)
6-8. Maurice apparently misinterpreted Richard Delbrueck, "Porträts byzantinischer Kaiserinnen," *Röm. Mitt.* 28 (1913) 310-52 at 327-30 and figs. 7a-c. Bankó, *op. cit.* 14, n. 26. Delbrueck, *Spätantike Kaiserporträts* 49 and ill. 19; Felletti Maj, "Contributo alia iconografia" 79, no. 10, and pl. 46.3; Elizabeth Alföldi-Rosenbaum, "Portrait Bust of a Young Lady of the Time of Justinian," *MMJ* 1 (1968) 19-40 at 38 and fig. 29; Helga von Heintze, "Ein spätantikes Mädchenporträt" 74, no. 11, and 75; Henning Wrede, *Die spätantike Hermengalerie von Welschbilig* (Berlin 1972) 94 and pls. 61.2 and 62.2; Raissa Calza, *Iconografia romana* 177-78, no. 92, and pl. LIX, nos. 187-88; Fittschen and Zanker, *op. cit.* 119-20, no. 181, and pls. 211-12; Max Wegner in L'Orange, *Das spätantike Herrscherbild* 145-46.

[28]Inv. no. C 76. Mohamed Yacoub, *Musée du Bardo* (Tunis 1970) 23; Charbonneaux, "Un portrait d'Hélène, mère de Constantin, au Musée du Bardo," *RArts* 2 (1952) 153-58; Raissa Calza, "Cronologia ed identificazione" 133; Maria R. Alföldi, *Die constantinische Goldprägung* 133, n. 1; Von Sydow, *op. cit.* 153; Raissa Calza, *Iconografia romana* 178, no. 93, and pl. LIX, no. 186. Max Wegner in L'Orange, *Das spätantike Herrscherbild* 147, rightly points out that the coiffure alone makes this identification very unlikely. Only Helga von Heintze, "Ein spätantikes Mädchenporträt" 67, deems Char-bonneaux's identification probable. Richard Klein in *RAC* XIV 365 quotes von Heintze.

[29]Helga von Heintze, *Die antiken Porträts der landgräflich-hessischen Sammlungen in Schloss Fasanerie bei Fulda* (Mainz 1968) 82-83, no. 55, and pls. 92, 93, and 140a and b (Helena?); Helga von Heintze, "Ein spätantikes Mädchenporträt" 74, no. 7, and pl. 10c (Helena?); Raissa Calza, *Iconografia romana* 267-68, no. 180, and pl. XCIII, nos. 327-30 (Constantia I); Max Wegner in L'Orange, *Das spätantike Herrscherbild* 143 (neither Helena nor Constantia). The head is now in the Villa Polissena, Rome, I have been informed by Mr. Andreas Dobler of the staff of Fasanerie Castle.

[30]Bernoulli, *op. cit.* II.3 86, nos. 13-14 (Elagabalus?); Alfred von Domaszewski *Die Religion des römischen Heeres* (Trier 1895) 65 (Monimos, an oriental god); Josef (Giuseppe) Wilpert, "Un capitolo di storia del vestiario," *L'arte* 1 (1898) 89-121 at 103-104 and fig. 21 (3rd or 4th century); Salomon Reinach, *Répertoire de la statuaire grecque et romaine* 2nd ed. II.1 (Paris 1908) 272, no. 8 (Cybele); Andreas Alföldi, "A Carnuntumi díszes ruhájú nöszobor," *Országos magyar régészeti társulat* 1 (1920-1922) 39-41 (Julia Domna); Andreas Alföldi, *Die monarchische Repräsentation* 145 with ill. 1 (an empress of the 3rd century); Sandro Stucchi, "Le due statue del praetorium di Cornuntum ed altri monumenti del museo di Deutsch Altenburg," *Bull. della commissione arch. communale di Roma* 73 (1949-1950), appendice 15-24 with ill. 1 (Fausta or, preferably, Helena); Erich Swoboda, *Carnuntum,* 2nd ed. (Vienna 1953) 108
(continued...)

A second head in the Ny Carlsberg Glyptotek in Copenhagen.[31]
A head in the Maison Carrée in Nimes.[32]
A bust in the Louvre.[33]
A statuette from Cyprus in the Cabinet des Médailles of the
Bibliothèque Nationale in Paris.[34]

[30](...continued)
and pl. XIV.2 (Julia Mamaea). But there is no mention of this statue in the 3rd ed.
(Graz 1958). Bianca Maria Folletti Maj, *Iconografia romana imperiale da Severo
Alessandro a M. Aurelio Carino* (Rome 1958) 113, no. 70 (uncertain); Max Wegner,
Das römische Herrscherbild III.1 (Berlin 1971) 149 and 206; Max Wegner in L'Orange,
Das spätantike Herrscherbild 144 (not pertinent).

[31]Inv. no. 835. Frederik Poulsen, *Catalogue* 538-39, no. 773, and Billedtavler, pl.
LXVI (end of the fourth century); Bernoulli, *op. cit.* II.3 203 (Helena); Bankó, *op. cit.*
13 and 14, n. 26 (not compelling); Frederik Poulsen, "Mellem Glyptotekets romerske
portraetter" 31 and ill. 44; Arnold Walter Lawrence, *Classical Sculpture* (London 1929)
398 and pl. 160a (doubtfully identified as St. Helena); Felletti Maj, "Contributo alla
iconografia" 82, no. 21 (ca. 360); Raissa Calza, "Cronologia ed identificazione" 132 (end
of the 3rd century); Rumpf, *op. cit.* 32 and pls. 28 and 122 (5th century); Helga von
Heintze, *Römische Porträtplastik aus sieben Jahrhunderten* (Stuttgart 1961) 17 and pl.
42 (middle of the 4th century); Maria R. Alföldi, *Die constantinische Goldprägung* 133,
n. 1 (Helena); Von Sydow, *op. cit.* 88 (ca. 440); Helga von Heintze, "Ein spätantikes
Mädchenbild" 76, no. 1, and pl. 11d (ca. 360); Raissa Calza, *Iconografia romana* 149-
50, no. 62; 178-79, no. 94; pls. XLII, no. 121, and XLIII, no. 122 (Galeria Valeria);
Vagn Poulsen, op. cit. II 195-96, no. 203, and pls. CCCXXXI-CCCXXXII (Aelia
Flaccilla?); Max Wegner in L'Orange, *Das spätantike Herrscherbild* 144-45 (*not*
Helena).

[32]Bankó, *op. cit.* 12 (similar to the head in Vienna); Reinach, *op. cit.* II.2 637, no.
4; Felletti Maj, "Contributo alla iconografia" 78, no. 6 (Constantinian); Raissa Calza,
"Cronologia ed identificazione" 126 (Helena); Raissa Calza, *Iconografia romana* 176,
no. 89, and pl. LVIII, nos. 179-80 (Helena); Max Wegner in L'Orange, *Das spätantike
Herrscherbild* 145 (*not* Helena).

[33]Salle des Saisons, no. 995. Eugénie Strong, La scultura romana I.2 (Florence 1923)
412 with ill. 253 (Helena); Eugénie Strong, *Art in Ancient Rome* II (New York 1928) 192
with fig. 550 (perhaps Helena); Étienne Coche de la Ferté, *La sculpture grecque et
romaine au Musée du Louvre*, 3rd ed. (Paris 1955) 70, ill. 71 (Julia Maesa); Jean
Charbonneaux, *La sculpture grecque et romaine au Musée du Louvre* (Paris 1963) 181
(Julia Maesa); Käte Buchholz, *Die Bildnisse der Kaiserinnen der severischen Zeit nach
ihren Frisuren* (Frankfurt 1963) 160 (3rd century); Max Wegner, *Das römische
Herrscherbild* III.1 157; Max Wegner in L'Orange, *Das spätantike Herrscherbild* 145
(not Helena).

[34]Carlo Albizzati, "Une statuette-portrait du Bas-Empire à la Bibliothèque Nationale,"
Aréthuse 5 (1928) 163-68, had dated this statuette to the 5th or 6th century. Delbrueck,
Spätantike Kaiserporträts 163-65 and pls. 62-64, claims this statuette for Helena. So
does Olof Vessberg, "Roman Portrait Art in Cyprus," *Opuscula Romana* 1 (1954) 160-65
(continued...)

A head in the Museo dell'Opera del Duomo in Pisa.[35]
A head in the magazine of the Museo Capitolino in Rome.[36]
A head known only from a drawing in the Barberini Codex (?) in the Vatican Library.[37]
The head on a (modern) statue on the grounds of the Villa Borghese in Rome.[38]

[34](...continued)
at 165 and figs. 14-15; *id.*, *Romersk Porträttkonst*, 3rd ed. (Göteborg 1985) 53 and fig. 71. The provenience of the statuette is no support for the attribution, since Helena's visit to Cyprus is no more than a possibility; see chapter VIII above. Others have not followed Delbrueck: Raissa Calza "Cronologia ed identificazione" 133 *(not* Constantinian); L'Orange, "Der subtile Stil" 72 and pl. 30, nos. 5-7 (probably Aelia Flaccilla); Wolfgang Friedrich Volbach, *Early Christian Art* (New York 1962) 323 and pl. 58 (Theodosian; Aelia Flaccilla?); Jale Inan and Elisabeth Rosenbaum, *Roman and Early Byzantine Portrait Sculpture in Asia Minor* (London 1966) 202, n. 2; Erika E. Schmidt, *op. cit.* 177 (ca. 400); Cornelius C. Vermeule, *Roman Imperial Art in Greece and Asia Minor* (Cambridge, Massachusetts, 1968) 405-406 (Aelia Flaccilla); Raissa Calza, *Iconografia romana* 175-76, no. 88, and pl. LVIII, nos. 182-83 (*not* Helena); Vodová, "La chronologie de la vie d'Hélène 70-71 and pl. X (end of the 4th century, probably Aelia Flaccilla or Eudoxia); James D. Breckenridge in Weitzmann, *Age of Spirituality* 26-27, no. 20, and pl. I; Max Wegner in L'Orange, *Das spätantike Herrscherbild* 145.

[35]Inv. 1963, no. 93 (9); formerly in the Camposanto, inv. no. 36; Bernoulli, *op. cit.* II.3 203 (Helena); Roberto Papini, *Catalogo delle cose d'arte e di antichità d'Italia: Pisa* (Rome 1912-1914) 11 102, no. 169 (Constantinian or later); Bankó *op. cit.* 12; Felletti Maj, "Contributo alla iconografia" 83, no. 26; Raissa Calza "Cronologia ed identificazione" 132 (not in the least like Helena); Raissa Calza, 176-77, no. 90, and pl. LIX, no. 184 (middle of the 4th century); Max Wegner in L'Orange, *Das spätantike Herrscherbild* 145; Lucia Faedo in Salvatore Settis, *Camposanto Monumentale di Pisa: Le antichità II* (Pisa 1984) 147-49, no. 72 (post-Constantinian).

[36]Former (Palazzo dei Conservatori) inv. no. 1005. Henry Stuart Jones, *A Catalogue of the Ancient Sculptures Preserved in the Municipal Collections of Rome: The Sculptures of the Palazzo dei Conservatori* (Oxford 1926) 228, no. 34, and pl. 86; L'Orange, "Der subtile Stil" 71 and pl. 29, ill. 5 and 6; Vermeule, "Greek, Etruscan, and Roman Sculptures" 340; Von Sydow, *op. cit.* 7; Max Wegner in L'Orange, *Das spätantike Herrscherbild* 146 (*not* Helena).

[37]Vat. lat, fol. 172 (An incomplete or erroneous citation?); Raissa Calza, *Iconografia romana* 174, no. 85, and pl. LVI, no 175 (no resemblance to Helena); Max Wegner in L'Orange, *Das spätantike Herrscherbild* 146 (concurs with Calza).

[38]Paul Arndt and Walter Amelung, *Photographische Einzelaufnahmen antiker Skulpturen* (Munich 1893-1940), series X, no 2842, with text by Paolina Mingazzini; Delbrueck, *Spätantike Kaiserporträts* 64; Felletti Maj, "Contributo alla iconografia 80, no 15; Raissa Calza, "Cronologia ed identificazione" 136 with ill. 24 (Helena); Helga von Heintze, "Ein spätantikes Mädchenporträt 66-67 with nn. 14 and 16 (a modern
(continued...)

A head in the Stathatos Collection in the National Museum in Athens.[39]

A head in the Archaeological Museum in Istanbul.[40]

It would appear then that there are only five pieces of Roman art of which we may say with some confidence that they provide us with portraits of Helena: the medallion in Nantes, the mosaic floor in Aquileia, the cameo in Trier, the seated statue in Rome, and the seated statue in Florence. Only the last two of these have features which are distinct enough to give us a sense of individual identity and character. We must allow for the tendency of imperial portraiture to idealize, and there is no suggestion of Helena's true age. Yet, the impression is one of noble beauty and keen intelligence. I do not see the "severity and seriousness of the Christian spirit" which Bankó attributed to the supposed head of Helena in Vienna. That Constantine held his mother in high regard and that she played an important role in his dynastic policy is confirmed.

Among the works of art here considered there is only one, it should be noted, in which we encounter a Christian symbol, namely the medallion in Nantes, and that dates from the final years of Helena's life. The imperial portraits in the mosaic floor in Aquileia, although set in a Christian context, are religiously neutral. No case can be made for the use of Christian symbols in the Trier cameo.[41] The two seated statues in Rome and Florence respectively are entirely in the tradition of pre-Christian Greek art. We have learned nothing about the date or circumstances of Helena's conversion.

[38](...continued)

copy); Raissa Calza, *Iconografia romana* 174-75, no 86, and pl LV, nos. 170-72 (Helena); Max Wegner in L'Orange, *Das spätantike Herrscherbild* 147 (*not* Helena); Bergmann, "Fälschung, Umarbeitung oder eigener Stil" 48-49 with ill. 9 (*not* Helena). The Villa Borghese is currently undergoing renovation and not accessible.

[39]Pierre Amandry in *Collection Hélène Stathotos* III (Strasbourg 1963) 48, no. 15, with fig. 20, and pls. IV bis and V (middle of the 3rd century); Helga von Heintze, "Ein spätantikes Mädchenporträt" 65, no. 6, 67, and pls. 5d, 7b, and 8b (Helena); Wessel, "Konstantin u. Helena" 358 (*not* Helena).

[40]Inv. n. 5318; found at Nicomedia (Izmit). Friedrich Karl Dörner, "Inschriften und Denkmäler aus Bithynien," *Istanbuler Forschungen* 14 (1941) 1-127 at 48, no. 7, and pl. 12; Inan and Rosenbaum, *op.cit.* 99-100, no.91,and pl. LVI (a private portrait, end of the 4th century); Vermeule, *Roman Imperial Art* 44, 58, and 354; not mentioned by Calza or Wegner.

[41]Engemann, *op. cit.* 304.

Chapter XIV.
The Numismatic and Epigraphic Evidence

Roman imperial coinage is of twofold interest to us in our study of Helena the empress. Coins minted in Helena's honor clearly demonstrate her rise to a position of honor and power, and they render her physiognomic features more faithfully than other media.

In the years before 325 the imperial mint of Thessalonike issued a bronze follis of Helena. The obverse shows a bust of a youthful looking woman, facing right and her hair gathered in a knot in the neck; the legends reads HELENA N(obilissima) F(emina). The reverse features an eight-pointed star in a laurel wreath. The mintmark TS or TSA is sometimes omitted. Two interpretations have been offered: one holds that the Helena in question is the mother of Constantine, the other that it is the younger Helena, the wife of Crispus.[1] The former view is, I think, the correct one, because it is not reported elsewhere that the younger Helena was granted the title of *nobilissima femina* and because no other coins were minted in her honor. Besides, the same mint at the same time issued a comparable coin of Fausta, and it is not likely that

---

[1]Cohen, VII² (1888) 97, no. 14, does not take a position in this matter. Maurice, *Numismatique Constantinienne* 1 (1908) 91 and pl. VIII, no. 1, assigns this coin to the elder Helena and to the years 313-324. But Maurice, *NC* II (1911) 452-54; 456, no. XIII; and pl. XIV, no. 5, proposes that the Helena in question is the wife of Crispus, and dates this issue to 323-324. Maurice defends this proposal in his "Portraits d'impératrices" (1914) against the criticism of Percy H. Webb, "Helena, N. F.," *NC* 1912, pp. 352-360. Delbrueck, *Spätantike Kaiserporträts* 47, 84, and pl. 10, no. 1, rejects Maurice's proposal and gives additional bibliography. Maria R. Alföldi, "Helena nobilissima femina" 82-84, revives Maurice's proposal and employs it to support the questionable identification of the younger Helena in the ceiling fresco in Trier (see chapter IV above). Carson, Hill, and Kent, *op. cit.*, part I, nos. 820 and 821-22, list this coin among those of the elder Helena. Patrick M. Bruun, *RIC VII* 493-94, 503-505, nos. 48 and 50, and pl. 15, no. 50, identifies the coin as one of Helena, the mother of Constantine, and dates it to 318-319, i. e. well before Crispus' marriage to the younger Helena; he specifically refutes the date proposed by Alföldi. Similarly Kent, *Roman Coins* 51, 330, and pl. 162, no. 638. Also Edwin Conrad, "A True Cross Bronze of Helena Sancta," *N Circ.* 86 (1978) 191-92 with fig. 2. Richard Klein in *RAC* XIV 362 appears to follow Bruun and Kent. Van Meter, *op. cit.* 293, lists this coin among those of the elder Helena, and so does Grünewald, *op. cit.* 142; but Kienast, *op. cit.* 302, seems to be persuaded by Alföldi.

the elder Helena would have been overlooked in favor of the younger Helena.[2]

Immediately after the defeat of Licinius, even before the end of the year 324, various mints began to issue coins which refer to Helena and Fausta respectively as Augusta and thus indicate equal rank for the two ladies.[3] In the coinage of Helena this type is far more common than the *nobilissima femina* type.

In 324-326 the mint of Ticinum in northwestern Italy issued a gold double-solidus or multiple which concerns us. The obverse features a bust of Helena facing right. She wears a diadem, earrings, and a necklace; her hair is combed back and then looped forward again.[4] The legend reads FL(avia) HELENA AVGVSTA. On the reverse there is an allegorical figure facing left, with a branch, the emblem of peace, in her right hand; the legend proclaims SECVRITAS REIPVBLICE (sic). The mintmark is SMT. There are specimens in Paris and in London.[5]

During the same years the mints of Ticinum, Sirmium, Thessalonike, and Nicomedia issued a gold solidus of the same design, both obverse and reverse. There are specimens in London, Belgrade, and

---

[2]Cohen, VII[2] (1888) 338, no. 25; Maurice, *NC* II 456, no. XIII, and pl. XIV, no. 6; Delbrueck, *Spätantike Kaiserporträts* 86-87, no. 2 (Sirmium?); Carson, Hill, and Kent, *op. cit.*, part I, nos. 824-25; *RIC* VII 504, no. 49; Kent, *Roman Coins* 51; Grünewald, *op. cit.* 143.

[3]Maurice, *NC* I pp. CXXXII-CXXXIII and 89-90; Maria R. Alföldi, *Die constantinische Goldprägung* 95 and 144; Reece, *op. cit.* 147; Raissa Calza, *Iconografia romana* 169 and pl. LI, no. 158; Charles Odahl, "Constantinian Coin Motifs in Ancient Literary Sources," *Journal of the Rocky Mountain Medieval and Renaissance Association* 7 (1986) 1-15 at 4-5 with figs. 3a-b; Richard Klein in *RAC* XIV 362; Robert (R. A. G.) Carson, *Coins of the Roman Empire*, (New York 1990) 170, not quite correctly, and pl. 45, nos. 669 and 670.

[4]Not an insigne of rank, but only a hairband, according to Maria R. Alföldi, *Die constantinische Goldprägung* 144-45.

[5]Cohen VII[2] (1888) 96-97, no. 10; Maurice, *NC* II 281, no. XV; Maurice erroneously assigns the coinage of Ticinum to a mint which he assumes to have existed at Tarraco (Tarragona) in Spain. His error is pointed out by C. H. V. Sutherland, *RIC* VI 6-7 and 43 with n. 1, and by Patrick M. Brunn, *RIC* VII 368, n. 53, but the same error is committed by Drijvers, *op. cit.* 42. Francesco Gnecchi, *I medaglioni Romani descritti ed illustrati* (Milan 1912) I 13 and pl. 6, no. 1; Delbrueck, *Spätantike Kaiserporträts* 85 and pl. 10, no. 10; J. M. C. Toynbee, *Roman Medallions* (New York 1944) 186 and p. XLVIII, no. 4; Maria R. Alföldi, *Die constantinische Goldprägung* 196, no. 462, and pl. 10, no. 155; *RIC* VII 383, no. 177; Kent, *Roman Coins* 330 and pls. 161-62, no. 639; Holum, *op. cit.* 33 and 35, fig. 3; Richard Klein in *RAC* XIV 362.

Vienna.[6] And bronze coins of similar design – an image of Helena, usually with diadem, and the legend FL(avia) HELENA AVGVSTA on the obverse and an allegorical figure with the legend SECVRITAS REIPVBLICE (sic) on the reverse – were put out between 324 and 330 by every mint then operating in the empire: London, Trier, Lyons, Arles, Ticinum, Rome, Siscia, Sirmium, Thessalonike, Heraclea, Constantinople, Nicomedia, Cyzicus, Antioch, and Alexandria.[7]

[6]Cohen VII[2] (1888) 97, nos. 11-13; Maurice, *NC* II 281 , no. XIV (Tarragona); II 407, no. II, and pl. XII, no. 15 (Sirmium); III 66, no. XXVI (Nicomedia); Delbrueck, *Spätantike Kaiserporträts* 85 and pl. 10, nos.7 (Nicomedia) and 11 (Sirmium); Maria R. Alföldi, *Die constantinische Goldprägung* 196, nos.463-65, and pl.10, no. 156; Picozzi, *op. cit.* 96; *RIC* VII 383, no. 183 (Ticinum); 476, no. 60 (Sirmium); 514-17, nos. 134 and 149 (Thessalonike); 613, nos. 79-80 (Nicomedia); Reece, *op. cit.*, p. 37, no. 621; Kent and Painter, *op. cit.* 166-67, no. 391 (Sirmium); Odahl, "Constantinian Coins Motifs" 5-6; National Museum, Belgrade, *Antički Portret u Jugoslaviji = Classical Portraits in Yugoslavia* (Belgrade 1987) 244, no. 245 (Thessalonike); Van Meter, *op. cit.* 293.

[7]Maurice, *NC* II 63, no. IV, and pl. II, no. 22; Gilbert Askew, *The Coinage of Roman Britain* (London 1951) 70, no. 834; Carson, Hill, and Kent, *op. cit.*, part I, no. 9; *RIC* VII 116, no 299; Carson, *op. cit.* 160; Van Meter, *op. cit.* 293, without listing the mints (London); Maurice, *NC* I 476, no. III, and pl. XXIII, no. 13; Delbrueck, *Spätantike Kaiserporträts* 85 and pl. 1O, nos. 9 and 12; Carson, Hill, and Kent, *op. cit.* part I, nos. 25, 35, 41, and 47; *RIC* VII 205-13, nos. 458, 465, 481, 508, and 515; Reece, *op. cit.*, pl. 54, nos. 877-78; Gilles, *op. cit.* 11 and 13, no. 15, and in Rheinisches Landesmuseum Trier, *Trier: Kaiserresidenz und Bischofssitz* 99, no. 22A 15 (Trier); Maurice, *NC* II 125, no. V, and pl. IV, no. 19; Carson, Hill, and Kent, *op. cit.*, part I, no. 177; *RIC* VII 137, no. 234 (Lyons); Maurice, *NC* II 185-86, no. V, and pl. VI, no. 21; Carson, Hill, and Kent, *op. cit.*, part I, nos. 287, 300, 309, 318, 327, 334, 338, and 351; *RIC* VII 264-70, nos. 278, 299, 307, 317, 324, and 340 (Arles); Maurice, *NC* II 276, no. IV, and pl. VIII, no. 16; Delbrueck, *Spätantike Kaiserporträts* 85 and pl. 1O, no. 6; Carson, Hill, and Kent, *op. cit.*, part I, nos. 474, 487, and 501; *RIC* VII 385-87, nos. 190, 202, and 209 (Ticinum); Maurice, *NC* I 240, no. IV, and pl. XVIII, no. 12; Delbrueck, *Spätantike Kaiserporträts* 85 and pl. 10, no. 3; Carson, Hill, and Kent, *op. cit.*, part I, nos. 514 and 520-21; *RIC* VII 325, no. 270, and 330, no. 291 (Rome); Maurice, *NC* II 352-53, no. III, and pl. X, no. 16; Carson, Hill, and Kent, *op. cit.*, part I, nos. 722, 728-29, 735, and 741; *RIC* VII 447-53, nos. 187, 196, 204, and 218; C. H. V. Sutherland, *Roman Coins* (New York 1974) 276-77, no. 545 (Siscia); Maurice, *NC* II 407, no. II, and pl. XII, no. 15; Carson, Hill, and Kent, *op. cit.*, part I, nos. 808-809; *RIC* VII 475-76, no. 54 (Sirmium); Maurice, *NC* II 461, no. III, and pl. XIV, no. 10; Carson, Hill, and Kent, *op. cit.*, part I, no. 823; *RIC* VII 519, no. 159 (Thessalonike); Maurice, *NC* II 597-98, no. VI, and pl. XVII, no. 16; Carson, Hill, and Kent, *op. cit.*, part I, nos. 873, 879, 886, 892-93, and 897; *RIC* VII 551-57, nos. 79, 85, 89, 95, and 109-10 (Heraclea); Maurice, *NC* II 494, no. III, and pl. XV, no. 3; Delbrueck, *Spätantike Kaiserporträts* 85 and pl. 10, no. 5; Carson, Hill, and Kent, *op. cit.*, part I, no. 975; *RIC* VII 571, no. 11 (Constantinople); Maurice, *NC* III 56, no. VI, and pl. II,

(continued...)

The Coin Cabinet of the British Museum holds a well-known and much-published bronze medallion of Helena. Some scholars believe that it was issued by the mint of Nicomedia, but Constantinople and Rome have also been suggested (there is no mintmark). The proposed dates range from 324 to 329. On the obverse the bust of Helena is again facing right and wearing a diadem; the legend reads FLAVIA AELENA (sic) AUGUSTA. On the reverse an allegorical figure, facing left, holds a child on her left arm and is offering a fruit to another child with her right hand; the legend reads PIETAS AVGVSTES (sic). The image of Helena on the obverse is of special interest to us because of its striking resemblance to the head of the statue of Helena in Rome's Capitoline Museum, as has been pointed out in the previous chapter. We may note a slightly curved nose, a small mouth with raised corners, and a strong chin; realistically Helena appears older than in most of her images.[8] The reverse happily bears out what Eusebius reports about the empress' charitable activities in the Holy Land (see chapter VIII above) and perhaps suggests that she engaged in such activities in other places as well. But *pietas* does not necessarily have Christian connotations; pagans would not be offended by it.

---

[7](...continued)
no. 23; Delbrueck, *Spätantike Kaiserporträts* 85 and pl. 10, no. 2; Carson, Hill, and Kent, *op. cit.*, part I, nos. 1082, 1091, and 1100; *RIC* VII 615-26, nos. 95, 129, 148, and 159 (Nicomedia); Maurice, *NC* III 128, no. III; Delbrueck, *Spätantike Kaiserporträts* 85 and p.10, no. 4; Carson, Hill, and Kent, *op. cit.*, part I, nos. 1168-69, 1176-77, 1184-85, 1194, 1199, and 1205; *RIC* VII 647-51, nos. 28, 39, 49, and 54, and pl. 22, no. 54 (Cyzicus); Maurice, *NC* III 203, no. V, and pl. VIII, no. 17; Delbrueck, *Spätantike Kaiserporträts* 85 and pl. 10, no. 8; Carson, Hill, and Kent, *op. cit.*, part I, nos. 1328, 1341, 1350, and 1355; *RIC* VII 689-91, nos. 67, 75, 80, and 82; Conrad, *op. cit.* with fig. 1. Another coin, Carson, Hill, and Kent, *op. cit.* part I, no. 1329, or *RIC* VII 687, no. 61, is unusual in that the legend FL(avia) HELENA AVGVSTA, together with a star in a crescent, is found on the reverse and the image of Helena without a legend on the obverse (Antioch). Maurice, *NC* III 274, no. V, and pl. X, no. 23; Carson, Hill, and Kent, *op. cit.*, part I, nos. 1406, 1412, 1416, 1417, 1422, 1423, and 1427; *RIC* VII 709-11, nos. 38, 44, 48, 53, and 57 (Alexandria).

[8]Cohen VII² (1888) 96, no. 7 (reverse legend erroneous); Maurice, *NC* I 92 and pl. VIII, no. 2; *ibid.* II 501, no. XX (reverse legend erroneous); Gnecchi, *op. cit.* II 131 and pl. 128 *(not* 129), no. 9; Maurice, St. Hélène 8; Delbrueck, *Spätantike Kaiserporträts* 47-48, ill. 17; 85-86 and pl. 11, no. 13; J. M. C. Toynbee, *Roman Medallions* 54, n. 93, and 100; Raissa Calza, "Cronologia ed identificazione" 128 with fig.20; Voelkl, *Der Kaiser Konstantin*, ill. 75; *RIC* VII 323, no. 250; Hans-Henning Lauer, *op. cit.* 23; Raissa Calza, *Iconografia romana* 169 and pl. LI, no. 159; Kent, *Roman Coins* 330 and pl. 162, no. 640; Bergmann, *Studien zum römischen Porträt* 185; Richard Klein in *RAC* XIV 362.

All the coins of Helena which were minted during her lifetime are religiously neutral. There is no reference to her conversion, her pilgrimage, or the *inventio* of the Cross. This is not entirely true of the commemorative coins of Helena which have already been considered in chapter XI above. The commemorative coins of Helena, and of Theodora, which were minted at Trier in 337 bear on the reverse, on the left side of the field, a small cross. This has been called the first use of a Christian symbol on coins minted at Trier.[9] But this cross appears neither in later emissions of the mint of Trier nor at other mints; it is therefore most likely a distinguishing sign, in addition to the mint mark, and of little or no religious significance.[10]

Helena makes her appearance in Byzantine coinage as well, but not very often, as a saint more than as empress, and in the company of Constantine.

During the Latin Empire of Constantinople (1204-1261) the mint of Thessalonike produced two types of "Latin imitative" coins which pertain to Helena. One is a billon trachy which features on the obverse an image of Christ and on the reverse full-length figures of Constantine (right) and Helena (left) in imperial dress and holding a double-barred cross between them.[11] The other is a copper half-tetarteron with a full-length figure of Helena on the obverse and a full-length figure of Constantine on the reverse.[12] In both types the identification is assured by legends.

We meet Constantine and Helena again on the reverse of copper coins minted under the Palaeologan emperors John V (1341-1391),

[9]Peter N. Schulten, *op. cit.* 30.

[10]*RIC* VIII 143, nos. 42 and 43. Guido Bruck, "Die Verwendung christlicher Symbole auf Münzen von Constantin I bis Magnentius," *NZ* 76 (1955) 26-32, does not consider this coin type.

[11]Billon is an alloy of copper and silver. At this time a billon trachy was worth 1/184 of a gold hyperpyron, the Byzantine standard coin. Michael F. Hendy, *Coinage and Money in the Byzantine Empire, 1081-1261* (Washington, D. C., 1969) 197 and pl. 28, nos. 9-10; Philip D. Whitting, *Byzantine Coins* (New York 1973) 220-21, nos. 360-61; Philip Grierson, *Byzantine Coins* (Berkeley and London 1982) 242, 259, and pl. 79, no. 1264.

[12]A tetarteron was a small-denomination copper coin; Michael F. Hendy, *op. cit.* 198 and pl. 28, nos. 12-14; Grierson, *op. cit.* 242, 259, and pl. 79, no. 1266.

Manuel II (1391-1425), and John VII (1399-1402).[13] Again Constantine and Helena are in imperial dress and hold a long cross between them.

In chapter VII above we have considered several inscriptions which document Helena's residence in Rome.[14] And in chapter II above we have briefly mentioned two inscriptions which refer to Helena as the legitimate wife of Constantius.[15] But we have not yet exhausted the epigraphic evidence.

The two inscriptions which refer to Helena as the legitimate wife of Constantius (I) are of further interest. The first of these was put up by a certain Alpinius Magnus, corrector of Lucania and Bruttium, at Salernum.[16] It stresses Helena's role as the mother of the ruling Augustus and grandmother of the Caesars Crispus, Constantine (II), and Constantius (II). Constantius was proclaimed Caesar on November 8, 324, while Crispus was executed at some time in 326; we thus have a fairly accurate date for this inscription. Interestingly enough the name of Crispus was subsequently erased but could still be read. The second inscription was put up by the senate and people of Naples and hails Helena as Augusta, thus giving us a date of 324 or later.[17] The Caesars are referred to only collectively rather than individually, so that only Helena's death can serve as a terminus ante quem. We can do no better for another Neapolitan inscription, which honors Helena wihout reference to her marital status.[18]

An inscription from Saepinum in Samnium, referring to Helena simply as the mother of Constantine, not as Augusta, must be dated to

---

[13]Grierson, *op. cit.* 317-10; Tommaso Bertelé, "Costantino il Grande e S. Elena su alcune monete bizantine," *Numismatica* 14 (1948) 91-106 at 95, fig. 12 bis, and 96, fig. 15; S. Bendall and P. J. Donald, *The Later Palaeologan Coinage, 1281-1453* (London 1979) 164-65, nos. 7 and 8. Warwick Wroth, *Imperial Byzantine Coins in the British Museum* (London 1908) 639 and pl. LXXVII, no. 6, gives a different interpretation; so does Hugh Goodacre, *Handbook of the Coinage of the Byzantine Empire* (London 1957) 349. Bertelé, *op.cit.* 96, figs. 13 bis and 14 bis; Bendall and Donald, *op. cit.* 170-71, no. 2.

[14]*CIL* VI 1134 (*ILS* 709), 1135, 1136, and 36950.

[15]*CIL* X 517 (*ILS* 706) and 1483.

[16]*CIL* X 517 = *ILS* 708; *PLRE* I 534; Richard Klein in *RAC* XIV 361; Drijvers, *op. cit.* 50-51 and 189; Robert M. Grant in Attridge and Hata, *op. cit.* 676. On the rank of corrector see A. H. Jones, *The Later Roman Empire* 145, 48, 106, and 525.

[17]*CIL* X 1483; E. D. Hunt, *op. cit.* 32, n. 25; Richard Klein in *RAC* XIV 361; Drijvers, *op. cit.* 51 and 189.

[18]*CIL* IX 1484; Drijvers, *op. cit.* 51-52 and 189.

Plate XIV

Obverse of a bronze coin minted in 324-330 at Antioch: FL HELENA AVGVSTA.

Coin in the author's possession.

Reverse of the same: SECURITAS REIPVBLICE (sic) and mintmork in the exergue.

Obverse of a bronze medallion of Helena, 324-329: FLAVIA AELENA (sic) AVGVSTA. Photo Coin Cabinet, British Museum.

Reverse of a commemorative coin of Helena minted at Trier in 337: PAX PVBLICA. Note the small cross in the left side of the field. Photo American Numismatic Society, New York.

Reverse of a commemorative coin of Theodora minted at Trier in 337: PIETAS ROMANA. Note the small cross in the left side of the field. Photo American Numismatic Society, New York.

324 or earlier.[19]   At Side in Pamphylia a statue of Helena must have been erected. The Greek inscription on the basis reads: Ἑλένην μη-τ[έ]ρα Αὐ[γ]ούστ[ου].[20]   A date prior to 325 must be assumed. Finally we must mention an inscription which a certain M. Valerius Gypasius set up at Sicca Veneria (El Kef) in Africa Proconsularis; in it Helena is called Augusta.[21]

When considered together the inscriptions tell us that Helena received the honor of public statues and inscriptions even before she was granted the rank of Augusta, and not only in Rome but even in small provincial towns; they also reveal Constantine's succession policy, that is, the advancement of the dynastic principle rather than the tetrarchic principle.[22]

---

[19]*CIL* IX 2446; E. D. Hunt, *op. cit.* 32, n. 25; Richard Klein in *RAC* XIV 361; Drijvers, *op. cit.* 50 and 189.

[20]*CIG* III 4349; Inan and Rosenbaum, *op. cit.* 52; Drijvers, *op. cit.* 53, n. 46.

[21]*CIL* VIII 1633; *PLRE* I 405; Richard Klein in *RAC XIV 361;* Drijvers, *op. cit.* 49.

[22]Thus correctly Richard Klein in *RAC* XIV 361, Grünewald, *op. cit.* 138-39, and Drijvers, *op. cit.* 52. But Klein, *loc. cit.,* is wrong in citing as additional evidence *CIL* X 678 = *ILS* 710: here *Faustae...uxori* must be read rather then Helenae ... matri. Drijvers, *op. cit.* 49, also misreads this inscription. E. D. Hunt, *op.* 32, n. 25.

Chapter XV.
Helena as Saint

In this chapter I propose to show how Helena joined the ranks of the saints, both in the Western church and in the Eastern church.

It is not surprising that those authors who report the *inventio* of the Cross have good things to say about Helena. To Ambrose Helena was *sanctae memoriae*;[1] to Rufinus she was *femina incomparabilis fide et religione animi*.[2]

The poet Venantius Fortunatus (ca. 530-610) was a friend of Gregory of Tours and ultimately bishop of Poitiers;[3] he had occasion to celebrate the Byzantine emperor Justin II (565-570) and his wife Sophia when, in 569, they sent a relic of the True Cross to Queen Radegund at Poitiers.[4] In the course of a long elegiac poem he compares them to

---

[1]*De Obitu Theodosii* 40 (Migne, *PL* XVI 1399 [ed. 1845] or 1462 [ed. 1866]; ed. Mannix 59; ed. Faller [*CSEL* LXXIIII] 393).

[2]*Hist. Eccl.* 1.7 in Migne, *PL* XXI 475; 10.7 in ed. Mommsen (*GCS* IX.2) 969; Mackes, *op. cit.* 190.

[3]Wilhelm Meyer, *Der Gelegenheitsdichter Venantius Fortunatus* (Berlin 1901); Bardenhewer, *op. cit.* V 367-77; Richard Koebner, *Venantius Fortunatus* (Leipzig 1915); Dominique Tardi, *Fortunat: Étude sur un dernier représentant de la poésie latine dans la Gaule mérovingienne* (Paris 1927); Manitius I 170-81; F. J. E. Raby, *A History of Christian-Latin Poetry in the Middle Ages*, 2nd ed.(Oxford 1953) 86-95; F.J. E. Raby, *A History of Secular Latin Poetry in the Middle Ages*, 2nd ed. (Oxford 1957) I 127-42; Laistner, *op. cit.* 127-29; Patrick Gerard Walsh, "Venantius Fortunatus," *The Month* 24 (1960) 292-302; Joseph Szövérffy, *Die Annalen der lateinischen Hymnendichtung* (Berlin 1964-1965) I 128-40; Prinz, *op. cit.* 484-85; Brunhölzl, *Geschichte de lat. Lit. des Mittelalters* I 118-28; Altaner-Stuiber, *op. cit.* 499-501; John Michael Wallace-Hadrill, *op. cit.* 82-87; Peter Godman, *Poets and Emperors* (Oxford 1987) 1-37; Judith George, *Venantius Fortunatus: A Latin Poet in Merovingian Gaul* (Oxford 1992).

[4]Gregory of Tours, *Hist. Franc.* 9.40 (Migne, *PL* LXXI 518; *MGH, SRM* I.1[2] 464); Meyer, *op. cit.* 90-108; Martin Conway, "St. Radegund's Reliquary at Poitiers," *Antiquaries Journal* 3 (1923) 1-12; Samuel Dill, *Roman Society in Gaul in the Merovingian Age* (London 1926) 382 and 431; Frolow, *La relique* 179-80, no. 33; Prinz, *op. cit.* 158; Frolow, *Les reliquaires* 147, 159, 178, and 241; František Graus, *Herrscher, Volk und Heiliger im Reich der Merowinger* (Prague 1965) 407-408; George Henderson, *Style and Civilization: Early Medieval* (Harmondsworth, Middlesex, 1972) 213-14; Averil Cameron, "The Early Religious Policies of Justin II," *Studies in Church History* 13 (1976) 51-67 at 55-59; Brian Brennan, "The Career of Venantius Fortunatus," *Traditio* 41 (1985) 49-78 at 61-63; Brian Brennan, "St. Radegund and the Early

(continued...)

Constantine and Helena, thus bestowing the ultimate compliment upon them.[5]

We have two *vitae* of Queen Radegund, one by Venantius Fortunatus, and the other, slightly later, by the nun Baudonivia, his contemporary. The latter not only reports the acquisition of the relic, but also refers to Helena thus: *beata Helena, sapientia imbuta, timore Dei plana, bonis operibus gloriosa*; it then compares Radegund to Helena: *quod fecit illa in orientali patria, hoc fecit beata Radegundis in Gallia.*[6]   We should note that Helena is called *beata* and said to hail from the East.

The *Liber Pontificalis* calls Helena *beatissima* already in the *vita* of Sylvester.[7]   And Helena is said to be *beata* in the so-called *Barbarus*

---

[4](...continued)
Development of Her Cult at Poitiers,' *JRH* 13 (1985) 340-54 at 345-46 and 350-51; Yvonne Labande-Mailfert, Robert Favreau, et. al., *Histoire de l'abbaye Sainte-Croix de Poitiers* (Poitiers 1986) 70-74; Herrin, *op. cit.* 84-85; George, *op. cit.* 30-31, 62-65, and 163-64. The event is commemorated at Poitiers on November 19.

[5]*Carmina*, Appendix 2.67 (ed. Leo [*MGH, AA* IV.1] 277).   Ewig, "Das Bild Constantins" 8; Joseph Szövérffy, *Weltliche Dichtungen des lateinischen Mittelalters* I (Berlin 1970) 228-32, esp. 231; Labande-Mailfert, Favreau, *et al., op. cit.* 39-40; Drijvers, *op. cit.* 183; Michael Whitby in Magdalino, *op. cit.* 89; John F. Haldon, *ibid.* 105.

[6]*Vita Sanctae Radegundis, Liber Secundus* 16 (*BHL* 7049; *Acta Sanct.* Aug. III [ed. 1867] 80; Migne, *PL* LXXII 673-74; *MGH, SRM* II 388); Labande-Mailfert, Favreau, *et. al., op. cit.* 39; Jo Ann McNamara, "*Imitatio Helenae*: Sainthood as an Attribute of Queenship," a paper given at the Twenty-third Annual Conference of the Center for Medieval and Early Renaissance Studies, State University of New York at Binghamton, in October, 1989. Professor McNamara kindly made her paper available to me prior to the publication of the conference proceedings. On Radegund see further: *Lyfe of St. Radegund*, attributed to Henry Bradshaw (ca. 1450-1513), ed. Frederick Brittain (Cambridge 1926); Émile Briand, *Histoire de sainte Radegonde, reine de France, et des sanctuaires et pèlerinages en son honneur* (Paris 1898); Wulf, *op. cit.* 376-87; Frederick Brittain, *St. Radegund: Patroness of Jesus College, Cambridge* (Cambridge 1925); René Aigrain, *Saine Radegonde* 2nd ed. (Poitiers 1952); MSS 250 and 252 of the Bibliothèque Municipale in Poitiers, of the 11th and 13th century respectively, each contain both of the *vitae* and offer interesting illuminations depicting scenes from St. Radegund's life. See Magdalena Elizabeth Carrasco, "Spirituality in Context: The Romanesque Illustrated Life of St. Radegund of Poitiers (Poitiers, Bibl. Mun., MS 250)," *ArtB* 72 (1990) 414-35; also, by the same author, "Sanctity and Experience in Pictorial Hagiography: Two Illustrated Lives of Saints from Romanesque France," in Renate Blumenfeld-Kosinski and Timea Szell, edd., *Images of Sainthood in Medieval and Renaissance Saints' Lives* (Ithaca 1991) 33-66 at 50-66.

[7]Ed. Mommsen (*MGH, GPR* I) 65-66; ed. Duchesne[2] I 182; Ewig, "Das Bild Constantins" 22; Cameron, *op. cit.* 58.

Scaligeri, which is a version of the *Consularia Italica* and in its original form to be assigned to the second half of the sixth century.[8]

In 601 Pope Gregory the Great compared the Anglo-Saxon king Ethelbert and his queen Bertha to Constantine and Helena.[9] Two years later the same pope reminded the empress Leontia – whose husband, the usurper Phocas, was on good terms with the papacy, as the column of Phocas in the Roman Forum reminds us to this day – that another empress, Pulcheria, had been acclaimed as the new Helena at the Council of Chalcedon.[10] Clearly Helena had become the role model for a special kind of saint, the saintly queen.[11]

Two pilgrims' itineraries of the seventh century call Helena *sancta*.[12] And in the Calendar of Willibrord (650-739) we find this entry for August 11: *deposito ... sanctae Haelinae*.[13] But whether this

---

[8]Ad annum 320 (*MGH, AA* IX = *Chron. Min.* I 292); Ewig, "Das Bild Constantins" 22; Theodor Mommsen in *MGH, AA* IX = *Chron Min.* I 272.

[9]*Reg. Epist.* 11.35 and 37 (Ed. Ewald-Hartmann [*MGH, Epist.*II] 304-306); in Migne, *PL* LXXVII 1141-42, the letter to Bertha is numbered 11.29, and *ibid.* 1201-1204 the letter to Ethelbert is numbered 11.66; Philipp Jaffé, *op. cit.* I 205, nos. 1825 and 1827; Frederick Homes Dudden, *Gregory the Great* (London 1905) II 124-25; Henry H. Howorth, *Saint Augustine of Canterbury* (London 1913) 135-37; Mann, *op. cit.* I.1² (1925) 162-63; Caspar, *op. cit.* II 506-507; Ewig, "Das Bild Constantins" 18; Godfrey, *op. cit.* 79-80; Jeffrey Richards, *Consul of God* (London 1980) 243-44; Frend, *op. cit.* 889; Drijvers, *op. cit.* 183; Michael Whitby in Magdalino, *op. cit.* 89. On Ethelbert and Bertha, see Bede, *Hist. Eccl.* 1.25-26; also Wulf *op. cit.* 414-15, and Stenton, *op. cit.* 105-106 and 109. On Gregory's Anglo-Saxon mission see Hodgkin, *op. cit.* I 257-69, Henry Mayr-Harting, *The Coming of Christianity to Anglo-Saxon England* (London 1972) 51-68, and Herrin, *op cit.* 169-71; on his missionary policy in general see Robert Austin Markus, "Gregory the Great and a Papal Missionary Strategy," *Studies in Church History*[6] (1970) 29-38.

[10]*Reg. Epist.* 13.42 (Ed. Ehwald-Hartmann [*MGH, Epist.* II] 405); in Migne, *PL* LXXVII 1288-89, this letter is numbered 13.39; Philipp Jaffé, *op. cit.* I 213, no. 1907; Dudden, *op. cit.* II 262-63, quotes the entire letter in English trl.; Mann, *op. cit.* I.1² (1925) 129; Caspar, *op. cit.* II 490; Eugen Heinrich Fischer, 'Gregor der Grosse und Byzanz,' *ZRG, K. Abt.* 36 (1950) 15-144 at 123 with n. 455; Ewig, "Das Bild Constantins" 8; Michael Whitby in Magdalino, *op. cit.* 89.

[11]McNamara, *op. cit.*; Drijvers, *op. cit.* 182; Michael Whitby in Magdalino, *op. cit.* 89.

[12]Chapter XII above, n. 7; Ewig, "Das Bild Constantins" 22; Michael Whitby in Magdalino, *op. cit.* 89.

[13]Ed. H. A. Wilson, *Henry Bradshaw Society* 55 (1918), pl. VIII and p. 10.

is a reference to our Helena is subject to question, in view of the date –
August 11 rather than 18 – and the spelling of the name.[14]

In 785 Pope Hadrian I acclaimed the emperor Constantine VI and
his mother Irene as the new Constantine and the new Helena respectively, referring to Helena as *beata*.[15] Helena is among the saints who
are invoked in a Carolingian Litany of All Saints which has been dated
to 783-787.[16] There is at this time no formal distinction between
beatus and *sanctus*.[17]

Nothing demonstrates Helena's acceptance as a saint more convincingly than the reported *translatio* in 840 of her relics from Rome to
Hautvillers, which we considered in chapter XII above. Whether or not
these relics were authentic is immaterial. But a feast day of St. Helena,
on August 18, is recorded for the first time only in the Martyrology of
Usuard, which we may date to 875 or slightly earlier.[18] This feast is
not mentioned in such earlier texts as the *Martyrologium Hieronymia-
num*, the *Sacramentarium Gregorianum*, or the Martyrology of Hrabanus
Maurus. From the Martyrology of Usuard it readily passed into the

[14]Sauerland, *op. cit.* 75; Ewig, "Das Bild Constantins" 24; Ewig, "Tradition" 159;
Linder, "The Myth of Constantine the Great" 87.

[15]Mansi XII 1055-58; Migne, *PL* XCVI 1217-18; Philipp Jaffé, *op. cit.* I 299, no.
2448; Mann, *op. cit.* I.2² (1925) 447-48; Ewig, "Das Bild Constantins" 8; Paul Speck,
Kaiser Konstantin VI. (Munich 1978) I 145; Gervais Dumeige, *Histoire des conciles
oecuméniques* IV: *Nicée II* (Paris 1978) 106-107; Kazhdan, "Constantin imaginaire" 246
and 248.

[16]Montpellier (Faculté de médicine) MS 409, folios 343-44; Victor Leroquais, *Les
psautiers manuscrits des bibliothèques de France* (Mâcon 1940-1941) I 273-77, esp. 275;
Lowe, *op. cit.* VI 29, no. 795, and facing ill.; Jean Mabillon, *Vetera Analecta*, 2nd ed.
(Paris 1723) 170-71; Migne, *PL* CXXXVIII 885-88; Bernhard Opfermann, *Die
liturgischen Herrscherakklamationen im Sacrum Imperium des Mittelalters* (Weimar 1953)
101 (partial); Ernst H. Kantorowicz, *Laudes Regiae* (Berkeley 1958) 33 and 37; Maurice
Coens, *Recueil d'etudes bollandiennes* (Brussels 1963) 282-88, esp. 286; Gamber, *op.
cit.* II 580, no. 1611; Gisbert Knopp, "Sanctorum nomina seriatim: Die Anfänge der
Allerheiligenlitanei und ihre Verbindung mit den 'laudes regiae'," *RömQ* 65 (1970) 185-
231 at 211-12. But Dietz, "St. Helena" 364, is wrong in stating that this is the first
instance of Helena's being called *sancta*.

[17]Hippolyte Delehaye, *Sanctus* (Brussels 1927) 69; Stephan Kuttner, "La réserve
papale du droit de canonisation," *RHDFE*, 4th ser. 17 (1938) 172-228 at 176.

[18]*Acta Sanct.* Iunii VII (ed. 1717) 474; Migne, *PL* CXXIV 373-74; ed. Dubois
(*Subsidia Hagiographica* 40) 285; Ewig, "Tradition" 159; Richard Klein in RAI XIV
373; Quentin, *op. cit.* 403; Manitius I 361, n. 6.

Martyrologium Romanum of 1584.[19] It is not found, however, in the *Calendarium Romanum* of 1969, having become a local rather than a universal feast.[20] On her feast day Helena is honored in the three prayers of the Proper of the Mass, i. e. the Collect, the Secret, and the Postcommunion. The Collect is of special interest to us: *Domine Jesu Christe, qui locum, ubi Crux tua latebat, beatae Helenae revelasti, ...*

It is apparent that Helena attained her status as a saint by a natural, informal, and gradual process rather than by formal pronouncement. This is only what one should expect. While canonization has been carefully regulated in modern times, this has not always been the case.[21] In the early church martyrs and confessors became saints by popular favor. Later bishops created new saints or transferred existing cults, often by *elevatio* or *translatio* of relics.[22] The first canonization of an individual by an extant papal bull is that, in 993 by Pope John XV, of Udalricus (Ulrich), the well-known bishop of Augsburg.[23] Only in

---

[19]*Mart. Rom.* (ed. 1586) 370; French trl. by J. Baudot and F. Gilbert (2nd ed., 1953) 306; English trl. by J. B. O'Connell (1962) 175; Karl Adam Heinrich Kellner, *Heartology: A History of the Christian Festivals from Their Origins to the Present Day* (London 1908) 248.

[20]Saint Andrew Daily Missal (1958) 1743-45.

[21]Canons 1999-2141 of the *Codex Iuris Canonici* of 1917; Raoul Naz, "Causes de béatification et de canonisation," in *DDrC* III (1942) 10-37. For the revised *processus de causis beatificationis et canonizationis,* announced by Pope Paul VI on March 19, 1969, see *AAS* 61 (1969) 149-53, and James I. O'Connor, *The Canon Law Digest* VII (Chicago 1975) 1015-19. In the new *Codex Iuris Canonici* of 1983 only canon 1403 pertains to canonization; see also James A. Coriden, Thomas J. Green, and Donald E. Heintschel, edd., *The Code of Canon Law: A Text and Commentary* (New York 1985) 947 and 951. Professor John E. Lynch, Department of Canon Law, The Catholic University of America, kindly answered my inquiry.

[22]Wulf, *op. cit.* 438-41; Delehaye, *Sanctus* 162-84; Kuttner, *op. cit.* 172-74; Naz, *op. cit.* 11-13; Erich Waldram Kemp, *Canonization and Authority in the Western Church* (London 1948) 3-55; Damian Joseph Blaher, (Washington, D. C., 1949) 1-5; Renate Klauser, "Zur Entwicklung des Heiligsprechungsverfahrens bis zum 13. Jahrhundert," *ZRG, K. Abt.* 40 (1954) 85-101 at 85-91; Bernhard Kötting, "Entwicklung der Heiligenverehrung und Geschichte der Heiligsprechung," in Peter Manns, ed., *Die Heiligen in ihrer Zeit,* 2nd ed. (Mainz 1966) I 27-39 with further bibliography; Hans Erich Feine, *Kirchliche Rechtsgeschichte: Die katholische Kirche,* 5th ed. (Cologne 1972) 339.

[23]*Incipit Cum conventus esset factus*; Giusto Fontanini, *Codex constitutionum ... in solemni canonizatione sanctorum* (Rome 1729), no. 1; Mansi XIX 169; *MGH, Script.* IV 378-79; Migne, *PL* CXXXVII 845-47; *Acta Sanct.* Iulii II (ed. 1867) 80; Baronio ad annum 993, *op. cit.* XVI 327-28; Philipp Jaffé, *op. cit.* I 488, no. 3648. Delehaye, (continued...)

1200, when Pope Innocent III canonized the empress Kunigunde (Cunegunda), did canonization become a prerogative of the papacy.[24]

We have seen in chapter II above that Helena's favorite saint was St. Lucian, who traditionally has been linked to Arianism. Moreover, the circumstances under which Eustathius, bishop of Antioch, was expelled from his see *may* suggest that Helena herself was inclined towards Arianism.[25] But *if* this was so it was not an obstacle on her way to sainthood. Neither was her humble background.

Mediaeval piety found expression in thousands of Latin hymns. Among these one finds a fair number of hymns to St. Helena. I counted 47 in Chevalier's *Repertorium Hymnologicum* – enough to be the subject of a separate study. We should not expect these hymns to provide reliable biographical data. Rather they celebrate events and deeds attributed to Helena by legend; some examples will serve to make the point:

---

[23](...continued)

Sanctus 185, erroneously gives 995. Theodor Klauser, "Die Liturgie der Heiligsprechung," in *Heilige Überlieferung*, Festschrift Ildefons Herwegen (Münster 1938) 212-33 at 220 and 229; Kuttner, *op. cit.* 179. Naz, *op. cit.* 12; Kemp, *op. cit.* 57; Blaher, *op. cit.* 5-6; Mikoletzky, *op. cit.* 119; Renate Klauser, *op. cit.* 91 and 97; Gerd Zimmermann in Manns, *op. cit.* I 483-86; Caterina Colafranceschi in *Bibl. Sanct.* XII (1969) 796-98; Feine, *loc. cit.* (n. 24); Friedrich Zoepfl in *LCI* VIII (1976) 507-10; Udalricus had died only 20 years earlier, in 973. He is the patron saint of Augsburg; his feast day is July 4. Bibliography in Leidl, *op. cit.* 147-48.

[24]The papal bull (Incipit *Cum secundum evangelicam veritatem*) found in full in Fontanini, *op. cit.*, no. 37, in *Acta Sanct.* Mart. I (ed. 1865) 279-80, and in Migne, *PL* CXL 219-22. A partial text is provided by Odorico Rinaldi, *Annales Ecclesiastici ab Anno 1198*, ed. Giovanni Domenico Mansi, I (Luca 1747) 92; August Potthast, *Regesta Pontificum Romanorum, 1198-1304* (Berlin 1874-1875) I 94, no. 1000; Johann Friedrich Böhmer, Julius Flicker, and Eduard Winkelmann, *Die Regesten des Kaiserreiches, 1198-1272* (Innsbruck 1892-1894) II 1067, no. 5705; Kuttner, *op. cit.* 225 and 228; Theodor Klauser, "Die Liturgie" 231; Kemp, *op. cit.* 104-105; Renate Klauser, *op. cit.* 100; Georg Beck, *St. Heinrich und St. Kunigunde* (Bamberg 1961) 48; Gian Domenico Gardini in *Bibl. Sanct.* IV (1964) 393-97; Hedwig Fritzen in Manns, *op. cit.* I 502-504; Feine, *loc. cit.* (n. 24); Georges Kiesel in *LCI* VII (1974) 357-60; Morris, *op. cit.* 228. For further literature on Kunigunde see Renate Klauser in *LThK*[2] VI (1961)) 680-81; her feast day is March 3. Kunigunde's husband, the emperor Henry II, had been previously canonized, in 1146; both lie buried in the cathedral of Bamberg.

[25]See chapter VIII above with nn. 9-17; Seeck, "Helena. 2," 2821; Holum, *op. cit.* 24 with n. 72; E. D. Hunt, *op cit.* 35-36. More cautiously Richard Klein in *RAC XIV* 358. Drijvers, *op. cit.* 38 and 71. Balsdon, *op. cit.* 169, surely goes too far in calling Helena a "rabid Arian."

One hymn, extent in several 14th and 15th century manuscripts, bids "holy Trier" to rejoice in being Helena's "mother."[26]   Another, preserved in a 15th century manuscript, calls Helena *Treverigena*, has her baptized by Sylvester, and credits her with finding the relics of the Magi.[27]   A third hymn, from a 15th century manuscript, knows that Helena was the daughter of a British king, that she was a convert from Judaism, that she founded 72 monasteries, that her head is in Trier, and that she brought the body of Matthias to Trier.[28]   References to the Invention of the Cross are frequent, as one might expect.

It can readily be shown that Helena was held in high regard throughout the history of the Byzantine Empire.[29]   Later Byzantine empresses emulated her as a model of humility, charity, and piety.[30]

Aelia Flaccilia, the wife of Theodosius I (379-395), was praised for cultivating the virtues of piety, humility, and charity.[31]   She personally served the poor and the sick, as Helena had served the consecrated virgins.   In 438-439 (Athenais-) Eudocia, the wife of Theodosius II (408-450), undertook a pilgrimage to Jerusalem, and on this occasion she caused a martyrium of St. Stephen Protomartyr to be built.[32]   Her acti-

---

[26]Incipit *Ad honorem summi regis nos qui sumus oves gregis;* Mone, *op. cit.* III 336, no.967; Kehrein, *op cit.* 542-43, no. 808; Chevalier, *Repertorium* I 11, no. 162; *AHMA* LV 182, no. 160.

[27]Incipit *In honorem summi regis psallant gregis novae legis; AHMA* IX 169, no. 226; Chevalier, *Repertorium* III 295, no. 28055.

[28]Incipit *Haec regina ter beata*; Mone, *op. cit.* III 337, no. 968; Kehrein, *op. cit.* 541-42, no. 807; Chevalier, *Repertorium* I 457, no. 7636; *AHMA* LV 183-84, no. 161.

[29]See chapter III above, n. 54.

[30]McNamara, *op. cit.*

[31]Ambr. *De Obitu Theodosii* 40 (Migne, *PL* XVI 1399 [ed. 1845] or 1462 [ed. 1866]; ed. Mannix 59; ed. Faller [*CSEL* LXXIII] 392); Gregory of Nyssa, *Oratio Funebris de Placilla Imperatrice* (Migne, *PG*, XLVI 877-92; ed. Jaeger IX. 1 475-90) *passim;* Theodoret, *Hist. Eccl.* 5.18.2-3 in Migne, *PG* LXXXII 1237-40; 5.19.2-3 in ed. Parmentier-Scheidweiler (*GCS* XLIV) 314; Hunger, *Reich der neuen Mitte* 176; Constantelos, *op. cit.* 89 and 120; Holum, *op. cit.* 25-26; Demandt, *op. cit.* 303 and 453; Drijvers, *op. cit.* 123 and 182; McNamara, *op. cit.*

[32]Antoninus Placentinus (6th c.), *Itinerarium* 25 (Migne, *PL* LXXII 908; ed. Geyer [*CSEL* XXXIX] 176 and 207; ed. Geyer *CC, Ser. Lat.* CLXXV] 142 and 166; ed. Milani [Milan 1977] 170-71). But Eudocia is erroneously called Eudoxia and said to be the wife of Justinian.   Evagrius, *Hist. Eccl.* 1.22 (Migne, *PG* LXXXVI. 2 2484; ed. Bidez-Parmentier 32); Marie-Joseph Lagrange, *Saint Étienne et son sanctuaire à Jérusalem* (Paris 1894) 61-72; Siméon Vailhé, "Les monastères et les églises Saint-Etienne à Jerusalem, *EO* 8 (1905) 78-86; Vincent and Abel, *Jerusalem* II. 4 745-51; Kötting, *op.*

(continued...)

vities were strikingly similar to those of Helena.[33] In 451, at the Council of Chalcedon, the emperor Marcian was called a new Constantine, a new Paul, and a new David, while his wife Pulcheria was hailed as a new Helena.[34] This same Pulcheria, who was the sister of the recently deceased Theodosius and had been his regent during the years of his minority, had made generous donations to charitable institutions and monasteries and had founded several churches.[35] In 518, when Justin I and Euphemia ascended to the throne, they were similarly hailed as a new

[32](...continued)
cit. 99-100 and 328; Armstrong, "Fifth and Sixth Century Church Buildings in the Holy Land" 18-19; Holum, op. cit. 186 and 219; E. D. Hunt, op. cit. 229-33; Peters, op. cit. 161-62; Maraval, op. cit. 69 and 266-67; Borgehammar, op. cit. 146; Drijvers, op. cit. 182. St. Stephen was Eudocia's favorite saint, and the martyrium was subsequently expanded into a basilica. The modern (Dominican) church stands on the site of the ancient church. Eudocia lived in Jerusalem permanently, estranged from her husband, from 444 until her death in 460; she was buried in the church which she had founded. A feast of St. Eudocia is observed in the East on August 13.

[33]Ferdinand Gregorovius, Athenaïs (Leipzig 1882) 250; Lagrange, op. cit. 69 and 71; Charles Diehl, Figures Byzantines I, 2nd ed. (Paris 1908) 42; Hunger, Reich der neuen Mitte 178; Gray, op. cit. 202; Harold Allen Drake, "A Coptic Version of the Discovery of the Holy Sepulchre," GRBS 20 (1979) 381-92 at 387-88; Harold Allen Drake in Orlandi, op. cit. 148 and 151; Gnilka, op. cit. 287; Timothy S. Miller, The Birth of the Hospital in the Byzantine Empire (Baltimore 1985) 93, 104, 125, and 126. Stemberger, op. cit. 251; Norwich, op. cit. 149; Averil Cameron, The Mediterranean World in Late Antiquity, AD 395-600 (London 1993) 18 and 68. McNamara, op. cit. But not everything about her is admirable; see Hans-Georg Beck in RAC VI (1966) 844-47.

[34]Mansi VII 169/170, 171/172, and 761. ACO II (Concilium Universale Chalcedonense) I.2 155 [351] (Greek) or II.2 9[101] (Latin); also ibid. III.2 176 [435] and 177 [436]. Hefele-Leclercq, op. cit. II.2 (1908) 732-33; Rhaban Haacke in Aloys Grillmeyer and Heinrich Bacht, edd., Das Konzil von Chalkedon (Würzburg 1951-1954) II 105. Ewig; "Das Bild Constantins" 6; Walter, L'iconographie 230; Linder, "The Myth of Constantine the Great" 59; Holum, op. cit. 216; E. D. Hunt, op. cit. 29; Frend, op. cit. 771; Drijvers, op. cit. 183; Grünewald, "Constantinus Novus" 473; Michael Whitby in Magdalino, op. cit. 89; McNamara, op. cit. On Pulcheria's role at the Council of Chalcedon see Eduard Schwartz, "Die Kaiserin Pulcheria auf der Synode von Chalkedon," in Festgabe für Adolf Jülicher (Tübingen 1927) 203-12.

[35]Sozomen, Hist. Eccl. 9.1 (Migne, PG LXVII 1593-97; ed. Bidez-Honsen f CCS LI 390-92); Theophones Homologetes, Chronographia ad annum mundi 5943 (Migne, PG CVIII 269; ed. de Boor I 105); Bury, History of the Later Roman Empire I 238-39; Donald Attwater, Saints of the East (New York, 1963) 67-74; Constantelos, op. cit. 157, 166, and 198; Gnilka, op. cit. 287; Timothy S. Miller, The Birth of the Hospital 92, 104, 123, and 125; McNamara, op. cit.

Constantine and a new Helena.[36] Euphemia, too, engaged in pious works, earning the acclamation after it had been bestowed upon her.[37] And again, at the Second Council of Nicaea (the Seventh Ecumenical Council) in 787, the emperor Constantine VI and his mother Irene were called a new Constantine and a new Helena.[38] Irene, too, is credited with having founded several philanthropic institutions.[39] We have had occasion previously to mention that Helena, the wife of Constantine VII Porphyrogenitus (913-959), established a nursing home.[40] One may assume that she was conscious of her namesake. Byzantine emperors, their ladies, and their officials often undertook charitable activities; in this and in other ways they followed the example set by Constantine and Helena.[41]

By the time of the Great Schism of 1054 Helena was universally recognized as a saint in both the West and the East. It is not surprising, therefore, that a formal pronouncement was not reqired and did not take place in the East any more than in the West.[42] But the cult of St. He-

---

[36]Mansi VIII 1058 (bis), 1062, 1063, and 1086; *ACO* III *(Collectio Sabbatica)* 72 (bis), 74, 75, and 86; Alexander Alexandrovich Yosiliev, *Justin the First* (Cambridge, Massachusetts, 1950) 141. See *ibid.* 68-74 for the circumstances surrounding Justin's election and coronation. Sévérien Salaville in Grillmeyer and Bacht, *op. cit.* II 684; Ewig, "Das Bild Constantins" 8.

[37]Vasiliev, *op. cit.* (n. 36 above) 91-92 with n. 69 and 378 with n. 90.

[38]Mansi XII 1153/54; XIII 129, 397, and 416; Hefele-Leclercq, *op. cit.* III.2 (1970) 773; Ewig, "Das Bild Constantins" 8; John F. Haldon in Magdalino, *op. cit.* 105; Walter, *L'iconographie* 230; Patrick Henry, "Initial Eastern Assessments of the Seventh Oecumenical Council," *JThS* N.S. 25 (1974) 75-92 at 75; Dumei, *op. cit.* 114; Speck, *op. cit.* II 576, n. 461; E.D. Hunt, *op. cit.* 29, n. 7; Joan Mervyn Hussey, *The Orthodox Church in the Byzantine Empire* (Oxford 1986) 49; Warren Treadgold, *The Byzantine Revival* (Stanford 1988) 60-126, esp. 82 and 87.

[39]*Patria* 3.85 (Migne, *PG* CLVII 581; ed. Preger II 246); Timothy S. Miller, *The Birth of the Hospital* 95.

[40]Chapter XI above, n. 11.

[41]Hunger, *Reich der neuen Mitte* 107 and 173-74. Constantelos, *op. cit.* 89. Klaus Wessel, "Kaiserbild" 734. Timothy S. Miller, "Byzantine Hospitals," *DOP* 38 (1984) 53-63 at 57, and *The Birth of the Hospital* 21 and 103-105. Demandt, *op. cit.* 453.

[42]The Orthodox churches have never developed formal procedures for ἁγιοποίησις comparable to the Catholic Church's *processus de causis beatificationis et canonizationis*; see the following: Hans-Georg Beck, *Kirche und theologische literatur* 274; P. Ioannou, s.v. Heiligsprechung II, in *LThK²* V (1960) 144; Constantine N. Tsirpanlis, *Introduction to Eastern Patristic Thought and Orthodox Theology* (Collegeville, Minnesota, 1991) 146-50. I owe this reference to the kindness of the late Professor John E. Rexine of

(continued...)

lena in the East differs somewhat from its counterpart in the West. In the East, much more so than in the West, Helena is associated closely with her son, and sometimes she is subordinated to him.[43] Cyril of Jerusalem, we have seen previously in his letter to Constantius, while silent about Helena, seems to say that Constantine found the wood of the Cross.[44] In a Coptic text called *The Discourse on the Cross*, erroneously ascribed to Cyril of Jerusalem but demonstrably of later date, it is Constantine who interrogates the Jews, has their chief priests cast into a pit, and commences the huge task of digging for the Tomb and the Cross; when he is called away by affairs of state Helena successfully completes the task.[45] Another Coptic text, the Eudoxia legend of the seventh century, attributes the discovery of the Cross to Helena, but the discovery of the Tomb to Eudoxia, an entirely fictitious sister of Constantine.[46] In the Menology of Basil II (Bulgaroktonos, 976-1025), for May 21, Constantine shares with his mother in the glory of having discovered the True Cross.[47] In the Greek Orthodox churches (but not in the Nestorian and Jacobite churches) Helena shares a feast day, May 21, with her son Constantine.[48] The Pierpont Morgan Library in New York

---

[42](...continued)
Colgate University.   But the Ecumenical Patriarch of Constantinople may grant ἀνακήρυξις, i.e. recognition of a saint by all the Orthodox churches rather than by one or more of the national churches only; see Richard Potz, *Patriarch und Synode in Konstantinopel* (Vienna 1971) 130.

[43]Harold Allen Drake in Orlandi, *Eudoxia and the Holy Sepulchre* 132, n. 1.

[44]Chapter IX above, n. 17.

[45]Quasten, *op. cit.* III 369; Tito Orlandi, "Cirillo di Gerusalemme nella letteratura copta," *Vet. Chr.* 9 (1972) 93-100 at 99; Harold Allen Drake, "A Coptic Version" 388. Text in E. A. Wallis Budge, *Miscellaneous Coptic Texts in the Dialect of Upper Egypt* (London 1915) I 183-230; English translation *ibid.* II 761-808.   Text now also in Antonella Campagnano, ed., *Ps. Cirillo di Gerusalemme: Omelie copte sulla passione, sulla Croce e sulla Vergine* (Milan 1980) 75-149 with Italian translation.

[46]Orlandi, *Eudoxia and the Holy Sepulchre*; Birger A. Pearson, *s. v.* Eudoxia, in *Copt. Enc.* IV 1067.

[47]Migne, *PG* CXVII 468. On the Menologion of Basil see Hans-Georg Beck, *Kirche und theologische Literatur* 251-52, and *cf.* chapter II above, n. 6.

[48]Dmitrievskii, *op. cit.* I 74; Von Maltzew, *op. cit.* II 332-33; *Synaxarium Constantinopolitanum*, ed. Delehaye (*Acta Sanct.*, Propylaeum Nov. [ed. 1902]) 697-700; Mateos, *op. cit.* I 297; Baumstark, *op. cit.* 219; Ewig, "Das Bild Constantins" 4; Werner Kaegi, "Vom Nachleben Constantins," *SZG* (1958) 289-326 at 294; Linder, "The Myth of Constantine the Great" 53; E. D. Hunt, *op. cit.* 29; Constantine also has a feast day of his own, September 3. In the Ethiopian Church the feast of Constantine and
(continued...)

City holds an Armenian lectionary which can be dated to 1334.[49] Among its many illuminations is one, for the feast of Constantine and Helena, which depicts Constantine alone.[50] On occasion the subordination of Helena to Constantine can be observed in Byzantine art.[51]

Among the thousands of hymns of the Greek Orthodox Church we can find a fair number which celebrate the feast of Sts. Constantine and Helena, while only a few honor Helena as they celebrate the *inventio* of the Cross.[52] Only two of the former will be briefly considered here. The first of these is by the obscure hymn-writer Byzantius of the seventh century (?).[53] His brief hymn for May 21, technically a *sticheron idiomelon*, makes no mention of Helena at all.[54] The second of these was composed by St. Methodius, the Patriarch of Constantinople in 843-847.[55] This brief hymn also a *sticheron idiomelon* honors Constantine far more than Helena; in fact Helena is identified only as Constantine's mother, not by her own name, and Constantine is said to have searched for and found the Cross "together with his mother."[56]

---

[48](...continued)
Helena falls on Genbôt 25 = May 30; see E. A. Wallis Budge, *The Book of the Saints of the Ethiopian Church* (Cambridge 1928) III 932. In the synaxarion of the Ethiopian Church Helena is cited repeatedly; see *ibid. passim*. In the Coptic Church Helena has a feast day of her own on Bashans 9 = May 4; see Atiya, "Synaxarion, Copto-Arabic" 2185.

[49]M. 803. Sirarpie Der Nersessian, "An Armenian Lectionary of the Fourteenth Century," in Dorothy Miner, ed., *Studies in Art and Literature for Bella de Costa Greene* (Princeton 1954) 231-37; Avedis K. Sanjian, *A Catalogue of Medieval Armenian Manuscripts in the United States* (Berkeley 1976) 610-25, no. 134; Thomas F. Mathews and Roger S. Wieck, edd., *Treasures in Heaven: Armenian Illuniated Manuscripts* (New York 1994) 195-96, no. 67.

[50]Folio 293r. Der Nersessian, "An Armenian Lectionary" 232, n. 5, in error; Sanjian, *op. cit.* 615, correctly.

[51]See chapter XVII below, n. 35.

[52]More than 60,000 incipits have been gathered by Enrica Follieri, *Initia Hymnorum Ecclesiae Graecae* (Vatican City 1960-1966). *Ibid.* V.2 200-201. *Ibid.* V.2 308.

[53]*AGCC*, p. XLIII; Hans-Georg Beck, *Kirche und theologische Literatur* 472; Egon Wellesz, *A History of Byzantine Music and Hymnography*, 2nd ed. (Oxford 1961) 237 and 443.

[54]*AGCC* 100. For a definition see Wellesz, *op. cit.* 243-44.

[55]*AGCA*, p. LI; H.J. W. Tillyard, *Byzantine Music and Hymnography* (London 1923) 34; Hans-Georg Beck, *Kirche und theologische Literatur* 498; Wellesz, *op. cit.* 236 and 443.

[56]*AGCC 99*.

In both the West and the East, apart from the official cult, St. Helena found her way into various popular beliefs and practices, only some of which shall be mentioned here.[57] Thus at Euren (Trier) it was believed of the "Helenenbrunnen" that Helena had produced it by striking the ground with her staff or that her likeness could be seen in its waters.[58] In France and Germany Helena's help was invoked to catch a thief and recover stolen goods.[59] In Languedoc her protection was sought against lightning, thunder, and fire.[60] At Hadres in the "Weinviertel" of Lower Austria there was once a chapel of St. Helena, where pilgrims expected to be cured of a fever.[61] In the Swiss and Austrian Alps and in the Rhineland Helena became the patron saint of miners, reasonably enough, since she had excavated the True Cross from the ground.[62] Just as reasonably, since she had recovered the nails of the Cross, she became the patron saint of nail-makers.[63] The lights which are sometimes seen after a storm at the masthead of a ship are commonly called St. Elmo's fire, but sometimes St. Helen's fire.[64] In Russia and the Ukraine Constantine's and Helena's feast day, May 21, was considered propitious for sowing flax.[65] On Cyprus there is a tradition

---

[57]For a fuller but flawed inventory see Bächtold-Stäubli III (1930-1931) 1702-1704.

[58]See chapter IV above, n. 100.

[59]Adolph Franz, *Die kirchlichen Benediktionen im Mittelalter* (Freiburg 1909) II 363-64; Réau, *Iconographie* III.2 634.

[60]Paul Sébillot, *Le folk-lore de France* I (Paris 1904) 107. Dietrich Heinrich Kerler, *Die Patronate der Heiligen* (Ulm 1905) 69 and 99.

[61]Gustav Gugitz, "Niederösterreichische Schalensteine im Volksglauben," *Österreichische Zeitschrift für Volkskunde* 53 = n. s. 4 (1950) 97-112 at 106. Gustav Gugitz, *Österreichs Gnadenstätten in Kult und Brauch* (Vienna 1955) II 40. Leopold Schmidt, *Volksglaube und Volksbrauch* (Berlin 1966) 194. The pilgrims hoped to effect a cure by lying down on a "Fieberstein," a bowl-shaped large stone. On the use of similar "Schalensteine" elsewhere see Bächtold-Stäubli VII (1935-1936) 990-92. The chapel has been torn down, but its site is marked by a Baroque statue of St. Helena.

[62]Georg Schreiber, "St. Helena als Inhaberin von Erzgruben," *Zeitschrift für Volkskunde* 53 (1956-1957) 65-76, esp. 69-72; Dietz, "St. Helena" 382.

[63]Kerler, *op. cit.* 257. Réau, *Iconographie* III.2 634.

[64]Paul Sébillot, *Légendes, croyances et superstitions de la mer* (Paris 1886) II 87-92; Bächtold-Stäubli II (1929-1930) 791; Réau, *Iconographie* III.1 438. In antiquity this phenomenon was associated with the Dioscuri and Helen of Troy; see Roscher, *Lexikon* I (1884-1886) 1163, and Hunger, *Reich der neuen Mitte* 190.

[65]Aukusti Vilho Rantasalo, *Der Ackerbau im Volksaberglauben der Finnen und Esten* (Sortavala 1919) 40, n. 1; V.I. Chicherov, *Zimnii period russkogo zemledel cheskogo*

(continued...)

which holds that Helena cleansed the island of poisonous snakes, either by fire or by introducing a large number of cats which devoured the snakes.[66]

In Greek Macedonia, specifically at Langadas and Agia Eleni (ca. ten km. south of Serres), the ancient ritual of fire-walking has long been practiced annually on the feast day of Sts. Constantine and Helena. In a state of religious ecstasy individuals, mostly women, known as Anastenarides dance barefoot on a bed of hot coals while carrying icons of Sts. Constantine and Helena. The practice can be traced back to the Thracian village of Kosti and to the year 1250: the church of St. Constantine was on fire, and courageous villagers entered the burning structure to rescue the holy icons when, so they thought, they heard them moaning. Hence in this context fire-walking is called Anastenaria, from ἀναστενάζω = to moan. Constantine plays a more significant role in the ritual than does Helena. Since the ritual is preceded by the sacrifice of a lamb or a bull its roots must be sought in pre-Christian practices. The hierarchy of the Greek Orthodox Church does not look with favor upon the Anastenaria.[67]

---

[65](...continued)
kalendaria XVI-XIX vekov (Moscow 1957) 12; Réau, *Iconographie* III.2 634; G. S. Maslova, *Narodnaia odezhda v vostochnoslavianskikh traditsionnykh obychaiakh i obriadakh XIX-nachala XX v* (Moscow 1984) 116.

[66]Stephanos D. Imelou, 'Από τὴν ἐπίσκεψιν τῆς ἁγίας 'Ελένης εἰς τὴν Κύπρον, Κυπριακὸς Λόγος, 12 (69-72), May-December 1980, pp. 367-71. This Cypriot tradition is comparable to similar traditions elsewhere: on Crete St. Paul is credited with having similarly cleansed the area of Archanai below Mt. Iuktas, and on Astypalaia in the Dodecanese such a feat is attributed to a disciple of St. John the Evangelist. But a different tradition gives credit for the introduction of the snake-eating cats to a certain Calocaerus, who was governor of Cyprus in 330-333; see Steven Runciman in David Hunt, ed., *Footprints in Cyprus*, 2nd ed. (London 1990) 139.

[67]Kostas Romaios, *Cultes populaires de la Thrace: Les Anasténaria: La cérémonie du Lundi pur* (Athens 1949) 17-118; Kaegi, *op. cit.* 323-26; Christos Evelpidis, "Anastenaria, un culte dionysiaque contemporain," *Cahiers du Sud* 51, no. 377 (1964), pp. [I-V], and no. 378/379 (1964), pp. [I-V]; Katerina Kakouri, *Dionysiaka: Aspects of Popular Thracian Religion of Today* (Athens 1965), esp. 9-32; Paul G. Brewster, "The Strange Practice of Firewalking," *Expedition* 19:3 (Spring 1977) 43-47 at 43; Loring M. Danforth, "The Role of Dance in the Ritual Therapy of the Anastenaria, *Byzantine and Modern Greek Studies* 5 (1979) 141-63 at 141-44; Loring M. Danforth, "Power through Submission in the Anastenaria," *Journal of Modern Greek Studies* 1 (1983) 203-223 at 211-12; Loring M. Danforth, *Firewalking and Religious Healing* (Princeton 1989) esp. 10-21, 85-86, and bibibliography. For additional bibliography see also Julia E. Miller,
(continued...)

It was long believed by native Christians in the Near East that Helena announced her discovery of the True Cross by means of a relay of bonfires.[68]   The late Professor Philip K. Hitti, a native of Lebanon, reports that "native Christians, particularly in Lebanon, still celebrate on September 14 a feast with bonfires re-enacting Helena's traditional announcement of the discovery to her son at Constantinople by means of bonfires from hilltop to hilltop."[69]   Professor Hitti's report is based on personal observation, one may assume, and has been independently verified.[70]   The feast, of course, is the exaltation of the cross.

In both the West and the East there were other women by the name of Helena who attained beatification or canonization. Four of these are of more than passing interest:

At Auxerre, the ancient Autisiodurum, in France (Yonne) the feast of St. Helena the Virgin is observed on May 22.[71]   This cult seems to be of local significance only. In 1215 the relics of the rather obscure St. Helena of Athyra were received in Troyes from Constantinople.[72]   The Russian Orthodox Church venerates another St. Helena on July 11 (by the Julian Calendar). This St. Helena was the princess Olga, widow of Prince Igor of Kiev, who visited Constantinople in 957, was baptized either before or during this visit, took the name of

---

[67](...continued)
Modern Greek Folklore: An Annotated Bibliography (New York 1985), s. v. Anastenaria. Professor Peter S. Allen of Rhode Island College has kindly provided additional information.

[68]Leontios Makharias, *Chronikon Kyprou* 1.6 (ed. R. M. Dawkins I 4.7). William Cowper Prime, *Holy Cross: A History of the Invention, Preservation and Disappearance of the Wood Known As the True Cross Known As the True Cross* (London and New York 1877) 52-54. I owe the reference to the kindness of Dr. Stephan Borgehammar, Uppsala.

[69]*The Near East in History* (Princeton 1961) 169.

[70]By my colleague Professor Abdo Baaklini, also a native of Lebanon, and by Professor Matti Moosa of Gannon University.

[71]Martyrology of Usuard (*Acta Sanct.* Iunii VI.2 [ed. 1714] 288; Migne, *PL* CXXIV 77-78; ed. Dubois [*Subsidia Hagiographica* 40] 233). *Mart. Rom.* (ed. 1586) 228; French trl. by J. Baudot and F. Gilbert (2nd ed. 1953) 199; English trl. by J. B. O'Connell (1962) 104. Ewig, "Tradition" 159.

[72]Giles Constable, "Troyes, Constantinople, and the Relics of St. Helen in the Thirteenth Century," in *Mélanges René Croset* (Poitiers 1966) II 1035-42; Patrick J. Geary, "Saint Helen of Athyra and the Cathedral of Troyes in the Thirteenth Century," *JMRS* 7 (1977) 149-68; Jean Marilier in *Bibl. Sanct.* IV (1964) 997-98.

Helena, and was later canonized.[73] By taking the name of Helena she probably expressed her respect for Helena Lecapena, the wife of Constantine VII and the reigning empress at the time, rather than for Helena, the mother of Constantine I. Helena, or Elin, of Skövde, in southern Sweden, was murdered at some time in the 12th century and acclaimed a saint some time later; her feast day is either July 30 or July 31.[74]

[73]Georg(e) Ostrogorsky, "Byzanz und die Kiewer Fürstin Olga," in his *Byzanz und die Welt der Slawen* (Darmstadt 1974) 35-52 (first published in Russian in 1967); Ostrogorsky, *History of the Byzantine State*[2] 283 with n. 1; A.P. Vlasto, *The Entry of the Slavs into Christendom* (Cambridge 1970) 249-51; Dimitri Obolensky, *The Byzantine Commonwealth* (New York 1971) 189, 195, and ill. 88; Dimitri Obolensky, *Byzantium and the Slavs: Collected Studies* (London 1971) II 511, IV 26, and X 48-49; Dimitri Obolensky, *The Byzantine Inheritance of Eastern Europe: Collected Essays* (London 1982) XV 3; Arnold Toynbee, *op. cit.* 437 with n. 2 and 518 with n. 3; Hussey, *op. cit.* 117-18; Richard A. Mason, "St. Olha's Christianity and Its Sources," in Nicholas L. Fr.-Chirovsky, ed., *The Millenium of Ukrainian Christianity* (New York 1988) 86-99. Olga's reception in Constantinople is described in the *Ceremonial Book of Constantine Porphyrogenitus: De Caerem.* 2.15 (ed. Reiske [*CSHB*] I 594-98; Migne, *PG* CXII 1108-12). Whether Olga received baptism before or during her visit cannot be decided here. Ostrogorsky, Vlasto, and Mason hold for the former, Obolensky for the latter; Toynbee and Hussey are undecided. For further literature on this question see Alexander P. Kazhdan, "Ol'ga," in *ODB* III 1522. A twelfth century Russian eulogy of Olga, in a German translation by F. Fritze, is found in Ernst Benz, ed., *Russische Heiligenlegenden* (Zürich 1953) 48-50. I am grateful to Dr. Ellen S. Hurwitz of Illinois Wesleyan University for her kind assistance.

[74]Her *vita (BHL* 3793) by Brynolf Algotsson (died 1317) is found in *Acta. Sanct. Iulii* VI (ed. 1868) 343-44 and in *Script. Rer. Suec.* III.2 (1876) 135-38. Algotsson also composed hymns to her; see *AHMA* XXVI 90-92 and XLIII 168-69. Hans Jägerstad in *LThK*[2] V (1960) 208. Alrik Gustafson, *A History of Swedish Literature* (Minneapolis 1961) 25; Tryggve Lundén, "Helena (el. *Elin*) av Skövde" in *Kulturhistoriskt Lexikon för Nordisk Medeltid* VI (Malmö 1961) 305-308. I owe the reference to the kindness of Dr. Stephan Borgehammar, Uppsala. Anna Lisa Sibilia in *Bibl. Sanct.* (1964) 996-97; Birgit Klockars in Eugéne Napoleon Tigerstedt, ed., *Ny illustrerad svensk litterhistoria*, 2nd ed. (Stockholm 1967) I 146.

Chapter XVI.
Helena in the Religious Literature
of the Middle Ages

Throughout the Middle Ages most Christians learned about the True Cross and about Helena not from the primary sources on which we rely today, but rather from religious poems, homilies, legendaries, breviaries, Books of Hours, and the liturgy of the Mass. We have already had occasion to examine the *Elene* of Cynewulf and *The Dream of the Rood.*[1] We shall next consider some other pieces of mediaeval religious literature, first from Western Europe and then from the Byzantine East.

First we return once more to the *vita* of St. Helena which Altmann of Hautvillers wrote *ca.* 850-860.[2] This is not only the longest but also the most important mediaeval text which deals with Helena, but it is largely disappointing. It is presented to us by the editor as a *vita seu potius homilia* and, indeed, it partakes of the character of a homily, or perhaps of a panegyric; certainly it contains much that is not history.[3] Nevertheless it merits a closer examination.

In the *epistola* which introduces the *vita* Altmann tells us that he is writing at the request of Archbishop Hincmar of Reims (845-882), in whose diocese Altmann's monastery was located.[4] The prologue which follows the *epistola* need not detain us.

In the first chapter Altmann surprises his readers by stating that Helena was a native of Trier, that her "house" became Trier's Church of St. Peter (the cathedral), and that Trier is to be called the *prima sedes*

---

[1]Chapter VI above.

[2]*BHL* 3772; *Acta Sanct.* Aug. III (ed. 1867) 580-99; Sigebert of Gembloux (llth century), *De Scriptoribus Ecclesiasticis* 98 (Migne, *PL* CLX 569).

[3]The shortcomings of Altmann's work are pointed out at length by the Bollandist editor Johannes Pinius in his commentary, pp. 548-80. Sauerland, *op. cit.* 61-79, esp. 62 and 73, is also sharply critical, but Ewig, "Tradition" 153-58, comes to his defense. We have seen in chapter IV above how Altmann has been shown to be correct on at least one important point: Helena's "house" in Trier. Gröber, *op. cit.* 138-39, and Richard Klein, in *RAC* XIV 372, do not pass judgment.

[4]*Acta Sanct.* Aug. III (ed. 1867) 581; Ewig, "Das Bild Constantins" 19, n. 102; Ewig, "Tradition" 155-56. On Hincmar see the following: Heinrich Schrörs, *Hinkmar, Erzbischof von Reims* (Freiburg 1884); Manitius I 339-44; Joseph de Ghellink, *Littérature latine au moyen âge* (Paris 1939) I 104-106; Duckett, *Carolingian Portraits* 202-64.

202 HELENA IN RELIGIOUS LITERATURE

Galliae Belgicae.[5]   This latter point is especially startling, considering at whose request Altmann was writing.[6] Altmann goes on to praise Helena for her faith, her modesty, and her sanctity, to say that she deserved to find the True Cross, and to call her the *mater imperii*. The rest of the chapter is a lengthy digression on the ten persecutions of the Church by the emperors. At the end of this digression Altmann gives credence to the erroneous tradition that the emperor Philip (the Arab; 244-249) was a Christian.

In the second chapter Altmann praises Constantine at length and tells of his conversion, following the *Actus S. Silvestri,* and of his vision, following the account of Eusebius (by way of Rufinus), apparently oblivious of the discrepancies between the two.[7]   His subsequent account of the *inventio* and *verificatio* of the Cross follows the *Tripartite History* of Cassiodorus. Once again Helena is praised enthusiastically: *quam mirabilis mater sancta Helena!*

The fulsome flattery continues in the third chapter, interrupted only by annoying digressions into Scripture.[8] Helena is compared at great length to the Queen of Sheba. Altmann then praises Helena for her humility in serving the consecrated virgins in Jerusalem, and finally assures his readers that she obtained a martyr's crown.

The fourth chapter offers no respite: more praise – *O venerabilis et omni modo spectabilis femina!* – and more digressions.[9] Helena is praised for gathering relics and, once more, for serving the consecrated virgins in Jerusalem.[10]   And Altmann is certain that from Jerusalem Helena returned to Rome, not to Constantinople. And again much praise is heaped on Constantine.

The fifth chapter credits Constantine with the construction of the Church of St. Irene and the Church of the Holy Apostles in Constantinople and praises Helena again for having found the True Cross and for her charitable deeds.[11] Altmann then tells this curious tale: Helena

---

[5]Pp. 583-85. The chapter divisions are those of the editor.

[6]See chapter II and chapter IV above. Ewig, "Tradition" 155, assures us that this passage is *not* a later interpolation. On the rivalry between Trier and Rheims see Hermann Schmitt, "Trier und Reims in der verfassungsgeschichtlichen Entwicklung bis zum Primatialstreit des 9 Jahrhunderts," *ZRG, K. Abt.* 18 (1929) 1-111.

[7]Pp. 586-88.

[8]Pp. 590-92.

[9]Pp. 592-94.

[10]See chapter X above.

[11]Pp. 595-97.

sent some relics to her *patria,* but the ship bearing these relics suffered shipwreck in the river Doubs (Duvius), near Besançon; at a later time some of the relics were recovered by the citizens of Besançon. One may suppose that Altmann learned about this tradition when he visited Besançon.[12] Turning then to the subject of Helena's death, Altmann treats us to an imaginary and tasteless conversation between Helena and Christ, but tells us nothing of substance.

Continuing on this subject in the sixth chapter, Altmann imagines that Helena on her deathbed encouraged Constantine in the faith; the assumption seems to be that *both* were then at Rome.[13] What Altmann then has to say about the place of Helena's burial is unintelligible: Constantine buried his mother *in Via Labicana inter duas lauros in vico Drepani*! There follows a naive and unsuccessful effort to explain the contradiction in terms of Greek and Latin etymology. Altmann imagines that Constantine and all the Romans shed many tears at Helena's funeral. Addressing Constantine as if he were still alive, he urges him to imitate his mother. He concludes thus: *haud dubium quin* [Helena] *adepta sit consortium angelorum in vita caelesti apud Deum.*

Altmann appends to his *vita* of Helena an account of the *translatio* of her remains to Hautvillers and an account of the miracles which took place during and after this event.[14]

In the eleventh century, more specifically in 1050-1072, an anonymous monk in Trier re-worked Altmann's *vita* of St. Helena and incorporated it in a double *vita* of Sts. Helena and Agritius.[15] No further examination of this text is necessary, since it has little of any value to offer to us.[16]

Hrabanus Maurus (ca. 780 - 856) was abbot of the Benedictine abbey of Fulda and later archbishop of Mainz. His passion for learning and teaching earned him the title of *praeceptor Germaniae.*[17] Among

---

[12]For Altmann's visit to Besançon see Sauerland, *op. cit.* 63-64, and Ewig, "Tradition" 156. Besançon also claims to have a church established by Helena; see chapter III above, n. 59.

[13]Pp. 597-99.

[14]See chapter XII above, n. 37 and n. 45.

[15]*BHL* 3776; text in Sauerland, *op. cit.* 172-84. For the *vita* of Agritius see chapter IV above, n. 6.

[16]Sauerland, *op. cit.* 57-60, 61, and 77.

[17]Manitius I 288-302; De Ghellinck, *op. cit.* 102-104; Raby, *A History of Christian-Latin Poetry*[2] 179-83; Brunhölzl, *Geschichte der lat. Lit. des Mittelalters* I 325-41; Klaus

(continued...)

his many writings are 162 Latin homilies, one of which concerns us here.[18]   Homily no. 70 briefly mentions Constantine's vision and victory and the *inventio* and *verificatio* of the True Cross by Helena; it then tells at length of the loss of the Cross to the Persians and of its recovery by Heraclius.[19]

Aelfric (ca. 955-1020) was first a Benedictine monk at Winchester and Cernel (Dorsetshire) and later abbot of Eynsham Abbey (Oxfordshire).   He was a prolific and accomplished writer of both Latin and Old English prose.   The first of his many writings is a collection, in two series, of vernacular homilies known as the *Catholic Homilies* and dating from the years 989-995.[20]   Among these homilies is one, in the second series, on the Invention of the Cross.[21]   It is concerned with Constantine more than with Helena; there is no mention of Macarius or of Judas, and the *verificatio* is only alluded to.

---

[17](...continued)
von See in Klaus von See, ed., *Europäisches Frühmittelalter* 32; Alf Önnerfors *ibid.* 168-69 and 173.   Hrabanus Maurus' *De Laudibus Sanctae Crucis,* a contrived *carmen figuratum,* is of only peripheral interest in our context.

[18]Gröber, *op. cit.* 127.

[19]Migne, *PL* CX 131-34.

[20]Eduard Dietrich, "Abt Aelfrik zur Literatur-Geschichte der angelsächsischen Kirche," *ZHT* 25 (1855) 487-594 and 26 (1856) 163-256, still useful; Caroline Louisa White, *AElfric: A New Study of His Life and Writings* (New Haven 1898) 101-105; S. Harvey Gem, *An Anglo-Saxon Abbot: AElfric of Eynsham* (Edinburgh 1912) 112-40; Gerould, *Saints' Legends* 115-21; Wardale, *op. cit.* 266-68; Marguerite-Marie Dubois, *AElfric: Sermonnaire, Docteur et Grammairien* (Paris 1943) 81-84.   Cyril L. Smetana, "Aelfric and the Early Medieval Homiliary," *Traditio* 15 (1959) 163-204, examines Aelfric's sources.   Peter Clemoes, "The Chronology of AElfric's Works," in Peter Clemoes, ed., *The Anglo-Saxons: Studies in Some Aspects of Their History and Culture Presented to Bruce Dickins* (London 1959) 212-47, esp. 244; Godfrey, *op. cit.* 332-42, esp. 333.   James E. Cross, *Aelfric and the Mediaeval Homiliary - Objection and Contribution* (Lund 1963), examines Aelfric's sources, responding to Smetana (above). Renwick and Orton, *op. cit.* 230-34; Peter Clemoes, "AElfric," in Eric Gerald Stanley, ed., *Continuations and Beginnings: Studies in Old English Literature* (London 1966) 176-209, esp. 181; Kemp Malone in Baugh, *op. cit.* 101-103; James Hurt, *AElfric* (New York 1972) 42-59; Greenfield and Calder, *op. cit.* 75-82.   Of broader interest: Milton McC. Gatch, *Preaching and Theology in Anglo-Saxon England: AElfric and Wulfstan* (Toronto 1977), and Paul E. Szarmach and Bernard F. Huppé, edd., *The Old English Homily and Its Background* (Albany 1978).

[21]Ed. Benjamin Thorpe, *The Homilies of the Anglo-Saxon Church: The First Part, Containing the Sermones Catholici or Homilies of AElfric* (London 1844-46) II 302-307, no. 19, with translation; ed. Malcolm Godden, AElfric's *Catholic Homilies. The Second Series: Text (EETS, SS* 5; London 1979) 174-76, no. 18.

The *History of the Holy Rood-tree* is an an Old English homily of the eleventh century.[22] It offers a peculiar variant on the *verificatio* of the Cross: there is only one "false" cross, and the scene has been transferred from Jerusalem to Constantinople.[23] Another Old English homily, *The Finding of the True Cross*, also dates from the eleventh century. It is ultimately derived from a Latin text of the Cyriacus version of the legend, but contains many additions.[24] Helena is said to return from the Holy Land to Rome, there to meet Constantine.[25]

Berengoz, or Berengosus, was abbot of Trier's Abbey of St. Maximinus *ca.* 1105-1125.[26] He wrote, among other *sermones*, a lengthy discourse under the title *De Laude et Inventione Sanctae Crucis*.[27] What he has to say on the *inventio* and *verificatio* of the Cross is nothing new.[28] Some other remarks of his are more noteworthy: the Jews are guilty of *impietas* and *invidia*, Helena was a native of Trier, Constantine was baptized by Pope Sylvester, Helena is more meritorious than Constantine, Helena's feast day is observed everywhere, and Trier is rightly called a second Rome.[29]

Hildebert of Lavardin (also known as Hildebert of Le Mans or Hildebert of Tours; 1056-1133) was first bishop of Le Mans and later archbishop of Tours. A prolific writer, he is counted among the most important literary figures of the Middle Ages.[30] Among his poems is

---

[22]Extant in a twelfth century manuscript in the Bodleian Library, Bodley 343; see Ker, *op. cit.* 368-75, no. 310; published by Arthur S. Napier, *EETS, OS* 103 (London 1894) 2-35.

[23]*Ibid.* 32-33.

[24]Extant in two manuscripts, Bodleian Library, Auct. F.4.32, and Cambridge, Corpus Christi College 303; see Ker, *op. cit.* 355, no. 297, and 99-105, no. 57, respectively. Ed. Richard Morris, *Legends of the Holy Rood (EETS, OS* 46; London 1871) 2-17; excellent new ed., with modern English translation, by Bodden, *op. cit.* 60-103.

[25]*Ibid.* 98-99.

[26]Marx, *op. cit.* II.1 95-102.

[27]*BHL* 4176; in three books, Migne, *PL* CLX 935-82; Gröber, *op. cit.* 197 and 201.

[28]2. 6-7 (Migne, *PL* CLX 957-58). For a convenient summary see Wiegel, *op. cit.* 8 with n. 38.

[29]1.2 (Migne, *PL* CLX 937-38); 2.1 (Migne, *PL* CLX 953); 2.2 and 3.7 (Migne, *PL* CLX 953 and 974); 2.11 (Migne, *PL* CLX 962); *ibid.*; 3.1 (Migne, *PL* CLX 965); William Hammer, "The Concept of the New or Second Rome in the Middle Ages," *Speculum* 19 (1944) 50-62 at 57-60.

[30]Gröber, *op. cit.* 375-76; Manitius III 853-65; De Ghellinck, *op. cit.* II 118-24; Raby, *A History of Christian Latin Poetry*[2] 265-73; Raby, *A History of Secular Latin*
(continued...)

one, in 391 hexameter lines, under the title *De Inventione Sanctae Crucis*, which tells the story of the *inventio* and *verificatio*, following the Cyriacus version.[31]

Jacobus de Voragine (or Jacopo da Varagine; ca. 1230-1290), Dominican priest, translator of the Bible, and finally Archbishop of Genoa, produced *ca.* 1260 a compilation of saints' legends, the *Legenda Sanctorum* or *Historia Lombardica*.[32] Under a changed title, *Legenda Aurea*, it quickly became one of the most widely read and circulated books in Western Europe, was before long translated into various vernacular languages, and inspired numerous works of art.[33] Extant manuscripts in Latin alone number approximately 1000.[34] The first

---

[30](...continued)
Poetry in the Middle Ages[2] I 317-29; Peter von Moos, *Hildebert von Lavardin, 1056-1133* (Stuttgart 1965).

[31]Migne, *PL* CLXXI 1315-22; Manitius III 860-61; see Wiegel, *op. cit.* 8 with n. 38, for a convenient summary.

[32]Edd. 1-3 Th. Graesse, Leipzig and Dresden 1846, 1850, and 1890; repr. Osnabrück 1965. Because of the deficiencies of this edition some modern translations into German, English, and French respectively ought to be noted: Richard Benz (Jena 1917-1925; repr. Heidelberg 1969 and 1975); Granger Ryan and Helmut Ripperger (London 1941; repr. New York 1969); Teodor de Wyzewa (Paris 1960; re-issue of the ed. of 1902); J. B. M. Roze (Paris 1967; re-issue of the ed. of 1902).

[33]Pierce Butler, *Legenda Aurea - Légende Dorée - Golden Legend* (Baltimore 1899) 10-12; Friedrich Wilhelm, *Deutsche Legenden und Legendare* (Leipzig 1907) 135-36; Gröber, *op. cit.* 279; Ernest C. Richardson, *Materials for a Life of Jacopo da Voragine* (New York 1935) I 40-59 and II 1-39; Maria von Nagy and N. Christoph de Nagy, *Die Legenda aurea und ihr Verfasser Jacobus de Voragine* (Bern and Munich 1971) 22-76; Wiegel; *op. cit.* 11-12; Franz Brunhölzl, "Die lateinische Literatur," in Willi Erzgräber, *Europäisches Spätmittelalter* (Wiesbaden 1978) 519-63 at 531-33; Kurt Ruh, "Geistliche Prosa," *ibid.* 565-605 at 585-86; Konrad Kunze, "Jacobus a Voragine," in *Verfasserlexikon*[2] IV (1982) 448-66 at 453-54; Alain Boureau, *La légende dorée* (Paris 1984); Sherry L. Reames, *The Legenda Aurea: A Reexamination of Its Paradoxical History* (Madison 1985) 3-5; Brenda Dunn-Lardeau, ed., *Legenda Aurea: Sept siècles de diffusion. Actes du colloque international sur la Legenda aurea* (Montreal and Paris 1986); Richard Klein in *RAC* XIV 371; Evelyn Birge Vitz, "From the Oral to the Written in Medieval and Renaissance Saints' Lives," in Blumenfeld-Kosinski and Szell, *op. cit.* 97-114 at 107-109.

[34]Konrad Kunze, "Katalog zur Überlieferung der Legenda Aurea des Jacobus de Voragine," *Anal. Boll.* 95 (1977) 168; Kurt Ruh in Erzgräber, *op. cit.* 585; Ulla Williams and Werner Williams-Krapp, *Die Elsässische Legenda Aurea* I (Tübingen 1980), p. XIII; Kunze in *Verfasserlexikon*[2] IV (1982/1983) 452; Barbara Fleith, "Le classement des quelque 1000 manuscrits de la *Legenda aurea* latine," in Dunn-Lardeau, *Legenda Aurea: Sept siècles de diffusion* 19-24 at 19-20; Georg Steer in Ingeborg Glier, ed., *Die deutsche Literatur im späten Mittelalter, 1250-1370* II (Munich 1987) 308.

printed edition appeared in Cologne in 1470; and by the end of the century there were 97 editions in Latin and additional editions in various vernacular languages, namely Italian, Czech, French, Dutch, English, and German.[35] The popularity of the work continued unabated until it came under intense attack at the time of the Protestant Reformation, and there have been intermittent attacks since then.[36]

The 182 chapters of the Latin version (in Graesse's edition) are arranged according to the church calendar, beginning with Advent. There are chapters on St. Sylvester (December 31), on the Invention of the Holy Cross (May 3), and on the Exaltation of the Holy Cross (September 14).[37] These chapters do not yield new biographical data or new hagiographical elements. Voragine used a wide variety of sources, but none to which we do not have direct access. He specifically mentions the *Ecclesiastical History* (of Rufinus), the *Tripartite History* (of Cassiodorus), the *Chronicle* of Jerome, St. Ambrose, and Gregory of Tours. At times he critically evaluates his sources.[38]

His chapter on Sylvester closely follows, as one might expect, the *Vita* or *Actus S. Silvestri*. But in his chapter on the Invention of the Holy Cross he is very much aware of different and conflicting reports on Constantine's baptism. Similarly he knows that several places claim to be Helena's birthplace. He remarks that Judas' father cannot possibly

[35]Pierce Butler, *op. cit.* 12; Robert Francis Seybolt, "Fifteenth Century Editions of the *Legenda Aurea*," *Speculum* 21 (1946) 327-38, erroneously including edd. of *Der Heiligen Leben* among vernacular edd. of the *Legenda Aurea*; Robert Francis Seybolt, "The *Legenda Aurea*, Bible, and *Historia Scholastica*," *Speculum* 21 (1946) 339-42 at 341-42; Williams and Williams-Krapp, *op. cit.* I, p. XIII. Paris' Bibliothèque Nationale alone boasts 64 incunabula of the *Legenda Aurea* (63 edd., 1472-1500); 44 in Latin, four in German, seven in French, three in Italian, and six in Dutch: *Catalogue des incunables* II.1 (Paris 1981) 85-96, J-61-124; Kunze in *Verfasserlexikon*[2] IV (1982/1983) 453; Georg Steer in Glier, *op. cit.* 308.

[36]Pierce Butler, *op. cit.* 13-16; Richardson, *op. cit.* II 19-20; Helen C. White, *Tudor Books of Saints and Martyrs* (Madison 1963) 67-95; Annemarie and Wolfgang Brückner in Wolfgang Brückner, ed., *Volkserzählung und Reformation* (Berlin 1974) 522-23; Josef Schmidt, "Golden Legends during the Reformation Controversy," in Dunn-Lardeau, *Legenda aurea: Sept siècles de diffusion* 267-75. Reames, *op. cit.* 11-43, argues that the reaction against the *Legenda Aurea* began in the ranks of orthodox Catholicism decades before the Reformation. Vitz, *op. cit.* 109-12; Pierce Butler, *op. cit.* 16-18.

[37]Chapter XII (ed. Graesse[3] 70-79); Chapter LXVIII (ed. Graesse[3] 303-11); Chapter CXXXVII (ed. Graesse[3] 605-11).

[38]Pierce Butler, *op. cit.* 7; Boureau, *op. cit.* 97,105, and 180; Marilyn Aronberg Lavin, *The Place of Narrative: Mural Decoration in Italian Churches, 431-1600* (Chicago 1990) 347, n. 130.

have been alive at the time of Christ's Passion. He knows of the two versions of the *verificatio* of the Cross. His chapter on the Exaltation of the Holy Cross, as far as it is of interest in our context, tells of Heraclius executing Chosroes, fighting the son of Chosroes in a duel on a bridge, and returning the Cross to Jerusalem.

From the early 14th century on, the *Legenda Aurea* was repeatedly translated into French.[39] The most famous of these translations into French is that which Jean de Vignay produced in the 1330's or 1340's.[40] This is extant in no fewer than 34 manuscripts, 29 of them illuminated, in French, Belgian, British, and American libraries, and in numerous early printed editions.[41]

We possess ten translations of the *Legenda Aurea* into German and Dutch.[42] One of these is the Alsatian prose translation of the *Legenda Aurea* which was produced in the first half of the 14th century by an anonymous translator at Strassburg. It is extant in 34 manuscripts, the oldest of which dates from 1362.[43] The first of two translations into Dutch dates from 1357.[44]

---

[39]Paul Meyer, "Notice du MS. Med.-Pal. 141 de la Laurentienne," *Romania* 33 (1904) 1-49 at 1-6. On the translation by a certain Jean Belet see Kurt Ruh in Erzgräber, *op. cit.* 585; but Pierce Butler, *op. cit.* 20-35, after a lengthy examination, was inclined to think that Belet's work is an independent compilation rather than a translation of Voragine's work.

[40]Pierce Butler, *op. cit.* 35; Christine Knowles, "Jean de Vignay: Un traducteur du XIVe siècle," *Romania* 75 (1954) 353-83 at 364-66; Kurt Ruh in Erzgräber, *op. cit.* 585-86.

[41]Pierce Butler, *op. cit.* 36-42; Paul Meyer, *op. cit.* 1-6; Brenda Dunn-Lardeau and Dominique Coq, "Fifteenth and Sixteenth-century Editions of the Légende dorée," *BHR* 47 (1985) 87-101; Christine Knowles, *op. cit.* 380-83; Hilary Maddocks, "Illumination in Jean de Vignay's *Légende dorée,"* in Dunn-Lardeau, *Legenda aurea: Sept siècles de diffusion* 155-69 at 155.

[42]Werner Williams-Krapp, "Die deutschen Übersetzungen der 'Legenda aurea' des Jacobus de Voragine," *BGDSL* 101 (1979) 252-76; Kunze in *Verfasserlexikon*[2] IV 456-63; Werner Williams-Krapp, "German and Dutch Translations of the *Legenda aurea,"* in Dunn-Lardeau, *Legenda aurea: Sept siècles de diffusion* 227-32 at 227.

[43]Konrad Kunze, Überlieferung und Bestand der Elsässischen Legenda aurea," *ZDA* 99 (1970) 265-309; Williams and Williams-Krapp, *op.cit.* I, pp. XIV-XXIV; critical edition of text *ibid.* 1-826; Kunze in *Verfasserlexikon*[2] IV 460-61; Georg Steer in Glier, *op. cit.* 309-10.

[44]Williams-Krapp, "Die deutschen Übersetzungen" 253; Kunze in Verfasserlexikon[2] IV 457-59; Williams-Krapp, "German and Dutch Translations" 228; Georg Steer in Glier, *op. cit.* 310.

A Czech translation and adaptation of the *Legenda Aurea* has been dated to 1357; two incunabula appeared before 1487 and in 1495 respectively.[45]

In *ca.* 1438 an anonymous translator produced the first English version, called *Gilte Legende*, which is much indebted to Jean de Vignay's French version.[46]

Among the many books produced by William Caxton, printer, translator, and editor, was his own not very precise English translation and expansion of the *Legenda Aurea* in editions of 1483, 1487, and 1493 (the last of these actually printed by Wynkyn de Worde).[47] The large number of extant copies gives evidence of its great popularity in its own days.[48]

There is another collection of saints' legends which also dates from the second half of the thirteenth century. This is the *South English Legendary*, a *liber festivalis* composed in rhymed couplets by an anony-

[45]Anežka Vidmomová, "La branche tchéque de la *Légende dorée,*" in Dunn-Lardeau, *Legenda aurea: Sept siècles de diffusion* 291-98 at 295 with n. 16; *ibid.* 297.

[46]Gerould, *Saints' Legends* 195-96; Sister Mary Jeremy, "The English Prose Translation of the *Legenda Aurea,*" *MLN* 59 (1944) 181-83; Wolpers, *Die englische Heiligenlegende* 373-76; Manfred Görlach, *The South English Legendary, Gilte Legende and Golden Legend* (Braunschweig 1972) 8; Kurt Ruh in Erzgräber, *op. cit.* 586. Pierce Butler, *op.cit.* 50-75, examines the extant manuscripts.

[47]Ed. F. S. Ellis, *The Golden Legend or Lives of the Saints as Englished by William Caxton* (7 vols. London 1900); Pierce Butler, *op. cit.* 75-87; Gerould, *Saints' Legends* 196; Henry R. Plomer, *William Caxton* (London 1925) 135-39; Nellie Slayton Aurner, *Caxton: Mirrour of Fifteenth-Century Letters* (Boston 1926) 115-29; Sister Mary Jeremy, "Caxton's *Golden Legend* and Varagine's *Legenda Aurea,*" *Speculum* 21 (1946) 212-21; Sister Mary Jeremy, "Caxton's *Golden Legend* and de Vignai's *Légende Dorée,*" *Mediaeval Studies* 8 (1946) 97-106; Henry Stanley Bennett, *op. cit.* 267-70; Helen C. White, *op. cit.* 31-66; Wolpers, *Die englische Heiligenlegende* 383-90; George D. Painter, *William Caxton: A Biography* (New York 1977) 143-46. The chapter on the Invention of the Holy Cross and the chapter on the Exaltation of the Cross have been reprinted from Caxton's 3rd ed. by Richard Morris in his *Legends of the Holy Rood* (*EETS, OS* 46; London 1871) 154-60 and 161-69 respectively.

[48]The Cambridge University Library alone has eight copies, Oxford's Bodleian Library four, and the British Library three; and there are several copies in American libraries. William Blades, *The Life and Typography of William Caxton* (London 1861-1863) II 151-156, 182-83, and 249-51; Edward Gordon Duff, *William Caxton* (Chicago 1905) 62-63, 71-72, and 81-83; Seymour de Ricci, *A Census of Caxtons* (Oxford 1909) 101-107, nos. 98-99, and 115-17, no.107; Edward Gordon Duff, *Fifteenth Century English Books* (Oxford 1917) 113-15, nos. 408-10; J. C. T. Oates, *A Catalogue of the Fifteenth-century Printed Books in the University Library Cambridge* (Cambridge 1954) 676-77, nos. 4087-91; 679, no. 4105; and 682-83, nos. 4131-32.

mous English poet. Since we have a firm date neither for this legendary nor for the *Legenda Aurea* it is difficult to know which of the two is the earlier. It has been held at one time that the two works are quite independent of each other, but more recently that the *South English Legendary* is dependent on or has drawn on the *Legenda Aurea*. The *South English Legendary* is extant in 51 manuscripts, but these vary greatly one from another in choice and arrangement of materials, suggesting a process of modification and accretion over a period of time.[49]

The oldest, but rather disorganized, manuscript of this legendary, Laud 108 in Oxford's Bodleian Library, contains the story of the Holy

---

[49]Carl Horstmann, ed., *The Early South-English Legendary or Lives of the Saints* (*EETS, OS* 87; London 1887), p. VIII, held that the *South English Legendary* and the *Legenda Aurea* were formed at the same time and independently of one another. Similarly Gerould, *Saints' Legends* 151-64, esp. 155-56, believes the work to be an original compilation from a number of different sources. Minnie E. Wells, "The South English Legendary in Its Relation to the *Legenda Aurea*," *PMA* 4 51 (1936) 337-60, dates the composition of the *Legenda Aurea* to 1255-1258 and that of the *South English Legendary* to 1275-1285 (see esp. p. 340) and concludes after lengthy examination that the compiler of the legendary used Voragine's collection as the basis of his work (see esp. p. 359). The same author seeks to strengthen her argument in a subsequent article, "The Structural Development of the South English Legendary," *JEGP* 41 (1942) 320-44 at 320-21 and 343-44. Beverly Boyd, "New Light on the *South English Legendary*," *TxSE* 37 (1958) 187-94, deems Horstmann's text to be merely a collection of miscellaneous material. Wolpers, *Die englische Heiligenlegende* 211 with n. 18, recognizes considerable influence of the *Legenda Aurea* on the *South English Legendary*. Albert C. Baugh in Baugh, *op. cit.* 206-207, notes the "family likeness" of the two works. Görlach, *The South English Legendary, Gilte Legende and Golden Legend* 7, dating the *Legenda Aurea* to ca. 1255-1270 and the *South English Legendary* to ca. 1270-1290, notes the influence of the former on the latter. Kurt Ruh in Erzgräber, *op. cit.* 586, holds that the author of the *South English Legendary* made use of the *Legenda Aurea*. Thomas J. Heffernan, "Additional Evidence for a More Specific Date of the South English Legendary," *Traditio* 35 (1979) 345-51, dates the South English Legendary, on the basis of calendar calculations, to either 1276 or 1279. J. A. W. Bennett, *Middle English Literature* (Oxford 1986) 60-62, calls the *South English Legendary* a "popular equivalent of the contemporary *Legenda Aurea*." Manfred Görlach, "The *Legenda aurea* and the Early History of *The South English Legendary*," in Dunn-Lardeau, *Legenda aurea: Sept siècles de diffusion* 301-16 at 304, admits the *Legenda Aurea* not as the major source but as a supplementary source of the *South English Legendary; ibid.* 307 he shows the influence of the *Legenda Aurea* on the story of the Invention of the Cross in the *South English Legendary*. For a more detailed study one must consult Görlach's *The Textual Tradition of the South English Legendary* (Leeds 1974). Klaus P. Jankofsky, "*Legenda aurea* Materials in *The South English Legendary*," in Dunn-Lardeau, *Legenda aurea: Sept siècles de diffusion* 317-29, explores the process of translation and adaptation. The same legendary is also known as the *Southern Legend Collection;* see Renwick and Orton, *op.cit.* 430.

Cross, following the Cyriacus version.[50] It also contains the story of St. Sylvester, but there is no mention of Sylvester having converted Constantine and Helena.[51] Another manuscript, Corpus Christi College, Cambridge, MS.145, gives us the Invention of the Cross and the Exaltation of the Cross in the order of the calendar, while the legend of St. Sylvester is omitted.[52]

A Swedish legendary, *Forsvenska Legendariet* or better *Skänningelegendariet*, which is largely based on the *Legenda Aurea*, dates from ca. 1300 and is the oldest collection of saints' legends in Swedish.[53] In the first quarter of the fourteenth century an anonymous poet in the north of England composed the *Cursor Mundi*.[54] This religious poem, ca. 30,000 lines long, contains mostly biblical material, but the author also shows familiarity with the *Legenda Aurea* and other sources.[55] The story of the Cross is told at length but in a most unusual variant: the location of the Cross is revealed by the familiar figure of the Jew demanding his pound of flesh, while Judas-Quiriacus is mentioned only at the end.[56]

It is not surprising that the *Legenda Aurea* was drawn upon as subject matter for homilies. A case in point is the *Northern English Homily Collection* which dates from the first half of the 14th century, is extant in three recensions, and appears to be dependent in part on the

[50]Ed. Carl Horstmann; see preceding note. In 614 lines; ed. Horstmann 1-19; summary *ibid.* pp. XXV-XXVI.

[51]In 66 lines; ed. Horstmann 391-92; summary *ibid.* p. XLVII.

[52]Charlotte D'Evelyn and Anna J. Mill, edd., *The South English Legendary (EETS, OS* 235, 236, and 244; Oxford 1956-1959). Nos. 38 and 63 respectively.

[53]Edd. George Stephens in *Samlingar utgivna av Svenska Fornskriftssällskapet* VII (Stockholm 1847-1865) and Valter Jansson *ibid.* LV (Stockholm 1938). Valter Jansson, "Forsvenska Legendariet," in *Kulturhistoriskt Lexikon för Nordisk Medeltid* IV (Malmö 1959) 518-22. I owe the reference to the kindness of Dr. Stephan Borgehammar, Uppsala. Gustafson, *op. cit.* 26-27; Birgit Klockars in Tigerstedt, *op. cit.* I 156-58; Kurt Schier in Henning Krauss, *op. cit.* 535 and 542. I have not examined this text.

[54]Ed. Richard Morris, *EETS, OS* 57, 59, 62, 66, 68 (text in four versions), 99, and 101 (editorial matter), London 1874-1893.

[55]Renwick and Orton, *op. cit.* 305; Albert C. Baugh in Baugh, *op. cit.* 206-207; J. A. W. Bennet, *op. cit.* 35-41.

[56]Ed. Morris *(EETS, OS* 66; London 1877) 1222-51; Richard Morris, ed., *Legends of the Holy Rood (EETS, OS* 46) 108-21.

Legenda Aurea.[57] It contains homilies both on the Invention and on the Exaltation of the Cross.[58] Another case in point is the *Festial* which John Mirk, a canon at Lilleshall in Shropshire, published in *ca.* 1400. This is a collection of about seventy vernacular homilies for various feasts of the year and based in part on the *Legenda Aurea.*[59] We find a homily both for the Invention of the Cross and for the Exaltation of the Cross.[60] In the former the author asserts that Helena was the daughter of King Cole, thus revealing his use of local (British) sources as well.[61]

In the German-speaking parts of central Europe the popularity of the *Legenda Aurea* was eventually eclipsed by that of another legendary, *Der Heiligen Leben.*[62] This was compiled by a Dominican friar at Nuremberg in *ca.* 1400. It draws upon the *Legenda Aurea* as one of its sources, but includes many more saints, especially from central Europe, among them St. Sebaldus, Nuremberg's patron saint. There is an impressive number of surviving manuscripts, and 29 printed editions appeared between 1471 and 1500.[63] The most successful of the early printed editions was that which Sebastian Brant produced at Strassburg

---

[57]Gordon Hall Gerould, *The North English Homily Collection* (Oxford 1902); Gerould, *Saints' Legends* 164-76; James E. Carver, *The Northern Homily Cycle* (New York 1941); Wolpers, *Die englische Heiligenlegende* 263-65; Renwick and Orton, *op. cit.* 429; Albert C. Baugh in Baugh, *op. cit.* 205.

[58]Text in Carl Horstmann, ed., *Altenglische Legenden: Neue Folge* (Heilbronn 1881) 56-62 and 128-31 respectively; also Richard Morris, ed., *Legends of the Holy Rood* (*EETS, OS* 46) 87-97 and 122-30 respectively.

[59]Gerould, *Saints' Legends* 184-88; Aurner, *op. cit.* 121; Henry Staley Bennett, *op. cit.* 119, 188, and 213; Wolpers, *Die englische Heiligenlegende* 370-71; Renwick and Orton, *op. cit.* 322-23; Görlach, *The South English Legendary, Gilte Legende and Golden Legend* 8; J. A. W. Bennett, *op. cit.* 300.

[60]Ed. Theodor Erbe (*EETS, ES* 96; London 1905) 142-46; *ibid.* 249-52.

[61]*Ibid.* 144.

[62]A critical and complete edition of the legendary is lacking. The edition of Severin Rüttgers, *Der Heiligen Leben und Leiden, anders genannt das Passional* (2 vols.; Leipzig 1913) is non-critical and offers a selection of legends only. It reproduces woodcuts from a 1492 edition.

[63]Wilhelm, *op. cit.* 174-212; Werner Williams-Krapp, "Studien zu 'Der Heiligen Leben'," *ZDA* 105 (1976) 274-303 at 291-94 and 298; Williams-Krapp, "Die deutschen Übersetzungen" 254; Konrad Kunze, "'Der Heiligen Leben'," in *Verfasserlexikon²* III, (1980/1981) 617-25; Williams-Krapp, "German and Dutch Translations" 229; Georg Steer in Glier, *op. cit.* 310-12; Werner Williams-Krapp, "Der Heiligen Leben," in *Literatur Lexikon* VI (1990) 122-24.

in 1502 for Johannes Grüninger.[64] *Der Heiligen Leben* contains chapters on Pope Sylvester, on the Invention of the Cross, and on the Exaltation of the Cross.[65] In the Invention Constantine is baptized not by Pope Sylvester but by Pope Eusebius, and the *verificatio* is performed twice, once on a dead young man and once on an ill woman.

Among the miracle plays which were popular in the Late Middle Ages we find the *Augsburger Heiligkreuzspiel*.[66] It was – the opening is lost – about 2000 verses long and was meant to be presented over two days. The first part, with 41 speaking roles, focuses on Constantine's victory over Maxentius and on Helena's *inventio* of the True Cross; the second part, with 42 speaking roles, on the loss of the Cross to Chosroes and on its recovery by Heraclius. In both parts the Jews are portrayed as the enemies of the Christian faith. The unknown author's major source was the *Legenda Aurea*.[67]

There are some breviaries which give a full account of the Invention of the Cross. One of these is the Breviary of Belleville, which dates from the 1320's.[68] Another is the Breviary of the Duke of Bedford, which dates from the 1430's.[69] Fairly concise accounts of the Invention and of the Exaltation of the Cross are given by the *Breviarium*

---

[64]Edwin H. Zeydel, *Sebastian Brant* (New York 1967) 115; Manfred Lemmer, "Brant, Sebastian," in *Verfasserlexikon*[2] I (1977/1978) 992-1005 at 994.

[65]Ed. Rüttgers I 237-42, II 48-53, and II 402-404.

[66]Staats- und Stadtbibliothek, Augsburg, 4° cod. H. 27 (before 1494), folios 47r-89v. The same manuscript contains the *Augsburger Georgsspiel,* folios 90r-135r. Wolf Gehrt in Helmut Gier and Johannes Janota, edd., *Von der Augsburger Bibelhandschrift zu Bertolt Brecht* (Weissenhorn 1991) 140-42; Adalbert von Keller, *Fastnachtspiele aus dem fünfzehnten Jahrhundert: Nachlese* (Stuttgart 1858) 54-122, no. 125; Elke Ukena, *Die deutschen Mirakelspiele des Spätmittelalters* (Bern 1975) II 453-559.

[67]Adalbert von Keller, *op. cit.* 331; Gerd Simon, *Die erste deutsche Fastnachtsspieltradition* (Lübeck 1970) 20-22; Ukena, *op. cit.* I 223-51; Heinrich Biermann, "'Augsburger (südbairisches) Heiligkreuzspiel'," in *Verfasserlexikon*[2] I (1977/1978) 528-30; Bernd Neumann, "Augsburger Heiligkreuzspiel," in *Literatur Lexikon* I (1988) 250-51. Such plays continued to be produced in the 16th century. In 1575 Renward Cysat, a citizen of Lucerne, wrote a *Spil dess heiligen Crützes Erfindung*, now only partially extant; see Ukena, *op. cit.* II 561-771. And in 1598 Wilhelm Stapfer, a citizen of Solothurn, produced in Zug a *Tragoedia von Erfindung dess heiligen Froncreützes wie auch dessen Erhöchung;* see Ukena, *op. cit.* II 773-954.

[68]Bibliothèque Nationale, Paris, Ms. lat. 10483-84, vol. I, folios 178r -178v; Wiegel, *op. cit.* 4 with n. 21.

[69]Bibliothèque Nationale, Paris, Ms. lat. 17294, folios 452v - 455r; Wiegel, *op. cit.* 141 with n. 203.

Romanum of 1568.[70] Mediaeval liturgical books of all kinds – sacramentaries, martyrologies, lectionaries, breviaries, graduals, and missals – are often richly illuminated for both feasts. A new kind of prayerbook, derived from the Book of Hours, made its appearance at the very end of the Middle Ages. This is the *Hortulus Animae* – or "Seelengärtlein," – of which more than 100 printed editions appeared between 1498 and 1523, mostly in Germany, in several languages and different versions.[71] Most of these editions are richly illustrated, as, for instance, the editions printed by Johannes Grüninger in Strassburg in 1498 and 1500.[72]

Turning to the Byzantine East, we must begin with a double *vita* of Constantine and Helena which is of an early but uncertain date, perhaps as early as the fifth or sixth century.[73] In this *vita* Helena, having been sent to Jerusalem by Constantine expressly for this purpose, finds both the Cross and the nails; there is no mention of Cyriacus or of a *verificatio*. Helena is said to have died in Rome and to have been buried in a porphyry sarcophagus in a round church.

Our second example from the Byzantine East is provided by one Alexander Monachos of Salamis on Cyprus (?), who, in the sixth century (or ninth century?), wrote a long treatise, *De Inventione Sanctae Crucis*, perhaps a homily delivered on the feast day of the Exaltation of the Cross.[74] In his account of the *inventio* Alexander makes no mention of

[70]Ed. Turin 1952, II (Spring) 1003-19, and IV (Autumn) 543-58.

[71]M. Consuelo Oldenbourg, *Hortulus animae (1494)-1523* (Hamburg 1973) 219-21; Peter Ochsenbein, "Hortulus animae," in *Verfasserlexikon*[2] IV (1982/1983) 147-54.

[72]Albert Schramm, *Der Bilderschmuck der Frühdrucke* XX.2 (Leipzig 1937), pls. 79-80, nos. 581-639.

[73]*BHG*[3] 365z, 366, and 366a; synoptic ed. by Friedhelm Winkelmann, "Die älteste erhaltene griechische hagiographische Vita Konstantins und Helenas (*BHG* Nr. 365z, 366, 366a)," in Jürgen Dummer, ed., *Texte und Textkritik: Eine Aufsatzsammlung* (*TU* 133 [1987]) 628-38. Borgehammar, *op. cit.* 71-73, thinks that this vita is an independent witness of the *inventio*.

[74]Greek: Λόγος εἰς τὴν εὕρεσιν τοῦ τιμίου καὶ ζωοποιοῦ σταυροῦ. *BHG*[3] 410; Migne, *PG* LXXXVII.3 4015-76; Albert Ehrhard in Krumbacher, *op. cit.* I 164; Sévérien Salaville, "Le moine Alexandre de Chypre," *EO* 15 (1912) 134-37; Straubinger, *op. cit.* 73-74; Bardenhewer, *op. cit.* V (1932) 144-45; Albert Ehrhard, *Überlieferung und Bestand der hagiographischen und homiletischen Literatur der griechischen Kirche* (Leipzig 1939-1952) I.1 236 and I.3 287; Hans-Georg Beck, *Kirche und theologische Literatur* 399; Wiegel, *op. cit.* 4; Michel van Esbroeck, "L'opuscule 'Sur la croix' d'Alexandre de Chypre et sa version géorgienne," *Bedi Kartlisa* 37 (1979) 102-32 at 102 and 119-20; Richard Klein in *RAC* XIV 371-72. Kazhdan, "Constantin imaginaire" 199-200, and "Alexander the Monk," in *ODB* I 60, is unable to resolve the question of date.

Judas-Cyriacus, and the *verificatio* takes place on an ill woman, not on a dead man. An encomium on the Cross follows.

Our third example is an anonymous double *vita* of Constantine and Helena which can be dated to the tenth century but made use of earlier sources. Once again there is no mention of Judas-Cyriacus and the *verificatio* of the Cross takes place on an ill woman.[75] Helena is credited with establishing numerous churches in the Holy Land; she returns to her son at Constantinople (not at Rome).[76]

Another *vita* of Constantine, also anonymous and also dating from the tenth century, will claim our attention next.[77] In this *vita* we read that Sylvester baptized both Constantine and Helena, that Helena found the True Cross – Judas-Cyriacus is not mentioned, – that the True Cross was verified on a dying woman and that Helena served the consecrated virgins in Jerusalem;[78] there follows a rather long account of the martyrdom of Lucian and of the founding of Helenopolis.[79]

Constantine Akropolites (died *ca.* 1321-1324) was both a statesman and a hagiographer.[80] Among some thirty encomia which he wrote there is one on Constantine and Helena.[81] A panegyric on Constantine

---

[75]*BHG*³ 364; ed. Michel Angelo Guidi, *Rendiconti della R. Accademia dei Lincei* V.16 (1907) 304-40 and 637-62; also published separately as *Un Bios di Costantino* (Rome 1908) 6-59; Nau, *op. cit.* 162-68; Ehrhard, *Überlieferung und Bestand* I.1 99, 367, and 430, and I.3 955; Alfons Maria Schneider, "Zur Datierung der Vita Constantini et Helenae," *ZNTW* 40 (1941) 245-49; Hans-Georg Beck, *Kirche und theologische Literatur* 509; Friedhelm Winkelmann, "Das hagiographische Bild Konstantins I in mittelbyzantinischer Zeit," in Vladimir Vavřinek, ed., *Beiträge zur byzantinischen Geschichte im 9.-11. Jahrhundert* (Prague 1978) 179-203 at 181-82; Kazhdan, "Constantin imaginaire" 201.

[76]Cf. chapter VIII above, nn. 60-64.

[77]*BHG*³ 365; Text in Hans Georg Opitz, "Die Vita Constantini des codex Angelicus 22," *Byzantion* 9 (1934) 535-93 at 545-90; Hans-Georg Beck, *Kirche und theologische Literatur* 566; Winckelmann, "Das hagiographische Bild Konstantins" 182; Kazhdan,"Constantin imaginaire" 201-202 and 225.

[78]Opitz, *op. cit.* 546-47, 577-78, and 579.

[79]Opitz, *op. cit.* 579-85.

[80]Donald M. Nicol, "Constantine Akropolites: A Prosopographical Note," *DOP* 19 (1965) 249-56; Alice-Mary Talbot, "Akropolites, Constantine," in *ODB* I 49.

[81]*BHG* ³ 368; ed. Konstantinos Simonides, Ὀρθοδόξων Ἑλλήνων Θεολογικαὶ γραφαὶ τέσσαρες (London 1853) 1-37; Albert Ehrhard in Krumbacher, *op. cit.* 204-205; Ehrhard, *Überlieferung und Bestand* I.3 60, 62, 64, 336, 457, and 878; Hans-Georg Beck, *Kirche und theologische Literatur* 698-99. I have not been able to examine this text.

and Helena was composed before 1431 by Bishop Ignatius of Selymbria in Thrace.[82]

Helena finds mention even in Islamic literature. Mujir al-Din (died in 1521), historian of the city of Jerusalem, reports that Helena found the Cross and built the Church of the Holy Sepulchre.[83]

[82]*BHG*³ 362; ed. Theophilos Ioannou, Μνημεῖα ἁγιολογικά (Venice 1884) 164-229; Albert Ehrhard in Krumbacher, *op. cit.* I 205, n. 4; Peter Heseler, "Zur Vita Constantini et matris Helenae des Ignatius von Selybria (*B. H. Gr.* 362)," *BNJ* 9 (1930) 320-37, esp. 320, n.1, and 326; Ehrhard, *Überlieferung und Bestand* I.3 253 and 256; Hans-Georg Beck, *Kirche und theologische Literatur* 779 (1481 erroneously for 1431) and 793. I have not been able to examine this text.

[83]A. Sebastianus Marmadji, *Textes géographiques arabes sur la Palestine* (Paris 1951) 35-36; Peters, *op. cit.* 194-95; Busse and Kretschmar, *op. cit.* 13.

Chapter XVII.
Helena in Religious Art

Helena and the story of the True Cross are richly represented in religious art. A survey aiming at completeness would readily fill a separate volume and is impossible in the present context.[1] I must regrettably limit myself to a limited number of representative examples from various regions of Europe and Asia Minor and from different genres. In chapter VI above we have already had occasion to consider two examples from English art. We shall turn next to Flemish and French art and begin with two works of Mosan art, i. e. art of the Meuse River valley.

The Pierpont Morgan Library in New York City owns a gilt silver portable altar of the middle of the 12th century which is known as the Stavelot Triptych, after the former abbey of Stavelot (Stablo) in Belgium, whose Abbot Wibald probably commissioned it. This triptych is a reliquary of the True Cross, incorporates both Western and Byzantine components, and illustrates various legends surrounding both Helena and Constantine. In the central panel of this triptych two smaller triptychs of Byzantine workmanship are mounted, one above the other. The decorative enamels of the lower one include Helena and Constantine, flanking the relic of the True Cross. The insides of the wings of the main triptych are adorned with three large, round enamels each. Those on the left portray, from bottom to top, Constantine's vision, his victory over Maxentius, and his baptism by Pope Sylvester. Those on the right tell, also from bottom to top, how Helena interrogates the Jews, threatening them with fire, how the Cross is found, and how it is verified, both in the presence of Helena. In three of the six medallions the hand of God appears above out of a cloud.[2]

---

[1]The most exhaustive study of the subject, up to and including Piero della Francesca, is that of Wiegel, *op. cit.*

[2]Falke and Frauberger, *op. cit.* 68, ill. 21, and pl. 117; Dalton, *Byzantine Art and Archaeology* 524 and figs. 309 and 310; H. P. Mitchell, "Some Enamels of the School of Godefroid de Claire," *Burlington Magazine* 34 (1919) 85-92 and 165-71 at 91 and pls. III and VI; Walters Art Gallery, *Early Christian and Byzantine Art* (Baltimore 1947) 109, no. 530, with earlier literature, and pls. LXX-LXXI; Suzanne Collon-Gevaert, *Histoire des arts du métal en Belgique* (Brussels 1951) 169-73 and pl. 28; Hanns Swarzenski, *Monuments of Romanesque Art*[2] 68 and pl.166; Frolow, *La relique* 335-36, no. 347; Klaus Wessel, *Byzantine Enamels* (Greenwich, Conn. 1968) 153-57, no. 47; Margaret
(continued...)

The second piece of Mosan art which we shall consider is in the treasury of the Church of Notre Dome in Tongres (Tongeren): a small triptych made of wood and copper and dating from ca. 1170-1180. The engravings on the inside of the wings concern us in the present context. In the upper part of the left wing there is a figure of Helena, with crown and nimbus and seated on a throne. At her feet there is a blazing fire. A bandelore reads: *inple desideriu(m) meu(m)*. She points, clear across the center panel of the triptych, to the upper part of the right wing. Here we have a group of Jews, with their pointed hats, and one of them is identified as Judas. In the lower part of the left wing two men are digging up a single cross, and one of these, too, is identified as Judas. In the lower part of the right wing St. Helena is engraved, with nimbus, crown, and scepter, and seated on a throne. In the upper right-hand corner of the outer frame, of related interest, we find Constantine's vision, among other scenes. In the center of the triptych there is a relic of the Holy Cross, flanked by the Virgin and St. John, with an image of Christ above and figures of the Church and the Synagogue below; in the four corners we find the symbols of the four evangelists.[3]

The great cathedral of Reims claims our attention next. Here, at the northern end of the west facade, in the tympanum of a blind arch, a relief dating from ca. 1250 tells a story: the interrogation of the Jews and the *inventio* of the True Cross in the lower register, and the *verifi-*

[2](...continued)
Frazer in Deuchler, *The Year 1200* II 188 and ill. 223; Andreas and Judith A. Stylianou, *By This Conquer* 44-49 and pls. 27, 27a, and 27b; Frolow, *Les reliquaires* 160 and figs. 11-12; Suzanne Collon-Gevaert, Jean Lejeune, and Jacques Stiennon, *A Treasury of Romanesque Art: Metalwork, Illuminations, and Sculpture from the Valley of the Meuse* (London 1972), pl. 27; Marie-Madeline S. Gauthier, *Émaux du moyen âge occidental*, 2nd ed. (Fribourg 1972) 124-25 and 343-44, no. 81; Lasko, *op. cit.* 187 and pl. 202; Schnütgen-Museum, *Rhein und Maas* II 156-57 and 200-201; Wiegel, *op. cit.* 101-107; William Voelkle in Pierpont Morgan Library, *The Stavelot Triptych: Mosan Art and the Legend of the True Cross* (New York 1980) 9-25 and ill. 1-9; bibliography *ibid.* 26; Marcel Durliat, *L'art roman* (Paris 1982) fig. 529; Marie-Madeline S. Gauthier, *Les routes de la foi* 50-53; Marilyn Aronberg Lavin, *The Place of Narrative* 103-105 with fig. 79.

[3]Joseph de Borchgrave d'Altena, "Inventaire archéologique de l'ancien pays de Liége, no. XCVI: Le triptyque reliquaire de la Vraie Croix à Tongres," *Chronique archéologique du pays de Liége* 16 (1925) 43-49; Collon-Gevaert, *op. cit.* 174, n. 1; Hanns Swarzenski, *Monuments*[2] 73 and pl. 187; Frolow, *La relique* 356-57, no. 395; Frolow, *Les reliquaires* 160 and fig. 17; Konrad Hoffmann, *The Year 1200* I (New York 1970) 171, no. 178; J. M. M. Timmers, *De kunst van het Maasland* (Assen 1971) 338-39 with ill. 485; Collon-Gevaert, Lejeune, and Stiennon, *op. cit.*, pl. 49; Schnütgen-Museum, *Rhein und Maas* II 211; Wiegel, *op. cit.*, 110-11.

Plate XV

The 12th century Stavelot Triptych, a reliquary of the True Cross. Two smaller Byzantine triptychs are mounted in the central panel of the main triptych. Photo Pierpont Morgan Library.

catio in the upper register.[4]   Additionally Helena has been identified among the sculptures of the left portal of the west facade, i.e. not very far from the relief.[5]   She wears a crown but is without the usual attributes of cross, nails, or book (both hands are lost).

In 1601 Archduke Albert (or Albrecht), governor of the Spanish Netherlands, commissioned Peter Paul Rubens, who was then just beginning his illustrious career, to produce three paintings for the Chapel of St. Helena in Rome's Church of Santa Croce in Gerusalemme,[6]   The Mocking of Christ, The Raising of the Cross, and St. Helena.   After various misfortunes the three paintings were acquired in 1827 for the chapel of the Municipal Hospital of Grasse in southern France, whence they were eventually transferred to the former Cathedral of Notre-Dame in the same city.   (The Raising of the Cross, however, is not Rubens' original, but only a copy.)   The St. Helena is slightly larger than the other two and decorated the main altar in its original location.   Rubens shows St. Helena in a state of rapture, with her eyes heavenward.   She carries a scepter, but is neither crowned nor nimbed.   To her right putti, some of whom are carrying emblems of Christ's passion, are holding up a large cross.   Neither the *inventio* nor the *verificatio* is visually shown; we must imagine Helena at some moment after the miracles have occur-

[4]Étienne Moreau-Nélaton, *La cathédrale de Reims* (Paris 1915) 68-69 and pls. 23 and 58-59; Maurice, *Sainte Hélène* 21; Arthur Gardner, *Medieval Sculpture in France* (Cambridge 1931) 308 and fig 311; Émile Mâle, *Religious Art in France: The Thirteenth Century* (Princeton 1984) 494, n. 29; Hans Reinhardt, *La cathédrale de Reims* (Paris 1963) 168 and ill. facing p. 137; Andreas and Judith A. Stylianou, *By This Conquer* 53-55 with fig. 29; Wiegel, *op. cit.* 59-64; Émile Mâle, *Art and Artists of the Middle* Ages (Redding Ridge, Connecticut, 1986) 166 and 171; Peter Kurmann, *La façade de la cathédrale de Reims* (Paris 1987) I 198-200 and II, pls. 401-404.

[5]Martin Hürliman and Jean Bony, *French Cathedrals,* 2nd ed. (London 1967) 97, no. 87; Wiegel, *op. cit.* 64; Mâle, *Art and Artists* 171; Kurmann, *op. cit.,* I 248 and II, pls. 831-34.

[6]The archduke had been a cardinal; the Church of Santa Croce had been his titular church. In 1609 the archduke appointed Rubens his court painter; Rubens' portraits of the archduke and of the archduchess Isabella are to be seen in the Kunsthistorisches Museum in Vienna; inv. nos. 6344 and 6345.

red.[7] Rubens' painting was copied by the French artist Jacques Callot in an etching dated to 1609-1611.[8]

Turning to Germany, we shall first visit the Cathedral of St. Blaise in Brunswick. Here, on the east and south walls of the south transept, late Romanesque wall paintings dating from the second quarter of the 13th century offer us a complete cycle of the legend of the True Cross. In the third register, from below, of the east wall we find the following scenes, from left to right:

1. Constantine, seated on a throne, holding a scepter, crowned, and nimbed, appears to instruct Helena to search for the Cross.
2. Helena and her companions are arriving in Jerusalem.
3. Helena, seated on a throne, is interrogating the Jews.
4. In the presence of a seated Helena two men are digging; two crosses have been found already.
5. Again in the presence of Helena, a dead person of indeterminable gender is restored to life by the touch of the True Cross, as two other crosses lie off to one side; a small devil is threatening Judas.

Helena is crowned and nimbed in scenes 2-5, but not in scene 1. In the second register, from below, of the east wall, on both sides of a transeptal apse, we find additional scenes. On the left Judas is baptized; he then is consecrated as bishop of Jerusalem. On the right Judas is seen praying; he then finds the nails, and the nails are venerated by Helena.

---

[7]Max Rooses, *L'oeuvre de Rubens* (Antwerp 1886-1892) II 278-84, nos. 444-46; Émile Michel, *Rubens* (London 1899) I 64-68; Max Rooses, *Rubens* (Philadelphia 1904) I 60-63; Hans Gerhard Evers, *Peter Paul Rubens* (Munich 1942) 40-42 with figs. 9-10; Heinrich Gerhard Franz, "Stileinflüsse im italienischen Frühwerk des Peter Paul Rubens," *Forschungen und Fortschritte* 24 (1948) 225-29; Marcel De Maeyer, "Rubens en de altaarstucken in het hospitaal te Grasse," *Gentse Bijdragen tot de Kunstgeschiedenis* 14 (1953) 75-87; Irving Lavin, "An Ancient Statue" 58 and fig. 3; Buchowiecki, *op. cit.* I 609 and 622-23; Christopher White, *Rubens and His World* (New York 1968) 17-18; Justus Müller Hofstede, "Rubens in Rom, 1601-1602," *Jb. der Berliner Museen* 12 (1970) 61-110, esp. ill. 2; Hans Vlieghe, *Saints* (*Corpus Rubenianum Ludwig Burchard* VIII; London 1973) II 58-68 and ill. 31; Frans Baudoin, *P. P. Rubens* (New York 1977) 55-58; Michael Jaffé, *Rubens and Italy* (Ithaca 1977) 10, 11, 16, 23-24, 53, 59, 61, and pls. 179, 182, and 187; Christopher White, *Peter Paul Rubens* (New Haven 1987) 23-25 and ill. 35. In the summer of 1989 the St. Helena was under restoration in Paris.

[8]Vlieghe, *op. cit.* 61 and fig. 32.

On the south wall there are several scenes of related interest depicting the veneration and the exaltation of the Cross.[9]

Our second example from German art shall be provided by Adam Elsheimer, who was born in 1578 in Frankfurt but established himself in Rome, where he died in 1610. *Ca.* 1603-1605 he painted a small altar of the Holy Cross. In 1619 this altar was acquired by Cosimo II, Grand Duke of Tuscany. Some time thereafter the altar seems to have been dismembered, and the whereabouts of the components were unknown for more than three centuries. Over a period of more than 30 years, 1950-1981, the Städelsches Kunstinstitut in Frankfurt has been able to acquire and reassemble all the component parts. The altar consists of seven copper panels which, arranged counter-clockwise, develop the theme of the Holy Cross. A central panel is flanked by two columns and two fixed wings; below these there is a predella of four panels.

In the left wing a youthful and beautiful Helena, richly dressed, and her attendants are embarking for the voyage to the Holy Land.[10] In the first panel of the predella (left to right) – the last of the seven parts to come to light – Helena is seen interrogating Judas, who is kneeling humbly before her.[11] In the second panel of the predella a cross is being lifted out of a pit, while digging continues in the presence of Helena, a bishop, and a third person (Constantine?).[12] In the third panel of the predella a male corpse has been restored to life and is sitting up on a large cross.[13] In the last panel of the predella the emperor Heraclius, on horseback and richly dressed, carries a large cross with the help of a page.[14] In the right wing the emperor is still dressed in the same rich robes, but he is now on foot, barefoot, and without his tur-

[9]V. Curt Habicht, *Die mittelalterliche Malerei Niedersachsens* I (Strassburg 1919) 39-40; Joachim Gerhardt, *Die spätromanischen Wandmalereien im Dome zu Braunschweig* (Hildesheim 1934) 13-14 and pls. V-VI; Kurt Seeleke and Friedrich Herzig, "Wiederherstellung der romanischen Wandmalereien im Südquerschiff des Braunschweiger Domes," *Niedersächsische Denkmalpflege* 2 (1955-1956) 25-28; Johann-Christian Klamt, *Die mittelalterlichen Monumentalmalereien im Dom zu Braunschweig* (Berlin 1968) 155-67; Otto Demus, *Romanesque Mural Painting* (London 1970) 616; Durliat, *L'art roman* 521; Wiegel, *op. cit.* 159-66; Legner, *Deutsche Kunst der Romanik* 161 and pl. 146.

[10]Inv. no. 2131.

[11]Inv. no. 2142.

[12]Inv. no. 2118.

[13]Inv. no. 2140.

[14]Inv. no. 2119.

ban.[15] The crowning piece of the entire composition is, of course, the central panel, an Exaltation of the Cross.[16] A large cross is surrounded by figures from the Old Testament, the New Testament, and ecclesiastical history. At the foot of the cross is St. Helena; in the upper left-hand corner a small Coronation of the Virgin. The combination of the two themes in a single panel is unusual; attention is drawn to the coronation by converging lines of light. The altar, both in conception and in execution, is a masterpiece.[17]

A renewed interest in St. Helena and in the story of the True Cross emerges in southern Germany and in Austria in the 18th century. Thus in 1753-1754 Christoph Thomas Scheffler decorated the Church of the Holy Cross, or Maltese Church, a former Jesuit church, in Landsberg am Lech (Upper Bavaria) with a series of ceiling frescoes. Three of these concern us. In the choir we find Constantine's victory over Maxentius in the sign of the cross. Above the organ loft we see the emperor Heraclius, as a penitent, returning the True Cross to Jerusalem. The largest of the ten paintings, in the nave, is a *verificatio:* the True Cross is tested on an ill woman, in the presence of Helena, Bishop Ma-

---

[15]Inv. no. 2054.

[16]Inv. no. 2024.

[17]Malcolm Waddingham and Christopher Wright, "Elsheimer: A Third Piece from the Frankfurt Tabernacle," *Burlington Magazine* 112 (1970) 192-94; I. G. Kennedy, "Elsheimer: Two Predellas from the Frankfurt Tabernacle," *Burlington Magazine* 113 (1971) 92-96; Margret Stuffmann, "Zu zwei Predellatafeln Elsheimers im Städelschen Kunstinstitut," *Städel-Jahrbuch* N. F. 4 (1973) 203-206; Keith Andrews, *Adam Elsheimer: Paintings - Drawings - Prints* (Oxford 1977) 25-27, 146-47, cat. no. 16, pls. 47-54, and color pl. II; Keith Andrews, "Once More Elsheimer," *Burlington Magazine* 121 (1979) 168-72; Christian Lenz, "Neuerwerbungen der Frankfurter Museen: Städelsches Kunstinstitut und Städtische Galerie," *Städel-Jahrbuch* N. F. 7 (1979) 300-301; Malcolm Waddingham, "Elsheimer's Frankfurt Tabernacle: Discovery of the Final Piece," *Burlington Magazine* 123 (1981) 346-50; A. Voretzsch, "Ende einer Odyssee: Eine kleine Kupfertafel von Adam Elsheimer ist den Frankfurtern teuer," *Artis* 33 (1981) 48-49; Hans-Joachim Ziemke, "Neuerwerbungen der Frankfurter Museen: Städelsches Kunstinstitut und Städtische Galerie," *Städel-Jahrbuch* N. F. 9 (1983) 259; Keith Andrews, *Adam Elsheimer: Werkverzeichnis der Gemälde, Zeichnungen und Radierungen* (Munich 1985) 25-27, 180-82, cat. no. 16, and pls. 59-66; also 197, cat. no. 41, and pl. 26; Paul Eich, "Das Kreuzretabel Adam Elsheimers im Städelschen Kunstinstitut zu Frankfurt am Main," in Werner Knopp, ed., *Spiegelungen* (Mainz 1986) 31-59; Städelsches Kunstinstitut und Städtische Galerie, Frankfurt, *Verzeichnis der Gemälde* (Frankfurt 1987) 44 with ill. 42; Gottfried Sello, *Adam Elsheimer* (Munich 1988) 43-56 and 114-26, ill. 18-30; Christian Lenz, *Adam Elsheimer: Die Gemälde im Städel,* 2nd ed. (Frankfurt 1989) 36-74. Dr. Christian Lenz, Bayerische Staatsgemäldesammlungen, Munich, has kindly provided helpful information.

Plate XVI

Altar of the Holy Cross, by Adam Elsheimer (1578-1610). To be "read" counter-clockwise, beginning with the left wing. Photo Städelsches Kunstinstitut, Frankfurt.

carius, and a large crowd of people, and with the Holy Trinity above.[18]

The story of the True Cross is encountered also in the arts of Spain. A case in point is a famous tapestry dating from the second half of the 11th century or the first quarter of the 12th century, exhibited in the treasury (museum) of the cathedral of Gerona in Catalonia, and known as the *Genesis of Gerona*. Along the bottom edge of this tapestry there are six scenes, unfortunately only half preserved, which tell the story of the True Cross.[19] The following scenes can be identified, notwithstanding the loss of the lower part, from left to right:

1. Helena, wearing a crown and standing in front of a building, possibly a church, is interrogating Judas; both Helena and Judas are identified by inscriptions.

2. Two figures, representing the Jewish elders summoned by Helena, seem to be entreating Helena with out-

---

[18]Joseph Braun, *Die Kirchenbauten der deutschen Jesuiten* II (Freiburg 1910) 283, 288, and pl. 13; Hermann Schmidt, *Landsberg am Lech* (Augsburg 1929) 22 and ill. 21, not very accurately; Alois Harbeck, *Die Fresken von Januarius Zick in Wiblingen und die Problematik illusionistischer Deckengestaltung* (Dissertation Munich 1966) 159-60; Hermann Bauer and Bernhard Rupprecht, *Corpus der barocken Deckenmalerei in Deutschland* I (Munich 1976) 132-36; Michael Meier, ed., *Die Kunst- und Kulturdenkmäler in der Region München* I (Munich 1977) 80-83; Wilhelm Braun, *Christoph Thomas Scheffler, ein Asamschüller* (Stuttgart 1939) 69-72; Sigfrid Hofmann, *Landsberg am Lech*, 3rd ed. (Munich 1983) 22 and 25-27; Holger H. Ehlert, *Die Deckenfresken von St. Paulin in Trier* (Mainz 1984) 43; Dagmar Dietrich in *Heilig-Kreuz-Kirche Landsberg a. Lech* (Munich and Zürich 1986) 25 and 29-35. Scheffler signed and dated his work; he died two years later.

[19]Louis de Farcy, *La broderie du Xi siècle à nos jours* II (Angers 1919) Suppl. II, pl. 181; Emilio Camps Cazorla, *El arte románico en España*, 2nd ed. (Barcelona 1945) 217; Lamberto Font, *Gerona: La Catedral y el Museo Diocesano* (Gerona 1952) 45-46 and figs. 88-91; José Gudiol i Ricart, *Arte de España: Cataluña* (Barcelona 1955) 41-42, fig.164, and pl. VIII; Pedro de Palol, "Une broderie catalane d'époque romane: La Genèse de Gérone," *Cah.Arch.* 8 (1956) 175-214 at 188-89 and 9 (1957) 219-51 at 237-46; Marie Schuette and Sigrid Müller-Christensen, *A Pictorial History of Embroidery* (London 1963) 299 and pls. 40-45; Pedro de Palol and Max Hirmer, *Early Medieval Art in Spain* (New York 1967) 174, pls. 132-33, and color pls. XXXV-XXXVI; J. M. Pita Andrade, *Treasures of Spain* (Geneva 1967) 118-21; Anton von Euw in Fillitz, *Das Mittelalter* I 264 and ill. 371; Wiegel, *op. cit.* 44-47; Mariano Oliver Alberti, *La catedral de Gerona* (León 1973) 57 and figs. 50-51; Santiago Alcolea, *Artes decorativas en la España Cristiana* (Madrid 1975) 380 and fig. 453; Josep Calzada i Oliveras, *La catedral de Gerona* (Barcelona 1979) 68-72 and 78-81; Joaquin Yarza in *Historia del arte hispánico* II² (Madrid 1982) 142-43; Núria de Dalmases and Antoni José i Pitarch, *Els inicis i l'art romànic* (Barcelona 1986) 169-70 and 196-97; Joan Ainaud de Lasarte, *Catalan Painting* (New York 1990) 15 and 37-38.

stretched arms; further to the right a large building representing Jerusalem.

3. A large cross, at an angle; below that is a much smaller cross, apparently atop an imperial crown. Was there a half-figure of Helena or of Constantine?

4. Judas is kneeling in prayer.

5. Judas is digging; one large cross has already been unearthed.

6. Judas is carrying a cross towards a man who is apparently kneeling before him; this is possibly a *verificatio*. Another building closes the composition.

A second case in point: at the Cartuja de Miraflores (a Carthusian monastery near Burgos in Old Castile), in the Chapel of the Holy Cross, there are five painted panels by a Renaissance pointer who, for want of a better name, has been called the Master of the Holy Cross.[20] These five panels tell the story of the True Cross as follows:

1. An *inventio*: three crosses are emerging from a paved floor, as a workman (right) is swinging his tool and Helena (left), crowned and nimbed, is standing by in an attitude of prayer.

2. A *verificatio*: an old man is sitting up on a bier, as the True Cross is applied to his body; two other crosses are held up by attendants (right background), as Helena (left) again stands by in an attitude of prayer.

3. Heraclius, on horseback, crowned, and carrying a large cross, is approaching the walls of Jerusalem; in the upper left corner an angel appears above a closed gate.

4. Heraclius is now dismounted, barefoot, and in penitent's dress, and his crown is carried by an attendant; the gate stands open.

5. An Exaltation: a cross is held up by angels on an altar, at the foot of which several people are kneeling; one of these is Heraclius, identified by the crown on a stool before him.

[20]Francisco Tarin y Juaneda, *La real Cartuja de Miraflores (Burgos)*, 2nd ed.(Burgos 1925) 213; Chandler Rathfon Post, *A History of Spanish Painting* IV (Cambridge, Massachusetts, 1933) 239; Diego Angulo Iñíguez, *Pintura del Renacimiento* (Madrid 1954) 111-12 and fig. 112.

The five panels are arranged on the walls of the chapel out of sequence. On one of the walls there is a small stone relief of the implements of the Passion.

The story of the True Cross was a popular one in Italian art through the centuries. One is especially apt to find pictorial representations of it in churches of the Franciscan order. This is so because St. Francis reportedly received the stigmata (in 1224) on or about September 14, the Feast of the Exaltation of the Cross, and because the Franciscans have long been the guardians of the holy sites of Palestine, including the Church of the Holy Sepulchre, for Latin Christianity.[21]

We visit first the Church of S. Croce in Florence, a Franciscan church, and proceed directly to the Alberti-Alamanni Chapel, the main chapel of the choir. Here, on the high south and north wells, Agnolo Gaddi created in *ca.* 1380 a complete cycle of frescoes which illustrate the legend, or legends, of the True Cross.[22] On each wall the space is

[21]St. Bonaventure, *Legenda maior S. Francisci* 13.3 (Ed. Clasen *[Franz. Quellenschr.* VII] 367); Raphael M. Huber, *A Documented History of the Franciscan Order, 1182-1517* (Milwaukee and Washington, D. C., 1944) 46; Michael de la Bedoyere, *Francis: A Biography of the Saint of Assisi* (New York 1962) 241-42; Piero Bargellinii, *S. Francisco d'Assisi* (Brescia 1964) 179-80; Omer Englebert, *Saint Francis of Assisi*, 2nd English ed. (Chicago 1966) 310; Adolf Holl, *The Last Christian* (Garden City, New York, 1980) 192-94; Colin Morris, *The Papal Monarchy* (Oxford 1989) 454; Marilyn Aronberg Lavin, *The Place of Narrative* 112 with n. 75. Today the Impression of the Stigmata is observed on September 17. Luke Wadding (1588-1657) and continuators, *Annales Minorum* VII[3] (Quaracchi 1932) 587-8; Heribert Holzapfel, *Handbuch der Geschichte des Franziskanerordens* (Freiburg 1909) 262-68; Giovanni Odoardi, "La custodia Francescana di terra santa nel VI centenario della sua costituzione (1342-1942)," *Miscellanea Francescana* 43 (1943) 217-56, esp. 233, 235, and 256; Giacinto Maria Faccio in Virgilio C. Corbo, ed., *Custodia di Terra Santa* (Jerusalem 1951) 12; John Moorman, *A History of the Franciscan Order from Its Origins to the Year 1517* (Oxford 1968) 436-38; Saul P. Colbi, *Christianity in the Holy Land* (Tel Aviv 1969) 62-63; Friedrich Heyer, *Kirchengeschichte des Heiligen Landes* (Stuttgart 1984) 137; Peters, *op. cit.* 369-70; Marilyn Aronberg Lavin, *The Place of Narrative* 113 with n. 78.

[22]Crowe and Cavalcaselle, *op. cit.* II (1903) 243; Adolfo Venturi, *Storia dell'arte italiana* V (1907) 817-26 with figs. 656-63; Mazzoni, *op. cit.* 101-14; Van Marle, *op. cit.* III (1924) 539-44 with figs 300-302; Pietro Toesca, *Die florentinische Malerei des vierzehnten Jahrhunderts* (Florence and Munich 1929) 63 and pls. 108-109; Tancred Borenius, *Florentine Frescoes* (London 1930) 35-37 and pl. 24; Maurice, *Sainte Hélène* 31 and 32 (erroneous attribution to Taddeo Gaddi); Roberto Salvini, *L'Arte di Agnolo Gaddi* (Florence 1936) 31-85, 183, and pls. VIII-XVII; Walter and Elisabeth Paatz, *Die Kirchen von Florenz* I (Frankfurt/Main 1940) 570-71; Pietro Toesca, *Il Trecento* (Turin 1951) 646-48 with fig. 560; George Kaftal, *Saints in Italian Art: Iconography of the*

(continued...)

organized in three registers and a tympanum. The tympanum and the two top registers on the south wall tell the apocryphal story of the wood of the Cross: the Tree of Life, Solomon, the Queen of Sheba, and the like. In our context the lowest register of the south wall is of more direct interest: here we have an *inventio* (right) and a *verificatio* (left) in a single composition; Helena appears in both scenes. Moving on to the tympanum of the north wall we see Helena and a man with a cross leading a procession, also a group of people kneeling in veneration. The three registers below the tympanum concern Chosroes and Heraclius.

In the top register Chosroes removes the Cross from Jerusalem. In the middle register Chosroes allows himself to be worshipped; Heraclius is visited by an angel; and Heraclius and the son of Chosroes are engaged in a duel on a bridge.[23] In the lowest register, on the left side, we see the decapitation of Chosroes. In the middle, continuing the composition without division, Heraclius, on horseback and carrying the Cross, is stopped before the gates of Jerusalem by an angel; and on the right side Heraclius appears barefoot and in penitent's dress, but still wearing his crown.

In 1466 Piero della Francesca completed his work on a famous and much-published cycle of frescoes on the walls of the main chapel in the choir of the Church of S. Francesco in Arezzo.[24] On the left and

---

[22](...continued)
Saints in Tuscan Painting (Florence 1952) 467-75 with figs. 555 and 557; Bernard Berenson, *Italian Pictures of the Renaissance: Florentine School,* 2nd ed. (London 1963) I 67 and pls. 343-47; Robert Oertel, *Early Italian Painting to 1400* (London and New York 1968) 315 and pl. 113; Millard Meiss, *The Great Age of Fresco* (New York 1970) 24-25; Andreas and Judith A. Stylianou, *By This Conquer* 57 and figs. 29a and 29b; Wiegel, *op. cit.* 184-88; Richard Fremantle, *Florentine Gothic Painters* (London 1975) 265-66, with extensive bibliography, and ill. 554-57, 559, and 561; Bruce Cole, *Agnolo Gaddi* (Oxford 1977) 21-26, 79-81, and pls. 25-33, dating the frescoes to 1388-1393; Alastair Smart, *The Dawn of Italian Painting* (Ithaca and Oxford 1978) 125-26 and pl. 62; Roberto Salvini, "Agnolo Gaddi," in Umberto Baldini and Bruno Nardini, *Santa Croce: Kirche, Kapellen, Kloster, Museum* (Stuttgart 1985) 184-209; Marilyn Aronberg Lavin, *The Place of Narrative* 99-103 with figs. 75-76, 105-10 with figs. 80-87, and pls. 10-11; Rab Hatfield in Timothy Verdon and John Henderson, edd., *Christianity and the Renaissance* (Syracuse 1990) 144-47 with figs. 5.5-5.8; Frederick Hartt, *History of Italian Renaissance Art,* 4th ed. (New York 1987) 140-42 and fig. 124.

[23]This visitation by an angel is comparable to the visions reportedly experienced by Constantine and Helena.

[24]Adolfo Venturi, *Storia dell'arte italianna* VII.1 (1911) 442-460 with figs. 240-53; Crowe and Cavalcaselle, *op. cit.* V (1914) 7-11 (with erroneous dates); Mazzoni, *op. cit.* 124-33 with pls. IX-X; Van Marle, *op. cit.* XI (1929) 30-49 with figs 16-29 and pl. I;

(continued...)

right wall the space has been organized in two registers and a tympanum. On the back wall smaller spaces are utilized on both sides of the window. The cycle of the True Cross begins in the tympanum on the right side with Adam's death and the Tree of Life; it ends in the tympanum on the left wall with the return of the Cross to Jerusalem by Heraclius.[25] In the upper register on the right wall the Queen of Sheba adores the sacred wood and is received by King Solomon (right); in the upper register on the left wall another royal lady, Helena, finds (left) and proves (right) the True Cross. In the lower register on the right wall Constantine's battle against Maxentius is depicted; in the lower register on the left wall Heraclius' battle against Chosroes. It has been pointed out that

[24](...continued)
Borenius, *op. cit.* 72-74 and pl. 45; Maurice, *Sainte Hélène* 40; Lionello Venturi and Rosabianca Skira-Venturi, *Italian Painting* (Geneva 1950-1952) I 138-48; Kaftal, *Tuscan Painting* 467-74 with fig. 556; Henri Focillon, *Piero della Francesca* (Paris 1952) 34-47, figs. 12-16, and pls. V-VIII; Lionello Venturi, *Piero della Francesca* (Geneva 1959) 25 and 51-92; pp. 56-57 are especially useful for orientation; Michel (Mikhail) Alpatov, "Les fresques de Piero della Francesca à Arezzo: Sémantique et stilistique," *Commentari* 14 (1963) 17-38; Roberto Longhi, *Piero della Francesca,* 3rd ed. (Florence 1963) 28-47, 210-14, color pls. VIII-XVII, and figs. 42-140; Enzo Carli, *Piero della Francesca: The Frescoes in the Church of San Francesco at Arezzo* (Milan 1967); Bernard Berenson, *Italian Pictures of the Renaissance: Central and North Italian Schools,* 3rd ed. (London 1968) I 340 and II, pl. 763; Philip Hendy, *Piero della Francesca and the Early Renaissance* (London and New York 1968) 79-92, ill. 28-44, and pls. XV-XXV; Kenneth Clark, *Piero della Francesca,* 2nd ed. (London 1969) 38-43, ill. 31-32, and pls. 28-92; Laurie Schneider, "The Iconography of Piero della Francesca's Frescoes Illustrating the Legend of the True Cross in the Church of San Francesco in Arezzo," *Art Quarterly* 32 (1969) 22-48 with figs. 1-2; Meiss, *op. cit.* 138-39 and 144-45; Andreas and Judith A. Stylianou, *By This Conquer* 57-63 with figs. 30-31; Wiegel, *op. cit.* 189-95; Pierluigi De Vecchi, *The Complete Paintings of Piero della Francesca* (New York 1970) 91-97 and pls. XIX-LII; Eugenio Battisti, *Piero della Francesca* (Milan 1971) I 132-259 and ill. 39-144; Mario Salmi, *La pittura di Piero della Francesca* (Novara 1979) 62-100; Paolo D'Ancona, *Piero della Francesca: Il cicle affrescato nella chiesa di S. Francesco in Arezzo* (Milan 1980); Eve Borsook, *The Mural Paintings of Tuscany,* 2nd ed. (Oxford 1980) 91-102 and pls. 112-19; James Beck, *Italian Renaissance Painting* (New York 1981) 134-41 with ill. 101-106; Alessandro Angelini, *Piero della Francesca* (Florence 1985) 20-47 with ill. 23-59; Carlo Ginzburg, *The Enigma of Piero* (London 1985) 27-51 and ill. 5-14; Marilyn Aronberg Lavin, *The Place of Narrative* 167-94 with figs. 137-63 and pls. 16-18; Rab Hatfield in Verdon and Henderson, *op. cit.* 145 and 148-54 with figs. 5.9-5.14; Carlo Bertelli, *Piero della Francesca* (New Haven 1992) 79-114; Marilyn Aronberg Lavin, *Piero della Francesca* (New York 1992) 30-37 and 74-103; Hartt, *op. cit.* 280-85 with figs. 282-86 and color pl. 36.

[25]Heraclius' approach to Jerusalem is depicted in a single scene, not two; he is dismounted, as are his attendants. A group of citizens, kneeling in prayer, is meeting him.

the artist has abandoned chronological narrative in order to arrange his
pictures in corresponding pairs. On the back wall, to the right of the
window, we see Solomon's workmen removing the sacred wood (middle), and Constantine's dream (bottom), a much-celebrated masterpiece.
To the left of the window we see Judas being raised from the well by
means of a windlass (middle), and an Annunciation (bottom).[26]

The *inventio* and the *verificatio*, in a single composition, on the
left wall call for further consideration. In the former, on the left, workmen have unearthed one huge cross and are lifting a second one out of
a pit, as Helena, wearing a curiously pointed crown, stands by; in the
background the city of Jerusalem. In the latter, on the right, against an
unusual architectural background, a third huge cross has been applied to
a young man who is now sitting up on his bier; Helena and her attendants are kneeling in prayer.

Paolo Veronese (1528-1588), the great Venetian master, has left
us two paintings titled *Vision of St. Helena*. One, believed to be the
earlier one, is in the National Gallery in London. We see a young and
beautiful Helena asleep in a chair before an open window; in the sky
outside there is a cross supported by two cherubs.[27] Helena's vision or
dream is an elaboration on the various reports, considered in chapter IX
above, which say that Helena was prompted by the Holy Spirit to undertake her search for the Cross. It is also a counterpart to Constantine's
vision before the Battle of the Mulvian Bridge. *Ca.* 1575-1580 Veronese painted a second *Vision of St. Helena,* now in the Pinacoteca Vati-

---

[26]The presence of an Annunciation in this cycle has been explained by Rainer
Kahsnitz, "Zur Verkündigung im Zyklus der Kreuzlegende bei Piero della Francesca,"
in Florens Deuchler and Reiner Hausherr, edd., *Schülerfestgabe für Herbert von Einem*
(Bonn 1965) 112-37. I have chosen not to consider in this context the two prophets who
flank the window in the uppermost spaces.

[27]Inv. no. 1041; Giuseppe Fiocco, *Paolo Veronese, 1528-1588* (Bologna 1928) 199
and pl. LVIII; Adolfo Venturi, *Paolo Veronese* (Milan 1928) 141-43 with fig. 96; Adolfo
Venturi, *Storia dell'arte italiana* IX.4 (1929) 881-83; Antoine Orliac, *Veronese* (London
1940) 109; Bernard Berenson, *Italian Pictures of the Renaissance: Venetian School*
(London 1958) I 132; Remigio Marini, *Tout l'oeuvre peint de Veronese* (Paris 1970) 112,
no. 145; National Gallery, London, *Illustrated General Catalogue* (1973) 783; Cecil
Gould, *National Gallery Catalogues: The Sixteenth Century Italian Schools* (London
1975) 324-26; Terisio Pignatti, *Veronese* (Venice 1976) 141, no. 206, and fig. 510; Kurt
Badt, *Paolo Veronese* (Cologne 1981) 128 and ill. 108. William R. Rearick, *The Art of
Paolo Veronese, 1528-1588* (Washington, D. C., and Cambridge 1988), no. 71, suggests
a date of 1558 for this painting. In Thomas Leman Hare, *The National Gallery: One
Hundred Plates in Colour* (London 1909) I 146 and pl. XXXV, this painting had been
attributed to Battista Zelotti.

Plate XVII

18327 - LONDRA - Paolo Veronese - La visione di S. Elena - National Gallery   Rip. Int. Anderson Roma

Vision of St. Helena, by Paolo Veronese (1528-1588).
Photo National Gallery, London.

cana. A beautiful Helena, richly dressed and wearing a crown, is asleep in a chair. A cross, supported by a cherub, appears before her in a dream.[28]

In the arts of the Byzantine East Helena and Constantine together, flanking a tall cross, become an almost ubiquitous motif, in keeping with the Byzantine preference for symbolic representation, while narrative cycles are less common.

The cathedral treasury of Esztergom (Gran) in Hungary houses a reliquary of the True Cross which invites comparison with the one in the cathedral treasury of Limburg, which we considered in Chapter X above.[29] Like the latter, it is of gilt silver and enameled, but somewhat smaller. In the middle register, of three, we find Constantine and Helena on the left and right, respectively, of the relic, which is in the shape of a double-barred cross.[30] Constantine and Helena are in the dress of Byzantine rulers and slightly turned towards each other. The reliquary is of Constantinopolitan provenience, but we do not know for certain how it reached Esztergom, and dates ranging from the 10th to the 13th century have been suggested for it.[31]

The Accademia of Venice now houses a staurothèque which the Greek cardinal Bessarion (1403-1472) presented in 1472 to the Scuola della Carità in Venice, as an inscription on the reverse records. This

[28]Inv. no. 352; Frank Preston Stearns, *Four Great Venetians* (London 1901) 337; Fiocco, *op. cit.* 193 and pl. LIX; Maurice, *Sainte Hélène* 47; Orliac, *op. cit.* 108; Ennio Francia, *Tesori della Pinacoteca Vaticana* (Milan 1964) 80. Berenson, *Italian Pictures of the Renaissance: Venetian School* I 135; Marini, *op. cit.* 119, no. 193; Pignatti, *op. cit.* 150, no. 256, and fig. 594; Badt, *op. cit.* 128 and ill. 109; Rearick, *op. cit.*, no. 71.

[29]Esztergom, situated ca. 40 km. northwest of Budapest on the right bank of the Danube, once was the residence of the kings of Hungary and still is the residence of the Catholic primate of Hungary. Nándor Knauz and C. L. Dedek, *Monumenta Ecclesiae Stringoniensis* (Esztergom 1874-1924).

[30]In the upper register there are two angels; in the lower register the Way of the Cross (left) and the Descent from the Cross (right). The whole composition is framed by a repoussé border of a later date.

[31]Dalton, *Byzantine Art and Archaeology* 525; Charles Diehl, *Manuel d'art byzantin*[2] II 691-93 with ill. 342; Maurice, *Sainte Hélène* 12; Elemér Varjú, "Az esztergomi sztaurotéka," *Magyar Müvészet* 7 (1931) 433-39; Joseph Braun, *Die Reliquiare* 263 and ill. 223; David Talbot Rice, *The Art of Byzantium* 321 and pl. 135; Frolow, *La relique* 331-32, no. 340; Frolow, *Les reliquaires* 96-97, 169, 219, 249, and fig. 41; Wessel, *Byzantine Enamels* 158-63, no. 49; Delvoye, *op. cit.* 292-93; Margaret Frazer in Deuchler, *The Year 1200* II, ill. 220; Beckwith, *Early Christian and Byzantine Art* 118; Bréhier, *op. cit.* 91-92 and pl. LXVII; Marie-Madeline S. Gauthier, *Les routes de la foi* 120, no. 69; Ulrich Henze in Legner, *Ornamenta Ecclesiae* III 116, no. H33; Kurt Weitzmann *et al.*, *The Icon* (New York 1987) 19 and 60.

reliquary is of Constantinopolitan provenience and dates from the late 14th or early 15th century. On the wooden cover there is a painted crucifixion, with seven other scenes of the Passion in the frame. On the inside there is a gilt-silver crucifix, flanked by figures of Constantine and Helena in niello.[32] Constantine holds a cross in his left hand, thus being given the greater honor, while Helena's hands are raised in a gesture of adoration; both are crowned and nimbed.

Cyprus offers us three cycles of Byzantine wall paintings narrating the story of the True Cross. Let us examine one of them: ca. five miles from the village of Platanistasa, in the Troodos Mountains, we find the Church of the Holy Cross of Agiasmati, a former monastery church. Its interior walls are decorated with a fine and complete cycle of wall paintings which have now been dated to 1494 and are the work of a painter named Philip Goul. On the wall of an arched recess on the north side of the church, arranged in the angles of a painted cross, there are ten miniature scenes depicting the story of the True Cross. We "read" from left to right and top to bottom:

1.   Helena, seated on a throne, crowned, and nimbed, is interrogating the Jews.
2.   Helena is interrogating Judas.

[32]Inv. no. 349; *CIG* IV 8765; Sandra Moschini Marconi, *Gallerie dell'Accademia di Venezia: Opere d'arte dei secoli XIV et XV* (Rome 1955) 191-94, no. 216; Evelyn Sandberg Vavalà, *La Croce dipinta italiana* (Verona 1943) passim; Frolow, *La relique* 563-65, no. 872. *Byzantine Art: An European Art,* 2nd ed. (Athens 1964) 246-47, no.187; Frolow, *Les reliquaires,* fig. 49, and see index. Volbach and Lafontaine-Dosogne, *op. cit.* 182 and ill. 50; Beckwith, *Early Christian and Byzantine Art*[2] 153 and pl. 291; Kurt Weitzmann, Manolis Chatzidakis, Krsto Miatev, and Svetozar Radojčić, *A Treasury of Icons* (New York 1968), p. XXXIV, no.76, on the cover only; *Venezia e Bisanzio* (Venice 1974) no. 112; Ginzburg, *op. cit.* 42 and ill. 28-30. The staurothèque was in Vienna from 1821 to 1921. The Accademia also owns, and displays directly above the staurothèque, a portrait of the cardinal by a Venetian painter of ca. 1540. The cardinal is seen holding the staurothèque in his hands. Cat. no. 876; see Ginzburg, *op. cit.,* ill. 80. Also, there is in Vienna's Kunsthistorisches Museum, Inv. Nr. 9101, a painting by Gentile Bellini (1429[?]-1507) in which Bessarion is seen kneeling before the staurothèque. See the following: Leo Planiscig, "Jacopo und Gentile Bellini: Neue Beiträge zu ihrem Werk," *Jb. der Kunsthistorischen Sammlungen in Wien,* n. s. 2 (1928) 41-62; Emerich Schaffran, "Gentile Bellini und das Bessarion-Reliquar," *Das Münster* 10 (1957) 153-57; Ginzburg, *op. cit.* 132 and ill. 78. Prof. Paul Wimmer, Vienna, has kindly verified the location of this painting. On Bessarion see the following: Ludwig Mohler, *Kardinal Bessarion als Theologe, Humanist und Staatsmann* (Paderborn 1923-1942); Raymond Joseph Loenertz, "Pour la biographie du cardinal Bessarion," *OCP* 10 (1944) 116-49; Joseph Gill, *Personalities of the Council of Florence* (Oxford and New York 1964) 45-54; Lotte Labowsky, "Bessarione," in *Dizionario biografico degli italiani* IX (1967) 686-96.

3. Judas is released from the well.
4. Judas is praying on Golgotha.
5. Five workmen are digging, but no cross is visible yet.
6. Three crosses are carried away.
7. Three crosses are presented to Helena.
8. The crosses are tested on a dying woman.
9. Judas-Cyriacus prays to find the Holy Nails.
10. Judas-Cyriacus presents the nails to Helena, who is kneeling in adoration.

Also, among six painted scenes in the soffit of the arched recess, there are three which are of related interest: Constantine's vision, Constantine's triumphal entry into Rome, and the Apotheosis of the Holy Cross (the cross being taken to heaven by two angels). Additionally, on the outside west wall of the church, south of the entrance, there is a fresco of Helena and Constantine in the traditional pose.[33]

We turn our attention next to Cappadocia. There, in an area extending some 100 km. west and southwest from Kayseri, the ancient Caesarea, nature has created some fantastic landscapes of steep cliffs and tall cones cut by erosion out of soft volcanic rock. Thousands of man-made cavities, hundreds of them chapels, churches, or monastic facilities, add to the strange effect. Many of the chapels and churches are decorated with architectural details and wall paintings. A few can be dated by inscriptions, while the dating of many remains problematical. It would appear that a period of relative stability from the late ninth century to the late eleventh century accounts for most of the decorated chapels and

---

[33]William Hepburn Buckler and Georgina Grenfell Buckler, "Dated Wall-paintings in Cyprus," *Annuaire de l'Institut de Philologie et Histoire Orientales et Slaves* 7 (1939-1944) 47-70 at 66-68; Robert B. Francis, *The Medieval Churches of Cyprus* (London 1948) 22; Andreas and Judith A. Stylianou, "Donors and Dedicatory Inscriptions, Suppliants and Supplications in the Painted Churches of Cyprus," *JÖB* 9 (1960) 97-128 at 111-12; Andreas Stylianou, "Some Wall-paintings of the Second Half of the 15th Century in Cyprus," *Actes du XII⁰ Congrès International des Études Byzantines* Ochride 1961 III (Belgrade 1964) 363-69 at 363-67; Athanasios Papageorgiou, *Icons of Cyprus* (New York 1970) 69-70; Andreas and Judith A. Stylianou, *By This Conquer* 67-72, 77-91, figs. 33-35, and figs. 39-49; Miltiadis Garidis, "La peinture Cypriote de la fin du XV⁰ - debut du XVI⁰ siècle, Πρακτικὰ τοῦ Πρώτου Διεθνοῦς Κυπρολογικοῦ Συνεδρίου (Nicosia 1972) II 25-32 at 27; Athanasios Papageorgiou, Κύπριοι Ζωγράφοι τοῦ 15ου καὶ 16οῦ αἰῶνα, *RDAC 1974*, pp. 195-209 at 202-203, without reference to the paintings in the arched recess; Andreas and Judith A. Stylianou, "A Re-examination of the Dates concerning the Painted Churches of St. Mamas, Louvaras, and the Holy Cross of Agias- mati, Platanistasa, Cyprus," *JÖB* 25 (1976) 279-82; Andreas and Judith A. Stylianou, *The Painted Churches of Cyprus* (London 1985) 39-40, 186-88, 198-205 with figs. 113-16, 216 with fig. 125, and 218.

churches.[34] The iconographical repertoir includes, as one would expect, Constantine and Helena. Of the 27 chapels or churches in which this motif can be found we can consider only one. This is Göreme Chapel 7, or Tokalı Kilise, the most elaborate of the Cappadocian cave churches. Once the katholikon of the Monastery of the Archangels, it is a complex consisting of, in chronological order, the Lower Church, the Old Church, and the New Church. The Old Church received a new program of painting in the early tenth century. A complete christological sequence covers the vault, and individual saints the walls. At the east end of the north wall, in the lower zone, Constantine and Helena are represented; next to them is St. Catherine. Constantine and Helena hold a tall cross between them; contrary to the usual practice Constantine is on the right and Helena on the left. The New Church was excavated and decorated in the second half of the tenth century. Constantine and Helena found places, facing each other, in the intrados of the central arch on the east side. Constantine carries a cross-staff in his right hand and an orb in his left hand, while Helena's hands are raised in the attitude of an *orans*.[35]

[34]Ugo Andolfato and Franco Zucchi in Luciano Giovannini, *Arts of Cappadocia* (London 1971) 51-61; Nicole Thierry, *op. cit.* 129-71; Spiro Kostof, *Caves of God* (Cambridge, Massachusetts, 1972) 9-24; Lyn Rodley, *Cave monasteries of Byzantine Cappadocia* (Cambridge 1985) 1-10; Annabel Jane Wharton, *Art of Empire: Painting and Architecture of the Byzantine Periphery* (University Park, Pennsylvania, 1988) 13-18. Marcell Restle, "Kappadokien B" in *RBK* III (1972-1978) 975-1115, provides a comprehensive and systematic survey of both architecture and painting.

[35]Dalton, *Byzantine Art and Archaeology* 273; Charles Diehl, *Manuel d'art byzantin*[2] II 574; Guillaume de Jerphanion, *Une nouvelle province de l'art byzantin: Les églises rupestres de Cappadoce* (Paris 1925-1942) I.1 267-68, I.2 316, and Album II, pl. 85.1. Weigand, *op. cit.* and in his review of Jerphanion's vol. I.2, in *BZ* 35 (1935) 131-35, challenged Jerphanion's dating of the New Church and argued at length for a 14th century date. Jerphanion defended his dating in "La date des plus récentes peintures de Toqale Kilissé en Cappadoce," *OCP* 2 (1936) 191-222. Weigand's views were refuted specifically by Manolis Chatzidakis, "A propos d'une nouvelle manière de dater les peintures de Cappadoce," *Byzantion* 14 (1939) 95-113. Ludwig Budde, *Göreme: Höhlenkirchen in Kappadokien* (Düsseldorf 1958)13-14 and pl. 48; Robin S. Cormack, "Byzantine Cappadocia: The Archaic Group of Wall Paintings," *JBAA* 3rd ser. 30 (1967) 19-36 at 22-23, 27, and 31; Marcell Restle, *Byzantine Wall Painting in Asia Minor* (Greenwich, Connecticut, 1968) I 111-16 and II, plan X and pl. 83; Nicole Thierry, "Un atelier de peintures du début du Xe siècle en Cappadoce: L'atelier de l'anciene église de Tokalı," *Bulletin de la Société des Antiquaires de France* 1971, pp. 170-78; Rodley, *Cave Monasteries* 213-15 with pl. 183; Ann Wharton Epstein, *Tokalı Kilise* (Washington, D.C., 1986), esp. 1,14-16, 29-30, 61, 67, fig. 42, and fig. 116; Wharton, *op. cit.* 21-23. The subordination of Helena to Constantine was noted by Guillaume de Jerphanion, "Les
(continued...)

We shall have to forego an examination of manuscript illuminations and of icons, as well as examples from the Balkans and Russia.
But the examples here presented are sufficient, I trust, to show the popularity of the motif. The demand for relics of Helena and for relics of the
True Cross and the frequency with which the motif is found in the religious literature easily account for this popularity.

[35](...continued)
caractéristiques et les attributs des saints dans la peinture cappadociènne," *Anal. Boll.* 55
(1937) 1-28 at 7, n. 1, and by Linder, "The Myth of Constantine the Great" 53, n. 51.

Chapter XVIII.
Conclusion

It is abundantly clear from the preceding chapters that Helena has left a rich legacy. This legacy is, not surprisingly, that of St. Helena more than that of Helena the empress, although sight was never lost of the fact that she was both. There are some further aspects of this legacy which it will be convenient to consider in this concluding chapter.

Two members of the imperial family flanking a cross are depicted on Byzantine coins with such frequency that it seems superfluous to cite specific examples. The ultimate source of this motif is to be seen, I think, in the statuary groups of Constantine and Helena first erected in the city of Constantinople.[1] And Constantine and Helena themselves are occasionally represented in this manner on Byzantine coins, as we have seen.[2] Other echoes can be found in the arts of both the East and the West.

Thus the Cabinet des Médailles of the Bibliothèque Nationale in Paris holds a Byzantine ivory plaque, once the center part of a triptych, in which Christ appears to be crowning or blessing an emperor and an empress who are flanking him on the left and right respectively.[3] An inscription identifies the emperor as Romanus and the empress as Eudocia (*not* Eudoxia); but it is difficult to know whether Romanus II or Romanus IV Diogenes is meant, since both emperors had a consort named Eudocia.[4] A very similar ivory plaque, probably once a book cover,

---

[1]See chapter XI above, nn. 20-21.

[2]Chapter XIV above, nn. 11 and 13.

[3]Inv. no. 300.

[4]The former reigned in 958-963, the latter in 1068-1071. (But some scholars date the ivory to the years 945-949.) Dalton, *Byzantine Art and Archaeology* 227 and fig. 139; Charles Diehl, *Manuel d'art byzantin*[2] II 660 and fig. 322; Andrew S. Keck and Charles Rufus Morey, review article in *ArtB* 17 (1935) 397-407 at 399-400; Grabar, *L'empereur dans l'art byzantin* 116 and pl. XXV.2; Bréhier, *op. cit.* 28, 73-74, and pl. XXX; Hayford Peirce and Royall Tyler, "An Ivory of the Xth Century," *DOP* 2 (1944) 11-18 at 15-16 and pl. 8; Bibliothèque Nationale, Paris, *Byzance et la France médiévale* (Paris 1958) 74, no. 146; David Talbot Rice, *The Art of Byzantium* 313 and pl. 97; Hunger, *Reich der neuen Mitte* 64 and 208; David Talbot Rice, *Art of the Byzantine Era* 87 and ill. 68; Delvoy, *op. cit.* 285-86 and ill. 160; Beckwith, *The Art of Constantinople*[2] 82 and fig. 101; Volbach and Lafontaine-Dosogne, *op. cit.* 201 and ill. 94b; Ostrogorsky, *History of the Byzantine State*[2], fig. 47; Otto Demus, *Byzantine Art and the*
(continued...)

may be seen in Paris' Musée de Cluny.[5] This time the imperial couple is the German emperor Otto II (972-983) and his wife, the Byzantine princess Theophano, daughter of Romanus II.[6]

In the south gallery of Constantinople's Hagia Sophia, at the east end, there is a mosaic which shows the Byzantine emperor Constantine IX Monomachus (1042-1055) and his wife Zoe on the left and right respectively of Christ enthroned.[7] Similarly, in another mosaic in the same

[4](...continued)

West (New York 1970) 85 and fig. 81; Joachim M. Plotzek in Schnütgen-Museum, *Rhein und Maas* I 169; Lasko, *op. cit.* 94; Adolph Goldschmidt and Kurt Weitzmann, *Die byzantinischen Elfenbeinskulpturen des X.-XIII. Jahrhunderts* (Berlin 1979) II 35, no. 34, and pl. XIV.

[5]Cl. 392.

[6]Dalton, *Byzantine Art and Archaeology* 22; Keck and Morey, *op. cit.* 399-400; Peirce and Tyler, *op. cit.* 16 and pl. 17; Bibliothèque Nationale, Paris, *Byzance et la France médiévale* 75, no. 148; Robert Holtzmann, *Geschichte der sächsischen Kaiserzeit (900-1024)*, 4th ed.(Munich 1961) 220-21 and ill. 25; *Byzantine Art: An European Art*, 2nd ed.(Athens 1964) 176-77, no. 82; Volbach and Lafontaine-Dosogne, *op. cit.* 18; Schramm and Mütherich, *op. cit.* 144, no. 73; Demus, *Byzantine Art and the West* 84 and fig. 80; Hans Wentzel, "Das byzantinische Erbe der ottonischen Kaiser: Hypothesen über den Brautschatz der Theophano," *Aachener Kunstblätter* 40 (1971) 15-39 at 16, and 43 (1972) 11-96 at 11, with ill. 1, and 85; Joachim M. Plotzek in Schnütgen-Museum, *Rhein und Maas* I 169; Lasko, *op. cit.* 94 and pl. 87; Goldschmidt and Weitzmann, *op. cit.* II 50, no. 85, and pl. XXXIV; Elisabeth Taburet-Delehaye, *Les ivories du Musée de Cluny* (Paris: Musée national de Cluny, 1978) 6-7; Danielle Gaborit-Chopin, *Elfenbeinkunst im Mittelalter* (Berlin 1978) 82 and 193, no. 74; Jean-Pierre Caillet, *L'antiquité classique, le haut moyen âge et Byzance au musée de Cluny* (Paris 1985) 141-43, no. 64.

[7]Grabar, *L'empereur dans l'art byzantin* 107-108; Thomas Whittemore, *The Mosaics of Hagia Sophia at Istanbul: Third Preliminary Report: The Imperial Portraits of the South Gallery* (Oxford 1942); Thomas Whittemore, "A Portrait of the Empress Zoe and of Constantine IX," *Byzantion* 18 (1946-1948) 223-27; André Grabar, *Byzantine Painting* (New York 1953) 98, 100, and 102; Charles Diehl, *Byzantium: Greatness and Decline* (New Brunswick, New Jersey, 1957) 28 and 132-33; Mango, *Materials* 27-28, diagram II, and and fig.14; David Talbot Rice, *The Art of Byzantium* 320 and pls. XIII and 133; David Talbot Rice, *Art of the Byzantine Era* 102 and ill. 90; Semavi Eyice, "Une nouvelle hypothese sur une mosaique de Sainte Sophie à Istanbul," in *Actes du XIIᵉ Congrès International d'Études Byzantines, Ochride 1961* (Belgrade 1964) III 99-101 and figs. 1-8; Cyril Mango in Heinz Kähler, *Die Hagia Sophia* (Berlin 1967) 60-62 and ill. 92; Delvoy, *op. cit.* 233 and ill. 113; Beckwith, *The Art of Constantinople*[2] 104-105 with fig. 130; Maclagan, *op. cit.* 99 and pl. 37; Volbach and Lafontaine-Dosogne, *op. cit.* 98 and 164; Ostrogorsky, *History of the Byzantine State*[2], figs. 44-45; Kinross, *op. cit.* 61 and 64; Ioannis Spatharakis, *The Portrait in Byzantine Illuminated Manuscripts* (Leiden 1976) 101, 256, and ill. 67; Cormack, *op. cit.* 184-89 with figs. 66-69.

gallery, the emperor John II Comnenus (1118-1143) and his wife Irene are shown flanking the Virgin and the Child.[8]

The First Cross of Matilda, or Otto-Mathilden-Kreuz, in the treasury of the cathedral of Essen can be dated to 973-982.[9] A small enamel at the foot of this cross depicts Matilda, Abbess of Essen, (left) and her brother Otto, Duke of Bavaria and Swabia, (right) holding a tall processional cross between them, like Constantine and Helena. This is a work of Rhenish art, but Byzantine influence is not to be excluded.

Reference has been made previously to a fresco in Karlstein Castle which depicts Emperor Charles IV and his wife with a large reliquary cross between them.[10] It has been suggested that Constantine and Helena served as model for this fresco.[11] And it would appear that the theme is passed from one generation to another. In Prague's National and University Library there is a manuscript dating from *ca.* 1410, the Breviary of one Benes (Benedict) of Waldstein.[12] One of the miniatures in this breviary shows Charles' son Wenzeslav and his wife (or

[8]Grabar, *L'empereur dans l'art byzantin* 107-108; Whittemore, *The Mosaics of Hagia Sophia at Istanbul;* Grabar, *Byzantine Painting* 99, 101, and 106; Charles Diehl, *Byzantium* 166; Mango, *Materials* 28, diagram II, and fig. 17; David Talbot Rice, *The Art of Byzantium* 328-29 and pls. XXIII and 164-65; Cyril Mango in Heinz Kähler, *Die Hagia Sophia* (Berlin 1967) 62; Delvoy, *op. cit.* 233; Beckwith, *The Art of Constantinople*[2] 121-22 with fig. 161; Maclagan, *op. cit.* 99-100; Volbach and Lafontaine-Dosogne, *op. cit.* 115, 170, and ill. 17; Ostrogorsky, *History of the Byzantine State*[2], figs. 51-52; Obolensky, *The Byzantine Commonwealth,* ill. 61c; Kinross, *op. cit.* 64; Spatharakis, *The Portrait* 29, 81-82, and ill. 48-49; Cormack, *op. cit.* 195-200 with figs. 73 and 75; Barbara Hill, Liz James, and Dion Smythe in Magdalino, *op. cit.* 223-25, with fig. 4.

[9]Paul Clemen, *Die Kunstdenkmäler der Stadt und des Kreises Essen* (Düsseldorf 1893) 43-44, no. 1, and pl. I; Georg Humann, *Die Kunstwerke der Münsterkirche in Essen* (Düsseldorf 1904) 115; Hermann Fillitz, *Die Insignien und Kleinodien des Heiligen Römischen Reiches* (Vienna 1954) 16; Walther Zimmermann, *Das Münster zu Essen* (Essen 1956) 55; Schnitzler, *Rheinische Schatzkammer* 32, no.43, and pls. 142-45; Marie-Madeline S. Gauthier, *Émaux du moyen âge occidental*[2] 50-51 with ill. 18 and 320, no. 18; Lasko, *op. cit.* 99 and pl. 93; Leonhard Küppers, *Essen: Dom und Domschatz* (Königstein im Taunus 1975) 54-56; Patrick M. De Winter, *The Sacral Treasure of the Guelphs* (Cleveland 1985) 36 with fig. 37; Ulrike Bergmann in Legner, *Ornamenta Ecclesiae* I 149-50, B1.

[10]Chapter XII, n. 69.

[11]Wammetsberger, *op. cit.* 82; Chadraba, *op. cit.* 68-69 and 108 (German summary).

[12]*CIM* E81; Joseph Truhlár, *Catalogus Codicum Manu Scriptorum Latinorum* (Prague 1905-1908), no. 1171.

possibly his mother, Anna von Schweidnitz) raising a large cross between them, again like Constantine and Helena.[13]

And in our own century there is Evelyn Waugh's novel *Helena*.[14] The novelist himself tells us that he has often "chosen the picturesque in preference to the plausible."[15] Thus we will not be surprised that once again Helena is the daughter of King Coel, that the wrong meaning is given to *stabularia* or that the marble steps of Pilate's praetorium are shipped off to Rome. A novel, of course, is to be judged not by its historical accuracy but by its literary qualities. Waugh himself thought that *Helena* was his masterpiece, but it has not enjoyed as much popularity as some of his other novels have.[16] Waugh was a convert to Catholicism, having finished *Helena* he visited the Holy Land, and he reflected deeply on the lives of the saints and their meaning in the modern world. Of Helena he says, in his essay "St. Helena Empress," that she was "at a time, literally, the most important woman in the world."[17] He admits that we do not know with absolute certainty that she found the True Cross and that we have no guarantee of the authenticity of her discovery. And yet he clearly wants to believe:

And at that crisis [the crisis of Christianity after the Edict of Milan] suddenly emerged God-sent from luxurious retirement in the far north a lonely, resolute old woman with a single concrete, practical task clear before

[13]Folio 504r; Chadraba, *op. cit.*, ill. 74. I am grateful to Professor Mojmir S. Frinta for his assistance.

[14]London and Boston 1951.

[15]Preface, p. IX.

[16]A. A. De Vitis, *Roman Holiday: The Catholic Novels of Evelyn Waugh* (New York 1956) 60-67; Frederick J. Stopp, *Evelyn Waugh: Portrait of an Artist* (Boston 1958) 123-29; James F. Carens, *The Satiric Art of Evelyn Waugh* (Seattle 1966) 111-19; Gene D. Phillips, *Evelyn Waugh's Officers, Gentlemen, and Rogues* (Chicago 1975) 89-99. I owe the reference to the courtesy of my colleague Professor Randall Craig; Calvin W. Lane, *Evelyn Waugh* (Boston 1981) 107-10; Robert Murray Davis, *Evelyn Waugh, Writer* (Norman, Oklahoma, 1981) 215-35; Jeffrey Heath, *The Picturesque Prison: Evelyn Waugh and His Writing* (Kingston and Montreal 1982) 198-205; Ian Littlewood, *The Writings of Evelyn Waugh* (Oxford 1983) 155-57; Jacqueline McDonnell, *Waugh on Women* (London 1986) 49, 101-102, and 116-17; Jacqueline McDonnell, *Evelyn Waugh* (London 1988) 110-14; Martin Stannard, *Evelyn Waugh: The Later Years 1939-1966* (New York 1992) 272-82; Martin Stannard has assembled five reviews of *Helena* in his *Evelyn Waugh: The Critical Heritage* (London 1984) 320-36.

[17]A talk first delivered on BBC radio in 1952; *Month*, January 1952, pp. 7-11; Clare Boothe Luce, ed., *Saints for Now* (New York 1952) 38-43; Donat Gallagher, ed., *The Essays, Articles and Reviews of Evelyn Waugh* (London 1983) 407-10.

her; to turn the eyes of the world back to the planks of wood on which their salvation hung. That was Helena's achievement. . . . What we can learn from Helena is something about the workings of God.[18]

The important role played by Helena is recognized and Helena sympathetically dealt with by Dorothy L. Sayers in her play *The Emperor Constantine: A Chronicle*.[19] The action of this play covers twenty-one years from 305 to 326, and an epilogue dramatically, but not quite truthfully, portrays Constantine's baptism and death in 337. Sayers, like Waugh, accepts the tradition of Helena's British birth and takes several other liberties with the historical facts. The play was written for and produced at the Colchester Festival in July, 1951. As theater the play was less than fully successful; it requires too many actors and too many scene changes and is too heavily laden with history, philology, and theology.[20]

European colonization carried Helena's name to the far corners of the world. A case in point is the Bay of St. Helena on the west coast of South Africa. On November 7, 1497, Vasco da Gama, on his first voyage to India, entered this bay with his fleet.[21] Why he chose to name it after St. Helena is not known.

The island in the South Atlantic which is best known today for having been Napoleon's place of exile in 1815-1821 was discovered by the Portuguese captain João de Nova on May 21, 1502, and so he called it St. Helena.[22] It was common enough practice of early navigators to name an island, cape, or bay according to the feast day on which they discovered it. Ascension Island, for instance, was so named on Ascen-

---

[18]*Ibid*.

[19]London and New York 1951; repr. Grand Rapids, Michigan, 1976.

[20]Colleen B. Gilbert, *A Bibliography of the Works of Dorothy L. Sayers* (Hamden, Connecticut, 1978) 215-16; Nancy L. Tischler, *Dorothy L. Sayers: A Pilgrim Soul* (Atlanta 1980) 107-109; Barbara Reynolds, *Dorothy L. Sayers: Her Life and Soul* (New York 1993) 362-63.

[21]Ernest George Ravenstein, trl. and ed., *A Journal of the First Voyage of Vasco da Gama, 1497-1499* (London 1898) 5 and 192; Kingsley Garland Jayne, *Vasco da Gama and His Successors: 1460-1580* (London 1910) 40; Edgar Prestage, *The Portuguese Pioneers* (London 1933) 253; Damião Peres, *História dos descobrimentos portugueses*, 3rd ed.(Porto 1983) 291.

[22]Thomas H. Brooke, *History of the Island of St. Helena*, 2nd ed. (London 1824) 46-47; Charles Prestwood Lucas, *A Historical Geography of the British Colonies* III³ (Oxford 1913) 387; Philip Gosse, *St. Helena, 1502-1938* (London 1938) 2; Peres, *op. cit.*, 397-98.

sion Day of 1503 (May 20);[23] St. Augustine, Florida, was so named by the Spanish explorer Pedro Menéndez de Avilés, because he first sighted the Florida coast on August 28, 1565, feast day of St. Augustine of Hippo;[24] and there are other examples.[25] But it is strange that a Portuguese captain should observe St. Helena's feast day on May 21 rather than on August 18.[26]

In 1526 the Spanish explorer Lucas Vásquez de Ayllón explored the eastern seaboard of North America.[27] When he come upon a headland on the coast of today's South Carolina his pilot, Pedro de Quexos, called it Punta de Santa Helena after his favorite saint.[28] Near this headland the aforementioned Menéndez founded forty years later the town of Santa Elena, which served as the capital of the Spanish territory

[23]Lucas, op. cit. 383; Peres, op. cit. 397-98.

[24]Gonzalo Solís de Merás, Pedro Menéndez de Avilés (Memorial, 1567), chapter X; English trl. by Jeannette Thurber Connor (Deland, Florida, 1923) 80-81 and 83; Bartolome Barrientos, Vida y hechos de Pedro Menéndez de Avilés (1567), chapter XIII; ed. Genaro Garcia (Mexico 1902) 39-40; English trl. by Anthony Kerrigan (Gainesville 1965) 37-38; George R. Fairbanks, The History and Antiquities of the City of St. Augustine, Florida (New York 1858) 19; Woodbury Lowery, The Spanish Settlements within the Present Limits of the United States: Florida 1562-1574 (New York and London 1905) 154; Alfonso Camín, El adelantado de la Florida, Pedro Menéndez de Avilés (Mexico 1944) 135 and 137; Michael V. Gannon, The Cross in the Sand (Gainesville 1965) 24-25; Michael V. Gannon, "Altar and Hearth: The Coming of Christianity, 1521-1565," The Florida Historical Quarterly 44 (1965-1966) 17-44 at 40-41; Luis Rafael Arana, "The Exploration of Florida and the Sources on the Founding of St. Augustine," The Florida Historical Quarterly 44 (1965-1966) 1-16 at 9-16; Charlton W. Tebeau, A History of Florida (Coral Gables 1971) 34 (erroneously June 28).

[25]Prestage, op. cit. 50, 124, 183, and 207; Samuel Eliot Morison, The Great Explorers (New York 1978) 182, 189, 218, 219, 442, 444, and 487; Peres, op. cit. 386-87. Similarly the towns of Santa Barbara and San Bernardino in California received their names, respectively, on a December 4, feast day of St. Barbara, and on a May 20, feast day of St. Bernardine of Siena, while San Antonio, Texas, owes its name to the feast day of St. Antony of Padua, June 13.

[26]On the feast days of St. Helena in the West and East respectively see chapter XV above, nn. 19 and 51. I doubt that de Nova was aware of St. Helena the Virgin, whose cult was observed at Auxerre in France and whose feast day was May 22; see chapter XV above, n. 77.

[27]Woodbury Lowery, The Spanish Settlements within the Present Limits of the United States, 1513-1561 (New York and London 1901) 164-67 and 447-48; Gannon, The Cross in the Sand 3; Tebeau, op. cit. 22.

[28]Writers' Program, South Carolina, Palmetto Place Names (Columbia, S. C. 1941) 140.

of La Florida until it was abandoned in 1587.[29] Parts of the modest town have been excavated on the golf course of the U.S. Marine Corps base at Parris Island.[30] The island just east of Parris Island still is called St. Helena Island.[31] The name of Santa Elena was perpetuated also by the Franciscan custody of Santa Elena de la Florida, which was organized in 1609 and raised to the rank of a province in 1612.[32]

In 1810 several new parishes were instituted in the territory which soon was to become the State of Louisiana.[33] Why one of these parishes was named St. Helena I have not been able to ascertain.

It is not known why, in 1864, a group of miners in western Montana chose the name of Helena for their small settlement.[34] Eventually that small settlement became the capital city of Montana and the see of a Catholic bishop. An impressive neo-Gothic cathedral was begun in 1908 and finally consecrated to the patronage of St. Helena in 1924.[35]

The gazetteers list numerous other places in the Americas and in Australia which bear the name of Helena, St. Helena, or St. Helens. I should think that in the case of most of these there is only a tenuous, perhaps secondary, or no link at all to our Helena.

Mr. Harold Perris of Schenectady, New York, called to my attention a small icon of St Helena, which is of interest in a different and

[29]Solís de Merá, op. cit., passim.; Barrientos, Vida, chapters XXXVII and IL; Spanish ed. 109-10 and 142; English trl. 103-104 and 134; Lowery, The Spanish Settlements within the Present Limits of the United States: Florida 1562-1574, pp. 247-49; Gannon, The Cross in the Sand 29 and 39; Tebeau, op. cit. 36-37; Eugene Lyon, The Enterprise of Florida: Pedro Menéndez de Avilés and the Spanish Conquest of 1565-1568 (Gainesville 1976) 156-57 and 166; Eugene Lyon, "Pedro Menéndez's Strategic Plan for the Florida Peninsula," The Florida Historical Quarterly 67 (1988-1989) 1-14 at 11-12.

[30]Joseph Judge, "Exploring Our Forgotten Century," National Geographic 173:3 (March, 1988) 330-63 at 340.

[31]Guion Griffis Johnson, A Social History of the Sea Islands, with Special Reference to St. Helena Island, South Carolina (Chapel Hill, North Carolina, 1930); Charles L. Blockson, "Sea Change in the Sea Islands," National Geographic 172:6 (December, 1987) 735-63. The island is situated between St. Helena Sound and Port Royal Sound.

[32]Wadding, op. cit. XXIV[2] (1934) 303 and XXV[2] (1934) 8; Holzapfel, op. cit. 393. Maynard J. Geiger, The Franciscan Conquest of Florida (1573-1618) (Washington, D.C., 1937) 36 and 45; Gannon, op. cit. 50.

[33]Charles Gayarré, History of Louisiana, 3rd ed.(New Orleans 1885) IV 243.

[34]Merrill G. Burlingame and K. Ross Toole, A History of Montana (New York 1957) I 126 and 129; Clark C. Spence, Montana: A Bicentennial History (New York 1978) 26.

[35]Victor Day, The Cathedral of St. Helena (Helena, Montana, 1938) I 35 and 108; II 142-43. Additional information was kindly provided by the Cathedral Parish office.

unexpected context. Mr. Perris, born Hipparchos Perdikis, came to the United States in 1921 with his parents, immigrants from Larnaka, Cyprus. The icon is one of several family keepsakes which Mr. Perdikis has donated to the new Ellis Island Immigration Museum on Ellis Island, New York, where it is now on display.[36]

Some modern historians have been very generous in their assessment of Helena's role in history and of her personality. Thus Francis Bond says that Helena was "one of the most noble and gracious women that ever stepped across the scene of history."[37] Otto Seeck praises the tact and dignity with which Helena performed the duties assigned to her by Constantine.[38] Henri Leclercq has this to say:

"Helena . . . seems to have been one of those rare women who are deserving of the first rank and capable of discharging their duties without fearing the judgment of posterity. If one grants her all the justice to which she is entitled one will mark her place in history among some princesses of exceptional merit ... This daughter of an innkeeper who became an empress seems to have brought from her humble background only beauty, purity, and all the noble ambitions of a naturally refined intelligence."[39]

Karl L. Mackes says of Helena: "She belongs ... to the outstanding personalities of Late Antiquity who laid the foundations of today's Christian and Western Civilization."[40]

I can only concur with these tributes to a remarkable woman. But Steven Runciman goes too far, it seems to me, when he calls Helena "the most exalted and most successful of the world's great archaeolo-gists."[41] (Treasure hunting, even if successful, is not archaeology.)

Helena has earned her place in history. I trust my readers will agree that she deserves to be remembered and respected. And to mil-lions who adhere to Roman Catholic or Eastern Orthodox traditions she continues to be not only empress but saint as well.

---

[36]Cat. no. STLI-6404, kindly supplied by the museum. Ivan Chermayeff, Fred Wasserman, and Mary J. Shapiro, *Ellis Island: An Illustrated History of the Immigrant Experience* (New York 1991) 182 and 234-35.

[37]*Dedications and Patron Saints* 73.

[38]Geschichte, I[4] 48.

[39]*DACL* VI.2 (1925) 2126-27; translation mine.

[40]*Op. cit.* 186; translation mine.

[41]*History of the Crusades* (Cambridge 1951) I 39. I owe the reference to the kindness of Professor Robert Wilken of the University of Virginia. Runciman similarly calls Helena a "holy archaeologist" in David Hunt, *op. cit.* 137.

BIBLIOGRAPHY

Abel, Felix-Marie. *Géographie de la Palestine.* 2 vols. 3rd ed. Paris 1967.

Adam, Adolf. *Das Kirchenjahr mitfeiern: Seine Geschichte und seine Bedeutung nach der Liturgie-erneuerung.* Freiburg 1979. English: *The Liturgical Year: Its History and Its Meaning after the Reform of the Liturgy.* New York 1981. Cited from the English ed.

Aigrain, René. *Sainte Radegonde.* 2nd ed. Poitiers 1952.

Aigrain, René. *L'hagiographie, ses sources, ses méthodes, son histoire.* Paris 1953.

Ainaud de Lasarte, Joan. *Pintura Catalana.* Geneva 1990. English: *Catalan Painting: The Fascination of the Romanesque.* New York 1990. Cited from the English ed.

Aland, Kurt. "Die religiöse Haltung Kaiser Konstantins." In *Studia Patristica* I = *TU* 63 (Berlin 1957) 549-600.

Alastos, Doros. *Cyprus in History.* London 1955.

Alberigo, Giuseppe, et al. *Conciliorum Oecumenicorum Decreta.* Freiburg 1962.

Albizzati, Carlo. "Une statuette-portrait du Bas-Empire à la Bibliothèque Nationale." *Aréthuse* 5 (1928) 163-68.

Alcolea, Santiago. *Artes decorativas en la España Cristiana. Ars Hispaniae: Historia universal del arte hispánico* XX. Madrid 1975.

Alexander, Suzanne Spain. "Studies in Constantinian Church Architecture." *RACrist.* 47 (1971) 281-330 and 49 (1973) 33-44.

Alexander, Suzanne Spain. See Spain, Suzanne.

Alföldi, Andreas (András). "A Carnuntumi díszes ruhájú nöszobar." *Országos magyar régészeti társulat* 1 (1920-1922) 39-41.

Alföldi, Andreas (Andrew). *The Conversion of Constantine and Pagan Rome.* Oxford 1948; 1969 impression.

Alföldi, Andreas. "Der grosse römische Kameo der Trierer Stadt-bibliothek." *TZ* 19 (1950) = *Aus der Schatzkammer des antiken Trier* (Trier 1951) 41-44.

Alföldi, Andreas. "Zur Erklärung der konstantinischen Deckengemälde in Trier." *Historia* 4 (1955) 131-50.

Alföldi, Andreas. *Die monarchische Repräsentation im römischen Kaiserreiche.* Darmstadt 1970. A reprint of two essays: "Die Ausgestaltung des monarchischen Zeremoniells am römischen Kaiserhofe," *Röm. Mitt.* 49 (1934) 3-118, and "Insignien und Tracht der römischen Kaiser," *Röm. Mitt.* 50 (1935) 3-158; both cited from the reprint.

Alföldi, Maria R. "Helena nobilissima femina: Zur Deutung der Trierer Deckengemälde." *JbNum.* 10 (1959-60) 79-90.

Alföldi, Maria R. *Die constantinische Goldprägung.* Mainz 1963.

Alföldi-Rosenbaum, Elisabeth. "Portrait Bust of a Young Lady of the Time of Justinian." *MMJ* 1 (1968) 19-40.

Aliprandis, Theologos Chr., and Nikos Chr. Aliprandis. Πάρος - 'Αντίπαρος. 2nd ed. Athens 1968.

Alpatov, Michel (Mikhail). "Les fresques de Piero della Francesca à Arezzo: Sémantique et stilistique." *Commentari* 14 (1963) 17-38.

Altaner, Berthold, and Alfred Stuiber. *Patrologie: Leben, Schriften und Lehre der Kirchenväter.* 8th ed. Freiburg 1978.

Amato, Pietro, ed. *Corrado Giaquinto: Atti del II Convegno Internazionale di Studi.* Molfetta 1985.

Amelung, Walter, and Georg Lippold. *Die Skulpturen des vaticanischen Museums.* Text 3 vols. in 4; plates 3 vols in 4. Berlin 1903-1956.

Ancient Portraits: Exhibition cat., Ackland Art Center, University of North Carolina. Chapel Hill 1970.

Anderson, Earl R. *Cynewulf: Structure and Theme in his Poetry.* London 1983.

Andresen, Carl. *Die Kirchen der alten Christenheit.* Stuttgart 1971.

Andrews, Keith. *Adam Elsheimer: Paintings - Drawings - Prints.* Oxford 1977.

Andrews, Keith. "Once More Elsheimer." *Burlington Magazine* 121 (1979) 168-72.

Andrews, Keith. *Adam Elsheimer: Werkverzeichnis der Gemälde Zeichnungen und Radierungen.* Munich 1985. An expanded version of *Adam Elsheimer: Paintings - Drawings - Prints* (Oxford 1977).

Angelini, Alessandro. *Piero della Francesca.* Florence 1985.

Angulo Iñíguez, Diego. *Pintura del Renascimento. Ars Hispaniae: Historia universal del arte hispánico* XII. Madrid 1954.

Anthony, Edgar Waterman. *A History of Mosaics.* Boston 1935; repr. New York 1968.

Anton, Hans Hubert. *Trier im frühen Mittelalter.* Paderborn 1987.

Arana, Luis Rafael. "The Exploration of Florida and the Sources on the Founding of St. Augustine." *The Florida Historical Quarterly* 44 (1965-1966) 1-16.

Arbeiter, Achim. *Alt-St. Peter in Geschichte und Wissenschaft: Abfolge der Bauten, Rekonstruktion, Architekturprogramm.* Berlin 1988.

Argan, Giulio Carlo. *Antonio Canova.* Rome 1969.

Armellini, Mariano. *Le chiese di Roma dal secolo IV al XIX.* 3rd ed. by Carlo Cecchelli. 2 vols. Rome 1942.

Armstrong, Gregory T. "Imperial Church Building in the Holy Land in the Fourth Century." *Biblical Archaeologist* 30 (1967) 90-102.

Armstrong, Gregory T. "Fifth and Sixth Century Church Buildings in the Holy Land." *Greek Orthodox Theological Review* 14 (1969) 17-30.

Arnaldi, Girolamo. "Andrea Dandolo Doge-Cronista." In Agostino Pertusi, ed., *La Storiografia Veneziana fino al secolo XVI* (Florence 1970) 127-252.

Arndt, Paul, and Walter Amelung. *Photographische Einzelaufnahmen antiker Skulpturen.* Munich 1893-1940.

Arnold-Forster, Frances. *Studies in Church Dedications.* 3 vols. London 1899. A revised ed. is being prepared by William Schipper, Memorial University, St. John's, Newfoundland.

Ashby, Thomas. *The Aqueducts of Ancient Rome.* Oxford 1935; repr. Washington, D. C., 1973.

Ashe, Geoffrey. *Mythology of the British Isles.* London 1990.

Askew, Gilbert. *The Coinage of Roman Britain.* London 1951.

Atiya, Aziz S. "Synaxarion, Copto-Arabic: The List of Saints." In *Copt. Enc.* VII 2173-90.

Attridge, Harold W., and Gohei Hata, edd. *Eusebius, Christianity, and Judaism.* Detroit 1992.

Attwater, Donald. *Saints of the East.* New York 1963.

Aubineau, Michel. "Les 318 serviteurs d' Abraham et le nombre des Pères au Concile de Nicée." *RHE* 61 (1966) 5-43.

Aurner, Nellie Slayton. *Caxton: Mirrour of Fifteenth-Century Letters.* London and Boston 1926; repr. New York 1965. Avi-Yonah, Michael. *The Holy Land from the Persian to the Arab Conquests (536 B.C. to A.D. 640): A Historical Geography.* Grand Rapids, Michigan, 1966.

Avi-Yonah, Michael. *Gazetteer of Roman Palestine.* Jerusalem

1976. Bachmann, Erich, ed. *Gotik in Böhmen.* Munich 1969. English: *Gothic Art in Bohemia.* New York 1977. Cited from the English ed.

Bachmann, Erich, ed. *Gotik in Böhmen.* Munich 1969. English: Gothic Art in Bohemia. New York, 1977. Cited from the English ed.

Bader, Walter. "Ausgrabungen unter dem Xantener Dom." *Germania* 18 (1934) 112-17.

Bader, Walter. *Die Stiftskirche des hl. Viktor zu Xanten* I.1. Kevelaer 1960.

Bader, Walter. "Das Xantener Grab der Märtyrer." *Der Niederrhein* 30 (1963) 168-80.

Bader, Walter, ed. *Sechzehnhundert Jahre Xantener Dom.* Cologne 1964.

Bader, Walter. *Der Dom zu Xanten* I. *Xantener Domblätter* 8. Kevelaer 1978.

Badt, Kurt. *Paolo Veronese.* Cologne 1981.

Bagatti, Bellarmino. *Gli antichi edifici sacri di Betlemme in seguito agli scavi e restauri praticati dalla Custodia di Terra Santa (1948-51).* Jerusalem 1952.

Bagatti, Bellarmino. *L'archeologia Cristiana in Palestina.* Florence 1962.

Bahat, Dan. "Does the Holy Sepulchre Mark the Burial of Jesus?" *Biblical Archaeology Review* 12 (1986) 26-45.

Baldini, Umberto, and Bruno Nardini, edd. *Il complesso monumentale di Santa Croce: La basilica, le capelle, i chiostri, il museo.* Florence 1983. German: *Santa Croce: Kirche, Kapellen, Kloster, Museum.* Stuttgart 1985. Cited from the German ed.

Baldwin, Charles Sears. *Three Medieval Centuries of Literature in England, 1100-1400.* New York 1968.

Balsdon, J. P. V. D. *Roman Women.* New York 1962.

Bankò, Julius. "Porträtkopf der heiligen Helena." *Jb. der Kunsthistorischen Sammlungen in Wien,* n. s. 1 (1926) 11-14.

Bárány-Oberschall, Magda von. *Die eiserne Krone der Lombardei und der lombardische Königsschatz.* Vienna 1966.

Bardenhewer, Otto. *Geschichte der altchristlichen Literatur.* 5 vols. 1st-2nd ed. Freiburg 1913-1932; repr. Darmstadt 1962.

Bardy, Gustave. *Recherches sur Saint Lucien d'Antioche et son école*. Paris 1936.

Bargellini, Piero. *S. Francesco d'Assisi*. Brescia 1964.

Barnard, Leslie W. "Church-State Relations, A.D. 313-337." *Journal of Church and State* 24 (1982) 337-55.

Barnes, Timothy D. "Emperor and Bishops, A.D. 324-344: Some Problems," *Am. Journ. of Anc. Hist.* 3 (1978) 53-75.

Barnes, Timothy D. *Constantine and Eusebius*. Cambridge, Massachusetts, 1981.

Barnes, Timothy D. *The New Empire of Diocletian and Constantine*. Cambridge, Massachusetts, 1982.

Baronio, Cesare. *Annales Ecclesiastici*. 38 vols. Ed. Augsburg 1738 ff.

Barrientos, Bartolome. *Vida y hechos de Pedro Menéndez de Avilés* (1567). Ed. Genaro Garcia. Mexico City 1902. English: Pedro Menéndez de Avilés, Founder of Florida, Anthony Kerrigan, trl., together with a facsimile reproduction of the Spanish ed. Gainesville 1965.

Bastet, Frédéric Louis. "Die grosse Kamee in Den Haag." *BAB* 43 (1968) 2-22.

Battisti, Eugenio. *Piero della Francesca*. 2 vols. Milan 1971.

Baudoin, Frans. *P. P. Rubens*. New York 1977.

Bauer, Hermann, and Bernhard Rupprecht. *Corpus der barocken Deckenmalerei in Deutschland*. 3 vols. to date. Munich 1976 ff.

Baugh, Albert C., ed. *A Literary History of England*. 2nd ed. New York 1967.

Baumgarten, Paul Maria. *Cartularium Vetus Campi Sancti Teutonicorum de Urbe*. *RömQ*, Suppl. 16. Rome 1908.

Baumstark, Anton. "Konstantinia aus syrischer Kunst und Liturgie." In Franz Josef Dölger, ed., *Konstantin der Grosse und seine Zeit*. (*RömQ*, Suppl. 19; Freiburg 1913) 217-54 and pls. VII-IX.

Baus, Karl. See Jedin, Hubert.

Beck, Georg. *St. Heinrich und St. Kunigunde: Das Leben des heiligen Kaiserpaares*. Bamberg 1961.

Beck, Hans-Georg. *Kirche und theologische Literatur im byzantinischen Reich*. *Byzantinisches Handbuch* II.1. *Handbuch der Altertumswissenschaft* XII.2.1. Munich 1959.

Beck, Hans-Georg, ed. *Studien zur Frühgeschichte Konstantinopels*. *Miscellanea Byzantina Monacensia 14*. Munich 1973.

Beck, James. *Italian Renaissance Painting.* New York 1981.

Beckwith, John. *The Art of Constantinople: An Introduction to Byzantine Art 330-1453.* 2nd ed. London 1968.

Beckwith, John. *Early Christian and Byzantine Art.* 1st ed. *The Pelican History of Art.* Harmondsworth, Middlesex, 1970.

Bedini, Balduino. *Le reliquie sessoriane della passione del Signore.* 3rd ed. Rome 1987.

Bedoyere, Michael de la. *Francis: A Biography of the Saint of Assisi.* New York 1962.

Beissel, Stephan. *Die Baugeschichte des heiligen Victor in Xanten. Ergänzungshefte zu den Stimmen aus Maria-Laach 23-24.* Freiburg 1883.

Beitz, Egid. *Das heilige Trier.* Augsburg 1927. English: *The Holy City of Trèves.* Augsburg 1928. Cited from the German ed.

Bellorini, Theophilus, and Eugene Hoade, translators. *Visit to the Holy Places of Egypt, Sinai, Palestine and Syria in 1384 by Frescobaldi, Gucci & Sigoli.* Jerusalem: Franciscan Press, 1948.

Belting-Ihm, Christa. "Das Justinuskreuz in der Schatzkammer der Peterskirche zu Rom: Bericht über die Untersuchungen des Römisch-Germanischen Zentralmuseums zu Mainz." *Jb. des Römisch-Germanischen Zentralmuseums, Mainz* 12 (1965) 142-66.

Bendall, S., and P. J. Donald. *The Later Palaeologan Coinage, 1282-1453.* London 1979.

Benham, W. Gurney, ed. and trl. *The Oath Book or Red Parchment Book of Colchester.* Colchester 1907.

Benham, W. Gurney. "Legends of Coel and Helena." *JBAS,* n. s. 25 (1919) 229-44.

Bennett, Henry Stanley. *Chaucer and the Fifteenth Century. The Oxford History of English Literature* II.1. Oxford 1947.

Bennett, J. A. W. *Middle English Literature. The Oxford History of English Literature* I.2. Oxford 1986.

Beny, Roloff, and Peter Gunn. *The Churches of Rome.* New York 1981.

Benz, Ernst, ed. *Russische Heiligenlegenden.* Zürich 1953.

Berenson, Bernard. *Italian Pictures of the Renaissance: Venetian School.* 2 vols. London 1958.

Berenson, Bernard. *Italian Pictures of the Renaissance: Florentine School.* 2nd ed. 2 vols. London 1963.

Berenson, Bernard. *Italian Pictures of the Renaissance: Central*

Italian and North Italian Schools. 3rd ed. 3 vols. London 1968.

Berger, Albrecht. *Untersuchungen zu den Patria Konstantinupoleos.* Bonn 1988.

Bergmann, Marianne. *Studien zum römischen Porträt des 3. Jahrhunderts n. Chr.* Bonn 1977.

Bergmann, Marianne. "Falschung, Umarbeitung oder eigener Stil: Beobachtungen zu einer konstantinischen Porträtbüste." *Städel-Jb.,* n. s. 10 (1985) 45-54.

Bernoulli, Johann Jakob. *Römische Ikonographie.* 2 vols. in 4. Stuttgart 1882-1894.

Bernstein, Burton. *Sinai: The Great and Terrible Wilderness.* New York 1979.

Bertelé, Tommaso. "Costantino il Grande e S. Helena su alcune monete bizantine." *Numismatica* 14 (1948) 91-106.

Bertelli, Carlo. *Piero della Francesca: La forza divina della pittura.* Milan 1991. English: *Piero della Francesca.* New Haven 1992. Cited from the English ed.

Bertrandon de la Broquière. *Voyage d'Outremer.* Ed. Charles Schefer. Paris 1892; repr. Westmead, Farnborough, Hants, England, 1972.

Besozzi, Raimondo. *La storia della basilica di Santa Croce in Gerusalemme.* Rome 1750. Besozzi was abbot of the Cistercian monastery of Santa Croce.

Betjeman, John. *Collins Pocket Guide to English Parish Churches: The North.* London 1968.

Beyer, Heinrich. *Urkundenbuch zur Geschichte der . . . mittelrheinischen Territorien* I. Koblenz 1860.

Bianchi Bandinelli, Ranuccio. *Rome: the Late Empire: Roman Art A.D. 200-400.* New York 1971. Also German and French edd. Cited from the English ed.

Bibliothèque Nationale, Paris. *Catalogus Codicum Manuscriptorum Bibliothecae Regiae.* 4 vols. Paris 1739-1744.

Bibliothèque Nationale, Paris. *Byzance et la France médiévale: Manuscrits à peintures du IIe au XVIe siècle.* Paris 1958.

Bibliothèque Nationale, Paris. *Catalogue des incunables* II. 4 fasc. Paris 1981-1985.

Bidinger, Andrea, ed. *Pfalzel: Geschichte und Gegenwart.* Trier: Arbeitsgemeinschaft Pfalzeler Chronik, 1989.

Biermann, Heinrich. "Augsburger (südbairisches) Heiligkreuzspiel." In *Verfasserlexikon*[2] I (1978) 528-30.

Bihain, Ernest. "L'épître de Cyrille de Jérusalem à Constance sur la vision de la croix *(BHG³* 413)." *Byzantion* 43 (1973) 264-96.

Black, Matthew. "The Festival of Encaenia Ecclesiae in the Ancient Church." *JEH* 5 (1954) 78-85.

Blades, William. *The Life and Typography of William Caxton.* 2 vols. London 1861-1863; repr. New York 1966.

Blaher, Damian Joseph. *The Ordinary Processes in Causes of Beatification and Canonization: A Historical Synopsis and a Commentary.* Washington, D. C., 1949.

Blatch, Mervyn. *A Guide to London's Churches.* London 1978.

Blockson, Charles L. "Sea Change in the Sea Islands." *National Geographic* 172:6 (December, 1987) 753-63.

Blümel, Carl. *Römische Bildnisse in Staatlichen Museen zu Berlin.* Berlin 1933.

Blumenfeld-Kosinski, Renate, and Timea Szell, edd. *Images of Sainthood in Medieval Europe.* Ithaca 1991.

Bodden, Mary-Catherine, ed. *The Old English Finding of the True Cross.* Cambridge 1987.

Böhmer, Johann Friedrich, Julius Flicker, and Eduard Winkelmann. *Die Regesten des Kaiserreiches unter Philipp, Otto IV, Friedrich II, Heinrich (VII), Conrad IV, Heinrich Raspe, Wilhelm und Richard: 1198-1272. Regesta Imperii V.* 3 vols. Innsbruck 1892-1894; repr. Hildesheim 1971.

Böhmer,Johann Friedrich, and Engelbert Mühlbacher. *Die Regesten des Kaiserreiches unter den Karolingern: 751-918. Regesta Imperii I.* Innsbruck 1889.

Böhner, Kurt, *Die fränkischen Altertümer des Trierer Landes.* 2 vols. Berlin 1958.

Bolton, Whitney F. *A History of Anglo-Latin Literature 597-1066.* I: 597-740. Princeton 1967.

Bond, Francis. *Dedications and Patron Saints of English Churches.* Oxford 1914.

Bondois, Marguerite. *La translation des saints Marcellin et Pierre: Étude sur Einhard et sa vie politique de 827 à 834.* Paris 1907.

Borchgrave d'Altena, Joseph de. "Inventaire archéologique de l'ancien pays de Liège, no. XCVI: Le triptyque reliquaire de la Vraie Croix de Notre Dame à Tongres." *Chronique archéologique du pays de Liège* 16 (1925) 43-49.

Borenius, Tancred. *Florentine Frescoes*. London 1930.

Borgehammar, Stephan. *How the Holy Cross Was Found: From Event to Medieval Legend*. Dissertation, Uppsala University. Stockholm: Almquist & Wiksell International, 1991.

Borger, Hugo. "Die Ausgrabungen im Bereich des Xantener Domes." *Neue Ausgrabungen in Deutschland* (Berlin 1958) 380-390. Römisch-Germanische Kommission des Deutschen Archäologischen Instituts, ed. W. Krämer.

Borger, Hugo. "Die Ausgrabungen unter der Stiftskirche des hl. Viktor zu Xanten in den Jahren 1945-1960 (Vorbericht II)." *BJ* 161 (1961) 396-448.

Borger, Hugo. "Die Ausgrabungen unter der Stiftskirche des hl. Viktor und in der Stifts-Immunität Xanten: Vorbericht." *Kunstchronik* 16 (1963) 117-37.

Borger, Hugo. "Die Ausgrabungen unter der Stiftskirche des hl. Viktor und in der Stifts-Immunität Xanten." *Der Niederrhein* 30 (1963) 181-86.

Borger, Hugo. *Xanten: Entstehung und Geschichte eines niederrheinischen Stiftes*. Xanten 1966.

Borger, Hugo. *Der Dom zu Köln*. Cologne 1980.

Borger, Hugo, and Friedrich Wilhelm Oediger. *Beiträge zur Frühgeschichte des Xantener Viktorstiftes. Rheinische Ausgrabungen* VI. Düsseldorf 1969.

Bornert, René. "La célébration de la sainte croix dans le rite byzantin." *La Maison-Dieu* 75 (1963) 92-108.

Borsi, Franco. *Bernini*. Italian: Milan 1980. English: New York 1984. Cited from the English ed.

Borsook, Eve. *The Mural Paintings of Tuscany*. 2nd ed. Oxford 1980.

Bosio, Antonio. *Roma sotterranea*. Rome 1632. Later edd. 1650 and 1710.

Boureau, Alain. *La Légende dorée*. Paris 1984.

Boussel, Patrice. *Des reliques et de leur bon usage*. Paris 1971.

Boussinesq, Georges, and Gustav Laurent. *Histoire de Reims depuis les origines jusqu' à nos jours*. 2 vols. in 3. Reims 1933.

Bovini, Giuseppe. *Edifici cristiani di culto d'età costantiniana à Roma*. Bologna 1968.

Bovini, Giuseppe. *Antichità cristane di Milano*. Bologna 1970.

Bovini, Giuseppe. *Mosaici paleocristiani di Roma*. Bologna 1971.

Bovini, Giuseppe. *L' antichità cristiane di Aquileia*. Bologna 1972.

Bowder, Diana. *The Age of Constantine and Julian*. London 1978.

Boyd, Beverly. "New Light on the South English Legendary." *TxSE* 37 (1958) 187-94.

Bracker, Jörgen. "Zur Ikonographie Constantins und seiner Söhne." *Kölner Jb.* 8 (1965-1966) 12-23.

Bracker, Jörgen. "Eine Kölner Kameenwerkstatt im Dienste konstantinisher Familienpolitik." *JbAC* 17 (1974) 103-108.

Brandenburg, Hugo. *Studien zur Mitra: Beiträge zur Waffen- und Trachtgeschichte der Antike.* Münster 1966.

Brandenburg, Hugo. "Meerwesensarkophage und Clipeusmotiv." *JDAI* 82 (1967) 195-245.

Brandenburg, Hugo. "Le pitture del soffitto del palazzo di Treviri e la loro interpretazione." *Corsi di cultura sull' arte Ravennate e Bizantina* 25 (1978) 29-32.

Brandenburg, Hugo. Review of Theodor Konrad Kempf, "Die Konstantinischen Deckenmalereien aus dem Trierer Dom," *Archäologisches Korrespondenzblatt* 7 (Mainz 1977) 147-59. *BZ* 72 (1979) 247.

Brandenburg, Hugo. *Roms frühchristliche Basiliken des 4. Jahrhunderts.* Munich 1979.

Brandenburg, Hugo. "Zur Deutung der Deckenbilder aus der Trierer Domgrabung." *Boreas: Münstersche Beiträge zur Archäologie* 8 (1985) 143-89.

Braun, Joseph. *Die Kirchenbauten der deutschen Jesuiten.* 2 vols. Freiburg 1908-1910.

Braun, Joseph. *Die Reliquiare des christlichen Kultes und ihre Entwicklung.* Freiburg 1940; repr. Osnabrück 1971.

Braun, Wilhelm. *Christoph Thomas Scheffler, ein Asamschüler: Beiträge zu seinem malerischen Werk.* Stuttgart 1939.

Braunfels, Wolfgang. *Die Kunst im Heiligen Römischen Reich.* 6 vols. Munich 1979-1989.

Bréhier, Louis. *La sculpture et les arts mineurs byzantins.* Paris 1936; repr. London 1973.

Brennan, Brian. "The Career of Venantius Fortunatus." *Traditio* 41 (1985) 49-78.

Brennan, Brian. "St. Radegund and the Early Development of Her Cult at Poitiers." *JRH* 13 (1985) 340-54.

Brennecke, Hanns Christof. "Synodum congregavit contra Euphratam nefandissimum episcopum: Zur angeblichen Kölner Synode gegen Euphrates." *ZKG* 90 (1979) 176-200.

Brennecke, Hanns Christof. "Lucian von Antiochien." In *TRE* XXI (1991) 474-79.

Brewster, Paul G. "The Strange Practice of Firewalking." *Expedition*

19:3 (Spring 1977) 43-47.

Briand, Émile. *Histoire de sainte Radigonde, reine de France, et des sanctuaires et pélerinages en son honeur.* Paris 1898.

Brittain, Frederick. *St. Radegund: Patroness of Jesus College, Cambridge.* Cambridge 1925.

Brooke, C. N. L. (Christopher). *The Saxon and Norman Kings.* New York 1963.

Brooke, Thomas H. *History of the Island of St. Helena.* 2nd ed. London 1824.

Broshi, Magen. "Evidence of Earliest Christian Pilgrimage to the Holy Land Comes to Light in Holy Sepulchre Church." *Biblical Archaeology Review* 3 (1977) 42-44.

Brower, Christopher. *Antiquitates et Annales Trevirenses.* Ed. Jacob Masen. 2 vols. Liège 1670.

Brown, Patricia Fortini. *Venetian Narrative Painting in the Age of Carpaccio.* New Haven 1988.

Bruck, Guido. "Die Verwendung christlicher Symbole auf Münzen von Constantine I bis Magnentius." *NZ* 76 (1955) 26-32.

Brückner, Wolfgang, ed. *Volkserzählung und Reformation.* Berlin 1974.

Brunhölzl, Franz. *Geschichte der lateinischen Literatur des Mittelalters* I (no more published). Munich 1975.

Brunhölzl, Franz. "Die lateinische Literatur." In Willi Erzgräber, ed., *Europäisches Spätmittelalter (Neues Handbuch der Literaturwissenschaft,* ed. Klaus von See, VIII. Wiesbaden 1978) 519-63.

Bruns, Gerda. *Staatskameen des 4. Jahrhunderts nach Christi Geburt. 104. Winckelmannsprogramm.* Berlin 1948.

Bruns, Gerda. "Der grosse Kameo von Frankreich." *Röm. Mitt.* 6 (1953) 71-115.

Buchholz, Käte. *Die Bildnisse der Kaiserinnen der severischen Zeit nach ihren Frisuren.* Dissertation Frankfurt 1963.

Buchowiecki, Walther. *Handbuch der Kirchen Roms.* 3 vols. Vienna 1967-1974.

Buckler, William H., and Georgina Grenfell. "Dated Wallpaintings in Cyprus." *Annuaire de l'Institut de Philologie et Histoire Orientales et Slaves* 7 (1939-1944) 47-50.

Budde, Ludwig. *Göreme: Höhlenkirchen in Kappadokien.* Düsseldorf 1958.

Budge, E. A. Wallis. *The Book of the Saints of the Ethiopian Church.* 4 vols. Cambridge 1928; repr. in 2 vols. Hildesheim 1976.

Büttner, Anita. "Die Trinkschale der Kaiserin Helena im Domschatz zu Trier." In *Festschrift Eugen von Mercklin* (Waldsassen, Bavaria, 1964) 27-31 and pls. 15-16.

Bunjes, Hermann, et al. *Die kirchlichen Denkmäler der Stadt Trier mit Ausnahme des Domes. Die Kunstdenkmäler der Rheinprovinz* XIII.3. Düsseldorf 1938; repr. Trier 1981.

Burlingame, Merrill G., and K. Ross Toole. *A History of Montana.* 3 vols. New York 1957.

Burney, Charles, and David Marshall Lang. *The Peoples of the Hills: Ancient Ararat and Caucasus.* New York 1971.

Burrow, John A. "An Approach to the Dream of the Rood." *Neophilologus* 43 (1959) 123-33.

Bury, J. B. "The Ceremonial Book of Constantine Porphyrogennetos." *EHR* 22 (1907) 209-27 and 417-39.

Bury, J. B. *History of the Later Roman Empire.* 2 vols. London 1923; repr. New York 1958.

Busse, Heribert, and Georg Kretschmar. *Jerusalemer Heiligtumstraditionen in altkirchlicher und frühislamischer Zeit.* Wiesbaden 1987.

Butler, Howard Crosby. *Early Churches in Syria.* Ed. E. B. Smith. Princeton 1929; repr. Amsterdam 1969.

Butler, Pierce. *Legenda Aurea - Légende Dorée - Golden Legend: A Study of Caxton's Golden Legend with Special Reference to Its Earlier English Prose Translation.* Baltimore 1899.

Byzantine Art: An European Art. 2nd ed. Exhibition catalogue, Athens 1964.

Cagiano de Azevedo, Michelangelo. "Ritratti o personificazioni le figure del soffitto dipinto di Treviri?" *Arch. Class.* 10 (1958) 60-63.

Cagiano de Azevedo, Michelangelo. "I palatia imperiali di Treviri, Milano e Ravenna." *Corsi di cultura sull' arte Ravennate e Bizantina* 25 (1978) 33-44.

Caillet, Jean-Pierre. *L'antiquité classique, le haut moyen âge et Byzance au musée de Cluny.* Paris 1985.

Calder, Daniel G. *Cynewulf. Twayne's English Authors Series.* Boston 1981.

Callu, J. P. "Pietas Romana: Les monnaies de l'impératrice Théodora." In *Melanges P. Boyancé* (Rome 1974) 141-51.

Calvesi, Maurizio. *Treasures of the Vatican.* New York 1962.

Calvin, John. *Traité des reliques.* In *Jean Calvin: Three French Treatises,* ed. Francis M. Higman (London 1970) 47-97.

Calza, Raissa. "Cronologia ed identificazione dell' 'Agrippina' capitolina." *MemPontAccad.* 8 (1955) 107-36.

Calza, Raissa. "Elena." In *Enciclopedia dell'arte antica* III (1960) 297-99.

Calza, Raissa. *Iconografia romana imperiale da Carausio a Giuliano (287-363 d. C.).* Rome 1972.

Calzada i Oliveras, Josep. *La catedral de Gerona.* Barcelona 1979.

Cameron, Averil. "The Early Religious Policies of Justin II." *Studies in Church History* 13 (1976) 51-67.

Cameron, Averil. *The Mediterranean World in Late Antiquity, AD 395-600.* London 1993.

Cameron, Averil, and Judith Herrin, edd. *Constantinople in the Early Eighth Century: The Parastaseis Syntomoi Chronikai.* Leiden 1984.

Camín, Alfonso. *El adelantado de la Florida, Pedro Menéndez de Avilés.* Mexico 1944.

Campagnano, Antonella, ed. *Ps. Cirillo di Gerusalemme: Omelie copte sulla passione sulla Croce e sulla Vergine.* Milan 1980.

Camps Cazorla, Emilio. *El arte Románico en España.* 2nd ed. Barcelona 1945.

Carandini, Andrea. Review of Kähler, *Die Stiftermosaiken.* In *Arch. Class.* 14 (1962) 310-13.

Carens, James F. *The Satiric Art of Evelyn Waugh.* Seattle 1966.

Carli, Enzo. *Piero della Francesca: The Frescoes in the Church of San Francesco at Arezzo.* Milan 1967.

Carra de Vaux, Bernard. *Le livre de l'avertissement et de la revision.* A translation from the Arabic *Tanbih* of al-Mas'udi. Paris 1896.

Carrasco, Magdalena Elizabeth. "Spirituality in Context: The Romanesque Illustrated Life of St. Radegund of Poitiers (Poitiers, Bibl. Mun., MS 250)." *ArtB* 72 (1990) 414-35.

Carrasco, Magdalena Elizabeth. "Sanctity and Experience in Pictorial Hagiography: Two Illustrated Lives of Saints from Romanesque France." In Renate Blumenfeld-Kosinski and Timea Szell, edd., *Images of Sainthood in Medieval Europe* (Ithaca 1991) 33-66.

Carrière, Auguste. *Nouvelles sources de Moïse de Khoren.* Vienna 1893; supplement 1894.

Carson, Robert (R. A. G.). *Coins of the Roman Empire.* New York 1990.

Carson, R. A. G., P. V. Hill, and J. P. C. Kent, *Late Roman Bronze Coinage, AD 324-498.* London 1960; repr. Chicago 1967.

Carver, James E. *The Northern Homily Cycle.* Abridgement of a New

York University Ph.D. dissertation. New York 1941.

Caspar, Erich. *Geschichte des Papsttums*. 2 vols. Tübingen 1930-1933.

Cassanelli, Roberto, ed. *Monza anno 1300: La basilica di S. Giovanni Battista e la sua fasciata*. Monza 1988.

Cecchelli, Carlo. "Il tesoro del Laterano II: Oreficerie, argenti, smalti." *Dedalo* 7 (1926) 231-56.

Cecchelli, Carlo, and Edoardo Persico. *SS. Marcellino e Pietro: La chiesa et la catacombe*. Le chiese di Roma illustrate 36. Rome 1936.

Cetto, Anna Maria. "Der Trierer Caesaren-Cameo: Eine neue Deutung." *Der kleine Bund* 30, no. 39 (Bern, Sept. 30, 1949).

Chadraba, Rudolf. *Staroměstká mostecká věž a triumfalní symbolika v uměnei Karla IV*. Prague 1971.

Chadwick, Hector Munro, et al. *Studies in Early British History*. Cambridge 1954; repr. 1959.

Chadwick, Henry. "The Fall of Eustathius of Antioch." *JThS* 49 (1948) 27-35. Repr. in Henry Chadwick, *History and Thought of the Early Church* (London 1982), chapter XIII. Cited from *JThS*.

Chadwick, Henry. "Conversion in Constantine the Great." *Studies in Church History* 15 (1978) 1-13.

Chadwick, Nora K. *Poetry and Letters in Early Christian Gaul*. London 1955.

Chahin, M. *The Kingdom of Armenia*. London 1987; New York 1991.

Chaine, Marius. *La chronologie des temps chrétiens de l'Égypte et de l'Éthiopie*. Paris 1925.

Chapot, Victor. *La frontière de l'Euphrate de Pompée à la conquête arabe*. Bibliothèque des écoles françaises d'Athènes et de Rome, fasc. 99. Paris 1907.

Charbonneaux, Jean. "Un portrait d'Hélène, mère de Constantin, au Musée du Bardo." *RArts* 2 (1952) 153-58.

Charbonneaux, Jean. *La sculpture grecque et romaine au Musée du Louvre*. Paris 1963.

Chatzidakis, Manolis. "A propos d'une nouvelle manière de dater les peintures de Cappadoce." *Byzantion* 14 (1939) 95-113; repr. in Manolis Chatzidakis, *Studies in Byzantine Art and Archaeology* (London 1972), section X.

Chatziioannou, Kyriakos. Ἡ ἀρχαία Κύπρος εἰς τὰς Ἑλληνικὰς πήγας. 5 vols. in 7. 1st-2nd edd. Nicosia 1971-1985.

Chenesseau, Georges Louis. *Monographie de la cathédrale d'Orléans*. Orléans 1925.

Chermayeff, Ivan, Fred Wasserman, and Mary J. Shapiro. *Ellis Island: An Illustrated History of the Immigrant Experience*. New York 1991.

Chevalier, Cyr Ulysse Joseph. *Repertorium Hymnologicum*. 6 vols. Louvain and Brussels 1892-1921.

Chicherov, V. I. *Zimnii period russkogo zemledel' cheskogo kalendaria XVI-XIX vekov*. Moscow 1957.

Clark, Kenneth. *Piero della Francesca*. 2nd ed. London 1969.

Classen, Wilhelm. *Das Erzbistum Köln: Archdiakonat von Xanten* I. *Germania Sacra* III.1.1. Berlin 1938.

Clemen, Paul. *Die Kunstdenkmäler des Kreises Moers. Die Kunstdenkmäler der Rheinprovinz*, ed. Paul Clemen, I.3. Düsseldorf 1892; repr. Moers 1979.

Clemen, Paul. *Die Kunstdenkmäler der Stadt und des Kreises Essen. Die Kunstdenkmäler der Rheinprovinz*, ed. Paul Clemen, II. 3. Düsseldorf 1893.

Clemen, Paul. *Die Kunstdenkmäler der Stadt und des Kreises Bonn. Die Kunstdenkmäler der Rheinprovinz*, ed. Paul Clemen, V.3. Düsseldorf 1905; repr. 1981.

Clemen, Paul. *Die romanische Monumentalmalerei in den Rheinlanden*. Text vol. and vol. of plates. Düsseldorf 1916.

Clemen, Paul. *Die gotischen Monumentalmalereien der Rheinlande*. Text vol. and vol. of plates. Düsseldorf 1930.

Clemen, Paul. *Der Dom zu Köln. Die Kunstdenkmäler der Stadt Köln* I.3. *Die Kunstdenkmäler der Rheinprovinz*, ed. Paul Clemen, VI.3. 2nd ed. Düsseldorf 1938; repr. 1980.

Clemoes, Peter. "The Chronology of Ælfric's Works." In Peter Clemoes, ed., *The Anglo-Saxons: Some Aspects of Their History and Culture Presented to Bruce Dickins* (London 1959) 212-47.

Clemoes, Peter. "Ælfric." In Eric Gerald Stanley, ed., *Continuations and Beginnings: Studies in Old English Literature* (London 1966) 176-209.

Coarelli, Filippo. *Roma. Guide archeologiche Laterza* VI. Rome 1980.

Coche de la Ferté, Étienne. *La sculpture grecque et romaine au Musée du Louvre*. 3rd ed. Paris 1955.

Coe, Brian. *Stained Glass in England: 1150-1550*. London 1981.

Coens, Maurice. *Recueil d'études bollandiennes*. *Subsidia Hagiographica* 37. Brussels 1963.

Colasanti, Arduino. *S. Maria in Aracoeli. Le chiese di Roma illustrate* 2. Rome 1923 (?).

Colbi, Saul P. *Christianity in the Holy Land: Past and Present.* Tel Aviv 1969.

Colchester: The Charters and Letters Patent Granted to the Borough by Richard I and Succeeding Sovereigns. Colchester 1904.

Cole, Bruce. *Agnoli Gaddi.* Oxford 1977.

Coleman, Christopher Bush. *Constantine the Great and Christianity.* Columbia University Ph.D. dissertation. New York 1914. Appendix I, 217-27, provides a partial text of the *Vita S. Silvestri* or *Actus S. Silvestri.* Appendix II, 228-37, provides the text of the Donation of Constantine.

Coletti, Luigi. *Pittura Veneta del Quattrocento.* Novara 1953.

Colini, Antonio Maria. "Horti Spei Veteris: Palatium Sessorianum." *MemPontAcc.* 8 (1955) 137-77.

Collection Hélène Stathatos. 3 vols. Strasbourg 1953-1963.

Collon-Gevaert, Suzanne. *Histoire des arts du métal en Belgique.* 2 vols. Brussels 1951.

Collon-Gevaert, Suzanne, Jean Lejeune, and Jacques Stiennon. *Art roman dans la vallée de la Meuse aux XIe, XIIe et XIIIe siècles.* 4th ed. Brussels 1966. English: *A Treasury of Romanesque Art: Metalwork, Illuminations, and Sculpture from the Valley of the Meuse.* London 1972. Cited from the English ed.

Comstock, Mary B., and Cornelius C. Vermeule. *Sculpture in Stone: The Greek, Roman, and Etruscan Collections of the Museum of Fine Arts, Boston.* Boston 1976.

Conant, Kenneth John, with the collaboration of Glanville Downey. "The Original Buildings at the Holy Sepulchre in Jerusalem." *Speculum* 31 (1956) 1-48.

Condé, Bruce. *See Lebanon.* Beirut 1960.

Conrad, Edwin, "A True Cross Bronze of Helena Sancta." *N. Circ.* 86 (1978) 191-92.

Constable, Giles. "Troyes, Constantinople, and the Relics of St. Helen in the Thirteenth Century." In *Mélanges René Crozet* (Poitiers 1966) II 1035-42.

Constantelos, Demetrios J. *Byzantine Philanthropy and Social Welfare.* 2nd ed. New Rochelle, New York, 1991.

Conti, Roberto, ed. *Il duomo di Monza.* 2 vols. 2nd ed. Milan 1989.

Conway, Martin. "St. Radegund's Reliquary at Poitiers." *Antiquaries Journal* 1923, pp. 1-12.

Corbo, Virgilio C., ed. *Custodia di Terra Santa, 1342-1942.* Jerusalem 1951.

Corbo, Virgilio C. *Il Santo Sepolcro di Gerusalemme: Aspetti archeologici dalle origini al periodo crociato.* 3 vols. Jerusalem 1982.

Coriden, James A., Thomas J. Green, and Donald E. Heintschel, edd. *The Code of Canon Law: A Text and Commentary.* New York 1985.

Cormack, Robin S. "Byzantine Cappadocia: The Archaic Group of Wall Paintings." *JBAA,* 3rd ser. 30 (1967) 19-36.

Cornaro (Corner),Flaminio. *Ecclesiae Venetae antiquis monumentis nunc etiam primum editis illustratae ac in decades distributae.* 18 vols. Venice 1749.

Cornet, Bertrand. "La fête de la croix du 3 mai." *RBPhil.* 30 (1952) 837-48.

Coüasnon, Charles. *The Church of the Holy Sepulchre in Jerusalem. British Academy Schweich Lectures.* London 1974.

Couzard, Remi. *Sainte Hélène d'après l'histoire et la tradition.* Paris 1911.

Cross, James E. *Aelfric and the Mediaeval Homiliary -- Objection and Contribution.* Lund 1963.

Crowe, Joseph A., and Giovanni Battista Cavalcaselle. *A History of Painting in Italy.* 6 vols. 2nd ed. London 1903-1914; repr. New York 1975.

Crowfoot, John Winter. *Early Churches in Palestine. British Academy Schweich Lectures.* London 1941; repr. College Park, Maryland, 1971.

Cüppers, Heinz, ed. *Die Römer in Rheinland-Pfalz.* Stuttgart 1990.

Dagron, Gilbert. "Les moines et la ville: Le monachisme à Constantinople jusqu'au concile de Chalcédoine (451)." *Travaux et Mémoires* 4 (1970) 229-76.

Dagron, Gilbert. *Naissance d'une capitale: Constantinople et ses institutions de 330 à 451.* Paris 1974.

Dagron, Gilbert. *Constantinople imaginaire: Études sur le recueil des Patria.* Paris 1984.

Dalmais, I.-H. "La glorification de la Sainte Croix dans l'église copte." *La Maison-Dieu* 75 (1963) 109-118.

Dalmases, Núria de, and Antoni José i Pitarch. *Els inicis i l'art romànic: s. IX-XII. Història de l'art català* I. Barcelona 1986.

Dalton, Ormonde M. *Byzantine Art and Archaeology.* Oxford 1911.

Dalton, Ormonde M. *East Christian Art: A Survey of the Monuments.* Oxford 1925; repr. New York 1975.

D'Ancona, Paolo. *Piero della Francesca: Il ciclo affrescato nella chiesa di S. Francesco in Arezzo*. Milan 1980. Text in Italian, French, English, and German; excellent pls.

Danforth, Loring M. "The Role of Dance in the Ritual Therapy of the Anastenaria," *Byzantine and Modern Greek Studies* 5 (1979) 141-63.

Danforth, Loring M. "Power through Submission in the Anastenaria." *Journal of Modern Greek Studies 1* (1983) 203-23.

Danforth, Loring M. *Firewalking and Religious Healing: The Anastenaria of Greece and the American Firewalking Movement*. Princeton 1989.

Davies, J. G. "Eusebius' Description of the Martyrium at Jerusalem." *AJA* 61 (1957) 171-73.

Davies, John. *A History of Wales*. London 1993. First published in 1990 in Welsh under the title *Hanes Cymru*.

Davis, Raymond. *The Book of Pontiffs (Liber Pontificalis)*. Liverpool 1989.

Davis, Robert Murray. *Evelyn Waugh, Writer*. Norman, Oklahoma, 1981.

Day, Victor. *The Cathedral of St. Helena*. Helena, Montana, 1938.

De Clercq, Victor C. *Ossius of Corduba: A Contribution to the History of the Constantinian Period*. Washington, D. C., 1954.

De Maeyer, Marcel. "Rubens en de altaarstukken in het hospital te Grasse." *Gentse Bijdragen tot de Kunstgeschiedenis* 14 (1953) 75-87.

De Rossi, Giovanni Battista, ed. *Inscriptiones Christianae Urbis Romae Septimo Saeculo Antiquiores*. 2 vols. Rome 1857-1888.

De Rossi, Giovanni Battista. *Roma sotterranea*. 3 vols. Rome 1861-1877.

De Vecchi, Pierluigi. *L'opera completa di Piero della Francesca*. Milan 1967. English: *The Complete Paintings of Piero della Francesca*. New York 1970. Cited from the English ed.

De Vitis, A. A. *Roman Holiday: The Catholic Novels of Evelyn Waugh*. New York 1956.

De Winter, Patrick M. *The Sacral Treasure of the Guelphs*. The Cleveland Museum of Art 1985.

Décarreaux, Jean. *Moines et monastères à l'époque de Charlemagne*. Paris 1980.

Deckers, Johannes G. "Die Decke eines Trierer Prunksaals." *Kölner Römer-Ilustrierte* 2 (1975) 176-79.

Deckers, Johannes G. "St. Gereon in Köln: Ausgrabungen 1978/79."

JbAC 25 (1982) 102-31.

Deichmann, Friedrich Wilhelm. "Untersuchungen an spätrömischen Rundbauten in Rom und Latium." *JDAI*, AA 1941, pp. 733-48.

Deichmann, Friedrich Wilhelm. *Frühchristliche Kirchen in Rom.* Basel 1948.

Deichmann, Friedrich Wilhelm. "Kassettendecken." *JÖB* 21 (1972) 83-107. Repr. in his *Rom, Ravenna, Konstantinopel, Naher Osten* (Wiesbaden 1982) 228-54. Cited from the original publication.

Deichmann, Friedrich Wilhelm, and Arnold Tschira. "Das Mausoleum der Kaiserin Helena und die Basilika der heiligen Marcellinus und Petrus an der Via Labicana vor Rom." *JDAI* 72 (1957) 44-110. Repr. in Deichmann, *Rom, Ravenna, Konstantinopel, Naher Osten* (Wiesbaden 1982) 305-374. Cited from the original publication.

Deichmann, Friedrich Wilhelm, Giuseppe Bovini, and Hugo Brandenburg. *Repertorium der christlich-antiken Sarkophage.* Text and pls. Wiesbaden 1967.

Delbrueck, Richard. "Porträts byzantinischer Kaiserinnen." *Röm. Mitt.* 28 (1913) 310-52.

Delbrueck, Richard. *Die Consulardiptychen und verwandte Denkmäler.* Berlin and Leipzig 1929.

Delbrueck, Richard. *Antike Porphyrwerke.* Berlin 1932.

Delbrueck, Richard. *Spätantike Kaiserporträts von Konstantinus Magnus bis zum Ende des Westreichs.* Berlin 1933; repr. 1978.

Delehaye, Hippolyte. "Saints de Chypre." *Anal. Boll.* 26 (1907) 161-297.

Delehaye, Hippolyte. *Sanctus: Essai sur le culte des saints dans l'antiquité.* Subsidia Hagiographica 17. Brussels 1927.

Delehaye, Hippolyte. *Les origines du culte des martyrs.* 2nd ed. *Subsidia Hagiographica* 20. Brussels 1933.

Delehaye, Hippolyte. *Les légendes hagiographiques.* 4th ed. Brussels 1955. English: *The Legends of the Saints.* New York 1962. Cited from the English ed.

Delvoye, Charles. *L'art byzantin.* Paris 1967.

Demandt, Alexander. *Die Spätantike: Römische Geschichte von Diocletian bis Justinian, 284-565 n. Chr. Handbuch der Altertumswissenschaft* III.6. Munich 1989.

Demus, Otto. *Byzantine Art and the West.* New York 1970.

Demus, Otto. *Romanische Wandmalerei.* Munich 1968. English:

Romanesque Mural Painting; London 1970. Cited from the English ed.

Der Nersessian, Sirarpie. "Remarks on the Date of the Menologium and Psalter Written for Basil II," *Byzantion* 15 (1940-1941) 104-25.

Der Nersessian, Sirarpie. "La fête de l'exaltation de la Croix." *In Mélanges Henri Gregoire* II, *Annuaire de l'Institut de Philologie et d'Histoire orientales et Slaves* 10 (1950) 193-98.

Der Nersessian, Sirarpie. "An Armenian Lectionary of the Fourteenth Century." In Dorothy Miner, ed., *Studies in Art and Literature for Bella de Costa Greene* (Princeton 1954) 231-37.

Deuchler, Florens, ed. *The Year 1200* II: *A Background Survey.* New York 1970.

Devos, Paul. "La date du voyage d'Égérie." *Anal. Boll.* 85 (1967). 165-94.

Devos, Paul. "Égérie à Bethléem." *Anal. Boll.* 86 (1968) 87-108.

Devreesse, Robert. "Le christianisme dans la péninsula sinaïtique, des origenes à l'arrivée des musulmans." *Rev. Bibl.* 49 (1940) 205-23.

Devreesse, Robert. Le Patriarcat d'Antioche depuis la paix de l'église jusqu'à la conquête arabe. Paris 1945.

Diehl, Charles. *Figures Byzantines* I. 2nd ed. Paris 1908; repr. Hildesheim 1965. Chapters I-VII in English: *Byzantine Portraits.* New York 1927. Also *Byzantine Empresses.* New York 1963. Cited from the French ed.

Diehl, Charles. *Manuel d'art byzantin.* 2 vols. 2nd ed. Paris 1925-1926.

Diehl, Charles. *Byzance: Grandeur et décadence.* 2nd ed. Paris 1926. English: *Byzantium: Greatness and Decline.* New Brunswick, New Jersey, 1957. Cited from the English ed.

Diel, Philipp. *Die St. Matthias-Kirche bei Trier und ihre Heiligthümer.* Trier 1881.

Dietrich, Eduard. "Abt Aelfrik zur Literatur-Geschichte der angelsächsischen Kirche," *ZHT* 25 (1855) 487-594 and 26 (1856) 163-256.

Dietz, Josef. *Aus der Sagenwelt des Bonner Landes.* Bonn 1965.

Dietz, Josef. "St. Helena in der rheinischen Überlieferung." In *Festschrift Matthias Zender* (Bonn 1972) I 356-83.

Dill, Samuel. *Roman Society in Gaul in the Merovingian Age.* London 1926.

Dmitrievskiı, Alekseı. *Opisanie liturgitseskich rukopisej.* 3 vols. Kiev 1895-1917; repr. Hildesheim 1965.

Dölger, Franz Joseph. "Die Taufe Konstantins und ihre Probleme." In his *Konstantin der Grosse und seine Zeit (RömQ,* Suppl. 19; Freiburg 1913) 377-447.

Dölger, Franz Joseph. "Das Anhängekreuzchen der hl. Makrina und ihr Ring mit der Kreuzpartikel." *Antike und Christentum* 3 (1932) 81-116.

Dörner, Friedrich Karl. "Inschriften und Denkmäler aus Bithynien." *Istanbuler Forschungen* 14 (1941) 1-127.

Domaszewski, Alfred von. *Die Religion des römischen Heeres.* Trier 1895; repr. New York 1975.

Dorigo, Wladimiro. *Pittura tardoromana.* Milan 1966. English: *Late Roman Painting.* New York 1971. Cited from the English ed.

D'Orsi, Mario. *Corrado Giaquinto.* Rome 1958.

Doubleday, H. Arthur, and William Page, edd. *A History of Hampshire and the Isle of Wight* II. *The Victoria History of the Counties of England.* London 1903.

Dowling, Theodore Edward (Archdeacon). "The Episcopal Succession in Jerusalem." *Palestine Exploration Fund Quarterly Statement for 1913,* pp. 164-77.

Downey, Glanville. "The Builder of the Original Church of the Apostles at Constantinople." *DOP* 6 (1951) 51-80.

Downey, Glanville. "The Tombs of the Byzantine Emperors at the Church of the Holy Apostles in Constantinople." *JHS* 79 (1959) 27-51.

Downey, Glanville. *A History of Antioch in Syria.* Princeton 1961.

Drake, Harold Allen. "A Coptic Version of the Discovery of the Holy Sepulchre." *GRBS* 20 (1979) 381-92.

Drake, Harold Allen. "Eusebius on the True Cross." *JEH* 36 (1985) 1-22.

Drijvers, Jan Willem. *Helena Augusta: The Mother of Constantine the Great and the Legend of Her Finding of the True Cross.* Leiden 1992. A revision and translation of the author's dissertation: *Helena Augusta: Waarheid en Legende;* Groningen 1989.

Du Cange, Charles Du Fresne. *Constantinopolis Christiana. Corpus Byzantinae Historiae* XXVI. Paris 1680; repr. Brussels 1964.

Dubois, François Noel Alexandre. *Notice historique et description de l'église cathédrale de Sainte-Croix d'Orléans.* Paris 1818.

Dubois, Marguerite-Marie. *Ælfric: Sermonnaire, docteur et grammairien.* Paris 1943.

Duby, Georges. *History of Medieval Art, 980-1440.* 2nd ed. 3 vols.

in 1. Geneva 1986.

Duchesne, Louis. *Fastes épiscopaux de l'ancienne Gaule.* 3 vols. lst - 2nd edd. Paris 1907-1915.

Duchesne, Louis. *Origines du culte chrétien.* 5th ed. Paris 1920. English: *Christian Worship: Its Origin and Evolution.* 5th ed. London 1949. Cited from the English ed.

Duckett, Eleanor Shipley. *Anglo-Saxon Saints and Scholars.* London 1947.

Duckett, Eleanor Shipley. *Carolingian Portraits.* Ann Arbor 1962.

Duckworth, H. T. F. *The Church of the Holy Sepulchre.* London 1923.

Dudden, Frederick Homes. *Gregory the Great: His Place in History and Thought.* 2 vols. London 1905; repr. New York 1967.

Dudley, Donald R. *Urbs Roma: A Source Book of Classical Texts.* London 1967.

Düwell, Kurt, and Franz Irsigler, edd. *Trier in der Neuzeit. 2000 Jahre Trier* III. Trier 1988.

Duff, Edward Gordon. *William Caxton.* Chicago 1905; repr. New York 1970.

Duff, Edward Gordon. *Fifteenth Century English Books.* Oxford 1917; repr. Frankfurt 1964.

Dugdale, William. *Monasticon Anglicanum.* 6 vols in 8. Ed. princeps London 1655 ff.; cited from the ed. London 1817-1830.

Dumeige, Gervais. *Histoire des conciles oecuméniques* IV: *Nicée II.* Paris 1978.

Dunlop, D. M. *Arab Civilization to A.D. 1500.* London, New York, and Beirut 1971.

Dunn-Lardeau, Brenda, ed. *Legenda aurea: Sept siècles de diffusion. Actes du colloque international sur la Legenda aurea: Texte latin et branches vernaculaires.* Montreal and Paris 1986.

Dunn-Lardeau, Brenda, and Dominique Coq. "Fifteenth and Sixteenth Century Editions of the *Légende dorée.*" *BHR* 47 (1985) 87-101.

Durliat, Marcel. *L'art romain.* Paris 1982.

Dussaud, René, Paul Deschamps, and Henri Seyrig. *La Syrie antique et médiévale illustrée.* Paris 1931.

Duval, Yvette. *Loca Sanctorum Africae: Le culte des martyrs en Afrique du IVe au VIIe siècle. Collection de l'école française de Rome* 58. 2 vols. Rome 1982.

Dvořáková, Vlasta, et al. *Gothic Mural Painting in Bohemia and Moravia, 1300-1378.* London 1964.

Dvořáková, Vlasta, and Dobroslava Menclová. *Karlstejn.* Prague 1965.

Ebersolt, Jean. "Sarcophages impériaux de Rome et de Constantinople." *BZ* 30 (1929-1930) 582-87.

Ebersolt, Jean. *Constantinople: Recueil d'études d'archéologie et d'histoire.* Paris 1951.

Eckenstein, Lina. *A History of Sinai.* London 1921.

Eden, Frederick Sydney. *Ancient Stained and Painted Glass.* 2nd ed. Cambridge 1933.

Egger, Rudolf. "Die Begräbnisstätte des Kaisers Konstantin." *ÖJh* 16 (1913) 212-30. Repr. in *Römische Antike und frühes Christentum: Ausgewählte Schriften von Rudolf Egger,* 1st-2nd ed. (Klagenfurt 1963-1967) I 1-21. Cited from *ÖJh.*

Egger, Rudolf. "Das Goldkreuz am Grabe Petri." *AAWW* 96 (1959) 182-202. Repr. in *Römische Antike und frühes Christentum: Ausgewählte Schriften von Rudolf Egger,* 1st-2nd ed. (Klagenfurt 1963-1967) II 304-20. Cited from *AAWW.*

Ehlert, Holger H. *Die Deckenfresken von St. Paulin in Trier: Das Dekorations-System eines barocken Kirchenbaues.* Mainz 1984.

Ehrhard, Albert. *Überlieferung und Bestand der hagiographischen und homiletischen Literatur der griechischen Kirche.* Part I in 3 vols. Leipzig 1937-1952.

Ehrhardt, Arnold. "Constantin d. Gr. Religionspolitik und Gesetzgebung." *ZRG, R. Abt.* 72 (1955) 127-90.

Ehrhardt, Arnold. "Constantine, Rome, and the Rabbis." *BRL* 42 (1959-1960) 288-312.

Eich, Paul. "Das Kreuzretabel Adam Elsheimers im Städelschen Kunstinstitut zu Frankfurt am Main." In Werner Knopp, ed., *Spiegelungen* (Mainz 1986) 31-59.

Elm, Kaspar, ed. *Norbert von Xanten: Adliger - Ordensstifter - Kirchenfürst.* Cologne 1984.

Encyclopedia of Archaeological Excavations in the Holy Land. English ed. by Michael Avi-Yonah and Ephraim Stern. 4 vols. Englewood Cliffs, New Jersey, 1975-1978.

The Encyclopaedia of Islam. 2nd ed. Leiden 1960 ff.

Engelskirchen, Heinrich. "Die Xantener Gereonskapelle in den Sümpfen." *AHVNrh.* 162 (1960) 130-34.

Engelskirchen, Heinrich. "Die Xantener Gereonskapelle innerhalb der Stadt." *AHVNrh.* 164 (1962) 197-204.

Engemann, Josef. "Glyptik." In *RAC* XI (1981) 270-313.

Englebert, Omer. *Saint Francis of Assisi.* 2nd English ed. Chicago

1966.

Epstein, Ann Wharton. *Tokali Kilise: Tenth Century Metropolitan Art in Byzantine Cappadocia. Dumbarton Oaks Studies 22.* Washington, D.C., 1986.

Epstein, Ann Wharton. See also Wharton, Annabel Jane.

Erasmus of Rotterdam. *Perigrinatio Religionis Causa.* In *Opera Omnia* I.3, ed. Halkin, Amsterdam 1972.

Erb, Ewald. *Geschichte der deutschen Literatur von den Anfängen bis 1160* II. *Geschichte der deutschen Literatur von den Anfängen bis zur Gegenwart,* ed. Klaus Gysi et al., I.2. Berlin 1965.

Erzgräber, Willi, ed. *Europäisches Spätmittelalter. Neues Handbuch der Literaturwissenschaft,* ed. Klaus von See, VIII. Wiesbaden 1978.

Esbroeck, Michel van. "L'opuscule 'Sur la croix' d'Alexandre de Chypre et sa version géorgienne." *Bedi Kartlisa* 37 (1979) 102-32.

Eschborn, Michael. *Karlstein: Das Rätsel um die Burg Karls IV.* Stuttgart 1971.

Evans, Joan. *A History of Jewellery, 1100-1870.* 2nd ed. London 1970.

Evelpidis, Christos. "Anastenaria, un culte dionysiaque contemporain," *Cahiers du Sud* 51, no. 377 (1964) pp. [I-V], and no. 378/379 (1964), pp.[I-V].

Evers, Hans Gerhard. *Peter Paul Rubens.* Munich 1942.

Ewald, Wilhelm, and Hugo Rahtgens. *Die Kunstdenkmäler der Stadt Köln* I.4. *Die Kunstdenkmäler der Rheinprovinz,* ed. Paul Clemen, VI.4. Düsseldorf 1916; repr. 1980 as *Die kirchlichen Kunstdenkmäler der Stadt Köln* I.

Ewig, Eugen. *Trier im Merowingerreich: Civitas, Stadt, Bistum. TZ* 21 (1952) 5-367. Also separately Trier 1954; repr. Aalen 1973.

Ewig, Eugen. "Das Bild Constantins des Grossen in den ersten Jahrhunderten des abendländischen Mittelalters." *Hist. Jb. der Goerres-Gesellschaft* 75 (1955) 1-46. Repr. in Herbert Hunger, ed., *Das byzantinische Herrscherbild* (Darmstadt 1975) 133-92. Repr. also in Eugen Ewig, *Spätantikes und fränkisches Gallien* I (Munich 1976) 72-113. Cited from *Hist. Jb.*

Ewig, Eugen. "Kaiserliche und apostolische Tradition im mittelalterlichen Trier." *TZ* 24-26 (1956-1958) 147-86. Repr. in Eugen Ewig, *Spätantikes und fränkisches Gallien* II (Munich 1979) 51-90. Cited from *TZ.*

Ewig, Eugen. See Jedin, Hubert.
Eyice, Semavi. "Une nouvelle hypothese sur une mosaique de Sainte
    Sophie à Istanbul. In *Actes du XIIe Congrès International
    d'Études Byzantines, Ochride 1961* (Belgrade 1964) III 99-
    101 and figs. 1-8.
Fabretti, Raphael. *De Aquis et Aquaeductibus Veteris Romae
    Dissertationes Tres.* Rome 1680.
Fagiolo dell'Arco, Maurizio and Marcello. *Bernini: Una introduzione
    al gran teatro del barocco.* Rome 1967.
Fairbanks, George R. *The History and Antiquities of the City of St.
    Augustine, Florida.* New York 1858; facsimile reproduction,
    Michael V. Gannon, ed., Gainesville 1975.
Falke, Otto von. *Der Dreikönigenschrein des Nikolaus von Verdun im
    Kölner Domschatz.* Mönchengladbach 1911.
Falke, Otto von, and Heinrich Frauberger. *Deutsche Schmelzarbeiten
    des Mittelalters.* Frankfurt/Main 1904.
Faral, Edmond. *La légende Arthurienne.* 3 vols. Paris 1929; repr.
    New York 1973.
Farcy, Louis de. *La broderie du XIe siècle jusqu'à nos jours.* With
    supplements 1-2. 2 vols. Angers 1890-1919.
Farmer, David Hugh. *The Oxford Dictionary of Saints.* Oxford
    1982.
Farmer, Hugh. "William of Malmesbury's Life and Works." *JEH* 13
    (1962) 39-54.
Farrer, William, and J. Brownbill, edd. *The Victoria History of the
    County of Lancaster* III and IV. *The Victoria History of the
    Counties of England.* London 1907-1911; repr. 1966.
Fedden, Robin. *Syria and Lebanon.* 3rd ed. London 1965.
Feine, Hans Erich. *Kirchliche Rechtsgeschichte: Die katholische
    Kirche.* 5th ed. Cologne 1972.
Felletti Maj, Bianca Maria. "Contributo alla iconografia del IV secolo
    d. C.: Il ritratto femminile." *Critica d'arte* 6 (1941) 74-90.
Felletti Maj, Bianca Maria. *Iconografia romana imperiale da Severo
    Alessandro a M. Aurelio Carino (225-285 d. C.).* Rome 1958.
*Festschrift zur 900-Jahrfeier der Pfarrei St. Helena im heiligen
    Jahr 1975.* Trier-Euren: Pfarrgemeinde St. Helena, 1975.
Fillitz, Hermann. *Die Insignien und Kleinodien des Heiligen
    Römischen Reiches.* Vienna 1954.
Fillitz, Hermann. *Das Mittelalter* I. *Propyläen Kunstgeschichte* V.
    Berlin 1969.
Finegan, Jack. *The Archeology of the New Testament: The Life of
    Jesus and the Beginning of the Early Church.* Princeton 1969.

Fiocco, Giuseppe. *Paolo Veronese, 1528-1588.* Bologna 1928.

Fischer, Balthasar. "Die Elfenbeintafeln des Trierer Domschatzes: Zu ihrer jüngsten Deutung durch Stylianos Pelekanides, 1952." *Kurtrierisches Jahrbuch* 9 (1969) 5-19.

Fischer, Eugen Heinrich. "Gregor der Grosse und Byzanz." *ZRG, K. Abt.* 36 (1950) 15-144.

Fittschen, Klaus, and Paul Zanker. *Katalog der römischen Porträts in den Capitolinischen Museen und den anderen kommunalen Sammlungen der Stadt Rom* III: *Kaiserinnen- und Prinzessinnenbildnisse, Frauenporträts.* Mainz 1983.

Fleith, Barbara. "Le classement des quelque 1000 manuscrits de la *Legenda aurea* latine en vue de l'établissement d'une histoire de la tradition." In Brenda Dunn-Lardeau, ed., *Legenda aurea: Sept siècles de diffusion* (Montreal and Paris 1986) 19-24.

Focillon, Henri. *Piero della Francesca.* Paris 1952.

Follieri, Enrica. *Initia Hymnorum Ecclesiae Graecae.* 5 vols. *Studi e Testi* 211-15 bis. Vatican City 1960-1966.

Font, Lamberto. *Gerona: La Catedral y el Museo Diocesano.* Gerona 1952.

Fontanini, Giusto. (Fontaninus, Iustus), *Codex constitutionum quas summi pontifices ediderunt in solemni canonizatione sanctorum.* Rome 1729.

Forsyth, George H. "The Monastery of St. Catherine at Mount Sinai: The Church and Fortress of Justinian." *DOP* 22 (1968) 1-19.

Forsyth, George H., and Kurt Weitzmann. *The Monastery of Saint Catherine at Mount Sinai: The Church and Fortress of Justinian.* I: Plates. Ann Arbor 1973.

Fowler, Alastair. *A History of English Literature.* Cambridge, Massachusetts, 1987.

Franchi de' Cavalieri, Pio Petro. "I funerali ed il sepolcro di Constantino Magno." *MEFR* 36 (1916-1917) 205-61.

Franchi de' Cavalieri, Pio Petro. "Il sarcofago di S. Helena prima dei restauri del secolo XVIII." *NBAC* 1921, pp. 15-38 and pls. 7-8.

Franchi de' Cavalieri, Pio Petro. See *Il menologio di Basilio II.*

Francia, Ennio. *Tesori della Pinacoteca Vaticana.* Milan 1964.

Francis, Robert B. *The Medieval Churches of Cyprus.* London 1948.

Franz, Adolph. *Die kirchlichen Benediktionen im Mittelalter.* 2 vols. Freiburg 1909; repr. Graz 1960.

Franz, Heinrich Gerhard. "Stileinflüsse im italienischen Frühwerk des Peter Paul Rubens." *Forschungen und Fortschritte* 24 (1948)

225-29.

Franzoi, Umberto, and Dina di Stefano. *Le chiese di Venezia.*
Venice 1976.

Fremantle, Richard. *Florentine Gothic Painters: From Giotto to
Masaccio.* London 1975.

Fremersdorf, Fritz. *Ältestes Christentum mit besonderer Berück-
sichtigung der Grabungsergebnisse unter der Severinskirche in
Köln.* Berlin 1956. Also in *Kölner Jb. für Vor- und
Frühgeschichte* 2 (1956) 7-26. Cited from the monograph.

Frend, W. H. C. *The Rise of Christianity.* Philadelphia 1984.

Frolow, Anatole. "La Vraie Croix et les expéditions d'Héraclius en
Perse." *REB* 11 (1953) 88-105.

Frolow, Anatole. *La relique de la Vraie Croix: Recherches sur le
développement d'un culte. Archives de l'Orient chrétien 7.*
Paris 1961.

Frolow, Anatole. *Les reliquaires de la Vraie Croix. Archives de
l'Orient chrétien 8.* Paris 1965.

Frühchristliche Kunst aus Rom. Exhibition catalogue, Essen 1962.

Führer zu vor- und frühgeschichtlichen Denkmälern 32: Trier. 2 vols.
Mainz 1977.

Führer zu vor- und frühgeschichtlichen Denkmälern 38: Köln II.
Mainz 1980. 191-204 by Hansgerd Hellenkemper. 204-11 by
Werner Schäfke.

Furtwängler, Adolf. *Die antiken Gemmen.* 3 vols. Leipzig 1900.

Gaborit-Chopin, Danielle, *Ivories du Moyen Âge.* Fribourg,
Switzerland, 1978. German: *Elfenbeinkunst im Mittelalter.*
Berlin 1978. Cited from the German ed.

Galbraith, Vivian Hunter. *Roger Wendover and Matthew Paris.*
Glasgow 1944.

Galey, John. *Sinai and the Monastery of St. Catherine.* Garden City,
New York, 1980.

Gallagher, Donat, ed. *The Essays, Articles and Reviews of Evelyn
Waugh.* London 1983.

Gallo, Rodolfo. *Il tesoro di San Marco e la sua storia.* Venice 1967.

Gams, Pius Bonifacius. *Series Episcoporum Ecclesiae Catholicae.*
Regensburg 1873; repr. Graz 1957.

Gannon, Michael V. *The Cross in the Sand: The Early Catholic
Church in Florida, 1513-1870.* Gainesville 1965.

Gannon, Michael V. "Altar and Hearth: The Coming of Christianity,
1521-1565." *The Florida Historical Quarterly* 44 (1965-1966)
17-44.

Gardner, Arthur. *Medieval Sculpture in France.* Cambridge 1931;

repr. New York 1969.

Gardner, Arthur. *English Medieval Sculpture.* Cambridge 1951. First published 1935 as *A Handbook of English Medieval Sculpture.* Cited from the 1951 ed.

Gardner, Helen. "The Dream of the Rood." In W. W. Robson, ed., *Essays and Poems presented to Lord David Cecil* (London 1970) 18-36.

Garenfeld, Victor. Die Trierer Bischöfe des vierten Jahrhunderts. Dissertation Bonn 1888.

Garidis, Miltiadis. "La peinture Cypriote de la fin du XVᵉ - debut du XVIᵉ siècle, et sa place dans les tendances générales de la peinture Orthodoxe après la chute de Constantinople." In Πρακτικὰ τοῦ Πρώτου Διεθνοῦς Κυπρολογικοῦ Συνεδρίου (Λευκωσία 1969), (Nicosia 1972) II 25-32.

Gatch, Milton McC. *Preaching and Theology in Anglo-Saxon England: Ælfric and Wulfstan.* Toronto 1977.

Gaudemet, Jean, ed. *Conciles Gaulois du IVᵉ siècle. Sources Chrétiennes* 241. Paris 1977.

Gauthier, Marie-Madeline S. Émaux du moyen âge occidental. 2nd ed. Fribourg 1972.

Gauthier, Marie-Madeline S. *Les routes de la foi.* Fribourg 1983. German: *Strassen des Glaubens.* Aschaffenburg 1983. Cited from the French ed.

Gauthier, Maximilien. *Palais et Musée du Louvre* II. Paris 1962. English: *The Louvre: Paintings.* New York 1964. Cited from the English ed.

Gauthier, Nancy. *L'évangélisation des pays de la Moselle.* Paris 1980.

Gauthier, Nancy. *Topographie chrétienne des cités de la Gaule des origines au millieu du VIIIᵉ siècle* I: *Province ecclésiastique de Trèves (Belgica Prima).* Paris 1986.

Gayarré, Charles. *History of Louisiana.* 4 vols. 3rd ed. New Orleans 1885; repr. New York 1972.

Geary, Patrick J. "Saint Helen of Athyra and the Cathedral of Troyes in the Thirteenth Century." *JMRS* 7 (1977) 149-68.

Geary, Patrick J. *Furta Sacra: Thefts of Relics in the Central Middle Ages.* Princeton 1978.

Geary, Patrick J. "The Ninth-Century Relic Trade." In James Obelkevich, ed., *Religion and the People 800-1700* (Chapel Hill 1979) 8-19.

Gedenkschrift zur Sechshundert-Jahrfeier der St. Helena Bruderschaft Xanten. Xanten 1963.

Geiger, Maynard J. *The Franciscan Conquest of Florida (1573-1618)*. Washington, D.C., 1937.

Gelderblom, Bernhard. "Die Kriegsschäden am Bonner Münster." *Bonner Geschichtsblätter* 3 (1947) 151-55. Also in *Bonn und sein Münster* (Festschrift Johannes Hinsenkamp; Bonn 1947) 151-55.

Gem, S. Harvey. *An Anglo-Saxon Abbot: Ælfric of Eynsham*. Edinburgh 1912.

George, Judith. *Venantius Fortunatus: A Latin Poet in Merovingian Gaul*. Oxford 1992.

Gerhardt, Joachim. *Die spätromanischen Wandmalereien im Dome zu Braunschweig*. Hildesheim 1934.

Gerkan, Armin von. "St. Gereon in Köln." *Germania* 29 (1951) 215-18.

Gerkan, Armin von. "Der Urbau der Kirche St. Gereon in Köln." In *Neue Beiträge zur Kunstgeschichte des 1. Jahrtausends* I.1: *Spätantike und Byzanz = Forschungen zur Kunstgeschichte und christlichen Archäologie* I (Baden-Baden 1952) 91-102.

Gerke, Friedrich. *Spätantike und frühes Christentum*. Baden-Baden 1967.

Gerould, Gordon Hall. *The North-English Homily Collection*. Oxford 1902.

Gerould, Gordon Hall. *Saints' Legends*. Boston 1916.

Ghellinck, Joseph de. *Littérature latine au moyen âge*. 2 vols. Paris 1939; repr. Hildesheim 1969.

Giannelli, Cyrus. *Codices vaticani Graeci: Codices 1485-1683*. Vatican City 1950.

Gibbon, Edward. *The Decline and Fall of the Roman Empire*. Modern Library ed. 2 vols. New York 1932.

Gier, Helmut, and Johannes Janota, edd. *Von der Augsburger Bibelhandschrift zu Bertolt Brecht*. Weissenhorn 1991.

Gierlich, Ernst. *Die Grabstätten der rheinischen Bischöfe vor 1200. Quellen und Abhandlungen zur mittelrheinischen Kirchengeschichte* 65. Mainz 1990.

Giesen, Josef. "Die HELENA DE BRITANIA des Meisters von St. Severin." *Jb. des Kölnischen Geschichtsvereins* 25 (1950) 145-52.

Gilbert, Colleen B. *A Bibliography of the Works of Dorothy L. Sayers*. Hamden, Connecticut, 1978.

Gill, Joseph. *Personalities of the Council of Florence*. Oxford and New York 1964.

Gilles, Karl-Josef. *Münzprägung im römischen und mittelalterlichen Trier*. Trier-Texte 3. Trier 1983.

Ginzburg, Carlo. *Indagini su Piero*. Turin 1981. English: *The Enigma of Piero: Piero della Francesca*. London 1985. Cited from the English ed.

Giovanni, Luciano, ed. *Arts of Cappadocia*. London 1971. German: *Kunst in Kappadokien*. Geneva 1972. Cited from the English ed.

Glaube, Heinz, and Eugen Wirth. *Aleppo*. Wiesbaden 1984.

Glier, Ingeborg. *Die deutsche Literatur im späten Mittelalter, 1250-1370*, II. *Geschichte der deutschen Literatur von den Anfängen bis zur Gegenwart*, founded by Helmut de Boor and Richard Newald, III. 2. Munich 1987.

Gnecchi, Francesco. *I medaglioni Romani descritti ed illustrati*. 3 vols. Milan 1912.

Gnilka, Christian. "Altersversorgung." In *RAC*, suppl. 1-2 (1985) 266-89.

Godfrey, John. *The Church in Anglo-Saxon England*. Cambridge 1962.

Godman, Peter. *Poets and Emperors: Frankish Politics and Carolingian Poetry*. Oxford 1987.

Görlach, Manfred. *The South English Legendary, Gilte Legende and Golden Legend*. Braunschweig 1972.

Görlach, Manfred. *The Textual Tradition of the South English Legendary*. Leeds 1974.

Görlach, Manfred. "The *Legenda aurea* and the Early History of *The South English Legendary*," in Brenda Dunn-Lardeau, *Legenda aurea: Sept siècles de diffusion* (Montreal and Paris 1986) 301-16.

Goerz, Adam. *Regesten der Erzbischöfe zu Trier von Hetti bis Johann II., 814-1503*. Trier 1861; repr. Aalen 1969.

Goffart, Walter. "The Fredegar-Problem Reconsidered." *Speculum* 38 (1963) 206-41.

Goldschmidt, Adolph, and Kurt Weitzmann. *Die byzantinischen Elfenbeinskulpturen des X.-XIII. Jahrhunderts*. 2 vols. 2nd ed. Berlin 1979.

Goodacre, Hugh. *Handbook of the Coinages of the Byzantine Empire*. 3 vols. London 1928-1933; repr. 1957 in 1 vol. Cited from the reprint.

Gordon, Arthur E. *Illustrated Introduction to Latin Epigraphy*. Berkeley 1983.

Gosse, Philip. *St. Helena, 1502-1938*. London 1938.

Goudard, Joseph. *La Sainte Vierge au Liban.* Paris 1908.
  Adaptation: Joseph Goudard and Henry Jalabert, *Lebanon:
  The Land and the Lady.* Beirut and Chicago 1966. Cited
  from the 1908 ed.

Gould, Cecil. *National Gallery Catalogues: the Sixteenth Century
  Italian Schools.* London 1975.

Grabar, André. *L'empereur dans l'art byzantin.* Paris 1936; repr.
  London 1971.

Grabar, André. *Martyrium: Recherches sur le culte de reliques et
  l'art chrétien antique.* 3 vols. Paris 1943-1946; repr. London
  1972.

Grabar, André. *La peinture Byzantine.* Geneva 1953. English:
  Byzantine Painting. New York 1953. Cited from the English
  ed.

Grabar, André. *Byzantium: From the Death of Theodosius to the Rise
  of Islam.* London 1966. U. S. ed.: *The Golden Age of
  Justinian: From the Death of Theodosius to the Rise of Islam.*
  New York 1967. Cited from the U.S. ed.

Gradara, Costanza. "I sarcofagi Vaticani di Sant' Elena e di Santa
  Costanza." *NBAC* 20: 3-4 (1914) 43-49.

Graf, Georg. *Geschichte der christlichen arabischen Literatur.* 5
  vols. Vatican City 1944-1953; repr. 1975.

Gransden, Antonia. Historical Writing in England. 2 vols. London
  and Ithaca 1974-1982.

Grant, Michael. *The Fall of the Roman Empire: A Reappraisal.*
  Radnor, Pennsylvania, 1976.

Graus, František. *Herrscher, Volk und Heiliger im Reich der
  Merowinger.* Prague 1965.

Gray, John. *A History of Jerusalem.* London and New York 1969.

Greenfield, Stanley B., and Daniel C. Calder. *A New Critical History
  of Old English Literature.* New York 1986.

Gregorietti, Guido. *Il gioiello nei secoli.* Milan 1969. English:
  Jewelry through the Ages. New York 1969. Cited from the
  English ed.

Gregorovius, Ferdinand. *Athenaïs: Geschichte einer byzantinischen
  Kaiserin.* Leipzig 1882. 3rd ed. 1892. Cited from the lst ed.

Gregorovius, Ferdinand. *Geschichte der Stadt Rom im Mittelalter.* 8
  vols. 4th-5th ed. Stuttgart 1903-1910. English: *History of
  the City of Rome in the Middle Ages.* 8 vols. in 13. London
  1896-1902. Cited from the English ed.

Gretz, Gertie, and Otto Koch. *St. Gereon zu Köln.* Bonn 1939.

Grierson, Philip. "The Tombs and Obits of the Byzantine Emperors

(337-1042)." *DOP* 16 (1962) 1-60.

Grierson, Philip. *Byzantine Coins.* Berkeley and London 1982.

Griffe, Élie. "Le *Liber Pontificalis* au temps du pape saint Grégoire," *BLE* 57 (1956) 65-70.

Grigioni, Carlo. *Marco Palmezzano.* Faenza 1956.

Grillmeyer, Aloys, and Heinrich Bacht, edd. *Das Konzil von Chalkedon: Geschichte und Gegenwart.* 3 vols. Würzburg 1951-1954; repr. 1962.

Grisar, Hartmann. *Il Sancta Sanctorum ed il suo tesoro sacro.* Rome 1907. German: *Die römische Kapelle Sancta Sanctorum und ihr Schatz.* Freiburg 1908. Cited from the German ed.

Griscom, Acton, ed. *The Historia Regum Britanniae of Geoffrey of Monmouth.* New York 1929.

Grodecki, Louis, Françoise Perrot, and Jean Talaron. *Les vitraux de Paris, de la région Parisienne, de la Picardie, et du Nord-Pas-de Calais. Corpus vitrearum Medii Aevi, Série complémentaire. Recensement des vitraux anciens de la France* I. Paris 1978.

Gröber, Gustav. *Übersicht über die lateinische Litteratur von der Mitte des VI. Jahrhunderts bis zur Mitte des XIV. Jahrhunderts.* First published as *Grundriss der romanischen Philologie* II.1, Strassburg 1902; repr. Munich 1963.

Grosche, Robert. "Zur Wiederherstellung des Inneren von St. Gereon zu Köln." *Das Münster* 15 (1962) 279-89.

Gross, Bredan J. "De H. Helena in de Aracoelikerk te Rome." *Clairlieu* 38 (1980) 101-103.

Grünewald, Thomas. *Constantinus Maximus Augustus: Herrschafts-propaganda in der zeitgenössischen Überlieferung. Historia Einzelschriften* 64. Stuttgart 1990.

Grünewald, Thomas. "'Constantinus Novus': Zum Constantin-Bild des Mittelalters." In Giorgio Bonamente and Franca Fusco, edd., *Costantino il Grande dall'antichità all'umanesimo* (Università degli studi di Macerata, *Publicazioni della facoltà di lettere e filosofia* 67; Macerata 1992) I 461-85.

Grumel, Venance. "A propos de la plaque d'ivoire de Trèves." *REB* 12 (1954) 187-90.

Grumel, Venance. "La reposition de la vraie Croix à Jérusalem par Héraclius: Le jour et l'année." *Byzantinische Forschungen* 1 (1966) 139-49.

Gudiol i Ricart, José. *Arte de España: Cataluña.* Barcelona 1955.

Gugitz, Gustav. "Niederösterreichische Schalensteine im Volksglauben." *Österreichische Zeitschrift für Volkskunde* 53,

n. s. 4 (1950) 97-112.

Gugitz, Gustav. *Österreichs Gnadenstätten in Kult und Brauch*. 2 vols. Vienna 1955-1958.

Guilland, Rodolphe. *Études de topographie de Constantinople byzantine*. 2 vols. Amsterdam 1969.

Guillou, André. "Le monastère de la Théotokos au Sinaï." *MélRome* 67 (1955) 217-58.

Gunnis, Rupert. *Historic Cyprus*. London 1936.

Gustafson, Alrik. *A History of Swedish Literature*. Minneapolis 1961.

Guyer, S. "La Madrasa al-Halâwiyya à Alep." *BIFAO* 11 (1914) 217-31.

Guyon, Jean. *Le cimetière aux deux lauriers: Recherches sur les catacombs romaines*. *Roma Sotterranea Cristiana* VIII. Vatican City 1987. Also *Bibliothèque des Écoles Françaises d'Athènes et de Rome* 264. Rome 1987.

Gwatkin, H. M., and J. P. Whitney, edd. *The Cambridge Medieval History* I. 2nd ed. Cambridge 1924; repr. 1967.

Haass, Robert. *Die Kreuzherren in den Rheinlanden*. *Rheinisches Archiv* 23. Bonn 1932.

Habicht, V. Curt. *Die mittelalterliche Malerei Niedersachsens* I: *Von den Anfängen bis um 1450*. *Beiträge zur niedersächsischen Kunstgeschichte* IV. Strassburg 1919.

Hackenbroch, Yvonne. *Italienisches Email des frühen Mittelalters*. Basel 1938.

Hackett, John. *A History of the Orthodox Church of Cyprus*. London 1901.

Hamilton, Robert William. "Excavations in the Atrium of the Church of the Nativity, Bethlehem." *QDAP* 3 (1934) 1-8.

Hamilton, Robert William. *The Church of the Nativity, Bethlehem*. Jerusalem 1947.

Hammer, Jacob, ed. *Geoffrey of Monmouth, Historia Regum Britaniae: A Variant Version*. Cambridge, Massachusetts, 1951.

Hammer, William. "The Concept of the New or Second Rome in the Middle Ages." *Speculum* 19 (1944) 50-62.

Hamza ibn al-Hasan, or Hamza al-Isfahani. *Annales*. Arabic text and Latin translation by J. M. E. Gottwaldt. 2 vols. in 1. St. Petersburg and Leipzig 1844-1849; repr. Beirut 1961.

Handbuch des Erzbistums Köln. 26th ed. I: *Geschichtlicher Teil*. Cologne: Erzbischöfliches Generalvikariat, 1966.

Hanfmann, George M. A. *From Croesus to Constantine*. Ann Arbor 1975.

Hanning, Robert W. *The Vision of History in Early Britain: From*

Gildas to Geoffrey of Monmouth. New York 1966.

Hanson, R. P. C. "The Fate of Eustathius of Antioch." *ZKG* 95 (1984) 171-79.

Hanson, R. P. C. *The Search for the Christian Doctrine of God: The Arian Controversy 318-381.* Edinburgh 1988.

Harbeck, Alois. *Die Fresken von Januarius Zick in Wiblingen und die Problematik illusionistischer Deckengestaltung.* Dissertation Munich 1966.

Hare, Thomas Leman. *The National Gallery: One Hundred Plates in Colour.* 2 vols. London 1909.

Harnack, Adolf von. *Lehrbuch der Dogmengeschichte.* 3 vols. 4th ed. Tübingen 1909-1910; repr. Darmstadt 1964.

Hartt, Frederick. *History of Italian Renaissance Art.* 4th ed. New York 1994.

Harvey, William. *Structural Survey of the Church of the Nativity, Bethlehem.* London 1935.

Hauptmann, Felix. "Die Helenakapelle in Bonn." *Bonner Archiv* 4 (1912) 60-62.

Hay, Denys, ed. *The Anglica Historia of Polydore Vergil, A.D. 1485-1537.* Camden Series LXXIV. London 1950.

Hay, Denis. *Polydore Vergil, Renaissance Historian and Man of Letters.* Oxford 1952.

Heath, Jeffrey. *The Picturesque Prison: Evelyn Waugh and His Writing.* Kingston and Montreal 1982.

Hefele, Karl Joseph von, and Henri Leclercq. *Histoire des conciles.* 11 vols. in 22. Paris 1907-1952: repr. Hildesheim 1973.

Heffernan, Thomas J. "Additional Evidence for a More Specific Date of the South English Legendary." *Traditio* 35 (1979) 345-51.

Hegel, Eduard. "Die rheinische Kirche in römischer und frühfränkischer Zeit." In Victor H. Elbern, ed., *Das erste Jahrtausend: Kultur und Kunst im werdenden Abendland an Rhein und Ruhr* (3 vols.; Düsseldorf 1962-1964) I 93-113.

Hegel, Eduard, ed. *Geschichte des Erzbistums Köln* I. 2nd ed. by Friedrich Wilhelm Oediger. Cologne 1972.

Hegemann, Hans-Werner. *Das Elfenbein in Kunst und Kultur Europas.* Mainz 1988.

Heid, Stefan. "Der Ursprung der Helenalegende im Pilgerbetrieb Jerusalems." *JbAC* 32 (1989) 41-71.

Heid, Stefan. "Zur frühen Protonike- und Kyriakoslegende." *Anal. Boll.* 109 (1991) 73-108.

Heilig-Kreuz-Kirche Landsberg a. Lech. Munich and Zurich 1986.

Heinen, Heinz. *Trier und das Trevererland in römischer Zeit.* 2000

Jahre Trier I. Trier 1985.

Heiniger, Ernst A., and Jean. *The Great Book of Jewels*. Lausanne 1974.

Heintze, Helga von. *Römische Porträt-Plastik aus sieben Jahrhunderten*. Stuttgart 1961.

Heintze, Helga von. *Die antiken Porträts der landgräflich-hessischen Sammlungen in Schloss Fasanerie bei Fulda*. Mainz 1968.

Heintze, Helga von. "Ein spätantikes Mädchenporträt in Bonn: Zur stilistischen Entwicklung des Frauenbildnisses im 4. und 5. Jahrhundert." *JbAC* 14 (1971) 61-91.

Heinzelmann, Martin. *Translationsberichte und andere Quellen des Reliquienkultes*. Turnhout 1979.

Heisenberg, August. *Grabeskirche und Apostelkirche: Zwei Basiliken Konstantins*. 2 vols. Leipzig 1908.

Helbig, Wolfgang. *Führer durch die öffentlichen Sammlungen klassischer Altertümer in Rom*. 4th ed. by Hermine Speier. 4 vols. Tübingen 1963-1972.

Henderson, George. *Style and Civilization: Early Medieval*. Harmondsworth, Middlesex, 1972.

Hendy, Michael F. *Coinage and Money in the Byzantine Empire, 1081-1261*. *Dumbarton Oaks Studies* XIII. Washington, D. C., 1969.

Hendy, Philip. *Piero della Francesca and the Early Renaissance*. London and New York 1968.

Henken, Elissa R. *The Welsh Saints: A Study in Patterned Lives*. Woodridge, Suffolk, 1991.

Henry, Patrick. "Initial Eastern Assessments of the Seventh Oecumenical Council." *JThS*, n.s. 25 (1974) 75-92.

Herrin, Judith. *The Formation of Christendom*. Princeton 1987.

Heseler, Peter. "Zur Vita Constantini et matris Helenae des Ignatius von Selymbra (*B. H. Gr.* 362)." *BNJ* 9 (1930) 320-37.

Heyer, Friedrich. *Kirchengeschichte des Heiligen Landes*. Stuttgart 1984.

Hibbard, Howard. *Bernini*. Harmondsworth, Middlesex, 1965.

Hilger, Hans Peter. *Der Dom zu Xanten*. *Die Blauen Bücher*. Königstein im Taunus 1984.

Hilger, Hans Peter. *Der Dom zu Xanten*. 3rd ed. *Rheinische Kunststätten* 275. Cologne 1985.

Hill, Sir George. *A History of Cyprus* I. Cambridge 1940; repr. 1949.

Historia del arte hispánico. 6 vols. in 7. 1st- 2nd ed. Madrid 1978-1982.

Hitti, Philip K. *The Near East in History: A 5000 Year Story.* Princeton 1961.

Hocker, Nikolaus. "Sagen von der Mosel." *Zeitschrift für deutsche Mythologie und Sittenkunde* 1 (1853) 189-95.

Hodgkin, Robert Howard. *A History of the Anglo-Saxons.* 2 vols. 3rd ed. London 1952.

Höroldt, Dietrich. "Das Stift St. Cassius in Bonn." *Bonner Geschichtsblätter* 11 (1957) 1-387.

Hoffmann, Konrad. *The Year 1200* I: *A Centennial Exhibition at the Metropolitan Museum of Art.* New York 1970.

Hofmann, Hans. *Die Heiligen Drei Könige: Zur Heiligenverehrung im kirchlichen, gesellschaftlichen und politischen Leben des Mittelalters.* Rheinisches Archiv 94. Bonn 1975.

Hofmann, Sigfrid. *Landsberg am Lech.* 3rd ed. Munich 1983.

Holder, Alfred. *Inventio Sanctae Crucis: Actorum Cyriaci Pars 1.* Leipzig 1889.

Holl, Adolf. *Der letzte Christ.* Stuttgart 1979. English: *The Last Christian.* Garden City, New York, 1980. Cited from the English ed.

Holtzmann, Robert. *Geschichte der sächsischen Kaiserzeit (900-1024).* 4th ed. Munich 1961.

Holum, Kenneth G. *Theodosian Empresses: Women and Imperial Dominion in Late Antiquity.* Berkeley 1982.

Holum, Kenneth G., and Gary Vikan. "The Trier Ivory, *Adventus* Ceremonial, and the Relics of St. Stephen." *DOP* 33 (1979) 113-33 with 11 figs.

Holzapfel, Heribert. *Handbuch der Geschichte des Franziskaner-ordens.* Freiburg 1909. Latin: *Manuale Historiae Ordinis Fratrum Minorum.* Freiburg 1909. English: *The History of the Franciscan Order.* Teutopolis, Illinois, 1948. Cited from the German ed.

Holzhausen, Walter. "Das Innere des Bonner Münsters: Zu einem Gemälde des 17. Jahrhunderts." *AHVNrh.* 155-56 (1954) 559-67.

Home, Gordon. *Roman York.* London 1924.

Home, Gordon. *Cyprus Then and Now.* London 1960.

Hontheim, Johann Nikolaus von. *Historia Trevirensis Diplomatica et Pragmatica.* 3 vols. Augsburg 1750.

Horstmann, Carl, ed. *Altenglische Legenden: Neue Folge.* Heilbronn 1881.

Hoster, Joseph. *Der Dom zu Köln.* Cologne 1965.

Howorth, Henry H. *Saint Augustine of Canterbury.* London 1913.

Huber, Paul. *Heilige Berge: Sinai, Athos, Golgota: Ikonen, Fresken, Miniaturen.* 2nd ed. Zürich 1982.

Huber, Raphael M. *A Documented History of the Franciscan Order, 1182-1517.* Milwaukee and Washington, D. C., 1944.

Hubert, Jean, Jean Porcher, and Wolfgang Friedrich Volbach. *L'empire carolingien.* Paris 1968. English: *The Carolingian Renaissance. The Arts of Mankind.* New York 1970. Cited from the English ed.

Hülsen, Christian. *La pianta di Roma dell'anonimo einsidlense.* Rome 1907.

Hülsen, Christian. *Le chiese di Roma nel medio evo: Cataloghi ed appunti.* Florence 1927; repr. Hildesheim 1975.

Hürliman, Martin, and Jean Bony. *French Cathedrals.* 2nd ed. London 1967.

Hugot, Leo. *Aachen-Kornelimünster.* 2nd ed. *Rheinische Kunststätten* 66. Cologne 1979.

Humann, Georg. *Die Kunstwerke der Münsterkirche in Essen.* Düsseldorf 1904.

Hunger, Herbert. *Reich der neuen Mitte.* Graz 1965.

Hunger, Herbert. *Die hochsprachliche profane Literatur der Byzantiner.* 2 vols. *Byzantinisches Handbuch* V. 1-2. *Handbuch der Altertumswissenschaft* XII.5.1-2. Munich 1978.

Hunt, David, ed. *Footprints in Cyprus: An Illustrated History.* 2nd ed. London 1990.

Hunt, E. D. *Holy Land Pilgrimage in the Later Roman Empire AD 312-460.* Oxford 1982.

Huppertz, Andreas. *Der Kölner Dom und seine Kunstschätze.* Cologne 1950.

Hurt, James. *Ælfric.* New York 1972.

Huse, Norbert, and Wolfgang Wolters. *Venedig: Die Kunst der Renaissance: Architektur, Skulptur, Malerei 1460-1590.* Munich 1986. English: *The Art of Renaissance Venice: Architecture, Sculpture and Painting, 1460-1590.* Chicago 1990. Cited from the English ed.

Hussey, Joan Mervyn. *The Orthodox Church in the Byzantine Empire.* Oxford 1986.

Ianulardo, Elena. *Santa Elena.* Foggia 1958.

Imelou, Stephanos D. Ἀπὸ τὴν ἐπίσκεψιν τῆς ἁγίας Ἐλένης εἰς τὴν Κύπρον. Κυπριακὸς Λόγος 12 (69-72), May-December 1980, pp. 367-71.

Inan, Jale, and Elisabeth Rosenbaum. *Roman and Early Byzantine Portrait Sculpture in Asia Minor.* London 1966.

Inglisian, Vahan. "Die armenische Literatur." In *Handbuch der Orientalistik,* ed. B. Spuler, I.7 (Leiden 1963) 156-250.

Irsch, Nikolaus. *Der Dom zu Trier. Die Kunstdenkmäler der Rheinprovinz* XIII.1. Düsseldorf 1931; repr. Trier 1984.

Iserloh, Erwin. "Der Heilige Rock und die Wallfahrt nach Trier." *Geist und Leben: Zeitschrift für Aszese und Mystik* 32 (Würzburg 1959) 271-79. Repr. in Erwin Iserloh, *Verwirklichung des Christlichen im Wandel der Geschichte,* ed. Klaus Wittstadt (Würzburg 1975) 24-32. Cited from the original.

Jaffé, Michael. *Rubens and Italy.* Ithaca 1977.

Jaffé, Philipp. *Regesta Pontificum Romanorum.* 2 vols. 2nd ed. Leipzig 1885-1888; repr. Graz 1956.

Janin, Raymond. "Les couvents secondaires de Psamathia." *EO* 32 (1932) 325-39.

Janin, Raymond. "Les églises byzantines des saints militaires." *EO* 34 (1935) 56-70.

Janin, Raymond. "Églises et monastères de Constantinople byzantine." *REB* 9 (1951) 143-53.

Janin, Raymond. *Constantinople byzantine. Archives de l'orient chrétien* 4. 2nd ed. Paris 1964.

Janin, Raymond. *La géographie ecclésiastique de l'empire byzantin* I: *Le siège de Constantinople et le patriarcat oecuménique.* 3: *Les églises et les monastères.* 2nd ed. Paris 1969.

Janin, Raymond. *Les églises et les monastères des grands centres byzantins. La géographie ecclésiastique de l'empire byzantin* II. Paris 1975.

Jankofsky, Klaus P. "*Legenda aurea* Materials in *The South English Legendary.*" In Brenda Dunn-Lardeau, *Legenda aurea: Sept siècles de diffusion* (Montreal and Paris 1986) 317-29.

Jansson, Valter. "Fornsvenska Legendariet." In *Kulturhistoriskt Lexikon för Nordisk Medeltid* IV (Malmö 1959) 518-22.

Jayne, Kingsley Garland. *Vasco da Gama and His Successors: 1460-1580.* London 1910; repr. New York and London 1970.

Jedin, Hubert, ed. *Handbuch der Kirchengeschichte.* 7 vols. in 10. Freiburg 1962-1979. Vol. I, 1962, by Karl Baus. Vol. II.1, 1973, by Karl Baus and Eugen Ewig.

Jedin, Hubert. *Kardinal Caesar Baronius: Der Anfang der katholischen Kirchengeschichtsschreibung im 16. Jahrhundert.* Münster 1978.

Jenkinson, Wilberforce. *London Churches before the Great Fire.* London 1917.

Jeremy, Sister Mary. "The English Prose Translation of the *Legenda Aurea.*" *MLN* 59 (1944) 181-83.

Jeremy, Sister Mary. "Caxton's *Golden Legend* and Varagine's *Legenda Aurea.*" *Speculum* 21 (1946) 212-21.

Jeremy, Sister Mary. "Caxton's *Golden Legend* and de Vignai's *Légende Dorée.*" *Mediaeval Studies* 8 (1946) 97-106.

Jerphanion, Guillaume de. *Une nouvelle province de l'art byzantin: Les églises rupestres de Cappadoce.* 2 vols. of text in 4; 3 vols. of pls. Paris 1925-1942.

Jerphanion, Guillaume de. "La date des plus récentes peintures de Toqale Kilissé en Cappadoce." *OCP* 2 (1936) 191-222.

Jerphanion, Guillaume de. "Les caractéristiques et les attributs des saints dans la peinture cappadociènne." *Anal. Boll.* 55 (1937) 1-28.

Jewell, Harry Herbert, and Frederick William Hasluck. *The Church of Our Lady of the Hundred Gates in Paros.* London 1920.

Joerres, P. *Urkundenbuch des Stiftes St. Gereon zu Köln.* Bonn 1893.

Johann Georg, Herzog zu Sachsen. *Der heilige Spyridon, seine Verehrung und Ikonographie.* Leipzig 1913.

Johnson, Guion Griffis. *A Social History of the Sea Islands, with Special Reference to St. Helena Island, South Carolina.* Chapel Hill, North Carolina, 1930; repr. New York 1969.

Johnson, Mark J. "Where Were Constantine I and Helena Buried?" *Latomus* 51 (1992) 145-50.

Jones, A. H. M. *Constantine and the Conversion of Europe.* London 1948; repr. New York 1962.

Jones, A. H. M. *The Later Roman Empire, 284-602.* 2 vols. Oxford 1964; repr. Baltimore 1986.

Jones, A. H. M. *The Cities of the Eastern Roman Provinces.* 2nd ed. Oxford 1971.

Jones, Henry Stuart. *A Catalogue of the Ancient Sculptures Preserved in the Municipal Collections of Rome: The Sculptures of the Museo Capitolino.* Oxford 1912.

Jones, Henry Stuart. *A Catalogue of the Ancient Sculptures Preserved in the Municipal Collections of Rome: The Sculptures of the Palazzo dei Conservatori.* Oxford 1926.

Jordan, Henri, and Christian Hülsen. *Topographie der Stadt Rom im Alterthum.* 2 vols. in 4. Berlin 1871-1907.

Jordan, William Chester. *Louis IX and the Challenge of the Crusade.* Princeton 1979.

Jounel, Pierre. "Le culte de la croix dans la liturgie romaine." *La*

Maison-Dieu 75 (1963) 68-91.

Judge, Joseph. "Exploring Our Forgotten Century." *National Geographic* 173:3 (March, 1988) 330-63.

Kaegi, Werner. "Vom Nachleben Constantins." *SZG* 8 (1958) 289-326.

Kähler, Heinz. *Die Stiftermosaiken in der konstantinischen Südkirche von Aquileia. Monumenta artis Romanae* 4. Cologne 1962.

Kähler, Heinz. *Die Hagia Sophia.* Berlin 1967.

Kähler, Heinz. *Die frühe Kirche: Kult und Kultraum.* Berlin 1972.

Kaftal, George. *Saints in Italian Art: Iconography of the Saints in Tuscan Painting.* Florence 1952.

Kaftal, George. *Saints in Italian Art: Iconography of the Saints in the Painting of North East Italy.* Florence 1978.

Kahsnitz, Rainer. "Zur Verkündigung im Zyklus der Kreuzlegende bei Piero della Francesca." In Florens Deuchler and Reiner Haussherr, edd., *Schülerfestgabe für Herbert von Einem* (Bonn 1965) 112-37.

Kaiser, Wilhelm Bernhard. "Der Trierer Ada-Kameo." In *Festgabe Wolfgang Jungandreas* (Trier 1964) 24-35.

Kajava, Mika. "Some Remarks on the Name and Origin of Helena Augusta." *Arctos* 19 (1985) 41-54.

Kakouri, Katerina I. Διονυσιακά. Athens 1963. English: *Dionysiaka: Aspects of Popular Thracian Religion of Today.* Athens 1965. Cited from the English ed.

Kaniuth, Agathe. *Die Beisetzung Konstantins des Grossen.* Breslau 1941; repr. Aalen 1974.

Kantorowicz, Ernst H. *Laudes Regiae.* Berkeley 1958.

Kaufmann, Hans. *Giovanni Lorenzo Bernini: Die figürlichen Kompositionen.* Berlin 1970.

Kazhdan, Alexander P. "Constantin imaginaire." *Byzantion* 57 (1987) 196-250.

Kazhdan, Alexander P. "Alexander the Monk." In *ODB* I 60.

Kazhdan, Alexander P. "Ol'ga." In *ODB* III 1522.

Keck, Andrew S., and Charles Rufus Morey. Review of Adolph Goldschmidt and Kurt Weitzmann, *Die byzantinischen Elfenbeinskulpturen des X.-XIII. Jahrhunderts,* vol. II. *ArtB* 17 (1935) 397-407.

Kee, Alistair. *Constantine versus Christ.* London 1982.

Kehrein, Joseph. *Lateinische Sequenzen des Mittelalters.* Mainz 1873; repr. Hildesheim 1969.

Keller, Adalbert von, ed. *Fastnachtspiele aus dem fünfzehnten Jahrhundert: Nachlese.* Stuttgart 1858; repr. Darmstadt 1965 and 1966.

Kellner, Karl Adam Heinrich. *Heortology: A History of the Christian Festivals from Their Origin to the Present Day.* London 1908.

Kelly, J. N. D. *Jerome: His Life, Writings, and Controversies.* New York 1975.

Kemp, Eric Waldram. *Canonization and Authority in the Western Church.* London 1948.

Kempf, Theodor Konrad. "Die altchristliche Bischofskirche Triers." *Trierer Theologische Zeitschrift, Pastor Bonus* 56 (1947) in 4 parts: 2-9, 33-37, 118-23, and 182-89.

Kempf, Theodor Konrad. "Die Deutung des römischen Kerns im Trierer Dom nach den Ausgrabungen von 1943-1946." *Das Münster* 1 (1947/48) 129-40.

Kempf, Theodor Konrad. "Jahresbericht 1941 bis 1944." *TZ* 18 (1949) 269-334.

Kempf, Theodor Konrad. "Die Erforschung einer altchristlichen Bischofskirche auf deutschem Boden." *Forschungen und Fortschritte* 26 (1950) 244-47.

Kempf, Theodor Konrad. "Neue Funde im Trierer Dombering." *Das Münster* 3 (1950) 52-53.

Kempf, Theodor Konrad. "Konstantinische Deckenmalereien aus dem Trierer Dom." *TZ* 19 (1950) 45-51. This volume of *TZ* was also published separately: *Aus der Schatzkammer des antiken Trier,* Trier 1951.

Kempf, Theodor Konrad. "Die vorläufigen Ergebnisse der Ausgrabungen auf dem Gelände des Trierer Domes." *Germania* 29 (1951) 47-58.

Kempf, Theodor Konrad. "Die konstantinische Doppelkirchenanlage in Trier und ihre Baugeschichte von 326 bis 1000." *Kunstchronik* 4 (1951) 107-109.

Kempf, Theodor Konrad. "Die altchristliche Bischofsstadt Trier." In *Trier: Ein Zentrum abendländischer Kultur. Rheinischer Verein für Denkmalpflege und Heimatschutz, Jb.* (1952) 47-64.

Kempf, Theodor Konrad. "Die Ausgrabungen am Trierer Dom und an der Liebfrauenkirche von 1943 bis 1950." In *Neue Beiträge zur Kunstgeschichte des 1. Jahrtausends* I.1: *Spätantike und Byzanz = Forschungen zur Kunstgeschichte und christlichen Archäologie* I (Baden-Baden 1952) 103-13.

Kempf, Theodor Konrad. "Neue Ergebnisse der Trierer Domgrabungen." *Kunstchronik* 6 (1953) 90-92.

Kempf, Theodor Konrad. "Trierer Domgrabungen 1943-1954." In:

Neue Ausgrabungen in Deutschland (Berlin 1958) 368-79.

Kempf, Theodor Konrad. Legende - Überlieferung - Forschung: *Untersuchungen über den Trierer Hl. Rock.* Trier: Bischöfliches Museum, 1959.

Kempf, Theodor Konrad. "Grundrissentwicklung und Baugeschichte des Trierer Domes." *Das Münster* 21 (1968) 1-32.

Kempf, Theodor Konrad. "Das Bild einer kaiserlichen Braut." *Kölner Römer-Illustrierte* 2 (1975) 175-76.

Kempf, Theodor Konrad. "Die Konstantinischen Deckenmalereien aus dem Trierer Dom." *Archäologisches Korrespondenzblatt* 7 (Mainz 1977) 147-59.

Kempf,Theodor Konrad. "Das Haus der heiligen Helena." *Neues Trierisches Jb.* 1979, Beiheft, 1-16.

Kempf, Theodor Konrad, and Wilhelm Reusch, edd. *Frühchristliche Zeugnisse im Einzugsgebiet von Rhein und Mosel.* Trier 1965.

Kennedy, Charles W. *The Earliest English Poetry.* London 1943; repr. 1971.

Kennedy, Charles W. *Early English Christian Poetry.* London 1952.

Kennedy, I. G. "Elsheimer: Two Predellas from the Frankfurt Tabernacle." *Burlington Magazine* 113 (1971) 92-96.

Kent, J. P. C. *Roman Coins.* London and New York 1978. A revised ed. of J. P. C. Kent, Bernhard Overbeck, and Armin U. Stylow, *Die römische Münze*, Munich 1973.

Kent, J. P. C., and K. S. Painter, edd. *Wealth of The Roman World: Gold and Silver AD 300-700.* London 1977.

Kentenich, Gottfried. *Geschichte der Stadt Trier.* Trier 1915; repr. 1979.

Kentenich, Gottfried. "Die älteste Nachricht über den Trierer Dom: Ein Beitrag zur Kritik Altmanns von Hautevillers." *TZ* 1 (1926) 87-92.

Kentenich, Gottfried. "Der Kult der Thebäer am Niederrhein: Ein Beitrag zur Heiligengeographie." *Rheinische Vierteljahrsblätter* 1 (1931) 339-50.

Ker, Neil R. *Catalogue of Manuscripts Containing Anglo-Saxon.* Oxford 1957.

Keresztes, Paul. *Constantine: A Great Christian Monarch and Apostle.* Amsterdam 1981.

Kerler, Dietrich Heinrich. *Die Patronate der Heiligen.* Ulm 1905.

Khitrovo, Sofia, ed. *Itinéraires russes en Orient* I.1. Geneva 1889.

Kienast, Dietmar. *Römische Kaisertabelle: Grundzüge einer römischen Kaiserchronologie.* Darmstadt 1990.

Kier, Hiltrud, and Ulrich Krings, edd. *Köln: Die romanischen*

Kirchen. 3 vols. *Stadtspuren: Denkmäler in Köln* I-III. Cologne 1984 ff. (vol. II not yet published).

Kightly, Charles. *Folk Heroes of Britain.* London 1982.

Kinross, Lord. *Hagia Sophia.* New York 1972.

Kirsch, Johann Peter (Giovanni). "Un cimitero romano cristiano con chiesa cimiteriale del IV° e V° secolo scoperto a Bonn sul Reno." *RACrist.* 9 (1932) 151-58.

Kirsch, Johann Peter (Giovanni). *Le catacombe romane.* Rome 1933. English: *The Catacombs of Rome.* Rome 1946. Cited from the English ed.

Kirschbaum, Engelbert. *Die Gräber der Apostelfürsten.* Frankfurt 1957. English: The Tombs of St. Peter and St. Paul. London 1959. Cited from the English ed.

Klamt, Johann-Christian. *Die mittelalterlichen Monumentalmalereien im Dom zu Braunschweig.* Berlin 1968.

Klapheck, Richard. *Der Dom zu Xanten und seine Kunstschätze.* Berlin 1930.

Klauser, Renate. "Zur Entwicklung des Heiligsprechungsverfahrens bis zum 13. Jahrhundert." *ZRG, K. Abt.* 40 (1954) 85-101.

Klauser, Theodor. "Die Liturgie der Heiligsprechung." In *Heilige Überlieferung,* Festschrift Ildefons Herwegen (Münster 1938) 212-33. Repr. in Theodor Klauser, Gesammelte Arbeiten (*JbAC,* Suppl. 3; Münster 1974) 161-76.

Klauser, Theodor. "Bemerkungen zur Geschichte der Bonner Martyrergräber." *Bonner Geschichtsblätter* 3 (1947) 35-41. Also in *Bonn und sein Münster (Festschrift Johannes Hinsankamp*; Bonn 1947) 35-41. Repr. in Theodor Klauser, *Gesammelte Arbeiten (JbAC,* Suppl. 3; Münster 1974) 310-13.

Klauser, Theodor. Review of Kähler, *Stiftermosaiken.* In *JbAC* 7 (1964) 158-61.

Klauser, Theodor. *Gesammelte Arbeiten zur Liturgiegeschichte, Kirchengeschichte und christlichen Archäologie.* Ed. Ernst Dassmann. *JbAC,* Suppl. 3. Münster 1974.

Klein, Adolf. *Der Dom zu Köln.* Cologne 1980.

Klein, Richard. "Helena II (Kaiserin)," in *RAC* XIV (1988) 355-75.

Klein, Richard. "Das Kirchenbauverständnis Constantins d. Gr. in Rom und in den östlichen Provinzen." In Christoph Börker and Michael Donderer, edd., *Das antike Rom und der Osten: Festschrift für Klaus Parlasca zum 65. Geburtstag* (Erlangen and Nuremberg 1990) 77-101.

Kleiner, Diana E. E. *Roman Sculpture.* New Haven 1992.

Kloos, Rudolf M. *Lambertus de Legia: De vita, translatione, inventione ac miraculis sancti Matthiae Apostoli libri quinque.* *Trierer theologische Studien* 8. Trier 1958.

Knauz, Nándor, and C. L. Dedek. *Monumenta Ecclesiae Stringoniensis.* 3 vols. Esztergom 1874-1924.

Knipping, Richard. *Die Regesten der Erzbischöfe von Köln im Mittelalter* II: *1100-1205.* Bonn 1901; repr. 1964.

Knopp, Gisbert. "Sanctorum nomina seriatim: Die Anfänge der Allerheiligen-litanei und ihre   Verbindung mit den 'laudes regiae.'" *RömQ* 65 (1970) 185-231.

Knowles, Christine. "Jean de Vignay: Un traducteur du XIVe siècle." *Romania* 75 (1954) 353-83.

Knowles, David, and R. Neville Hadcock. *Medieval Religious Houses: England and Wales.* 2nd ed. New York 1972.

Koebner, Richard. *Venantius Fortunatus: Seine Persönlichkeit und seine Stellung in der geistigen Kultur des Merowinger-Reiches.* Leipzig 1915.

Kölzer, Theo. "Zu den Fälschungen für St. Maximin in Trier." In *Fälschungen im Mittelalter* (*MGH*, Schriften 33. I-V, 1988) III 315-26.

König, Ingemar. "Die Berufung des Constantius Chlorus und des Galerius zu Caesaren." *Chiron* 4 (1976) 567-76.

König, Ingemar. *Origo Constantini: Anonymus Valesianus. Teil 1: Text und Kommentar. Trierer Historische Forschungen* 11. Trier 1987.

Kötting, Bernhard. *Peregrinatio Religiosa: Wallfahrten in der Antike und das Pilgerwesen der alten Kirche.* Münster 1950.

Kolb, Frank. *Diocletian und die erste Tetrarchie: Improvisation oder Experiment in der Organisation monarchischer Herrschaft?* Berlin 1987.

Korres, Georgios N. ʿΗ ʾΕκατονταπυλιανὴ τῆς Πάρου. Athens 1954.

Kostof, Spiro. *Caves of God: The Monastic Environment of Byzantine Cappadocia.* Cambridge, Massachusetts,1972.

Kraus, Franz Xaver. *Der heilige Nagel in der Domkirche zu Trier. Beiträge zur Trierischen Archäologie und Geschichte* I. Trier 1868.

Kraus, Franz Xaver. *Die christlichen Inschriften der Rheinlande.* 2 vols. Freiburg 1890-1894.

Krauss, Henning, ed. *Europäisches Hochmittelalter. Neues Handbuch der Literaturwissenschaft,* ed. Klaus von See, VII. Wiesbaden 1981.

Krautheimer, Richard. *Corpus Basilicarum Christianarum Romae:*

The Early Basilicas of Rome. 5 vols. Vatican City 1937-1977.

Krautheimer, Richard. "Zu Konstantins Apostelkirche in Konstantinopel." In *Mullus: Festschrift Theodor Klauser, JbAC,* suppl. 1 (1964) 224-29. Repr. in his *Studies in Early Christian, Medieval and Renaissance Art* (New York 1969) 27-34. Cited from the original.

Krautheimer, Richard. "The Constantinian Basilica." *DOP* 21 (1967) 115-40.

Krautheimer, Richard. *Rome: Profile of a City, 312-1308.* Princeton 1980.

Krautheimer, Richard. *Three Christian Capitals: Topography and Politics.* Berkeley 1983.

Krautheimer, Richard. *Early Christian and Byzantine Architecture. Pelican History of Art.* 4th ed. Harmondsworth, Middlesex, 1986.

Kretschmayr, Heinrich. *Geschichte von Venedig.* 3 vols. Gotha 1905-1934; repr. Aalen 1964.

Krug, Antje. *Antike Gemmen im Römisch-Germanischen Museum Köln.* Frankfurt 1981.

Krumbacher, Karl. *Geschichte der Byzantinischen Litteratur.* 2 vols. *Handbuch der klassischen Altertumswissenschaft* IX.1-2. 2nd ed. Munich 1897; repr. New York 1958.

Kubach, Hans Erich, and Albert Verbeek. *Romanische Baukunst an Rhein und Maas.* 3 vols. Berlin 1976.

Kubitschek, Wilhelm. "Gedächtnismünzen der Kaiserinnen Helena und Theodora." *Numismatische Zeitschrift* (Vienna) N. F. 8 (1915) 180-84.

Künstle, Karl. *Ikonographie der christlichen Kunst.* 2 vols. Freiburg 1926-1928.

Küppers, Leonhard. *Essen: Dom und Domschatz.* Königstein im Taunus 1975.

Kuhn, Hans Wolfgang. "Zur Geschichte des Trierer und des Limburger Domschatzes." *Archiv für mittelrheinische Kirchengeschichte* 28 (1976) 155-207.

Kunze, Konrad. "Überlieferung und Bestand der Elsässischen Legenda aurea: Ein Beitrag zur deutschsprachigen Hagiographie des 14. und 15. Jahrhunderts." *ZDA* 99 (1970) 265-309.

Kunze, Konrad. "Katalog zur Überlieferung der Legenda Aurea des Jacobus de Voragine." *Anal. Boll.* 95 (1977) 168.

Kunze, Konrad. "'Der Heiligen Leben' ('Prosa-',

'Wenzelpassional')." In *Verfasserlexikon²* III (1981) 618-25.

Kunze, Konrad. "Jacobus a (de) Voragine (Varagine)." In Verfasserlexikon² IV (1982) 448-66.

Kurmann, Peter. *La façade de la cathédrale de Reims.* 2 vols. Paris 1987.

Kuttner, Stephan. "La réserve papale du droit de canonisation." *RHDFE,* 4th ser. 17 (1938) 172-228.

Labande-Mailfert, Yvonne, Robert Favreau, et. al. *Histoire de l'abbaye Sainte-Croix de Poitiers.* Poitiers 1986.

Labarge, Margaret Wade. *Saint Louis: Louis IX, Most Christian King of France.* Boston 1968.

Labowsky, Lotte. "Bessarione." In *Dizionario biografico degli italiani* IX (1967) 686-96.

Lafaurie, Jean. "Médaillon Constantinien." *RN,* 5th ser. 17 (1955) 227-50.

Lafaurie, Jean. "Un médaillon conservé au Musée Thomas Dobrée à Nantes." *Bull. Soc. des Antiqu. de France* 1956, pp. 20-21.

Lafontaine-Dosogne, Jacqueline. *Histoire del'art byzantin et chrétien d'Orient.* Louvain-La-Neuve 1987.

Lagrange, Marie-Joseph. *Saint Étienne et son sanctuaire à Jérusalem.* Paris 1894.

Laistner, M. L. W. *Thought and Letters in Western Europe, A.D. 500-900.* 2nd ed. Ithaca 1957.

Lanciani, Rodolfo. *Topografia di Roma antica: I comentarii di Frontino intorno le acque e gli acqedotti.* Rome 1880.

Lanciani, Rodolfo. *L'itinerario di Einsiedeln e l'ordine di Benedetto canonico.* Rome 1891.

Lanciani, Rodolfo. *Pagan and Christian Rome.* London 1892.

Lanciani, Rodolfo. *Forma Urbis Romae.* Milan 1893-1901.

Lanciani, Rodolfo. *The Ruins and Excavations of Ancient Rome.* New York 1897; repr. 1967.

Lanciani, Rodolfo. *Storia degli scavi di Roma.* 3 vols. in 2. Rome 1902-1907.

Lanciani, Rodolfo. *Wanderings through Ancient Roman Churches.* Boston 1924.

Lane, Calvin W. *Evelyn Waugh.* Boston 1981.

Lane Fox, Robin. *Pagans and Christians.* Harmondsworth, Middlesex, 1986; New York 1987.

Laskin, Myron. "Corrado Giaquinto's St. Helena and the Emperor Constantine Presented by the Virgin to the Trinity." *Museum Monographs* (The Saint Louis Art Museum) 1 (1968) 28-40.

Lasko, Peter. *Ars Sacra, 800-1200. The Pelikan History of Art.*

Harmondsworth, Middlesex, 1972.

Lassus,Jean. *Sanctuaires chrétiens de Syrie.* Paris 1947.

Lauer, Hans-Henning. *Kaiserin Helena: Leben und Legenden.* Munich 1967.

Lauer, Philippe, ed. *Les annales de Flodoard.* Paris 1905.

Lavin, Irving. "The Ceiling Frescoes in Trier and Illusionism in Constantinian Painting." *DOP* 21 (1967) 97-113 with 61 ill.

Lavin, Irving. "An Ancient Statue of the Empress Helena Reidentified?" *ArtB* 49 (1967) 58-59.

Lavin, Irving. *Bernini and the Crossing of Saint Peter's. Monograph of the College Art Association of America.* New York 1968.

Lavin, Irving. *Bernini and the Unity of the Visual Arts.* 2 vols. New York and London 1980.

Lavin, Marilyn Aronberg. *Seventeenth-Century Barberini Documents and Inventories of Art.* New York 1975.

Lavin, Marilyn Aronberg. *The Place of Narrative: Mural Decoration in Italian Churches, 431-1600.* Chicago 1990.

Lavin, Marilyn Aronberg. *Piero della Francesca* New York 1992.

Lawrence, Arnold Walter. *Classical Sculpture.* London 1929.

Le Couteur, John D. *English Mediaeval Painted Glass.* 2nd ed. London 1978.

Leeb, Rudolf. *Konstantin und Christus. Arbeiten zur Kirchengeschichte 58.* Berlin 1992.

Lees-Milne, James. *Saint Peter's: The Story of Saint Peter's Basilica in Rome.* Boston 1967.

Legner, Anton. *Deutsche Kunst der Romanik.* Munich 1982.

Legner, Anton, ed. *Ornamenta Ecclesiae: Kunst und Künstler de Romanik.* 3 vols. Exhibition catalogue, Cologne 1985.

Lehner, Hans, and Walter Bader. "Baugeschichtliche Untersuchungen am Bonner Münster." *BJ* 136/137 (1932) 1-216.

Leidl, August, ed. *Bistumspatrone in Deutschland.* Munich 1984.

Lemaire, François. *Histoire et antiquitez de la ville et duché d'Orleans.* 2 vols. in 1. 2nd ed. Orléans 1648.

Lemmer, Manfred. "Brant, Sebastian." In *Verfasserlexikon*[2] I (1978) 992-1005.

Lenz, Christian. "Neuerwerbungen der Frankfurter Museen: Städelsches Kunstinstitut and Städtische Galerie." *Städel-Jahrbuch* N. F. 7 (1979) 300-301.

Lenz, Christian. *Adam Elsheimer: Die Gemälde im Städel.* 2nd ed. Frankfurt 1989.

Leonardy, Johann. *Geschichte des Trierischen Landes und Volkes.* 2nd ed. Trier 1877; repr. 1982.

Leroquais, Victor. *Les psautiers manuscrits latins des bibliothèques publiques de France.* 2 vols. and vol. of pls. Mâcon 1940-1941.

Levison, Wilhelm. *Aus rheinischer und fränkischer Frühzeit.* Düsseldorf 1948. A collection of essays previously published elsewhere; the following essays are cited from this collection: "Die Anfänge rheinischer Bistümer in der Legende." *AHVNrh.* 116 (1956) 5-28. "Bischof Eberigisil von Köln." In *Festschrift Albert Brackmann* (Weimar 1931) 40-63. "Konstantinische Schenkung und Silvester-Legende." In *Miscellanea Francesco Ehrle* II = *Studi e Testi* 38 (Vatican City 1924; repr. 1972) 159-247.

Levison, Wilhelm. "Die Bonner Urkunden des frühen Mittelalters." *BJ* 136/137 (1932) 217-70.

Lewis, Clive Staples. *English Literature in the Sixteenth Century, Excluding Drama. The Oxford History of English Literature* III. Oxford 1954.

Licht, Fred, and David Finn. *Canova.* New York 1983.

Lieberman, Ralph. *Renaissance Architecture in Venice, 1450-1540.* New York 1982.

Linder, Amnon. "The Myth of Constantine the Great in the West: Sources and Hagiographic Commemoration." *Studi Medievali,* 3rd ser. 16 (1975) 43-95.

Linder, Amnon. "Jerusalem as a Focal Point in the Conflict between Judaism and Christianity." In Hebrew with English summary. In Benjamin Z. Kedar, ed., *Jerusalem in the Middle Ages: Selected Papers* (Jerusalem 1979) 5-26.

Lipinsky, Angelo. "Crux Vaticana, Kaiser Justinus' II Kreuz." *RömQ* 63 (1968) 185-203.

Littlewood, Ian. *The Writings of Evelyn Waugh.* Oxford 1983.

Llewellyn, Peter. *Rome in the Dark Ages.* London 1971.

Lloyd, John Edward. *A History of Wales.* 2 vols. 3rd ed. London 1939.

Loenertz, Raymond Joseph. "Pour la biographic du cardinal Bessarion." *OCP* 10 (1944) 116-49.

Longhi, Roberto. *Piero della Francesca.* 3rd ed. Florence 1963.

Loomis, Louise Ropes. *The Book of the Popes.* New York 1916; repr. 1965.

Looshorn, Johann. *Die Geschichte des Bisthums Bamberg.* 7 vols. Bamberg 1886-1910; repr. Bamberg 1967.

L'Orange, Hans Peter. "Der subtile Stil: Eine Kunstströmung aus der Zeit um 400 nach Christus." *Antike Kunst* 4 (1961) 68-74.

Repr.in Hans Peter L'Orange, *Likeness and Icon* (Odense 1973) 54-71. Cited from *Antike Kunst.*

L'Orange, Hans Peter. *Das spätantike Herrscherbild von Diokletian bis zu den Konstantin-Söhnen: 284-361 n. Chr. Das römische Herrscherbild,* ed. Max Wegner, III.4. Berlin 1984.

Lorenz, Rudolf. "Die Anfänge des abendländischen Mönchtums im 4. Jahrhundert." *ZKG* 77 (1966) 1-61.

Lorenzetti, Giulio. *La 'Scuola Grande' di S. Giovanni Evangelista a Venezia.* Venice 1929.

Lowe, Elias Avery. *Codices Latini Antiquiores* V. Oxford 1950.

Lowery, Woodbury. *The Spanish Settlements within the Present Limits of the United States, 1513-1561.* New York and London 1901; repr. New York 1959.

Lowery, Woodbury. *The Spanish Settlements within the Present Limits of the United States: Florida 1562-1574.* New York and London 1905; repr. New York 1959.

Lucas, Charles Prestwood. *A Historical Geography of the British Colonies* III: *West Africa.* 3rd ed. Oxford 1913.

Luce, Clare Boothe, ed. *Saints for Now.* New York 1952.

Lucot, Paul. *Sainte Hélène, mère de l'empereur Constantin.* Paris 1876.

Lugli, Giuseppe. *I monumenti antichi di Roma e suburbio.* 3 vols. and suppl. Rome 1931-1940.

Lugli, Giuseppe. *Fontes ad topographiam veteris urbis Romae pertinentes.* 8 vols. Rome 1952-1962.

Lugli, Giuseppe. *Itinerario di Roma antica.* Milan 1970.

Lundén, Tryggve. "Helena (el. *Elin*) av Skövde." In *Kulturhistoriskt Lexikon för Nordisk Medeltid* VI (Malmö 1961) 305-308.

Luthmer, Ferdinand. *Die Bau- und Kunstdenkmäler des Lahngebietes. Die Bau- und Kunstdenkmäler des Regierungsbezirkes Wiesbaden* III. Frankfurt 1907; repr. Walluf bei Wiesbaden 1973.

Lyon, Eugene. *The Enterprise of Florida: Pedro Menéndez de Avilés and the Spanish Conquest of 1565-1568.* Gainesville 1976.

Lyon, Eugene. "Pedro Menéndez's Strategic Plan for the Florida Peninsula." *The Florida Historical Quarterly* 67 (1988-1989) 1-14.

Mabillon, Jean. *Museum Italicum.* 2 vols. Paris 1687-1689; repr. Rome 1971 (?).

Mabillon, Jean. *Vetera Analecta.* 2nd ed. Paris 1723; repr. Farnborough, Hants, England, 1967.

MacCormack, Sabine G. *Art and Ceremony in Late Antiquity.*

Berkeley 1981.

MacDonald, William L. *Early Christian and Byzantine Architecture.* New York 1962.

Mackes, Karl L. "Das Werden der Helenalegende." In his *Aus der Vor-, Früh- und Siedlungsgeschichte der Stadt Viersen* (Viersen 1956) 182-202.

Maclagan, Michael. *The City of Constantinople.* New York 1968.

MacMullen, Ramsay. *Constantine.* New York 1969; repr. 1987.

MacMullen, Ramsay. *Christianizing the Roman Empire.* New Haven 1984.

MacMullen, Ramsay. *Corruption and the Decline of Rome.* New Haven 1988.

Maddocks, Hilary. "Illumination in Jean de Vignay's Légende dorée." In Brenda Dunn-Lardeau, ed., *Legenda aurea: Sept siècles de diffusion* (Montreal and Paris 1986) 155-69.

Magdalino, Paul, ed. *New Constantines: The Rhythm of Imperial Renewal in Byzantium, 4th - 13th Centuries.* Aldershot, Hampshire, 1994.

Majeska, George P. *Russian Travelers to Constantinople in the Fourteenth and Fifteenth Centuries. Dumbarton Oaks Studies* 19. Washington, D.C., 1984.

Mâle, Émile. *L'art religieux après le Concile de Trente.* Paris 1932.

Mâle, Émile. *Art et artists du Moyen Âge.* 4th ed. Paris 1947. English: *Art and Artists of the Middle Ages.* Redding Ridge, Connecticut, 1986. Cited from the English ed.

Mâle, Émile. *Rome et ses vieilles églises.* Paris 1950. English: *Early Churches of Rome.* London 1960. Cited from the English ed.

Mâle, Émile. *L'art religieux du XIIe siècle en France: Étude sur l'origine de l'iconographie du moyen âge.* 7th ed. Paris 1966. English: *Religious Art in France: The Twelfth Century.* Princeton 1978. Cited from the English ed.

Mâle, Émile. *L'art religieux du XIIIe siècle en France: Étude sur l'iconographie du moyen âge et sur ses sources d'inspiration.* 9th ed. Paris 1958. English: *Religious Art in France: The Thirteenth Century.* Princeton 1984. Cited from the English ed.

Maltzew, Alexios (Aleksei) von. *Menologion der Orthodox-Katholischen Kirche des Morgenlandes.* 2 vols. Berlin 1900-1901. Text in German and Russian.

Manceaux, Jean Baptiste. *Histoire de l'abbaye et du village d'Hautvillers.* 3 vols. Epernay 1880.

Mango, Cyril. "Le Diippion: Étude historique et topographique." *REB* 8 (1950) 152-61.

Mango, Cyril. *The Brazen House: A Study of the Vestibule of the Imperial Palace of Constantinople.* Copenhagen 1959.

Mango, Cyril. *Materials for the Study of the Mosaics of St. Sophia at Istanbul. Dumbarton Oaks Studies* VIII. Washington, D. C., 1962.

Mango, Cyril. *Art of the Byzantine Empire, 312-1453: Sources and Documents.* Englewood Cliffs, New Jersey, 1972.

Mango, Cyril. *Byzantium: The Empire of New Rome.* New York 1980.

Mango, Cyril. *Le développement urbain de Constantinople (IV*e*-VII*e *siècles). Travaux et Mémoires du Centre de recherche d'Histoire et Civilisation de Byzance, Collège de France, Monographies* 2. Paris 1985.

Mann, Horace K. *Lives of the Popes in the Early Middle Ages.* 16 vols. 1st-2nd ed. London 1902-1932.

Manns, Peter, ed. *Die Heiligen in ihrer Zeit.* 2 vols. 2nd ed. Mainz 1966.

Mansi, Joannes Dominicus (Giovanni Domenico), ed. *Sacrorum Conciliorum Nova et Amplissima Collectio.* 31 vols. Ed. Paris 1901; repr. Graz 1960.

Mansuelli, Guido A. *Galleria degli Uffizi: Le sculture.* 2 vols. Rome 1958-1961.

Maraval, Pierre. *Lieux saints et pèlerinages d'Orient: Histoire et géographie des origines à la conquêste arabe.* Paris 1985.

Marini, Remigio. *Tutta la pittura di Paolo Veronese.* Milan 1968. French: *Tout l'oeuvre peint de Veronese.* Paris 1970. Cited from the French ed.

Markus, Robert Austin. "Gregory the Great and a Papal Missionary Strategy." *Studies in Church History* 6 (1970) 29-38. Repr. in Robert Austin Markus, *From Augustine to Gregory the Great* (London 1983), chapter XI. Cited from the original publication.

Marle, Raimond van. *The Development of the Italian Schools of Painting.* 19 vols. The Hague 1923-1938; repr. New York 1970.

Marmadji, A. Sebastianus. *Textes géographiques arabes sur la Palestine.* Paris 1951.

Martin, Geoffrey Haward. *The Story of Colchester from Roman Times to the Present Day.* Colchester 1959.

Martin, Geoffrey Haward. *Colchester: Official Guide.* 5th ed.

Colchester 1982.

Marucchi, Orazio. *Éléments d'archéologie chrétienne.* 3 vols. Paris 1899-1903.

Marx, Jacob. *Geschichte des heiligen Rockes in der Domkirche zu Trier.* Trier 1844.

Marx, Jacob. *Geschichte des Erzstifts Trier.* 3 vols. in 5. Trier 1858-1864; repr. Aalen 1970.

Maslova, G. S. *Narodnaia odezhda v vostochnoslavianskikh traditsionnykh obychaiakh i obriadakh XIX-nachala XX v.* Moscow 1984.

Mason, Richard A. "St. Olha's Christianity and Its Sources." In Nicholas L. Fr.-Chirovsky, ed., *The Millenium of Ukrainian Christianity* (New York 1988) 86-99.

Mateos, Juan, ed. *Le Typicon de la Grande Église.* 2 vols. *Orientalia Christiana Analecta* 165-66. Rome 1962-1963; repr. 1977.

Mathews, Thomas F. *The Early Churches of Constantinople: Architecture and Liturgy.* University Park, Pennsylvania, 1971.

Mathews, Thomas F. *The Byzantine Churches of Istanbul: A Photographic Essay.* University Park, Pennsylvania, 1976.

Mathews, Thomas F., and Roger S. Wieck, edd. *Treasures in Heaven: Armenian Illuminated Manuscripts* (Exhibition catalogue, The Pierpont Morgan Library). New York 1994.

Matt, Leonard von, Georg Daltrop, and Adriano Prandi. *Art Treasures of the Vatican Library.* New York 1974.

Matthews, John Frederick. *Western Aristocracies and the Imperial Court, A.D. 364-425.* Oxford 1975.

Matthews, John Frederick. "Mauretania in Ammianus and the Notitia." *British Archaeological Reports, Supplementary Series* 15 (1976) 157-86. Repr. in John Frederick Matthews, *Political Life and Culture in Late Roman Society* (London 1985), chapter XI.

Matthews, John Frederick. "Macsen, Maximus and Constantine." The *Welsh Historical Review* 11 (1983) 431-48. Repr. in John Frederick Matthews, *Political Life and Culture in Late Roman Society* (London 1985), chapter XII.

Maurice, Jules. *Numismatique Constantinienne.* 3 vols. Paris 1908-1912; repr. Brussels 1965.

Maurice, Jules. "Portraits d'impératrices de l'epoque constantinienne." *NC* 1914, pp. 314-29 and pl. 20.

Maurice, Jules. *Sainte Hélène.* Paris 1930.

Mayerson, Philip. "Procopius or Eutychius on the Construction of the Monastery at Mt. Sinai: Which is the More Reliable Source?" *BASOR* 230 (1978) 33-38.

Mayr-Harting, Henry. *The Coming of Christianity to Anglo-Saxon England.* London 1972.

Mazzoni, Piero. *La leggenda della Croce nell'arte italiana.* Florence 1914.

McAndrew, John. *Venetian Architecture of the Early Renaissance.* Cambridge, Massachusetts, 1980.

McDonnell, Jaqueline. *Waugh on Women.* London 1986.

McDonnell, Jaqueline. *Evelyn Waugh.* London 1988.

McNamara, Jo Ann. *"Imitatio Helenae:* Sainthood as an Attribute of Queenship." A paper delivered at the Twenty-third Annual Conference of the Center for Medieval and Early Renaissance Studies, State University of New York at Binghamton, in October, 1989; forthcoming.

Meer, Frederik van der. *Oudchristelijke Kunst.* Zeist, Netherlands, 1959. English: *Early Christian Art.* Chicago 1967. Cited from the English ed.

Meier, Michael, ed. *Die Kunst- und Kulturdenkmäler in der Region München* I. Munich 1977.

Meinardus, Otto. "A Study of the Relics of Saints of the Greek Orthodox Church." *Or. Chr.* 54 (1970) 130-278.

Meiss, Millard. *The Great Age of Fresco.* New York 1970.

Il Menologio di Basilio II. Facsimile ed. by Pio Pietro Franchi de' Cavalieri. *Codices e Vaticanis selecti phototypice expressi* VIII. 2 vols. Turin 1907.

Merati, Augusto. *Storia architettonica del duomo di Monza.* Monza 1962.

Merati, Augusto. *Il tesoro del duomo di Monza.* 2nd ed. Monza 1969.

Merriman, Joseph Francis. "The Empress Helena and the Aqua Augustea." *Arch. Class.* 29.2 (1977) 436-46.

Metford, J. C. J. *Dictionary of Christian Lore and Legend.* London 1983.

Metz, Peter. *Elfenbein der Spätantike.* Munich 1962.

Meyer, Paul. "Notice du MS. Med.-Pal. 141 de la Laurentienne." *Romania* 33 (1904) 1-49.

Meyer, Wilhelm. *Der Gelegenheitsdichter Venantius Fortunatus. Göttinger Abhandlungen, Philologisch-historische Klasse, N.F.* IV.5. Berlin 1901.

Michel, Émile. *Rubens: His Life, His work, and His Times.* 2 vols.

London 1899.

Michel, Walter. "Die Inschriften der Limburger Staurothek." *Archiv für mittelrheinische Kirchengeschichte* 28 (1976) 23-43.

Mielsch, Harald. "Zur stadtrömischen Malerei des 4. Jahrhunderts n. Chr." *Röm. Mitt.* 85 (1978) 151-207.

Miesges, Peter. *Der Trierer Festkalender. Trierisches Archiv, Ergänzungsheft* 15. Trier 1915.

Mikoletzky, Hanns Leo. "Sinn und Art der Heiligung im frühen Mittelalter." *MIÖG* 57 (1949) 83-122.

Milburn, Robert L. *Early Christian Art and Architecture.* Berkeley 1988.

Milik, Joséf Tadeusz. "Notes d'epigraphie et de topographie palestiniennes." *Rev. Bibl.* 67 (1960) 354-67 and 550-91.

Miller, Julia E. *Modern Greek Folklore: An Annotated Bibliography.* New York 1985.

Miller, Timothy S. "Byzantine Hospitals." *DOP* 38 (1984) 53-63.

Miller, Timothy S. *The Birth of the Hospital in the Byzantine Empire.* Baltimore 1985.

Millet, Gabriel. "*Parastaseis Syntomoi Chronikai*: Essai sur la date." *BCH* 70 (1946) 393-402.

Mitchell, H. P. "Some Enamels of the School of Godefroid de Claire." *Burlington Magazine* 34 (1919) 85-92 and 165-71.

Mohler, Ludwig. *Kardinal Bessarion als Theologe, Humanist und Staatsmann.* 3 vols. Paderborn 1923-1942; repr. Aalen 1967.

Mombritius, Boninus (Mombrizio, Bonino). *Sanctuarium seu Vitae Sanctorum.* 2 vols. Ed. Paris 1910. Editio princeps Milan 1480.

Monceaux, Paul. "Enquête sur l'epigraphie chrétienne d'Afrique." *MémAcInscr.* 12 (1908) 161-399.

Mone, Franz Joseph. *Lateinische Hymnen des Mittelalters.* 3 vols. Freiburg 1853-1855; repr. Aalen 1964.

Montini, Renzo Uberto. *Le tombe dei papi.* Rome 1957.

Moore, Stuart A., ed. *Cartularium Monasterii Sancti Johannis Baptiste de Colecestria.* 2 vols. London 1897.

Moorman, John. *A History of the Franciscan Order from Its Origins to the Year 1517.* Oxford 1968.

Moos, Peter von. *Hildebert von Lavardin, 1056-1133.* Stuttgart 1965.

Morant, Philip. *The History and Antiquities of the Most Ancient Town and Borough of Colchester in the County of Essex.* London 1748; repr. Wakefield 1970.

Morant, Philip. *The History and Antiquities of the County of Essex.*

2 vols. London 1763-1768; repr. Chelmsford 1816 and East
Ardsley 1978.
Moreau-Nélaton, Étienne. *La cathédrale de Reims.* Paris 1915.
Morey, Charles Rufus. "The Inscription on the Enameled Cross of
Paschal I." *ArtB* 19 (1937) 595-96 and figs. 1-2.
Moricca, Umberto. *Storia della letteratura latina cristiana.* 3 vols.
in 5. Turin 1928-1934.
Morison, Samuel Eliot. *The Great Explorers: The European
Discovery of America.* New York 1978.
Morris, Colin. *The Papal Monarchy: The Western Church from 1050
to 1250. The Oxford History of the Christian Church.* Oxford
1989.
Moschini Marconi, Sandra. *Gallerie dell'Accademia di Venezia:
Opere d'arte dei secoli XIV e XV.* Rome 1955.
Moschini Marconi, Sandra. *Gallerie dell'Accademia di Venezia:
Opere d'arte del secolo XVI.* Rome 1962.
Müller Hofstede, Justus. "Rubens in Rom, 1601-1602: Die
Altargemälde für Sta. Croce in Gerusalemme." *Jb. der
Berliner Museen* 12 (1970) 61-110, esp. ill. 2.
Müller-Wiener, Wolfgang. *Bildlexikon zur Topographie Istanbuls.*
Tübingen 1977.
Mulligan, Winfried Joy. "The British Constantine: An English
Historical Myth." *JMRS* 8 (1978) 257-79.
Munier, Charles, ed. *Concilia Galliae A. 314 - A. 506. CC, Ser.
Lat.* CXLVIII. Turnhout 1963.
Murman, Robert. "The Monument to Vittore Cappello of Antonio
Rizzo." *Burlington Magazine* 113 (1971) 138-45 with figs. 21-
32.
Muratori, Lodovico Antonio. *De Corona Ferrea.* Milan 1719.
Murphy-O'Connor, Jerome. *The Holy Land: An Archaeological
Guide from Earliest Times to 1700.* 2nd ed. Oxford 1986.
Museum of Fine Arts, Boston. *Greek & Roman Portraits, 470 BC -
AD 500.* Boston 1972.
Nagy, Maria von, and N. Christoph de Nagy. *Die Legenda aurea
und ihr Verfasser Jacobus de Voragine.* Bern and Munich
1971.
Nash, Ernest. *Pictorial Dictionary of Ancient Rome.* 2 vols. 2nd ed.
New York 1968.
Natanson, Joseph. *Early Christian Ivories.* London 1953.
National Gallery, London. *Illustrated General Catalogue.* London
1973.
National Museum, Belgrade. *Antički Portret u Jugoslaviji =*

Classical Portraits in Yugoslavia. Exhibition catalogue. Belgrade 1987.

Nattermann, Johannes Christian. *Die goldenen Heiligen: Geschichte des Stiftes St. Gereon zu Köln.* Cologne 1960.

Nau, François Nicolas. "Les constructions palestiniennes dues à Sainte Hélène." *Rev. Or. Chr.* 10 (1905) 162-68.

Naz, Raoul. "Causes de béatification et de canonisation." In *DDrC* III (1942) 10-37.

Nektarios, Patriarch of Jerusalem. 'Επιτομὴ τῆς ἱεροκοσμικῆς ἱστορίας. Ed. princeps Venice 1677. Another ed. Venice 1805.

Nelson, Marie. *Judith, Juliana, and Elene: Three Fighting Saints.* New York 1991.

Nelson, Philip. *Ancient Painted Glass in England, 1170-1500.* London 1913.

Nelson, Philip. "The Fifteenth Century Glass in the Church of St. Michael, Ashton-under-Lyne." *Archaeological Journal* 70 (n. s. 20; 1913) 1-10.

Nestle, Eberhard. *De Sancta Cruce: Ein Beitrag zur christlichen Legendengeschichte.* Berlin 1889.

Neuss, Wilhelm. *Die Anfänge des Christentums im Rheinlande.* 2nd ed. Bonn 1933.

Neuss, Wilhelm. "Eine altchristliche Märtyrerkirche unter dem Chor der St. Viktorskirche in Xanten." *RömQ* 42 (1934) 177-82.

Neuss, Wilhelm, ed. *Rheinische Kirchen im Wiederaufbau.* Verein für christliche Kunst im Erzbistum Köln und Bistum Aachen, Jahresgabe 1949-51. Mönchen-Gladbach 1951.

Newman, Philip. *A Short History of Cyprus.* 2nd ed. London 1953.

Nicol, Donald M. "Constantine Akropolites: A Prosopographical Note," *DOP* 19 (1965) 249-56.

Nicol, Donald M. *Byzantium and Venice: A Study in Diplomatic and Cultural Relations.* Cambridge 1988.

Norwich, John Julius. *Byzantium: The Early Centuries.* London 1988.

Oates, J. C. T. *A Catalogue of the Fifteenth-Century Printed Books in the University Library Cambridge.* Cambridge 1954.

Oberhummer, Eugen. *Die Insel Cypern* I. Munich 1903.

Obolensky, Dimitri. *The Byzantine Commonwealth: Eastern Europe, 500-1453.* New York 1971.

Obolensky, Dimitri. *Byzantium and the Slavs: Collected Studies.* London 1971. Articles previously published in 1945-1967.

Obolensky, Dimitri. *The Byzantine Inheritance of Eastern Europe: Collected Essays.* London 1982. Articles previously

published in 1970-1981.
Ochsenbein, Peter. "Hortulus animae." In *Verfasserlexikon²* IV (1982/1983) 147-54.
O'Connor, James I. *The Canon Law Digest* VII. Chicago 1975.
Odahl, Charles. "Constantinian Coin Motifs in Ancient Literary Sources." *Journal of the Rocky Mountain Medieval and Renaissance Association* 7 (1986) 1-15.
Odahl, Charles. "Constantine's Epistle to the Bishops at the Council of Arles: A Defense of Imperial Authorship." *JRH* 17 (1993) 274-89.
Odahl, Charles. *Early Christian Latin Literature: Readings from the Ancient Texts.* Chicago 1993.
Odahl, Charles. "The Christian Basilicas of Constantinian Rome." *AncW* 26 (1995) 3-28.
Odahl, Charles. "God and Constantine: Divine Sanction for Imperial Rule in the First Christian Emperor's Early Letters and Art." Forthcoming in *CHR* 81 (1995).
Odoardi, Giovanni. "La custodia Francescana di terra santa nel VI centenario della sua costituzione (1342-1942)." *Miscellanea Francescana* 43 (1943) 217-56.
Oediger, Friedrich Wilhelm. *Die Regesten der Erzbischöfe von Köln im Mittelalter* I: *313-1099.* Bonn 1954; repr. Düsseldorf 1978.
Oediger, Friedrich Wilhelm. *Vom Leben am Niederrhein.* Düsseldorf 1973. A collection of essays previously published elsewhere; the following essays are cited from this collection: "Die Heimat der Annales Xantenses." *AHVNrh.* 144/145 (1946-1947) 32-38. "Noch einmal die 'Annales Xantenses'." *AHVNrh.* 157 (1955) 181-90. "Monasterium beati Christi martyris: Zur Frühgeschichte des Xantener Stiftskapitels (vor 1300)." *Rheinische Ausgrabungen* 6 (1969) 207-67.
Oediger, Friedrich Wilhelm: see Hegel, Eduard.
Oelmann, Franz. Untitled report on excavations under the Münster in Bonn. *BJ* 149 (1949) 334-35 and 356-61.
Oertel, Robert. *Die Frühzeit der italienischen Malerei.* 2nd ed. Stuttgart 1966. English: *Early Italian Painting to 1400.* London and New York 1968. Cited from the English ed.
Oldenbourg, M. Consuelo. *Hortulus animae: (1494)-1523.* Hamburg 1973.
Oliver Alberti, Mariano. *La catedral de Gerona.* León 1973. Republished in *Catedrales de España: Lugo - Toledo - Gerona*

- *Pamplona - Almeria* (Madrid 1981?) 209-71.

Opfermann, Bernhard. *Die liturgischen Herrscherakklamationen im Sacrum Imperium des Mittelalters.* Weimar 1953.

Oppenheimer, Francis. *Frankish Themes and Problems.* London 1952. Contains "The Tympanum of the Church of St. John in Monza," 105-70 with pls. 4 and 14.

Oppermann, Otto. *Rheinische Urkundenstudien.* 2 vols. Utrecht 1922-1951.

Orlandi, Tito. "Cirillo di Gerusalemme nella letteratura copta." *Vet. Chr.* 9 (1972) 93-100.

Orlandi, Tito, ed. *Eudoxia and the Holy Sepulchre: A Constantinian Legend in Coptic.* Milan 1980.

Orlando, Francesco Saverio. *Il tesoro di San Pietro.* Milan 1958.

Orliac, Antoine. *Veronese.* London 1940.

Orsi, Mario d'. *Corrado Giaquinto.* Rome 1958.

Ortolani, Sergio. *S. Giovanni in Laterano. Le chiese di Roma illustrate* 13. Rome 192-?.

Ortolanik Sergio. *S. Croce in Gerusalemme. Le chiese di Roma illustrate.* 106. 2nd ed. Rome 1969.

Ostrogorsky, Georg(e). "Vizantija i kievskaja knjaginja Olga." In *To Honor R. Jakobson* (The Hague 1967) 1458-73. German: "Byzanz und die Kiewer Fürstin Olga." In Georg Ostrogorsky, *Byzanz und die Welt der Slawen* (Darmstadt 1974) 35-52. Cited from the German ed.

Ostrogorsky, Georg(e). *Geschichte des byzantinischen Staates.* 3rd ed. *Byzantinisches Handbuch* I.2. *Handbuch der Altertumswissenschaft* XII.1.2. Munich 1963. English: *History of the Byzantine State.* 2nd ed. New Brunswick, New Jersey, 1969. Cited from the English ed.

Ovadiah, Asher. *Corpus of the Byzantine Churches in the Holy Land.* Bonn 1970.

Paatz, Walter and Elisabeth. *Die Kirchen von Florenz.* 5 vols. Frankfurt 1940-1953.

Page, William, ed. *The Victoria History of the County of Norfolk* II. *The Victoria History of the Counties of England.* London 1906; repr. 1975.

Painter, George D. *William Caxton: A Biography.* New York 1977.

Palmer, E. H. *The Desert of the Exodus.* New York 1872.

Palol, Pedro de. "Une broderie catalane d'époque romane: La Genèse de Gérone." *Cah. Arch.* 8 (1956) 175-214 and 9 (1957) 219-51.

Palol, Pedro de, and Max Hirmer. *Early Medieval Art in Spain.*

New York 1967.
Papageorgiou, Alekos. "Κύπριοι Ζωγράφοι τοῦ 15ου καὶ 16ου αἰώνα." *RDAC* 1974, pp. 195-209 and pls. XXX-XXXV.
Papageorgiou, Athanasios. *Icons of Cyprus.* New York 1970.
Papini, Roberto. *Catalogo delle cose d'arte e di antichità d'Italia: Pisa.* 2 vols. Rome 1912-1914.
Pardyová-Vodová see Vodová.
Parks, George Bruner. *Richard Hakluyt and the English Voyages.* New York 1928.
Parrot, André. *Golgotha et Saint-Sépulcre.* Neuchâtel 1955. English: *Golgotha and the Church of the Holy Sepulchre. Studies in Biblical Archaeology* 6. New York 1957. Cited from the English ed.
Parry, Thomas. *A History of Welsh Literature.* Translated from the Welsh by H. Idris Bell. Oxford 1955.
Pascher, Joseph. *Das liturgische Jahr.* Munich 1963.
Paschoud, François. *Cinq études sur Zosime.* Paris 1975.
Pastor, Ludwig von. *Geschichte der Päpste seit dem Ausgang des Mittelalters.* 16 vols. in 21. Freiburg 1866 ff. English: *The History of the Popes from the Close of the Middle Ages.* 40 vols. London 1891 ff.; repr. 1952. Cited from the English ed.
Paulin, Antoine. *Saint Cyrille de Jérusalem, catéchète.* Paris 1959.
Pauls, Emil. "Beiträge zur Geschichte der grösseren Reliquien und der Heiligtumsfahrten zu Cornelimünster bei Aachen." *AHVNrh.* 52 (1891) 157-74.
Peirce, Hayford, and Royall Tyler. "An Ivory of the Xth. Century." *DOP* 2 (1941) 11-18 and pls. 1-22.
Pelekanides, Stylianos. "Date et interprétation de la plaque en ivoire de Trèves." *Mélanges Henri Grégoire* IV = *AIPHOS* 12 (1952) 361-71.
Peres, Damião. *História dos descobrimentos portugueses.* 3rd ed. Porto 1983.
Peters, F. E. *Jerusalem: The Holy City in the Eyes of Chroniclers, Visitors, Pilgrims, and Prophets from the Days of Abraham to the Beginnings of Modern Times.* Princeton 1985.
Petri, Franz, and Georg Droege, edd. *Rheinische Geschichte.* 4 vols. in 6. Düsseldorf 1976-1983. Vol. I.1 by Harald von Petrikovits; vol. I.2 by Eugen Ewig; vol. I.3 by Egon Boshof, Odilo Engels, and Rudolf Schieffer; vol. of ill. by Klaus Ring.
Petrignani, Achille. *Il santuario della Scala Santa.* Vatican City 1941.

Petrikovits, Harald von. *Das römische Rheinland: Archäologische Forschungen seit 1945. Arbeitsgemeinschaft für Forschung des Landes Nordrhein-Westfalen: Geisteswissenschaften* 86. Cologne 1960.

Petrikovits, Harald von. "Die Zeitstellung der ältesten frühchristlichen Kultanlage unter dem Bonner Münster." *Kölner Jb.* 9 (1967-1968) 112-19. Repr. in Harald von Petrikovits, *Beiträge zur römischen Geschichte und Archäologie 1931 bis 1974 (Beihefte der Bonner Jahrbücher* 36; Bonn 1976) 463-72. Cited from *Kölner Jb.*

Pevsner, Nikolaus. *The Buildings of England: Lancashire* I. Harmondsworth, Middlesex, 1967.

Pevsner, Nikolaus. *The Buildings of England: County Durham.* 2nd ed., rev. by Elizabeth Williamson. Harmondsworth, Middlesex, 1984.

Phillips, Gene D. *Evelyn Waugh's Officers, Gentlemen, and Rogues: The Fact behind His Fiction.* Chicago 1975.

Pick, Joachim. *Dom und Domschatz in Limburg an der Lahn -- Lubentiuskirche in Dietkirchen.* 3rd ed. Königstein im Taunus 1986.

Picozzi, Vittorio. *La monetazione imperiale Romana.* Rome 1966.

Pierpont Morgan Library. *The Stavelot Triptych: Mosan Art and the Legend of the True Cross.* New York 1980.

Pietri, Charles. *Roma Christiana.* 2 vols. *Bibliothèque des Écoles Françaises d'Athènes et de Rome* 224. Paris 1976.

Piganiol, André. *L'empire chrétien (325-395).* 2nd ed. *Histoire Romaine* IV.2. Paris 1972.

Pignatti, Terisio. *Veronese.* 2 vols. Venice 1976.

Pita Andrade, J. M. *Treasures of Spain.* Geneva 1967.

Planiscig, Leo. *Venezianische Bildhauer der Renaissance.* Vienna 1921.

Planiscig, Leo. "Jacopo und Gentile Bellini: Neue Beiträge zu ihrem Werk." *Jb. der Kunsthistorischen Sammlungen in Wien,* n. s. 2 (1928) 41-62.

Plomer, Henry R. *William Caxton.* London 1925; repr. New York 1968.

Poche, Emanuel. *Böhmen und Mähren. Kunstdenkmäler in der Tschechoslowakei,* ed. Reinhardt Hootz. Munich 1986.

Pohlsander, Hans A. "Crispus: Brilliant Career and Tragic End." *Historia* 33 (1984) 79-106.

Pope-Hennessy, John. *Italian High Renaissance and Baroque Sculpture. An Introduction to Italian Sculpture* III. 2nd ed.

London 1970.

Pope-Hennessy, John. *Italian Renaissance Sculpture. An Introduction to Italian Sculpture* II. 2nd ed. London 1971.

Post, Chandler Rathfon. *A History of Spanish Painting.* 14 vols. in 16. Cambridge, Massachusetts, 1930-1966; repr. New York 1970.

Potthast, August. *Regesta Pontificum Romanorum, 1198-1304.* 2 vols. Berlin 1874-1875; repr. Graz 1957.

Potz, Richard. *Patriarch und Synode in Konstantinopel.* Vienna 1971.

Poulsen, Frederik. "Mellem Glyptotekets romerske portraetter." *Kunstmuseets Aarsskrift* 13-15 (1926-1928) 1-55.

Poulsen, Frederik. *Catalogue of Ancient Sculptures in the Ny Carlsberg Glyptotek.* Copenhagen 1951.

Poulsen, Vagn. *Les portraits romains.* 2 vols. in 3. Copenhagen 1962-1974.

The Prayerbook of Michelino da Besozzo. A facsimile ed., Colin Eisler and Patricia Corbett, edd. New York 1981; German ed. Munich 1981.

Praz, Mario, and Giuseppe Pavanello. *L'opera completa del Canova.* Milan 1976.

Preger, Theodor. "Konstantinos-Helios." *Hermes* 36 (1901) 457-69.

Preger, Theodor, ed. *Scriptores Originum Constantinopolitanarum.* 2 vols. Leipzig 1901-1907; repr. New York 1975.

Prestage, Edgar. *The Portuguese Pioneers.* London 1933; repr. New York 1967.

Prime, William Cowper. *Holy Cross: A History of the Invention, Preservation, and Disappearance of the Wood Known As the True Cross.* London and New York 1877.

Prinz, Friedrich. *Frühes Mönchtum im Frankenreich.* Munich 1965.

Prior, Edward S., and Arthur Gardner. *An Account of Medieval Figure-Sculpture in England.* Cambridge 1912.

Prokopp, Mária. *Italian Trecento Influence on Murals in East Central Europe, particularly Hungary.* Budapest 1983.

Pugh, George Augustus. "The Old Glass Windows of Ashton-under-Lyne Parish Church." *Transactions of the Lancashire and Cheshire Antiquarian Society* 20 (1902) 130-38.

Quantrill, Malcolm and Esther. *Monuments of Another Age: The City of London Churches.* London 1975.

Quasten, Johannes. *Patrology.* 3 vols. Westminster, Maryland, 1950; repr. 1960-1963. Vol. IV, ed. Angelo di Berardino, 1986; from the Italian ed. of 1978.

Quentin, Henri. *Les martyrologes historiques du moyen âge.* 2nd ed. Paris 1908; repr. Aalen 1969.

Rabino, Hyacinth Louis. *Le monastère de Sainte-Cathérine du Mont Sinaï.* Cairo 1938.

Raby, F. J. E. *A History of Christian-Latin Poetry from the Beginning to the Close of the Middle Ages.* 2nd ed. Oxford 1953.

Raby, F. J. E. *A History of Secular Latin Poetry in the Middle Ages.* 2 vols. 2nd ed. Oxford 1957.

Radó, Polycarpus. *Enchiridion Liturgicum.* 2 vols. Rome 1966.

Rahtgens, Hugo. *Die Kunstdenkmäler der Stadt Köln* II.1. *Die Kunstdenkmäler der Rheinprovinz,* ed. Paul Clemen, VII.1. Düsseldorf 1911; repr. 1980 as *Die kirchlichen Kunstdenkmäler der Stadt Köln* II.

Rahtgens, Hugo, and Hermann Roth. *Die Kunstdenkmäler der Stadt Köln* II.2. *Die Kunstdenkmäler der Rheinprovinz,* ed. Paul Clemen, VII.2. Düsseldorf 1929; repr. 1980 as *Die kirchlichen Kunstdenkmäler der Stadt Köln* III.

Rantasalo, Aukusti Vilho. *Der Ackerbau im Aberglauben der Finnen und Esten.* 5 vols. *FF Communications* 30-32, 55, and 62. Sortavala 1919-1925.

Rauch, Jakob, Schenk zu Schweinsberg, and Johann Michael Wilm. "Die Staurothek von Limburg." *Das Münster* 8 (1955) 201-40.

Ravenstein, Ernest George, trl. and ed. *A Journal of the First Voyage of Vasco da Gama, 1497-1499.* London 1898; repr. New York 1963 (?).

Read, Herbert Edward. *English Stained Glass.* London and New York 1926; repr. Millwood, New York, 1973.

Reames, Sherry L. *The Legenda Aurea: A Reexamination of its Paradoxical History.* Madison 1985.

Rearick, William R. *The Art of Paolo Veronese, 1526-1588.* Washington, D. C., and Cambridge 1988.

"Recent Museum Acquisitions." *Apollo* 77 (1963) 348.

Reece, Richard. *Roman Coins.* London 1970.

Reekmans, Louis. *La tombe du pape Corneille et sa région cémétériale.* *Roma Sotterranea Cristiana* IV. Vatican City 1964.

Regan, Catharine. "Evangelicalism as the Informing Principle of Cynewulf's *Elene.*" *Traditio* 29 (1973) 27-52.

Reinach, Salomon. *Répertoire de la statuaire grecque et romaine.* 2nd ed. 3 vols. in 4. Paris 1908-1909.

Reiners, Heribert. *Die Kunstdenkmäler der Landkreise Aachen und Eupen. Die Kunstdenkmäler der Rheinprovinz* IX.2. Düsseldorf 1912.

Reinhardt, Hans. *La cathédrale de Reims.* Paris 1963.

Renwick, W. L., and Harold Orton. *The Beginnings of English Literature to Skelton, 1509.* 3rd ed. London 1966.

Restle, Marcell. *Die byzantinische Wandmalerei in Kleinasien.* 3 vols. Recklinghausen 1967. English: *Byzantine Wall Paintings in Asia Minor.* Greenwich, Connecticut, 1968. Cited from the English ed.

Restle, Marcell. "Konstantinopel." In *RBK,* fasc. 27/28 (1989) 366-639 and fasc. 29/30 (1990) 641-737.

Reusch, Wilhelm. See Kempf, Theodor Konrad.

Reynolds, Barbara. *Dorothy L. Sayers: Her Life and Her Soul.* New York 1993.

Reynolds, Beatrice R. "Latin Historiography: A Survey, 1400-1600." *Studies in the Renaissance* 2 (1955) 7-66.

Rheinisches Landesmuseum Bonn. *Führer durch die Sammlungen.* 2nd ed. Cologne 1985.

Rheinisches Landesmuseum Trier. *Trier: Kaiserresidenz und Bischofssitz.* Mainz 1984.

Riant, Paul Édouard Didier. *Exuviae Sacrae Constantinopolitanae.* 3 vols. Geneva 1877-1904.

Ricci, Seymour de. *A Census of Caxtons.* Oxford 1909.

Ricciotti, Guiseppe. *The Age of Martyrs: Christianity from Diocletian to Constantine.* Milwaukee 1959.

Rice, David Talbot. *The Art of Byzantium.* New York 1961.

Rice, David Talbot. *Art of the Byzantine Era.* London 1963.

Richards, Jeffrey. *Consul of God: The Life and Times of Gregory the Great.* London 1980.

Richardson, Ernest C. *Materials for a Life of Jacopo de Voragine.* New York 1935. 1 vol., but 4 parts, each with its own pagination.

Richardson, L., Jr. *A New Topographical Dictionary of Ancient Rome.* Baltimore 1992.

Richmond, E. T. "Basilica of the Nativity: Discovery of the Remains of an Earlier Church." *QDAP* 5 (1936) 75-81.

Richmond, E. T. "The Church of the Nativity: The Plan of the Constantinian Church." *QDAP* 6 (1938) 63-66, and "The Church of the Nativity: The Alterations Carried Out by Justinian," *ibid.* 67-72.

Richter, Gisela M. A. *The Engraved Gems of the Romans. The*

Engraved Gems of the Greeks, Etruscans and Romans, Part II. London 1971.

Richter, Jean Paul. *Quellen der byzantinischen Kunstgeschichte*. Vienna 1897.

Rinaldi, Odorico (Raynaldus, Odoricus). *Annales Ecclesiastici ab Anno 1198*. Ed. Giovanni Dominico Mansi. 15 vols. Luca 1747-1756.

Robinson, Joseph Armitage. *The Times of Saint Dunstan*. Oxford 1923.

Rodenwaldt, Gerhard. "Der Belgrader Kameo." *JDAI* 37 (1922) 17-38.

Rodenwaldt, Gerhard. "Zum Sarkophag der Helena." In *Scritti in onore di Bartolomeo Nogara* (Vatican City 1937) 389-93 and pls. LIV-LVI.

Rodley, Lyn. *Cave Monasteries of Byzantine Cappadocia*. Cambridge 1985.

Rohault de Fleury, Charles. *Mémoire sur les instruments de la passion de N.-S. J.-C.* Paris 1870.

Rollason, David W. "Relic-cults as an Instrument of Royal Policy, c. 900 - c. 1050." *ASE* 15 (1986) 91-103.

Romaios, Kostas. *Cultes populaires de la Thrace: Les Anastenaria; La cérémonie du Lundi pur. Collection de l'Institute Français d'Athènes* 18. Athens 1949.

Ronig, Franz J. "Die Ausstattung des Trierer Domes." *Das Münster* 21 (1968) 33-48.

Ronig, Franz J., ed. *Der Trierer Dom. Rheinischer Verein für Denkmalpflege und Landschaftsschutz, Jb.* 1978/79. Neuss 1980.

Ronig, Franz J., ed. *Schatzkunst Trier: Forschungen und Ergebnisse.* (Trier 1991).

Ronig, Franz J. "Der heilige Rock im Dom zu Trier: Eine kurze Zusammenfassung seiner Geschichte, seiner Bedeutung und der Wallfahrten." In *Zwischen Andacht und Andenken: Kleiodien religiöser Kunst und Wallfahrtsandenken aus Trierer Sammlungen* (Trier 1992) 117-36.

Rooses, Max. *L'oevre de Rubens.* 5 vols. of text; 5 vols. of pls. Antwerp 1886-1892.

Rooses, Max. *Rubens.* 2 vols. Philadelphia 1904.

Ross, Marvin C. "Basil the Proedros: Patron of the Arts." *Archaeology* 11 (1958) 271-75.

Rouillon, A.-M. *Sainte Hélène.* Paris 1908.

Round, John Horace. *St. Helen's Chapel, Colchester.* London 1887.

Royal Commission on Historical Monuments, England. *An Inventory of the Historical Monuments in Essex* II. London 1922.

Royal Commission on Historical Monuments, England. *An Inventory of the Historical Monuments in London* IV: *The City*. London 1929.

Rubin, Ze'ev. "The Church of the Holy Sepulchre and the Conflict between the Sees of Caesarea and Jerusalem." In L. I. Levine, ed., *The Jerusalem Cathedra* II (Jerusalem 1982) 79-105.

Ruh, Kurt. "Geistliche Prosa." In Willi Erzgräber, ed., *Europäisches Mittelalter* (*Neues Handbuch der Literaturwissenschaft*, ed. Klaus von See, VIII. Wiesbaden 1978) 565-605.

Rumpf, Andreas. *Stilphasen der spätantiken Kunst: Ein Versuch. Arbeitsgemeinschaft für Forschung des Landes Nordrhein-Westfalen, Geisteswissenschaften* 44. Cologne 1957.

Runciman, Steven. *History of the Crusades*. 3 vols. Cambridge 1951.

Sacra Congregatio Rituum. "Instructio de Calendariis Particularibus." *Eph. Lit.* 75 (1961) 143-54.

Sacra Congregatio Rituum. *Calendarium Romanum*. Vatican City 1969.

Sacra Congregatio Rituum. "Calendarium Romanum Generale." *Eph. Lit.* 83 (1969) 202-23.

Salaville, Sévérien. "Le moine Alexandre de Chypre." *EO* 15 (1912) 134-37.

Salmi, Mario. *La pittura di Piero della Francesca*. Novara 1979.

Salvini, Roberto. *L'arte di Agnolo Gaddi*. Florence 1936.

Sanderson, Warren. "Die frühmittelalterlichen Krypten von St. Maximin in Trier." *TZ* 31 (1968) 7-172.

Sanjian, Avedis K. *A Catalogue of Medieval Armenian Manuscripts in the United States*. 2 vols. Berkeley 1976.

Sansovino, Francesco. *Venetia città nobilissima et singolare*. Ed. Venice 1663; repr. Farnborough, Hants, England, 1968.

Sauerland, Heinrich Volbert. *Trierer Geschichtsquellen des XI. Jahrhunderts*. Trier 1889.

Sauser, Ekkart. *Heilige und Selige im Bistum Trier*. Trier 1987.

Sauvaget, Jean. *Alep*. Paris 1941.

Saxl, Fritz. *English Sculptures of the Twelfth Century*. Ed. Hanns Swarzenski. Boston 1956.

Sayers, Dorothy Leigh. *The Emperor Constantine: A Chronicle*. London and New York 1951; repr. Grand Rapids, Michigan, 1976.

Schäfke, Werner. *Kölns romanische Kirchen.* 5th ed. Cologne 1985.

Schäfke, Werner. *St. Gereon in Köln.* Cologne 1985. Previously published as *Rheinische Kunststätten* 300, Cologne 1984. Cited from the 1985 ed.

Schaffran, Emerich. "Gentile Bellini und das Bessarion-Reliquar." *Das Münster* 10 (1957) 153-57.

Schaskolsky, P. "La leggenda di Costantino il Grande e di Papa Silvestro." *Roma e l'oriente* 6 (1913) 12-25.

Schatzkunst Trier. Exhibition catalogue, Bischöfliches Generalvikariat Trier, 1984. Trier 1984.

Scheibler, Ludwig, and Carl Aldenhoven. *Geschichte der Kölner Malerschule.* Lübeck 1902.

Schmidt, Erika E. *Römische Frauenstatuen.* N. p., 1967.

Schmidt, Hermann. *Landsberg am Lech.* Augsburg 1929.

Schmidt, J. H. "Der Schrein des heiligen Viktor." *Xantener Domblätter* 3.2 and 4 (1952) 75-84.

Schmidt, Josef. "Golden Legends during the Reformation Controversy: Polemical Trivialization in the German Vernacular." In Brenda Dunn-Lardeau, ed., *Legenda Aurea: Sept siècles de diffusion* (Montreal and Paris 1986) 267-75.

Schmidt, Leopold. *Volksglaube und Volksbrauch.* Berlin 1966.

Schmitt, Hermann. "Trier und Reims in der verfassungsgeschichtlichen Entwicklung bis zum Primatialstreit des 9. Jahrhunderts." *ZRG, K. Abt.* 18 (1929) 1-111.

Schneider, Alfons Maria. *Byzanz: Vorarbeiten zur Topographie und Archäologie der Stadt.* Berlin 1936; repr. Amsterdam 1967.

Schneider, Alfons Maria. Review of K. Hönn, *Konstantin der Grosse. GGA* 202 (1940) 208-10.

Schneider, Alfons Maria. "Zur Datierung der Vita Constantini et Helenae." *ZNTW* 40 (1941) 245-49.

Schneider, Carl. *Geistesgeschichte des antiken Christentums.* 2 vols. Munich 1954.

Schneider, Laurie. "The Iconography of Piero della Francesca's Frescoes Illustrating the Legend of the True Cross in the Church of San Francesco in Arezzo." *Art Quarterly* 32 (1969) 22-48 with figs. 1-22.

Schnitzler, Hermann. *Der Dreikönigenschrein.* Bonn 1939.

Schnitzler, Hermann. *Rheinische Schatzkammer.* Düsseldorf 1957.

Schnütgen-Museum, Cologne. *Rhein und Maas: Kunst und Kultur 800-1400.* 2 vols. Exhibition catalogue, Cologne 1972.

Schramm, Albert. *Der Bilderschmuck der Frühdrucke.* 23 vols. Leipzig 1920-1943.

Schramm, Percy Ernst, and Florentine Mütherich. *Denkmale der deutschen Könige und Kaiser*. Munich 1962.

Schreiber, Georg. "St. Helena als Inhaberin von Erzgruben." *Zeitschrift für Volkskunde* 53 (1956-57) 65-76.

Schrörs, Heinrich. *Hinkmar, Erzbischof von Reims*. Freiburg 1884; repr. Hildesheim 1967.

Schubring, Paul. *Die italienische Plastik des Quattrocento*. *Handbuch der Kunstwissenschaft* VII. Berlin 1919.

Schuette, Marie, and Sigrid Müller-Christensen. *Das Stickereiwerk*. Tübingen 1963. English: *A Pictorial History of Embroidery*. London 1963. Cited from the English ed.

Schulten, Peter N. *Die römische Münzstätte Trier von der Wiederaufnahme ihrer Tätigkeit unter Diocletian bis zum Ende der Folles-Prägung*. Frankfurt 1974.

Schulten, Walter. *Die heilige Stiege auf dem Kreuzberg in Bonn*. Düsseldorf 1964.

Schulten, Walter. *Der Schrein der Heiligen Drei Könige*. Cologne 1975.

Schulten, Walter. *Der Kölner Domschatz*. Cologne 1980.

Schulten, Walter. *Die heilige Stiege und Wallfahrtsstätte auf dem Kreuzberg in Bonn*. 5th ed. *Rheinische Kunststätten* 20. Cologne 1986.

Schulten, Walter. *Der Dom zu Köln*. 7th ed. Cologne 1986.

Schulz, Anne Markham. *Niccolò di Giovanni Fiorentino and Venetian Sculpture of the Early Renaissance*. New York 1978.

Schulz, Anne Markham. *Antonio Rizzo: Sculptor and Architect*. Princeton 1983.

Schumacher, Walter N. "Cubile Sanctae Helenae." *RömQ* 58 (1963) 196-222.

Schumacher, Walter N. *Hirt und 'Guter Hirt': Studien zum Hirtenbild in der römischen Kunst vom 2. bis zum Anfang des 4. Jahrhunderts. RömQ*, suppl. 34 (Freiburg 1977) 217-303.

Schwab, Otmar. "St. Gereon." In *Frühchristliches Köln (Schriftenreihe der Archäologischen Gesellschaft Köln* 12. Cologne: Römisch-Germanisches Museum, 1965) 34-37.

Schwab, Ute. "Das Traumgesicht vom Kreuzesbaum: Ein ikonologischer Interpretationsansatz zu dem ags. Dream of the Rood." In Ute Schwab and Elfriede Stutz, edd., *Philologische Studien: Gedenkschrift für Richard Kienast* (Heidelberg 1978) 131-92.

Schwartz, Eduard. "Die Kaiserin Pulcheria auf der Synode von Chalkedon." In *Festgabe für Adolf Jülicher* (Tübingen 1927)

203-12.

Sébillot, Paul. *Légendes, croyances et superstitions et la mere.* 2 vols. Paris 1886.

Sébillot, Paul. *Le folk-lore de France.* 4 vols. Paris 1904-1907; repr. 1968.

See, Klaus von, ed. *Europäisches Frühmittelalter. Neues Handbuch der Literaturwissenschaft,* ed. Klaus von See, VI. Wiesbaden 1985.

Seeck, Otto. "Constantius. 1." In *RE* IV.1 (1900) 1039-1043.

Seeck, Otto. "Helena. 2." In *RE* VII.2 (1912) 2820-23.

Seeck, Otto. *Regesten der Kaiser und Päpste für die Jahre 311 bis 476 n. Chr.* Stuttgart 1919; repr. Frankfurt 1964.

Seeck, Otto. *Geschichte des Untergangs der antiken Welt.* 4th ed. 6 vols. Stuttgart 1921; repr. 1966.

Seeleke, Kurt, and Friedrich Herzig. "Wiederherstellung der romanischen Wandmalereien im Südquerschiff des Braunschweiger Domes." *Niedersächsische Denkmalpflege* 2 (1955-1956) 25-28.

Segal, J. B. *Edessa: 'The Blessed City.'* Oxford 1970.

Seibt, Ferdinand, ed. *Bohemia Sacra: Das Christentum in Böhmen, 973-1973.* Düsseldorf 1974.

Seibt, Ferdinand. *Karl IV.: Ein Kaiser in Europa, 1346-1378.* Munich 1978.

Seibt, Ferdinand, ed. *Kaiser Karl IV.: Staatsmann und Mäzen.* 2nd ed. Munich 1978.

Sellers, Robert Victor. *Eustathius of Antioch and His Place in the Early History of Christian Doctrine.* Cambridge 1928.

Sello, Gottfried. *Adam Elsheimer.* Munich 1988.

Settis, Salvatore, ed. *Camposanto Monumentale di Pisa: Le antichità II.* Pisa 1984.

Setton, Kenneth M. *The Papacy and the Levant (1204-1571).* 4 vols. Philadelphia 1976-1984.

Ševčenko, Ihor. "The Early Period of the Sinai Monastery in the Light of Its Inscriptions." *DOP* 20 (1966) 255-64.

Seybolt, Robert Francis. "Fifteenth-Century Editions of the *Legenda Aurea.*" *Speculum* 21 (1946) 327-38.

Seybolt, Robert Francis. "The *Legenda Aurea,* Bible and Historia Scholastica." *Speculum* 21 (1946) 339-42.

Siering, Theo. *Das Münster im Herzen der Stadt Bonn.* Bonn 1980.

Sigal, Pierre-André. "Les miracles de Saint-Hélène à l'abbaye d'Hautvillers au Moyen-Âge et à l'époque moderne." In *Assistance et assistés jusqu'à 1610: Actes du 97ᵉ Congres national des sociétés savantes, Nantes 1972, Section de philologie et d'histoire jusque'à 1610* (Paris 1979) 499-513.

Simon, Erika. *Die konstantinischen Deckengemälde in Trier. Kulturgeschichte der antiken Welt 34. Trierer Beiträge zur Altertumskunde* 3. Mainz 1986.

Simon, Gerd. *Die erste deutsche Fastnachtsspieltradition. Germanische Studien,* Heft 240. Lübeck 1970.

Sirmond, Jacques, ed. *Concilia Antiqua Galliae.* 3 vols. Paris 1629; repr. Aalen 1970.

Sivan, Hagith. "Who was Egeria? Piety and Pilgrimage in the Age of Gratian." *HThR* 81 (1988) 59-72.

Sjöqvist, Erik, and Alfred Westholm. "Zur Zeitbestimmung der Helena-und Constantiasarkophage." In Swedish Institute in Rome, *Opuscula Archaeologica* I (Lund 1935) 1-46 and pls. I-VIII. Skrobucha, Heinz. *Sinai.* German ed. Olten and Freiburg 1959. English ed. London 1966. Cited from the English ed.

Smart, Alastair. *The Dawn of Italian Painting, 1250-1400.* Ithaca and Oxford 1978.

Smetana, Cyril L. "Ælfric and the Early Medieval Homiliary." *Traditio* 15 (1959) 163-204.

Smith, Robert Houston. "The Tomb of Jeus." *Biblical Archaeologist* 30 (1967) 74-90.

Smith, Toulmin, and Lucy Toulmin Smith. *English Gilds. EETS, OS,* no. 40. Oxford 1870; repr. 1963.

Solís de Merás, Gonzalo. *Pedro Menéndez de Avilés (Memorial 1567).* English trl. by Jeannette Thurber Connor. Deland, Florida, 1923; facsimile reproduction Gainesville 1964.

Soper, Alexander Coburn. "The Italo-Gallic School of Early Christian Art." *ArtB* 20 (1938) 145-92.

Sotiriou, Georgios A. and Maria. *Icones du Mont Sinaï* = Εἰκόνες τῆς μονῆς Σινᾶ (text in Greek; French summary). 2 vols. *Collection de l'Institut Français d'Athènes* 100 and 102. Athens 1956-1958.

    Spätantike und frühes Christentum. Exibition catalogue, Frankfurt 1983.

Spain, Suzanne. "The Translation of Relics Ivory, Trier." *DOP* 31 (1977) 279-304.

Spain, Suzanne. See Alexander, Suzanne Spain.

Spatharakis, Ioannis. *The Portrait in Byzantine Illuminated Manuscripts.* Leiden 1976.

Speck, Paul. *Kaiser Konstantin VI.* 2 vols. Munich 1978.

Spence, Clark C. *Montana: A Bicentennial History*. New York 1978.

Spyridakis, Constantinos. *A Brief History of Cyprus*. Rev. ed. Nicosia 1974.

The St. Louis Art Museum. *Handbook of the Collections*. St. Louis 1975.

Städelsches Kunstinstitut und Städtische Galerie, Frankfurt. *Verzeichnis der Gemälde*. Frankfurt 1987.

Stange, Alfred. *Deutsche Malerei der Gotik*. 11 vols. Berlin and Munich 1934-1961; repr. Nendeln 1969.

Stannard, Martin, ed. *Evelyn Waugh: The Critical Heritage*. London 1984.

Stannard, Martin. *Evelyn Waugh: The Later Years 1939-1966*. New York 1992.

Stearns, Frank Preston. *Four Great Venetians*. London 1901; repr. Freeport, New York, 1969.

Steer, John. *A Concise History of Venetian Painting*. London 1970; repr. 1979.

Steffens, Arnold. "Die alten Wandgemälde auf der Innenseite der Chorbrüstungen des Kölner Domes." *ZChrK* 15 (1902) in 6 parts: 129-43, 161-70, 193-206, 225-34, 257-64, and 289-98.

Stegenśek, August. "Architektonische Untersuchung von S. Croce in Gerusalemme in Rome." *RömQ* 14 (1900) 177-86.

Steidle, Wolf. "Die Leichenrede des Ambrosius für Kaiser Theodosius und die Helena-Legende." *Vig. Chr.* 32 (1978) 94-112.

Stemberger, Günter. *Juden und Christen im heiligen Land: Palestina unter Konstantin und Theodosius*. Munich 1987.

Stenton, Frank Merry. *Anglo-Saxon England*. 3rd ed. Oxford 1971.

Stephenson, David. *The Book of Colchester: A Portrait of the Town*. Chesham 1978.

Stepsis, Robert, and Richard Rand. "Contrast and Conversion in Cynewulf's *Elene*." *NM* 70 (1969) 273-82.

Stevens, Courtenay Edward. "Magnus Maximus in British History." *Études celtiques* 3 (1938) 86-94.

Stevenson, James. *The Catacombs: Rediscovered Monuments of Early Christianity*. London 1978.

Stohlman, W. Frederick. *Gli smalti del Museo Sacro Vaticano*. Vatican City 1939.

Stoll, Robert Thomas, and Jean Roubier. *Britannica Romanica*. Vienna 1966. English: *Architecture and Sculpture in Early Britain: Celtic, Saxon, Norman*. London 1967. Cited from the English ed.

Stone, Lawrence. *Sculpture in Britain: The Middle Ages.* Pelican *History of Art.* 2nd ed. Harmondsworth, Middlesex, 1972.

Stopp, Frederick J. *Evelyn Waugh: Portrait of an Artist.* Boston 1958.

Stratmann, Franziskus Maria. *Die Heiligen und der Staat.* 5 vols. Frankfurt 1949-1958.

Straubinger, Johannes. *Die Kreuzauffindungslegende. Forschungen zur christlichen Literatur- und Dogmengeschichte* 11.3. Paderborn 1912.

Strong, Eugénie. *La scultura romana da Augusto a Constantino.* 2 vols. Florence 1923-1926.

Strong, Eugénie. *Art in Ancient Rome.* 2 vols. New York 1928.

Stucchi, Sandro. "Le due statue del praetorium di Carnuntum ed altri monumenti del museo di Deutsch Altenburg." *Bull. della* commissione arch. comunale di Roma 73 (1949-1950), appendice 15-24.

Stuffmann, Margret. "Zu zwei Predellentafeln Elsheimers im Städelschen Kunstinstitut." *Städel-Jahrbuch, N. F.* 4 (1973) 203-206.

Styger, Paul. *Die römischen Martyrergrüfte.* 2 vols. Berlin 1935.

Stylianou, Andreas. Αἱ περιηγήσεις τοῦ Βάρσκου ἐν Κύπρῳ, Κυπριακαὶ Σπουδαί 21 (1975) 1-158.

Stylianou, Andreas. "Some Wall-paintings of the Second Half of the 15th Century in Cyprus." *Actes du XIIᵉ Congrès International des Études Byzantines (Ochride 1961)* III (Belgrade 1964) 363-69 and pls. I-IX.

Stylianou, Andreas and Judith A. "Donors and Dedicatory Inscriptions, Supplicants and Supplications in the Painted Churches of Cyprus." *JÖB* 9 (1960) 97-128.

Stylianou, Andreas and Judith A. *By This Conquer.* Nicosia 1971.

Stylianou, Andreas and Judith A. "A Re-examination of the Dates concerning the Painted Churches of St. Mamas, Louvaras, and the Holy Cross of Agiasmati, Platanistasa, Cyprus." *JÖB* 25 (1976) 279-82.

Stylianou, Andreas and Judith A. *The Painted Churches of Cyprus.* London 1985.

Sulzberger, Max. "Le symbole dela croix et les monogrammes de Jésus chez les premiers Chrétiens." *Byzantion* 2 (1925) 337-448.

Sutherland, C. H. V. *Roman Coins.* New York 1974.

Swanton, Michael J. "Ambiguity and Anticipation in 'The Dream of the Rood'." *NM* 70 (1969) 407-25.

Swarzenski, Hanns. *Monuments of Romanesque Art.* 2nd ed.

Chicago and London 1967.

Swoboda, Erich. *Carnuntum: Seine Geschichte und seine Denkmäler.* 2nd ed. Vienna 1953.

Sydow, Wilhelm von. *Zur Kunstgeschichte des spätantiken Porträts im 4. Jahrhundert n. Chr.* Bonn 1969.

Symeonides, Sibilla. *Fourteenth and Fifteenth Century Paintings in the Accademia Gallery, Venice.* Florence 1977.

Szarmach, Paul E., and Bernard F. Huppé, edd. *The Old English Homily and Its Background.* Albany 1978.

Szövérffy, Joseph. *Die Annalen der lateinischen Hymnendichtung.* 2 vols. Berlin 1964-1965.

Szövérffy, Joseph. *Weltliche Dichtungen des lateinischen Mittelalters* I. Berlin 1970.

Taburet-Delehaye, Elisabeth. *Les ivories du Musée de Cluny.* Paris: Musée de Cluny, 1978.

Talbot, Alice-Mary. "Akropolites, Constantine." In *ODB* I 49.

Tardi, Dominique. *Fortunat: Étude sur un dernier représentant de la poésie latine dans la Gaule mérovingienne.* Paris 1927.

Tarin y Juaneda, Francisco. *La real Cartuja de Miraflores (Burgos).* 2nd ed. Burgos 1925.

Tebeau, Charlton W. *A History of Florida.* Coral Gables 1971.

Tesei, Giovanni Paolo. *Le chiese di Roma.* Rome 1986.

Testini, P. "L'Anastasis alla luce delle recenti indagini." *OA* 3 (1964) 263-92.

Thierry, Nicole. "Un atelier de peintures du début du Xe siècle en Cappadoce: L'atelier del'ancienne église de Tokali." *Bulletin de la Société nationale des Antiquaires de France* 1971, pp. 170-78. Repr. in Nicole Thierry, *Peintures d'Asie Mineure et de Transcaucasie aux Xe et XIe s.* (London 1977), IV, pagination unchanged.

Thoby, Paul. *Le crucifix des origines au concile de Trent.* Nantes 1959.

Thomas, Charles. *Christianity in Roman Britain to AD 500.* London 1981.

Thomas, Heinz. *Studien zur Trierer Geschichtsschreibung des 11. Jahrhunderts, insbesondere zu den Gesta Treverorum. Rheinisches Archiv* 68. Bonn 1968.

Thomas, Heinz. "Gesta Treverorum." In *Verfasserlexikon²* III (1981) 34-37.

Thomson, Robert W., trl. and comment. *Moses Khorenats'i: History of the Armenians.* Cambridge, Massachusetts, 1978.

Thomson, Rodney. *William of Malmesbury.* Woodbridge, Suffolk,

1987.

Thubron, Colin. *The Hills of Adonis: A Quest in Lebanon.* Boston 1968.

Tiftixoglu, Victor. "Die Helenianai nebst einigen anderen Besitzungen im Vorfeld des frühen Konstantinopel." In *Studien zur Frühgeschichte Konstantinopels,* ed. Hans-Georg Beck (*Miscellanea Byzantina Monacensia* 14; Munich 1973) 49-120.

Tigerstedt, *Eugène Napoleon,* ed. *Ny illustrerad svensk litteraturhistoria.* 2 vols. 2nd ed. Stockholm 1967.

Tillemont, Louis Sébastien le Nain de. *Mémoires pour servir à l'histoire ecclésiastique de six premiers siècles.* 16 vols. Paris 1693-1712.

Tillyard, H. J. W. *Byzantine Music and Hymnography.* London 1923.

Timmers, J. J. M. *De kunst van het Maasland.* Assen, Netherlands, 1971.

Tischler, Nancy M. *Dorothy L. Sayers: A Pilgrim Soul.* Atlanta 1980.

Tittoni, Maria Elisa, and Sergio Guarino, edd. *Invisibilia: Riedere i capolavori, vedere i progetti.* Exhibition catalogue. Rome 1992.

Toesca, Pietro. *Il medioevo.* 2 vols. *Storia dell'arte italiana* I. Turin 1927; repr. 1965.

Toesca, Pietro. *Die florentinische Malerei des vierzehnten Jahrhunderts.* Florence and Munich 1929. English: *Florentine Painting of the Trecento.* Florence and New York 1929. Cited from the German ed.

Toesca, Pietro. *Il Trecento. Storia dell'arte italiana* II. Turin 1951; repr. 1965.

Toynbee, Arnold. *Constantine Porphyrogenitus and His World.* London 1973.

Toynbee, J. M. C. *Roman Medallions. Numismatic Studies* V. New York 1944; repr. 1985.

Toynbee, J. M. C. "Der römische Kameo der Stadtbibliothek Trier." *TZ* 20 (1951) 175-77.

Toynbee, Jocelyn (J. M. C.), and John Ward Perkins. *The Shrine of St. Peter and the Vatican Excavations.* New York 1957.

Treadgold, Warren. *The Byzantine Revival 780-842.* Stanford 1988.

Truhlář, Joseph. *Catalogus Codicum Manu Scriptorum Latinorum qui in C. R. Bibliotheca Publica atque universitatis Pragensis Asservantur.* 2 vols. Prague 1905-1906.

Tsafrir, Yoram, ed. *Ancient Churches Revealed.* Jerusalem and

Washington, D.C., 1993.
Tsafrir, Yoram. "Ancient Churches in the Holy Land," *Biblical Archaeology Review* 19 (1993) 26-39.
Tsirpanlis, Constantine N. *Introduction to Eastern Patristic Thought and Orthodox Theology.* Collegeville, Minnesota, 1991.
Tümmers, Horst-Johs. *Die Altarbilder des älteren Bartholomäus Bruyn.* Cologne 1964.
Türr, Karina. *Fälschungen antiker Plastik seit 1800.* Berlin 1984.
Ukena, Elke. *Die deutschen Mirakelspiele des Spätmittelalters: Studien und Texte.* 2 vols. Bern 1975.
United States Catholic Conference. *The Roman Calendar: Text and Commentary.* Washington, D.C., 1976.
Vailhé, Siméon. "Les monastères et les églises Saint-Etienne à Jérusalem." *EO* 8 (1905) 78-86.
Valentini, Roberto, and Giuseppe Zuchetti. *Codice Topografico della Città di Roma.* 4 vols. Rome 1940-1953.
Van Deman, Esther Boise. *The Building of the Roman Aqueducts.* Washington, D.C., 1934; repr. 1973.
Van den Bosch, P. "Sancta Helena, nobilissima femina." *Clairlieu* 38 (1980) 71-88.
Van Heck, Adrian. *Breviarium Urbis Romae Antiquae.* Leiden and Rome 1977.
Van Meter, David. *The Handbook of Roman Imperial Coins.* Nashua, New Hampshire: Laurion Numismatics, 1991.
Van Millingen, Alexander. *Byzantine Churches in Constantinople.* London 1912; repr. 1974.
Varjú, Elemér. "Az esztergomi sztaurotéka." *Magyar Művészet* 7 (1931) 433-39. Brief review (in German) by E. Darkó in *BZ* 32 (1932) 230-31.
Vasiliev, Alexander Alexandrovich. "Imperial Porphyry Sarcophagi in Constantinople." *DOP* 4 (1948) 1-26 and ill. 1-18.
Vasiliev, Alexander Alexandrovich. *Justin the First: An Introduction to the Epoch of Justinian the Great.* Cambridge, Massachusetts, 1950.
Vavalà, Evelyn Sandberg. *La Croce dipinta italiana.* Verona 1943.
Ven, Paul van den. *La légende de S.Spyridon, évêque de Trimithonte.* Louvain 1953.
Venezia e Bisanzio. Exhibition catalogue, Venice 1974.
Venturi, Adolfo. *Storia dell'arte italiana.* 11 vols. in 24. Milan 1901-1939; repr. Nendeln, Liechtenstein, 1967.
Venturi, Adolfo. *Musaici cristiani in Roma.* Rome 1925.
Venturi, Adolfo. *Paolo Veronese.* Milan 1928.

Venturi, Lionello. *Piero della Francesca*. Geneva 1959.

Venturi, Lionello, and Rosabianca Skira-Venturi. *Italian Painting*. 3 vols. Geneva 1950-1952.

Verbeek, Albert. *Das Münster in Bonn*. 2nd ed. *Rheinische Kunststätten* 213. Cologne 1983.

Verdon, Timothy, and John Henderson, edd. *Christianity and the Renaissance*. Syracuse 1990.

Vermeule, Cornelius C. "Greek, Etruscan, and Roman Sculptures in the Museum of Fine Arts, Boston." *AJA* 68 (1964) 323-41.

Vermeule, Cornelius C. *Roman Imperial Art in Greece and Asia Minor*. Cambridge, Massachusetts, 1968.

Vessberg, Olof. "Roman Portrait Art in Cyprus." *Opuscula Romana* 1 (1954) 160-65.

Vessberg, Olof. *Romersk Porträttkonst*. 3rd ed. Göteborg 1985.

The Victoria History of the Counties of England. For individual volumes cited see the respective editors:
Hampshire and the Isle of Wight II: H. Arthur Doubleday and William Page.
Lancaster III-IV: William Farrer and J. Brownbill.
Norfolk II: William Page.

Vidmonová, Anežka. "La branche tchècque de la *Légende dorée.*" In Brenda Dunn-Lardeau, *Legenda aurea: Sept siècles de diffusion* (Montreal and Paris 1986) 291-98.

Vimont, Maurice. *Histoire de l'église et de la paroisse Saint-Leu-Saint-Gilles à Paris*. Paris 1932.

Vincent, Hugues. "L'Éléona, sanctuaire primitif de l'ascension." *Rev. Bibl.* 64 (1957) 48-71.

Vincent, Hugues, and F.- M. Abel. *Jérusalem: Recherches de topographies d'archéologie et d'histoire*. 2 vols. in 4. Paris 1912-1926.

Vincent, Hugues, and F.- M. Abel. *Bethléem: Le sanctuaire de la Nativité*. Paris 1914.

Visconti, Carlo Lodovico. *Les monuments de sculpture antique du Musée Torlonia*. Rome 1884.

Vitz, Evelyn Birge. "From the Oral to the Written in Medieval and Renaissance Saints' Lives." In Renate Blumenfeld-Kosinski and Timea Szell, edd., *Images of Sainthood in Medieval Europe* (Ithaca 1991) 97-114.

Vlasto, A. P. *The Entry of the Slavs into Christendom*. Cambridge 1970.

Vlieghe, Hans. *Saints. Corpus Rubenianum Ludwig Burchard* VIII. 2 vols. London 1973.

Vodová, Marie. "La chronologie de la vie d'Hélène, mère de l'empereur Constantin, et ses portraits." (In Czech with summaries in French and Russian) *SPFB* 24 (1979) 63-72.

Vodová (also Pardyové-Vodová), Marie. "L'impératrice Hélène et l'invention de la Sainte-Croix." *SPFB* 25 (1980) 235-40.

Voelkl, Ludwig. "Die konstantinischen Kirchenbauten nach Eusebius." *RACrist.* 29 (1953) 49-66 and 187-206.

Voelkl, Ludwig. *Der Kaiser Konstantin: Annalen einer Zeitenwende.* Munich 1957.

Voelkle, William M. *The Iconography of the Legend of the Finding of the True Cross in Mosan Art of the Last Half of the Twelfth Century.* Columbia University M.A. thesis, 1965. (Not cited.)

Vogt, Joseph. "Die Bedeutung des Jahres 312 für die Religionspolitik Konstantins des Grossen." *ZKG,* 3rd ser. 61 (1942) 171-90. Repr. in Heinrich Kraft, ed., *Konstantin der Grosse* (Darmstadt 1974) 247-72. Cited from *ZKG.*

Vogt, Joseph. "Streitfragen um Konstantin den Grossen." Röm. Mitt. 58 (1943) 190-203.

Vogt, Joseph. "Berichte über Kreuzeserscheinungen aus dem 4. Jahrhundert n. Chr." *Annuaire de l'Institut de philologie et d'histoire orientales et slaves* 9 (1949) 593-606.

Vogt, Joseph. "Der Erbauer der Apostelkirche in Konstantinopel." *Hermes* 81 (1953) 111-17.

Vogt, Joseph. "Constantinus der Grosse." In *RAC* III (1957) 306-79.

Vogt, Joseph. *Constantin der Grosse und sein Jahrhundert.* 2nd ed. Munich 1960.

Vogt, Joseph. "Heiden und Christen in der Familie Constantins des Grossen." In *Eranion: Festschrift für Hildebrecht Hommel* (Tübingen 1961) 149-68. English: "Pagans and Christians in the Family of Constantine the Great." In Arnaldo Momigliano, ed., *The Conflict between Paganism and Christianity in the Fourth Century* (Oxford 1963) 38-55. Cited from *Eranion.*

Vogt, Joseph. "Helena Augusta, das Kreuz und die Juden: Fragen um die Mutter Constantins des Grossen." *Saeculum* 27 (1976) 211-22. English: "Helena Augusta, the Cross and the Jews: Some Enquiries about the Mother of Constantine the Great." *Classical Folia* 31 (1977) 135-51. Cited from *Saeculum.*

Vogüé, Melchior de. *Les églises de la Terre Sainte.* Paris 1860; repr. Toronto 1973.

Volbach, Wolfgang Friedrich. *Frühchristliche Kunst.* Munich 1958. English: *Early Christian Art.* New York 1962. Cited from the English ed.

Volbach, Wolfgang Friedrich. *Elfenbeinarbeiten der Spätantike und des frühen Mittelalters.* 3rd ed. Mainz 1976.

Volbach, Wolfgang Fritz, and Jacqueline Lafontaine-Dosogne. *Byzanz und der christliche Osten. Propyläen Kunstgeschichte* III. Berlin 1968.

Volpi, Marisa. "Corrado Giaquinto e alcuni aspetti della cultura figurativa del' 700 in Italia." *BdA* 43 (1958) 263-82.

Voretzsch, A. "Ende einer Odyssee: Eine kleine Kupfertafel von Adam Elsheimer ist den Frankfurtern teuer." *Artis* 33 (1981) 48-49.

Wachsmann, Ute. *Die Chorschrankenmalereien im Kölner Dom.* 2 vols. Dissertation Bonn 1985.

Wackenroder, Ernst, and Heinrich Neu. *Die Kunstdenkmäler des Landkreises Trier. Die Kunstdenkmäler der Rheinprovinz* XV.11. Düsseldorf 1936; repr. Trier 1981.

Wadding, Luke (1588-1657) and continuators. *Annales Minorum.* 2nd-3rd ed. Quaracchi 1931 ff.

Waddingham, Malcolm. "Elsheimer's Frankfurt Tabernacle: Discovery of the Final Piece." *Burlington Magazine* 123 (1981) 346-50.

Waddingham, Malcolm, and Christopher Wright. "Elsheimer: A Third Piece from the Frankfurt Tabernacle." *Burlington Magazine* 112 (1970) 192-94.

Walker, Peter (P. W. L.). *Holy City, Holy Places? Christian Attitudes to Jerusalem and the Holy Land in the Fourth Century.* Oxford 1990.

Wallace-Hadrill, David S. *Christian Antioch.* Cambridge 1982.

Wallace-Hadrill, John Michael. *The Frankish Church.* Oxford 1983.

Wallraf-Richartz-Museum, Cologne. *Die Heiligen Drei Könige: Darstellung und Verehrung.* Exhibition catalogue, Cologne 1982.

Wallraf-Richartz-Museum, Cologne. *Vollständiges Verzeichnis der Gemäldesammlung.* Cologne and Milan 1986.

Walser, Gerold. *Die Einsiedler Inschriftensammlung und der Pilgerführer durch Rom (Codex Einsidlensis 326). Historia Einzelschriften* 53. Stuttgart 1987.

Walsh, Patrick Gerard. "Venantius Fortunatus." *The Month* 24

(1960) 292-302.

Walter, Christopher. *Art and Ritual of the Byzantine Church.* London 1982.

Walter, Christopher. *L'iconographie des conciles dans la tradition byzantine.* Paris 1970.

Walters Art Gallery. *Early Christian and Byzantine Art.* Baltimore 1947.

Wammetsberger, Helga. "Individium und Typ in den Porträts Kaiser Karls IV." *Wissenschaftliche Zeitschrift der Friedrich-Schiller-Universität Jena, Gesellschafts- und sprachwissenschaftliche Reihe* 16 (1967) 79-95.

Wankenne, André. "Constantin et Hélène à Trèves." *Et. Cl.* 52 (1984) 313-16.

Ward Perkins, John. "The Shrine of St. Peter and Its Twelve Spiral Columns." *JRS* 42 (1952) 21-33.

Wardale, E. E. *Chapters on Old English Literature.* London 1935; repr. 1965.

Waugh, Evelyn. *Helena: A Novel.* London and Boston 1951.

Waugh, Evelyn. "St. Helena Empress." *The Month,* January 1952, pp. 7-11.

Weber, Peter. *Der Domschatz zu Trier.* Augsburg 1928.

Weber, Winfried. "Die Reliquienprozession auf der Elfenbeintafel des Trierer Domschatzes und das kaiserliche Hofzeremoniell." *TZ* 42 (1979) 135-51.

Weber, Winfried. *Die Heiligkreuz-Kapelle in Trier.* Trier 1982.

Weber, Winfried. *Constantinische Deckengemälde aus dem römischen Palast unter dem Trierer Dom. Museumsführer* 1. 2nd ed. Trier: Bischöfliches Museum, 1986.

Wegner, Max, ed. *Das römische Herrscherbild* III.1. Berlin 1971. For vol. III. 4 see L'Orange, Hans Peter.

Weigand, Edmund. "Zur Datierung der kappadokischen Höhlenmalereien." *BZ* 36 (1936) 337-97.

Weiland, Albrecht. *Der Campo Santo Teutonico in Rom und seine Grabdenkmäler. Der Campo Santo Teutonico in Rom,* ed., Erwin Gatz, I. *RömQ,* Supplementheft 43. Rome 1988.

Weiler, Peter. *Urkundenbuch des Stiftes Xanten* I. Bonn 1935.

Weinfurter, Stefan, and Odilo Engels. *Series Episcoporum Ecclesiae Catholicae Occidentalis.* V.1. Stuttgart 1982.

Weitzmann, Kurt. "The Ivories of the So-called Grado Chair." *DOP* 26 (1972) 43-91 plus plates. Repr. in *Studies in the Arts of Sinai: Essays by Kurt Weitzmann* (Princeton 1982) 119-65. Cited from *DOP.*

Weitzmann, Kurt, ed. *Age of Spirituality: Late Antique and Early Christian Art, Third to Seventh Century.* Exhibition catalogue, New York 1979.

Weitzmann, Kurt, ed. *Age of Spirituality: A Symposium.* New York 1980.

Weitzmann, Kurt, et al. *Le icone.* Milan 1981. English: *The Icon.* New York 1987. Cited from the English ed.

Weitzmann, Kurt, Manolis Chatzidakis, Krsto Miatev, and Svetozar Radojčić. *Ikone sa Balkana.* Belgrade 1966. English: *A Treasury of Icons: Sixth to Seventeenth Centuries.* New York 1968. Also German and French edd. Cited from the English ed.

Wellesz, Egon. *A History of Byzantine Music and Hymnography.* 2nd ed. Oxford 1961.

Wells, Minnie E. "The South English Legendary in Its Relation to the *Legenda Aurea.*" *PMLA* 51 (1936) 337-60.

Wells, Minnie E. "The Structural Development of the South English Legendary." *JEGP* 41 (1942) 320-44.

Wentzel, Hans. "Das byzantinische Erbe der ottonischen Kaiser: Hypothesen über den Brautschatz der Theophano." *Aachener Kunstblätter* 40 (1971) 15-39 and 43 (1972) 11-96.

Wessel, Klaus. *Die byzantinische Emailkunst.* Recklinghausen 1967. English: *Byzantine Enamels from the 5th to the 13th Century.* Greenwich, Connecticut, 1968. Cited from the English ed.

Wessel, Klaus. "Kaiserbild." In *RBK* III (1972-1978) 722-854.

Wessel, Klaus. "Konstantin u. Helena." In *RBK,* fasc. 27/28 (1989) 357-66.

Westermann-Angerhausen, Hiltrud. *Die Goldschmiedearbeiten der Trierer Egbertwerkschaft. TZ* 36 (1973) Beiheft.

Westermann-Angerhausen, Hiltrud. "Überlegungen zum Trierer Egbertschrein." *TZ* 40-41 (1977-78) 201-20.

Westlake, H. F. *The Parish Gilds of Medieval England.* London 1919.

Wharton, Annabel Jane. *Art of Empire: Painting and Architecture of the Byzantine Periphery: A Comparative Study of Four Provinces.* University Park, Pennsylvania, 1988.

Wharton, Annabel Jane. See also Epstein, Ann Wharton.

White, Caroline Louisa. *Ælfric: A New Study of His Life and Writings.* New Haven 1898; repr. Hamden, Connecticut, 1974.

White, Christopher. *Rubens and His World.* New York 1968.

White, Christopher. *Peter Paul Rubens: Man and Artist.* New

Haven 1987.

White, Helen C. *Tudor Books of Saints and Martyrs*. Madison 1963.

Whittemore, Thomas. *The Mosaics of Hagia Sophia at Istanbul: Third Preliminary Report: The Imperial Portraits of the South Gallery*. Oxford 1942.

Whittemore, Thomas. "A Portrait of the Empress Zoe and of Constantine IX." *Byzantion* 18 (1946-1948) 223-27.

Whitting, Philip D. *Byzantine Coins*. New York 1973.

Wiegel, Karl Adolf. *Die Darstellungen der Kreuzauffindung bis zu Piero della Francesca*. Dissertation Cologne 1973.

Wightman, Edith Mary. *Roman Trier and the Treveri*. London 1970.

Wightman, Edith Mary. *Gallia Belgica*. Berkeley 1985.

Wilhelm, Friedrich. *Deutsche Legenden und Legendare: Texte und Untersuchungen zu ihrer Geschichte im Mittelalter*. Leipzig 1907.

Wilken, Robert L. *The Land Called Holy*. New Haven 1992.

Wilkinson, John. *Egeria's Travels to the Holy Land*. Rev. ed. Jerusalem and Warminster, England, 1981.

Williams, Rowan D. *Arius: Heresy and Tradition*. London 1987.

Williams, Stephen. *Diocletian and the Roman Recovery*. New York 1985.

Williams, Ulla, and Werner Williams-Krapp. *Die Elsässische Legenda Aurea* I. Tübingen 1980.

Williams-Krapp, Werner. "Studien zu 'Der Heiligen Leben'." *ZDA* 105 (1976) 274-303.

Williams-Krapp, Werner. "Die deutschen Übersetzungen der 'Legenda aurea' des Jacobus de Voragine." *BGDSL 101* (1979) 252-76.

Williams-Krapp, Werner. "German and Dutch Translations of the Legenda aurea." In Brenda Dunn-Lardeau, *Legenda aurea: Sept siècles de diffusion* (Montreal and Paris 1986) 227-32.

Wilpert, Josef (Giuseppe). "Un capitolo di storia del vestiario." *L'arte* 1 (1898) 89-121.

Wilpert, Josef. *La cripta dei Papi e la cappella di santa Cecilia*. Rome 1910.

Wilpert, Joseph. *Die römischen Mosaiken und Malereien der kirchlichen Bauten vom IV. bis XIII. Jahrhundert*. 4 vols. 3rd ed. Freiburg 1924.

Wilson, Laurie J. " The Trier Procession Ivory: A New Interpretation." *Byzantion* 54 (1984) 602-14.

Wilson, Stephen. "Cults of Saints in the Churches of Central Paris." In Stephen Wilson, ed., *Saints and Their Cults: Studies in*

Religious Sociology, Folklore and History (Cambridge 1983) 233-60.

Winheller, Ernst. *Die Lebensbeschreibungen der vorkarolingischen Bischöfe von Trier. Rheinisches Archiv* 27. Bonn 1935.

Winkelmann, Friedhelm. "Zur Geschichte des Authentizätsproblems der Vita Constantini." *Klio* 40 (1962) 147-243.

Winkelmann, Friedhelm. "Charakter und Bedeutung der Kirchengeschichte des Gelasios von Kaisareia." *Byzantinische Forschungen* 1 (1966) 346-385.

Winkelmann, Friedhelm. *Untersuchungen zur Kirchengeschichte des Gelasios von Kaisareia. Sb. der deutschen Ak. der Wissensch. zu Berlin* 1965:3. Berlin 1966.

Winkelmann, Friedhelm. "Das hagiographische Bild Konstantins I in mittelbyzantinischer Zeit." In Vladimir Vavřinek, ed., *Beiträge zur byzantinischen Geschichte im 9.-11. Jahrhundert* (Prague 1978) 179-203.

Winkelmann, Friedhelm. "Die älteste erhaltene griechische hagiographische Vita Konstantins und Helenas (BHG Nr. 365z, 366, 366a)." In Jürgen Dummer, ed., *Texte und Textkritik: Eine Aufsatzsammlung (TU* 133 [1987]) 623-38.

Wisplinghoff, Erich. *Untersuchungen zur frühen Geschichte der Abtei S. Maximin bei Trier von den Anfängen bis etwa 1150.* Mainz 1970.

Wistrand, Erik (E. K. H.). *Konstantins Kirche am Heiligen Grab in Jerusalem nach den ältesten literarischen Zeugnissen.* Göteborg 1952.

Witte, Fritz. *Die Schatzkammer des Domes zu Köln.* Augsburg 1927.

Witte, Fritz. *Der goldene Schrein: Ein Buch über Köln.* Cologne 1928.

Wittkower, Rudolf. *Gian Lorenzo Bernini: The Sculptor of the Roman Baroque.* 2nd ed. London 1966.

Wittkower, Rudolf. *Art and Architecture in Italy 1600-1750.* 3rd ed. *The Pelican History of Art.* Harmondsworth, Middlesex, 1973.

Wolpers, Theodor. *Die englische Heiligenlegende des Mittelalters: Eine Formgeschichte des Legendenerzählens von der spätantiken lateinischen Tradition bis zur Mitte des 16. Jahrhunderts.* Tübingen 1964.

Woodforde, Christopher. *English Stained and Painted Glass.* Oxford 1954.

Woolf, Rosemary. "Doctrinal Influences on the *Dream of the Rood.*" *MÆ* 27 (1958) 137-53.

Wormald, Francis. "The Rood of Bromholm." *JWarb.* 1 (1937-1938) 31-45.

Wortley, John. "The Trier Ivory Reconsidered." *GRBS* 21 (1986) 381-94.

Wrede, Henning. *Die spätantike Hermengalerie von Welschbillig.* Berlin 1972.

Writers' Program, South Carolina. *Palmetto Place Names.* Columbia, South Carolina, 1941; repr. Spartansburg, South Carolina, 1975.

Wroth, Warwick. *Imperial Byzantine Coins in the British Museum.* 2 vols. in 1. London 1908; repr. Chicago 1966.

Wüstenfeld, Heinrich Ferdinand, translator. *Synaxarium, das ist Heiligen-Kalender der Coptischen Christen.* Gotha 1879.

Wulf, Max von. *Über Heilige und Heiligenverehrung in den ersten christlichen Jahrhunderten.* Leipzig 1910.

Yacoub, Mohamed. *Musée du Bardo.* Tunis 1970.

Yale University Art Gallery. *A Taste for Angels: Neapolitan Painting in North America, 1650-1750.* Exhibition catalogue, New Haven, Connecticut, 1987.

Young, Elizabeth and Wayland. *Old London Churches.* London 1956.

Zadoks-Josephus Jitta, A. N. "De grote camee in het Kon. Penningkabinet." *Hermeneus* 22 (1951) 182-85.

Zadoks-Josephus Jitta, A. N. "Imperial Messages in Agate, II." *BAB* 41 (1966) 91-104.

Zaunert, Paul. *Rheinland Sagen.* 2 vols. Jena 1924.

Zender, Matthias. *Räume und Schichten mittelalterlicher Heiligenverehrung in ihrer Bedeutung für die Volkskunde.* 2nd ed. Cologne and Bonn 1973.

Zenz, Emil. *Geschichte der Stadt Trier im 19. Jahrhundert.* 2 vols. Trier 1979-1980.

Zenz, Emil. *Die Stadt Trier im 20. Jahrhundert: 1. Hälfte, 1900-1950.* Trier 1981.

Zeydel, Edwin H. *Sebastian Brant.* New York 1967.

Ziemke, Hans-Joachim. "Neuerwerbungen der Frankfurter Museen: Städelsches Kunstinstitut und Städtische Galerie." Städel-Jb., N. F. 9 (1983) 259.

Zilliken, Georg. "Der Kölner Festkalender." *BJ* 119 (1910) 13-157.

Zimmermann, Walther. *Das Münster zu Essen.* Essen 1956.

Zwischen Andacht und Andenken: Kleinodien religiöser Kunst und Wallfahrtsandenken aus Trierer Sammlungen (exhibition catalogue). Trier: Bischöfliches Dom- und Diözesanmuseum Trier and Städtisches Museum Simeonstift Trier, 1992.

INDEX
OF
GEOGRAPHICAL LOCATIONS

INDEX
OF
SOURCES

INDEX
OF
MODERN AUTHORITIES

GENERAL INDEX

Hermann, Bishop of Metz, 161
Hincmar, Archbishop of Reims, 201
Honoria, sister of Valentinian III, 80
Hugh, Duke of the Franks , 66
hymns, Greek , 196
hymns, Latin, 59, 191-92
Igor, Prince of Kiev, 199
Innocent II, Pope, 159, 160
Innocent III, Pope, 191
Innocent IV, Pope, 34, 60
inscriptions, 6-7, 13, 73-74, 75-76, 79-80, 80-81, 103-104, 118, 160, 164, 184-85, 223, 229, 231, 234
Irene, mother of Constantine VI, 189, 194
Irene, wife of John II Comnenus, 236
Iulius Maximilianus, 75, 76
Iuventas, 46
Jesuit order, 222
Jews, Judaism, 6, 7, 26, 63, 109, 110, 192, 195, 205, 211, 213, 217, 218, 220, 223, 230
Joâo de Nova, 238
Johann I, Archbishop of Trier, 131
John XV, Pope, 190
John XXIII, Pope, 115
John II Comnenus, Byzantine emperor, 236
John V, Byzantine emperor, 183
John VII, Byzantine emperor, 184
John, Bishop of Constantinople, 130
Judaism, see Jews
Judas, Bishop of Jerusalem, 110
Judas (Cyriacus, Quiriacus, Κυριακός), 2, 63, 109, 110, 111, 204, 207, 211, 214, 215, 218, 220, 221, 223, 224, 228, 230, 231

Julia, daughter of Augustus, 17
Julian the Apostate, 20, 108
Julius Constantius, 20
Justin I, 193
Justin II, 118, 186
Justinian I, 3, 93, 97, 144
Kunigunde (Cunegunda), Saint, Empress, 191
Kuno von Falkenstein, Archbishop of Trier, 163
Κυριακός, see Judas
laurel wreath, 21, 170, 179
Lazarus, 163
Leontia, wife of Phocas, 188
Licinius, 21, 139, 180
lignum crucis, 104, 114, 195
Longinus, Saint, 82, 118
Louis the Pious, 34
Louis, Saint, 120, 121
Lucian, Saint, of Antioch, 3-4, 22, 29, 191, 215
Macarius, Bishop of Jerusalem, 87, 90, 101, 102, 106, 107, 204, 222-23
Macrina the Younger, Saint, 104
Macson Wledig, see Magnus Maximus
Magi, see Three Kings
Magnus Maximus (Macsen Wledig or Maxen Wledig), 69
Malusius, Saint, Theban martyr, 55
Manuel II, Byzantine emperor, 184
Marcellinus and Peter, martyrs, 149, 150
Marcian, Byzantine emperor, 193
Mark, Saint, 137, 155
Mary, Virgin, 79, 91, 145, 218, 222, 236
Master of the Holy Cross, 224
Maternus, Bishop of Cologne, reportedly Bishop of Trier, 32, 51, 52, 134